Choice, Decision, and Measurement: Essays in Honor of R. Duncan Luce

Edited by

A. A. J. Marley

LEA LAWRENCE ERLBAUM ASSOCIATES, PUBLISHERS
1997   Mahwah, New Jersey   London

Lawrence Erlbaum Associates, Inc., Publishers
10 Industrial Avenue
Mahwah, New Jersey 07430

Library of Congress Cataloging-in-Publication Data

Choice, decision, and measurement : essays in honor of R. Duncan Luce
/ edited by A.A.J. Marley.
    p. cm.
  Papers originally presented at a conference held at the University
of California, Irvine, Aug. 2-3,1995.
  Includes bibliographical references and indexes.
  ISBN 0-8058-2234-8 (alk. paper)
  1. Psychometrics--Congresses. 2. Choice (Psychology)--Congresses.
3. Decision-making--Congresses. I. Luce, R. Duncan (Robert Duncan)
II. Marley, A. A. J.
BF39.C49 1966
153.8'3--dc20   96-41621
                           CIP

Books published by Lawrence Erlbaum Associates are printed
on acid-free paper, and their bindings are chosen
for strength and durability.

Printed in the United States of America

10 9 8 7 6 5 4 3 2 1

Choice, Decision, and Measurement
A. A. J. Marley (Ed.),
©Lawrence Erlbaum Associates, NJ, 1997.

CONTENTS

Choice, Decision, and Measurement
A. A. J. Marley (Ed.),
©Lawrence Erlbaum Associates, NJ, 1997.

PREFACE

This volume arose from a conference held August 2-3, 1995, at the University of California Irvine (UCI) on the topics that provide its title: Choice, Decision, and Measurement. The conference was organized by Professor Louis Narens (UCI) and sponsored by the School of Social Sciences and the Institute for Mathematical Behavioral Sciences. Financial support for it was provided to the Institute by UCI, a National Science Foundation Research and Training Grant, and by funds from UCI's Committee on Research and Graduate Studies obtained for this purpose by Professor Mary-Louis Kean, Chair of the Department of Cognitive Sciences.

The conference was held, and the volume prepared, in honor of Professor R. Duncan Luce on his 70th birthday. The social climax of the conference was a banquet held to pay tribute to Professor Luce, his wife Carolyn Scheer, and daughter Aurora. The banquet was arranged by Janet Phelps and Dee Yox (UCI) and hosted by Professor Jack Yellott (UCI). Warm speeches were given by Professor Richard Atkinson, then Chancellor of the University of California San Diego, now President of the University of California; Professor David Green, member of the National Academy of Sciences; Professor William McGill, former President of Columbia University and former Chancellor of the University of California San Diego; Professor A. A. J. Marley, Chair of the Department of Psychology at McGill University, who received his Ph. D. under Professor Luce's supervision; and Professor P. Suppes, recipient of the National Medal of Science. Professor Suppes' talk was especially delightful, covering both scientific and personal aspects of Professor Luce's career; he was assisted by Carolyn Scheer with material and slides on significant events in Professor Luce's life. Finally, and apparently following a Russian custom of honoring illustrious professors with a song written specially for them, Professor Barbara Mellers and Professor Elke Weber, who received her Ph. D. under Professor Luce's supervision, sang a charming and amusing song that had been created especially for the occasion, with words by Serguei Tichtenko and music by Professor Jerome Busemeyer.

The volume begins with a short autobiographical statement by Luce covering the years 1988 to 1995; an earlier piece covered the years prior to 1988 (Luce, 1989 – see *Scientific Publications of R. Duncan Luce*, this book). The remainder of the volume is organized into four topics, to each of which Luce has made significant contributions.

The goal of the book is to provide the reader with some overview of current issues in each area and to present some of the best recent relevant theoretical and empirical work. Personal reflections on Luce and his work begin each section, these reflections being written by outstanding senior researchers: Peter Fishburn (*Decision Making and Risk*), Patrick Suppes (*Preference, Measurement Theory, and Axiomatic Systems*), William J. McGill (*Psychophysics and Response Time*), W. K. Estes (*Choice and Categorization*).

The first section, *Decision Making and Risk*, presents recent theoretical and empirical work on descriptive models of decision making. Luce's recent theoretical and empirical work on rank- and sign-dependent utility theory is important in many of these contributions. The second section, *Preference, Measurement Theory, and Axiomatic Systems*, presents theoretical results on general probabilistic models of choice and ranking, probabilistic measurement, psychophysics, test theory, and aggregation. The third section, *Psychophysics and Response Time*, presents various process oriented models, with supportive data, for tasks such as redundant signal detection, forced choice, and absolute identification. The final section, *Choice and Categorization*, contains theory and data on categorization and attention, and general theoretical results for developing and testing models in these domains.

Luce has made major contributions to every area discussed in this book. A small indicator of this fact is that 19 of the 22 chapters make direct substantive reference to his work. These references range over – but are not limited to – his work on: rank- and sign-dependent utility theory; the possible psychophysical laws; the representational theory of measurement; attention-based psychophysical models; and, of course, the choice model. I now comment briefly on some of Luce's contributions, the full extent of which can be seen in the bibliography of his work that appears as the final chapter of the book.

In addition to almost 200 scientific articles, Luce has written seven books and edited eleven, either alone or with colleagues. These books give an indication of the breadth of his interests over the years. His first book *Games and Decisions* (with H. Raiffa) was one of the first major integrations of that field and is a classic. His second book *Individual Choice Behavior* presents the very elegant axiomatization of his choice model and applies it to domains such as psychophysics, learning, and utility. This model, now generally known as *Luce's choice model*, continues to be extensively applied in psychology and other behavioral sciences, and is a special case of many of the more general models that have been developed over the intervening years. The next important books were the three volume *Handbook of Mathematical Psychology* and the two volume *Readings in Mathematical Psychology* (edited with R. R. Bush and E. Galanter). These volumes included surveys and new contributions about the most exciting work of the early sixties on psychophysics, learning, language, and utility; preparing these volumes would be a major enterprise for many scientists, but for Luce they were something one does in spare moments. The next major book enterprise, spanning a twenty year period, was the three volume *Foundations of Measurement* (written with D. H. Krantz, P. Suppes, and A. Tversky). This important work contains significant new results on the representational theory of measurement, and continues to be a foundation and source for challenging work in measurement theory. Finally, his book *Response Times*, published in 1986, masterfully integrates the theoretical and empirical literature on that topic, and will remain the standard reference for years to come; and his textbook *Sound and*

Hearing, published in 1993, makes a similar contribution with respect to work in those areas.

The chapters in this volume by Fishburn, Suppes, McGill, and Estes expand further on Luce's contributions, both past and present, to the above and other areas. Alongside his current work on general theoretical work in measurement, Luce is developing and testing fascinating new ideas on utility theory, returning to interests first explored by him in the 1950's. As always, this work is the best in the field, challenging others to meet the superior standard that Luce sets himself in both theoretical and empirical endeavors.

I thank the authors for promptly preparing and revising their chapters, and especially for complying with our rigid formatting guidelines. I also thank the authors and the other referees (listed on a separate page) for their extensive evaluation of contributions. I received necessary financial support for the preparation of the book from the School of Social Sciences at the University of California Irvine and from the Department of Psychology and the Faculty of Science at McGill University. Finally, there is absolutely no way I could have completed this task without the tremendous work of Carlos Mario Martínez-Mascarúa. Carlos was responsible for the entire production of the book from the initial preparation of the guidelines sent to the authors to the completion of the camera-ready copy. Carlos and I also received invaluable assistance from Carlos Zamora-Cura, Margarita Sanchez and Chantale Bousquet.

Montréal, Canada, April 1997   A. A. J. MARLEY

LIST OF CONTRIBUTORS

János Aczél. *Faculty of Mathematics, University of Waterloo, Waterloo, Ontario N2L 3G1, Canada.* Email: jdaczel@math.uwaterloo.ca

F. Gregory Ashby. *Department of Psychology, University of California, Santa Barbara, CA 93106, USA.* Email: ashby@psych.ucsb.edu

Donald Bamber. *Naval Command, Control & Ocean Surveillance Center, Research, Development, Test & Evaluation Division, NCCOSC RDTE DIV 44215, 53355 Ryne Road, Rm. 222, San Diego, CA 92152-7252, USA.*
Email: bamber@nosc.mil

Patricia M. Berretty. *Department of Psychology, University of California, Santa Barbara, CA 93106, USA.* Email: berretty@psych.ucsb.edu

Michael H. Birnbaum. *Department of Psychology, California State University, P.O. Box 6846, Fullerton, CA 92834-6846, USA.* Email: mbirnbaum@fullerton.edu

Robert L. Carlson. *Department of Cognitive Sciences, University of California, Irvine, CA 92697, USA.* Email: rcarlson@aris.ss.uci.edu

Hans Colonius. *Institut für Kognitionsforschung, Universität Oldenburg, D-26111 Oldenburg/Germany.* Email: colonius@psychologie.uni-oldenburg.de

Ehtibar N. Dzhafarov. *Beckman Institute, University of Illinois, 405 North Mathews, Urbana, IL 61801, USA.* Email: edzhafar@s.psych.uiuc.edu

W. K. Estes. *Department of Psychology, William James Hall, Harvard University, 33 Kirkland St. Cambridge, MA 02138, USA.* Email: wke@wjh.harvard.edu

Jean-Claude Falmagne. *School of Social Sciences, University of California, Irvine, CA 92717, USA.* Email: jcf@uci.edu

Peter C. Fishburn. *AT&T Labs-Research, Murray Hill, NJ 07974, USA.* Email: fish@research.att.com

Bernard N. Grofman. *Department of Politics and Society, School of Social Sciences, University of California, Irvine, CA 92697, USA.* Email: bgrofman@uci.edu

Dieter Heyer. *Institut für Psychologie, Universität Kiel, D-24098 Kiel, Germany.* Email: heyer@psychologie.uni-kiel.de

Geoffrey Iverson. *Department of Cognitive Sciences and the Institute for Mathematical Behavioral Sciences, University of California, Irvine, CA 92717, USA.* Email: giverson@.aris.ss.uci.edu

Peter Karpiuk, Jr. *OPTUM Software, 3330 Harbor Blvd., Costa Mesa, CA 92626, USA.* Email: pkarpiuk@atkc.com

David LaBerge. *Department of Cognitive Sciences, University of California, Irvine, CA 92717, USA.* Email: dlaberge@vmsa.oac.uci.edu

Yves Lacouture. *Laboratoire de Recherche en Psychologie Cognitive, Ecole de Psychologie, Faculté des Sciences Sociales, Université Laval, Québec G1K 7P4, Canada.* Email: yves@psy.ulaval.ca

Michael V. Levine. *Department of Educational Psychology, University of Illinois and ADAMS (Algorithm Design and Measurement Services), 905 Shurts St, Urbana, IL 61801, USA.* Email: m-levine@ux1.cso.uiuc.edu

R. Duncan Luce. *Institute for Mathematical Behavioral Sciences, Social Science Plaza, University of California, Irvine, CA 92697-5100, USA.* Email: rdluce@uci.edu

A. A. J. Marley. *Department of Psychology, McGill University, 1205 Avenue Dr. Penfield, Montreal, Quebec H3A-1B1, Canada.* Email: tony@hebb.psych.mcgill.ca

William J. McGill. *9500 Gilman Drive/0109, University of California, San Diego, La Jolla, CA 92093-0109, USA.* Email: wjmcgill@psy.ucsd.edu

Barbara A. Mellers. *Department of Psychology, The Ohio State University, 1885 Neil Avenue, Columbus, OH 43210, USA.* Email: mellers.1@osu.edu

Louis Narens. *School of Social Sciences, University of California Irvine, Irvine, CA 92717, USA.* Email: lnarens@uci.edu

Reinhard Niederée. *Institut für Psychologie, Universität Kiel, D-24098 Kiel, Germany.* Email: niederee@psychologie.uni-kiel.de

Robert M. Nosofsky. *Department of Psychology, Indiana University, Bloomington, IN 47405, USA.* Email: nosofsky@indiana.edu

Michel Regenwetter. *Department of Psychology, McGill University, 1205 Ave. Dr. Penfield, Montréal, Québec H3A 1B1, Canada.* Email: regenwet@maude.psych.mcgill.ca

Alan Schwartz. *Department of Psychology, University of California, Tolman Hall, Berkeley, CA 94720-1650, USA.* Email: alansz@cogsci.berkeley.edu

Richard M. Shiffrin. *Department of Psychology, Indiana University, Bloomington, IN 47405, USA.* Email: shiffrin@indiana.edu

Patrick Suppes. *Ventura Hall, Stanford University, Stanford, CA 94305-4115, USA.* Email: suppes@ockham.stanford.edu

James T. Townsend. *Department of Psychology, Indiana University, Bloomington, IN 47405, USA.* Email: jtownsen@ucs.indiana.edu

Sherman Tsein. *Model Based Measurement Laboratory, Department of Education, 210 Education Bldg., Champaign, IL 61820, USA.* Email: stsien@s.psych.uiuc.edu

Detlof von Winterfeldt. *Decision Insights, Inc., 4590 MacArthur Blvd., Suite 500 Newport Beach, CA 92660, USA.* Email: detlof@aol.com

Elke U. Weber. *Department of Psychology, The Ohio State University, 1885 Neil Avenue, Columbus, OH 43210.* Email: weber.211@osu.edu

John K. Williams. *Department of Cognitive Sciences, University of California, Irvine, CA 92697, USA.* Email: jwilliam@aris.ss.uci.edu

John I. Yellott, Jr. *Department of Cognitive Sciences, University of California, Irvine, CA 92697, USA.* Email: jyellott@uci.edu

Choice, Decision, and Measurement
A. A. J. Marley (Ed.),
©Lawrence Erlbaum Associates, NJ, 1997.

LIST OF REFEREES

F. G. Ashby

J. Balakrishan

M. H. Birnbaum

B. Bloxom

A. Brothers

J. Busemeyer

Y.-H. Cho

J.-P. Doignon

E. N. Dzhafarov

W. K. Estes

J.-Cl. Falmagne

D. Heyer

H. Hughes

D. H. Krantz

D. Laberge

Y. Lacouture

K. Lamberts

C. Lewis

L. Lopes

R. D. Luce

B. A. Mellers

J. Miyamoto

A. Munnich

R. M. Nosofsky

S. Pekec

M. Regenwetter

F. S. Roberts

R. M. Shiffrin

R. Suck

J. T. Townsend

D. von Winterfeldt

P. P. Wakker

E. U. Weber

J. I. Yellott

PART 1

INTRODUCTION

Choice, Decision, and Measurement
A. A. J. Marley (Ed.),
©Lawrence Erlbaum Associates, NJ, 1997.

THE PAST SEVEN YEARS: 1988-95

R. DUNCAN LUCE

University of California, Irvine

ABSTRACT. In 1989 my then scientific autobiography (Luce, 1989) concluded:
"At that point [early 1988] I did take early retirement from Harvard, but the
next five to ten years promise not to be idle." These few pages take up the
ensuing seven years, which indeed have not been idle. (Perhaps the problem
is that I've never taken up golf.) For example, 32 papers have appeared in
journals and book chapters, half a dozen are in various pre-publication stages,
and three books have appeared: the much belated volumes II and III of the
Foundations of Measurement (Luce, Krantz, Suppes, & Tversky, 1990; Suppes,
Krantz, Luce, & Tversky, 1989) and a textbook, based on the core course given
at Harvard and repeated several times at UCI, *Sound & Hearing* (Luce, 1993).
Although favorably reviewed, it has not spawned the courses I had hoped it
might.

1. RESEARCH THEMES

During the period from 1975 through the late 1980's roughly half of my work
centered on the representational (or axiomatic or algebraic) theory of measurement.
Although we are far from completing that program of research – witness the list of 15
open problems suggested in Luce and Narens (1994) – much of my research energy
has shifted from the abstract themes to more concrete attempts to apply what
we have learned about measurement theory to empirically interesting problems.
Several things lay behind the shift: criticism of representational measurement as
seemingly irrelevant to substantive issues, e.g. Cliff (1992), but also see Narens and
Luce (1993), my own scientific disposition to develop theory that makes empirical
predictions and to test these, and perhaps some attenuation of my abstract skills
which is said to occur with age – although occasionally it seems to be less of an issue
than is commonly believed, witness, e.g., Patrick Suppes. In any event, beginning
with Luce (1988), I began participating in the rather lively developments in our
understanding of how to measure utility.

Key words and phrases. Scale type, joint receipt, rank-dependent utility, sign-dependent
utility, relation of riskless and risky utility, weighting functions.

Acknowledgments. I thank A. A. J. Marley and Peter Fishburn for useful comments on
an earlier draft of these remarks. Also, I appreciate Dr. Marley's efforts in bringing about this
volume.

Address for correspondence. R. Duncan Luce, Institute for Mathematical Behavioral Sciences,
Social Science Plaza, University of California, Irvine, CA 92697-5100. Email: rdluce@uci.edu

Applications of Measurement Theory to Utility Theory. Much recent economic literature on individual decision making under risk[1] and under uncertainty has focused on how to adapt the subjective expected utility (SEU) model of Savage (1954) to some of the empirical findings that seem to undermine the basic tenets of rationality embodied in that model. Two main avenues have been pursued. One, mostly followed by economists and well summarized by one of its originators J. Quiggin (Quiggin, 1993), focused on weakening what economists call the independence axiom, which is explicated below, and deriving from modifications of that axiom and the other axioms new forms of the numerical representation. The other tack, mostly pursued by psychologists, involved directly modifying the SEU representation to accommodate some of the empirical anomalies. The most important example of this approach was D. Kahneman and A. Tversky's prospect theory (Kahneman & Tversky, 1979) which, beyond doubt, has been more widely cited than any other paper in this area in the past few decades. It seemed to me that both approaches had significant difficulties, and part of my effort was to try to overcome them.

Economists often begin by restricting the domain of alternatives to lotteries: money consequences with known probabilities. They interpret such lotteries as random variables with probability distributions over money. That seems innocent enough, a mere mathematical notation for a lottery. But, empirically, it isn't innocent at all for the following simple reason. Suppose X and Y are random variables and λ is a probability, i.e., a number between 0 and 1. Then

$$Z = \lambda X + (1 - \lambda)Y$$

is the mixture random variable having the distribution

$$\Pr[Z = z] = \lambda \Pr[X = z] + (1 - \lambda) \Pr[Y = z].$$

The mathematics of random variable theory automatically reduces any compound mixture lottery to its equivalent first order form. No distinction is made among compound random variables having the same bottom line. It is unlikely that people treat them as the same, and substantial empirical data support differential treatment except for the simplest reductions. Nonetheless, that strong assumption is built into the meaning of random variables.

The problem is illustrated vividly by the following example of consequence monotonicity and its reduced form in the case of random variable representations. Suppose g, g', and h are lotteries (not interpreted as random variables) and λ, $0 < \lambda < 1$, is a probability. Then a compound lottery can be formed as $(g, \lambda; h)$, meaning that when the chance experiment underlying λ is run, one receives g with probability λ and h with probability $1 - \lambda$. Let $g \succsim h$ denote a weak preference ordering, where $g \succ h$ denotes that g is strictly preferred to h, $g \sim h$ denotes that g and h are indifferent, and $\succsim = \succ \cup \sim$. A major assumption of rational behavior

---

[1] *Risk* is the term used when the consequences in the gamble have known probabilities of arising, whereas *uncertainty* refers to cases involving chance events for which their probabilities are either not known or appear to be inherently unknowable. *Riskless* choice concerns cases where chance plays no role in the consequence received.

in many theories, called *consequence monotonicity*, is:

$$g' \succsim g \text{ if and only if } (g', \lambda; h) \succsim (g, \lambda; h). \tag{1}$$

In words, replacing one consequence by another that is viewed as better improves matters. Now, suppose we think of g, g', and h as random variables, say $\mathbf{X}$, $\mathbf{X}'$, and $\mathbf{Y}$, respectively. Then in the usual random variable notation we write the above condition as:

$$\mathbf{X}' \succsim \mathbf{X} \text{ if and only if } \lambda\mathbf{X}' + (1-\lambda)\mathbf{Z} \succsim \lambda\mathbf{X} + (1-\lambda)\mathbf{Z}. \tag{2}$$

This property is called the *independence axiom*. The problem is that although it seems equivalent to consequence monotonicity, it really is not because it also assumes that one can reduce the compound form to its equivalent first order form. No such property holds for consequence monotonicity unless it is explicitly assumed.

Early in the history of utility theory for lotteries, M. Allais (Allais, 1953) described a compelling thought experiment where people violate independence; subsequently this and variants on it were confirmed experimentally (for summaries of much empirical work concerning the SEU model, see Schoemaker, 1982, 1990). Despite the fact that others, e.g. Brothers (1990) and Kahneman and Tversky (1979), provided evidence that, when the compound lotteries are presented without reduction to their first order form, consequence monotonicity holds, economists have continued to model alternatives as random variables and attempted to weaken the independence property. It seemed obvious to me that one should be very cautious, indeed, about invoking the reduction property of random variables, in which case it might be possible to retain the highly rational property of consequence monotonicity[2]. That observation has been one of three foundation stones of my work.

A second foundation stone, hardly original, is that the distinction between gains and losses matters greatly. The economist H. Markowitz (Markowitz, 1952) and the psychologist W. Edwards (Edwards, 1962) were among the first to emphasize that fact and to point out that the extant theories ignored it. But once again the paper that made a real difference on this score was Kahneman and Tversky (1979). The issue of how gains and losses are to be defined is still far from resolved. In experiments we typically treat no exchange of money to define the status quo, and any addition to the status quo is a gain and any reduction from it is a loss. But we are acutely aware that this is inadequate. For a person desperately in need of $100, a "net win" of $50 in an evening at a casino may functionally seem more like a loss than a gain. More commonly, a choice set of gambles may define a temporary status quo somewhere between the smallest and largest possible consequences.

---

[2]This is not the place to go into much detail, but it should be mentioned that M. H. Birnbaum and B. A. Mellers (Birnbaum, 1992b; Mellers, Weiss, & Birnbaum, 1992b) have argued from their data that consequence monotonicity fails when one of the consequences is no exchange of money and the consequences are evaluated in terms of a judged monetary certainty equivalence – the sum of money the person judges to be indifferent to the gamble. von Winterfeldt, Chung, Luce, and Cho (1997) questioned their use of judged certainty equivalents and provided choice-based data that cast in some doubt the conclusion that monotonicity fails in these cases. Various sources of evidence should make one very wary of assuming judged certainty equivalents are really the same as monetary indifferences to gambles.

So the problem has been partitioned into developing theories in which the status quo is assumed to exist and gains and losses are carefully distinguished and in working out theories to describe how the status quo or reference levels are constructed. The former theories are by now rather well developed. But, for all practical purposes, no work on the latter has begun in any serious way. I have been unable to come up with a useful empirical way to estimate reference levels and, beyond what is in Luce, Mellers, and Chang (1993), I know of no theoretical proposals. L. L. Lopes has studied experimentally the impact of various distributions of money on reference levels (Lopes, 1984, 1987).

The third foundation stone is the observation that utility can be constructed for riskless consequences[3] using a binary operation rather than studying the trade-off between consequences and chance, which has been the basis of all theories of weighted or expected utilities. The operation, which I have called *joint receipt*, is the simplest thing in the world. You often receive two or more things at once: checks and bills in the mail, gifts on birthdays and holidays, purchases when shopping, etc. The key fact is that if x and y are valued objects, then their joint receipt, which I denote by $x \oplus y$, is also a valued "object." This basis for measurement is much like that underlying the measurement of mass, and indeed the pan balance analogy seems quite close.

These are the ideas that I have been able to pursue with some success. The details are far too complex to cover here in detail, but the main outlines are describable. Let e denote the status quo and consider for the moment just gains, i.e., consequences x such that $x \succsim e$. We assume, in all cases, that $e \sim (e, E; e)$ and that the utility function U has the property $U(e) = 0$, where e is the status quo. (In many cases this is forced by assumed properties.) Observe that we have potentially four distinct ways to construct such a utility function:

(1) The first measure is based on binary gambles of gains. Much of the recent literature, including experimental papers, suggests that a *rank-dependent weighted average* form works in which the weight assigned to an event depends not only on that event, as in SEU, but also on the rank order position of its consequence among all of the consequences of that gamble. In the binary case, where $(x, E; y)$ means a chance device is run and x is received if the event E occurs and y is received if E fails to occur, the utility for gains x, y ($\succsim e$) has the rank-dependent form

$$U_1(x, E; y) = \begin{cases} U_1(x)W_1^+(E) + U_1(y)[1 - W_1^+(E)] & \text{if } x \succ y \\ U_1(x) & \text{if } x \sim y \\ U_1(x)[1 - W_1^+(\neg E)] + U_1(y)W_1^+(\neg E) & \text{if } y \succ x, \end{cases} \qquad (3)$$

where $\neg E$ denotes the complement of E relative to the chance device. P. P. Wakker has provided an axiomatization (Wakker, 1989) of this form which basically rests

---

[3]Such a riskless utility measure can be extended to gambles by finding their certainty equivalents, the sum of money perceived by the subject as indifferent to the gamble. But as Cho and Luce (1995) showed empirically, this may not be without difficulties for it appears that the joint receipt of two gambles may not be indifferent to the joint receipt of their respective certainty equivalents. We do not yet know whether this is a significant finding or simply evidence that our estimates of certainty equivalents are biased, which I suspect can occur for skewed psychometric functions and/or skewed gambles. This possibility is under investigation.

on assuming the usual SEU-type axioms separately for the two regions of $x \succ y$ and $y \succ x$.

Generalizations of the rank-dependent form are found in many articles, many of which are summarized in Quiggin (1993). Others include Liu (1995), Luce and Fishburn (1991, 1995), and Tversky and Kahneman (1992). The treatment by Liu is especially economical.

(2) The second measure is also based on binary gambles, but now of a gain and a loss. Here two different weighting functions arise, one when the consequence attached to an event is a gain and a different one when it is a loss:

$$U_2(x^+, E; y^-) = U_2(x^+)W_2^+(E) + U_2(y^-)W_2^-(\neg E) \tag{4}$$

Because in general $W_2(E) + W_2(\neg E) \neq 1$ and $e \sim (e, E; e)$, it follows immediately that Equation 4 forces $U(e) = 0$. The form in Equation 4 was first postulated in Kahneman and Tversky (1979). It, together with a generalization of Equation 3 to gambles with finitely many consequences, has been axiomatized in Luce and Fishburn (1991, 1995), and Wakker and Tversky (1993). The trick used in the latter paper is basically to assume the SEU axioms hold in the regions defined by gains and losses and by order among the consequences. The former one builds the axiom system in terms of joint receipts (see below).

Some of the properties of binary systems with $U_1 = U_2$ are discussed in Luce and von Winterfeldt (1994). Of course, an obvious question is when does $U_1 = U_2$ and $W_1^+ = W_2^+$? This is easily seen to come down to consequence monotonicity of the gambles.

There is another property of binary gambles, which is appreciably weaker than Equations 3 and 4, that plays an important role. A utility function U is said to be *separable* if there exist functions $W^{(k)}, k = +, -$, over events such that

$$U(x, E; e) = U(x)W^{(k)}(E), \quad k = \begin{cases} + & \text{if } x \succsim e, \\ - & \text{if } x \precsim e. \end{cases} \tag{5}$$

If $\mathcal{C}$ denotes the set of consequences and $\mathcal{E}$ the set of events, Equation 5 means that $\langle \mathcal{C} \times \mathcal{E}, \succsim \rangle$ satisfies the axioms of additive conjoint measurement (Krantz, Luce, Suppes, & Tversky, 1971, see Chapter 3). Tversky (1967) provided a direct test of this representation and found it held; however, W was not finitely additive, which of course was inconsistent with SEU. The key axioms of additive conjoint measurement are monotonicity and the Thomsen condition. The latter can be shown to be equivalent to the empirically testable condition called *status-quo event commutativity*[4]:

$$((x, E; e), D; e) \sim ((x, D; e), E; e)) \tag{6}$$

The empirical literature on this property is somewhat mixed. Using a forced choice procedure between the two sides, Ronen (1971, 1973) showed a pronounced preference for the side in which the first event is more probable. Since the choice is forced, the only distinction available is the order of events: apparently most subjects agreed to resolve the quandary in the same way. Results of Brothers (1990) are complex, but using choice-based certainty equivalents, Brothers found some

---

[4]It is called just *event commutativity* if Equation 6 holds for an arbitrary y in place of e.

support for Equation 6. And pursuing the same approach more carefully, Chung, von Winterfeldt, and Luce (1994) found support for it in 22 of 25 subjects. One advantage of using certainty equivalents is that one avoids forcing subjects to make a choice.

(3) A quite different way to measure utility of gains is based on the ordering and joint receipt of just gains. Assuming that joint receipt, denoted by $\oplus$, is commutative, Luce and Fishburn (1991, 1995) have modeled joint receipts of gains as an extensive structure – the same type of structure as underlies much physical measurement such as mass, length, and charge. This is surely the case if, for money consequences, it is true that $x \oplus y = x + y$, as Tversky and Kahneman (1992) claimed and as Cho and Luce (1995) established experimentally for gains and losses separately. However, Thaler (1985), using a classroom questionnaire, found evidence that additivity of money held for losses but not for gains. I do not really understand the inconsistency in these empirical results, although I suspect that the scenarios used in Thaler (1985) carry a lot of extraneous meaning beyond the simple concept of joint receipt.

Although the assumption of an extensive structure means there is an additive numerical representation, we do not take that to be the utility measure, but rather a representation of the form

$$U_3(x \oplus y) = U_3(x) + U_3(y) - U_3(x)U_3(y)/C, \qquad C > 0 \qquad (7)$$

where $0 \leq U_3(x) \leq C$ follows from monotonicity of $\oplus$. It may seem odd to use a bounded, non-additive representation when an additive one exists, but the reason is that the non-additive one is compatible with other measures of utility and the additive one is not. Note that by assuming $e \sim e \oplus e$, $U(e) = 0$ is forced by Equation 7.

(4) The fourth and last measure is based on the trade-off of joint receipts between gains and losses. Let x^+ denote a gain and y^- a loss. Then we assume that the underlying operation has the properties of an additive conjoint structure and so has a representation

$$U_4(x^+ \oplus y^-) = U_4(x^+) + U_4(y^-). \qquad (8)$$

As noted earlier, there is a well-known axiomatization for such a representation.

Some interesting properties of joint receipt coupled with certainty equivalents of gambles are described in Luce (1995b) and tested in Cho and Luce (1995).

The basic theoretical questions my colleagues and I have worked on are: What properties lead to the various possible equalities among the measures: $U_1 = U_3, U_2 = U_4$, and $U_3 = U_4$? And how do these properties fare empirically? Of course, completely analogous questions arise for the utility of losses, and the same empirical questions have to be explored. The mathematics for gains and losses is essentially the same, except for parameter differences, and so it need not be duplicated, but of course we cannot take for granted that gains and losses exhibit the same properties empirically. To outline fully all of the properties and what is known about them would take far too much space. An example concerns the relation of U_1 and U_3.

The following empirical property is called *segregation*: For gains x and y,

$$(x, E; e) \oplus y \sim (x \oplus y, E; y). \tag{9}$$

Note the highly rational character of this reduction condition. On both sides it says that $x \oplus y$ is the consequence if E occurs and $e \oplus y \sim y$ if E does not occur. Empirical evidence supporting segregation is provided by both Cho and Luce (1995) and Cho, Luce, and von Winterfeldt (1994).

Segregation was implicitly invoked in Kahneman and Tversky (1979), and Pfanzagl (1959) explored its implications without any constraint on the domain of consequences, leading to a result too strong for our purposes.

Consider now the following properties:

(a) Segregation (Equation 9).

(b) U_1 satisfies Equation 3 and weak subadditivity $U_1(x \oplus x) \le 2U_1(x)$.

(c) U_3 is separable (Equation 5) and satisfies the representation of Equation 7.

Luce and Fishburn (1991, 1995) have shown that any two imply the third with $U_1 = U_3$. The fact that (a) and (b) imply Equation 7 is, of course, a good reason for using the non-additive representation rather than the additive one. This is analogous to the fact that physicists use a non-additive representation of relativistic velocity despite the fact that an additive one exists (in which the "speed" of light is ∞). They do this for several reasons, one being that a defining property of velocity (namely, velocity equals distance travelled divided by time taken) holds for the non-additive representation but not the additive one.

One feature of the above result is that (a) plus (c) provides an axiomatization of the rank-dependent form that does not presuppose knowing that rank dependence will arise. But as an axiomatization it has the major weakness that U is assumed to be separable as well as satisfying Equation 7. Why should this be? I show in Luce (1996) that if U is separable and satisfies Equation 7, then the following property holds: For any gains x, y, and event E, there is an event $D = D(x, E)$ such that

$$(x \oplus y, E; e) \sim (x, E; e) \oplus (y, D; e) \tag{10}$$

Moreover, using mathematical results of Aczél, Luce, and Maksa (1996), I have shown[5] that if Equation 10 holds and if there are separable utility functions and also ones that satisfy Equation 7 and a pair is related by a function that along with its inverse is differentiable, then there are ones that are both separable and satisfy Equation 7.

The case of separable utility for joint receipt of mixed consequences results in a condition similar to Equation 10.

Neither of these behavioral properties has yet been explored empirically, and it may prove difficult to do so because of their existential character.

The major linking property between U_2 and U_4, analogous to segregation, is called *duplex decomposition*:

$$(x, E; y) \sim (x, E', e) \oplus (e, E''; y) \tag{11}$$

---

[5]As stated, this is misleading. I reduced this and two other problems like it to solving functional equations. After some very partial progress, I posed them to J. Aczél and after some e-mail and FAX correspondence he and Gy. Maksa did solve them.

where E' and E'' mean that E arises in two independent realizations of the underlying chance experiment. Slovic and Lichtenstein (1968) first noted that this property was sustained empirically, and Cho et al. (1994) reconfirmed that it held using somewhat different methods. Note that it is a decidedly non-rational property: on the left either x^+ or y^- but not both must arise whereas on the right there are additional possibilities, $x^+ \oplus y^-$ and $e \oplus e \sim e$. Nevertheless it seems to hold. It is worth emphasizing that this is the sole source of non-rationality, and so deviation from SEU, in this entire complex of ideas.

Representational Theory of Measurement. Although utility has been my greatest focus during this period, general measurement issues have not been completely abandoned. First, Luce (1992a) presented a general theory of ordered structures with a monotonic[6] operation of order n and with finitely many singular points, where an element is singular if it is fixed under all automorphisms[7] of the structure. If the structure is homogeneous[8] between adjacent singular points, then one can show that there are most three singular points: a minimum, a maximum, and an interior one. Some of their properties were established, and a numerical representation was developed by patching together ones from the theory with no singular points (Alper, 1987; Narens, 1981a, 1981b). This work was heavily motivated by the models that had arisen in utility theory, and it offers a possible generalization of the linear weighted forms should they prove inadequate.

Second, a major finding in the representational theory of measurement was the formulation and partial results of Narens (1981a, 1981b), later completed in Alper (1987), to the effect that when a structure on the real continuum is homogeneous and finitely unique[9], then it has a numerical representation in which the admissible scale types lie between ratio (i.e., similarity) transformations and interval (i.e., positive affine) transformations. I have considered the question of whether one can dispense with the real continuum and replace it by Archimedean assumptions. With the help of T. M. Alper, this has been done. Let a *translation* be any automorphism with no fixed point and a *dilation* be one with at least one fixed point. The conditions are that, for the asymptotic order on the group of automorphisms, the order is connected, the set of translations is Archimedean relative to itself, the set of dilations is Archimedean relative to all automorphisms, and the structure is homogeneous. I had hoped that, as is true for theories of additive structures, the continuum case could be shown to be a special case of the Archimedean one, but so far this proof has eluded us.

Third, given our better understanding of measurement structures I reopened the issue I first approached in Luce (1959b), namely why are psychophysical matching functions of various sorts so often power functions. The trouble with the 1959

---

[6]The definition of monotonicity requires some delicacy at singular points.

[7]An *automorphism* is an isomorphism of the structure onto itself or what physicists refer to as a *symmetry*.

[8]Homogeneity means, intuitively, that elements cannot be distinguished by their properties. Formally, it is defined as follows: For any two elements x and y between a pair of adjacent singular points, there is an automorphism of the structure that takes x into y.

[9]A structure is finitely unique if there is an integer N such that whenever an automorphism has N fixed points it must be the identity.

paper, and more generally of many presentations of dimensional analysis, is a difficulty in distinguishing at the representational level between a change of units and a translation of the stimuli. These are far from the same thing – the one being a systematic change of stimuli and the other a systematic change of notation – and yet in ratio scale representations both appear at the representational level simply as multiplication by positive constants.[10] In Luce (1990b) I showed that if a matching relation exhibited what I called *translation consistency*, which was formulated entirely in terms of translations of the two physical continua involved, then a power function had to hold in the physical ratio scale representations. This result has been subsumed in the much deeper work that Narens reports in a chapter of this volume.

2. PERSONS, PLACES, AND EVENTS

Mathematical Behavioral Sciences at University of California, Irvine (UCI). From UCI's perspective, my major role in coming was to bring some structure to the existing interdisciplinary strength in mathematical modeling in the School of Social Sciences, to help augment it with new appointments, and to achieve greater national and international recognition. This effort began with the creation in 1988 of the Irvine Research Unit (IRU) in Mathematical Behavioral Sciences of which I was appointed director. These IRUs are five year creations of the campus that either sunset or are converted, via a somewhat tortuous process, to Organized Research Units (ORU) of the University of California, which are pretty much assured a 15 year or greater lifetime. A great many of them are focused on fairly explicit research topics, but some, like ours, are more generic. We went through the hurdles and became an ORU in 1992 with the name Institute for Mathematical Behavioral Sciences.

The basic organization of the Institute is into five distinct (but somewhat overlapping) subgroups:

> Axiomatic measurement theory and foundational issues.
> Statistical modeling.
> Individual decision making.
> Perception and psychophysics.
> Social and economic phenomena:
> > social networks,
> > public choice,
> > macroeconomics and game theory.

We do not cover the important area of complex, adaptive systems. There is some work of this type on campus – in computer science, engineering, and psychobiology – but we have no such focus of strength in the Institute. This lack is one we have so far failed to overcome, due in part to budgetary problems discussed below and

---

[10]This is not always the case. For example, Equation 7 is invariant under a change of unit – multiplication by a positive constant – provided the dimensional constant C is also changed in this way. But this transformation does not correspond to an automorphism of the underlying operation which for this representation is of the form $U \to U' = C[1-(1-U/C)^k]$ for some $k > 0$. An analogous situation holds for relativistic velocity.

in part to the difficulty of beginning something new of this degree of popularity by making one appointment at a time.

An IRU or an ORU lies on one dimension of a matrix organization in which the other dimension is departments. Almost all appointments are in departments, which of course carry much of the burden of teaching, especially at the undergraduate level. Some teaching, mostly at the graduate level, arises from the existence of interdisciplinary Ph.D. programs. We proposed one in mathematical behavioral sciences, with membership nearly co-extensive to that of the Institute (which technically supports only research – as if teaching and research are clearly distinguishable at the graduate level), and it was approved in 1989. To get this started, we applied for and received in 1990 a five year NSF Research and Training grant.

One consequence of this matrix structure is that I report jointly to the Vice Chancellor for Research, who provides the budget, and the Dean of Social Sciences, who provides all sorts of support, including space, and who controls the allocation of faculty positions. I have been very fortunate to have extremely cordial relations with William Schonfeld, our dean. He is not the least bit quantitative – except for being a master of budgets – or mathematical, and yet he has been an enthusiastic supporter of the Institute. During the past seven years we have had three Vice Chancellors for Research. The position is currently held by an applied mathematician, Frederick Wan, who has some understanding of and, I believe, sympathy for what we do.

The major activities of the Institute have been a colloquium series (about 25 per year), 7 conferences (mostly in the summer) in various areas of mathematical behavioral sciences, partial support of visiting scholars, and the development and maintenance of a somewhat elaborate computer system. In addition, during the period of the training grant, we had a number of Institute postdoctoral fellows.

All of these activities were initiated in an era when the campus, and the whole UC system, was planning a then demographically plausible 40% expansion by the year 2005. We were hiring at all levels and some of those added strength to the Institute, for example, Chew Soo-Hong and Stergios Skaperdas in Economics and Barbara Dosher, Jean-Claude Falmagne, and George Sperling in Cognitive Sciences. No one at the time anticipated the collapse of the Soviet Union and the resulting massive cut back of jobs in California defense industries, which was a major factor in sharp reductions in state funds to UC – roughly a drop of 25%. Another major contributing factor was ballot initiatives, passed by the voters, that have long-term adverse consequences for the UC system by shifting the balance of funds away from higher education into K-12 education and into the criminal justice system ("Three strikes and you're out"). As this transfer increases, per force UC is increasingly becoming a private institution.

It is unclear to what degree UC, and UCI in particular, will be altered in accomplishing the necessary adjustment. The impacts of these changes and, more generally, of somewhat similar national trends are already significant. I will cite several that concern us. Until academic year 1995-96, faculty growth was decidedly attenuated and, what growth there was, was mostly at the junior level. The applicant pool of graduate students, except for foreign ones, seems reduced, especially in areas involving mathematics. And academic job placement is difficult.

This seems to be a significant problem for students with an interdisciplinary bent because departments seem to be narrowing their disciplinary foci.

One impact, personally favorable, was that UC reacted to the budget cuts by offering generous "early retirement" to senior faculty, thus transferring them from the operating budget to the apparently over-funded retirement fund, and replacing them by less expensive junior faculty. Once retired, I and others were recalled to continue in various capacities, in my case, to continue directing the Institute, to teach some graduate seminars, and to continue supervising the four (now three after one received a Ph.D. in December of 1995) graduate students working with me. This strongly appealed to me because increasingly I found myself out of touch with the undergraduates. Nominally I am 49% time; functionally, full time.

National Scene. During this period I continued to participate in several national activities: 1987-90 as a member of the Executive Committee of the Society for Judgment and Decision Making; 1988-91, President of the Federation of Behavioral, Psychological, and Cognitive Sciences; 1989-91 on the Board of Directors of the American Psychological Society; 1992-94 as a member of the National Research Council's Committee on National Needs for Biomedical and Behavioral Research; 1993-95, Outside Visiting Committee for the Beckman Institute, University of Illinois; 1993-95 on the American Psychological Association's Board of Scientific Affairs; and 1994-97 on the NRC's Board for the Mathematical Sciences. Much of this effort has focused on creating and managing subgroups that worked on various intellectual problems having some sort of widespread implications. At times I found the lack of content and the political battles of various constituencies frustrating, but that seems to be in the nature of this kind of service.

Personal. Despite some of the problems arising from the UC cutback and some background anxiety about earthquakes, I have been very pleased by our move to southern California. I greatly enjoy the kind of outdoor living that is possible year round. Even in winter, unless it is raining, Carolyn, our cat Heidi[11], and I regularly lunch out of doors. Our garden and patio, although of modest size, has an expansive view of over 180 degrees looking out over all of Orange and (on clear days) Los Angeles counties and to the mountain range including Mount Baldy, some 80 miles away. Despite the garden's small size, it somehow manages to absorb more of our time tending and revising it than we had expected. Perhaps that is good given that gardening is my sole form of exercise.

I had been somewhat apprehensive about how Carolyn, a tried and true New Englander, would take to life here. After some months of adjustment, she began to take a lively interest in the incredibly varied landscape of California and the southwest. We quite regularly take automobile trips to various places, sometimes staying a week in one place and venturing forth from there. This has been fostered by our buying a time share condominium in Palm Springs. We never use it ourselves, but bank it for exchange with similar condominia located in spots we would like to visit – Kauai, Flagstaff, Santa Fe, and the like.

---

[11] Her name is a terrible pun on the fact that she, the shyest cat I've ever known, hides when anyone new comes into the house.

Since 1991 it has been marvelous to have my daughter, Aurora, in California, first at Marymount College in Palo Verdes and then St. Mary's College in Moraga. We have seen a good deal more of her than when she was in Brazil and, of course, she has become thoroughly acculturated.

A number of honors have been bestowed on me. In 1994 UCI awarded me a Distinguished Lectureship for Research and I was elected to the American Philosophical Society. That summer a conference was held in Keil, Germany, which jointly honored the memory of Herman von Helmholtz and me – hardly comparable contributors, but flattering. 1995 was my 70th year – a chronological fact decidedly at variance with my internal self image. In May, Carolyn hosted a lovely birthday luncheon of friends from the area. In August, UCI, in conjunction with the Society for Mathematical Psychology, honored me with a symposium and banquet at which some past students, A. A. J. Marley and Elke Weber, and some old professional colleagues, Richard Atkinson, David Green, William McGill, and Patrick Suppes, spoke, each in his or her own way reminding me of past associations and work. Jack Yellott of UCI served as the suave master of ceremonies. The present volume arose, in part, from this symposium. And in September, the European Mathematical Psychology Group, meeting in Regensberg, Germany also held a symposium and banquet in my honor, both arranged by Jan Drössler, and with charming remarks at the banquet by Edward (Eddy) Roskam. Although flattering and a source of lovely memories, all in all I'm happy this phase is over. Shy people become uneasy with such attention.

PART 2

DECISION MAKING AND RISK

Choice, Decision, and Measurement
A. A. J. Marley (Ed.),
©Lawrence Erlbaum Associates, NJ, 1997.

BOOKENDS: RECOLLECTIONS OF A DECISION THEORIST

PETER FISHBURN

AT&T Research

ABSTRACT. Duncan Luce's enduring contributions to several fields of inquiry have helped define their present configurations and will continue to challenge other researchers to explore new directions. My own work on decision theory and related areas illustrates the point. Duncan's influence on that work since the early 1960s has manifested itself in ways both obvious and subtle. It is a pleasure to recount a few of my personal and intellectual debts to a good friend and master craftsman.

1. INTRODUCTION

The invitation to write about Duncan Luce's influence on my research in decision theory during a career that began thirty-five years ago is both an honor and a source of apprehension. The honor of thanking one of this century's pre-eminent decision theorists needs no amplification. But I am apprehensive about adequately expressing my debt to a man and his work that have affected my own research so powerfully for so many years. Perhaps I can best convey the measure of his influence by recalling a few statistics and sharing a few thoughts on mutual research interests.

I first met Duncan in the mid-1960s at the University of Pennsylvania, where he invited me to give a seminar, and at a summer workshop on mathematical psychology at the University of Michigan. By then I was familiar with Duncan's *Individual Choice Behavior* (1959) and *Games and Decisions* (1957), the latter written jointly with Howard Raiffa. Although the details of our first contacts are now vague, I recall with pleasure meeting the person whose ideas and extraordinary ability to clearly express them in writing have influenced me and many others in the intervening years.

That influence was already evident in my first publication, *Decision and Value Theory* (1964), which referenced his 1957 and 1959 books along with other seminal works by Russ Ackoff, West Churchman, Frank P. Ramsey, Jimmie Savage, and the game-theory duo John von Neumann and Oskar Morgenstern. Many years later, in the acknowledgments to my eighth and perhaps final book, *Nonlinear Preference and Utility Theory* (1988), I paid tribute to Duncan and others in the following words:

Key words and phrases. Decision theory, interval orders, joint receipt.

Address for correspondence. Peter Fishburn, AT&T Labs-Research, Murray Hill, NJ 07974. Email: fish@research.att.com

It is a distinct pleasure to acknowledge and thank teachers and colleagues who have shared their interest and expertise in decision theory with me during the past three decades. Russ Ackoff and Jimmie Savage were my two great teachers in the subject. In more recent years I have been strongly influenced by the careful experimental research and incisive thinking of Duncan Luce and Amos Tversky.

I could add that the formative guidance of Russ and Jimmie had subsided by the late 1960s, whereas Duncan's influence and encouragement has remained strong for the past thirty years. It is almost certainly true, for example, that he has been an associate editor or referee for more of my articles than any other person. That has been no small task, and in so far as one can discern such things, Duncan has always handled it with respect and care.

A more visible statistic came to light when I checked my books' citations. Only Duncan and Pat Suppes are referenced in all eight. Von Neumann and Morgenstern and Savage have greater citation totals because of frequent references to their pathbreaking axiomatizations of expected utility in *Theory of Games and Economic Behavior* (1944) and *The Foundations of Statistics* (1954), but my overall research interests have intersected more with those of Duncan and Pat than with the others.

Another telling statistic concerns joint authorship. I have been blessed by scores of co-authors over the years, but Duncan is the only one included in the preceding list of major influences. Russ Ackoff and Jimmie Savage were instrumental in several early publications but preferred to remain in the background. This might be true also of Duncan, but in any case our jointly authored work is quite recent. I say more about it in Section 4 after recalling events that involved Duncan and significantly affected my life and research career.

2. INTERVALS

While employed in the Advanced Research Department at the Research Analysis Corporation (RAC) in the 1960s, I set out to learn what I could about preference and utility theory. Among hundreds of articles examined, one that intrigued me was Duncan's 1956 paper *Semiorders and a theory of utility discrimination*. It is his earliest work that I have cited, and its impact has been huge.

Semiorders showed that the traditional idea of precise preference orders could be relaxed to accommodate imprecision and just noticeable differences in a way that still allows nicely structured utility representations. An economist, W. E. Armstrong, had discussed similar ideas several years earlier, but Duncan coined the term *semiorder* and provided it with an elegant axiomatic foundation. Dean and Keller (1968), who were unaware of the earlier work, used the phrase "normal natural partial ordering" for the same concept, but fortunately their name did not catch on.

A few years after Duncan wrote *Semiorders*, Scott and Suppes (1958) proved that if the set X on which a strict preference relation $\succ$ is defined is finite, then $(X, \succ)$ is a semiorder if and only if there is a mapping u from X into the reals such that, for all $x, y \in X$,

$$x \succ y \Leftrightarrow u(x) > u(y) + 1 .$$

That is, x is preferred to y if and only if a unit interval $[u(x), u(x) + 1]$ for x everywhere exceeds a unit interval $[u(y), u(y) + 1]$ for y. In this representation 1, which is easily converted to any constant $c > 0$ by rescaling u, measures a just noticeable difference so that x and y are judged indifferent, or $x \sim y$, if and only if $|u(x) - u(y)| \leq 1$. Intransitive indifference arises when one interval overlaps two disjoint intervals:

$$x \sim z \sim y \text{ but } x \succ y.$$

A semiorder combines intransitive indifference and the notion of a uniform threshold of discriminability. This may be appropriate for a unidimensional source of discriminability, such as the number of grains of sugar in one's coffee, but is problematic when multiple factors affect a person's ability to distinguish differences between objects, or even when a single source manifests itself in different degrees. A generalization of the semiorder representation that retains its lineal feature and allows multiple inclusions and nested intervals, for example

models a wider range of judgmental phenomena than the uniform-threshold model, including some aspects just noted.

The more general variable-threshold model was developed in my *Intransitive indifference with unequal indifference intervals* (1970). It is a modest paper but has probably been cited more than any other I've written. The name for the partial order $(X, \succ)$ underlying the model, which was proposed by a still-anonymous referee, is "interval order".

Formally, $(X, \succ)$ is an *interval order* if $\succ$ on X is irreflexive (we never have $x \succ x$) and if, for all $x, y, a, b \in X$,

$$x \succ y \text{ and } a \succ b \Rightarrow x \succ b \text{ or } a \succ y.$$

When X is finite, $(X, \succ)$ is an interval order if and only if there are mappings u and ρ from X into the reals with ρ positive such that, for all $x, y \in X$,

$$x \succ y \Leftrightarrow u(x) > u(y) + \rho(y).$$

Here ρ is the threshold function and x's indifference interval is $[u(x), u(x) + \rho(x)]$. If we add the condition that $x \succ y \succ z \Rightarrow (x \succ a \text{ or } a \succ z)$ whenever $a, x, y, z \in X$, the interval order turns into Duncan's semiorder and we can take $\rho \equiv 1$.

Although I have received credit for introducing interval orders, their structure would not have been unfamiliar in fields that assign time intervals to events such as the birth-to-death periods of civilizations or species. I learned well after 1970 that interval orders had in fact been discussed much earlier as "relations of complete sequence" by the young Norbert Wiener (1894–1964) in *A contribution to the theory of relative position* (1914). This was the first of three papers by Wiener on the relational theory of measurement which, until recently, lay in obscurity because they used the arcane notation of Whitehead and Russell's *Principia Mathematica* and were overshadowed by Wiener's brilliant contributions to other subjects such as stochastic processes, harmonic analysis and ergodic theory. Interpretations and commentaries on those three papers are available in Fishburn and Monjardet (1992).

Semiorders and interval orders are a small but important piece of a constellation of specialized relational structures in graph theory and ordered sets investigated in recent years. Some of my own research for the 1970 paper and many that followed is described along with work by others in *Interval Orders and Interval Graphs: A Study of Partially Ordered Sets* (1985). Numerous other contributions to the field appear in Tom Trotter's *Combinatorics and Partially Ordered Sets* (1992). In the preface to the 1985 book I wrote that

> I am indebted to many people for guidance and encouragement over the years in my work on ordered sets. Special thanks go to Fred Roberts, Duncan Luce, Peter Hammer, Ronald Graham, and Thomas Trotter.

Two things strike me as I re-read these words. First, Duncan is the only person named here who is mentioned in the preceding section. Second, unlike the co-authorship note at the end of that section, I have published jointly with all five people just named, some many times. Duncan is more than partly responsible for such good fortune as I will indicate in the next few pages.

3. THE INSTITUTE FOR ADVANCED STUDY

As my education in preference and utility continued at RAC in the late 1960s, the company decided that its advanced research budget should be spent to drum up new business for the firm. It was time to leave. The possibility of a year at Stanford was in the works when Duncan, who had relocated to The Institute for Advanced Study, invited me to spend 1970–71 there. When I told Jimmie Savage about accepting Duncan's offer, he wrote that a year "at the navel of the universe" sounded great. It was a lovely, stimulating year.

In the summer of 1970 we moved our furniture into storage and ourselves into a furnished garden apartment on von Neumann Drive next to the famous Institute woods. This allowed me to indulge my love of nature as I wrote *The Theory of Social Choice* (1973) and related articles on the mathematics of voting, an interest developed at RAC to go along with individual decision theory. Although social choice theory was not high on Duncan's personal agenda, Luce and Raiffa (1957) includes an excellent chapter on group decision making, and Duncan fully supported my new direction.

My year at the Institute was special in ways beyond nature and social choice. It gave Duncan and me many opportunities to become better acquainted and brought me into contact with other distinguished people, among them Kurt Gödel, Clifford Geertz, and George A. Miller, a fine golfer and even better psychologist. George had his own Princeton University ID to gain access to their course; I had none and, in a gender reversal unrecognized at the pro shop, signed in with Clifford's wife's card as H. Geertz.

Quite possibly the most important event of the year for us was my wife's return to school. Jan had decided many years earlier to pursue a church-related vocation but put it on hold, as was customary at that time, to raise a family. When our youngest child entered kindergarten the year we moved to Princeton, Jan enrolled at Princeton Theological Seminary. She never looked back.

During the year I accepted a position for the fall of 1971 as research professor in the College of Business Administration at The Pennsylvania State University, and Jan was accepted into their new doctoral program in religious studies. She completed her degree in 1978 with a dissertation on the social gospel in American church history and was offered a position in the Theological School of Drew University in Madison, New Jersey. A few months later I had the good fortune to be offered a job in economic and mathematical research at Bell Laboratories in Murray Hill, and we moved to Madison in the summer of 1978. We are deeply indebted to Duncan for initiating the chain of events that led us back to New Jersey.

4. INTERACTIONS

The years have been kind to us since 1978. Jan went on to become a full professor at Drew, was ordained a teaching elder by the Presbyterian church in 1988, published two pathbreaking books, and completed the Drew part of her career in 1995 after a year's service as Dean of the Theological School. The move to Bell Labs breathed new life into my career by bringing me into contact with some of the world's finest mathematicians. The opportunity to work with Paul Erdős, Ron Graham, Larry Shepp, Andrew Odlyzko, and many other first-rate mathematicians would have been unimaginable elsewhere.

Duncan and I have kept in touch over the years through correspondence on diverse matters and visits to each other's institutions, which for Duncan included three years at the University of California at Irvine, 12 at Harvard, and a return to UCI in 1988. Although I have moved ever deeper into combinatorial and discrete mathematics, my old love of decision theory persists. Three aspects of the old in new directions stand out.

The first has been an extensive investigation into nonlinear and sometimes nontransitive preferences in decision under risk and uncertainty that led to my 1988 book. An offshoot has involved serious consideration of cyclic preferences such as $x \succ y$, $y \succ z$ and $z \succ x$. Although cogent examples argue for the reasonableness of preference cycles, especially when judgments are affected by multiple factors, traditionalists raised on transitivity as the sine qua non of rational preference structures have often looked askance at this work. I mention it here because I have felt Duncan's respect for the work even when his loyalties lay elsewhere.

The second new direction is a continuing long-term collaboration with Irving LaValle on facets of utility theory with special emphasis on multidimensional utilities ordered lexicographically. One interesting feature of our research is the emergence of matrix probabilities in place of real-valued probabilities in a modified Savage formulation of decision under uncertainty (LaValle & Fishburn, 1995). Irv, like Duncan, has been gracious about my intransitivity views while demonstrating that certain commitments to coherent decisions in dynamic choice imply that preferences are transitive (LaValle, 1992).

The third direction brings us to my collaboration with Duncan. In 1989, Duncan invited me to think with him about utility structures that incorporate a notion of joint receipt. How, for example, do people process the simultaneous occurrence of several gains, or a loss and a gain, or a portfolio of risky options? And what types of utility representations are appropriate for plausible joint receipt preferences? The main results of our collaboration are described in Luce and Fishburn (1991, 1995) and Fishburn and Luce (1995).

The first paper focuses on a joint receipt operation $\oplus$ between uncertain prospects g, h, ... with monetary outcomes. We let e denote the status quo outcome and assume that $e \oplus e = e$. The fundamental representation axiomatized in the paper has $g \succ h \Leftrightarrow u(g) > u(h)$ with $u(e) = 0$ and

$$u(g \oplus h) = \begin{cases} a^+ u(g) + b^+ u(h) + c^+ u(g)u(h) & \text{if } g \succsim e, \ h \succsim e \\ a^+ u(g) + b^- u(h) & \text{if } g \succsim e \succsim h \\ a^- u(g) + b^+ u(h) & \text{if } h \succsim e \succsim g \\ a^- u(g) + b^- u(h) + c^- u(g)u(h) & \text{if } e \succsim g, \ e \succsim h, \end{cases}$$

where $\succsim$ is the union of $\succ$ and $\sim$, and a^+ through c^- are constants with a^+, a^-, b^+ and b^- positive. Assuming u unbounded and $\oplus$ monotonic, we showed also that $c^+ \geq 0$ and $c^- \leq 0$. In Luce and Fishburn (1995), based on questions raised in Tversky and Kahneman (1992) about the model if $x \oplus y = x + y$, we explored the interesting possibility that u is bounded and $\oplus$ is monotonic, leading to $c^+ \leq 0$ and $c^- \geq 0$. Our weighted additive forms for $g \succsim e \succsim h$ and $h \succsim e \succsim g$ are a compromise between the simplest additive form $u(g \oplus h) = u(g) + u(h)$ and more complex possibilities. Further assumptions that involve uncertain events show how the fundamental representation gives rise to a rank-dependent utility model with sign-dependent event probabilities in a tradition of rank-dependent utility associated with earlier work of Quiggin (1982) and Schmeidler (1989) among others.

Our other main paper concentrates on the conceptually simpler joint receipt of two quantities x and y of a real variable such as money. We assume in Fishburn and Luce (1995) that preferences for quantities of the variable are represented by a continuous increasing utility function u with $u(0) = 0$, and denote by $x \oplus y$ the joint receipt of x and y. We refer to $x \geq 0$ as a *gain*, $x \leq 0$ as a *loss*, and investigate structures for u which satisfy the *hedonic editing rule*

$$u(x \oplus y) = \max\{u(x + y), u(x) + u(y)\}$$

introduced in Thaler (1985). The rule says that the utility of the joint receipt of x and y is the larger of the utility of the integrated sum of x and y, and the sum of the utilities of x and y considered separately.

The paper analyzes hedonic editing under the assumption that u is concave in gains, increasing at a decreasing rate, and either convex in losses or concave in losses. Of particular interest for these two main cases is the behavior of u in the mixed gain/loss region where $x > 0$ and $y < 0$, which is related to the mixed cases that have $g \succsim e \succsim h$ and $h \succsim e \succsim g$ in the first paper. A principal result is that each main case has six subcases determined by the limiting relations among the slopes of u at ± 0 and $\pm \infty$. Each subcase partitions the behavior of u in the mixed region into subregions of integration, where $u(x \oplus y) = u(x + y)$, and segregation, where $u(x \oplus y) = u(x) + u(y)$. The subregions have substantially different shapes depending on whether u is convex or concave in losses. We also identify conditions on preferences under joint receipt that correspond to our assumptions about u for the two main cases and their subcases.

Duncan's investigation of joint receipt preferences and choice has involved other theoretical avenues (Luce, 1995b) along with empirical research (Cho et al., 1994; Cho & Luce, 1995), and he continues to explore this intriguing new area. It has been a joy for me to participate in his research program and, more broadly, to voice my thanks for so many things over so many years.

Choice, Decision, and Measurement
A. A. J. Marley (Ed.),
©Lawrence Erlbaum Associates, NJ, 1997.

EMPIRICAL TESTS OF LUCE'S RANK- AND SIGN-DEPENDENT UTILITY THEORY

DETLOF VON WINTERFELDT

Institute of Safety and Systems Management
University of Southern California
and
Decision Insights, Inc.

ABSTRACT. In a series of papers (Luce, 1988, 1991; Luce & Fishburn, 1991, 1995), Duncan Luce developed a descriptive theory of decision making under uncertainty that accounts for many empirical challenges to the subjective expected utility theory. In Luce's theory, the weights assigned to events depend on the rank of the consequences and on the position of consequences relative to the status quo. Because of these dependencies, Luce called his theory a rank- and sign-dependent utility (RSDU) theory. This paper describes RSDU theory, discusses its assumptions, and reviews the experimental results that tested them. Two key issues emerged in the review of the experimental literature: whether two formally equivalent gambles (e.g., the normal and the extended form) are also psychologically equivalent and whether choice procedures to determine certainty equivalents lead to the same results as direct judgments of certainty equivalents. The experimental tests provide support for the assumptions of RSDU theory, provided that 1) only the most obvious formal equivalences are assumed to be psychologically equivalent, and 2) certainty equivalents are derived from sequential choices rather than being directly judged. Some questions remain, however, about the validity of two assumptions: that the sequence of events does not matter as long as the same consequences obtain (event commutativity), and that preferences among gambles do not change when a sure thing is added as a joint receipt to each gamble (monotonicity of joint receipts).

1. INTRODUCTION

This paper reviews experiments that tested assumptions of Duncan Luce's rank- and sign dependent utility (RSDU) theory (Luce, 1988, 1991; Luce & Fishburn, 1991, 1995). Together with prospect theory (Kahneman & Tversky, 1979; Tversky & Kahneman, 1986, 1992; Wakker & Tversky, 1993), RSDU theory is the major descriptive competitor of the subjective expected utility (SEU) theory (von Neumann & Morgenstern, 1947; Savage, 1954; Fishburn, 1980). To the extent that

---

Key words and phrases. Utility theory, rank dependence, sign dependence, subjective expected utility, prospect theory.

Acknowledgments. Support for this paper was provided by the National Science Foundation under grant No. SES-9308915 to The University of Southern California. I would like to thank Alan Brothers, Younghee Cho, and Duncan Luce for helpful comments on an earlier draft of this paper.

Address for correspondence. Detlof von Winterfeldt, Decision Insights, Inc., 4590 MacArthur Blvd., Suite 500 Newport Beach, CA 92660, USA. Email: detlof@aol.com

the experimental findings shed light on the distinctions between RSDU theory and SEU theory, this paper also reviews the empirical foundation of SEU theory.

Following a series of experiments that cast doubt on the descriptive validity of SEU theory, Kahneman and Tversky (1979) wrote a seminal paper that introduced prospect theory. It differed from SEU theory by identifying the status quo as the major reference point, by postulating separate value functions for gains and losses, by using non-linear probabilities, and by assuming a series of editing operations that simplify the judgment of gambles. Tversky and Kahneman (1992) generalized prospect theory to a cumulative representation including multiple outcomes, and Wakker and Tversky (1993) provided an axiomatization of this generalization.

Meanwhile, Luce took a different approach to the same problem. Building on the general theory of concatenation structures (e.g, Luce & Narens, 1985), he developed first a rank dependent utility (RDU) theory and then a rank- and sign-dependent utility (RSDU) theory (Luce, 1988, 1991; Luce & Fishburn, 1991, 1995). The results were very similar to prospect theory: RSDU theory involves a status quo and possibly non-linear probabilities. It also includes formal definitions of the editing operations postulated in prospect theory.

Thus, the differences between RSDU theory and prospect theory on one hand and SEU on the other are:

(a) *Status quo dependence*: In SEU theory, the status quo plays no special role. In RSDU and prospect theory, the status quo defines two domains (gains and losses) with possibly different value functions for each.

(b) *Non-additive weights*: In SEU theory, weights are interpreted as probabilities and they are additive. In RSDU and prospect theory, they are interpreted as possibly non-additive weights that depend on the consequences of events.

(c) *Editing operations*: In SEU theory, gambles and their consequences are combined and separated according to the laws of probability and arithmetic. In RSDU and prospect theory, editing operations are postulated that do not necessarily correspond to these laws.

There also are several differences between RSDU and prospect theory.

(a) *Formalization of the editing process*: Prospect theory postulates a set of qualitative editing operations, by which subjects simplify gambles (e.g., elimination of common elements). RSDU theory formalizes these editing operations through a joint receipt operation $\oplus$. Formally the joint receipt $g \oplus h$ of two gambles g and h means that both gambles are played, possibly successively.

(b) *Value functions for gains and losses*: Prospect theory itself is silent about the form of the value function, but to account for observed risk aversion in gains and risk seeking in losses, an additional assumption is usually made that the value function is concave in gains and convex in losses. In RSDU theory, the value functions can be shown to be either two-piece exponential functions or two-piece linear functions, and, with some minor additional assumptions, to be weakly concave in gains and weakly convex in losses.

(c) *Weighting functions*: Prospect theory is also silent about the shape of the weighting function, but its usual interpretation defines a weighting function to be concave for low probabilities to about .40 and convex for higher probabilities. RSDU theory makes no assumptions about the shape of the weighting function.

The most controversial of these differences is the introduction of the joint receipt operation $\oplus$. Tversky and Kahneman (1992) criticize the use of the joint receipt operation in RSDU theory, since, applied to sure amounts of money, it appears to imply that

$$x \oplus y \sim x + y.$$

In Tversky and Kahneman's words: "...we expect a decision maker to be indifferent between receiving a \$10 bill or receiving a \$20 bill and returning \$10 in change" (Tversky & Kahneman, 1992, p. 302). They also concluded that this additivity assumption, in conjunction with the 1991 version of RSDU theory, implied linear value functions for money, which is clearly wrong descriptively. Luce and Fishburn (1995) later relaxed the assumptions of RSDU and it now implies exponential rather than linear value functions.

The interpretation of the joint receipt operation is very important in this context. Luce (personal communication, March 25, 1996) prefers to interpret joint receipts to be either simultaneous (e.g., playing two gambles at the same time) or in immediate succession. With this interpretation, the additivity assumption is probably reasonable and the form of the value function is, as a consequence, limited. However, receipts that are separated in time and/or obtained in different contexts may not have the additivity property. Consider the following case. On Monday, you receive an unexpected state tax bill for \$10,000. On the following Wednesday, you receive an equally unexpected federal tax refund of \$10,000. Would you prefer this sequence of events over not having received either notification? Would you prefer to receive the notifications in reverse sequence? The answers to these questions are not obvious and they certainly deserve empirical testing.

This paper will describe RSDU theory, its assumptions, and the experimental results that bear on them. The presentation of RSDU theory and its assumptions in Section 2 will follow closely an earlier presentation by Luce and von Winterfeldt (1994). The experimental sections (Sections 3-5) will emphasize recent studies that were conducted as part of a collaborative National Science Foundation project by Duncan Luce and myself. Section 6 provides the conclusion about the empirical status of RSDU theory to date.

2. THE RSDU REPRESENTATION AND ITS ASSUMPTIONS

When considering an event F (such as rolling a die), and an algebra of events $\mathcal{E}$ (such as all possible outcomes of rolling a die, their unions and intersections) one can create binary gambles by identifying two mutually exclusive and exhaustive subevents of F, E, and $\neg E$ (the complement of E), and by assigning a consequence x to E and a consequence y to $\neg E$. When the context makes the conditioning on the event F clear, the binary gambles thus created will be denoted as $x o_E y$ or $(x, E; y)$. When x and y are pure consequences from a set C, e.g., monetary gains and losses, $x o_E y$ is called a first order binary gamble. Second-order and higher-order binary gambles can be created recursively. A generalized mixture operation

o is defined as the set $\{o_E\}_{E\in\mathcal{E}}$. An operation $\oplus$ denotes the joint receipt of pure consequences and/or gambles. For two gambles, $g \oplus h$ denotes the joint receipt of g and h played independently at the same time or in immediate succession. The convolution of g and h is also sometimes used and referred to by the operation $*$. Thus, when $g = (xo_Ey)$ and $h = (vo_Fw)$, then $g * h$ is the quaternary gamble $(x + v, E \cap F; x + w, E \cap \neg F; y + v, \neg E \cap F; y + w, \neg E \cap \neg F)$. G is the set of all pure consequences and gambles recursively created by the operations o and $\oplus$. The element e in G is the pure consequence or gamble such that the decision maker is indifferent between receiving it or not receiving it. A preference relation $\succeq$ is defined over G and $\succ$ and $\sim$ are defined as the strict preference and indifference subsets of $\succeq$. The set of consequences for which $x \succ e$ holds is called gains, the set of consequences for which $e \succ y$ holds is called losses.

The relational structure $(G, o, \oplus, \succeq)$ is said to have an RSDU representation if for any two gambles $g = (xo_Ey)$ and $h = (vo_Fw)$ in G,

$$g \succeq h \text{ if and only if } u(g) \succeq u(h)$$

and

$$u(xo_Ey) = \begin{cases} w^+(E)u(x) + [1 - w^+(E)]u(y) & \text{if } x \succeq y \succeq e, \\ w^+(E)u(x) + [(1 - w^-(\neg E)]u(y) & \text{if } x \succeq e \succeq y, \\ w^-(\neg E)u(x) + [1 - w^-(\neg E)]u(y) & \text{if } e \succeq x \succeq y, \end{cases}$$

(plus the equivalent forms if the roles of x and y are reversed), and

$$u(g \oplus h) = \begin{cases} a^+u(g) + b^+u(h) - c^+u(g)u(h) & \text{if } g, h \succeq e, \\ a^+u(g) + b^-u(h) & \text{if } g \succeq e \succeq h, \\ a^-u(g) + b^+u(h) & \text{if } h \succeq e \succeq g, \\ a^-u(g) + b^-u(h) - c^-u(g)u(h) & \text{if } e \succeq h, g. \end{cases}$$

The axiomatic basis for this representation is provided in Luce (1991) and in Luce and Fishburn (1991, 1995).

This representation has several important features. First, both the utility for mixtures xo_Ey and for the joint receipts $g \oplus h$ depend on the relative position of the consequences to the status quo element e. In addition, the weight for the events depend on the order of x and y and their relative position to the status quo. This is the reason for the name "rank- and sign-dependent utility" theory.

Second, it is not necessarily true that $w^+(E) + w^-(\neg E) = 1$. Luce and von Winterfeldt (1994) describe a simple condition which leads to equality in this equation and reduces the RSDU representation to a representation that depends on the status quo only. If status quo dependency is dropped as well, the standard SEU model obtains.

Third, the structure of the joint receipt utility function is somewhat peculiar. It is additive for consequences or gambles with opposite signs, but not necessarily additive for consequences with identical signs. If one makes the fairly trivial assumption that $g \oplus e \sim e \oplus g \sim g$, then $a^+ = a^- = b^+ = b^-$. The implication of this assumption is that sequencing of the joint receipt does not matter. If one assumes, in addition, that C consists of monetary consequences, that $c^+ = c^- = 0$, and that $x \oplus y = x + y$, then u is proportional to money.

The next three sub-sections describe several assumptions that are necessary for the above representation to hold. Following Luce and von Winterfeldt (1994), the assumptions are grouped into three categories: structural rationality assumptions, preference rationality assumptions, and quasi-rationality assumptions.

Structural Rationality Assumptions. Structural rationality assumptions involve formal transformations of gambles which, from a normative perspective, should not make a difference to a decision maker. As a result, it is often assumed that formally equivalent gambles are also psychologically equivalent, and that the decision maker should be indifferent between the two formally equivalent gambles.

For example, the extended form of a gamble (an event tree with consequences attached to the end nodes) can be reduced to the normal form (a probability distribution over a random variable), when probabilities are prescribed and consequences are defined as a random variable. The extended form of the gamble is transformed to the normal form by multiplying the probabilities down the tree and thereby creating a probability distribution over the random variable that characterizes the consequences. It is often implicitly assumed that these two formal representations are psychologically equivalent, and, therefore, that decision makers should be indifferent between a gamble represented in its extended form and a gamble represented in its normal form. However, some features of the gamble are changed in the transformation from the extended form to the normal form which may in fact make a difference to the decision maker. For example, the sequencing and the label of the events is suppressed in the normal form. Furthermore, the assumption is made that the subjective probability of joint events is equal to the product of the probability of each component event. Both the irrelevance of sequencing and the multiplication of probabilities are descriptively suspect assumptions.

RSDU theory makes the structural rationality assumptions explicit and subject to testing. The four simplest structural rationality assumptions are idempotence, complementarity, event commutativity, and auto-distributivity.

Idempotence. This assumption states that a gamble with identical consequences for the events is indifferent to the consequence itself:

$$x o_E x \sim x.$$

Complementarity. According to the complementarity assumption, the decision maker recognizes that associating x with an event E and y with the non-occurrence of the event is the same as associating y with the non-occurrence of the event E and x with the complement of the non-occurrence E:

$$x o_E y \sim y o_{\neg E} x.$$

Event commutativity. This assumption states that the order of events is irrelevant as long as the same consequences are associated with the same event combinations. Formally, event commutativity requires that

$$(x o_D y) o_E y \sim (x o_E y) o_D y.$$

Auto-distributivity. Auto-distributivity assumes that, when a gamble $xo_E y$ is mixed with a sure consequence z, then it does not matter whether the uncertainty about z is first resolved vis à vis x and y separately, or after the uncertainty about x and y is resolved:

$$(xo_E y)o_E z \sim (xo_E z)o_E(yo_E z).$$

Preference Rationality Assumptions. The three preference rationality assumptions are transitivity, consequence monotonicity, and event monotonicity.

Transitivity. Transitivity requires that for any three gambles or sure consequences f, g, and h

$$\text{if } f \succeq g \text{ and } g \succeq h, \text{ then } f \succeq h.$$

Without transitivity, it would not be possible to establish a complete ranking of gambles and consequences.

Consequence monotonicity. According to this assumption, if one consequence of a gamble is replaced by a preferred consequence, the new gamble is preferred to the original one:

$$x \succeq y \text{ if and only if } xo_E z \succeq yo_E z,$$

where x, y, and z are pure consequences. The gamble $xo_E z$ includes a consequence x that is preferred to or indifferent to the consequence y which is in the gamble $yo_E z$. Therefore, the gamble that includes x must be preferred or indifferent to the gamble that includes y.

Event monotonicity. This assumption states that, for three events C, D, and E, with C disjoint from both D and E, and consequences $x \succeq y$,

$$xo_D y \succeq xo_E y \text{ if and only if } xo_{C \cup D} y \succeq xo_{C \cup E} y.$$

In other words, if the preferred consequence x is made more likely, the preference order cannot change.

These preference rationality assumptions, together with the structural rationality assumptions and some technical assumptions that assure the richness and smoothness of the representation imply the SEU theory. In turn, SEU theory implies all forms of structural rationality, including the equivalence of the normal and extended form of gambles.

Quasi-Rationality Assumptions. The remaining assumptions are related to the editing of gambles, the decomposition of gambles into those involving gains and those involving losses, and the interplay between the joint receipt operation $\oplus$ and the mixture operation o. They are called quasi-rational, because they are not necessarily consistent with the normative principles embodied in SEU theory.

Aggregation into gains and losses. This assumption states that a first order gamble with gains and losses can be re-structured as a second order gamble in which the gains are pitted separately against the losses and against the zero (status quo) consequence. Let $E(+)$, $E(0)$, and $E(-)$ be the union of all events in the first order gamble g that have gains, status quo, or losses as consequences. Let $g(+)$ be the restriction of g to $E(+)$ and let $g(0)$ and $g(-)$ be the similar restrictions to the status quo consequences and losses. g^2 is the sign partitioned second order gamble

$[g(+), E(+); g(0), E(0); g(-), E(-)]$. The assumption of aggregating into gains and losses states that this second order gamble is indifferent to the original first order gamble, i.e.

$$g^2 \sim g.$$

Monotonicity of joint receipts. The first assumption related to the joint receipt of gambles is the monotonicity of joint receipts:

$$g \succeq h \text{ if and only if } g \oplus z \succeq h \oplus z.$$

Duplex decomposition. This assumption states that a gamble that involves gains and losses is indifferent to the joint receipt of two gambles, one that pits the gains against the status quo and one that pits the losses against the status quo. Thus, in terms of the sign partitioned second order gamble g^2:

$$g^2 \sim [g(+)o_{E(+)'}e] \oplus [g(-)o_{E(-)''}e],$$

where e is the status quo consequence and $E(+)'$ and $E(-)''$ denote two independent realizations of $E(+)$ and $E(-)$. Because the gamble on the right has consequences that are not possible in the gamble on the left (i.e., those that involve both a gain and a loss), this assumption introduces a major element of quasi-rationality.

Segregation. The purpose of the segregation assumption is to allow a recursive editing of gambles by "subtracting" least preferred ("smallest") gains or most preferred ("smallest") losses from each consequence. Let $x_1, x_2, \ldots, x_m$ be the gains, ordered by preference, that are associated with m events in a gamble. Thus, x_m is the least preferred gain. Let y_i be the consequence such that $y_i \oplus x_m \sim x_i$ (i.e., y_i replaces x_i after "subtracting out" x_m). Let g^x be the original gamble and g^y be the gamble in which the x_i's are replaced by the y_i's. The segregation assumption then requires that

$$g^y \oplus x_m \sim g^x.$$

A similar segregation assumption is assumed to hold for losses, except that the most preferred ("smallest") loss is subtracted first.

RSDU theory requires the following assumptions: idempotence, complementarity, event commutativity, transitivity, and consequence monotonicity and all quasi-rationality assumptions. It does *not* require auto-distributivity and event monotonicity. A set of assumptions of RSDU theory, not listed here, have to do with the form of the utility function over joint receipts: additive in the mixed quadrants and multi-linear in the same-sign quadrants. The assumptions for this form are complex and not more intuitive than the result itself (stated in the RSDU representation above).

3. EXPERIMENTAL TESTS OF STRUCTURAL RATIONALITY ASSUMPTIONS

Idempotence and Complementarity. There have been no tests of the idempotence and complementarity assumptions – for the obvious reason that they are almost certainly valid.

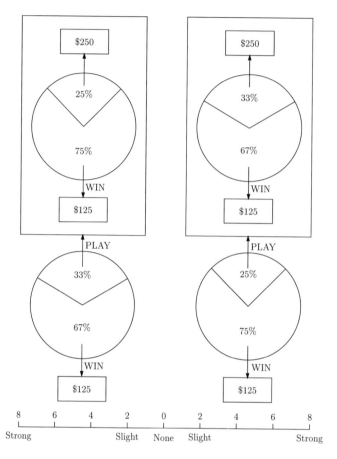

FIGURE 1. Display of gambles for an event commutativity test
(from Brothers, 1990. Reproduced with the author's permission).

Event Commutativity. Event commutativity has been tested by Ronen (1971,
1973), Brothers (1990), Chung et al. (1994). Ronen conducted two experiments.
In the first, he presented 22 subjects with a series of 20 compound gamble pairs.
In each gamble two mutually exclusive events occurred in sequence and each event
could either be "positive" or "negative". If both events were "positive", the subject
was paid $0.40. If one or both of the events was "negative", the consequence was
$0. Each gamble pair consisted of two gambles that were identical, except that
the order of the positive events was switched. Subjects were asked for a choice
between the two gambles (an indifference response was not allowed). Gambles were
actually played in accordance with subjects' expressed preferences after all choices
were made, and subjects were paid the resulting winnings.

Ronen observed a systematic violation of event commutativity in that subjects
chose the gamble with a higher probability of obtaining the positive event in the first
stage rather than in the second stage. In a second experiment, he asked 96 business
students to evaluate hypothetical business ventures which, if two sequential events

were positive, would either lead to success (described in words, not dollars), otherwise to no improvement (described as the status quo). As in his first experiment, the majority of the subjects (70%) more often selected the gamble with the higher probability of obtaining the positive event in the first stage.

Brothers (1990) conducted three experiments to test event commutativity. In the first experiment 30 subjects made side-by-side comparisons of pairs of gambles designed to test event commutativity (see Figure 1). Consequences were hypothetical dollar amounts ranging from -$1,000 to +$1,000. Subjects indicated a preference and a strength of preference (on a ruler below the displays of the gambles) for one of the gambles in each test. About 20% of the subjects recognized the equivalence of the two gambles and stated little or no preference. Another 20% of the subjects showed a preference for the gamble with a higher chance of entering the second stage gamble (the upper part of Figure 1). The remaining subjects showed no clear pattern of responses.

In the second experiment, Brothers asked subjects to assign certainty equivalents (CEs) to the gambles separately and he compared the CEs of the event commutativity gambles. The result showed that there was a tendency to assign somewhat higher certainty equivalents to the gamble with the lower probability of entering the second stage gamble.

Believing that this was a result of a response mode bias, Brothers then used a sequential choice procedure to elicit certainty equivalents as well as directly judged certainty equivalents in his third experiment. The sequential choice procedure was first applied by Bostic, Herrnstein, and Luce (1990) who called it PEST for "Parameter Estimation by Sequential Testing." In PEST subjects compare sure things with gambles and state a preference. The sure thing is then sequentially increased or decreased until subjects reverse their preferences. After the reversal occurs, the direction of the change is reversed and the step size to determine the next sure thing is reduced. Eventually, the certainty equivalent is defined within a narrow band of sure things. Because the sequential choice procedure is lengthy, Brothers used only four pairs of gambles. He again found lower directly judged certainty equivalents for the gamble with the higher probability of entering the second stage. However, he found no systematic differences between the certainty equivalents when they were elicited with the PEST procedure.

Chung et al. (1994) tested a larger set of twelve event commutativity stimuli using the PEST procedure. Twenty-five subjects were presented with a court case scenario, in which two witnesses were assumed to testify for or against the subject. If both witnesses testified in the subject's favor, the subject would win the case and receive $9,600, otherwise the subject would receive or lose an amount x (x varied between $4,800 and -$2,400). The results of 22 of the 25 subjects supported the event commutativity assumption. The other three subjects preferred the gamble with the higher probability of entering the second stage.

These tests of event commutativity are not conclusive. The most disturbing results are those by Ronen, with some support in Brothers' first study and by a few subjects in the Chung et al. experiment. Some subjects appear to prefer a sequence of events that gives them a better chance to continue the gamble to obtain the gain. For example, they would prefer a 90% chance of entering the second stage and a 10% chance of winning in the second stage over a 10% chance of entering the second stage and a 90% chance of winning in the second stage. However, when directly judged certainty equivalents were used to determine preferences, the effect was small or even reversed. When sequential choice procedures were used to elicit certainty equivalents, the effect all but disappeared.

Auto-distributivity. Brothers (1990) provided the only tests of the auto-distributivity assumption to date. He created 36 gamble pairs patterned after the auto-distributivity assumption. Gambles had monetary gains and losses between $200 and -$200. The probability $p(E)$ in the gambles was always .33. The two gambles were presented in the form of pie charts next to each other on a page (see Figure 2). Thirty subjects were asked to state a preference and to indicate their strength of preference on a ruler below the displays of the gambles. Subjects appeared to fall into three categories: six subjects had no appreciable preference for either of the two gambles, thirteen subjects showed a clear preference pattern and justified their preference with some heuristic, and twelve subjects showed no clear pattern and could not justify their preferences by a consistent heuristic. Only one subject recognized the formal equivalence between the two gambles. Brothers concluded that auto-distributivity failed largely because the complexity of the stimuli invited subjects to use simplifying heuristics when comparing them. These heuristics, in turn, led them to a preference, even though the gambles are formally equivalent.

4. EXPERIMENTAL TESTS OF PREFERENCE RATIONALITY ASSUMPTIONS

Transitivity. There have been numerous empirical studies challenging the transitivity assumption. The primary challenge has been the preference reversal phenomenon, first reported by Lichtenstein and Slovic (1971); for reviews, see Loomis (1990), Pommerehne, Schneider, and Zweifel (1982), Slovic and Lichtenstein (1983). The effect is well established: judged certainty equivalents and direct preference orders of gambles do not always yield the same order, and, in some cases, systematic order reversals occur between the two response modes. In recent years, there has been a tendency to attribute this reversal phenomenon to a response mode bias. In particular, the judged certainty equivalent method appears to lead to responses that are influenced by the consequences of the gambles, while choice procedures appear to lead to responses that are influenced by the probabilities (Tversky, Slovic, & Kahneman, 1990).

Bostic et al. (1990) tested the preference reversal phenomenon using the PEST procedure. They found no evidence of a preference reversal phenomenon with this procedure, confirming the hypothesis that the preference reversal phenomenon is a response mode effect.

Other evidence against the transitivity assumption come from studies of context effects and from observing preferences in response to incremental changes to gambles. MacCrimmon, Stanburg, and Wehrung (1980) showed that the preference ordering of two gambles reversed, when these two gambles were embedded in different context gambles. Tversky (1969) showed that small changes to a gamble

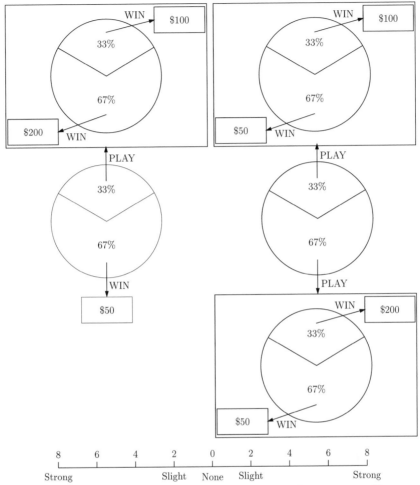

FIGURE 2. Display of gambles for an auto-distributivity test (from Brothers, 1990. Reproduced with the author's permission).

(e.g., changing the probabilities by a small amount) are ignored until the difference is large enough to produce a reversal. Budescu and Weiss (1987), Montgomery (1977), and Raynard (1977) found similar evidence.

There is little doubt that violations of transitivity occur as a result of response mode effects, context effects, and stimulus presentation effects. It would be disturbing if such violations would persist with efforts at engineering against them (e.g., using sequential choice procedures). It would be even more disturbing if subjects would insist on intransitivities. Fortunately, the evidence to date suggests that neither is the case.

Consequence Monotonicity. The Allais paradox (Allais, 1953; Allais & Hagen, 1979; von Winterfeldt & Edwards, 1986) was the first evidence against the consequence monotonicity assumption. Violations of consequence monotonicity have also been found by Kahneman and Tversky (1979), who referred to them as the common ratio effect. In a typical demonstration of this effect, subjects show the following preference pattern:

$$\$5,000 \succeq \$10,000 o_{.50} \$0$$

and

$$\$10,000 o_{.05} \$0 \succeq \$5,000 o_{.10} \$0,$$

where $o_{.50}$ stands for the mixture operation using an event with prescribed probability .50. Presumably, subjects focus on the sure win of \$5,000 in the first choice, since in the gamble $\$10,000 o_{.50} \$0$ they may win nothing at all. In the second choice, their attention shifts to the larger amount to win (\$10,000), since both gambles involve fairly low probabilities of winning.

This preference violates compound monotonicity, if we assume that $p(E) = .50$, $p(F) = .10$, and $p(E \cap F) = .05$, since

$$\$5000 \succeq \$10,000 o_E \$0$$

implies by compound monotonicity that

$$\$5000 o_F \$0 \succeq (\$10,000 o_E \$0) o_F \$0.$$

To recognize the monotonicity relationship, note that if F occurs, the gambles in the second choice have the sure thing (\$5,000) or the gamble ($\$10,000 o_E \$0$) in the first choice as consequences. If F does not occur, the consequences in the second choice are zero.

The Allais paradox and the common ratio effect only violate compound monotonicity, not monotonicity expressed in terms of pure consequences, and, to conclude a violation, one must make the additional structural rationality assumption that

$$(\$10,000 o_E) o_F \$0 \sim \$10,000 o_{E \cap F} \$0$$

and that $p(E \cap F) = .50 * .10 = .05$. When consequence monotonicity is disentangled from this structural rationality assumption, fewer or no violations were found (Keller, 1985a; Tversky & Kahneman, 1986).

Several recent experiments tested consequence monotonicity in its pure form. Brothers (1990) tested this assumption for gambles with amounts of money x and y with $x > y$. Making the trivial assumption that more money is preferred to less, consequence monotonicity implies that

$$x o_E z \succeq y o_E z$$

and

$$z o_E x \succeq z o_E y.$$

Brothers showed subjects pairs of gambles represented by pie charts on the same page and asked for a preference and a rating of the strength of preference. Only 5 out of 540 judgments showed a violation of consequence monotonicity and the few subjects who showed any violations (four out of 30) recognized them as mistakes in the debriefing session.

Brothers also tested compound monotonicity. First, he established a preference or indifference between two first order gambles that had close to identical expected values, but were otherwise dissimilar. Next, he created two second order gambles which mixed the first order gambles with a common sure consequence. The test stimuli were presented side-by-side on a page and subjects were asked for a preference and a rating of their strength of preference. About 35% of the subjects' responses violated compound monotonicity. However, in test-retest responses to the same gamble pair, also about 34% of the responses were reversed. Thus, the violations of compound monotonicity seemed to be mainly attributable to noise.

A series of experiments by Birnbaum, Mellers, and their colleagues cast a more serious doubt on consequence monotonicity. In the first study, Birnbaum, Coffey, Mellers, and Weiss (1992) asked subjects to assign certainty equivalents to binary gambles with consequences between $0 and $96. Gambles were presented using pie charts with stated probabilities and dollar consequences. Several of these gambles had a dominance relationship, for example, the gamble 96o_E$$0 was dominated by the gamble 96o_E$$6. For most pairs of gambles the dominated gamble received a lower certainty equivalent than the dominating one, as predicted by consequence monotonicity. However, whenever $p(E)$ was large, e.g. .95, more than 50% of the subjects assigned a higher certainty equivalent to the dominated gamble.

Mellers et al. (1992b) replicated this result using pie charts only (to avoid use of probabilities), odd dollar amounts (to avoid the use of calculations), mixed gains and losses, and larger stakes. They found the same type of violation of consequence monotonicity, except when the gambles had mixed consequences and when the set of test gambles was smaller than thirty. Birnbaum and Sutton (1992) replicated the effect, but also showed that subjects adhered to consequence monotonicity, when the dominated and dominating gamble was shown to them side-by-side on a page. Mellers, Berretty, and Birnbaum (1995) showed that the effect also occurs with three outcome gambles.

One explanation for these results is a response mode effect. For gambles of the form 96o_E$$0 with a large $p(E)$, subjects may estimate the certainty equivalent by ignoring the zero amount, anchoring on the $96 amount and revising this amount down to account for the probability which is less than one. For gambles of the form 96o_E$$6, subjects may instead estimate the certainty equivalent by anchoring on the average of $96 and $6 and adjusting upward to account for the probability which is larger than .50. If subjects' adjustment is insufficient, this process would lead to higher certainty equivalents for the gambles of the form 96o_E$$0.

Birnbaum (1992b) examined an alternative response mode in which subjects compared a gamble to an ordered list of 27 monetary amounts. The task was to make pairwise comparisons between the gamble and each monetary amount and circle all monetary amounts preferred to the gamble. The violations of consequence monotonicity persisted. However, the task still resembled the task of directly judging a certainty equivalent more than making sequential choices.

von Winterfeldt et al. (1997) considered two questions: First, to what extent would the violations of consequence monotonicity disappear, when sequential choices are used to elicit the certainty equivalents; second, to what extent can the results be predicted by noise alone? In three experiments, they replicated the previous consequence monotonicity violations using judged certainty equivalents. However, the percentage of violations was smaller (about 30% to 40%), especially when using the PEST procedure for eliciting certainty equivalents.

In a fourth experiment, von Winterfeldt et al. (1997) obtained test-retest judgments of the certainty equivalents and used the variability of these judgments to construct a noise model that predicted random violations of consequence monotonicity. This noise model predicted about 35-40% violations, 40-50% non-violations, and 15-20% ties. The observed percentages of violations were not significantly different from those predicted by the noise model. Moreover, because of the test-retest design, it was possible to count whether subjects violated consequence monotonicity twice, once, or not at all in two tests with the same gamble pair. When using the PEST procedure to obtain certainty equivalents, subjects almost never violated consequence monotonicity twice for the same gamble pair.

In summary, the Allais and common ratio violations of consequence monotonicity are likely due to the failure of structural rationality assumptions like reduction of compound gambles, not to genuine violations of pure consequence monotonicity. The violations found by Birnbaum, Mellers, and their colleagues are undoubtedly real violations of pure consequence monotonicity. However, they seem likely to be a result of response mode effects compounded with a fair amount of noise. When choice procedures were used and when the noise in estimating CEs was accounted for when interpreting observed proportions of violations, the consequence monotonicity assumption could not be rejected.

Event Monotonicity. Ellsberg's paradox is the most compelling evidence against the descriptive validity of event monotonicity (Ellsberg, 1961; von Winterfeldt & Edwards, 1986). In his example, subjects are presented with two decision problems. In the first problem, they face an urn with 90 balls, 30 of which are known to be red (event R) and 60 of which are either yellow (Y) or black (B), but it is unknown how many yellow and black balls there are. A first choice is presented to subjects:

$$\$100 o_R \$0 \quad \text{vs.} \quad \$100 o_B \$0.$$

In this choice, most subjects prefer the left hand gamble, because the probability of winning is known.

A second choice is presented as follows:

$$\$100 o_{R \cup Y} \$0 \quad \text{vs.} \quad \$100 o_{B \cup Y} \$0.$$

Most subjects prefer the right hand gamble for the same reason that they preferred the left hand gamble in the first choice: the probability of winning is known. This violation of event monotonicity is apparently rooted in an aversion against ambiguity – subjects prefer bets in which probabilities are known.

This type of violation of event monotonicity has been demonstrated in several experiments (for summaries, see Camerer & Weber, 1993; von Winterfeldt & Edwards, 1986) and there is little doubt that the phenomenon is real. Since event monotonicity is a major requirement for SEU theory (but not for RSDU or prospect theory), this violation is a significant point of departure between the RSDU theory and prospect theory on the one hand and SEU theory on the other.

5. EXPERIMENTAL TESTS OF QUASI-RATIONALITY ASSUMPTIONS

The quasi-rationality assumptions, especially those related to joint receipts, offer a rich and fascinating area of experimental exploration. So far, only a handful of experiments have studied these assumptions.

Aggregation into Gains and Losses. No experiment has yet tested the assumption that mixed consequence gambles can be re-cast as three sub-gambles representing the losses, status quo, and the gains of the original gamble and that this re-cast gamble is indifferent to the original one. It is fairly hard to imagine, however, how such recasting of a gamble would produce a preference.

Commutativity of Joint Receipts. Commutativity of joint receipts is not a necessary assumption of RSDU theory, but it is implied by the seemingly trivial assumption that $g \oplus e \sim e \oplus g \sim g$. It seems hard to imagine violations of commutativity, if, as Luce prefers (personal communication, March 25, 1996), the joint receipt operation involves only simultaneous receipts or consequences received in rapid succession. Relaxing this interpretation to allow receipts that are further separated in time and perhaps received in different contexts, makes the commutativity assumption less trivial. In such situations the order of the consequences may indeed matter. For example, would you rather receive the good news (a tax refund of $10,000) or the bad news (a loss in an investment of $5,000) first? The timing of the events and the similarity of the transactions involved may make this a non-trivial assumption. For example, if the first event is a loss and the second is a gain and they are separated in time, there will be a period of mental anguish. If the two consequences involve very different accounts (e.g., tax losses vs. long-term investment gains), they may involve different mental accounting processes. Empirically, the issue of commutativity of joint receipts is fascinating and largely unresolved.

Monotonicity of Joint Receipts. There have been no experimental tests of the monotonicity of joint receipts (although Cho & Luce, 1995, tested a stricter version of this assumption as part of testing additivity of joint receipt, see below). Possible violations may occur through an endowment effect: consider two gambles, with equal expected value, but one having a very small variance, the other having a large one, such that most subjects would prefer the low variance gamble. Now add a joint receipt to each gamble consisting of a substantial gain. It is possible that a preference reversal would occur, violating monotonicity of joint receipts.

For example, consider the following two gambles:

$$\$10,000o_{.50}\$0 \text{ vs. } \$6,000o_{.50}\$4,000.$$

Many subjects will prefer the gamble on the right, because it has lower variance and because it guarantees the gain of $4,000. Now consider the same two gambles with a joint receipt of $10,000:

$$(\$10,000o_{.50}\$0) \oplus \$10,000 \text{ vs. } (\$6,000o_{.50}\$4,000) \oplus \$10,000.$$

Now, many subjects are likely to prefer the left-hand side gamble, because it offers a solid low end ($10,000) but a higher upside ($20,000 vs. $16,000) than the right-hand side gamble.

Duplex Decomposition. Slovic and Lichtenstein (1968) used the joint receipt of two gambles as a device to control their expected value, while manipulating the variance. Their intention was to study variance preferences. Their data suggested that the duplex decomposition assumption is valid.

Cho et al. (1994) studied duplex decomposition explicitly. Their stimuli were hypothetical gambles involving gains of up to $96 to losses of up to $160. The response modes were direct judgments of certainty equivalents and certainty equivalents derived by a sequential choice procedure. To test the duplex decomposition assumption, the median certainty equivalents of the gambles $xo_E y$ and $(xo_E 0) \oplus (0o_E y)$ were compared. The value of x was always $96. The value of y and the probability $p(E)$ was systematically varied. The certainty equivalents for $xo_E y$ were not significantly different from those for $(xo_E 0) \oplus (0o_E y)$ either for the judged certainty equivalent method or for the PEST method. Thus, the duplex decomposition assumption was sustained.

Segregation. Cho et al. (1994) tested segregation by comparing certainty equivalents for gambles of the form $(x \oplus y)o_E y$ with the joint receipt $(xo_E 0) \oplus y$. In this experiment they assume that $x \oplus y \sim x + y$. The value of $x = \$96$ was paired with $y = \$70$ and the one of $x = -\$96$ with $y = -\$70$). The probabilities $p(E)$ were .2, .5, and .9. Ninety-one subjects directly judged the certainty equivalents for the gambles or joint receipt and one hundred and forty-four subjects used the PEST procedure to determine a choice based certainty equivalent. The median judged certainty equivalents for the two conditions were significantly different for $p(E) = .2$ for both $y = +\$70$ and $y = -\$70$. In all other cases the medians were not significantly different. There was a tendency of subjects to prefer the gamble $(x \oplus y)o_E y$ over the joint receipt in the gains condition (x and y positive), but to prefer the joint receipt in the loss condition (both x and y negative). When using the sequential choice procedure to elicit certainty equivalents, almost all tests supported segregation. Thus, it appears that segregation holds, when using choice procedures for eliciting certainty equivalents.

Cho and Luce (1995) also tested segregation and found no systematic violations of it. In addition, they found support for a special form of segregation, which is additive in certainty equivalents (CE's):

$$CE[(x + y)o_E y] = CE(xo_E 0) + y.$$

Additivity of Joint Receipts. Additivity of joint receipts is not a necessary assumption of RSDU theory, but it would simplify the theory substantially. A form of additivity can be tested in terms of certainty equivalents:

$$CE(x \oplus y) = CE(x) + CE(y)$$

and, for gambles

$$CE(g \oplus h) = CE(g) + CE(h).$$

Experimental results by Thaler (1985), Thaler and Johnson (1990), Linville and Fischer (1991) question the additivity assumption for sure consequences. Thaler asked subjects whether a person would be happier (or unhappier, in the case of losses), if he or she received two consequences jointly or separately. For example, person A might receive two prizes in two lotteries, one for $25 and one for $75. Person B might receive one prize in one lottery for $100. If both consequences were gains, subjects indicated that the person who receives two separate gains would be happier than the person who received one combined gain. If both consequences were losses, subjects indicated that the combined loss was preferred to two separate losses. When a large gain was mixed with a smaller loss, the joint (small) gain was preferred to the separate gain and loss. When a small gain was combined with a larger loss, the preference was for separating the two.

Thaler and Johnson (1990) asked subjects questions like the following: "When does losing $9 upset you more, when it occurs by itself, or when it occurs after winning $30?" Subjects generally stated that the former event hurt more than the latter. They also said that losing $9 would hurt more if it occurred after losing $30 than if it occurred just by itself.

Linville and Fischer (1991) asked subjects whether they would prefer two consequences on the same day or on different days. For example, subjects were asked to imagine that they lost a non-refundable airline ticket worth $250 and they accidentally damaged their stereo system with repair cost of $200. Not all questions involved monetary consequences. Others included receiving grades, social interactions, etc. The pairs of situations were either two large gains, two small gains, two large losses, two small losses, a large gain combined with a small loss, or a large loss combined with a small gain. Similar to Thaler (1985) and Thaler and Johnson (1990), they found that subjects tended to prefer to separate large gains over receiving them as a joint consequence. In contrast to the previous findings, they found that subjects also prefer to separate large losses over receiving them as a joint receipt. For mixed gains and mixed losses, subjects generally preferred the separate receipt over the joint receipt.

Cho et al. (1994), studied the assumption of additivity of joint receipts directly. Subjects and stimuli were the same as the ones used in the segregation and the duplex decomposition tests. The judged certainty equivalents $CE[(xo_E0) \oplus y]$ were significantly different from the sum $CE(xo_E0) + y$ for most gamble pairs, with a tendency for the joint receipt gamble to receive a smaller certainty equivalent, when x and y were positive (sub-additivity in gains). However, when both x and y were negative, the joint receipt gamble received a larger certainty equivalent (super-additivity in losses). The judged certainty equivalents $CE[(xo_E0) \oplus (0o_Ey)]$ were not significantly different from the sum of the judged certainty equivalents for each component gamble $CE(xo_E0) + CE(0o_Ey)$, consistent both with additivity of joint receipts and duplex decomposition.

When using the sequential choice procedure to elicit certainty equivalents, several gamble pairs showed significantly non-additive results. In general, there was a tendency for sub-additivity in gains and super-additivity in losses. Thus, additivity of joint receipt seems to be systematically violated for some gambles.

Cho and Luce (1995) studied additivity of joint receipts and several other related assumptions. For sure things, they found the additivity assumption to hold, but for gambles, they found sub-additivity in gains. In addition, certainty equivalents for the convolution of two gambles tended to be larger than the certainty equivalent for the joint receipt for subjects that they classified as gamblers (i.e., subjects that gave relatively high certainty equivalents for most gambles). For subjects classified as non-gamblers, however, the equality of convolution and joint receipt seemed to hold.

These results create a somewhat confusing picture of the status of the several types of additivity assumptions. Clearly, more research is needed in this area. To begin with, the simplest forms of additivity of joint receipt for sure things need to be tested more thoroughly. If this type of additivity fails, alternative forms that are compatible with the RSDU theory need to be explored.

6. CONCLUSIONS

Table 1 summarizes the assumptions of RSDU theory and their current empirical status. Among the structural rationality assumptions required for RSDU, the key issue is whether event commutativity is satisfied. The effects found by Ronen (1971, 1973) and in one experiment by Brothers (1990) are somewhat disturbing in this regard. However, this effect appeared to vanish when using certainty equivalents derived from sequential choices. Auto-distributivity, a necessary assumption of SEU theory, but not for RSDU theory, was studied in only one experiment. While there were many violations, there are no coherent psychological explanations for these violations. Since auto-distributivity is one of the two points of departure between the descriptive RSDU theory and the normative SEU theory (event monotonicity being the other), its failure should be studied more systematically.

Among the preference rationality assumptions transitivity and consequence monotonicity appear to hold for choice data. The effects demonstrated in studies of preference reversals, the Allais paradox, the common ratio effect, and dominance violations are no doubt real. But, on balance, these findings are more likely to be a result of compounding pure rationality tests with structural rationality assumptions, response mode effects and noisy data rather than of a genuine violation of the assumptions. In any case, there is plenty of evidence that subjects, when confronted with their violations of transitivity and consequence monotonicity quickly recognize them as "errors" and make adjustments to resolve the inconsistency. Event monotonicity is required by SEU theory, but not by RSDU theory. Its failure up to now has been attributed to versions of the Ellsberg paradox, with the most compelling explanation being an aversion towards ambiguity. It would be interesting to test the Ellsberg paradox with certainty equivalents and choice procedures.

The quasi-rationality assumptions are special to RSDU theory. Aggregation and commutativity of joint receipts have not been studied, but they do not seem likely to be violated. Monotonicity of joint receipts has not been systematically studied, but it may be violated by the endowment effect. Duplex decomposition has been studied quite extensively, and it seems to hold up rather well. Segregation has also been studied twice and seems to be reasonably well supported.

Assumption	Required by RSDU	Empirical Results
Structural Rationality		
Idempotence	Yes	Not tested, assumed to be trivially valid
Complementarity	Yes	Not tested, assumed to be trivially valid
Event Commutativity	Yes	Valid for choice data, some questions remain
Auto-Distributivity	No	Not valid, needs testing with choice data
Preference Rationality		
Transitivity	Yes	Valid for choice data
Consequence Monotonicity	Yes	Valid for choice data
Event Monotonicity	No	Not valid, needs testing with choice data
Quasi Rationality		
Aggregation	Yes	Not tested, assumed to be trivially valid
Commutativity of Joint Receipt	Yes	Not tested, assumed to be trivially valid
Monotonicity of Joint Receipt	Yes	Mixed results
Duplex Decomposition	Yes	Valid for choice data
Segregation	Yes	Valid for choice data

TABLE 1. Summary of tests of assumptions of RSDU Theory.

Additivity of joint receipts is not required by RSDU theory. The experiments on additivity are mixed. Earlier studies suggest that additivity may not hold even for sure outcomes, and the recent studies clearly show sub-additivity for gambles with gains and super-additivity for gambles with losses. Luce and Fishburn (1995) provide an axiomatization that does not require the joint receipt operation to be additive in utilities.

Future research. Luce's introduction of the joint receipt operation in RSDU theory created one of the most fascinating areas of theoretical and experimental exploration in utility theory today. Open questions are whether this operation is commutative, monotone, and additive. In addition, RSDU theory pinpoints the departure between generalized utility theories and SEU theory in event monotonicity and auto-distributivity. Both assumptions should be tested more thoroughly with sequential choice procedures.

Choice, Decision, and Measurement
A. A. J. Marley (Ed.),
©Lawrence Erlbaum Associates, NJ, 1997.

THE UTILITY OF MEASURING AND MODELING PERCEIVED RISK

ELKE U. WEBER

The Ohio State University

ABSTRACT. This chapter argues that measures of subjective risk perception are important for the following three reasons: (a) perceived risk is an important dependent variable in its own right, independent from choice, and governmental and corporate risk managers and policy makers need to track public risk perception; (b) decompositions of risky choice alternatives into a risk and a return component that originated in the theory of finance may provide us with a better understanding of the psychology of risky choice, and recent work has suggested measures of risk that depart from the standard equation of risk and variance; and (c) conceptualizing risk perception as a psychological variable that can be affected by decision context or problem framing allows for a definition of risk attitude that has shown greater stability across situations than conventional operationalizations and thus might measure a stable personality trait.

1. INTRODUCTION

The 1980's saw a large volume of work on axiomatic measures of subjective risk, much of it conducted and/or inspired by R. Duncan Luce. Until recently, this work has largely existed in parallel to work on risky choice, and the investigation of risk perception as a psychological variable has been considered suspect by researchers subscribing to the expected utility framework and the tenets of consequentialism. Ward Edwards, for example, only somewhat tongue-in-cheek, has likened the measurement of perceived risk to the collection of judgments about "orthosonority", a nonsense construct invented by S. S. Stevens for which people nevertheless provided systematic ratings.

Outside of the expected utility framework, the concept of risk is not a newcomer. The pioneering work of Markowitz (1959) in the theory of finance as well as the subsequent work of Coombs (1975) on the psychology of risky decision making conceptualized risky choice as a compromise between the riskiness and the value of options. In contrast to the assumption pervasive in the theory of finance that people should and will strive to minimize risk, Coombs assumed that people have

Key words and phrases. Risk perception, risk preference, risk attitude, risky choice, utility theory, individual differences.

Acknowledgments. I would like to thank Duncan Luce for triggering and sustaining my interest in risk perception, and Michael Birnbaum, Ward Edwards, Robin Keller, Barbara Mellers, Rakesh Sarin, and Martin Weber for stimulating conversations related to issues discussed in this chapter.

Address for correspondence. Elke U. Weber, Department of Psychology, The Ohio State University, 1885 Neil Avenue, Columbus, OH 43210. Email: weber.211@osu.edu

an ideal point for risk that may or may not be at the zero point, and that – ceteris paribus – they will prefer options that come closest to this ideal point. Coombs hypothesized that a risk order over a set of options and a given individual's ideal point for risk could be obtained from his or her preference order.

Regardless of the success of such unfolding (Lehner, 1980), one may join Coombs in questioning the assumption of the rationality of risk minimization. In most formalizations[1], risk implies upside potential at the cost of downside potential. Whether risk – again ceteris paribus – is considered desirable or something to be avoided will thus depend on the relative emphasis one places on the upside potential relative to the downside potential. Lopes (e.g., 1987) has provided ample evidence that people differ in the extent to which they weigh those two factors when making decisions under risk. This differential weighting of upside vs. downside potential may either be an individual difference characteristic, as argued by Lopes, or a function of the situation or role people find themselves in. Thus Birnbaum and Stegner (1979) found that participants assigned to a seller's role put greater weight on the upper values of a range of price estimates for a used car than those assigned to the buyer's role who put greater weight on the lower estimates.

When upside and downside potential receive differential weight, they can do so in two logically distinct ways. The weights can affect people's perception of the riskiness of different options, such that options with a large downside potential seem proportionately more risky to individuals who put a larger weight on the downside potential. Alternatively, the weights might affect risk preference, rather than (or in addition to) risk perception. That is, keeping perceived risk constant, people who put a larger weight on the downside potential of risky options will find them less acceptable. In other words, the choice between two risky prospects can be different for two individuals either because they differ in their perception of the relative riskiness of the two options but have the same preference for risk (e.g., both are risk averse) or because they perceive the riskiness of the options in the same way but differ in their preference for risk, with one being risk averse and the other risk seeking. To differentiate between these two reasons for the difference in choice, we must be able to assess how both individuals subjectively perceived the riskiness of the two choice options.

In this chapter I will thus address the following two questions: (1) How do people perceive the riskiness of risky options, and is there evidence of individual and/or situational differences in risk perception? (2) Is risk preference also affected by these individual or situational differences or does the traditional economic assumption of universal risk aversion actually hold, after we factor out differences in risk perception?

2. MODELING RISK PERCEPTION

R. Duncan Luce, to whom this volume is dedicated, has contributed substantially to an answer to the first of those questions. Luce (1980, 1981) suggested

---

[1]In those formalizations that prefer to restrict the term risk to the downside potential of options (see Yates & Stone, 1992a, e.g.), risky choice is subsequentially characterized as a tradeoff between risk as downside potential and other considerations, including attractive benefits.

several possible axiomatic models of risk perception, adding to the literature on risk measurement that had been started by Coombs and his collaborators (e.g., Coombs & Bowen, 1971; Coombs & Huang, 1970; Coombs & Lehner, 1984; Pollatsek & Tversky, 1970). For a review of this history, see Weber (1988). The final modification of this theory, in response to Weber's (1984) and Keller, Sarin, and M. Weber's (1986) empirical work, was the conjoint expected risk (CER) model by Luce and Weber (1986). The CER model captures both similarities in people's risk judgments (by a common functional form by which probability and outcome information of risky options is combined) as well as individual differences (with the help of model parameters that reflect the relative weight given to positive and negative outcome and probability information). Thus the perceived riskiness R of risky option X is described as:

$$R(X) = A_0 \Pr[X = 0] + A_+ \Pr[X > 0] + A_- \Pr[X < 0] \qquad (1)$$
$$+ B_+ \mathrm{E}[X^{k_+} | X > 0] \Pr[X > 0] + B_- \mathrm{E}[X^{k_-} | X < 0] \Pr[X < 0],$$

i.e., it is a linear weighted combination of the probability of breaking even, the probability of a positive outcome, the probability of a negative outcome, the conditional expectation of positive outcomes raised to the power of k_+, and the conditional expectation of negative outcomes raised to the power of k_-, where $k_+, k_- > 0$. Weber and Bottom (1989, 1990) submitted the behavioral axioms on which the CER model is based to empirical tests and found support for the transitivity and monotonicity assumptions. Some violations of the expectation principle for risk judgments in the gain domain (also reported by Keller et al., 1986) were shown to be the result of nonnormative probability accounting, similar to that observed for preferences (e.g. Luce, 1990a). Finally, Weber and Bottom's (1989) results supported the additive combination of gain and loss components hypothesized by the CER model and ruled out, at least as descriptive models, other risk functions (e.g. Fishburn, 1982) that are multiplicatively separable in their loss and gain components. Yates and Stone (1992b) recently described the CER model as the "most viable model to describe single-dimensional risk appraisal" (p. 72), as for example the risk appraisal of financial gambles.

In addition to Fishburn's (1982, 1984) work, several alternative axiomatic models of risk take an exponential form. Sarin (1984) extended Luce's (1980, 1981) work and derived the model

$$R(X) = \mathrm{E}[e^{-cX}]. \qquad (2)$$

This model was modified by M. Weber (1990) into a form that made the risk measure location free, by subtracting the mean of the risky option from all outcomes:

$$R(X) = \mathrm{E}[e^{-c(X - \overline{X})}]. \qquad (3)$$

3. INDIVIDUAL DIFFERENCES IN RISK PERCEPTION

The CER model or other models of risk allow us to identify individual differences in risk perception. In addition to simply finding such differences (e.g. Weber, Anderson, & Birnbaum, 1992), it allows us to pinpoint the locus of such differences. Thus Weber (1988) found that college students and high school teachers differed in their perceptions of financial risks, an effect that was mediated by differences in the parameters k_+ and k_-, with teachers being more sensitive to the magnitude of gains and losses in their risk judgments (i.e., having larger k_+ and k_- parameters). Bontempo, Bottom, and Weber (in press) found cross-cultural differences in the risk judgments of MBAs and security analysts from the United States, the Netherlands, Hong Kong, and Taiwan, in the direction that the risk perception of members of the two Asian countries relative to that of members from the two Western countries was less meliorated by the probability of positive outcomes (A_+) and depended more on the magnitude (k_-) rather than the probability (B_-) of negative outcomes.

4. REASONS TO MEASURE PERCEIVED RISK

A wealth of evidence suggests that the perceived riskiness of an option is not an immutable characteristic of that option (as is, for example, its variance) that is perceived in a similar way by different observers and in different contexts. Instead, perceived riskiness appears to be a psychological variable that differs between individuals and possibly across situations. With that in mind, we will now revisit the question of why one should be concerned with the measurement of this variable. In the remainder of the chapter, I will provide a tripartite answer to the question of why researchers as well as practitioners should care about risk perception, and in particular about the identification of individual and situational differences by a descriptive model of risk perception. I will argue that (1) people's perceptions of subjective risk are an important dependent variable in their own right; that (2) the decomposition of risky choice into a tradeoff between a risk and a return component may provide us with a better understanding of the psychology of risky choice; and that (3) the measurement of individual and situational differences in risk perception provides for a new measure of risk preference which holds the promise of restoring the possibility of risk attitudes as stable individual dispositions.

Perceived Risk as a Dependent Variable. The perceptions of the riskiness of new or existing technologies by ordinary citizens or the perceptions of the riskiness of products by consumers are an ever more powerful force that private companies and government regulatory bodies have to reckon with. While business or government experts may have clear quantitative definitions of the risks of products or technologies based on objective data or models, members of the general public often seem to evaluate the same options in very different ways. Much of the early work by Slovic, Lichtenstein, and Fischhoff on psychological risk dimensions (e.g., Fischhoff, Lichtenstein, Derby, & Keeney, 1981) was funded by the Nuclear Regulatory Commission to help them in their bafflement about how public perception of the riskiness of nuclear technology could differ so drastically from the estimates provided by their engineers.

Holtgrave and Weber (1993) were concerned by the lack of connection between the literature on the perception of financial risks, described above, and the literature on the perception of health and safety risks. To remedy this situation, they took a set of risky activities that included both financial risks (e.g., "investing 80% of savings in the stock of a new medical research firm") and health and safety risks (e.g., "riding a bicycle 1 mile daily in an urban area," or "working on a special weapons and tactics police team") and compared the fit of a simplified version of the CER model, originally developed to describe financial risk perception, with the fit of the psychometric risk dimension model by Slovic, Fischhoff, and Lichtenstein (e.g., 1986), originally developed for the perception of health and safety risks. Respondents provided their overall evaluation of the riskiness of these different activities as well as evaluations of the component variables of the two models (probability of a loss or a gain, and expected loss or gain for the CER model; voluntariness, dread, control, knowledge, catastrophic potential, novelty, and equity for the Slovic et al. model). Contrary to expectations, the CER model actually provided a better fit for the health and safety risks than for the financial risks ($R^2 = .64$ vs. .46) and also provided a better fit than the psychological risk dimension model for both financial risks ($R^2 = .46$ vs. .36) and health and safety risks ($R^2 = .64$ vs. .39). Holtgrave and Weber (1993) speculated that the reason for the superior fit of the CER model might be that its dimensions such as probability of negative consequences or harm and expected value of harm come close to the way people naturally think about the overall risk in a given activity or situation. The psychological risk dimension model may need a dimension or dimensions reflecting the probability of harm to provide a better fit, since this dimension is highly correlated with risk ratings. Another reason might be that people consider the pros and cons of activities when judging riskiness; they may use CER dimensions such as the probability of positive outcomes and the expected value of positive outcomes to counter the impact of negative outcomes. The psychometric model focuses exclusively on the downside of activities.

Not surprisingly, a hybrid model that added three of Slovic et al.'s (1986) seven psychological risk dimensions to the CER model ("dread," the degree to which the negative consequences of the risky options were dreaded, which accounted for most of the additional explained variance; but also "catastrophic potential," the worst-case disaster severity of the activity, and perceived "control," the degree to which the person engaging in the activity had control over the consequences) turned out to do the best job in describing the risk perceptions of University of Chicago MBAs for financial risks. Holtgrave and Weber's (1993) results demonstrate that risk perception in different content domains can be captured by the same model. It also suggests that risk perception of financial stimuli can have an "emotional" component for some observers that is not completely described by the "objective" components of the CER model. This result may well have implications in some areas of finance, for example in the identification of noise traders, that is traders who base their investment decisions partly on irrational factors (Lee, Shleifer, & Thaler, 1991). By modeling and comparing, for example, the risk judgments of institutional investors for a set of investment options with those of small private investors, one should be able to determine whether the risk judgments of the latter group (suspected to be noise traders) showed greater evidence of being affected by such emotional risk dimensions as dread or catastrophic potential above and beyond the effects of the objective information about the investment options.

In addition to financial and health and safety risks, the CER model has been shown to describe risk judgments in the domain of lifestyle choices. Palmer (1994) applied it in the context of genetic counseling to successfully model and characterize the judgments made by members of a clinical population of dwarfs about the riskiness of different procreative alternatives available to them. Palmer and Sainfort (1993) argue that the genetic counseling literature has been misguided in equating the perceived riskiness of an adverse event (e.g., the birth of a child with a genetic disorder) with the perceived probability of the event's occurrence. In a review of the literature on the impact of genetic counseling on the reproductive decisions made by couples, the authors submit that the failure of these studies to find a clear relationship between changes in risk perception as the result of genetic counseling and subsequent reproductive decisions is the result of these studies conceiving of "risk" primarily as probability of occurrence. Palmer and Sainfort argue that the risk of different reproductive alternatives perceived by counselees will also reflect the severity of consequences and that, therefore, conceptualizations and measures of risk that combine both probability and outcome information (such as the CER model) ought to be employed.

Given the growing political influence of grassroots organizations and consumer activism, it is becoming increasingly more important to be able to characterize and predict people's intuitive subjective risk judgments. Public perception of the risks of silicone implants (in causing autoimmune diseases), for example, led Dow Corning to stop production of implants in 1992 and file for bankruptcy in 1995, despite two major medical reports of no evidence of silicone-related illnesses and a clean bill of health from the American College of Rheumatology (Cowley, 1995). Controversies about the licensing of technologies such as genetic engineering, or the siting of facilities such as landfills, incinerator plants, or halfway houses for the mentally handicapped, tend to be fueled primarily by disagreements about present or future levels of risk, rather than about disagreements about the acceptability of specific risk levels.

Along the same lines, risk communication and public education campaigns succeed best when they manage to alleviate people's fears, i.e., when they reduce the *perception* of riskiness rather than attempt to influence people's risk-benefit tradeoffs (Long, 1988). Affirmative action or other legal injunctions can, in this context, be seen as an opportunity to expose people, against their will but for the greater social good, to information that will disprove those of their fears that are based on irrational prejudices and stereotypes. Having the halfway house operate in their neighborhood for a year without incidents, for example, will likely result in a lower level of perceived risk than residents had anticipated. To gauge the subjective risk perceptions of members of the general public and to evaluate shifts in perceived risk as a function of educational and other interventions, it is necessary to have a measure of these perceptions. I argued in this section that axiomatic models of risk perception developed for financial stimuli, such as the CER model, augmented perhaps with some of the variables detected by the psychometric work on risk perception, have a broader range of applicability than the domain for which they were originally designed.

New Interest in Risk-Return Models. In contrast to the expected utility framework for modeling risky choice, the risk-return framework commonly found in the theory of finance (e.g., Markowitz, 1959) introduces risk and risk preference as constructs central to risky choice. Some theorists consider risk-return tradeoff models "more intuitively satisfying ... than expected utility"(see Bell, 1995, p. 3). Sarin and M. Weber, (1993, p. 148) describe the "intuitive appeal of risk-value models" as due to the fact that they require that "choice should depend on the riskiness of the gamble and its value." The early risk-return models of finance equated risk with variance, a formalization that is compatible with a quadratic utility function (Levy & Markowitz, 1979). Recent work by Sarin and M. Weber (1993), Jia and Dyer (in press), Bell (1995), and Franke and M. Weber (1996) has shown that a broad range of utility functions have risk-return interpretations. Different utility functions imply different measures of risk, under the assumption of risk aversion and the equating of return with expected value.

The psychological and axiomatic research on subjective risk perception discussed in the introduction can be characterized as taking a *bottom-up* approach, by starting with absolute or comparative risk judgments and fitting models to them. In contrast, the decomposition of choice into a risk and a return component can be described as providing a *top-down* approach, by starting with choices and utility functions and inferring perceived risk functions from them. Ideally, the two approaches will provide converging evidence for a model or a class of models of subjective risk that describes all observed empirical regularities of both risk perception *and* risky choice. Some such integration is already underway. Thus Jia and Dyer (in press) describe the following measure of perceived risk:

$$R(X) = be^{c\overline{X}}\mathrm{E}[e^{-c(X-\overline{X})} - 1] \tag{4}$$

This measure is (a) consistent with exponential and linear plus exponential utility functions and (b) has properties that are consistent with existing empirical tests of axioms about perceived risk. Their risk function has the implication that the Archimedean assumption (i.e., that when the riskiness of X exceeds that of Y, there exists a positive real number a such that the riskiness of aY exceeds that of aX) need only hold for negative outcome lotteries, consistent with the empirical results of Weber and Bottom (1990). This is the case because Equation 4 can be rewritten as

$$R(X) = b(\mathrm{E}[e^{-cX}]e^{-c\overline{X}}). \tag{5}$$

Only for lotteries with negative expected values will the two components of Equation 5 point in the same direction, guaranteeing that the riskiness of aY exceeds that of aX.

Implicit in the class of generalized risk-return models is the realization that it is possible to define risk in different ways. The framework suggests that differences in choice patterns that can be modelled by different utility functions can also be interpreted as differences in the definition of risk. Sarin and M. Weber (1993) discuss the fact that risk (just as preference) is a learned concept, and that people with different experiences or training may perceive risk in different ways. Weber and Milliman (1997) recently showed that people's perceptions of the risks of a small set of stocks changed over the course of only ten investment periods as a function of whether they consistently made money or lost money. Whether we are considering individual differences in choice or situational differences where the same individual chooses differently as a function of a different context or a different set of previous experiences, risk-return conceptualizations of risky choice suggest that what is changing from choice to choice is the perception of the *riskiness* of the choice alternatives, not the perception of the return (which is assumed to remain equal to the expected value of the options), nor the preference for risk (which is assumed to remain risk averse).

Perceived-Risk Attitude as a Stable Trait. The assumption of risk aversion as the dominant attitude towards risk in the population and its association with a decreasing marginal utility function for money has been around since Bernoulli in the 18th century. Decreasing marginal utility would, of course, result in greater weight being given to the downside rather than to the upside of a risky option. Even though, within the expected utility framework, risk attitudes only serve as descriptive labels for the shape of the utility function that describes the choices (i.e., with risk seeking/avoiding behavior being described by a convex/concave utility function and the corresponding Arrow (1971) – Pratt (1964) index $\frac{-u''(x)}{u'(x)}$), the popular as well as managerial folklore tends to interpret risk preference as a personality trait. While most people are assumed to be risk averse, some – for example, entrepreneurs – are assumed to be risk takers. In addition, risk taking, perhaps because of its rarity, is assumed to be associated with personal and corporate success, an assumption for which there is a small amount of empirical support (MacCrimmon & Wehrung, 1990).

Unfortunately, there are two problems with the interpretation of risk preference as a personality trait. First, different methods of assessing risk preference can result in different classifications (Slovic, 1964; MacCrimmon & Wehrung, 1990). Second, individuals do not appear to be consistently risk seeking or risk averse across different domains or situations, either in laboratory studies or in managerial contexts. Thus people have been shown to be risk averse for gains but risk seeking for losses (e.g. Payne, Laughhunn, & Crum, 1980), a phenomenon sufficiently stable that Kahneman and Tversky's (1979) prospect theory describes it as an empirical regularity which they model by a value function that is concave for gains, but convex for losses. In addition, choice- and utility-function inferred risk attitudes have not been stable across domains, with people appearing, for example, risk averse in their financial decisions but risk seeking in their recreational choices or vice-versa (e.g. MacCrimmon & Wehrung, 1986).

Weber and Milliman (1997) recently showed that a measure of risk attitude that takes into consideration situational and contextual differences in the perception of the riskiness of options has much greater potential to be consistent for a given individual across situations, and thus to qualify as a measure of a stable personality trait. They called their measure *perceived-risk attitude*, since it measures whether – ceteris paribus – a person tends to seek out options that he or she perceives to be more risky (perceived-risk seeking) or less risky (perceived-risk averse). It is easy to see why such a measure could (but need not, necessarily) lead to greater cross-situational consistency. Our approach is similar to the logic behind Dyer and Sarin's (1982) measure of relative risk attitude, which was to remove differences in marginal value functions from utility functions, to see whether any remaining curvature (the relative risk attitude which reflected solely one's attitude towards uncertainty) was more consistent for a given individual across domains (unfortunately, it was not; see Keller, 1985b). Instead of factoring differences in marginal value out of choice, the perceived-risk attitude measure factors differences in perceived risk out of choice. If an individual's choices appear to be the risk seeking when she is deciding between investment options but appear to be the risk averse when she is deciding between recreational sports possibilities, it may well be that she has a positive attitude towards risk for money, but a negative attitude towards safety risks. On the other hand, it is also possible that her perception and definition of a risky investment option does not coincide with that implied by the expected-utility interpretation of her choices (e.g., risk equal to variance). Assume, for example, that she needs to pay off a balloon mortgage next year and otherwise risks losing her house. In this case, a risky investment option is one that does not provide her with any chance of earning that balloon payment by next year, which may be true for low-variance options. Thus it is at least possible that the woman in our example is consistently perceived-risk averse in both the financial and the recreational decision, that is, she is choosing the option that she perceives to be less risky in both domains. What is different in the two domains and hence affects the option that she chooses is her definition of what constitutes risk in the two domains.

What success does such a measure of perceived-risk attitude (that unconfounds situational differences in risk perception from situational differences in risk prefer-ence) have in bringing about greater cross-situational consistency in risk preference? The answer is overwhelmingly positive. In the first investigation of this issue, We-ber and Bottom (1989) asked their respondents to choose between pairs of lot-teries that either had only positive outcomes or had only negative outcomes and, at a later point in time, asked them to rate which lottery in each pair was riskier. They classified those individuals as perceived-risk averse who consistently chose the option that they had designated as less risky, and those individuals as perceived-risk seeking who consistently chose the option that they had designated as more risky. Consistency was defined statistically by a sign-test, and those individuals who showed no significant relationship between perceived risk and preference were classified as perceived-risk neutral. Each individual's perceived-risk attitude for the set of positive outcome lotteries was compared to his or her perceived-risk attitude for the set of negative outcome lotteries. Even though choices had reflected for most people in the direction predicted by prospect theory (Kahneman & Tversky, 1979), perceived-risk attitudes were quite stable across the two domains. 76% of all participants were either perceived-risk averse or perceived risk neutral for both sets of lotteries. Only one person with a negative perceived-risk attitude in the gain domain displayed perceived-risk seeking in the loss domain.

In a follow-up study, Weber and Milliman (1997) looked at the stability of three different definitions of risk attitude across decisions in the gain vs. the loss domain. Using commuter trains with risky arrival times as choice alternatives, Weber and Milliman asked respondents to choose between pairs of trains that had either only positive arrival times (faster than or equal to the status quo) or only negative arrival times (slower than or equal to the status quo). The same pairs

of trains were also shown again at a later point in time with the request to judge
which of those two trains was the riskier one. In addition, respondents answered
questions that allowed for the construction of their utility functions for faster and
slower commuting time as well as their marginal value functions for gains vs. losses
in commuting time. Choices again reflected from pairs with faster arrival times
(gains) to pairs with slower arrival times (losses), though in the direction opposite
from the pattern commonly observed for monetary gambles. Consistent with this
difference in choice pattern, there was little consistency in people's risk attitude
across the gain and the loss domain when risk attitude was defined by the shape
of an individual's utility functions for gains and losses in commuting time. Only
22% of commuters had consistent utility-function risk attitudes in both domains,
about evenly divided between risk seeking (convex utility functions) and risk aversion (concave utility functions). Consistency improved some, but not dramatically,
to 37% when differences in marginal value for gains vs. losses were factored out,
and people's relative risk attitudes for gains vs. losses in commuting time were compared. However, consistency jumped to 87% when differences in the perceptions
of the riskiness of gains vs. losses in commuting time were factored out, in other
words, when perceived-risk attitudes for gains vs. losses were compared. About
two-thirds of the individuals who showed a consistent perceived-risk attitude in the
gain and the loss domain were consistently risk averse, i.e., choosing trains that
they perceived to be less risky; the other third was consistently perceived-risk seeking, i.e., preferring trains that they perceived to be riskier (expected values were
approximately the same in each pair).

In a second study, Weber and Milliman (1997) tested MBA students with stock
market experience in two sessions of an investment game where they had to pick
one of six stocks (described by standard financial indicators) in each of ten investment periods. In one session of the game, participants lost money in most of the
ten periods, whereas in the other session (with order of sessions, of course, counter-
balanced) they made money in most of the ten periods. Choice patterns were quite
different for the two sessions (with more switching in the failure session), as were
the ratings of the riskiness of the six stocks, as mentioned earlier. When controlling
for those changes in the perceived riskiness of the stocks from the successful to the
unsuccessful investment session, perceived-risk attitudes again showed remarkable
consistency across sessions. Overall, 83% of the investors had the same perceived-
risk attitude in both sessions, with three-quarters of them consistently investing in
stocks that they perceived to be less risky and one-quarter consistently investing in
stocks that they perceived to be more risky.

Finally, Weber and Hsee (in press) obtained risk judgments as well as minimum
buying prices for risky options in both the money domain (investments) and the
time domain (time management plans that may save or cost working hours per
week). Respondents lived in one of four countries: the United States, Germany,
the People's Republic of China, or Poland. While both risk judgments and buying
prices showed significant between-country differences (with Americans perceiving
the most risk and the Chinese the least risk in both domains, and the Chinese
paying the highest prices for the financial options and the Germans the highest
prices for the time options), after differences in risk perception were factored out of

the choices of every respondent, the proportion of individuals who were perceived-risk averse or perceived-risk seeking were not significantly different in either the four countries or the two domains (money vs. time). Around 70% of respondents tended to pay more for options perceived to be less risky (i.e., were perceived-risk averse), whereas the other 30% tended to pay more for those options perceived to be riskier (i.e., were perceived-risk seeking). When perceived-risk attitudes of the same individual in the two domains were compared, 76% of respondents showed the same perceived-risk attitude in this within-subject comparison.

5. SUMMARY AND IMPLICATIONS

Risk perception appears to be a useful construct in all three applications examined in this chapter. Deviations of subjective risk perception from objective definitions of risk (e.g., risk equals variance) are firmly established, as are interpretable individual and situational differences in risk perception. Many measures of subjective risk exist in the literature and researchers continue their efforts to find the measure that best describes absolute and relative risk judgments as well as satisfying other theoretical restrictions.

Individual, situational, and domain differences in risk perceptions do not mean, however, that a single model of subjective risk will be insufficient. As I showed, the CER model has been able to describe the perception of the riskiness of financial, health and safety, and lifestyle choices, and captured domain and respondent similarities (in the functional form of the integration of probability and outcome information) as well as domain and individual differences (in the weighting of different types of information) by differences in its parameter values. This makes risk judgments qualitatively different from judgments of "orthosonority," where each respondent provided judgments in an orderly fashion without any consistency in information weighting or integration across respondents.

The risk perceptions of ordinary citizens and consumers are becoming an ever more powerful factor in the economic and political decisions made in the United States. Whether they "make sense" or approximate nonsensical "orthosonority," they need to be measured to track trends, make comparisons between segments of the population of the United States or cross-national comparisons, and to assess the impact of communications, actions, and interventions.

In addition, perceived risk also appears to be a useful intervening construct. Similar to other subjective self-report measures such as, for example, consumer confidence, it may help to predict subsequent behavior. Current work on generalized risk-return models implies that, as choice patterns change, so does the definition of risk. If so, then an individual's or a group's attitude towards risk may be a constant, even though behavior changes. If choice can differ either because of differences in perceived risk or because of differences in risk attitude, both cannot be simultaneously inferred from choice. In a series of studies that assessed people's perception of the subjective risk of risky options independently from choice, the overwhelming result was that risk perception tended to change alongside with choices and that perceived-risk attitude (either seeking or avoiding options perceived to be riskier) was remarkably constant for a given individual across situations or domains. In line with traditional economic wisdom, the majority risk attitude (between 70% to 80% of the respondents in different studies) was that of perceived-risk aversion.

A final topic worthy of some consideration is the relationship between the conceptualization of risky choice presented in this chapter and its conceptualization in a currently very popular class of models that model risky choice as the maximization of rank- and sign-dependent utility. In this chapter, risky choice was conceptualized as a perceived risk-return tradeoff, with perceived risk as a variable open to individual and situational differences and perceived-risk attitude as determining the desirability of perceived risk in the tradeoff. People can make different choices between a given pair of risky options either because they differ in their perception of the options' riskiness or because they differ in their perceived-risk attitudes (see Mellers, Schwartz, & Weber, this volume). In rank- and sign-dependent utility conceptualizations of risky choice (e.g., Luce & Fishburn, 1991; Tversky & Kahneman, 1992; for a review see Weber & Kirsner, 1996), people can make different choices either because they have different utilities for the outcomes of the choice alternatives or because they differ in the rank- and sign-dependent redistribution of decision weights assigned to those outcomes. The correspondence between individual or situational differences in the components of these two frameworks is essentially an empirical question, and unfortunately no empirical comparison has yet been conducted. One may, however, speculate about the outcome of such a comparison. In a series of studies of rank-dependent utility theory (a special case of a class of models Birnbaum refers to as configural weight models, where the weight given to a particular outcome depends on the configuration of other possible outcomes), Birnbaum (e.g., Birnbaum et al., 1992) has reported excellent model fits with the use of an identity function for the mapping of objective dollar outcomes into the utility function component of his rank-dependent models. This suggests that the utility transformation of outcomes in rank-dependent models is secondary to their success in accounting for people's deviations from an expected value evaluation of risky prospects. Nonlinearity in the utility function of rank- and sign-dependent models may map into nonlinearity in the (riskless) marginal value functions of (positive and negative) outcomes in a particular outcome domain, but probably has little to do with either risk perceptions or risk attitudes. I would suspect that, similar to expected utility models, rank-dependent utility models contain both effects of risk perception and effects of perceived-risk attitudes in their outcome weighting function. The "pessimism" of a particular rank-dependent weighting scheme that assigned disproportionate weights to low outcomes, for example, may be the result (a) of choices based on an equally pessimistic evaluation of the riskiness of choice alternatives paired with a relatively neutral attitude towards perceived risk or (b) of choices based on a relatively rank-neutral evaluation of the riskiness of choice alternatives paired with a negative or aversive attitude towards downside risk. Risk perception and perceived-risk attitudes will be confounded in any utility model estimated exclusively on the basis of choice data. To obtain a psychological interpretation of either utility functions or weighting functions, it is therefore advisable to obtain and model perceived risk judgments in addition to choices.

Choice, Decision, and Measurement
A. A. J. Marley (Ed.),
©Lawrence Erlbaum Associates, NJ, 1997.

DO RISK ATTITUDES REFLECT IN THE EYE OF THE BEHOLDER?

BARBARA A. MELLERS
The Ohio State University

ALAN SCHWARTZ
University of California, Berkeley

ELKE U. WEBER
The Ohio State University

ABSTRACT. Research in risky decision making has shown that choices between gambles with monetary outcomes often reflect around the status quo: preferences are "risk averse" in the gain domain and "risk seeking" in the loss domain. These "economic" risk attitudes are based on an a priori definition of risk: riskier gambles are those with greater variance. We contrast economic risk attitudes with "perceived-risk" attitudes in which the decision maker defines the riskiness of gambles. Those who choose a gamble they judge as less risky than another gamble are perceived-risk averters, and those who choose a gamble they judge as riskier are perceived-risk seekers. We presented subjects with pairs of gambles and obtained both choices and judgments of relative riskiness. We replicated earlier results with economic risk attitudes by showing that the most frequent overall pattern was risk averse preferences in the gain domain and risk seeking preferences in the loss domain. When we examined perceived-risk attitudes in the same set of data, we found that the most frequent overall pattern was perceived-risk aversion in *both* domains. perceived-risk attitudes do *not* tend to reflect in the eye of the beholder. These risk attitudes show considerably more stability across domains than do economic risk attitudes.

1. INTRODUCTION

For over 200 years, expected utility theory has provided a normative framework for decision making under risk. The rule is simple: When making risky choices, people should select the option with the greatest expected utility. Within this framework, two individuals who select different options are assumed to differ in their utilities. Differing utility functions imply differing risk attitudes. We will refer to these risk attitudes, defined by the shape of the utility function, as economic risk attitudes, because they were originally proposed by economists (Pratt, 1964; Arrow, 1965). Later, we distinguish between economic risk attitudes and perceived-risk attitudes, a psychological approach to risky choice described below.

Key words and phrases. Risk attitudes, reflection effect, risk perceptions, risky decision making.

Acknowledgments. These studies were supported by an NSF Grant (SBR-9409698) to Barbara Mellers. We thank Alan Cooke, Duncan Luce, Tony Marley, and Philip Tetlock for comments on an earlier draft.

Address for correspondence. Barbara Mellers, Department of Psychology, Ohio State University, Columbus, Ohio 43210. Email: mellers.1@osu.edu

Consider a choice between a sure thing and a gamble of equal expected value. A person who prefers the sure thing is said to be "risk averse" and is assumed to have a negatively-accelerated utility function. A person who prefers the gamble is called "risk seeking" and is assumed to have a positively-accelerated utility function. Research over the past several years has shown that people are often risk averse in their preferences. Why? The most common explanation has been that people have diminishing marginal utility over wealth. That is, a dollar means less to a millionaire than a pauper. In recent years, this explanation has been challenged by those who theorize that risk averse preferences arise from a nonlinear, rank-dependent probability-weighting function, in addition to, or instead of, a negatively-accelerated utility function (Birnbaum et al., 1992; Lopes, 1987, 1990; Luce, 1991; Luce & Fishburn, 1991; Quiggin, 1982; Yaari, 1987; Tversky & Kahneman, 1992).

Although risk aversion is often considered the norm, people do have risk seeking preferences, especially in the domain of losses (Laughhunn, Payne, & Crum, 1980). To some, a sure loss may be less desirable than a gamble with *some* chance of breaking even, despite the possibility of an even greater loss. In a classic paper on risky choice, Kahneman and Tversky (1979) showed that risk attitudes often reflect around the status quo; people have risk averse preferences in the domain of gains and risk seeking preferences in the domain of losses. They called this reversal of risk attitudes the reflection effect.

Kahneman and Tversky (1979) offer many examples of the reflection effect. In one case, they asked Israeli respondents to choose between A and B, where A was an 80% chance of winning 4,000 Israeli pounds, otherwise nothing, and B was 3,000 Israeli pounds for sure. Eighty percent of respondents exhibited risk aversion for gains by preferring B over A. Another group of respondents chose between C and D, where C was an 80% chance of losing 4,000 pounds and D was a sure loss of 3,000 pounds. Ninety-two percent of respondents displayed risk seeking preferences for losses by preferring C over D. These results suggest that, when the probabilities of winning and losing are large, people have risk averse preferences for gains and risk seeking preferences for losses[1].

What accounts for the reflection effect? Kahneman and Tversky (1979) proposed a theory of risky choice known as prospect theory. People evaluate risky options by means of a value function and a probability-weighting function. The value function is concave for gains and convex for losses; furthermore, it is steeper for losses than gains. The probability-weighting function is convex and implies that smaller probabilities are overweighted and larger probabilities are underweighted. In addition, riskless outcomes are weighted more heavily than risky outcomes. Taken together, these functions imply that when gambles with large probabilities are compared to sure things, economic risk attitudes should reflect around the status quo.

---

[1]Other studies have not found the same degree of support, and there is some debate about the magnitude of the reflection effect in both between-subject and within-subject designs (Cohen, Jaffray, & Said, 1987; Hershey & Schoemaker, 1980; Laughhunn et al., 1980; Schneider & Lopes, 1986).

2. PERCEIVED-RISK ATTITUDES

Weber and Bottom (1989) and Weber and Milliman (1997) took a different approach to understanding the reflection effect. They proposed that risk attitudes might not reflect around the status quo if risk is defined by the decision maker. Risk attitudes that treat risk as a psychological variable are called "perceived-risk" attitudes. Perceived-risk attitudes are based on the assumption that choices between risky options depend both on peoples' perceptions of risk and their preferences for risk. The perceived riskiness of a gamble is *not* based on an apriori definition, such as variance or mean-preserving spread (Rothschild & Stiglitz, 1970). Rather, it is elicited from the decision maker. Preferences for perceived risk express one's taste for risk. Some people are attracted to risk, while others are repelled by it. Those who avoid perceived risk are called perceived-risk averters, and those who seek it out are called perceived-risk seekers.

Perceived-risk attitudes differ from economic risk attitudes in a fundamental way: Risk is a perceptual variable that may differ across individuals and decision contexts. Weber (this volume) describes both individual differences and situational differences in risk perceptions. If risk is assumed to be a psychological variable rather than an a priori characteristic of choice alternatives, then choices are no longer sufficient to infer a person's perceived attitude toward risk. Perceived-risk attitudes require knowledge about both choices *and* perceptions of risk.

A wide range of studies suggest that people have different perceptions of risk. Bromiley and Curley (1992) pointed out that many individuals who appear to be risk takers based on their decisions and actions do not perceive themselves as such. Keyes (1985) quoted a wire walker as saying, "I have no room in my life for risk. You can't be both a risk taker and a wire walker. I take absolutely no risks" (p. 10). He argued that people who believe in their ability to manage or control the events in their lives (i.e., those with an internal, rather than an external, locus of control) often take large risks, but that they do not believe they are taking such risks. In support of this hypothesis, Miller, Kets de Vriess, and Toulouse (1982) found that risk taking in a sample of CEOs was primarily associated with an internal locus of control. By implication, a CEO with an internal locus of control may engage in risky options without perceiving them as risky. In addition, Cooper, Woo, and Dunkelberg (1988) found that risk seeking entrepreneurs were best differentiated from risk averse managers by their overly optimistic perceptions about risks. An outside observer who perceives risks differently (and perhaps more realistically) might be less likely to assume those risks. After differences in risk perceptions are factored out, entrepreneurs have a preference for situations with only moderate perceived risk (Brockhaus, 1982).

Table 1 illustrates how one can infer perceived-risk attitudes from observed choice and judgments of comparative risk (risk perceptions). Consider a choice between two gambles with identical expected values. One gamble has higher variance (HV), and the other has lower variance (LV). Columns refer to risk perceptions; either the LV gamble or the HV gamble could be perceived as riskier. Rows refer to preferences; either the LV gamble or the HV gamble could be chosen. Cell entries

Perceived Risker
LV   HV

	LV	HV
Preferred LV	PRS	PRA
Preferred HV	PRA	PRS

TABLE 1. Illustration of how choices (rows) between a pair of gambles with identical expected values but different variances (LV = low variance gamble, and HV = high variance gamble) and risk perceptions produce different perceived attitudes, shown as cell entries (PRA = perceived-risk averse, and PRS = perceived-risk seeking).

designate perceived-risk attitudes. Perceived-risk averters (PRA) choose the gamble they judge to be less risky, and perceived-risk seekers (PRS) select the gamble they perceive as riskier.

Table 2 presents the framework from Table 1 in a slightly different fashion. Choices (cell entries) are the result of risk perceptions (columns) and perceived-risk attitudes (rows). When might two people select the *same* option? Not surprisingly, two people with identical risk perceptions and identical perceived-risk attitudes will pick the same gamble. Perhaps less obvious is the fact that two people with different risk perceptions *and* different perceived-risk attitudes will also pick the same option. For example, a perceived-risk averter could choose the LV gamble because he perceives the HV gamble as riskier, and a perceived-risk seeker could also choose the LV gamble if he perceives the LV gamble as riskier. Two people make identical choices when they share both risk perceptions and perceived-risk attitudes or when they share neither.

Perceived Risker
LV   HV

Perceived-Risk Attitude		LV	HV
	PRA	HV	LV
	PRS	LV	HV

TABLE 2. Illustration of how different perceived-risk attitudes (rows) and risk perceptions (columns) produce different choices. Cell entries represent the preferred gamble in a choice between a LV and HV gamble.

When might two people select *different* options? Two people would select different options if they have different risk perceptions and identical perceived-risk attitudes. For example, two perceived-risk averters could perceive either the LV gamble or the HV gamble as riskier. The one who judged the LV gamble as riskier would choose the HV gamble, and the one who thought the HV gamble was riskier would select the LV gamble. Second, two people would select different options if they have different perceived-risk attitudes and identical risk perceptions. For example, a perceived-risk averter and a perceived-risk seeker could agree that the LV gamble seemed riskier. If so, the perceived-risk averter would choose the HV gamble and the perceived-risk seeker would choose the LV gamble. Differing choices imply that people differ *either* in their risk perceptions or their perceived-risk attitudes, but not both.

To summarize, perceived-risk attitudes are based on the premise that choices depend on both risk perceptions and preferences for perceived risk. Two people who select identical options have either identical risk perceptions and identical perceived-risk attitudes or different risk perceptions and different perceived-risk attitudes. Two people who select different options have either identical risk perceptions and differing perceived-risk attitudes or differing risk perceptions and identical perceived-risk attitudes.

The reflection effect is usually a demonstration that the same person has differing economic risk attitudes in the domain of gains and losses. Why might the same person have risk averse preferences in the gain domain and risk seeking preferences in the loss domain? In Weber and Milliman's framework, that person might have different risk perceptions and identical perceived-risk attitudes or different perceived-risk attitudes and identical risk perceptions across domains.

Weber and Bottom (1989) suggested that people with reflecting economic risk attitudes might have identical perceived-risk attitudes for gains and losses, but differing risk perceptions. This account would mean that perceived-risk attitudes are more stable and consistent across domains than traditional risk attitudes. In two experiments, Weber and Milliman (1997) asked subjects to choose between risky options and judge the comparative risk of each. One experiment examined decisions between commuter trains varying in arrival times, and the other investigated financial decisions between stock market investments. They found that, in both experiments, a large percentage of subjects had preferences that reflected around the status quo. Furthermore, an even larger percentage of subjects had identical perceived-risk attitudes across domains, and most of them were perceived-risk averters. That is, people chose the option that they perceived as less risky in both domains; however, the low variance option was judged to be less risky in the gain domain, and the high variance option judged to be less risky in the loss domain. The following experiment further examines perceived-risk attitudes using familiar stimuli in the field of decision making – namely, gambles with monetary outcomes.

3. METHOD

People made choices and comparative risk judgments between pairs of risky options described as gambles, with two nonnegative outcomes (in the gain domain) or two nonpositive outcomes (in the loss domain). Gambles in the gain domain had expected values of $40, and those in the loss domain had expected values of -$40.

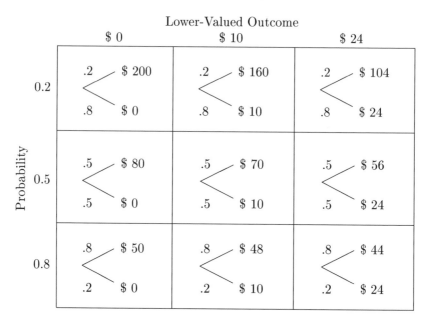

TABLE 3. Experimental design. Each cell represents a gamble. Rows are probabilities of high-valued outcomes, and columns are lower-valued outcomes. Expected values for all 9 gambles are $40.

Gambles with positive expected values were constructed from a factorial design of Probability by Outcome, and these gambles are shown in Table 3. Gambles with negative expected values had the same structure, except the signs of the outcomes were negative. Each set of options included the nine gambles and a sure thing equal to the expected value of the gambles.

Participants made choices and reported the strength of their preference for all possible pairs of options with the same expected value (45 pairs in each set). After stating all of their preferences, subjects were presented with the same pairs and indicated which option was riskier[2]. There were 90 choices and 90 comparative risk judgments in total.

Gambles were displayed as pie charts on IBM computers. People were told to imagine a spinner attached to the center of the pie chart. An example is shown in Figure 1. For this gamble, if the imaginary spinner was spun and the pointer landed in the white region, the outcome would be a win of $70. If the pointer landed in the grey region, the outcome would be a win of $10.

One hundred and thirty seven undergraduates at the University of California at Berkeley served as subjects and received credit in a psychology course for their participation. A few additional subjects who did not follow instructions were excluded from the analyses.

---

[2]Pilot work suggested no effect of task order.

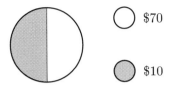

FIGURE 1. Gamble display. The white region corresponds to a 0.50 chance of winning $70. The grey region corresponds to a 0.50 chance of winning $10.

4. RESULTS

Consider a choice between a sure win of $40 and a gamble with an 80% chance of winning $50. Which would you prefer? Now consider a choice between a sure loss of $40 and a gamble with an 80% chance of losing $50. Although neither option is desirable, which would you prefer? The left-hand panel in Table 4 shows our subjects' choices for this pair of questions[3].

In the gain domain, 95 out of 133 subjects (71%) preferred the sure thing; these subjects were risk averse according to the economic definition. In the loss domain, the majority of subjects (69%) preferred the gamble; these subjects were risk seekers in the traditional sense. These percentages provide between-subject support for the reflection effect. Within-subject support can be found in the lower-left cell; 67 subjects (50%) were both risk averse for gains and risk seeking for losses.

The right-hand panel of Table 4 shows *perceived*-risk attitudes for these subjects. In the gain domain, 93 subjects (70%) were perceived-risk averters, and in the loss domain, 59% of the subjects were also perceived-risk averters. These percentages provide between-subject support for the notion that people are perceived-risk averters in both domains. Within-subject support can be found in the upper-right cell; 59 subjects (44%) were perceived-risk averters in both domains. For this gamble, 60% of the subjects (59 + 21) had consistent perceived-risk attitudes across domains.

Table 5 takes an even closer look at the perceived-risk attitudes for each pattern of economic risk attitudes (from Table 4). For example, the 28 subjects in the upper-left cell of Table 4 appear in the upper-left panel of Table 5. Almost all of these people (21 out of 28) were perceived-risk averters in both domains.

The most interesting panel is the one in the lower left that shows perceived-risk attitudes for people whose choices reflected around the status quo in the familiar way. Of these, 54% had identical perceived-risk attitudes in both domains, and the overwhelming majority (36 of 37) were perceived-risk averters. An additional 30 subjects (45%) had perceived-risk attitudes that resembled their economic risk attitudes; these subjects selected the less risky gamble in the gain domain and the riskier gamble in the loss domain.

---

[3]Four subjects who could not be classified because they were indifferent between the gamble and the sure thing have been excluded.

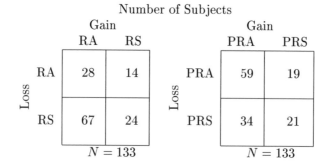

Number of Subjects

	Gain				Gain	
	RA	RS			PRA	PRS
RA	28	14		PRA	59	19
RS	67	24		PRS	34	21
	N = 133				N = 133	

TABLE 4. Numbers of subjects with different economic risk attitudes in the gain and loss domain (RA = risk averse, and RS = risk seeking).

Number of Subjects

		RA Gain Gain		*RS Gain* Gain	
		PRA	PRS	RA	RS
RA Loss Loss	PRA	21	1	1	11
	PRS	4	2	0	2
RS Loss Loss	PRA	36	0	1	7
	PRS	30	1	0	16

TABLE 5. Numbers of subjects with different *perceived*-risk attitudes in the gain and loss domain for each cell in Table 4.

In summary, why did preferences in our study reflect around the status quo? Preferences reflected for two different reasons. About half of the respondents had perceived-risk attitudes that resembled their economic risk attitudes; these people avoided gambles they perceived as risky in the gain domain, but were attracted to those gambles in the loss domain. The other half of the respondents were perceived-risk averters in both domains. Their taste for risk did not reflect, but their *perceptions* of risk varied around the status quo.

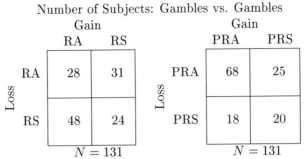

TABLE 6. Numbers of subjects with different economic risk attitudes in the gain and loss domains based on all of the data for gambles vs. gambles.

How robust is this pattern? To answer this question, we classified individuals into one of four patterns of economic risk attitudes using all of their choices. Since reflection has been shown to occur more frequently with gambles versus sure things than with gambles versus gambles (Schneider & Lopes, 1986), we present the two types of comparisons separately. There were 36 gamble-vs.-gamble pairs, and nine gamble-vs.-sure thing pairs. For each individual, we classified each choice in the gain and loss domain according to the four economic risk attitudes. Then we categorized each person based on the most frequently occurring pattern of economic risk attitudes (e.g., RA in the gain domain and RS in the loss domain)[4].

Table 6 shows numbers of subjects with different economic risk attitudes (left-hand panel) and different perceived-risk attitudes (right-hand panel) for the gamble-vs.-gamble comparisons. Although there are many individual differences, the most common pattern of economic risk attitudes was the familiar reflection effect: 48 out of 131 subjects (37%) had risk averse preferences for gains and risk seeking preferences for losses[5]. The right-hand panel shows perceived-risk attitudes. The majority of subjects (67%) had identical perceived-risk attitudes across domains, and the overwhelming majority were perceived-risk averters.

Table 7 shows perceived-risk attitudes for each pattern of economic risk attitudes. One can see that, for those subjects whose preferences reflected in the familiar way (lower-left panel), 29 were perceived-risk averters in both domains and 15 had perceived-risk attitudes that matched their economic risk attitudes. To the perceived-risk averters, the *high* variance gamble was riskier in the gain domain, and the *low* variance gamble was riskier in the loss domain. To the group with different perceived-risk attitudes across domains, the riskier gamble was always the high variance gamble.

Table 8 shows the same analyses as Table 6 for the gamble-vs.-sure thing comparisons, where the reflection effect is usually stronger. In our study, we found that a greater percentage of subjects showed reflection in these comparisons than in

[4]Subject classifications can also be done statistically, as in Weber and Bottom (1989).
[5]Six subjects in the gamble-vs.-gamble comparisons and 25 subjects in the gamble-vs.-sure thing comparisons could not be classified because they had identical numbers of RA or RS choices in one or both domains.

Number of Subjects: Gambles vs. Gambles

	RA Gain Gain PRA	PRS	RS Gain Gain RA	RS
RA Loss Loss PRA	23	1	9	19
PRS	3	1	0	3
RS Loss Loss PRA	29	4	7	1
PRS	15	0	0	16

TABLE 7. Numbers of subjects with different perceived-risk attitudes in the gain and loss domains for each cell in Table 6.

Number of Subjects: Gambles vs. Sure Things

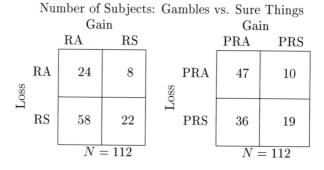

	Gain RA	RS		Gain PRA	PRS
Loss RA	24	8	Loss PRA	47	10
RS	58	22	PRS	36	19
	$N = 112$			$N = 112$	

TABLE 8. Numbers of subjects with different economic risk attitudes in the gain and loss domains based on all of the data for gambles vs. sure things.

the gamble-vs.-gamble comparisons using both between-subject and within-subject tests. Fifty-two percent of subjects were risk averse in the gain domain and risk seeking in the loss domain. The right-hand panel shows, once again, that the reflecting economic risk attitudes were not perceived to reflect by the majority of subjects. Fifty-nine percent of subjects (47+19) had consistent perceived-risk attitudes across domains, and the majority were perceived-risk averters.

Table 9 presents the same information as Table 7 for gamble-vs.-sure thing comparisons. Perceived-risk attitudes for those subjects whose preferences reflected in the familiar way (lower-left corner) tend to fall into one of two groups. Either

Number of Subjects: Gambles vs. Sure Things

	RA Gain Gain			RS Gain Gain	
	PRA	PRS		RA	RS
RA Loss — Loss — PRA	20	0		0	6
PRS	3	1		1	1
RS Loss — Loss — PRA	25	1		2	3
PRS	32	0		0	17

TABLE 9. Numbers of subjects with different perceived-risk attitudes in the gain and loss domains for each cell in Table 8.

their perceived-risk attitudes resembled their economic risk attitudes (and they perceived the gamble as riskier in both domains) or they were perceived-risk averters in both domains and their perceptions of risk varied.

These two groups of subjects had the same patterns of choices (risk averse preferences for gains and risk seeking preferences for losses) for two different reasons. For one group (the perceived-risk averters) risk was unattractive. These people selected the option they perceived as less risky in both domains. In the gain domain, the risky option was the gamble, and in the loss domain, the risky option was the sure thing (with a guaranteed loss). For the other group, perceived-risk attitudes paralleled economic risk attitudes. Their risk perceptions were identical across domains; the risky option was always the gamble.

We now focus on the two groups of subjects from Table 7 whose preferences reflected – namely, the 29 subjects who were always perceived-risk averters and the 15 subjects who were perceived-risk averters for gains and perceived-risk seekers for losses. For each group, we derived two sets of preference orders (one for the gain and one for the loss domain) and two sets of riskiness orders over the nine gambles. Preference orders were obtained by counting the number of times the majority of subjects preferred one gamble to the other eight gambles. Riskiness orders were obtained in a similar fashion.

Figure 2 shows preference orders (left panel) and risk orders (right panel) for people with identical perceived-risk attitudes and different risk perceptions. Gambles on the abscissa are ordered from least preferred to most preferred in the gain

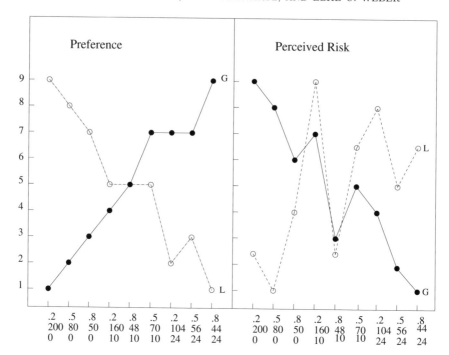

FIGURE 2. Preference orders (left panel) and perceived-risk orders (right panel) plotted against gambles for subjects with reflecting economic risk attitudes who were perceived-risk averse for both gains and losses ($n = 29$). Solid curves labeled "G" are for gains; dashed curves labeled "L" are for losses.

domain. There is a dramatic crossover interaction of preference orders in the gain (G) and loss (L) domains; this is the reflection effect. The correlation between these preference orders was -0.97; what is liked in the gain domain is disliked in the loss domain. Risk perceptions also show a crossover interaction, although not quite so dramatic. Figure 3 plots preference and risk orders for those with different perceived-risk attitudes and identical risk perceptions. Once again, the crossover interaction in the left panel shows the reflection effect. Risk orders in the right panel are almost identical in the gain and loss domains.

Figure 4 replots the information shown in Figures 2 and 3 to highlight additional features of the data. Orders are presented as a function of outcome with a separate curve for each level of the probability of that outcome. Upper panels show preference and risk orders for those people who had different risk perceptions, but identical perceived-risk attitudes. Perceived-risk attitudes can be inferred from comparisons of preference and risk orders within a domain. Correlations were -0.89 and -0.58 for gains and losses, respectively; negative correlations mean that subjects preferred the gambles they perceived as less risky. In both domains, these subjects were perceived-risk averters. The fact that their risk perceptions differed between gains and losses can be seen by comparing the risk orders across domains; this correlation was -0.31.

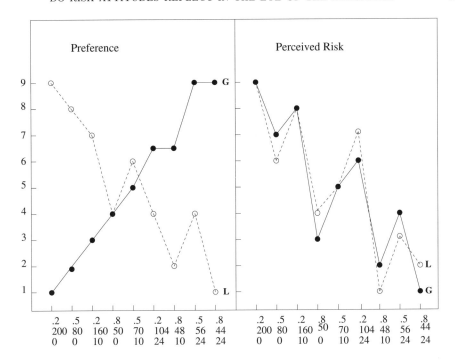

FIGURE 3. Preference orders (left panel) and perceived-risk orders (right panel) plotted against gambles for subjects with reflecting economic risk attitudes and reflecting perceived-risk attitudes ($n = 15$). Solid curves labeled "G" are for gains; dashed curves labeled "L" are for losses.

Lower panels show preference and risk orders for those individuals with different perceived-risk attitudes and identical risk perceptions (i.e., those for whom perceived-risk attitudes resembled economic risk attitudes). The fact that they had different perceived-risk attitudes can be seen by comparing preference and risk orders within a domain. Correlations were -0.86 and 0.85 for gains and losses, respectively. These individuals disliked perceived risk in the gain domain, but liked it in the loss domain. The fact that their risk perceptions were identical for gains and losses can be seen by comparing risk orders across domains; this correlation was 0.95.

Did perceptions of risk correlate with the a-priori definition of risk as variance for either group? For those whose perceived-risk attitudes resembled their economic risk attitudes, risk perceptions were quite similar to the order derived from the variance of the gambles. Correlations between risk order and variance order were 0.95 and 1.0 for gains and losses, respectively. For those with different risk perceptions across domains, perceived risk correlated with variance in the gain domain ($r = 0.90$), but not in the loss domain ($r = 0.0$). In the loss domain, gambles perceived as most risky were those with two negative outcomes, and those with the largest negative outcomes were perceived to be the riskiest. Gambles allowing the

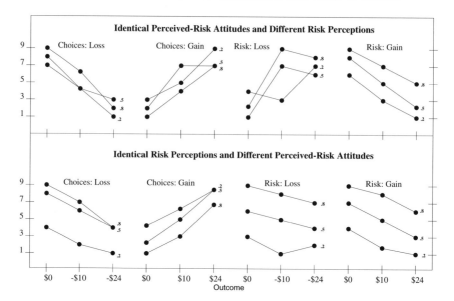

FIGURE 4. This figure replots preference orders and risk orders for the subjects in Figure 2 (upper panels) and Figure 3 (lower panels). Orders are shown as a function of one outcome, with a separate curve for that outcome's probability. The largest differences between the two groups can be seen in their perceptions of risk in the loss domain.

opportunity to break even (i.e., those with one zero outcome) were judged as less risky.

In sum, risk perceptions for the two groups whose choices reflected around the status quo were similar in the gain domain, and those perceptions were well-described by the variance of the gambles. In the loss domain, risk perceptions differed for the two groups. For the perceived-risk seekers, risky gambles were those with greater variance. For the perceived-risk averters, risky gambles were those with lower variance which translated into a guaranteed loss, combined with the threat of an even larger loss.

5. DISCUSSION

A widely-accepted result in the literature on risky choice is that economic risk attitudes reflect around the status quo (Kahneman & Tversky, 1979). When the probabilities of winning and losing are large, people often have risk averse preferences in the gain domain and risk seeking preferences in the loss domain. Weber and Milliman (1997) suggested that this apparent inconsistency in economic risk attitudes might be reduced by treating risk as a psychological variable. They suggested that perceived-risk attitudes, based on people's perceptions of risk, might reveal greater consistency across domains. In our experiment, the most common pattern of economic risk attitudes was reflection – risk aversion for gains and risk seeking for losses. The reflection effect was stronger for gambles vs. sure things than for gambles vs. gambles, consistent with previous results (Schneider & Lopes, 1986). Furthermore, the majority of subjects (in both types of comparisons) had identical perceived-risk attitudes across domains, and most of these subjects were perceived-risk averters.

A careful look at *only* those people whose preferences reflected around the status quo revealed two groups who made the same choices for quite different reasons. Differences appeared in the loss domain. One group tried to avoid risk, which was perceived as a guaranteed loss, with the potential for an even greater loss. The other group preferred risk. For these people, the riskier option was not synonymous with the "bad" option. Risk was desirable because it offered the chance to break even.

Economic risk attitudes are not an explanation of choice; they provide an a posteriori classification of individuals. Similarly, perceived-risk attitudes are not an explanation; they provide a categorization of people based on the conjunction of choices and perceptions of risk. What is needed is a theory of risky choice and a theory of comparative risk judgment that can simultaneously account for both economic and perceived-risk attitudes, and the individual differences that occur with both. Rank- and sign-dependent theory (Luce, 1991; Luce & Fishburn, 1991) may be a reasonable contender for risky choice[6]. Several theories of risk judgment have been proposed, including conjoint expected risk theory (Luce & Weber, 1986), the bilinear model of risk (Coombs & Lehner, 1984) and the additive model (Mellers & Chang, 1994), but none of these theories directly addresses the individual differences in the loss domain.

In conclusion, we find that economic risk attitudes often reflect around the status quo, but perceived-risk attitudes are more stable and consistent across domains. People tend to avoid what they perceive as risky regardless of the sign of the outcomes, but their perceptions of risk vary for positive and negative outcomes. Results from the present study show that risk perceptions give us a broader, though not entirely simple, picture of the psychology of risky choice.

---

[6]We constructed a set of predictions based on Tversky and Kahneman's cumulative prospect theory. However, the correlations between choice proportions and binary predictions were quite low for both groups of subjects in the gain and loss domains. Predictions were derived from the parameters given by Tversky and Kahneman (1992). Those were estimated from certainty equivalents rather than choice proportions, and we suspect that the parameters for choice proportions may be quite different.

Choice, Decision, and Measurement
A. A. J. Marley (Ed.),
©Lawrence Erlbaum Associates, NJ, 1997.

VIOLATIONS OF MONOTONICITY IN JUDGMENT AND DECISION MAKING

MICHAEL H. BIRNBAUM

California State University, Fullerton
and Institute for Mathematical Behavioral Sciences, Irvine

ABSTRACT. Monotonicity is a fundamental assumption of axiomatic decision theories. According to this principle, if two alternatives are otherwise identical, except one has an outcome for at least one nonempty state of nature that is preferred to the corresponding outcome for the other alternative, then the alternative with the better outcome should be preferred. Applied to judgments of the value of gambles, the principle states that the judged value of a gamble should increase monotonically as a function of each outcome, holding everything else constant. As appealing as this axiom is for normative theory, it has been systematically violated in experiments in which subjects judge cash values of gambles. The violation has not been observed in transparent, direct comparisons, but it has been replicated when the gambles are compared to a fixed set of cash values. The violations can be explained by the assumption that decision weights in judgment differ depending on the rank and also on the augmented sign (which is negative, zero, or positive). Violations of branch independence can also be explained by rank-dependent configural weighting. The pattern observed rules out the theory that subjects cancel common outcomes in comparison. The pattern is also opposite that predicted by the inverse-S weighting function used in cumulative prospect theory. Testable properties are suggested to distinguish different models of configural weighting.

1. INTRODUCTION

The principle of consequence monotonicity can be stated briefly as follows: If two alternatives are otherwise identical but one alternative has a consequence for one nonempty state of nature that is preferred to the corresponding consequence for that state of nature given the other alternative, then the alternative with the better consequence should be preferred.

For gambles defined as probability distributions whose consequences are monetary outcomes, outcome monotonicity can be defined as follows:

Key words and phrases. Decision making and judgment, axiomatic theories of decision-making, monotonicity, Savage's axiom, subjective expected utility theory, cumulative prospect theory, configural weighting, rank-dependent utility theory, dominance, choice, preference, utility.

Acknowledgments. Research summarized in this paper was supported by a National Science Foundation Grant, SES 8921880, to California State University, Fullerton Foundation. Preparation of this chapter was facilitated by SBR-9410572. I thank R. Duncan Luce, Barbara Mellers, John Miyamoto, Peter Wakker, Elke Weber, and an anonymous reviewer for helpful comments on an earlier draft.

Address for correspondence. Prof. Michael H. Birnbaum, Department of Psychology, California State University, P.O. Box 6846, Fullerton, CA 92834-6846. E-mail: mbirnbaum@fullerton.edu

Suppose gambles A and A' differ in their outcomes on one branch as follows:

$$A = (x, p(x); a_2, p(a_2); \ldots ; a_i, p(a_i); \ldots ; a_m, p(a_m))$$
$$A' = (y, p(x); a_2, p(a_2); \ldots ; a_i, p(a_i); \ldots ; a_m, p(a_m))$$

where $p(x)$ is the probability to receive outcome x (or y), given choice A (or A'), respectively; and the sum of the probabilities is 1 within each gamble. Monotonicity requires that gamble A is preferred to A' if and only if gamble B is preferred to B' where:

$$B = (x, p'(x); b_2, p(b_2); \ldots ; b_j, p(b_j); \ldots ; b_n, p(b_n))$$
$$B' = (y, p'(x); b_2, p(b_2); \ldots ; b_j, p(b_j); \ldots ; b_n, p(b_n))$$

for all gambles so defined.

The term *stochastic dominance* refers to the relation between nonidentical gambles, A and B, such that gamble A stochastically dominates gamble B if and only if the probability of receiving x or less given gamble A is less than or equal the probability of receiving x or less given gamble B, for all x. Tversky and Kahneman (1986) reported a violation of stochastic dominance, when the relation was not transparent.

Stochastic dominance combines monotonicity with respect to outcomes and monotonicity with respect to probabilities. A violation of outcome monotonicity also violates stochastic dominance, but a violation of stochastic dominance is not necessarily a violation of monotonicity, unless other assumptions are made (Luce, 1986a, 1988). Luce and von Winterfeldt (1994) noted that it is therefore useful to decompose the concept of dominance into consequence (outcome) monotonicity and event monotonicity. In Luce's (1988) approach, the Ellsberg paradox can be interpreted as a violation of event monotonicity, but is not a test of outcome monotonicity.

This chapter deals with outcome monotonicity, concerning which Luce (1992c) remarked, "Because monotonicity is a keystone to all existing theories of choices among uncertain alternatives, it is essential that we decide whether or not it is generally applicable. If not, it's back to the drawing boards." (*p. 23*)

The next section reviews research showing that certain types of judgments systematically violate outcome monotonicity. A configural weight model is presented in the third section to describe the violations. The fourth section presents experimental replications and extensions of the research paradigm. The fifth section takes up choice-based certainty equivalents, which give mixed results, depending on the method used. The sixth section reviews experiments that have estimated the configural weighting function for positive, negative, and zero outcomes. The seventh section takes up a related phenomenon, violations of branch independence, which can be used to test among different configural weighting models. The eighth section summarizes the current status of evidence and describes testable properties that can be used to compare different classes of configural weighting models, and the ninth section gives a summary of conclusions.

2. VIOLATIONS OF MONOTONICITY IN JUDGMENT

Although outcome monotonicity seems a very reasonable axiom for the rational decision maker, recent experiments have found situations in which mean judgments violate the principle systematically. Birnbaum and Gregory Coffey designed and conducted two experiments in 1986, following the approach of Birnbaum and Stegner (1979). Their first experiment showed violations of monotonicity that appeared to indicate that the outcome of zero receives less weight than nonzero outcomes, similar to results previously reported by Anderson and Birnbaum (1976). Birnbaum and Coffey designed a stronger test for violations in their second experiment. Their results were reported by Birnbaum (1987a, 1987b, 1987c).

At this time, collaborative projects were under way with Elke Weber, Barbara Mellers, Carolyn Anderson, and Lisa Ordóñez to investigate whether principles of judgment, inferred from judgments in other domains, also applied to judgments of gambles. Weber et al. (1992) applied the approach of Birnbaum and Stegner (1979) to model the relationships between ratings of the risk and attractiveness of gambles. One line of research was devoted to testing the models of preference reversals of Goldstein and Einhorn (1987) and Tversky, Sattath, and Slovic (1988), using the criterion of scale convergence (Birnbaum, 1974, 1982). Although the expression theory of Goldstein and Einhorn (1987) can accommodate violations of monotonicity, neither it nor the contingent weighting theory of Tversky et al. (1988) correctly accounts for changes in rank order between ratings and prices using the same scale of utility (Mellers, Ordóñez, & Birnbaum, 1992a).

The experiments of Birnbaum and Coffey had been designed to test several predictions of configural weighting models, including a specific pattern of changes in rank order of judgments that should be produced by point of view if point of view affects configural weights, as postulated in Birnbaum and Stegner (1979). The violations of monotonicity, confirmed in their second experiment, excited interest and became the focus of new research.

Sara Sutton, Barbara Mellers, Patricia Berretty, and Robin Weiss soon joined in the study of these phenomena, fitting the data to models and exploring the effects of different subjects, different values, different stimulus formats, and other variations. Results of these investigations were published in several papers (Birnbaum, 1992b; Birnbaum et al., 1992; Birnbaum & Sutton, 1992; Mellers et al., 1992b; Weber et al., 1992). That research led to further investigations (Birnbaum & Thompson, 1996; Mellers et al., 1995; von Winterfeldt et al., 1997). This chapter will review this body of empirical research.

Let (x, p_x, y) represent the binary gamble to receive x with probability p_x and otherwise receive y ($p_y = 1 - p_x > 0$). Monotonicity requires that (x_1, p_1, y) is preferred to (x_2, p_1, y) if and only if (x_1, p_2, y) is preferred to (x_2, p_2, y); in other words, if and only if x_1 is preferred to x_2. Birnbaum et al. (1992) found that (\$0, .05, \$96) receives a higher mean judgment than (\$24, .05, \$96), although (\$24, .5, \$96) receives a higher mean judgment than (\$0, .5, \$96); indeed, we assume that \$24 is better than \$0.

Figure 1 illustrates the pattern of results observed by Birnbaum et al. (1992). Mean judgments from the buyer's point of view (the "most a buyer should pay" for each gamble), the neutral's point of view ("fair" price), and the seller's point of view (the "least a seller should accept to sell the gamble") are plotted in separate panels as a function of the probability to win $96, with open circles for gambles in which the lowest outcome was $0, and filled circles for gambles in which the worst outcome was $24. According to outcome monotonicity, filled symbols ($24) should exceed the open symbols ($0), for all values of p. Instead, the data values cross for three levels of $1 - p \geq .8$ in each point of view. The percentage of subjects who violated monotonicity when $1 - p = .95$ was 53%, 60%, and 36% in the buyer's, neutral's and seller's points of view, compared with 34%, 25%, and 36% who conformed to it, respectively, and the rest were ties. Similar results were observed when $72 replaced $96.

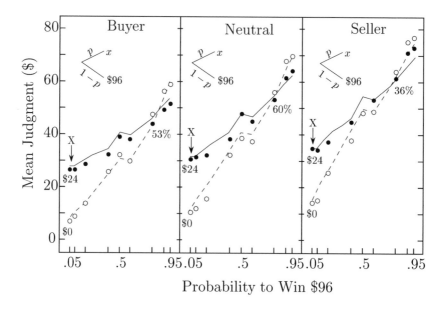

FIGURE 1. Mean judgments of binary gambles (x, p, y) as a function of the probability to win $96 ($1 - p$), with unfilled circles showing results when $x = $0, and filled circles showing results when $x = $24. Separate panels show judgments in the buyer's, neutral's, and seller's points of view. Crossing of the curves indicates violation of outcome monotonicity. Lines show predictions of configural weight model. Data from Birnbaum et al. (1992).

3. CONFIGURAL WEIGHT MODEL OF VIOLATIONS AND POINT OF VIEW

The term *configural* is used to indicate that the parameter representing a stimulus component depends on the relationships between that component and others that comprise the stimulus array presented on each trial (Birnbaum, 1974). Subjective expected utility (SEU) theory (Savage, 1954), for example, is not configural because the weight of each outcome's utility is independent of the value of the outcome and its relationships to other outcomes in the same gamble, and the utility of each outcome is independent of the other outcomes. Similarly, Edwards (1954) version of SEU using a weighting function for probabilities is also not configural, for the same reason. "Configural weighting" models allow the weights of the outcomes to depend on the configuration of outcomes and probabilities that comprise the gambles, but assume that the utility function is independent of context and configuration.

Birnbaum's (1974, *p. 559*) configural weight model allows the weight of a stimulus component to depend on its rank among the other components that comprise the stimulus array. Applied to gambles, the weight of the same outcome with the same probability can be different in different gambles depending on the other outcomes in those gambles (Birnbaum, 1982, 1992a, 1992b; Birnbaum et al., 1992; Birnbaum & Sotoodeh, 1991; Birnbaum & Stegner, 1979; Weber et al., 1992; Weber, 1994).

Configural weighting models, such as Birnbaum's (1974) range model, are closely related to rank-and sign-dependent utility models (Chew & Wakker, 1996; Lopes, 1990; Luce, 1992b, 1992c, 1995b; Luce & Fishburn, 1991, 1995; Luce & Narens, 1985; Quiggin, 1982; Tversky & Kahneman, 1992; Yaari, 1987), which were developed independently [see review by Wakker (1993)].

Rank-dependent utility theory and rank-and sign-dependent utility theories are configural weight models that allow violations of outcome independence (see Section 7), but assume monotonicity. The model of cumulative prospect theory is a special case of rank- and sign-dependent theory with a restricted weighting function; this model implies stochastic dominance. To account for violations of monotonicity, the numerical representation of rank- and sign-dependent utility theory (Luce & Fishburn, 1991), for example, would have to be modified to allow different weights for different outcomes. Luce (1992b) noted that the violations observed thus far have been restricted to gambles including the outcome zero, and suggested how a rank- and sign-dependent representation of certainty equivalents could be modified to accommodate the violations. In the eighth section of this chapter, empirical properties are described that can test among various configural weight models. In this section, we present the model of Birnbaum et al. (1992) to account for violations of monotonicity and which also describes changes in rank order that depend on the judge's point of view.

Birnbaum et al. (1992) represented judgments of binary gambles, (x, p_x, y), by the following configural weight model:

$$U_V(x, p_x, y) = \frac{Au(x) + Bu(y)}{A + B} \tag{1a}$$

where $U_V(x, p_x, y)$ is the utility of the gamble in point of view V; $u(x)$ and $u(y)$ are the utilities (subjective values) of the lower- and higher-valued outcomes $(x < y)$; and A and B are their absolute configural weights, which depend on the judge's point of view, on probability, and value as in the following equations:

$$A = a_V S_x(p_x) \tag{1b}$$

$$B = (1 - a_V)[1 - S_x(1 - p_y)] \tag{1c}$$

where a_V is the configural weighting parameter for point of view V; p_x and p_y are the probabilities to receive x or y, respectively; and $S_x(p_x)$ is a function of the probability of the lower-valued outcome, x, that depends on its value.

Birnbaum et al. (1992) posited two different S_x functions for the cases in which $x > 0$ and for $x = 0$. For $.04 < p < .96$, $S_x(p)$ can be approximated by $S_x(p) = .59p+.29$, for $x > 0$; however, for $x = 0$, $S_0(p)$ is approximated by $S_0(p) = .74p+.14$. Note that $S_0(p)$ is less than $S_x(p)$, especially for small values of p. In this model, monotonicity violations occur because the lowest outcome of zero has less weight than a lowest outcome that is a small positive amount (for the same low probability).

For three-outcome gambles $(x, p_x; y, p_y; z, p_z)$, where $0 \leq x < y < z$, and $p_z = 1 - p_x - p_y$, Birnbaum et al. (1992) used the following expression:

$$U_V(x, p_x; y, p_y; z, p_z) = \frac{Au(x) + Bu(y) + Cu(z)}{A + B + C} \qquad (1d)$$

where

$$C = (1 - a_V)[1 - S_x(1 - p_z)]. \qquad (1e)$$

A and B are as defined in Expressions 1b and 1c.

In this model, $u(x)$ and $S_x(p_x)$ are assumed to be independent of point of view, context, and configuration. Birnbaum et al. (1992) assumed that the weights of the middle and highest stimuli are equal when they are of equal probability (i.e., $C = B$ when $p_y = p_z$), an assumption that will be reconsidered in Section 7.

This model can be derived from the assumption that the subject is minimizing an asymmetric loss function, assuming that the stimuli are spaced so that the response is between the lowest and middle stimuli (Birnbaum et al., 1992; Birnbaum & McIntosh, 1996). When the response is between the middle and highest stimuli, however, the weight of the middle stimulus would equal that of the lowest outcome, a switch of configural weights that allows violations of comonotonic independence (Birnbaum & McIntosh, 1996). Thus, the loss function approach implies that configural weights will depend not only on rank but also on the spacing of the stimuli. Experiments to test these interpretations are proposed in Section 8.

The loss function concept also provides a rationale to explain why configural weights would depend on the judge's point of view (Birnbaum & Stegner, 1979). Judge's "point of view" refers to instructions that may affect the relative costs of judgment errors in different directions. Examples of viewpoint manipulations are instructions to the judge to identify with the buyer or seller in a transaction, to judge the morality of others or to consider being judged, or to identify with the prosecution or defense in a trial. If point of view affects the relative costs of over- or under-estimating a value, and if judges choose responses to minimize costs, then configural weights should depend on viewpoint. If weights change in different viewpoints, the models predict special patterns of reversals of preference due to changes in point of view (Birnbaum, 1982; Birnbaum & Beeghley, 1997).

Previous research that fit configural weight models to judgments concluded that weights also differ for neutral, or zero-valued outcomes (Anderson & Birnbaum, 1976); such an assumption allows configural weighting to explain violations of monotonicity. Configural weight models assume scale convergence, the principle that the utility (or value) function is independent of point of view and configuration. The assumption of scale convergence was used to test rank dependent models against the nonconfigural models (Birnbaum et al., 1992; Birnbaum & Sutton, 1992).

The configural weight parameters, a_V, predict how the rank order of gambles change in different points of view. For the seller's point of view, a_V was set to .5, and the values estimated for the neutral's and buyer's points of view were approximately .6 and .7, respectively. Configural weight theory (Expressions 1a-1e) led to an estimated $u(x)$ function that was invariant with respect to point of view (Birnbaum et al., 1992); nonconfigural theories require different $u(x)$ functions in different viewpoints. This model led to an estimated $u(x)$ function that was also compatible with estimates of $u(x)$ based on judgments of "ratios" and "differences" of riskless utility (Birnbaum & Sutton, 1992).

4. REPLICATIONS AND EXTENSIONS

Monotonicity Satisfied in Direct Comparisons. Birnbaum and Sutton (1992), as part of their study of scale convergence, included a partial replication of the tests of monotonicity from Birnbaum et al. (1992). They also asked subjects to choose between pairs of gambles, including pairs involving tests of monotonicity. Although mean and median judgments violated monotonicity, replicating the findings of Birnbaum et al. (1992), few subjects violated monotonicity when asked to make direct comparisons.

Figure 2 shows mean judgments from Birnbaum and Sutton (1992) in the seller's point of view. [Medians for both buyer's and seller's viewpoints are similar, as shown in Birnbaum & Sutton (1992, Figure 9)]. Mean judgments for ($0, p, $96) and for ($0, p, $72) are shown as open squares and circles, respectively, connected by dashed lines; mean judgments of ($24, p, $96) and ($24, p, $72) are shown as filled squares and circles, respectively, connected by solid lines. The crossing of open and filled symbols represent violations of monotonicity. Figure 2 also shows that judgments of ($24, p, $96) are not simply $24 plus the judgments of ($0, p, $72).

Equations 1a-1e fit the data of Birnbaum et al. (1992), and predicted the patterns of monotonicity violations obtained by Birnbaum and Sutton (1992) and Birnbaum (1992b). The gambles in these studies were presented as in the following example:

$$\frac{.2 \qquad .8}{\$24 \qquad \$96}$$

which represents ($24, .2, $96). One possibility was that subjects were violating monotonicity because of some numerical algorithm induced by the particular stimulus display.

Violations with Pie charts, Negative Outcomes, and Cash Incentives. Mellers et al. (1992b) replicated and extended the investigation, using a graphical display of probability, different numerical values, and different subjects. Whereas Birnbaum et al. (1992) and Birnbaum and Sutton (1992) had used numerical probabilities, Mellers et al. (1992b) represented probability by means of pie charts, to see

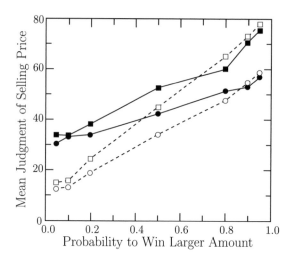

FIGURE 2. Mean judgments of selling prices plotted against the probability to win either $96 (squares) or $72 (circles) with unfilled and filled symbols showing results when the lower outcome is $0 or $24, respectively. Data from Birnbaum and Sutton (1992).

if the violations would persist when probability was presented graphically. Figure 3 shows an example display.

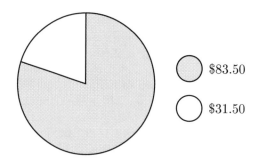

FIGURE 3. An example stimulus display, using a pie chart to represent probability. This stimulus represents ($31.50, .2, $83.50)

With these stimuli, similar violations were observed. Mellers et al. (1992b) studied judgments of gambles of the form (x, p, y) and $(0, p, y)$ as a function of x and p. Judgments were made from an ownership point of view, in which the subject judged either the lowest selling price (to give up playing favorable gambles) or the most they would pay (to avoid playing unfavorable gambles, like buying insurance).

Mean judgments are shown in Figure 4, with negative numbers representing offers to pay to avoid the gamble. With y set to $83.50, judgments are plotted as a function of x with a separate curve for each level of the probability to win

$83.50 $(1-p)$. A violation of monotonicity is observed for all seven levels of p, comparing mean judgments of ($0, p, 83.50), shown as unfilled circles, compared with ($5.40, p, 83.50), shown as filled circles connected by dashed lines. (Note that all seven dashed curves have negative slope.) There were also significantly more individual violations of monotonicity between ($0, .05, 83.50) and ($31.50, .05, 83.50) than between ($5.40, .05, 83.50) and ($31.50, .05, 83.50), even though the former comparison has a greater difference in expected value.

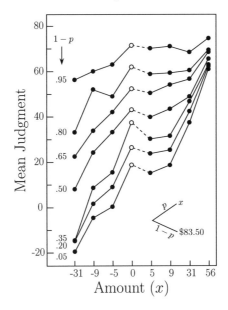

FIGURE 4. Mean judgments of binary gambles of the form $(x, p, $83.50)$, plotted as a function of x with a separate curve for each level of $1 - p$, the probability to win $83.50. The nonmonotonic "kink" at $x = 0, shown as unfilled circles and dashed lines, depicts a violation of monotonicity for each probability used. Data from Mellers, et al. (1992b)

In another experiment, Mellers et al. (1992b) used monetary incentives, instructing subjects that they would play for real cash payoffs one of two selected gambles, the one to which they assigned the higher value. Violations of monotonicity in judgment persisted even when real money was used as an incentive. They also found that violations were observed when both x and y are negative; for example, subjects offered to pay more on the average to *avoid* the gamble ($0, .05, -$85.50$) than the gamble ($-$31.50, .05, -$85.50$). Similar violations were obtained when the absolute magnitudes of the stakes were changed by multiplying both outcomes by the same constant (see Mellers, et al., 1992b, Figures 6-8 and Tables 1 and 2). Violations were rare, however, when x and y were of opposite sign.

Violations in Three Outcome Gambles. One interpretation of the configural weighting explanation of monotonicity violations was that subjects adopt a simplifying strategy with two-outcome gambles, so zero outcomes would receive a reduced weight only in simple, two-outcome gambles. For these two outcome gambles only (this idea assumes), people multiply probability and value, ignoring the outcome of zero. When there are two nonzero outcomes or three outcomes, they average the outcomes using weights that are more "regressed" than probabilities. This interpretation implies that violations of monotonicity should not occur with three-outcome gambles having two nonzero outcomes. Nevertheless, the same equations and approximated parameters from Birnbaum et al. (1992) successfully predicted violations of monotonicity in a new set of three-outcome gambles (Mellers et al., 1995), using the assumption of Birnbaum et al. (1992) that the lowest outcome receives the same absolute weight in both two- and three-outcome gambles, and the other two outcomes each receive the weight that a higher outcome receives in a two-outcome gamble (Expressions 1a-1e).

In later work with three outcome gambles, this simplifying assumption was revised (as will be discussed in Section 7); nevertheless, the simple assumption and extrapolation of parameters from Birnbaum et al. (1992) to three outcomes did a fair job predicting violations of monotonicity with the new gambles.

Although violations of monotonicity have been found consistently in judgment studies in which the key gambles are judged separately, conditions that facilitate comparisons among the gambles appear to reduce violations. Mellers et al. (1992b) found that when the two gambles involving a dominance relation are presented for judgment in a short list of gambles, the frequency of violations is reduced. Because direct choices yield a different ordering from that obtained from judgment, Birnbaum and Sutton (1992) identified their finding as a new type of preference reversal between judgment and choice.

5. MONOTONICITY AND CHOICE-BASED CERTAINTY EQUIVALENTS

The certainty equivalent is the amount of cash that is psychologically indifferent to a gamble. Some preference reversals can be reduced when choice rather than judgment is used to find certainty equivalents (Bostic et al., 1990), so it is reasonable to ask if the choice task itself, rather than the transparency of the choices presented, induces conformity to monotonicity.

Choices between Gambles and Fixed Set of Cash Values. Birnbaum (1992b) offered subjects choices between gambles and a list of cash values that was the same for all gambles. By examining how each gamble stacked up against a fixed set of cash amounts, this procedure separates choice from transparent comparison. Birnbaum (1992b) found that violations of monotonicity persisted even when gambles are ordered by choice-based certainty equivalents (based on comparisons between gambles and a list of sure amounts of money).

The following model is useful for discussing choices between gambles and cash:

$$P(c, \text{G}) = F[u(c) - U(\text{G})] \tag{2}$$

where $P(c, \text{G})$ is the probability of choosing the sure cash, c, over the gamble $\text{G} = (x, p, y)$; U is a function that assigns an overall utility to each gamble; u is the utility function for money; F is a monotonic function that maps a given utility difference into a choice probability.

The certainty equivalent, c^*, of gamble G is defined as the value of cash that would be indifferent to the gamble in the sense that it would be preferred half the time; i.e., the value of c^* for which $P(c^*, G) = 1/2$. Birnbaum (1992b) found that values of c^* violate monotonicity, when certainty equivalents are determined by a choice procedure in which each gamble is compared to a fixed set of comparison cash amounts.

Contextual Effects in Choice. Birnbaum (1992b) also found that the value of c^* depends on the particular set of comparisons used; higher values of c^* are observed when the average value of the cash amounts offered for comparison are higher than when the cash amounts are lower on the average. An example of contextual effects found by Birnbaum (1992b) is illustrated in Figure 5. Note that the inferred certainty equivalent for this gamble, ($0, .95, $48), is larger when the context of comparison cash values has a median of $77 (filled circles) than in the context of comparisons with a median of $14 (open circles). The fact that choice indifference points depend on the context of comparisons makes the interpretation of choice-based certainty equivalents more complicated.

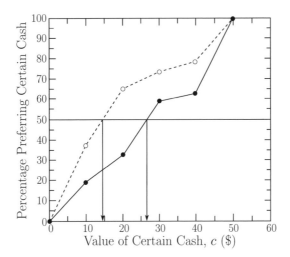

FIGURE 5. Percentage choosing cash over the gamble ($0, .95, $48) as a function of the value of cash, with a separate curve for each context. Each context used a different set of cash values; filled circles show results when median of cash values was $77; open circles show results when median of comparisons was $14. Note that the certainty equivalents (abscissa projections of 50%) are larger when the context of cash values has a higher median. Redrawn from Birnbaum (1992b).

PEST-based Certainty Equivalents. von Winterfeldt et al. (1997) found different rates of violations of monotonicity when certainty equivalents were obtained from different procedures. Using PEST, a staircase method in which different gambles receives different cash comparisons, depending on each subject's choices, they concluded monotonicity violations are less frequent than they are in judgment. Procedures such as PEST confound the distribution of cash values offered with the gambles to be assessed. Because the same gamble can receive different indifference points when different contexts of comparisons are used, when different gambles are presented with different sets of comparisons, it is difficult to know what would have happened if the gambles had been compared to the same standards.

One (overly simple) model of contextual effects is to assume that on some portion of the trials, the subject chooses randomly. If so, then the observed choice indifference point will be a compromise between the "true" choice indifference point and the median of the comparison cash values offered. Thus, the finding by von Winterfeldt et al. (1997) that certainty equivalents in the PEST method obey monotonicity may be due either to the subjective values of the gambles obeying monotonicity, or the fact that on the average higher cash values are presented for comparison to the dominant gambles in this method.

Unfortunately, the PEST algorithm (and the algorithm used by Tversky and Kahneman, 1992, as well) allows a gamble of higher expected value to receive comparisons of higher average value than a gamble of lower expected value. Such a procedure may thus find greater satisfaction of monotonicity because it capitalizes on contextual effects and the monotonicity of expected values rather than because the procedure itself reveals a "truer" measure of certainty equivalents. Although an attempt was made by von Winterfeldt et al. (1997) to statistically correct for differences in context, statistical partialling does not properly correct for confounded variables (Birnbaum & Mellers, 1989).

It would be useful to explore a variation of the PEST procedure using the same values of sure cash for both gambles being compared. One approach would be to study directly contextual effects by systematic variation of the algorithm. Another approach would be to "yoke" two gambles, such as ($0, .05, $96) and ($24, .05, $96), so that the same cash comparisons were presented on different trials against these two gambles. Such an experiment could provide the same context for both gambles being compared.

Scalability and Monotonicity in Choices between Cash and Gambles.
Birnbaum and Thompson (1996) considered the following set of relations. For each value of c, operationally define the relation, $\succ_c$, as follows:

$$A \succ_c B \text{ if and only if } P(c, A) < P(c, B) \tag{3}$$

where $P(c, A)$ represents the proportion of subjects preferring cash amount c over gamble A in a context in which the distribution of cash amounts is fixed for all gambles.

If Equation 2 held with a single function F, then all of the relations in Expression 3 should agree (i.e., the comparison between two gambles would be independent of the cash value c). The agreement of the relations in Expression 3 is termed *scalability*. If F were subscripted for each gamble, then the inferred ordering of gambles in this set of relations can depend on the value of c, violating scalability. Busemeyer (1985) found violations of scalability that suggest that F in Equation 2 depends on the variance of the outcomes within the gamble. Birnbaum and Thompson (1996) found that observed choice proportions violate both monotonicity and scalability.

Figure 6 illustrates these violations by plotting the proportion of choices favoring the cash over ($0, .2, 96) and ($48, .2, 96), shown as open and filled circles, against the value of cash, c. Crossing of curves in Figure 6 represent violations of scalability. Monotonicity is violated in Figure 6 when the open circles are below and to the right of the filled circles. For values of c less than $48 (the lowest positive outcome), monotonicity of $\succ_c$ is satisfied, but when $c > 55, it is systematically violated. For these gambles, certainty equivalents (abscissa projections of c^* corresponding to ordinate $= 50\%$) and the $\succ_c$ relationship (for $c > 55) violate monotonicity.

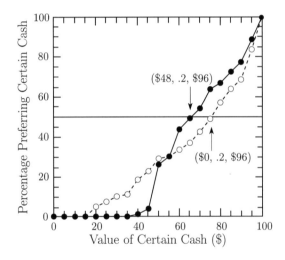

FIGURE 6. Percentage of choices preferring cash to gambles, plotted as a function of the amount of cash, using solid circles for ($48, .2, 96), and open circles for ($0, .2, 96). Crossing of the curves represents violation of scalability. When solid circles are above open circles, there is a violation of monotonicity for that value of c. In this case, monotonicity is satisfied for $c < 55, but not for $c > 55. Certainty equivalents (abscissa projections of 50%) also violate monotonicity. Similar results were obtained for other gambles. Data from Birnbaum & Thompson (1996).

6. WEIGHTING FUNCTIONS

The violations of outcome monotonicity can be predicted by different weighting functions for gambles with or without the outcome zero. This section explores determinants of the weighting functions as a function of the number, rank, and sign of the outcomes.

Weights of Equally Likely Outcomes as a Function of Number. Birnbaum and McCormick (1991) used yet another procedure for investigating violations of monotonicity in judgment. Their experiment was also designed to estimate weighting functions for positive, negative, and zero outcomes presented with different frequencies. Gambles were presented in the form of a list of equally likely outcomes that would be placed into an urn, from which one would be drawn at random to determine the outcome. For example,

$$(\$24, \$96, \$96, \$96, \$96)$$

represents an urn with five equally-likely tickets, from which one will be selected at random to determine the prize. This gamble offers a probability of .2 to win \$24 and a .8 probability to win \$96. However, in this procedure, the probabilities are not stated, but left to the subject to infer from the lists of values.

Gambles were judged from the viewpoint of "receipt indifference". Subjects were instructed to judge the amount of money that was equal to each gamble in the sense that they would be indifferent between receiving (or paying) that amount or receiving (or paying out) the outcome of the gamble. Forty-three undergraduates judged the values of 230 distinct gambles, consisting of from 2 to 32 outcomes that were positive, zero, or negative, of different frequencies. The gambles were constructed from the union of four subdesigns.

The first subdesign used 55 gambles composed of two equally-likely outcomes, using all pairs of the following 11 values, -\$96, -\$72, -\$48, - \$24, -\$12, \$0, \$12, \$24, \$48, \$72, \$96. The second subdesign used 150 gambles containing from 2 to 32 equally likely outcomes of exactly two different values $(x, n_x; y, n_y)$; there were six pairs of values (x, y): $(-\$96, -\$48)$, $(-\$96, \$0)$, $(-\$96, \$96)$, $(-\$48, \$48)$, $(\$0, \$96)$, $(\$48, \$96)$; there were 5 different values of n_y ($n_y = 1, 2, 4, 8,$ or 16 tickets) combined with 5 different values of n_x ($n_x = 1, 2, 4, 8,$ or 16). The third subdesign contained 25 gambles of the form $(x, 1; \$96, n_y)$ with one ticket having one of 5 values of x $(-\$96, -\$48, \$0, \$24, \$48)$, factorially combined with 5 different values of n_y for $y = \$96$ ($n_y = 1, 2, 4, 8, 16$), producing probabilities, $n_x/(n_x + n_y)$, of .5, .667, .8, .889, or .941, to receive \$96. The fourth subdesign combined 5 different values of n_x for $x = \$0$, ($n_x = 1, 2, 4, 8, 16$) with 5 single values of $y = -\$96, -\$48, \$24, \$48, \$96$.

Birnbaum and McCormick fit the following model to the data:

$$U_I(x, n_x; y, n_y) = \frac{Au(x) + Bu(y)}{A + B} \qquad (4a)$$

where $U_I(x, n_x; y, n_y)$ is the utility of the gamble from the receipt "indifference" point of view; $u(x)$ and $u(y)$ are the utilities of the outcomes; A and B are the weights of the outcomes, which depend on the number of outcomes of each value (n_x and n_y), the rank of the outcomes in the gamble (either lower or higher), and the augmented sign of the outcomes (the three levels of augmented sign, s_x, are +, 0, and −, for $x > 0$, $x = 0$, and $x < 0$, respectively):

$$A = W(n_x, r_x, s_x) \qquad (4b)$$

$$B = W(n_y, r_y, s_y) \qquad (4c)$$

where n_x and n_y are the number of outcomes; r_x and r_y are the ranks of the outcomes (i.e., either least or most in the gamble); s_x and s_y are the augmented signs of outcomes x and y, respectively. Because this experiment used five levels of number of outcomes, two levels of rank, and three levels of augmented sign, there are 30 weights to estimate (one of which can be fixed). Consistent with previous results (Birnbaum & Beeghley, 1997; Birnbaum et al., 1992; Birnbaum & McIntosh, 1996), the data could be as well fit with $u(x) = x$ as with a general power function, and the relationship between overt judgments and subjective values of Equation 4a could be approximated as linear.

The need to estimate the weight of the zero outcome separately from those for nonzero outcomes can be seen in Figure 7. Figure 7 shows mean judged indifference values for gambles with one ticket that is either \$0 (open circles) or \$24 (filled circles) and either 1, 2, 4, 8, or 16 tickets to win \$96 [(\$0, 1; \$96, n_y) and (\$24, 1; \$96, n_y)]. Mean judgments are plotted as a function of the probability to win \$96 [i.e., $n_y/(1 + n_y)$]. Crossing of the curves in Figure 7 replicates the violation of monotonicity in Figure 1, using a yet another procedure for representing probability. The crossover in Figure 7 can be described by Expressions 4 if the weighting function depends on whether x is zero or positive.

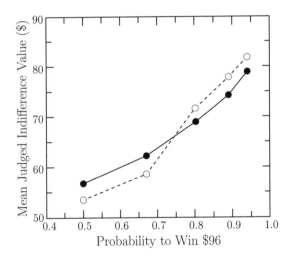

FIGURE 7. Mean judgment of receipt cash indifference value, as a function of probability to win \$96, with open and closed circles showing judgments when the lowest outcome was \$0 and \$24, respectively. Probabilities were manipulated by including one outcome of \$0 or \$24 with 1, 2, 4, 8, or 16 equally-likely outcomes of \$96. From Birnbaum and McCormick (1991).

The 30 weights of Expression 4 were estimated from the mean judgments of the 230 gambles used in the experiment. The estimated values of A (and B) in Equations 4b and 4c can be further simplified because they fit closely to the following multiplicative model:

$$W(n_x, r_x, s_x) = f(n_x)a_V(r_x, s_x) \tag{5}$$

where $f(n_x)$ is a function of number of outcomes, and $a_V(r_x, s_x)$ are six weights for two ranks and three augmented signs; these would be expected to depend on point of view, V. Fit of this model to the estimated weights can be assessed in Figure 8, which plots the estimated weights as a function of the estimated values of $f(n_x)$, with a separate curve for each level of rank and augmented sign. According to the multiplicative model of Equation 5, estimated weights should be linearly related to each other, with different slopes for different ranks and augmented signs, but they should share a common point of intersection. The estimated weights, shown as symbols, fall close to the bilinear fan predicted by the multiplicative model of Equation 5, shown as straight lines that intersect at a common point.

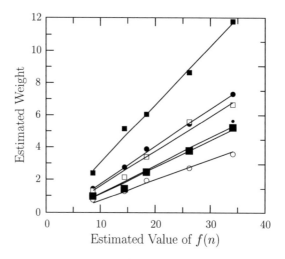

FIGURE 8. Estimated weights of $n = 1, 2, 4, 8,$ or 16 equally likely outcomes, fit to judgments of 230 gambles in the "indifference" viewpoint, plotted as a function of the number of outcomes of a type, with a separate symbol for each combination of rank (circles = lower outcome, squares = higher outcome) and augmented sign (small = negative, unfilled = zero, large = positive) of outcomes. Lines show predictions of multiplicative model of $f(n)$ by a function of rank and augmented sign. From Birnbaum and McCormick (1991).

For rank $= 1$ (lower outcome), the estimated configural parameters, a_V in Equation 5, are .172, .127, and .232, for negative, zero, and positive outcomes, respectively. For rank $= 2$ (higher outcome), the parameters are .359, .216, and .165, respectively. Thus, for two positive outcomes, the relative weights of the lower and higher outcomes are .58 and .42, respectively, consistent with previous findings of "risk aversion" (greater weight on lower positive outcomes) in the neutral viewpoint. The smallest weight (.127) is for zero outcomes when zero is the low-est outcome; this reduced weight for zero accounts for violations of monotonicity. When the highest outcome is negative, it has greater weight (.359) than the low-est negative outcome (.172), consistent with previous findings of "risk seeking" for purely negative gambles (e.g., Tversky & Kahneman, 1992).

Equation 5 simplifies the treatment of monotonicity violations. Instead of two $S_x(p)$ functions, there is only one $f(n_x)$ function, the analog of $S(p)$, and the effects of rank and augmented sign are assumed to be multiplicative changes only, produced by different values of a_V.

If the a_V parameters were all equal, and if $f(n_x) = n_x$, then Equations 4 and 5 would reduce to expected utility theory. Instead, the estimated $f(n_x)$ function can be approximated as the square root of n_x. The fact that $f(n_x)$ follows this function implies that the relationship between relative weight $[A/(A + B)]$ and probability [averaged over different combinations with the same probability, $n_x/(n_x + n_y)$], will have an inverse-S relationship.

Varey, Mellers, and Birnbaum (1990) asked subjects to judge the proportion of dots of one color as a function of the numbers of dots of each color, and found a similar inverse-S relationship between average judged "proportion" and actual proportion. This function was explained by Varey et al. (1990) in terms of the psychophysical functions relating subjective number to actual number of dots in a relative ratio model. The psychophysical functions in that study were constrained to also account for judgments of "differences" and "ratios" of the numbers of dots (using subtractive and ratio models), as well as "proportions." A similar inverse-S weighting function has also been postulated by Tversky and Kahneman (1992) in their model of cumulative prospect theory, but it has a different interpretation in that theory. The difference in interpretations will be taken up in the next sections.

Cumulative Prospect Model of Binary Gambles. Tversky and Kahne-man (1992) presented a special case of rank- and sign-dependent utility theory in which the weights of positive outcomes depend on the decumulative probability of each outcome in the gamble. For binary gambles of the form, $(z, 1 - p, x)$, where $0 \leq z < x$ and p is the probability to receive the higher outcome, the cumulative prospect model represents the value of the gamble as follows:

$$V(z, 1 - p, x) = (1 - \pi(x))u(z) + \pi(x)u(x) \qquad (6a)$$

where $\pi(x) = W(p)$ is the weight of the higher outcome; the values of the two outcomes are $u(z)$ and $u(x)$.

Tversky and Kahneman (1992) approximated the value function with $u(x) = x^\beta$, where $\beta = .88$. In their model, the weight of the higher outcome, x, in a two outcome gamble is given by the following expression,

$$\pi(x) = W(p) = \frac{p^\gamma}{[p^\gamma + (1 - p)^\gamma]^{1/\gamma}} \qquad (6b)$$

where the estimate of $\gamma = .61$ for positive outcomes. The certainty equivalent of a gamble is calculated from the inverse of the value function in Expression 6a,

$$CE(z, 1 - p, x) = V(z, 1 - p, x)^{1/\beta}. \qquad (6c)$$

Tversky and Kahneman (1992) fit their model to transformed certainty equivalents, as shown in Figure 9. Each symbol represents a median certainty equivalent from Tversky and Kahneman (1992, Table 3), subtracting z, and divided by $x - z$. Unfilled squares, large circles, triangles, and small circles show adjusted certainty equivalents for $(\$0, p, x)$, where $x = \$50$, $\$100$, $\$200$, and $\$400$, respectively. The solid squares show results for gambles of the form $(\$50, 1 - p, \$150)$. The solid curve in the figure shows Equation 6b, transformed by Equation 6c.

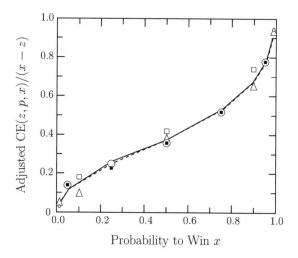

FIGURE 9. Median adjusted certainty equivalents of binary gambles plotted against the probability to win the larger outcome (Data from Tversky & Kahneman, 1992). Two weighting functions are compared. The solid line is the curve fit by Tversky and Kahneman (1992). The dashed curve shows that the configural weight model makes nearly identical predictions.

The experiment of Tversky and Kahneman (1992) was not designed to test for violations of monotonicity. Because of the confound between expected value and the set of comparisons offered for each gamble, and because of the use of relatively large lower positive outcomes (\$50), their experiment is not well-suited for this purpose. However, if $u(x) = x$, for $\$0 \leq x \leq \$150$, if the solid squares fall on the same function, then there is no evidence of a different weighting function for zero outcomes for these data. If $u(x) = x^{.88}$, as suggested by Tversky and Kahneman, however, then the filled and unfilled circles in Figure 9 should not coincide unless the weighting function differs for these cases. That experiment cannot distinguish these interpretations.

The dashed curve plots the configural weight equations, Equations 4a and 5, assuming that the weight of the lower and higher outcomes are $A = a_V f(p)$ and $B = (1 - a_V)f(1 - p)$, where $f(p) = p^{.56}$ and $a_V = .63$ for the lower outcome. Equations 4a and 5 can be derived from the theory that subjects act as if they are minimizing an asymmetric squared loss function (weighted by a_V and $1 - a_V$ for squared overestimation and underestimation, respectively), by substituting $f(p)$ for p, and $f(1 - p)$ for $1 - p$ in Equation 6 of Birnbaum et al. (1992). The solid and dashed curves are virtually identical, but the implications are quite different, as becomes apparent for three-outcome gambles.

It is interesting that the value of $a_V = .63$, which fits the data of Tversky and Kahneman (1992) under the configural weighting interpretation, has also been obtained in two other experiments. It agrees with the weight of the lower positive outcome estimated in the neutral ("fair price") point of view by Birnbaum et al. (1992). The same value of a_V was also estimated from experiments testing interval independence (Birnbaum, Thompson, & Bean, in press). In one experiment, subjects judged the amount they would pay to receive one gamble rather than another. Subjects offered to pay an average of \$44 to play (\$74, \$100) rather than (\$8, \$100) but they offered to pay only \$24 to play (\$6, \$74) rather than (\$6, \$8). Ratings of strength of preference also showed that the judged strength of preference was greater when the common outcome was the highest than when it was the lowest outcome. Such violations of interval independence can be explained by greater weight on the lower outcome, and this experiment led to the value of .63 for that relative weight.

For two outcome gambles, the cumulative prospect model and the configural weight model (Equations 4a-4c and 5) make virtually identical predictions, as shown in Figure 9. However, for three outcome gambles, the theories make very different predictions for violations of branch independence, as will be shown in the next section.

When there are more than two outcomes, cumulative prospect theory postulates that the weights can be represented as differences in the $W(p)$ function for decumulative probability,

$$\pi(x_i) = W(P_i) - W(Q_i) \tag{7}$$

where $\pi(x_i)$ is the weight of outcome x_i in the gamble, P_i is the decumulative probability that the outcome in the gamble is $\geq x_i$; Q_i is the probability that the outcome exceeds x_i. For three, equally likely positive outcomes, the middle outcome would have the least weight, because $\pi(x) = W(2/3) - W(1/3)$ is the smallest of the three vertical differences (weights) in an inverse-S function, such as Figure 9.

7. VIOLATIONS OF BRANCH INDEPENDENCE

Savage's *sure thing principle* states that if two alternatives yield the same consequence for some state of the world, the value of that consequence should not make a difference for the preference due to other aspects of the alternatives. *Branch independence* corresponds to the "weak independence" condition that Cohen and Jaffray (1988) find more plausible than Savage's axiom. It states that if two gambles have the same outcome produced by the same event with a known probability, the value of that outcome should have no effect on the preference order. For three-outcome gambles $(x, p; y, q; z)$, in which the outcome is x with probability p, y with probability q and z otherwise $(1 - p - q)$, branch independence can be written as follows:

$$(x, p; y, q, z) \succ (x', p'; y', q'; z)$$

$$\text{if and only if} \tag{8}$$

$$(x, p; y, q; z') \succ (x', p'; y', q', z')$$

where $0 < p + q = p' + q' < 1$, and $\succ$ is the preference relation. Changing the common branch of z (with probability $1 - p - q$) to z' (at the same probability) should not affect the preference order produced by the other components of the gamble.

Branch independence is required by Savage's (1954) SEU theory, and is also implied by Edwards' (1954) psychological version of SEU that uses a weighting function of probability. It would also be observed if subjects were to edit the gambles being compared by canceling common branches, as discussed by Tversky (1969, 1972a), Kahneman and Tversky (1979), and Tversky and Kahneman (1992).

However, rank dependent utility theories allow violations of branch independence. For example, suppose that the rank-dependent utility of a gamble composed of three equally-likely outcomes (z, x, y), with outcomes chosen such that $0 < z < x' < x < y < y' < z'$, is given by the following expression,

$$\text{RDU}(z, x, y) = w_L u(z) + w_M u(x) + w_H u(y) \tag{9a}$$

where $\text{RDU}(z, x, y)$ is the rank-dependent utility of gamble (z, x, y); w_L, w_M, and w_H are the weights of the lowest, medium, and highest of three equally likely positive outcomes, respectively. When the common outcome is changed from lowest to highest (z to z'), then the weights of the low, medium, and highest outcomes are associated with x, y and z', respectively, as follows:

$$\text{RDU}(x, y, z') = w_L u(x) + w_M u(y) + w_H u(z'). \tag{9b}$$

Violations of Branch Independence in Choice. Birnbaum and McIntosh (1996) showed that Expressions 9a-9b imply that branch independence can be violated in two opposite ways. In the first case,

$$\frac{w_L}{w_M} < \frac{u(y') - u(y)}{u(x) - u(x')} < \frac{w_M}{w_H}$$

$$\text{if and only if} \tag{10}$$

$$(z, x, y) \succ (z, x', y') \text{ and } (x, y, z') \prec (x', y', z').$$

In the other case,

$$\frac{w_L}{w_M} > \frac{u(y') - u(y)}{u(x) - u(x')} > \frac{w_M}{w_H}$$

$$\text{if and only if} \tag{11}$$

$$(z, x, y) \prec (z, x', y') \text{ and } (x, y, z') \succ (x', y', z').$$

Experimentally, the tactic is to systematically vary x, y, x', and y' to find an intermediate value for the ratio of differences in utility, which should produce a reversal of preferences due to the change from z to z' (a violation of branch independence).

Birnbaum and McIntosh (1996) found systematic violations of branch independence in choices between gambles composed of three equally likely outcomes. They found that most people prefer ($2, $40, $44) to ($2, $10, $98); however, most people also prefer ($10, $98, $136) to ($40, $44, $136). This pattern was replicated with many different combinations of values. This pattern of preferences is consistent with Expression 10 but it is opposite that implied by Expression 11, which follows from the inverse-S weighting function of the cumulative prospect model of Tversky and Kahneman (1992).

According to the inverse-S (Equations 6b and 7), the middle of three equally likely outcomes should have the least weight. If the middle outcome had the least weight, then Expression 11 would follow because $w_L/w_M > 1$ and $1 > w_M/w_H$. These systematic violations are also not consistent with the theory that subjects edit and cancel common components when making choices, which implies that any violations of branch independence would be due to error (and should therefore be unsystematic).

Violations of Branch Independence in Judgment. Birnbaum and Beeghley (1997) found similar (but distinct) violations for buyer's and seller's prices. The violations of branch independence were again opposite those predicted by the inverse-S weighting function in both points of view. For example, ($4, $39, $45) was judged higher than ($4, $12, $96) yet ($39, $45, $148) was judged lower than ($12, $96, $148) in both viewpoints. However, judgments in the buyer's point of view of (x, y, z) decrease as $|x - y|$ is increased, holding $x + y$ constant, for all values of z; whereas, in the seller's point of view, these judgments increase as a function of $|x - y|$ when z is the highest outcome, but decrease when z is not highest. These changing violations and preference orders are consistent with the theory that the utility function of money is independent of the task, but that configural weights depend on the judge's point of view (Birnbaum et al., 1992; Birnbaum & Stegner, 1979; Birnbaum & Sutton, 1992).

Weights estimated from these three studies are presented in Table 1. In all three experiments, the different rank orders of the data could be well fit with the same utility function, $u(x) = x$ for $0 \leq x \leq 150$. Although the weights differ in different tasks and viewpoints, all three sets of weights satisfy Expression 11. Weights from the choice task are intermediate between those obtained from judgments of buyer's prices and seller's prices, apparently closer to the buyer's viewpoint. The finding that all three experiments share the same utility function and weights that satisfy Expression 10 suggests that the pattern of violations is not due to something peculiar to either choice or judgment.

8. TESTING AMONG CONFIGURAL WEIGHT MODELS

Until recently, most empirical work has been designed to distinguish configural weight theories from simpler, nonconfigural theories, rather than to test among alternative configural weight models. This section describes several properties that can be tested to distinguish among various models that have been suggested. These empirical properties are stochastic dominance, comonotonic independence, distribution independence, cumulative independence, and asymptotic independence.

Stochastic Dominance. Cumulative prospect theory implies stochastic dominance, whereas original prospect theory violates stochastic dominance (Kahneman

Experiment	Lowest	Middle	Highest
Buyer's Prices	.56	.36	.08
Seller's Prices	.27	.52	.21
Preferences	.51	.33	.16

TABLE 1. Estimated relative weights of three equally likely outcomes as a function of rank. Relative weights are normalized to sum to one by dividing by the sum of weights in each case. Weights for Preferences were estimated by Birnbaum and McIntosh (1996); Weights for Buyer's and Seller's Prices are from Birnbaum and Beeghley (in press). All three studies were fit with the same utility function $u(x) = x$ for $0 < x < \$150$.

& Tversky, 1979; Tversky & Kahneman, 1986, 1992). The configural weight model presented here violates monotonicity, therefore, it violates stochastic dominance. As shown below, this model also implies other violations of stochastic dominance that have not yet been tested.

According to the configural weight model presented here, for example, using the parameters of Birnbaum and McIntosh (1996), $U(\$12, .05; \$14, .05; \$96) = 53.6$, which is less than $U(\$12, .10; \$90, .05; \$96) = 61.1$, so the latter gamble should be judged better, even though the former stochastically dominates it. It seems worthwhile to test such predictions for violations of dominance using judged prices, using indirect comparisons in which each of the above gambles would be compared against a third gamble such as (\$55, .5; \$59, .5), and using direct comparisons between the two gambles. Note that this prediction of a violation of dominance does not rely on the presumed lower weighting for zero-valued outcomes, but follows instead from the configural weight model's weighting scheme for positive outcomes.

Although there have been occasional demonstrations of violations of stochastic dominance (e.g., Tversky & Kahneman, 1986), aside from the program of research reviewed here on violations of monotonicity, we do not yet have an adequate empirical description of more general types of violations of stochastic dominance.

Comonotonic Independence. Comonotonic independence is a special case of branch independence in which the preference order is assumed invariant when the common branch does not change rank order in the gambles to be compared.

For example, for three outcomes, comonotonic independence is the special case of Expression 8 where z and z' maintain the same rank in all four gambles (i.e., z and z' are either lowest in all four, middle in all four, or highest in all four gambles). A related property, ordinal (or "tail") independence, was tested by Wu (1994), who reported systematic violations that he attributed to a cancellation process specific to choice. Comonotonic independence has been tested in pure form (keeping the number of distinct outcomes equal in both gambles compared) in only a few papers (Birnbaum & Beeghley, 1997; Birnbaum & McIntosh, 1996; Wakker, Erev, & Weber, 1994; Weber & Kirsner, 1996), and it has not yet been reported to be systematically violated.

As noted by Birnbaum and McIntosh (1996), however, comonotonic independence has not yet received a strenuous test. Testing comonotonic independence evaluates the class of rank- and sign-dependent utility theories (Luce & Fishburn, 1991, 1995). This class includes cumulative prospect theory (Tversky & Kahneman, 1992) and the model presented here, both of which satisfy comonotonic independence when the probability distribution is fixed.

Chew and Wakker (1996) discuss the comonotonic sure thing principle as characterizing "all existing rank-dependent forms," but it is important to note that their treatment does not include all configural forms. If configural weights depend on the spacing of the outcomes as well as their ranks, as they would according to the minimum loss theory presented by Birnbaum et al. (1992), then comonotonic independence can be violated (Birnbaum & McIntosh, 1996, Appendix A).

Distribution Independence. Distribution independence assumes that preferences should be independent of the (common) probability distribution of common branches. For four outcome gambles, with outcomes chosen such that $0 < z < x' < x < y < y' < v$, and nonzero probabilities, p, q, r, and $s = 1 - p - q - r$, distribution independence requires:

$$(z, r; x, p; y, q; v, s) \succ (z, r; x', p; y', q; v, s)$$

$$\text{if and only if} \qquad (12)$$

$$(z, s; x, p; y, q; v, r) \succ (z, s; x', p; y', q; v, r)$$

Distribution independence asserts that the trade-off between $(x, p; y, q)$ and $(x', p; y', q)$ should be independent of the probability distribution of the common branches (r and s vs. s and r), holding (p, q) fixed. Note that in Expression 12, the common outcomes are the same, but their probabilities differ; whereas, in branch independence the probabilities of the common branches are the same and their outcomes differ.

The configural weight model presented in this chapter can violate branch independence but must satisfy distribution independence. The revised configural weight model of Birnbaum and Stegner (1979, Equation 10), however, violates distribution independence. This model will be discussed further in the section below on asymptotic independence.

Cumulative prospect theory implies systematic violations of distribution independence, with the pattern of violations dependent on the $W(p)$ function of Equation 7. For example, the model of Tversky and Kahneman (1992) implies that

$$(\$2, .59; \$10, .2; \$98, .2; \$108, .01) \succ (\$2, .59; \$50, .2; \$54, .2; \$108, .01);$$

however,

$$(\$2, .01; \$10, .2; \$98, .2; \$108, .59) \prec (\$2, .01; \$50, .2; \$54, .2; \$108, .59),$$

violating distribution independence.

Birnbaum and Chavez (1996) tested distribution independence, and found small but systematic violations in the opposite direction from those predicted by cumulative prospect model. For example, they found that the percentage choosing $(z, .59; x, .2; y, .2; v, .01)$ over $(z, .59; x', .2; y', .2; v, .01)$ is greater than the percentage choosing $(z, .01; x, .2; y, .2; v, .59)$ over $(z, .01; x', .2; y', .2; v, .59)$ for all six different contrasts of (x, y) vs. (x', y') used, contrary to the prediction of the inverse-S function, which predicts the opposite pattern of shifting preferences. Similar results were obtained when $(r, s) = (.55, .05)$.

Cumulative Independence. If the weights depend entirely on the cumulative (or decumulative) distribution of outcomes, as in Equation 7, then the weights of outcomes should be independent of how that cumulative (decumulative) distribution is produced. Cumulative independence holds for cumulative prospect theory and is systematically violated by configural weight models.

Cumulative prospect theory makes the following predictions for two and three-outcome gambles, with nonzero probabilities, p, q, and r that sum to one, and $0 < z < x' < x < y < y' < z'$:

If $(z, r; x, p; y, q) \succ (z, r; x', p; y', q)$, then $(x', r; y, p + q) \succ (x', r + p; y', q)$. (13)

Similarly,

If $(x', p; y', q; z', r) \succ (x, p; y, q; z', r)$, then $(x', p; y', q + r) \succ (x, p + q; y', r)$. (14)

These tests of cumulative independence do not assume a particular form of $W(p)$, such as the inverse-S, but hold for any cumulative (or decumulative) weighting function. These tests are not "pure" tests of a single axiom, as they can be viewed as a combination of comonotonic independence, monotonicity, transitivity, and the "accounting equivalence" that equal outcomes can be coalesced by adding their probabilities. [For example, one can deduce Expression 13 as follows: If $(z, r; x, p; y, q) \succ (z, r; x', p; y', q)$ then $(x', r; x, p; y, q) \succ (x', r; x', p; y', q)$ by comonotonic independence; by monotonicity, $(x', r; y, p; y, q) \succ (x', r; x, p; y, q)$; therefore, by transitivity, $(x', r; y, p; y, q) \succ (x', r; x', p; y', q)$; finally, by the coalescing equivalence, $(x', r; y, p + q) \succ (x', r + p; y', q)$.] The key idea of cumulative independence is that increasing the probability of an outcome should have the same effect on weights as adding another distinct outcome with the same probability, if that outcome preserves comonotonicity.

Configural weight theory, on the other hand, distinguishes increasing the probability of an outcome from adding a new outcome. If $S(p)$ is negatively accelerated, then a new outcome will have greater weight than the marginal increase in weight due to the same increase in probability of an existing outcome. The configural weight model presented here implies violations of the cumulative independence conditions described above. For example, with $p = q = r = 1/3$, using parameters from Birnbaum and McIntosh (1996), the model implies the following violations of cumulative independence:

$$U(\$2, 1/3; \$40, 1/3; \$44, 1/3) = 21.3 > U(\$2, 1/3; \$10, 1/3; \$98, 1/3) = 20.0;$$

however,

$$U(\$10, 1/3; \$44, 2/3) = 25.9 < U(\$10, 2/3; \$98, 1/3) = 35.4,$$

in contradiction to Expression 13.
Similarly,

$$U(\$10, 1/3; \$98, 1/3; \$108, 1/3) = 55.7 > U(\$40, 1/3; \$44, 1/3; \$108, 1/3) = 52.2;$$

however,

$$U(\$10, 1/3; \$98, 2/3) = 51.2 < U(\$40, 2/3; \$98, 1/3) = 56.7,$$

contradicting Expression 14.

This property appears to give a sharp distinction between cumulative prospect theory and the configural weight model presented here. Although the property has not yet been tested in a single experiment with the same subjects, data by Wu and Gonzalez (1996) combined with data of Birnbaum and McIntosh (1996) suggest indirectly that the property might be violated.

Asymptotic Independence. Birnbaum and Stegner (1979, Equation 10) presented a revised configural weight model in which the transfer of weights among outcomes of different ranks depends on the point of view of the judge and is also proportional to the weight of the outcome losing weight. This revised model differs from the previous rank-dependent configural weight model of Birnbaum (1974), extended by Birnbaum et al. (1992), and presented here. The revised configural weight model of Birnbaum and Stegner (1979) violates both distribution independence and asymptotic independence.

For two outcome gambles, asymptotic lower independence can be defined as follows: as $p \to 0$, $U(x, p, y) \to u(y)$, for all x. Asymptotic upper independence is defined as follows: as $1 - p \to 0$, $U(x, p, y) \to u(x)$, for all y. Thus, the value of an improbable outcome should become less and less relevant as the probability of the other outcome approaches 1.

For moral judgment (Birnbaum, 1973; Riskey & Birnbaum, 1974), likeableness judgments (Birnbaum & Rose, 1973), and buying prices (Birnbaum & Stegner, 1979), however, the value of the worst deed, trait, or estimate appears to set an upper limit on a person's morality, likeableness, or buying price. Given a person has done a single very immoral deed, for example, it appears that the person's judged morality is bounded to be low, no matter how many good deeds that person does. However, a single good deed appears to set no such limit on the lower bound of judged morality.

For gambles, asymptotic independence says that no matter how bad an outcome is, it should approach irrelevance as it becomes less and less probable. A contrary notion, for example, is that some outcomes are so bad that no matter how small their probabilities, the utility of a gamble with such a possible outcome is bounded to a lower value unless its probability is zero. Discussions of insurance and risk of accidental nuclear war, for example, often seem to express this notion. The aversion that people have toward probabilistic insurance (a less than half-priced policy in which the insurance agent flips a coin to decide if the company will pay off in the event of a fire) suggests that asymptotic independence may be violated. People often express the idea that the purpose of insurance is to eliminate the possibility of bad outcomes, rather than to merely reduce their probabilities.

The revised configural weight model presented by Birnbaum and Stegner (1979, Equation 10) allows an outcome of near zero probability to place an upper (or lower) bound on the response as the probability of that outcome approaches (but does not equal) zero. For buying prices of two outcome gambles, (x, p, y), $x < y$, $0 < p < 1$, assuming that the lower outcome receives greater weight, this revised model retains Equation 1a, but it replaces Equations 1b and 1c with the following:

$$A = S_x(p) + a_V S_x(1-p) \tag{15a}$$

$$B = (1 - a_V)S_x(1-p) \tag{15b}$$

where A and B are the absolute configural weights of the lower and higher outcomes, respectively, as in Equation 1a; and a_V is the configural weight parameter that in this model represents the proportion of weight taken from the higher valued outcome (for buying prices) and given to the lower valued outcome. The other terms are as defined in Expressions 1.

For example, if $S(p) = p$, and $a_V > 0$, Equations 15 imply that $U(x,p,y) = [p + a_V(1-p)]u(x) + [(1-a_V)(1-p)]u(y)$. As $p \to 0$, $U(x,p,y) \to a_V u(x) + (1-a_V)u(y)$, which indicates that as long as the lower outcome is possible, it limits the utility of the gamble. However, as $1 - p \to 0$, $U(x,p,y) \to u(x)$. Thus, this model violates asymptotic lower independence, but satisfies asymptotic upper independence.

When weight is transferred from the lower to the higher value, as for example in selling prices, then the weight transferred is proportional to the weight of the lower value, as follows:

$$A = (1 - a_V)S_x(p) \tag{16a}$$

$$B = S_x(1-p) + a_V S_x(p). \tag{16b}$$

In this case, a possible good outcome sets a lower limit on the selling price, but a low outcome sets no such upper limit.

The models in Equations 15-16 violate asymptotic independence, implying that the worst outcome places an upper bound on the buying price and the best outcome sets a lower bound on the selling price of a gamble. This revised model gave a better fit (than the simple configural model) to judgments of buying and selling prices of used cars based on estimates given by sources (Birnbaum & Stegner, 1979), and it can describe judgments of likeableness and morality. However, implications of asymptotic independence have not been tested for judgments or choices among gambles.

9. DISCUSSION AND CONCLUSIONS

Violations of monotonicity add to a growing literature in judgment and decision making of phenomena that trouble the theoretician. Taking the results from different studies together, what might be considered a single empirical effect, the pattern of results in Figure 1, might show up as violations of three axioms: monotonicity, transitivity, and consistency.

Birnbaum and Sutton (1992) noted that because the monotonicity violation is obtained in judgment but not direct choice, there is a reversal of preference, violating consistency. Let $A = (\$0, .05, \$96)$ and $B = (\$24, .05, \$96)$. Birnbaum and Sutton found that A is judged higher than B, but in a direct comparison, the vast majority choose B over A.

Birnbaum and Thompson (1996) found evidence suggesting that there is a value of cash that is intermediate between A and B, such that $P(A, c) > 1/2$

and $P(c, B) > 1/2$. However, from Birnbaum and Sutton, $P(B, A) > 1/2$, which might be taken as a violation of transitivity. It is unclear if such cross-experiment comparisons predict what a single individual would do when faced with all three comparisons, but it should be clear that the theoretician has a problem accounting for all of the choices in terms of a single, transitive preference order.

The axioms of monotonicity, transitivity, and consistency appear quite reasonable from a normative standpoint. Luce and von Winterfeldt (1994) regard transitivity as "nonnegotiable" from the normative perspective. In judgment experiments, where the subject assigns a number to each gamble, transitivity is automatically satisfied (because the numbers are transitive). However, Tversky (1969) concluded that there are situations in which transitivity is systematically violated in choice. If choices can be made to violate transitivity, therefore, one might argue that judgment should be preferred as a mode of response because it satisfies transitivity.

On the other hand, this chapter reviews evidence that monotonicity can be violated in judgment, but has not been violated systematically in transparent choices. Because monotonicity is an axiom that seems compelling to both theoreticians and subjects, who rarely try to defend their violations, choice might seem a preferred method because it seems to obey the axiom of monotonicity.

Thus, if we try to enforce the most cherished of normative axioms by our selection of procedure, we are torn between choice, which presumably satisfies monotonicity but might violate transitivity, and judgment, which automatically satisfies transitivity but may systematically violate monotonicity.

The intermediate method of choice-based certainty equivalents might therefore seem a good compromise between choice and judgment. Certainty equivalents satisfy transitivity. Some evidence suggests that certainty equivalents based on PEST may reduce violations of monotonicity (von Winterfeldt et al., 1997). However, violations of scalability (Birnbaum & Thompson, 1996) indicate that violations of monotonicity depend on the value of cash against which the gambles are compared. Furthermore, contextual effects in choices (Birnbaum, 1992b) suggest that we need more data and better theory on this procedure before we can know how to distinguish the value of a gamble from the context of cash values presented in the procedure.

The classic form of preference reversals (Bostic et al., 1990; Lichtenstein & Slovic, 1971; Lindman, 1971; Slovic, Lichtenstein, & Fischhoff, 1988) are but a small portion of the reversals of preference that have now been demonstrated. The problems at hand are to explain how and why the apparent rank order of gambles changes depending on the task (choice vs. judgment), the judge's point of view (buyer's vs. neutral's, vs. seller's), the common outcome (branch independence), the context, and whether outcomes are negative, positive, or zero.

Because so many factors appear to affect preferences, Tversky and Kahneman (1992) concluded with the "pessimistic" assessment that no decision theory will successfully account for all of the phenomena. Indeed, this chapter has reviewed results that go beyond even the list of problems discussed by Tversky and Kahneman. Nevertheless, analogies from the history of science give us room for hope of devising a single theory that can account for all of the phenomena.

What can at first appear to be many exceptions and complications in one theory can suddenly fall into place when a better theory is devised. For example, planetary positions calculated from Ptolemy's geocentric model with uniform circular motion required many "fudge" factors of offset epicycles to fit the data. The heliocentric model of Copernicus was simpler, but still required "fudge" factors to account for departures from uniform circular motion. Kepler's elliptical models (Kepler's "laws") produced a more accurate description with a simpler unifying set of equations.

In decision research, changes in preference order due to the subject's viewpoint, for example, would be interpreted as evidence of changing $u(x)$ functions in the framework of nonconfigural models. However, configural weight models allow one to retain the premise that the $u(x)$ function is invariant with respect to viewpoint (Birnbaum et al., 1992; Birnbaum & Sutton, 1992). Furthermore, configural weight models can account for violations of branch independence in different viewpoints, again using a single $u(x)$ function. Evidence so far does not yet require the rejection of a single $S(p)$ function, if configural weights are allowed to depend on the number of outcomes, their augmented signs, and ranks.

The configural weight models, on the other hand, contain these configural weighting parameters, which until they can be explained by deeper primitives, seem to have the character of the epicycles used early in Astronomy. Different ideas about the origin of the configural weights – that they depend on asymmetric costs of over- or under-estimation (Birnbaum et al., 1992; Birnbaum & McIntosh, 1996; Weber, 1994), that they depend on subject's conformance to the comonotonic "sure thing" principle (e.g., Chew & Wakker, 1996), or properties of joint receipt (Luce, 1995b; Cho et al., 1994) – lead to distinct testable implications. These implications, some of which are described in Section 8, have the potential to make the world seem even more complicated, and hopefully, they may also lead to new theory that will make it seem simpler.

PART 3

PREFERENCE, MEASUREMENT THEORY, AND AXIOMATIC SYSTEMS

Choice, Decision, and Measurement
A. A. J. Marley (Ed.),
©Lawrence Erlbaum Associates, NJ, 1997.

DUNCAN LUCE AS MEASUREMENT THEORIST

PATRICK SUPPES

Stanford University

ABSTRACT. This article records significant aspects of Duncan Luce's work as a measurement theorist. Its rather personal slant is based on our friendship of more than four decades.

1. FIRST ACQUAINTANCE

I first met Duncan in 1954 when he was a first-year fellow at the Center for Advanced Study in the Behavioral Sciences at Stanford. We talked some that year but our acquaintance really became much closer in the summer of 1957 when several of us, including Duncan, organized a family of summer institutes in various topics in mathematical social science at Stanford under the auspices of the Social Sciences Research Council. It was at this 1957 summer meeting that Duncan circulated the first draft of *Individual Choice Behavior* (1959).[1] At first I thought his formulation of the choice axiom was wrong, and we had some very intense arguments about it that summer. Out of our disagreement about this, and my recognition that I was wrong in my views about Duncan's formulation, we became not just acquaintances but close friends.

When Duncan, Bob Bush, and Gene Galanter decided to edit the *Handbook of Mathematical Psychology* in the early 60's, they invited me to write the first article on measurement, which I did jointly with Jerry Zinnes. In connection with that article, Duncan and I began discussions about the theory of measurement. As Volume III of the *Handbook of Mathematical Psychology* was organized, Duncan invited me to write jointly with him a long chapter entitled "Preference, Utility and Subjective Probability." This chapter actually contains a substantial amount of material on measurement theory, as is evident from the title, because its focus is an area in which a good deal of the modern research on measurement theory has been conducted. Duncan and I talked about this chapter a lot and out of that grew a strong common interest in measurement concepts.

2. THE THREE-VOLUME FOUNDATIONS OF MEASUREMENT

Following the publication of the *Handbook of Mathematical Psychology*, in 1968 Duncan and I wrote with Bob Bush the article on mathematical models in the social sciences for the *International Encyclopedia of the Social Sciences*, and in the same

---

Key words and phrases. Measurement, semiorders, conjoint measurement, psychophysics.

Address for correspondence. Patrick Suppes, Ventura Hall, Stanford University, Stanford CA 94305-4115. Email: suppes@ockham.stanford.edu

[1] The many books and papers of Duncan referred to here can be found in his bibliography given at the end of this volume.

year Duncan and I also wrote the article on mathematics for it. At about the same time, we got the idea of writing a substantial treatise on the foundations of measurement that would be aimed at covering most developments in the subject at that time. We agreed that we needed help in areas we did not know well, so we invited Dave Krantz and Amos Tversky to join us. Each of the four authors may have a slightly different recollection of how it got organized, but I think this is approximately correct. Certainly Duncan, as always, was the pacemaker in getting his parts of the treatise written. I have some further remarks about that in the last section.

Of the three volumes of *Foundations of Measurement*, Volume I appeared in 1971 – the only volume originally intended – Volume II in 1989 and Volume III in 1990. The final decision to have three rather than two volumes came quite late, as we realized there was too much material for a single second volume. Completing the work occupied all four of us over a good many years. Not certainly our only occupation, but still a major preoccupation to get it finished.

I can remember well the couple of weeks that Duncan moved in with me and my family to complete the chapters I was still lagging on in Volume I. This was probably sometime in the summer or early fall of 1970. He knew that one way to get them written was to come and stay until they were finished. Naturally the chapters, or parts of chapters, he had taken primary responsibility for were long since in finished draft. We had a somewhat similar experience in the writing of Volumes II and III. Duncan was always first off the mark with the parts he was committed to drafting and he was good at pestering the rest of us to get something finished. As is evident both from the articles referenced and from other features of the volume, most of Volume III was actually put together by Duncan and a good many parts of it reflect his particular interests in the theory of measurement that continue into the present, a subject which I remark on later.

Writing a joint work of the length of *Foundations of Measurement*, with a composition that extended over many years, is a strain without any doubt, but I am happy to say that Duncan and I are still talking in friendly terms and continue to see each other. We are of course all relieved, not just Duncan and me, but Dave Krantz[2] as well, that after many years the work is finally finished. It is clear that for each of us this will probably be the longest publication we participate in directly as an author in our entire academic career.

3. LUCE'S RESEARCH IN MEASUREMENT

I have already remarked on Duncan's central and leading role in the writing of *Foundations of Measurement* (*FM*). I want to stress now the importance of the research in the theory of measurement that he has done over many years, much of which is included in *FM* in systematic review of the subject. But *FM* is primarily a report of research already completed and so it is appropriate to give a separate account of Duncan's many papers in measurement. I will not try to cover everything. There are really too many to comment on each one in depth. What is

---

[2]Sadly for all of us Amos Tversky died May 26, 1996.

important is to comment on those that in my view have had a significant impact on research in the field.

The place for me to begin is his famous 1957 paper on semiorders. The idea of just noticeable differences had been around in psychology for a good many decades, going back at least to early work of Thurstone, but a qualitative non-statistical theory of just noticeable differences, particularly at the level of simple orderings, had not been well worked out prior to Duncan's paper. He carefully developed the relation between just noticeable differences and utility discriminations. The algebraic work on semiorders now probably has a research literature of as many as 500 papers. Duncan's article is the beginning of that rich and fertile concept.

There followed in 1958 the article with Ward Edwards on the derivation of subjective scales from just noticeable differences, and in 1959, the article "A probabilistic theory of utility and its relationship to Fechnerian scaling" in a volume on measurement theory edited by Churchman and Ratoosh (1959). And then in the same year his important paper "On the possible psychophysical laws" which like the paper with Edwards a year earlier appeared in *Psychological Review*. Duncan's work on these related topics of subjective scales, psychophysical laws, and closely related matters such as Fechnerian scaling has contained some of his most original and interesting ideas. He has subsequently published several papers on the possible psychophysical laws. I have always felt myself that this work is among the most interesting from a theoretical standpoint of any that has appeared in psychophysics.

In fact, I think one of the problems I have in writing about Duncan's work on measurement is not to try to cover a large part of the research papers he has written, because so many of the things that he has focused on in psychophysics and decision theory, both theoretical and experimental, have been closely related to issues of measurement. For example, many of his experimental papers on preference and choice have tested particular measurement axioms for preferences, utility or subjective probability.

A theoretical paper of Duncan's with John Tukey in 1964 is another example of a paper squarely in the theory of measurement that has had a significant impact both on measurement theory and several other areas of psychology. I refer to the well-known article of that year on conjoint measurement, which appeared in the first volume of the *Journal of Mathematical Psychology* (*JMP*). Duncan has continued to write papers on conjoint measurement, but perhaps more important, a large number of other people have as well. The literature on conjoint measurement, taken in both its theoretical and experimental aspects, is even larger in my judgment, though I have not attempted a serious quantitative comparison, than that on semiorders.

As another aspect of Duncan's fundamental work on possible psychophysical laws I mention also his 1965 paper that appeared in the journal *Philosophy of Science* entitled "A 'fundamental' axiomatization of multiplicative power relations among three variables." Duncan's work in this area is extraordinarily interesting. As written up by Duncan in Chapter 10 in Volume I, it is some of the most permanent material in terms of significance to be found in *FM*.

Another direction of Duncan's work in measurement is reflected in his 1967 paper in the *Annals of Mathematical Statistics* on sufficient conditions for the existence of a finitely additive probability measure. The axiom that really does the work here is complicated, but it is typical of Duncan that he kept at the topic until he got to something that indeed provided a reasonable sufficient condition. This was followed up in 1968 by a related article in the *Annals of Mathematical Statistics* on the numerical representation of qualitative *conditional* probability. In many ways the article on conditional probability, because of its greater complexity, marked a more substantial advance in the subject. In the same year, 1968, Duncan published in *Synthese* with Fred Roberts an article that I have always admired, and consider fundamental, on axiomatic thermodynamics and extensive measurement. Again, much of this work was included in Volume I of *FM*.

Then in the next year, 1969, Duncan published with Tony Marley another extension of extensive measurement, namely, extensive measurement when the concatenation operation is restricted and maximal elements may exist, a subject of considerable conceptual interest from the standpoint of the actual practice of extensive measurement. Again, the core results were included in Volume I of *FM*. Then in 1971 Duncan published three measurement articles, with results that mostly were also reorganized and put in Volume 1 of *FM*. I have in mind, first, the article on periodic extensive measurement, in itself an interesting conceptual problem. This article appeared in *Composito Mathematica*. Next was the article on conditional expected utility with Dave Krantz, which appeared in *Econometrica*, and third was Duncan's article "Similar systems and dimensionally invariant laws" which appeared in *Philosophy of Science*.

In 1972 and in the years that followed, with Volume I of *FM* out of the way, Duncan in many ways accelerated his publications in the theory of measurement. First in 1972 appeared "Conditional expected, extensive utility" in *Theory and Decision*. Then in 1973, the paper "Three axiom systems for additive semi-ordered structures" in the *SIAM Journal of Applied Mathematics* and the article "Measurement and psychophysics" in the volume *Notes of Lectures on Mathematics in the Behavioral Sciences*, published by the Mathematical Association of America. This is a long article reviewing much of the work that Duncan had done on measurement in psychophysics.

In the second half of the 70's Duncan began publishing an important series of articles with Louis Narens on the theory of measurement. In 1976 two articles appeared with Narens, first "The algebra of measurement" in the *Journal of Pure and Applied Algebra* and "A qualitative equivalent to the relativistic additive law for velocities" in *Synthese*, and then two years later, again with Narens, "Qualitative independence in probability theory" in *Theory and Decision*. Duncan and Louis come at the theory of measurement from a somewhat different perspective. Duncan, with a broad scientific experience in mathematical psychology, and originally Louis with a background in mathematics and a focus on abstract theory of measurement as he moved into the mathematical social sciences. Certainly it has been a very fruitful and productive collaboration. I will not have space to mention all of their joint work but it has been one of the important collaborations in the theory of measurement in the last two decades.

To mention some of the important papers in this long collaboration, there is a 1983 paper with Louis on interpersonal comparability of utility in *Theory and Decision* and the long paper entitled "Symmetry, scale types, and generalizations of classical physical measurement" in *JMP*. Then in the next year, 1984, with Louis "Classification of real measurement representations by scale type" in *Measurement*, and in 1985 with Louis "Classification of concatenation structures according to scale type" in *JMP*, and in 1986 "Uniqueness and homogeneity of real relational structures" in *JMP*. I like to think in many ways of this leading up to a central interest of both Duncan's and Louis', namely, obtaining very general theorems about the scale type of the relational structures that have numerical representations and satisfy a few quite general conditions. This tendency is very much brought out in the 1987 article with Louis "The mathematics underlying measurement on the continuum" in *Science*, and Duncan's article "Measurement structures with Archimedean ordered translation groups" in *Order*.

Toward the latter part of the 80's Duncan became intensely concerned with revising the classical axioms for subjective expected utility to provide an axiomatization reflecting in a more sensitive way many of the descriptive aspects of choice behavior that had been found in a number of experimental studies, several of which Duncan was himself involved in as author or co-author. I have in mind for example his 1988 article "Rank-dependent, subjective-utility representations" in *The Journal of Risk and Uncertainty*. This same direction of work is to be seen in his 1991 article "Rank- and sign-dependent linear utility models for binary gambles" in the *Journal of Economic Theory*, his article in the same year with Peter Fishburn "Rank- and sign-dependent linear utility models for finite first-order gambles" in the *Journal of Risk and Uncertainty*, and a number of articles in the 90's that continue this line of investigation. I mention especially Duncan's 1992 article "Where does subjective expected utility fail descriptively?" in the *Journal of Risk and Uncertainty*, and even more recent work that is still in the process of being published at the time of my writing this article.

During the last few years in the 90's Duncan has also continued the line of investigation with Louis I mentioned that I thought was particularly important in terms of reaching for the greatest level of generality in characterizing measurement structures. I mention here their 1992 article "Intrinsic Archimedeanness and the continuum" in the measurement volume edited by Savage and Ehrlich (1992).

Although I will not really finish this survey, I will just stop with the comment that it is evident enough from looking at my file of papers soon to be published by Duncan, and by talking with him, that his interest in measurement continues unabated. We may expect a host of papers in the years ahead, particularly now that he has retired and has even more time to pursue the many measurement ideas I know he feels are not yet put in proper order.

In closing my survey of Duncan's research on measurement I should mention some areas in which we have had many discussions and about which we do not entirely agree.

To begin with, Duncan has been very much more attracted to the continuum as a framework for theories of measurement than I have. He has made a good case for his views, especially in much of his recent abstract work with Louis Narens. Our very disagreement has, on the other hand, inspired me to further work and I have been motivated to take the long route of setting up a constructive system of axioms for the foundations of mathematics within which one can prove a certain kind of isomorphism between standard continuous models and finite models. I will not try to give a technical description of this work (see Suppes & Chuaqui, 1993; Chuaqui & Suppes, 1995; Sommer & Suppes, in press a, in press b). The important point is that one does not have to agree with Duncan about what are the very best approaches to the theory of measurement to recognize how important his work has been in pushing forward the frontiers of the subject, especially in a general mathematical setting.

The second remark is that we have also had many discussions about the theory of error, and we both agree that this is without question the biggest omission in the kind of work on the foundations of measurement that he and I have engaged in for many years. Where we do not entirely agree is how the theory of error should be approached from the standpoint of the theory of measurement. Again, I will not try to enter into the details of where we have a different kind of emphasis. It may well be that when the problems are really straightened out we will find we very much agree about their solutions.

Third, although I have respected and admired Duncan's detailed work on rank-order models and the like for preferences and decision theory, my own view is that the deficiencies of decision theory and of subjective expected utility theory are to be found more in the thinness of the psychological assumptions about preference at a more general level. In this case, Duncan and I have not really discussed our differences of view with any thoroughness, mainly because my own ideas about how to modify the classical approach have only recently begun to head in a new direction. Duncan would certainly be entitled at this stage to tell me to put some axioms on the table because I have not as yet done anything like the detailed work he has on modifying the classical framework. I do hope to do so and to bring in such matters as the way in which unconscious associations have an effect on choices immediately following them, and how such matters of association can be integrated into a theory of what it means to be rational. Some skeptics may call this the Freudian view of the ideal consumer. But elaboration of these ideas must be left for another time, when I am sure Duncan will be there to give me a proper set of criticisms.

4. SOME PERSONAL REMARKS

From what I said at the beginning, it is evident that my friendship with Duncan extends over more than forty years, and so I feel entitled to comment on my perceptions of Duncan as a working scientist. The remarks I want to make are similar to ones that I made at a dinner in honor of his retirement at Irvine on August 3, 1995. As everybody knows, Duncan is smart and hard working. He has been one of the most influential mathematical social scientists of his generation.

He is compulsive in two ways, both of which are almost necessary for a really successful scientific career. How is he compulsive? First, he is the best person I have ever met at meeting deadlines. My own list of collaborators is long and no one in that list is his equal. He simply gets the job done in a quicker and more thorough fashion than anyone else I know. Secondly, he is also compulsive about making headway on a problem once he has decided to work on it. He does not give up easily. If he knows that there is something to be done that should be done and that is important for a given area, whether it is a very general theorem in the theory of measurement or new axioms for choice behavior in preference situations, you can count on Duncan to stay with the matter for a very long time to get something that is workable and useful.

Third, he is stubborn. He has very definite ideas of his own and he is not easily persuaded that other ideas are better. This is, it seems to me, again an excellent quality for a good scientist to have, although it may not be the best quality for a parent or spouse. I will say that Duncan is willing to listen and is not so stubborn as to hold out against all odds.

A fourth quality is that he has had a large number of collaborators, many of them former students, working with him. This extensive network has amplified considerably the total amount of work he has done, especially in the experimental direction. It is my impression that his collaborators have found Duncan highly constructive in his approach to joint work, even if he is at times demanding and impatient at the lateness of delivery of work by others. He really understands well the psychology of collaboration, he brings a lot to the table, and he has the capacity to appreciate what others are offering as well. These to me are the important characteristics of someone who has a long and successful career of collaboration with many different kinds of colleagues.

Finally I will mention that he has been a good and loyal friend over many years. It has been an honor and a pleasure to work with him and to enjoy his friendship for more than four decades.

Choice, Decision, and Measurement
A. A. J. Marley (Ed.),
©Lawrence Erlbaum Associates, NJ, 1997.

A STOCHASTIC MODEL FOR THE EVOLUTION OF PREFERENCES

J.-CL. FALMAGNE, M. REGENWETTER, AND B. GROFMAN

University of California, Irvine

ABSTRACT. This chapter presents a model describing the evolution of preferences as a stochastic process. These preferences are represented by weak
orders, i.e. rankings with possible ties, on a set of alternatives, and can be
modified under the influence of 'tokens' of information delivered by the environment according to a stochastic mechanism. The parameters of this mechanism
can be estimated from the data and are descriptive of the environment. The
potential effect of a token is to move an alternative up or down in an agent's
ranking. Attitude change is modeled by the stepwise transitions between the
weak orders, which takes the form of a Markov process. The model permits
exact predictions (up to a small number of parameters) of panel data in which
the judges have been required to repeatedly evaluate the alternatives at times
$t_1, \ldots, t_n$. An illustrative application of this model is described in a companion paper (Regenwetter, Falmagne, & Grofman, 1995). That illustration uses
NES Thermometer (Rating) data on the 1992 presidential candidates.

1. INTRODUCTION

A few quantitative models are available, in the political science and economics
literature, that deal with attitude change (e.g., Anderson, 1971; Converse, 1964,
1975; Zaller, 1992).

Some of these models are intended to apply to panel data (Converse & Markus,
1979; Markus, 1982; McPhee, Andersen, & Milholland, 1962) where the same individuals in a large sample have been questioned repeatedly, at times $t_1, t_2, \ldots, t_n$.
On each occasion, the panel members have been asked to express their preference
concerning a fixed set of alternatives. While some of the published models have a
probabilistic component (modeling for example the measurement error), they typically do not cast such data as a manifestation of a stochastic process in the specific
sense of this term in the theory of stochastic processes (e.g., Parzen, 1962; Norman,
1972). As a result, the predictions, and the ensuing analysis of the data, are not
as complete and revealing as they could be. In particular, we cannot compute,
in terms of the parameters of these models, the joint probability of observing the
preference relations $P_1, P_2, \ldots, P_n$ at times $t_1, t_2, \ldots, t_n$ (for any choice of n-tuples
of preference relations and times of observation).

Key words and phrases. Attitude change, public opinion, preferences, strict weak order,
Markov process.

Acknowledgments. This work was supported by NSF grant No SBR 9307423 to Jean-Claude
Falmagne at the University of California, Irvine. We thank two referees for helpful comments.

Address for correspondence. J.-Cl. Falmagne, School of Social Sciences, University of California, Irvine CA 92717. Email: jcf@uci.edu

This paper offers a stochastic model of attitude change that is closely related to recent work in mathematical behavioral science (Falmagne, 1996; Falmagne & Doignon, in press). The key idea is consistent with social choice theory in that, at any time $t > 0$, an individual's attitude is represented by a preference relation on the set of alternatives. These preference relations are formalized by 'weak orders,' that is, rankings with possible ties. A current ranking may be altered by 'tokens' of information delivered by the environment in a probabilistic fashion. The potential effect of a token is to move an alternative up or down in the current ranking. The axioms specifying the model ensure that detailed predictions can be obtained. In particular, we can derive an exact expression for the asymptotic probability of any ranking $\succ$ (see Theorem 3). We can also compute the joint probability of observing rankings $\succ$ and $\succ'$ at time t and $t + \delta$, respectively, for any pair of rankings $\succ$ and $\succ'$ and for large t (see Theorem 4). Moreover, the model lets us explicitly solve for the degree of relative negativity/positivity in the information token environment (see Regenwetter et al., 1995), e.g., to evaluate the extent of negative campaigning by reasoning backwards from observed changes in voter preferences. Negative campaigning has been studied by, for instance, Garramone (1985), Skaperdas and Grofman (1995), Ansalobehere, Iyengar, Simon, and Valentino (1994). For concreteness, our attention will be focused on the special case of three alternatives. A followup paper (Regenwetter et al., 1995) provides an illustrative test of the model with National Election Study (NES) panel data on voter evaluations of political figures, with a focus on the Bush-Clinton-Perot 1992 contest. That paper also contains a detailed discussion of the statistical issues associated with the practical application of the model.

Sections 1 and 2 respectively contain an informal outline of the model, and a point by point comparison of its assumptions with other concepts and approaches. A formal statement of the assumptions is given in Section 3 in the guise of three Axioms. The predictions are listed and examined in Section 4. Section 5 discusses some limitations of the present model and possible elaborations. Section 6 contains a summary of the work, and some suggestions for further research.

2. OVERVIEW OF THE MODEL

We write $\mathcal{A}$ for the set of alternatives. By a *preference relation* on the set $\mathcal{A}$, we mean here a binary relation in the usual sense of set theory, i.e., a set of ordered pairs of elements of $\mathcal{A}$. We restrict consideration to those preference relations $\succ$ which satisfy the following condition: for all i, j and k in $\mathcal{A}$,

[SW]   if $i \succ j$, then $\begin{cases} \text{not } j \succ i \text{ and} \\ \text{either } i \succ k \text{ or } k \succ j \text{ (or both).} \end{cases}$

A preference relation satisfying this condition is sometimes called a *strict weak order* (Roberts, 1979), and we conform to this terminology. Condition [SW] induces a strict weak order on the set $\mathcal{A}$. In fact, it is well known that if the set $\mathcal{A}$ is finite or countable and the relation $\succ$ satisfies [SW], then we can assign a number $u(i)$ to each alternative i in such a way that

$$i \succ j \quad \text{if and only if} \quad u(i) > u(j) \tag{1}$$

(see e.g. Krantz et al., 1971). Note that the scale u is only defined up to an arbitrary strictly increasing transformation. The empty relation $\emptyset$ – i.e., the relation containing no ordered pairs – is a special case of a preference relation. Indeed, [SW] 'vacuously' holds in that case because the case $i \succ j$ never arises. In the case of a set $\mathcal{A} = \{1, 2, 3\}$, there are exactly 13 different strict weak orders on that set. They are represented by their graphs (Hasse diagrams) in the 13 rectangles of Figure 3. (Ignore the other features of that Figure for the moment. Note that the empty strict weak order is represented by the empty rectangle in the middle of the figure.) We only consider the case of three alternatives for the rest of this paper.

The model is organized around four basic ideas.

1. The latent strict weak orders. We suppose that the responses of an individual to some questions of a survey are governed by a latent personal strict weak order which we call the 'state' of that individual. In the case of three alternatives, there are thus 13 possible states. The empty strict weak order is referred to as the *neutral* state. The set of all states will be denoted by $\mathcal{S}$.

2. The naive state. We also assume that an individual is initially naive, in the sense that, when first confronted with the set $\mathcal{A}$, he or she does not prefer any alternative to any other one. In other words, the state of a naive individual is the neutral state.

3. The probabilistic environment. Starting from this initial state, successive transformations may take place over time. Specifically, we assume that the individual is immersed in a probabilistic environment delivering at certain random times $t_1, t_2, \ldots, t_n, \ldots$ 'tokens' of information regarding the alternatives. These tokens represent events occuring in the environment and having a positive or negative connotation regarding particular alternatives.

4. The tokens. Examples of token generators are T.V. programs, newspaper articles, or conversations with acquaintances convincingly extolling or criticizing some alternative (Iyengar & Kinder, 1987; Iyengar, Peters, & Kinder, 1982). In our model, however, the occurrence of the tokens is not regarded as part of the recorded data. They are not necessarily observable, or controllable by the social scientist. Nevertheless, these tokens play a crucial role in the mechanism responsible for the evolution of the preferences and deserve close attention. In fact, we shall see that the analysis of the data will reveal statistical aspects of the occurrence of the tokens, thereby providing useful indications regarding the information flow.

As indicated above, a token can be *positive* or *negative*. Moreover, to each of these two types of tokens corresponds its *opposite* token. We shall indulge in some idealization and gather all the positive tokens pertaining to alternative i into one class, which will be denoted by $[i]$. For convenience, we shall refer to that class as 'token $[i]$.' A similar idealization will apply to all token types. Table 1 summarizes this notation.

The potential effect of a positive token $[i]$ is to modify the current state so as to move alternative i to the top position of the strict weak order, that is, the position in which i dominates the two other alternatives. There are three such

Types of Tokens	Representing Symbol
alternative i is good	$[i]$
i is not (necessarily) good	$\widetilde{[i]}$
i is bad	$[-i]$
i is not (necessarily) bad	$\widetilde{[-i]}$

TABLE 1. The four types of tokens and their notation.

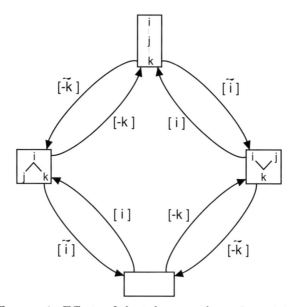

FIGURE 1. Effects of the tokens on the various states.

states, namely[1]:

$$[i \succ j, i \succ k], \quad [i \succ k \succ j], \quad \text{and} \quad [i \succ j \succ k]. \tag{2}$$

(Note the convenient abuse of notation committed in Equation 2: since each of the three formulas specifies a different strict weak order, different symbols – e.g., $\succ$, $\succ'$ and $\succ''$ – should have been used. Our convention simplifies the writing and will be used whenever the context makes clear what is intended.) For example, an individual in state $[i \succ k, j \succ k]$ (that is, preferring both i and j to k) and perceiving token $[i]$ would end up in state $[i \succ j \succ k]$. This transition is represented by the upward arrow in the upper right corner of Figure 1. (The generic graph of Figure 1 illustrates all the possible transitions and will be useful for the rest of this Section.)

The opposite of token $[i]$ is denoted by $\widetilde{[i]}$. As indicated, the occurrence of such a token will modify the current state by removing alternative i from its top position

---

[1]The notation should be self explanatory. For example, $[i \succ j, i \succ k]$ means that i is preferred to both j and k, which are indifferent to each other, and $[i \succ k \succ j]$ has the same meaning, with moreover k preferred to j.

(if it occupies it). Two instances of such a transition are represented in Figure 1. The downward arrow in the upper right corner represents the transition which is the opposite of the one we just described. The downward arrow in the lower left corner represents the transition from the state $[i \succ j, i \succ k]$ to the neutral state. Note that the opposite tokens, when they are effective, always transform a state into one nearer the neutral state. Note also that a token is not always effective. The states are endowed with some rigidity, in the sense that transformations only take place between adjacent states. For example, the occurrence of token $[i]$ has no effect on state $[j \succ i, k \succ i]$ because each of the states having i in its top position (the three states in Equation 2) is far removed from $[j \succ i, k \succ i]$. The intuition underlying the assumption of partial rigidity of the states is that extensive changes in preferences cannot be triggered by a single token of information. (For example, a piece of negative information concerning an alternative at the top of someone's ranking is likely to be discarded.) This relation of 'adjacency' of the states could be formalized, but we shall refrain from doing so here. In any event, its meaning is made clear by the graph of Figure 1 in the case of three alternatives.

The effect of a token ζ on a state $\succ$ will be captured by an operation $\circ$ which is defined by the graph of Figure 1. Thus, the operation $\circ$ maps the pair $(\succ, \zeta)$ to some strict weak order $\succ' = \succ \circ \zeta$. For example:

$$[2 \succ 3 \succ 1] \circ \widetilde{[-1]} \;=\; [2 \succ 3, 2 \succ 1]$$
$$[2 \succ 3 \succ 1] \circ \widetilde{[-3]} \;=\; [2 \succ 3 \succ 1]$$
$$\emptyset \circ [-3] \;=\; [2 \succ 3, 1 \succ 3].$$

One rationale for the transformations illustrated by Figure 1 is to imagine that the alternatives are implicitly evaluated by the respondents on a 3-point scale having -1, 0 and +1 as possible values, with 0 serving as a reference point. Equivalent alternatives are always rated 0. (This means that at most one alternative can be rated 1, or -1.) The value 1 corresponds to the top position of the state, when only one alternative occupies that position (cf. alternative i in the last two cases of Equation 2). A value -1 corresponds to the bottom position, with the same proviso. The value 0 given to some alternative j corresponds to the remaining three pairs of cases, namely:

$$[i \succ j \succ k], \qquad [k \succ j \succ i],$$
$$[j \succ k, i \succ k], \qquad [k \succ i, j \succ i],$$
$$[i \succ j, i \succ k], \qquad [k \succ j, k \succ i].$$

The 0 position on the 3-point scale will sometimes be referred to as the *middle* position (even though j may be a maximal or a minimal element in the state, as in the last four examples above). It is easy to check that exactly 13 strict weak orders can be generated by these rules, via Equation 1. The effect of a positive token $[i]$ or a negative token $[-i]$ is to add or substract 1 to (from) the current value of alternative i if that value is currently 0. The corresponding opposite tokens $\widetilde{[-i]}$ and $\widetilde{[i]}$ have the reverse effect and set the current value of an alternative to 0 when it has been -1 or 1, respectively.

We shall exercise these concepts with an illustrative hypothetical sequence of tokens gradually transforming the states, starting from the neutral state. These transformations are represented in Figure 2. The time axis is in the first column, the horizontal bars marking the occurrence of the tokens, with time flowing from the top to the bottom of the figure. The tokens themselves are indicated in the second column. The current state is pictured in the third column by its Hasse diagram. At time 0, the agent is in the neutral state, and remains in that state until the occurrence of token $[1]$ at time t_1. This results in transforming the neutral state $\emptyset$ into state

$$[1 \succ 2, 1 \succ 3] = \emptyset \circ [1].$$

Next comes the negative token $[-2]$ at time t_2. Its effect is to move alternative 2 to the bottom of the state, resulting in the state

$$[1 \succ 3 \succ 2] = [1 \succ 2, 1 \succ 3] \circ [-2].$$

Token $\widetilde{[1]}$ occurs at time t_3, displacing alternative $[1]$ from its top position, and moving the state closer to the neutral state. Note that token $[2]$, occuring at time t_4, has no effect on the current state $[1 \succ 2, 3 \succ 2]$. The reason is that changing that state into a state having alternative 2 in the top position would be a major transformation, which cannot be realized by a single token. We leave to the reader to ponder the effect of token $\widetilde{[-2]}$ occuring at time t_5.

At first blush, the opposite tokens may appear superfluous. Intuitively, it may perhaps seem that their role could be reassigned – via some appropriate modification of the rules of the model – to the positive and negative tokens. They were introduced to give the model some flexibility in capturing important effects. For example, a prevalence of opposite tokens in the environment would induce a high probability of the neutral state, in other words, a high proportion of uncommitted individuals. In particular, in a political context, a high proportion of opposite tokens of the types $\widetilde{[i]}$ or $\widetilde{[-i]}$ could yield a large number of uncommitted voters.

Finally, we suppose that the delivery of the tokens by the medium during the period of reference is, at least to a first approximation, a stable process in the sense that the probabilities of occurrence of the various tokens in any interval of time $[t, t + \delta]$, $t > 0$, $\delta > 0$, do not vary with t. (This idea will be specified in Section 3.) An important consequence of the Axioms is that the temporal succession of the states is a homogeneous random walk on the family of all states, with the probabilities of the transition between the states being governed by the probabilities of the tokens. A graph of this random walk is displayed in Figure 3.

To simplify the graph, only the centrifugal transitions – i.e., away from the neutral state – are indicated. The centripetal transitions can be obtained by reversing the arrows and capping each of the symbols representing tokens by a '~' sign. (The symbols β_i and τ_i refer to the transition probabilities between the states and should be ignored for the moment. They will be explained in Section 3.) One useful feature of this random walk is that asymptotic results can be obtained (see Section 3). In particular, it can be shown that the asymptotic probabilities of the

TIME	EVENTS (TOKENS)	STRUCTURE AT TIME t	COMMENTS

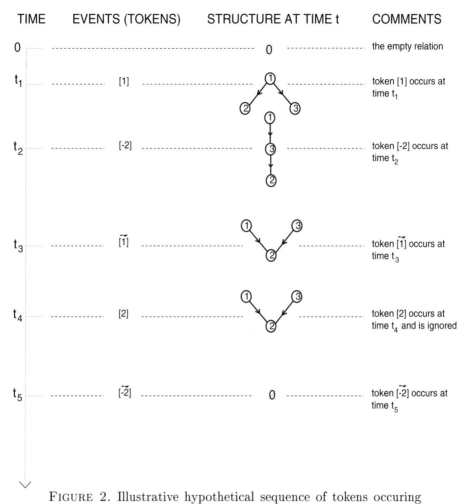

FIGURE 2. Illustrative hypothetical sequence of tokens occuring at times $t_1, \ldots, t_5, \ldots$ and the resulting preference relations.

states satisfy the following regularity condition. In words:

> *The asymptotic probabilities of two adjacent states $\succ$ and $\succ \circ \zeta$ differ by a factor which depends on the token ζ, but not on the state $\succ$.* (3)

To state this condition more precisely, some notation is required. For any state $\succ$, let $p_\succ$ be the asymptotic probability of that state[2]. Take any two distinct states $\succ$ and $\succ'$ and let ζ be some token. Suppose that the four states

$$\succ, \quad \succ \circ \zeta, \quad \succ', \quad \succ' \circ \zeta$$

---

[2]In other words, suppose that the population of reference has been exposed to the tokens for a long time. Then, $p_\succ$ is the probability that, if an agent is sampled from the population, then this agent will be in state $\succ$.

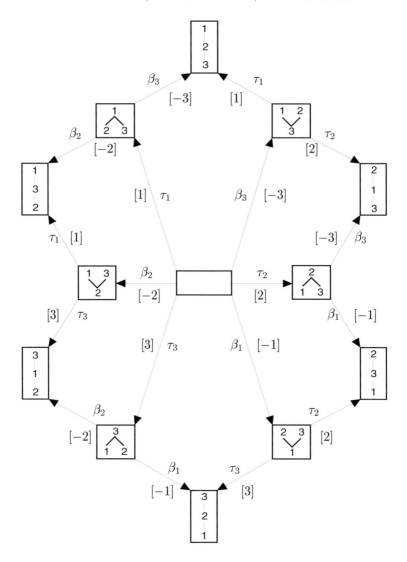

FIGURE 3. Transition diagram of the random walk on $\mathcal{S}$. The positive or negative token producing a transition is marked next to the corresponding edge, with its probability. To simplify the graph, only the centrifugal transitions (that is, away from the neutral state) are indicated. The centripetal transitions are obtained by reversing the arrows and by capping the symbols by '$\sim$' (tildes). This graph contains 6 different instances of the generic graph of Figure 1 which are obtained by setting i, j and k equal to 1, 2 and 3 in the 6 possible ways.

are all distinct. As a straightforward consequence of Theorem 3 (see Section 8 at the end of this chapter), we must have

$$\frac{p_\succ}{p_{\succ \circ \zeta}} = \frac{p_{\succ'}}{p_{\succ' \circ \zeta}}. \tag{4}$$

For example:

$$\frac{p_\emptyset}{p_{\emptyset \circ [-3]}} = \frac{p_{[1 \succ 2, 1 \succ 3]}}{p_{[1 \succ 2, 1 \succ 3] \circ [-3]}} = \frac{p_{[2 \succ 1, 2 \succ 3]}}{p_{[2 \succ 1, 2 \succ 3] \circ [-3]}},$$

that is,

$$\frac{p_\emptyset}{p_{[1 \succ 3, 2 \succ 3]}} = \frac{p_{[1 \succ 2, 1 \succ 3]}}{p_{[1 \succ 2 \succ 3]}} = \frac{p_{[2 \succ 1, 2 \succ 3]}}{p_{[2 \succ 1 \succ 3]}}.$$

(cf. the three edges marked $[-3]$ at the upper right of Figure 3). Equation 4 means that the ratio $p_\succ / p_{\succ \circ \zeta}$ does not depend on the state $\succ$. Writing $G(\zeta)$ for the right member of Equation 4, and multiplying both members by $p_{\succ \circ \zeta}$, we get

$$p_\succ = p_{\succ \circ \zeta} \times G(\zeta)$$

which is a formalization of Equation 3. The invariance of ratios condition specified by Equation 4 is of interest because it has received some empirical support (see Regenwetter et al., 1995).

Another result in the same vein deals with two successive polls separated by a time interval δ. This result, which is too technical to state here (see Equation 14) concerns the joint probability $p_{\succ, \succ'}(\delta)$ of observing strict weak order $\succ$ at time t and strict weak order $\succ'$ at time $t + \delta$, for large t and for any pair of strict weak orders $\succ, \succ'$. This type of result provides a quantitative prediction of the effect of the passage of time on the correlation between successive judgments given by the same individuals.

An axiomatic presentation of this model is given in Section 3. It is worth pointing out that this model is only one of a fairly large class based on the same ideas. In these models, the successive preference relations of an individual are also seen as a realization of a stochastic process, and similar mechanisms manufacturing the changes are postulated. The models differ by the type of tokens considered, by the particular type of preference relations adopted for the states and by the transformations of the states induced by the tokens (i.e., the operation∘ of this paper). We chose to present the strict weak order case in view of the good fit to the data obtained by Regenwetter et al. (1995). Other models, centered on different relations – linear orders in Falmagne (1996), and semiorders, partial orders and interval orders in Doignon and Falmagne (in press) (see also Doignon & Falmagne, in press) were less successful. Note that, even though all these models are conceptually related, the technical differences between them are not trivial.

3. COMPARISON WITH OTHER MODELS OF ATTITUDE CHANGE

There are two prominent differences between the model that we propose and other models of attitude change, such as those encountered in the literature on survey research dealing with panel data (Converse, 1964), or in the social psychology and political science literatures on persuasion and attitude change[3] (Fishbein & Ajzen, 1981; Iyengar & Kinder, 1987; Zaller, 1992).

One concerns the type of preference relation considered. Measures of attitudes are often regarded as providing cardinal (i.e., numerical) information. For instance, thermometer data or Likert scales are treated as instances of interval scale measurement. A much more conservative viewpoint is taken here, in which only the order information contained in the numerical responses is retained: we suppose that an agent's attitude is represented by some strict weak order $\succ$, which may change over time. As indicated by Equation 1 such a relation can be given a numerical interpretation, but the numerical scale contains no cardinal information. (For example, the difference $u(i) - u(j)$ between two scale values has no empirical meaning.) However, the potential loss caused by discarding cardinal information is largely compensated by the comprehensive analysis of the data made possible by the model, which relates to the second of the two differences. In contrast to other models, attitude change in our model is explicitly cast as a (real time) stochastic process, and as such takes into account the full history of the responses provided by each agent. In the case of a sample of agents tested at times $t_1, t_2, \ldots, t_n$, these data correspond to the observed frequencies of all the n-tuples $(\succ_1, \succ_2, \ldots, \succ_n)$ of strict weak orders. For three alternatives, and with agents having provided their preferences on three occasions, the data comprises $13^3 - 1 = 2196$ independent frequencies, to be explained with only a dozen or so parameters.

We must also mention in passing the vast literature in psychology dealing with mathematical learning theory (Bush & Mosteller, 1955; Atkinson, Bower, & Crothers, 1965; Norman, 1972). There is a parentage between the learning models developed by the mathematical psychologists and that of this paper. In fact, there was an early attempt to apply mathematical learning theory to social choice theory (Suppes, 1961). The empirical context is quite different, however. The mathematical learning models apply primarily to highly controlled situations in experimental psychology. A representative example is a task in which a respondent is asked to predict which of two lights will come on. The respondent indicates his or her prediction, at the beginning of each trial, by pressing one of two keys. The trial ends up with a probabilistic event providing feedback. Three aspects of this approach are relevant here. For one, the occurrence of the stimuli (e.g., lights) is controlled by the experimenter (while the tokens are hypothetical constructs, having probabilities that have to be estimated from the data.) For another, with very few exceptions, the learning models are 'discrete parameter stochastic processes', that is, they are formalized in terms of a sequence of discrete trials (while the model of this paper formalizes a process taking place in real time, that is, a 'continuous parameter stochastic process'). Finally, the class of possible 'states of the subject' in the learning models does not resemble that postulated here, namely, a family of preference relations. These empirical and theoretical differences prevent a wholesale importation of the mathematical learning models.

---

[3]There is also a vast literature on propaganda and persuasion (Petty & Cacioppo, 1981; Hastie, 1986). With some adaption, the sequential features at the focus of that work could be incorporated in our approach.

4. FORMAL STATEMENT OF THE MODEL

We consider three basic sets. We recall that $A = \{1, 2, 3\}$ is the set of alternatives. Each of the 13 strict weak orders on A is a possible *state* of an individual, and we write S for the set all such states. Note that S contains the empty relation $\emptyset$. The set of all tokens is denoted by T. Thus, T contains the positive and negative tokens and their respective opposites. We have

$$T = \{\zeta | \zeta = [i] \text{ or } \zeta = \widetilde{[i]} \text{ or } \zeta = [-i] \text{ or } \zeta = \widetilde{[-i]}, \text{ for } i = 1, 2, 3\}.$$

The effect of a token ζ on a state $\succ$ will be captured by the operation $(\succ, \zeta) \mapsto \succ \circ \zeta$ already encountered and defined by the graph of Figure 1

We suppose that there exists a probability distribution $\theta : \zeta \mapsto \theta_\zeta$, with $\theta > 0$, on the set T of all tokens. This probability constrains the delivery of the tokens via a Poisson process governing their times of occurrence (see Axiom [T]). The model is cast in terms of three collections of random variables. We write:

S_t to signify the state of the individual at time $t > 0$,

$N_{t,t+\delta}$ to specify the number of tokens arising in the half open interval of time $]t, t + \delta]$, with $t > 0$. In the sequel, we write $N_t = N_{0,t}$,

T_t to mean the last token presented before or at time t. We set $T_t = 0$ if no tokens were presented, that is, if $N_t = 0$.

Thus, S_t takes its values in the set S of states, $N_{t,t+\delta}$ is a nonnegative integer, and $T_t \in T \cup \{0\}$. Notice that N_t will turn out to be the 'counting random variable' of a Poisson process, specifying the number of Poisson events occuring in the interval $]0, t]$. The three axioms below recursively define the stochastic process (S_t, N_t, T_t) in terms of the parameters θ_ζ and one parameter λ specifying the Poisson process governing the times of occurrence of the tokens.

Axioms

[I] (*Initial state.*) Initially, the state of the agent is the neutral state $\emptyset$. The agent remains in state $\emptyset$ until the realization of the first token. That is,

$$\mathbb{P}(S_t = \emptyset | N_t = 0) = 1.$$

The notation $\mathcal{E}_t$ stands for any arbitrarily chosen history of the process before time $t \geq 0$; $\mathcal{E}_0$ denotes the empty history.

[T] (*Occurrence of the tokens.*) The occurrence of the tokens is governed by a homogeneous Poisson process of intensity λ. When a Poisson event is realized, the token ζ occurs with probability θ_ζ, regardless of past events. Thus, for any nonnegative integer k, any real numbers $t \geq 0$ and $\delta > 0$, and any history $\mathcal{E}_t$,

$$\mathbb{P}(N_{t,t+\delta} = k) = \frac{(\lambda\delta)^k e^{-\lambda\delta}}{k!} \tag{5}$$

$$\mathbb{P}(T_{t+\delta} = \zeta | N_{t,t+\delta} = 1, \mathcal{E}_t) = \mathbb{P}(T_{t+\delta} = \zeta | N_{t,t+\delta} = 1) = \theta_\zeta. \tag{6}$$

[L] (*Change of state.*) If an individual is in the state $\succ$ at time t, and a single token ζ arises between times t and $t + \delta$, then the individual will be in state $\succ \circ \zeta$ at time $t + \delta$, regardless of past events before time t. Formally:

$$\mathbb{P}(\boldsymbol{S}_{t+\delta} = \succ' \, | \boldsymbol{T}_{t+\delta} = \zeta, \boldsymbol{N}_{t,t+\delta} = 1, \boldsymbol{S}_t = \succ, \boldsymbol{N}_t = k, \mathcal{E}_t)$$

$$= \quad \mathbb{P}(\boldsymbol{S}_{t+\delta} = \succ' \, | \boldsymbol{T}_{t+\delta} = \zeta, \boldsymbol{N}_{t,t+\delta} = 1, \boldsymbol{S}_t = \succ)$$

$$= \quad \begin{cases} 1 & \text{if } \succ' = \succ \circ \zeta, \\ 0 & \text{if } \succ' \neq \succ \circ \zeta. \end{cases}$$

For the rest of this paper, we assume that these three Axioms hold.

Remarks. Three types of objections can be raised against these axioms. One concerns the stability inherent in the homogeneous Poisson process postulated in Axiom [T]. In the case of a political election, it may appear quite unrealistic to suppose that the intensity of the campaign does not significantly vary over time. Actually, it is well known that the opposite is true. The second objection is that, in the framework of the model, the only difference between the agents polled lies in the chance occurrence of the tokens, the distribution of which is the same for all agents. This is implausible, since the agents read different newspapers, watch different TV programs, live in different neighborhoods, all of which should reasonably affect the individual distributions of the tokens[4]. A third potential criticism is that the model requires that all the tokens are 'processed' by the agent, without allowing for possible selective perception/selective attention effects (Iyengar, 1990; Zaller, 1992).

All of these objections are well taken, but less critical than they may appear, because they only bear on superficial aspects of the theory. Relatively minor changes in the assumptions are easy to conceive, which would go a long way toward eliminating these shortcomings, leaving the basic machinery of the model intact. We return to some of these issues in Section 5.

5. RESULTS

We first consider a particular realization of the Poisson process at times t_1, t_2, $\ldots$, t_n, $\ldots$. The ensuing sequence of states is a discrete stochastic process, which turns out to be a random walk. Let us state this formally.

We partition the time axis into the segments

$$]0, t_1[, \ [t_1, t_2[, \ \ldots, \ [t_n, t_{n+1}[, \ \ldots \tag{7}$$

such that $\boldsymbol{N}_t = 0$ for $t < t_1$, $\boldsymbol{N}_t = 1$ for $t_1 \leq t < t_2$, and in general $\boldsymbol{N}_t = n$ for $t_n \leq t < t_{n+1}$. Fixing the sequence (t_n), we define the discrete parameter process $\boldsymbol{S}_n^* = \boldsymbol{S}_{t_n}$ with state space $\mathcal{S}$. The process $(\boldsymbol{S}_n^*)$ is called the *discrete companion* of $\boldsymbol{S}_t$. Even though this discrete parameter process is implicitly indexed by the particular sequence of times of occurrence of Poisson events, in some important sense it does not depend on it. In fact, we have the following situation:

---

[4]Still more elaborate differences between agents have been considered (and modeled, for the case of two agents) by McKelvey and Ordeshook (1986).

Theorem 1. *With t_1, t_2, ..., t_{n+1} as in (7), the discrete companion $(\boldsymbol{S}_n^*)$ of $(\boldsymbol{S}_t)$ is a homogeneous random walk on the set $\mathcal{S}$ of all states, with transition probabilities defined, for any $\succ, \succ'$ in $\mathcal{S}$, by*

$$p_{\succ,\succ\circ\zeta}^* = I\!\!P(\boldsymbol{S}_{n+1}^* = \succ\circ\zeta | \boldsymbol{S}_n^* = \succ) = I\!\!P(\boldsymbol{S}_{t_{n+1}} = \succ\circ\zeta | \boldsymbol{S}_{t_n} = \succ) = \theta_\zeta.$$

This result follows immediately from the definitions. (All proofs are contained in Section 8. Proofs.) We call the Markov chain $(\boldsymbol{S}_n^*)$ a random walk because its transitions only take place between neighbor states, where $\succ' \neq \succ$ is a *neighbor* of $\succ$ if $\succ' = \succ \circ \zeta$ for some token ζ. The graph of this random walk is pictured in Figure 3. Note that only the centrifugal transitions and their probabilities are marked. A simplified mnemonic notation is used for these probabilities. We write:

$$\theta_\zeta = \begin{cases} \tau_i & \text{if } \zeta = [i] \\ \tilde{\tau}_i & \text{if } \zeta = \widetilde{[i]} \\ \beta_i & \text{if } \zeta = [-i] \\ \tilde{\beta}_i & \text{if } \zeta = \widetilde{[-i]}. \end{cases} \tag{8}$$

Thus, the movements to and from the top of the state are induced by tokens with probabilities τ_i and $\tilde{\tau}_i$, respectively, and the movements to and from the bottom of the state are induced by tokens with probabilities β_i and $\tilde{\beta}_i$, respectively.

We define by

$$p_{\succ,\succ'}^*(k) = I\!\!P(\boldsymbol{S}_{n+k}^* = \succ' | \boldsymbol{S}_n^* = \succ) \tag{9}$$

the k-step transition probability of the random walk $(\boldsymbol{S}_n^*)$. We also have:

Theorem 2. *The stochastic process $(\boldsymbol{S}_t)$ is a homogeneous Markov process, with transition probability function*

$$p_{\succ,\succ'}(\delta) = I\!\!P(\boldsymbol{S}_{t+\delta} = \succ' | \boldsymbol{S}_t = \succ) = \sum_{k=0}^{\infty} p_{\succ,\succ'}^*(k) \frac{(\lambda\delta)^k e^{-\lambda\delta}}{k!}. \tag{10}$$

The 'long term' probability of any state $\succ$ exists and can be computed. Specifically:

Theorem 3. *For any state $\succ$, we have the asymptotic probabilities*

$$p_\succ = \lim_{t \to \infty} I\!\!P(\boldsymbol{S}_t = \succ) = \lim_{n \to \infty} I\!\!P(\boldsymbol{S}_n^* = \succ) \tag{11}$$

$$= \frac{\xi_1(\succ)\xi_2(\succ)\xi_3(\succ)}{\sum_{\succ' \in \mathcal{S}} \xi_1(\succ')\xi_2(\succ')\xi_3(\succ')}, \tag{12}$$

with, for every $\succ \in \mathcal{S}$ and distinct $i, j, k \in \{1, 2, 3\}$,

$$\xi_i(\succ) = \begin{cases} \tau_i\tilde{\beta}_i & \text{if } i \succ j \text{ and } i \succ k, \\ \tilde{\tau}_i\beta_i & \text{if } j \succ i \text{ and } k \succ i, \\ \tilde{\tau}_i\tilde{\beta}_i & \text{in the remaining cases.} \end{cases} \tag{13}$$

Writing K for the denominator of Equation 12, we have thus for the four generic cases:

$$p_{[i \succ j \succ k]} \quad = \quad \frac{1}{K} \tau_i \tilde{\beta}_i \tilde{\tau}_j \tilde{\beta}_j \tilde{\tau}_k \beta_k \tag{14}$$

$$p_{[i \succ j, i \succ k]} \quad = \quad \frac{1}{K} \tau_i \tilde{\beta}_i \tilde{\tau}_j \tilde{\beta}_j \tilde{\tau}_k \tilde{\beta}_k \tag{15}$$

$$p_{[j \succ i, k \succ i]} \quad = \quad \frac{1}{K} \tilde{\tau}_i \beta_i \tilde{\tau}_j \tilde{\beta}_j \tilde{\tau}_k \tilde{\beta}_k \tag{16}$$

$$p_{[\emptyset]} \quad = \quad \frac{1}{K} \tilde{\tau}_i \tilde{\beta}_i \tilde{\tau}_j \tilde{\beta}_j \tilde{\tau}_k \tilde{\beta}_k. \tag{17}$$

Remarks. 1) The conclusion of Theorem 3 in the guise of Equations 12-13 would hold under much more general assumptions on the process governing the delivery of the tokens. The homogeneity of the Poisson process plays no useful role in establishing the result. In fact, a general class of renewal counting process would do as well. On the other hand, this homogeneity is critical for the next theorem (for the second time interval, of duration δ).

2) The 13 asymptotic probabilities $p_\succ$ are expressed by Equation 12 in terms of 12 parameters: τ_i, $\tilde{\tau}_i$, β_i, $\tilde{\beta}_i$, $i = 1, 2, 3$, with a sum equal to 1. However, these probabilities only depend upon the probabilities of the tokens via the products $\xi_i(\succ)$, with $i \in \{1, 2, 3\}$ and $\succ \in \mathcal{S}$. There are nine such products. In fact, a still more economical reparametrization of the model is available, involving only 6 parameters (see Section 8. Proofs). Suppose that the frequencies of all 13 strict weak orders in a sample of respondents have been collected experimentally. This remark means that the $13 - 1$ independent frequencies of the strict weak orders can be predicted by 6 parameters. This kind of prediction, while not trivial if the number of respondents polled is large, is not breathtaking. The predictive power of the model is more impressive in the case of the sequential statistics to which we now turn.

Using Theorem 2 and Theorem 3, an explicit expression can be obtained for the joint probability of observing the states $\succ$ and $\succ'$ at time t and time $t + \delta$, respectively, for large t.

Theorem 4. *Let $p^*_{\succ, \succ'}(k)$ be as in Equation 9, i.e. the k-step transition probability between the states $\succ$ and $\succ'$ in the random walk $\boldsymbol{S}^*_n$ on $\mathcal{S}$. Then, successively*

$$\lim_{t \to \infty} \mathbb{P}(\boldsymbol{S}_t = \succ, \boldsymbol{S}_{t+\delta} = \succ') = \lim_{t \to \infty} [\mathbb{P}(\boldsymbol{S}_t = \succ) \cdot \mathbb{P}(\boldsymbol{S}_{t+\delta} = \succ' | \boldsymbol{S}_t = \succ)]$$

$$= \quad p_\succ \cdot p_{\succ, \succ'}(\delta)$$

$$= \quad \frac{\xi_1(\succ)\xi_2(\succ)\xi_3(\succ)}{\sum_{\succ'' \in \mathcal{S}} \xi_1(\succ'')\xi_2(\succ'')\xi_3(\succ'')} \sum_{k=0}^{\infty} p^*_{\succ, \succ'}(k) \frac{(\lambda\delta)^k e^{-\lambda\delta}}{k!}, \tag{18}$$

with $\xi_i(\succ)$ ($i \in \{1, 2, 3\}, \succ \in \mathcal{S}$) as in 13.

Remark. Suppose that, on two occasions separated by a time interval of δ days, the respondents in a sample have been asked to provide rankings of the three alternatives, allowing for possible ties. This means that $13^2 - 1 = 168$ independent frequencies of all the possible pairs of strict weak orders have been collected. Assuming that the first poll took place after the respondent had an extended exposure to the flow of tokens (that is, at a sufficiently large time t), Equation 18 provides a prediction of these 168 independent frequencies in terms of 12 parameters: 12-1 token probabilities, plus the parameter λ of the Poisson process[5]. In the case of three successive polls, we would have $13^3 - 1 = 2196$ independent frequencies predicted by the same number of parameters. Further discussion on statistical issues for models of this kind can be found in Doignon and Falmagne (in press) or Regenwetter et al. (1995).

6. LIMITATIONS OF THE MODEL AND POSSIBLE ELABORATIONS

Examining the assumptions of the model from a common sense standpoint leads to several possible criticisms. One concerns the homogeneity of the Poisson process governing the times of occurrence for the tokens. Consider the case of three political candidates running for an elective office. It is unrealistic to suppose that the intensity of the campaign – which is measured in the model by the density of the tokens – would not vary over time. A more sensible assumption is that campaigning starts slowly, then builds up to culminate just before the election. Remember however that some key predictions of the model do not depend upon this homogeneity assumption. In particular, the formula for the asymptotic probabilities $p_\succ$ of the states in Equation 12 would be valid for a general class of renewal counting processes, including non-homogeneous ones. On the other hand, Equation 18 in Theorem 4 critically depends upon the homogeneity of the Poisson process. What this means is that, from the viewpoint of these homogeneity considerations, the model as stated here would be appropriate for the following situation involving two polls. One poll taken just before a major event taking place long after the beginning of the campaign, such as a debate between the candidates, while the second poll is taken, a short time later, to assess the effect of the debate. Two different sets of token probabilities θ_ζ and θ'_ζ would be required. The first set of probabilities θ_ζ would be used for the computation of the asymptotic probabilities $p_\succ$ in the first factor of Equation 18, which does not depend upon homogeneity. The second set of probabilities θ'_ζ reflects the effect of the debate, and are used in the computation of the k-step transition probabilities $p^*_{\succ,\succ'}(k)$ in the summation part of Equation 18. The assumption of homogeneity is critical for the prediction of these transition probabilities, but not implausible since it only covers a short interval of time.

In any event, while the assumption of homogeneity greatly simplifies the computation of the predictions, it is by no means essential to the basic mechanisms driving the model. We could assume, for example, that the intensity parameter λ of the Poisson process is a function of time, the analytic form of which may depend upon a couple of parameters. In the case of the three political candidates mentioned above, the estimated value of these parameters would be revealing of the general course of the campaign.

---

[5]This supposes that the probabilities of the tokens do not vary for the period considered. If we assume that the probabilities of the tokens change, we can split the time period into two periods with different parameters. For example as a result of a political debate between the candidates that took place just after the first poll, a new process may start right after the first poll. Then the number of parameters increases to $6 + 11 + 1 = 18$.

Another possible criticism concerns the assumption of homogeneity of the population of individuals. Three objections must be distinguished here.

1. All the individuals are initially in the same (neutral) state.
2. They have the same chance of being exposed to the tokens.
3. All the individuals have the same reactions to the tokens.

It is easy to take care of Objection [1]. Rather than assuming that any individual is initially, with probability one, in the neutral state, we could postulate an a priori distribution on the set of states, which would be representative of the population of agents under consideration. This added touch of realism would change very little in the model, but would come at the cost of 12 ($= 13 - 1$) extra parameters. This would not be prohibitive, if the data consist in several polls. Objection [2] can be met, for example, by considering different subpopulations of individuals. The model can then be applied separately to the samples selected from each subpopulation. The estimated values of the probabilities θ_ζ of the tokens can be compared, and may reveal informative differences between the subpopulations. As for Objection [3], notice that the model is not exactly stating that the effect of a token is the same for all agents, since this effect depends on the current state. Nevertheless, it may be of interest to complicate the model by introducing an extra mechanism modulating the effect of a token that has occurred, thus modifying the transition probabilities between the states. This type of elaboration of the model would be in the spirit of the work of Sniderman, Glaser, and Griffin (1990), who allow for different categories of voters to use the same information differently, and the work of Iyengar (1990) that deals with selectivity biases in information monitoring.

There are various ways of developing our model in that direction. We shall outline two of them. For concreteness, suppose that the data allow one to sort the agents into two categories labeled R and D. In some situations, the effect of a token may depend on the category of the agent. To model such a dependency, we could index the operation $\circ$ by R or D. Thus, the effect of a token ζ on a individual in state $\succ$ and belonging to category D would be $\succ \circ_D \zeta$. In this version, the tokens are perceived the same way by all agents, but the definition of the operation $\circ$ depends upon the agent's category.

Another possibility involves the assumption of different screening mechanisms on the part of the agents. A token presented may be ignored with some probability depending on the category of the agent. From a formal viewpoint, this assumption is equivalent to supposing that the probability distribution on the tokens is not the same for the two categories of agents. Accordingly, only very minor changes of the model are required.

Further elaborations of the model can be gathered from the discussion in Falmagne and Doignon (in press). While the class of models considered in their paper does not include the model developed here, their remarks can readily be adapted.

7. SUMMARY

At the core of the model described here is the concept that an individual's preferences are driven by his or her latent state, which we idealize as a strict weak order. The empty set, a special kind of strict weak order, is the 'neutral state', and

serves as a reference: likes and dislikes are evaluated with respect to the neutral
state. Over time, the state of an individual may change under the influence of
quanta of information delivered by the environment. A quantum is called a 'token.'
The potential effect of a token is to transform one state into another, neighboring
the first. Profound changes may gradually result from the accumulation of such
quantum changes. The tokens were classified into four categories: 'positive', 'negative', and their 'opposites', depending on their impact on the current state. The
possible effect of a positive or negative token is to drive an alternative to the top or
to the bottom of the strict weak order representing the state. The possible effect
of the opposite is to drive the state toward the neutral state.

This qualitative version of the model was specialized, for the special case of
three alternatives, by axioms casting the model as a (continuous parameter) Markov
process, the succession of states being a homogeneous random walk on the collection
of states. We supposed that the times of occurence of the tokens is governed by a
homogeneous Poisson process. The effect of a token τ on a state $\succ$ was formalized by
an operation $\succ \circ \tau = \succ'$ defined by Figure 1 (see also Figure 3). Quantitative results
were stated in the form of four Theorems, which together yield exact predictions
for the frequencies of pairs $(\succ, \succ')$ of strict weak orders obtained from a sample
of respondents in two successive polls taken at times t and $t + \delta$, for large t (see
Equation 18). Similar predictions could easily be derived for the general case of n
polls taken at some arbitrarily chosen times $t_1 < t_2 < \cdots < t_n$, for large t_1.

Finally, we recall our earlier remark that the model presented here is but one
of many possibilities falling under the same basic principles. Other related models
are considered in Falmagne (1996) and Falmagne and Doignon (in press) (see also
Doignon & Falmagne, in press). A general theory is presented in Falmagne (in
press). We chose to present this particular model in view of its successful application
to some important data, as reported in Regenwetter et al. (1995). As demonstrated
in this paper, this type of model offers a powerful class of tools for the analysis of
rich data. Further research along the lines of this paper would proceed first by
analyzing a number of available panel data. The result of these analyses would
dictate appropriate theoretical elaborations of these models such as those outlined
in Section 5.

8. PROOFS

Sketch of Proofs of Theorems 1–4. These proofs are similar to those of
corresponding results in Falmagne and Doignon (in press). Accordingly, only an
outline of the arguments is included here.

We suppose that the three Axioms [I], [T] and [L] hold. Theorem 1 is a straightforward consequence. To prove Theorem 2, notice that

$$\mathbb{P}(S_{t+\delta} = \succ' \mid S_t = \succ)$$

$$= \sum_{k=0}^{\infty} \mathbb{P}(S_{t+\delta} = \succ' \mid N_{t,t+\delta} = k, S_t = \succ) \, \mathbb{P}(N_{t,t+\delta} = k \mid S_t = \succ)$$

$$= \sum_{k=0}^{\infty} \mathbb{P}(S_{n+k}^* = \succ' \mid S_n^* = \succ) \, \mathbb{P}(N_{t,t+\delta} = k) \, .$$

With $p^*_{\succ,\succ'}(k)$ defined by Equation 9 and using Equation 5, Theorem 2 obtains.

The proof of Theorem 3 follows standard lines. The Markov chain (S^*_n) is irreducible and aperiodic, and thus has a unique stationary distribution. To prove that this stationary distribution is that given by Equation 12, we use the well known fact that if $(m_{R,S})_{R,S \in S}$ is the transition matrix of a regular Markov chain on a finite set S, and $\pi : R \mapsto \pi_R$ is a probability distribution on S satisfying the condition:

$$\forall R, S \in S, \quad \pi_R \cdot m_{R,S} = \pi_S \cdot m_{S,R},$$

then π is the unique stationary distribution of the Markov chain. Writing K for the denominator of Equation 12 we only have to show that, for all $\succ, \succ' \in S$ and distinct $i, j, k \in \{1, 2, 3\}$, we have

$$\frac{1}{K} \xi_i(\succ)\xi_j(\succ)\xi_k(\succ)p^*_{\succ,\succ'} = \frac{1}{K} \xi_i(\succ')\xi_j(\succ')\xi_k(\succ')p^*_{\succ',\succ}. \tag{19}$$

We check the case

$$\succ = [i \succ j, i \succ k], \qquad \succ' = [i \succ' j \succ' k]$$

and leave the others to the reader. Cancelling the denominators, Equation 19 specializes into

$$\tau_i \tilde{\beta}_i \tilde{\tau}_j \tilde{\beta}_j \tilde{\tau}_k \tilde{\beta}_k \cdot \beta_k = \tau_i \tilde{\beta}_i \tilde{\tau}_j \tilde{\beta}_j \tilde{\tau}_k \beta_k \cdot \tilde{\beta}_k,$$

which is trivial. The proof of Theorem 4 is immediate.

The Reparametrization in Remark 2 after Theorem 3. Dividing the numerator and the denominator of Equations 14-17 by $\tilde{\tau}_i \tilde{\beta}_i \tilde{\tau}_j \tilde{\beta}_j \tilde{\tau}_k \tilde{\beta}_k$ and defining

$$T_i(\succ) = \begin{cases} \frac{\tau_i}{\tilde{\tau}_i} & \text{if } \xi_i(\succ) = \tau_i \tilde{\beta}_i \\ 1 & \text{otherwise,} \end{cases}$$

$$B_i(\succ) = \begin{cases} \frac{\beta_i}{\tilde{\beta}_i} & \text{if } \xi_i(\succ) = \tilde{\tau}_i \beta_i \\ 1 & \text{otherwise,} \end{cases}$$

Equation 12 becomes

$$p_\succ = \frac{\Pi^3_{i=1} T_i(\succ)B_i(\succ)}{\sum_{\succ' \in S} \Pi^3_{i=1} T_i(\succ)B_i(\succ)}.$$

More explicitly, writing C for the denominator in the above equation, the four generic expressions, Equations 14-17, become

$$p_{[i \succ j \succ k]} = \frac{1}{C} T_i(\succ)B_k(\succ),$$

$$p_{[i \succ j, i \succ k]} = \frac{1}{C} T_i(\succ),$$

$$p_{[j \succ i, k \succ i]} = \frac{1}{C} B_i(\succ)$$

$$p_{[\emptyset]} = \frac{1}{C}.$$

The right members in these four expressions can be computed from the 6 parameters $T_i(\succ)$, $B_i(\succ)$, $i = 1, 2, 3$, which must be estimated from the data. Note, however, that when the data of two or more polls is considered, then the full quota of parameters is involved in the computation of the transitions probabilities $p^*_{\succ,\succ'}$ between states (c.f. Theorem 4).

Choice, Decision, and Measurement
A. A. J. Marley (Ed.),
©Lawrence Erlbaum Associates, NJ, 1997.

PREFERENCE MODELS AND IRREVERSIBILITY

JOHN I. YELLOTT, JR.

University of California, Irvine

ABSTRACT. When preferences for a set of alternatives are expressed by rank ordering, rankings can be made from best to worst or from worst to best. Intuition suggests that if the same person repeatedly ranks the same alternatives, sometimes in one direction and sometimes the other, rank orders that signify the same preference ordering should occur with the same probability in both cases. However, it is well known that when Luce's Choice Axiom is extended to ranking behavior in what seems the most natural way, that requirement is only satisfied in the special case of complete indifference. This paper investigates the prevalence of this 'irreversibility' property within a family of random utility models that generalizes Case V of Thurstone's theory of comparative judgment. The analysis focuses on the case of three alternatives. The basic question is whether irreversibility is unique to the Choice Axiom model (i.e., to the generalized Case V random utility model based on the double exponential probability distribution). The answer is no, because the same property characterizes the Case V model based on the exponential distribution. Moreover at least a partial form of irreversibility proves to be common to many models in this family – e.g., all models based on one-sided probability density functions that are square integrable.

1. INTRODUCTION

The term 'irreversibility' is used here to refer to a curious property of certain models for probabilistic ranking behavior that was first described by Duncan Luce in the (1959a) monograph which introduced his famous Choice Axiom. That monograph included a brief section on the problem of extending the Choice Axiom to situations where a person's preferences for a set of alternatives are expressed not by choosing a single alternative from the set, but instead by rank ordering all of them. When alternatives are ranked, there is always the question of whether the direction of ranking should be from best to worst (*forward ranking*) or from worst to best (*backward ranking*). Intuitively one expects that if the same person ranks the same alternatives first in one direction and then the other, rank orders that mean the same thing should occur with the same probability. That is, if $r(i,j,k)$ is the probability of the 3-alternative forward ranking 'i better than j better than k' and $r^*(k,j,i)$ is the probability of the backward ranking 'k worse than j worse than i' for the same alternatives, it seems reasonable to expect $r^*(k,j,i) = r(i,j,k)$. But

Key words and phrases. Choice, ranking, preference.

Acknowledgments. I thank Ram Kakarala for proving Lemma 5

Address for correspondence. John I. Yellott, Jr., Cognitive Sciences Department, University of California, Irvine, CA 92697. Email: jyellott@uci.edu

Luce showed that when the Choice Axiom is extended to ranking behavior in what seems the most natural way, this requirement can only be satisfied if the person doing the ranking is completely indifferent about the alternatives, i.e., only if both the forward ranking and backward ranking probabilities all equal 1/6.

This irreversibility property of the Choice Axiom model for ranking is the topic of this paper. Because it seems such a strong and surprising property, it is natural to wonder whether it is unique to the Choice Axiom within some broader class of preference models that includes the Choice Axiom as a special case. That is the basic question addressed here. The answer we arrive at is that within a class of models called *Generalized Case V Thurstone models*, irreversibility is not unique to the Choice Axiom, and in fact is shared – in a sense – by many models in the class.

The paper focuses on the case of three preference alternatives. Other papers dealing with the concept of irreversibility include Fishburn (1994), Marley (1968, 1982), and Yellott (1980).

2. IRREVERSIBILITY AND THE CHOICE AXIOM

Of course there is no necessary logical or psychological relationship between ranking and choosing, so when we say 'the Choice Axiom model for ranking' we have to explain how the Choice Axiom has been extended from choice behavior to ranking behavior. Luce's (1959a) analysis focused on the idea that rankings are produced by a sequence of covert independent choices, each one governed by the probability that applies when the same choice is made overtly – probabilities that themselves satisfy the Choice Axiom.

To express this idea precisely we need notation. Consider first forward ranking. Suppose a person is repeatedly confronted with some set of alternatives $\{a_1, a_2, a_3\}$ (three restaurants, for example) and required to express his preferences about them, on some occasions ('trials') by ranking them from best to worst, and on other trials by choosing a single best alternative. We suppose that on some trials only two of the alternatives are available (one restaurant happens to be closed). Ranking trials with three alternatives generate six forward ranking probabilities $r(i, j, k)$ corresponding to the six permutations of 1,2,3, and ranking trials with two alternatives generate three pairs of probabilities of the form $r(i, j), 1 - r(i, j)$, where $r(i, j)$ is the probability that i is ranked better than j when only $\{a_i, a_j\}$ is available. Choice trials with three alternatives generate three choice probabilities $p(i), i = 1, 2, 3$, where $p(i)$ is the probability of choosing a_i as best from the set $\{a_1, a_2, a_3\}$, and choice trials with two alternatives generate three pairs of probabilities of the form $\langle p(i, j), 1 - p(i, j) \rangle$, with $p(i, j)$ being the probability of choosing i as best when only the pair $\{a_i, a_j\}$ is available. The entire set of p and r probability distributions constitute a *system of forward preference probabilities* for three alternatives, and we denote such a system by $\langle p, r \rangle$.

A special case that will occur often enough to merit a special name and symbol is the *indifferent preference system*, denoted I and defined by $p(i, j) = r(i, j) \equiv \frac{1}{2}$; $p(i) \equiv \frac{1}{3}$; and $r(i, j, k) \equiv \frac{1}{6}$ for all i, j, k.

Logically, of course, beyond the constraints imposed by probabilities summing to one, there are no necessary relationships between these choice and ranking probabilities; modeling is a matter of imposing them. By definition, the choice probabilities satisfy Luce's Choice Axiom if and only if for all i and j,

$$p(i,j) = \frac{p(i)}{p(i) + p(j)}. \tag{i}$$

Now we need to connect choice and ranking. It is natural to think of pairwise ranking and pairwise choice as identical operations, so we can readily assume

$$r(i,j) = p(i,j). \tag{ii}$$

It is not so obvious how the three-way ranking probabilities $r(i,j,k)$ should be related to choice probabilities, but the idea proposed by Luce in (1959a) seems very natural and appealing. It is that

$$r(i,j,k) = p(i)p(j,k). \tag{iii}$$

i.e., to rank order $\{a_1, a_2, a_3\}$ the subject first chooses a best object from the full set and then makes a second independent choice from the remaining pair, and in both cases these covert choices on ranking trials are governed by the same probabilities that apply when the same choices are made overtly on choice trials. This assumption has sometimes been called *decomposition* (e.g. in Strauss, 1979; Yellott, 1980); we will use that term here. A preference system $\langle p, r \rangle$ will be said to *satisfy the Choice Axiom* if it satisfies assumptions (i), (ii), and (iii).

Now for irreversibility. First we broaden the scope of our experiment to include trials on which the subject is asked to give backward rankings, sometimes of all three alternatives, and sometimes of pairs. Then $r^*(i,j,k)$ denotes the probability of the ranking 'i worse than j worse than k' when all three alternatives are available, and $r^*(i,j)$ the probability of ranking 'i worse than j' when only a_i and a_j are available. And finally, we include worst-choice trials, with either two or three alternatives, and let $p^*(i)$ be the probability of choosing a_i as the worst alternative when three alternatives are available and $p^*(i,j)$ the probability of choosing a_i as worst from the set $\{a_i, a_j\}$. The entire set of p^* and r^* probabilities constitute a *system of backwards preference probabilities* for three alternatives, denoted $\langle p^*, r^* \rangle$. The backwards choice probabilities p^* satisfy the Choice Axiom iff

$$p^*(i,j) = \frac{p^*(i)}{p^*(i) + p^*(j)} \tag{i*}$$

and the backwards preference system $\langle p^*, r^* \rangle$ *satisfies the Choice Axiom* if in addition

$$r^*(i,j) = p^*(i,j) \tag{ii*}$$

and

$$r^*(i,j,k) = p^*(i)p^*(j,k). \tag{iii*}$$

Now suppose $\langle p, r \rangle$ and $\langle p^*, r^* \rangle$ are forward and backward preference systems for the same subject judging the same three alternatives. Our intuitive belief that rankings expressing the same preference order should occur with the same probability, regardless of whether ranking is done forwards or backwards, means that r and r^* should satisfy the following *reversibility relations*

$$r^*(i,j) = r(j,i) \tag{iv}$$
$$r^*(i,j,k) = r(k,j,i). \tag{v}$$

But as Luce showed in (1959a), the following lemma holds:

Lemma 1. *Relations (iv) and (v) are consistent with assumptions (i), (i*), (ii), (ii*), and (iii), (iii*) only in the special case of complete indifference, i.e. if and only if* $\langle p, r \rangle = \langle p^*, r^* \rangle = I.$

The proof of this result is brief, and we repeat it here for completeness.

Proof. First, the Choice Axiom assumptions (i) and (i*) imply the existence of ratio scale values v_i and v_i^*, for $i = 1, 2, 3$, which determine all the choice probabilities via the relations

$$p(i,j) = v_i/[v_i + v_k] \qquad p(i) = v_i/[v_i + v_j + v_k]$$
$$p^*(i,j) = v_i^*/[v_i^* + v_j^*] \qquad p^*(i) = v_i^*/[v_i^* + v_j^* + v_k^*]$$

Then assumptions (ii) and (ii*) combined with the first reversibility relation (iv) imply that $v_i^*/v_j^* = v_j/v_i$ for all i and j, and the second reversibility relation (v) combined with the decomposition ranking assumptions (iii) and (iii*) gives us the equation

$$
\begin{aligned}
r(i,j,k) &= \frac{v_i}{v_i + v_j + v_k} \frac{v_j}{v_j + v_k} \\
&= r^*(k,j,i) \\
&= \frac{v_k^*}{v_i^* + v_j^* + v_k^*} \frac{v_j^*}{v_j^* + v_i^*} \\
&= \frac{1}{v_k/v_i + v_k/v_j + 1} \frac{1}{1 + v_j/v_i}.
\end{aligned}
$$

Simplifying this we find that $v_j^2 = v_i v_k$, and thus $v_j/v_i = v_k/v_j$. But for some choice of indices i, j, k it must be true that $v_j \leq v_i \leq v_k$, so that $v_j/v_i \leq 1$ and $v_k/v_j \geq 1$. Consequently the only general solution to the equation is $v_1 = v_2 = v_3$, and thus $v_1^* = v_2^* = v_3^*$ as well, so $\langle p, r \rangle = \langle p^*, r^* \rangle = I.$ $\qquad \square$

3. RANDOM UTILITY PREFERENCE SYSTEMS

In Luce's (1959a) approach to relating ranking and choice, the Choice Axiom (i) and the decomposition assumption (iii) were logically independent of one another. A year later (Block & Marschak, 1960) pointed out that if we assume that the choice and ranking probabilities satisfy a common random variables model, decomposition and the Choice Axiom are actually equivalent assumptions. Suppose that associated with each alternative a_i there is a random variable U_i, that $P(U_i = U_j) = 0$ for all i, j, with $i \neq j$ (ties never occur), and that the random variables U_1, U_2, U_3 determine the preference system $\langle p, r \rangle$ via the relations

$$p(i, j) = r(i, j) = P(U_i > U_j) \tag{vi}$$

$$p(i) = P(U_i = \max\{U_1, U_2, U_3\}) \tag{vii}$$

$$r(i, j, k) = P(U_i > U_j > U_k). \tag{viii}$$

In this case we say that $\langle p, r \rangle$ is a *random utility preference system* for three alternatives. (It might be more usual to say that $\langle p, r \rangle$ is a 'random utility model', but we reserve the term 'model' to refer to collections of preference systems, as explained later in Section 5. From that perspective, a random utility preference system is a random utility preference model with only a single member.)

Random utility is a very general concept; the joint distribution of the U_i random variables is unrestricted except for the no-ties assumption (which we need to ensure that our probabilities sum to one). Nevertheless, it is far from vacuous. First, of course, it implies that the choice and ranking probabilities must be probabilistically consistent, in the sense that

$$p(i) = r(i, j, k) + r(i, k, j) \tag{ix}$$

$$r(i, j) = p(i, j) = r(i, j, k) + r(i, k, j) + r(k, i, j). \tag{x}$$

(Conversely, (ix) and (x) together actually imply (vi) – (viii), as shown originally by Block & Marschack, 1960. We do not use that fact here, and will not prove it.) Obviously, in a random utility preference system, the three-alternative ranking probabilities determine all the choice probabilities.

Not quite so obviously, using (ix) and (x) we can show that for any three-alternative random utility preference system the choice probabilities uniquely determine the ranking probabilities:

$$p(j, k) - p(j) = r(i, j, k) + r(j, i, k) + r(j, k, i) - r(j, i, k) - r(j, k, i)$$
$$= r(i, j, k).$$

This fact will prove useful later, so we state it formally as

Lemma 2. *If a preference system $\langle p, r \rangle$ is a random utility system then for all i, j, k*

$$r(i, j, k) = p(j, k) - p(j). \tag{1}$$

(For more than three alternatives it is no longer true that the choice probabilities of a random utility preference system uniquely determine its ranking probabilities. Yellott, 1980, gives a counterexample with four alternatives.)

Next, combining the decomposition assumption (iii) with (x) we have

$$p(i, j) = p(i)p(j, k) + p(i)p(k, j) + p(k)p(i, j)$$

which implies

$$p(i, j) = \frac{p(i)}{p(i) + p(j)}$$

i.e., the Choice Axiom. Conversely, the Choice Axiom and Lemma 1 imply

$$r(i, j, k) = p(j, k) - p(j)$$
$$= \frac{p(j)}{p(j) + p(k)} - p(j)$$
$$= p(i)p(j, k)$$

so we have Block and Marschak's (1960) result:

Lemma 3. *If a three-alternative preference system $\langle p, r \rangle$ is a random utility system, its choice probabilities satisfy the Choice Axiom (i) if and only if its ranking probabilities satisfy the decomposition condition (iii).*

4. Opposite preference systems

So far we have been reviewing history; now we begin to introduce something new. If $\langle p, r \rangle$ is a preference system for three alternatives, we define its *opposite* to be the preference system $\langle p^\circ, r^\circ \rangle$ defined by

$$r^\circ(i, j) = r(j, i)$$
$$r^\circ(i, j, k) = r(k, j, i)$$
$$p^\circ(i, j) = r^\circ(i, j) \tag{xi}$$
$$p^\circ(i) = r^\circ(i, j, k) + r^\circ(i, k, j).$$

(Note that the indifferent system I is its own opposite.) One way an opposite preference system might arise would be if preferences for the same set of alternatives are determined both by best-to-worst rankings and best-choices and by worse-to-best rankings and worst-choices; the reversibility conditions (iv) and (v) express the idea that a backwards preference system $\langle p^*, r^* \rangle$ should be the opposite of the forwards system $\langle p, r \rangle$ for the same alternatives. Another way is to imagine that two people A and B both repeatedly rank order the same alternatives, and B perversely tries to be as different as possible from A, so that whenever A produces a ranking $a_i > a_j > a_k$ (or $a_i > a_j$), B produces the reverse ranking $a_k > a_j > a_i$ (or $a_j > a_i$). In this case if A's ranking probabilities form the ranking part of a preference system $\langle p, r \rangle$, B's ranking probabilities will form the ranking part of the opposite system $\langle p^\circ, r^\circ \rangle$.

Using the concept of opposite preference systems we can now restate Luce's (1959a) irreversibility result as

Theorem 1. *If a preference system $\langle p, r \rangle \neq I$ satisfies the Choice Axiom, its opposite $\langle p^\circ, r^\circ \rangle$ cannot satisfy the Choice Axiom.*

And combining the opposite concept with Lemmas 1 and 3 we have the following

Theorem 2. *If a random utility preference system $\langle p, r \rangle \neq I$ satisfies decomposition (assumption (iii)), its opposite $\langle p^\circ, r^\circ \rangle$ cannot satisfy decomposition.*

Theorem 2 is a prototype of the kind of general results we would like to obtain: it shows that the inability of the Choice Axiom to accommodate both forward and backward ranking extends to a class of models that is (or seems to be) more general than the Axiom itself. But of course here the extra generality is only an illusion, because the class of models described by the theorem is exactly the same as the Choice Axiom model itself. We turn now to classes of models that are truly more general.

5. PREFERENCE MODELS, REVERSIBILITY, AND IRREVERSIBILITY

First we need a definition of 'model.' At the most abstract level a *preference model* for three alternatives is simply a set of one or more preference systems – typically, but not necessarily, systems that are related to one another in some natural way. As examples, we have the set of all preference systems that satisfy the Choice Axiom in the sense defined in Section 1 (which we will call the *Choice Axiom preference model*), and the set of all random utility preference systems (which might be called the *general random utility preference model*. Any arbitrary set of random utility preference systems will be called a *random utility model*). We say that a preference system $\langle p, r \rangle$ 'satisfies' a model M (or that M 'admits' $\langle p, r \rangle$) if $\langle p, r \rangle$ is a member of M. And we will say that two preference models M and M' are *equivalent* if they are identical as sets – i.e., whenever a preference system satisfies one model, it also satisfies the other. For example, Lemma 3 shows that the Choice Axiom model is equivalent to the model consisting of all random utility preference systems that satisfy the decomposition assumption (iii).

Equivalence is an important concept, and it is sometimes useful to distinguish two subtypes: *equivalence for choice*, where whenever one model M contains a preference system $\langle p, r \rangle$ the other model M' contains a system $\langle p, r' \rangle$ whose choice probabilities are the same as those of $\langle p, r \rangle$ but not necessarily its ranking proba- bilities; and *equivalence for ranking*, defined in the analogous way for the ranking probabilities. For the random utility models that concern us here this refinement is generally superfluous, because for these models the ranking probabilities of a system $\langle p, r \rangle$ always determine its choice probabilities by construction, and Lemma 2 shows that its choice probabilities determine its ranking probabilities. So two random utility preference models are equivalent for choice iff they are equivalent for ranking. (This identity does not extend to the case of four or more alternatives: Yellott (1980) gives an example of two random utility preference systems for four alternatives that are equivalent for choice but not for ranking.)

Now suppose a model M contains a preference system $\langle p, r \rangle$. We will say that M *is reversible for* $\langle p, r \rangle$ if M also contains the opposite system $\langle p^\circ, r^\circ \rangle$; otherwise M *is irreversible for* $\langle p, r \rangle$. We note that if a model contains the indifferent preference system I it must be reversible for at least that one system, since I is its own opposite. We will say that a preference model is *completely reversible* if it contains the opposites of all of its preference systems, or *completely irreversible* if it contains none of the opposites of its preference systems except for at most I, or *partially irreversible* if it is irreversible for some of its preference systems but not for all of them. In a moment we will encounter many examples of completely reversible preference models; an example of a completely irreversible preference model is the Choice Axiom model. Partially irreversible models are easy to construct artificially, so to speak, (e.g., take any completely reversible model and delete the opposite of any one of its non-I preference systems) but as we shall see it is not so easy to create them in a natural way.

6. GENERALIZED CASE V THURSTONE MODELS

We now define the general class of preference models that will concern us from here on. This is the class of *Generalized Case V Thurstone (GT-V) models*, so-called because they represent generalizations of Case V of Thurstone's (1927) theory of comparative judgment – generalized in the sense that Thurstone's assumption of normally distributed 'discriminal process' random variables is broadened to allow for a range of possible probability distributions. (Recall that in Thurstone's Case V the normal discriminal processes are independent and identically distributed except for shifts. The somewhat ponderous label 'GT-V' was used earlier in Yellott (1977, 1980); we retain it here for consistency. Marley (1982) calls the same class 'independent Thurstonian models'.) A GT-V model is a random utility model in which the utility random variables U_i all take the form $U_i = X_i + s_i$, where the s_i are real constants (*scale values*) and the X_i are independent random variables, all identically distributed as some fixed random variable X. We assume X has a probability density function, and that if X' is another independent random variable identically distributed as X, the distribution function of the difference $X - X'$, $D_X(x) = P(X - X' \le x)$, is continuous and strictly increasing for all x. If a random variable X has both these properties we call it a *Thurstone random variable*. A preference system $\langle p, r \rangle$ satisfies the GT-V model M_X corresponding to a Thurstone random variable X if there are scale values s_1, s_2, s_3 such that for all i, j, k

$$p(i,j) = r(i,j) = P(X_i + s_i > X_j + s_j)$$
$$p(i) = P(X_i + s_i = \max\{X_1 + s_1, X_2 + s_2, X_3 + s_3\}) \qquad \text{(xii)}$$
$$r(i,j,k) = P(X_i + s_i > X_j + s_j > X_k + s_k)$$

where X_1, X_2, and X_3 are independent random variables all identically distributed as X. The requirement that the difference distribution D_X be continuous and strictly increasing guarantees that probabilities sum to one, because ties never occur, and also that the probability of choosing alternative a_i over a_j, for $p(i,j) = P(X_j - X_i < s_i - s_j) = D_X(s_i - s_j)$, is a strictly increasing function of the scale value difference $s_i - s_j$ for all possible scale values. (An implication of this is that the distribution of X itself cannot be concentrated on a finite interval.)

A given GT-V model M_X then is the set of all preference systems that can be generated by applying rule (xii) to arbitrary sets of scale values s_i, using random variables X_i identically distributed as a fixed random variable X; different GT-V models correspond to different choices for (the distribution of) X. We note that the preference system generated by M_X for a given set of scale values s_1, s_2, s_3 is unchanged if we add a constant c to each value, and that for any pair of constants a, b, with $a > 0$, the events $X_i + s_i > X_j + s_j$ and $aX_i + as_i + b > aX_j + as_j + b$ are identical, so for any random variable X the GT-V models M_X and $M_{aX+b}(a > 0)$ are always equivalent. In other words, all probability distributions of the same type give rise to equivalent GT-V models, so we need not distinguish between them.

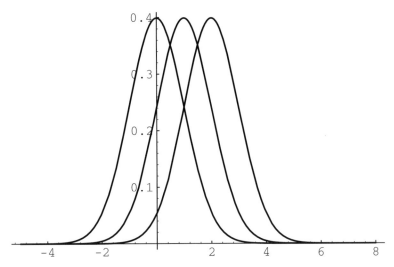

FIGURE 1. Typical probability density functions for the utility random variables of the normal GT-V model.

Thus, for example, we can speak of 'the' *normal GT-V model* M_X, meaning the model generated by assuming that X is any normal random variable. This is the natural extension of Thurstone's Case V choice model to ranking. Figure 1 illustrates probability density functions for typical $X_i + s_i$ utility random variables for this model. The normal model provides an example of a GT-V model M_X based on a random variable with a *symmetric distribution*, i.e., a random variable X with the property that $X - E(X)$ and $-X + E(X)$ are identically distributed. Symmetry plays an important role in understanding the reversibility properties of GT-V models.

The Choice Axiom preference model is equivalent to the GT-V model M_X in which X has the *double exponential distribution*: $F(x) = P(X \leq x) = e^{-e^{-x}}$, whose density function is $f(x) = e^{-x}e^{-e^{-x}}$. Figure 2 illustrates double exponential density functions. Note that the densities are *asymmetric* and extend over the whole line. Holman and Marley (cited in Luce & Suppes, 1965) originally showed that this distribution creates a GT-V model whose choice probabilities obey the Choice Axiom, so the two models are equivalent for choice, and Yellott (1977) showed that this choice equivalence is unique, because a GT-V model M_X is equivalent to the double exponential model iff X has a distribution of the double exponential type. Since for random utility models equivalence for choice implies equivalence for ranking and conversely, the double exponential model is the unique GT-V preference model that is equivalent to the Choice Axiom model. (To prove that the double exponential GT-V model is equivalent to the Choice Axiom preference model we write out the GT-V choice probabilities explicitly:

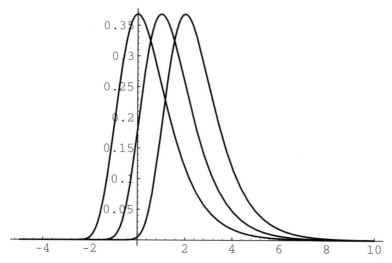

FIGURE 2. Typical density functions for the double exponential GT-V model.

$$p(i,j) = P(X_i + s_i > X_j + s_j)$$

$$= \int_{-\infty}^{\infty} F(x + s_i - s_j) f(x) dx$$

$$= \int_{-\infty}^{\infty} e^{-e^{-(x+s_i-s_j)}} e^{-x} e^{-e^{-x}} dx$$

$$= \frac{e^{s_i}}{e^{s_i} + e^{s_j}}$$

and similarly

$$p(i) = P(X_i + s_i > X_j + s_j, X_i + s_i > X_k + s_k)$$

$$= \int_{-\infty}^{\infty} F(x + s_i - s_j) F(x + s_i - s_k) f(x) dx$$

$$= \frac{e^{s_i}}{e^{s_i} + e^{s_j} + e^{s_k}}.$$

We see that the choice probabilities of a preference system $\langle p, r \rangle$ satisfy the double exponential GT-V model with the scale values s_i iff they also satisfy the Choice Axiom with v scale values $v_i = e^{s_i}$. For both models those choice probabilities determine the system's ranking probabilities, via decomposition (iii) for the Choice Axiom model and via Lemma 2 for the GT-V model, and one can quickly show that the resulting ranking probabilities are the same in both cases.)

Figure 3 illustrates the probability density functions of the utility random variables of a third GT-V model, the *exponential model*, where $P(X \leq x) = 1 - e^{-x}$

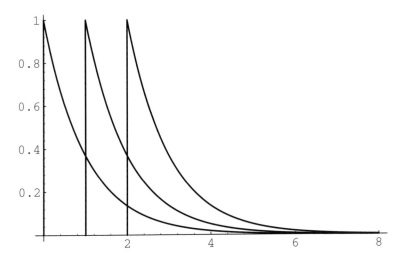

FIGURE 3. Density functions for the exponential GT-V model.

for $x \geq 0$, and $P(X < 0) = 0$. (Yellott, 1977, shows that for pair comparison choice experiments this model is equivalent to a 'threshold' model proposed by Dawkins, 1969). This provides an example of a GT-V model based on a random variable with a *one-sided distribution*, i.e., a random variable X such that either $P(X < c) = 0$ for some lower bound c (the distribution is one sided to the right – e.g., the exponential distribution, where $c = 0$) or $P(X > c) = 0$ for some upper bound c (one-sided to the left, e.g., $-X$ when X is exponential).

7. REVERSIBILITY PROPERTIES OF THE GT-V MODELS

We begin by noting a simple relationship between the GT-V models based on a random variable X and on its negative $-X$. Clearly if X is a Thurstone random variable then $-X$ is also, and if M_X admits a preference system $\langle p, r \rangle$ using scale values s_i, then

$$r(i, j, k) = P(X_i + s_i > X_j + s_j > X_k + s_k)$$
$$= P(-X_k - s_k > -X_j - s_j > -X_i - s_i)$$

so the model M_{-X} must admit the opposite system $\langle p^\circ, r^\circ \rangle$ using the scale values $-s_i$. It follows that M_X is reversible for a system $\langle p, r \rangle$ iff M_{-X} is also, and consequently that the general reversibility properties of M_X and M_{-X} are always the same:

Lemma 4. *A GT-V model M_X is completely reversible (completely irreversible, partially irreversible) if and only if the model M_{-X} is also completely reversible (completely irreversible, partially irreversible).*

Then Lemma 4 and Theorem 1 imply

Theorem 3. *If X is a double exponential random variable, the GT-V models M_X (the Choice Axiom model) and M_{-X} are both completely irreversible.*

The complete irreversibility of the 'negative double exponential' GT-V model in Theorem 3 (which had been noted earlier by Marley, 1982) provides an answer of sorts to our original question about whether the property of complete irreversibility is unique to the Choice Axiom, since the choice probabilities of that model do not obey the Axiom. But if this were the only other completely irreversible GT-V model we would still be justified in thinking of that property as uniquely tied to the Choice Axiom. The next result shows this is not the case:

Theorem 4. *If X is an exponential random variable, the GT-V models M_X and M_{-X} are both completely irreversible.*

Proof. Suppose the exponential model admits both a preference system $\langle p, r \rangle$ with scale values s_1, s_2, s_3, and also its opposite $\langle p^\circ, r^\circ \rangle$ with scale values $s_1^\circ, s_2^\circ, s_3^\circ$. Then for all i, j

$$r(i,j) = P(X_i + s_i > X_j + s_j) = r^\circ(j,i) = P(X_j + s_j^\circ > X_i + s_i^\circ)$$

i.e.,

$$P(X_j - X_i < s_i - s_j) = P(X_i - X_j < s_j^\circ - s_i^\circ)$$

or

$$D_X(s_i - s_j) = D_X(s_j^\circ - s_i^\circ)$$

and because the cumulative distribution function D_X is strictly increasing, this implies

$$s_i^\circ - s_j^\circ = s_j - s_i \tag{2}$$

for all i and j. Then we examine the three-alternative ranking probabilities. We can assume the ordering $s_1 \geq s_2 \geq s_3$, and we consider the particular relationship

$$r(2,3,1) = r^\circ(1,3,2). \tag{3}$$

From Lemma 2 this can be written as

$$r(3,1) - p(3) = r^\circ(3,2) - p^\circ(3) \tag{4}$$

and after a bit of calculation (keeping in mind our assumed ordering of the scale values and using (2) to substitute $s_i - s_j$ values for $s_j^\circ - s_i^\circ$ values on the right side) we find that (4) becomes

$$\frac{e^{(s_2+s_3+2s_1)}}{6} = \frac{e^{(s_2-s_1)}}{2} - \frac{e^{(2s_3-s_1-s_2)}}{3}. \tag{5}$$

Then since our scale values are only unique up to the addition of a constant, we are free to set $s_3 = 0$, and (5) simplifies to

$$2e^{-2s_2} + e^{-s_1} = 3. \tag{6}$$

But because $s_2 \geq s_3 = 0$ and $s_1 \geq s_3 = 0$, (6) can only be true if $s_2 = s_1 = s_3 = 0$, i.e., only if $\langle p, r \rangle = I$, and consequently $\langle p°, r° \rangle = I$ as well. So M_X is completely irreversible, and Lemma 4 implies that M_{-X} must be as well. □

The completely irreversible GT-V models of Theorems 3 and 4 all involve random variables with asymmetric distributions. That asymmetry is a necessary condition for irreversibility, as shown by the following

Theorem 5. *If a Thurstone random variable X has a symmetric distribution (i.e., $X - E(X)$ and $-X + E(X)$ are identically distributed), the GT-V model M_X is completely reversible.*

Proof. Suppose M_X admits the preference system $\langle p, r \rangle$ with scale values s_1, s_2, s_3, and consider the M_X system $\langle p^-, r^- \rangle$ corresponding to the scale values $-s_1$, $-s_2$, $-s_3$. We have

$$
\begin{aligned}
p^-(i,j) = r^-(i,j) &= P(X_i - s_i > X_j - s_j) \\
&= P(X_j - X_i < s_j - s_i) \\
&= r(j,i) = r°(i,j) = p°(i,j)
\end{aligned}
$$

and

$$
\begin{aligned}
r^-(i,j,k) &= P(X_i - s_i > X_j - s_j > X_k - s_k) \\
&= P(-X_k + s_k > -X_j + s_j > -X_i + s_i) \\
&= P(-X_k + E(X) + s_k > -X_j + E(X) + s_j > \\
&\qquad - X_i + E(X) + s_i) \\
&= P(X_k - E(X) + s_k > X_j - E(X) + s_j > X_i - E(X) + s_i) \\
&= P(X_k + s_k > X_j + s_j > X_i + s_i) \\
&= r(k,j,i) = r°(i,j,k).
\end{aligned}
$$

So M_X always admits the opposite system $\langle p°, r° \rangle$, using the scale values $-s_1$, $-s_2$, $-s_3$. □

Thus, for example, the normal GT-V model is completely reversible.

Now that we have examples of completely reversible GT-V models and completely irreversible models, it is natural to wonder about partially reversible GT-V models. I have not been able to find any, and have come to suspect that there are none. Theorem 5 shows that if there are partially reversible GT-V models they must be based on asymmetric probability distributions, but it turns out that symmetry itself is not quite the key to reversibility. Instead, the key is a somewhat more subtle property, as the following theorem shows.

Theorem 6. *A GT-V model M_X is completely reversible if and only if it is equivalent to the model M_{-X}.*

Proof. As noted earlier in proving Lemma 4, $\langle p, r \rangle \in M_X$ implies $\langle p°, r° \rangle \in M_{-X}$, so if M_X is completely reversible, $\langle p, r \rangle \in M_X$ implies $\langle p°, r° \rangle \in M_X$, which implies $\langle p, r \rangle \in M_{-X}$. The same argument in reverse shows that $\langle p, r \rangle \in M_{-X}$ implies $\langle p, r \rangle \in M_X$. Thus M_X and M_{-X} are equivalent. Conversely, suppose M_X

is equivalent to M_{-X} and $\langle p, r \rangle \in M_X$. Then M_{-X} also admits $\langle p, r \rangle$ using some set of scale values s_i and we have

$$r(i, j, k) = P(-X_i + s_i > -X_j + s_j > -X_k + s_k)$$
$$= P(X_k - s_k > X_j - s_j > X_i - s_i).$$

So M_X generates the opposite system $\langle p^\circ, r^\circ \rangle$ using the scale values $-s_i$. □

8. REVERSIBILITY AND THE BISPECTRUM

Theorems 5 and 6 together imply that if a GT-V model M_X is based on a symmetric distribution, it is always true that M_X is equivalent to M_{-X}. But symmetry is not a necessary condition for that equivalence. To show this we examine the relationship between M_X, M_{-X} equivalence and the characteristic function of the random variable X. If M_X and M_{-X} are equivalent the preference system $\langle p, r \rangle$ admitted by M_X using any set of scale values $s1, s2, s3$ is also admitted by M_{-X} using the same scale values, so we have

$$P(X_1 + s_1 > X_2 + s_2 > X_3 + s_3) = P(-X_1 + s_1 > -X_2 + s_2 > -X_3 + s_3)$$

i.e.,

$$P(X_2 - X_1 < s_1 - s_2, X_3 - X_2 < s_2 - s_3) =$$
$$P(X_1 - X_2 < s_1 - s_2, X_2 - X_3 < s_2 - s_3).$$

Since this is true for all values of the s_i, the random vectors $(X_2 - X_1, X_3 - X_2)$ and $(X_1 - X_2, X_2 - X_3)$ are identically distributed. Conversely, if those random vectors are identically distributed, we can run the same argument backwards to show that for any scale values s_i

$$P(X_i + s_i > X_j + s_j > X_k + s_k) = P(-X_i + s_i > -X_j + s_j > -X_k + s_k)$$

so M_X and M_{-X} are equivalent.

Now let $c_X(u)$ denote the characteristic function of X: $c_X(u) = E[e^{-i2\pi u X}]$ for a real argument u (in other words, $c_X(u)$ is the Fourier transform of the probability density function of X). Since the random vectors $(X_2 - X_1, X_3 - X_2)$ and $(X_1 - X_2, X_2 - X_3)$ are identically distributed, they must have the same characteristic function:

$$E[e^{(-i2\pi(u(X_2-X_1)+v(X_3-X_2)))}] = E[e^{(-i2\pi(u(X_1-X_2)+v(X_2-X_3)))}]$$

and using the independence of the X_i, this equation can be rewritten in terms of c_X:

$$c_X(-u)c_X(v)c_X(u - v) = c_X(u)c_X(-v)c_X(v - u).$$

This relationship holds for all u and v, so we can replace $-u$ with u to obtain the more symmetric form

$$c_X(u)c_X(v)c_X(-u - v) = c_X(-u)c_X(-v)c_X(u + v). \tag{7}$$

What we have just shown is that

Theorem 7. *A GT-V model M_X is completely reversible if and only if the characteristic function of X, $c_X(u)$, satisfies Equation 7 for all u and v.*

The entities that appear in Equation 7 have a name and a sizable literature in optics and image processing; Yellott and Iverson (1992) provide references. The left side of Equation 7 is the so-called *bispectrum* of the random variable X, defined as the expectation

$$E[e^{(-i2\pi(uX_1+vX_2+(-u-v)X_3))}] \tag{8}$$

where X_1, X_2, X_3 are independent and identically distributed as X. (Usually the term 'bispectrum' is applied to functions rather than random variables; in that case the left side of Equation 7 is the bispectrum of the probability density function of the random variable X. Our terminology is a shorthand way of saying that.) And the right side of Equation 7 is the same expectation for the random variable $-X$. So another way to express Theorem 7 is to say that *a GT-V model M_X is completely reversible if and only if X and $-X$ have the same bispectrum.*

(The bispectrum of an integrable real function $f(x)$ is the Fourier transform of its *triple correlation*, which is the function defined by the integral

$$\int_{-\infty}^{\infty} f(x)f(x+y)f(x+z)dx.$$

The triple correlation is the first in a series of 'higher-order autocorrelations' which generalize the ordinary concept of autocorrelation, as explained in Yellott & Iverson, 1992.)

The usefulness of the bispectrum in practical applications depends on the fact that under rather general conditions the bispectrum of a function f uniquely determines that function up to a translation (i.e., another function g has the same bispectrum as f iff $g(x) = f(x + a)$ for some constant a). Yellott and Iverson (1992) provide an extensive analysis of conditions under which 1-dimensional and 2-dimensional 'image functions' are determined by their bispectra. These functions, which represent optical images, are nonnegative locally integrable functions, so the class of 1-dimensional image functions includes probability density functions as a special case. To review their results here in any detail would take us too far afield, but the essential point is that the key to whether or not a probability density function is determined by its bispectrum lies in the zeros of its characteristic function, which cannot extend over intervals above a certain length. Here we will use without proof the following result, which R. Kakarala (personal communication in 1994) has shown to be a corollary of Theorem 4 in Yellott and Iverson (1992):

Lemma 5. *A probability density function is uniquely determined up to a translation by its bispectrum if its characteristic function never vanishes on an interval (i.e., there is no interval (a, b) in which the characteristic function is zero at every point).*

Lemma 5 implies that the exponential and double exponential densities are both determined by their bispectra, because in both cases the characteristic function is nonvanishing. (To avoid repetition, from now on when we say that a function is determined by its bispectrum, we mean determined up to a translation.)

Now suppose X is an asymmetric Thurstone random variable whose probability density function is determined by its bispectrum. In this case Equation 7 cannot hold, because if it did the densities of X and $-X$ would be the same except for a translation, making X symmetric rather than asymmetric. Consequently

Theorem 8. *If a Thurstone random variable X has an asymmetric probability density function, the GT-V model M_X can only be completely reversible if that density function is not determined by its bispectrum.*

Most asymmetric density functions one is likely to think of offhand will be determined by their bispectrum, which means that their GT-V models cannot be completely reversible. But it is quite possible to construct asymmetric densities whose GT-V models are completely reversible. The trick for doing this is to construct an asymmetric probability density function whose bispectrum is the same as that of some symmetric density. In that case the bispectrum of the asymmetric density will satisfy Equation 7, and by Theorem 7 the corresponding GT-V model will be completely reversible. As an example, the asymmetric probability density function $\text{sinc}^2(x)(1 + \sin 6\pi x)$ can be shown to have the same bispectrum as the symmetric probability density function $\text{sinc}^2(x)(1 + \cos 6\pi x)$, where $\text{sinc}(x) = \sin(\pi x)/\pi x$. (This is proved in Rockwell & Yellott, 1979.) Figure 4 illustrates the two densities. Both have only isolated zeros and extend over the whole line, so their difference distributions satisfy the Thurstone condition. And the same is true of all pairs of densities of the same form with 6 replaced by any larger number, so there is no shortage of completely reversible GT-V models based on asymmetric probability distributions (though admittedly none will have much practical appeal).

So within the class of GT-V models based on asymmetric probability distributions we find both completely irreversible models (the exponential and double exponential models), and, rather surprisingly, completely reversible models. However we note that our examples of asymmetric but reversible models all involve probability distributions that extend over the whole line. When we restrict our attention to asymmetric distributions that are one-sided (the most extreme form of asymmetry, in a sense), it turns out to be much harder to create completely reversible GT-V models. The reason for this is that one-sided probability density functions are essentially *causal functions*, and under rather general conditions, the Fourier transforms of causal functions can have only isolated zeros. A function $f : R \to R$ is said to be causal if $f(x) = 0$ for $x < 0$, and it is well known (e.g., Champeney, 1987) that if such a function belongs to the class L^2 (i.e. f^2 is integrable) its Fourier transform can only vanish on a null set – hence, not on any interval. (This is a consequence of the famous Paley-Wiener theorem – Paley & Wiener, 1934.) Now suppose M_X is a GT-V model based on a random variable X whose probability density function $f(x)$ is one-sided to the right (if to the left we can use $-X$ to the same effect). Then either $f(x)$ is already causal, or we can translate X to make it so without changing the model M_X, and if $f \in L^2$, its characteristic function cannot vanish on any interval. In light of Lemma 5 then, f must be determined by its bispectrum, which means that X and $-X$ cannot have the same bispectrum and thus M_X and M_{-X} cannot be equivalent, so M_X cannot be completely reversible. Thus we have the following

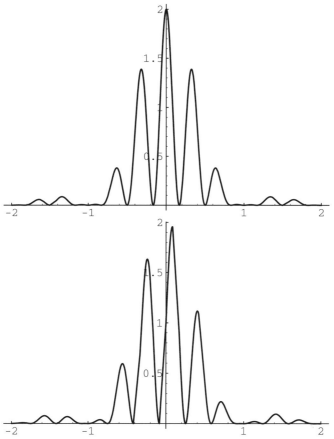

FIGURE 4. Top panel: the symmetric probability density function $\text{sinc}^2(x)(1+\cos 6\pi x)$. Bottom panel: the asymmetric density function $\text{sinc}^2(x)(1 + \sin 6\pi x)$.

Theorem 9. *If a GT-V model M_X is based on a random variable whose probability density function f is one-sided, and $f \in L^2$, M_X cannot be completely reversible.*

The condition $f \in L^2$ is equivalent to the density function of the difference $X - X'$ being finite at the origin, since

$$D_X(x) = P(X - X' \le x) = \int_{-\infty}^{\infty} F(y + x)f(y)dy$$

making the density function at $x = 0$ be $\int_{-\infty}^{\infty} f(x)^2 dx$. It is not impossible for a one-sided GT-V model to violate this condition (the one-sided density $f(x) = e^{-x}/\sqrt{\pi x}$ does so, but it has a nonvanishing characteristic function and thus cannot be completely reversible), but it is certainly not easy to find an example of a one-sided density whose characteristic function vanishes on an interval, and thus escapes the constraint of Theorem 8.

9. IMPLICATIONS OF PARTIAL IRREVERSIBILITY

Theorem 8 provides many examples of GT-V models that cannot be completely reversible – i.e., any model based on an asymmetric probability distribution that is not determined by its bispectrum. But we have only identified a handful of these models as completely irreversible – those described in Theorems 3 and 4. About the rest, all we know is that they are at least partially irreversible. I have not found any examples of GT-V models that are truly only partially irreversible, and my hunch is that there are none, i.e., that every GT-V model is either completely reversible or completely irreversible. But I have not been able to prove this conjecture, and must leave it as an open problem.

We can, however, show that if a GT-V model is not completely reversible, and thus irreversible for at least one of its preference systems, it must be irreversible for infinitely many. To prove this we construct a function that measures the extent to which any given preference system $\langle p, r \rangle$ violates reversibility – a function whose arguments are any two independent pairwise choice probabilities, say $p(1,2)$ and $p(2,3)$. (As will be shown in a moment, these two probabilities determine all the other probabilities in the system, so there is a one to one mapping between the preference systems of a model M_X and the probability pairs $(p(1,2), p(2,3))$ – i.e., the points of the open unit square.) This function is zero when the system $\langle p, r \rangle$ corresponding to a given $p(1,2), p(2,3)$ pair is reversible, has some value greater than zero when it is not, and is a continuous function of its arguments. Consequently if a model is irreversible for some pair $p(1,2) = p$, $p(2,3) = q$, it must be irreversible for all pairs within some neighborhood of the point (p, q) – i.e., for an infinite number of preference systems. (Moreover it will be apparent that irreversibility for the pair $p(1,2)$, $p(2,3)$ implies irreversibility for the pair $1 - p(1,2)$, $1 - p(2,3)$, so each irreversible system $\langle p, r \rangle$ creates two neighborhoods containing infinitely many irreversible preference systems.)

To construct our irreversibility index, we first show that for any GT-V model M_X, all of the choice and ranking probabilities of any preference system are determined by any two of its three independent pair-comparison probabilities, say $p(1,2)$ and $p(2,3)$ (as pointed out by Marley, 1982). To show that these two determine the remaining pair-comparison probability $p(1,3)$ we note that

$$
\begin{aligned}
p(1,3) &= P(X_1 + s_1 > X_3 + s_3) = D_X(s_1 - s_3) \\
&= D_X((s_1 - s_2) + (s_2 - s_3)) \\
&= D_X(D_X^{-1}(p(1,2)) + D_X^{-1}(p(2,3)))
\end{aligned}
\tag{9}
$$

where D_X^{-1} is the inverse of D_X (which must exist because D_X is strictly increasing). Because D_X is continuous, D_X^{-1} is also, making $p(1,3)$ a continuous function of $p(1,2)$ and $p(2,3)$. Then to show that the three-alternative choice probabilities are determined by $p(1,2)$ and $p(2,3)$ we write

$$
\begin{aligned}
p(i) &= P(X_i + s_i > X_j + s_j, X_i + s_i > X_k + s_k) \\
&= P(X_j - X_i < s_i - s_j, X_k - X_i < s_i - s_k) \\
&= P(D_X(X_j - X_i) < p(i,j), D_X(X_k - X_i) < p(i,k)).
\end{aligned}
\tag{10}
$$

The objects on the left sides of the inequalities in Equation 10 are the cumulative distribution functions of random variables applied to those random variables, so each is itself a random variable uniformly distributed on the interval $(0,1)$, and the right side of Equation 10 is the cumulative distribution function of the 2-dimensional random vector $(D_X(X_1-X_2), D_X(X_3-X_2))$, evaluated at the point $(p(i,j), p(i,k))$. Letting $G(x,y)$ denote that distribution function, we can write Equation 10 as

$$p(i) = G(p(i,j), p(i,k)). \qquad (11)$$

Marley (1982) points out that since both marginals of G are continuous (both are the uniform distribution function on $(0,1)$), G itself is continuous. It is easy to see that G is strictly increasing in both arguments, and that $G(p,q) = G(q,p)$. So all the choice probabilities are continuous functions of the pair $(p(1,2), p(2,3))$, and since the ranking probabilities are continuous functions of the choice probabilities (Equation 1), they too are continuous functions of that pair. Thus every preference system admitted by a GT-V model corresponds to some unique pair $(p(1,2), p(2,3))$, and conversely.

Now we suppose a model M_X admits a system $\langle p, r \rangle$ using some set of scale values $\{s_i\}$, and ask how close M_X comes to being reversible for that system, i.e., how close M_X comes to admitting the opposite system $\langle p^\circ, r^\circ \rangle$. An M_X system with scale values s_i' has the same pairwise choice probabilities as $\langle p^\circ, r^\circ \rangle$ iff $s_i' - s_j' = s_j - s_i$, i.e. iff $p'(i,j) = p^\circ(i,j) = p(j,i)$. Call that system $\langle p^-, r^- \rangle$; M_X is reversible for $\langle p, r \rangle$ iff $\langle p^-, r^- \rangle = \langle p^\circ, r^\circ \rangle$. By construction the pairwise choice probabilities of those two systems are the same, so the degree to which reversibility is violated depends on the difference between the ranking probabilities $r^-(i,j,k)$ and $r^\circ(i,j,k)$, i.e., on the difference $r^-(i,j,k) - r(k,j,i)$. The probability $r^-(i,j,k)$ is given by

$$r^-(i,j,k) = p^-(j,k) - p^-(j)$$
$$= p(k,j) - P(X_i - X_j < s_i - s_j, X_k - X_j < s_k - s_j)$$
$$= p(k,j) - G(p(i,j), p(k,j))$$

so a measure of the degree of irreversibility for the ranking probability $r^-(i,j,k)$ is the squared difference

$$[r^-(i,j,k) - r(k,j,i)]^2 =$$
$$[(p(k,j) - G(p(i,j), p(k,j))) - (p(j,i) - G(p(j,i), p(j,k)))]^2. \quad (12)$$

We note that the difference in (12) is always a continuous function of the pair-comparison probabilities $(p(1,2), p(2,3))$.

Now we define the *total irreversibility*, $V_X[p(1,2), p(2,3)]$, of the M_X system $\langle p, r \rangle$ corresponding to a given pair $p(1,2), p(2,3)$, to be

$$V_X(p(1,2), p(2,3)) = \sum_{i,j,k} [r^-(i,j,k) - r(k,j,i)]^2$$

where the sum is taken over all six permutations of $1, 2, 3$. V_X is a nonnegative function whose domain is the open unit square; it equals zero iff M_X is reversible for the preference system corresponding to the pair of choice probabilities $(p(1,2), p(2,3))$ and it is a continuous function of those probabilities. So if $V_X(p,q)$ is nonzero for some pair $p(1,2) = p, p(2,3) = q$, it must be nonzero within a neighborhood of (p,q). In other words, a GT-V model can never be irreversible for just one of its preference systems; if it is irreversible for one, it is irreversible for infinitely many. Moreover it is easy to see that $V_X(p,q) = V_X(q,p)$ (since the M_X preference system corresponding to (q,p) is identical to that of (p,q) except for a relabeling of the alternatives), and also that $V_X(1-p, 1-q) = V_X(p,q)$ (since the difference $[r^-(i,j,k) - r(k,j,i)]^2$ for the M_X system corresponding to $p(1,2) = 1-p$, $p(2,3) = 1-q$, is the same as the difference $[r^-(k,j,i) - r(i,j,k)]^2$ for the system corresponding to $p(1,2) = p, p(2,3) = q$. So whenever a model is irreversible for a preference system corresponding to a single pair $(p(1,2)p(2,3)) = (p,q)$, it must also be irreversible for infinitely many points in neighborhoods around $(p,q), (q,p), (1-p, 1-q)$, and $(1-q, 1-p)$.

Finally, we note that the right side of Equation 12 is always tautologically zero if $p(j,i) = p(k,j)$. In terms of the s_i scale values this is the case when $s_j - s_i = s_k - s_j$, i.e., $s_j = (s_i + s_k)/2$: the scale value of the middle alternative in $r(k,j,i)$ is midway between the scale values of the other two. But when $s_j \leq s_i \leq s_k$ this can only be true if $s_j = s_i = s_k$. So if Equation 12 only vanishes when $p(j,i) = p(k,j)$, the model in question must be completely irreversible. This is really how we established the complete irreversibility of the double exponential (Choice Axiom) model in Section 2 (since the critical v scale relationship $v_j/v_i = v_k/v_j$ is the same as $p(j,i) = p(k,j)$), and of the exponential model in Section 7. And in general we can see that if the vanishing of the right side of Equation 12 implies a one-to-one functional relationship between $p(k,j)$ and $p(j,i)$ (i.e., for any fixed value of $p(j,i)$ there is only one value of $p(k,j)$ that makes (12) zero) then the model in question must be completely irreversible.

At the other extreme, it is easy to show that the right side of Equation 12 vanishes for all $p(j,i), p(k,j)$ pairs when X has a symmetric distribution. To do this we rewrite the expression in terms of the cumulative distribution function $F(x)$ of X and its density function $f(x)$: in that case the vanishing of the right side of Equation 12 means that

$$\int_{-\infty}^{\infty} F(x + s_k - s_j)(1 - F(x + s_i - s_j))f(x)dx =$$
$$\int_{-\infty}^{\infty} F(x + s_j - s_i)(1 - F(x + s_j - s_k))f(x)dx. \quad (13)$$

Writing y for $s_k - s_j$ and z for $s_i - s_j$, Equation 13 becomes

$$E[F(X + y)(1 - F(X + z)] = E[F(X - z)(1 - F(X - y))]. \quad (14)$$

Then if X is symmetric, we can always shift it to make its distribution symmetric around the origin, without altering the preference model M_X, making X and $-X$ identically distributed and $1 - F(x) = F(-x)$. Then in Equation 13 we have

$$E[F(X + y)F(-X - z)] = E[F(-X + y)F(X - z)] \quad (15)$$

and since X and $-X$ are identically distributed, Equation 15 is true for all y and z, making the model completely reversible.

A model M_X then can only be partially irreversible if for some preference systems $\langle p, r \rangle \neq I$ (i.e., some pair of $p(1,2), p(2,3)$ values not both equal to $1/2$) the right side of Equation 12 only vanishes for the tautological solution $p(k,j) = p(j,i)$ (implying irreversibility for $\langle p, r \rangle$), while for other systems Equation 12 has a non-tautological solution for all indices i, j, k. Given the structure of GT-V models, this seems to me unlikely, hence my conjecture that all such models are either completely reversible or completely irreversible. If that is true, then of course all models based on asymmetric distributions not determined by their bispectrum will share the complete irreversibility of the Choice Axiom model.

10. SUMMARY

Section 1 promised that we would exhibit a large class of preference models that all share ('in a sense') the irreversibility property of the Choice Axiom model. To accomplish this we introduced the concept of the opposite of a preference system, and used it to define what it means for a preference model to be completely reversible, completely irreversible, or partially irreversible. In that terminology the Choice Axiom model is the prototype of a completely irreversible model. Then we showed that within the class of Generalized Case V Thurstone models, the property of complete irreversibility is not intrinsically unique to the Choice Axiom model (i.e., the double exponential GT-V model) because it is shared by the exponential model. And we showed that a large subset of GT-V models are at least partially irreversible – irreversible for an infinite number of their preference systems, if not for all. This is precisely the class of models based on asymmetric probability density functions that are not determined by their bispectrum. ('In a sense' in Section 1 referred to this partial irreversibility.) In general, then, it turns out that typical GT-V models based on asymmetric probability distributions will exhibit at least some degree of irreversibility (especially if the distribution is one-sided), and it is only in artificially constructed special cases that such a model can be completely reversible. Finally, it seems likely that all partially reversible GT-V models are actually completely irreversible, but that conjecture remains to be decided. One way or the other, the answer would provide a neat completion to our understanding of the reversibility properties of GT-V models.

Choice, Decision, and Measurement
A. A. J. Marley (Ed.),
©Lawrence Erlbaum Associates, NJ, 1997.

GENERALIZED RANDOM UTILITY MODELS AND THE REPRESENTATIONAL THEORY OF MEASUREMENT: A CONCEPTUAL LINK

REINHARD NIEDERÉE AND DIETER HEYER

University of Kiel, Germany

ABSTRACT. Extending the concept of a binary choice system, this chapter considers finite systems of probabilities of qualitative experimental observations. These probabilities are conceived as being assigned to corresponding formal statements (Boolean combinations of basic relational statements). Mixture models are discussed which assume that subjects' responses are based on underlying finite algebraic structures of a certain type, each of which occurs with a certain probability. It is shown that for each system of probabilities on formal statements the following are equivalent: (i) it is explainable by a mixture model, (ii) it is explainable by a generalized (distribution-free) random utility model, and (iii) it satisfies a finite set of testable linear inequalities. A detailed account is provided of the role of noncoincidence (which may or may not be satisfied by the generalized random utility models considered). A general procedure is described that allows one to derive some simple necessary linear inequalities. In our approach elementary concepts of random utility theory, axiomatic measurement theory and the theory of convex polytopes are connected. Various examples are discussed to illustrate the wide range of possible applications covered by the theorems presented.

1. INTRODUCTION

In mathematical psychology two important concepts of measurement are encountered. On the one hand, there is the tradition of axiomatic measurement theory (see e.g., Krantz, Luce, Suppes, Tversky, 1971; Narens, 1985), which deals with deterministic relational structures and their numerical representation. On the other

---

Key words and phrases. Random utility models, measurement theory, probabilistic measurement, probabilistic mixture models.

Acknowledgments. Material related to this paper was presented at the Workshops on Measurement and the Mathematical Representations of Empirical Structures (August 1990) and on Mathematical Systems Underlying Axiomatic Measurement Theories (July 1992) at the University of California, Irvine. We are grateful to the organizers R. D. Luce, A. A. J. Marley, and L. Narens for the invitations, and we appreciate the numerous fruitful discussions we had at these meetings. We thank M. Regenwetter, an anonymous referee, and A. A. J. Marley for their comments on earlier drafts of this chapter.

This paper was written while the authors were fellows at the Center for Interdisciplinary Research (ZiF), University of Bielefeld, Germany.

Address for correspondence. Reinhard Niederée, Institut für Psychologie, Universität Kiel, D-24098 Kiel, Germany. Email: niederee@psychologie.uni-kiel.de

hand, concepts of 'probabilistic measurement' have been intensively studied, particularly in psychophysics and utility theory (e.g., Luce & Suppes, 1965; Falmagne, 1985). The present paper describes a general framework which brings together basic concepts of both traditions.

To illustrate the kind of situations that are covered by this approach, let us briefly outline a simple and well-known example which belongs to the theory of binary choices (further details are given below). Under certain conditions systems of choice probabilities p_{ab} ($a, b \in A$, A being some finite set, p_{ab} denoting the probability that a is chosen over b) can be conceived as being induced by rankings, that is, they can be 'explained' by a probability mass on a set of (strict) linear orders on A. Block and Marschak (1960) showed that choice probabilities p_{ab} can be explained by such a 'probabilistic mixture' of linear orders if and only if they can be explained by a random utility model, which means that the elements a of A can be represented by real random variables U_a in such a way that $p_{ab} = \Pr[U_a > U_b]$. It is known that such a 'random representation' is possible if and only if the choice probabilities p_{ab} satisfy a finite system of testable linear inequalities (the number of which depends on the cardinality of A; one of these is the *triangle inequality* $p_{ca} \leq p_{cb} + p_{ba}$). Major progress in understanding such systems of inequalities has been achieved recently by taking up a geometrical perspective, that is, by using methods of the theory of convex polytopes (for a historical overview and a discussion of the relation between the probabilistic and the geometrical aspects of these issues see Fishburn, 1992; for a recent account and further references see Koppen, 1995). In sum, for systems of choice probabilities p_{ab} on a finite set A, the following three properties are known to be equivalent (omitting technical details): (i) the p_{ab}'s are explainable by a probabilistic mixture of (strict) linear orders, (ii) the p_{ab}'s are explainable by a random utility model, and (iii) the p_{ab}'s satisfy some finite set of linear inequalities.

It turns out that both the concept of a *probabilistic mixture* of linear orders and the just-mentioned *random utility* concept can be generalized to a wide class of finite relational structures, and it can be shown that the equivalence of (i), (ii) and (iii) extends to most of these cases (Heyer & Niederée, 1989, 1992).[1] The approach presented in these papers is based on some simple general definitions and theorems which give a unified account for a variety of situations, so there is no further need to prove the equivalence of the corresponding counterparts to (i), (ii) and (iii) for each such situation individually. In particular, virtually all standard finitary structures considered in measurement theory (as discussed e.g., in Roberts, 1979) are covered by that approach, such as linear orders, weak orders, semiorders, partial orders, equivalence relations, betweenness relations, algebraic difference structures, (finite fragments of) extensive structures, and the like.

In Heyer and Niederée (1992) the above issues were illustrated by the example of additive conjoint structures. Assume that subjects have to choose between pairs (a, b), (c, d) of objects from a finite set A. For the corresponding choice probabilities $p_{ab;cd}$ the following conditions are equivalent: (i) the $p_{ab;cd}$'s are explainable by a

---

[1] The term 'random utility model' refers here to a variety of models based on random variable representations, which need not be related to concepts of utility. The term is used here for historical reasons.

probabilistic mixture of additive conjoint structures, (ii) the $p_{ab;cd}$'s are explainable by a (distribution-free) random utility model, that is, there is a family U_a ($a \in A$) of real random variables such that $p_{ab;cd} = \Pr[U_a + U_b \geq U_c + U_d]$, (iii) the $p_{ab;cd}$'s satisfy a certain finite set of linear inequalities. This example is used throughout the present paper to illustrate the various concepts and results presented.

In principle the approach introduced in Heyer and Niederée (1989, 1992) can also be applied to more complex cases such as choice probabilities p_{aB} ($B \subseteq A$) where p_{aB} is the probability that a subject selects a as the preferred element out of B, as discussed in Falmagne (1978). To do this, however, one has to introduce additional, and somewhat 'artificial', relations (see Appendix A in Section 9). The present paper develops a general, unifying framework which canonically extends our former approach and allows such situations to be treated in a much more natural manner. One feature of this extension is that probabilities on simple formal statements describing experimental events are considered which may include logical connectives such as 'and', 'or' and 'not': A choice probability p_{aB} can for instance be represented as the probability[2] assigned to the formalized version of the statement 'a is preferred to b_1 and ... and a is preferred to b_k' where $\{b_1, \ldots, b_k\} = B \setminus \{a\}$. Using such an approach, suitable generalizations of the above-mentioned equivalence between (i), (ii) and (iii) can easily be shown. Note that formal statements are introduced here simply because they provide a convenient tool for setting up corresponding general theorems. In Section 7 we demonstrate how these theorems can be applied to more complex situations such as the just-mentioned example and an extension of Regenwetter's (1996) topset voting model.

The general perspective introduced in Heyer and Niederée (1989, 1992) has recently been taken up by Regenwetter (1996) (see also Regenwetter & Marley, 1996) and Suck (1995a, 1995b). Related concepts are also found e.g. in Schweizer and Sklar (1983) for the special case of metric spaces. Regenwetter (1996) deals with issues related to equivalences of type '(i) $\Leftrightarrow$ (ii)', using a construction which is essentially equivalent to the one employed in Heyer and Niederée (1989, 1992). Suck's above-mentioned forthcoming papers discuss the cases of semiorders, partial orders, interval orders, and equivalence relations, the emphasis being placed on the (often nontrivial) geometrical problem of determining facet-defining linear inequalities for the corresponding polytopes. This paper, in contrast, is not concerned with the problem of determining facet-defining linear inequalities for individual cases. However, in pursuing our above-mentioned goal, geometrical concepts are referred to in our proof of the general equivalence of (i) and (iii). Furthermore, we will describe a very easy general method that allows one to derive some necessary linear inequalities (the method will be applied to some examples, such as the above-mentioned case of additive conjoint measurement; compare Table 2 below).

In our opinion, the results presented here, which are potentially applicable to a plethora of empirical situations, provide a fruitful method for probabilistic modeling, regardless of whether or not one takes up a measurement-theoretic perspective.

---

[2]In probabilistic logic, which will not be used here, there is in fact a long tradition of considering probabilities on logical formulae (or, more generally, on abstract Boolean algebras; see e.g., Łoś, 1967, and for a general discussion Heyer, 1990).

At the same time, however, our approach provides one way of 'probabilizing' concepts of the representational theory of measurement, thereby establishing a link between the two traditions mentioned in the beginning.

   This paper, which is largely self-contained, is structured as follows. In Section 2 the basic concept of a probability assignment is introduced, which generalizes the concept of a system of binary choice probabilities. Section 3 and Section 4 introduce probabilistic mixture models and generalized (distribution-free) random utility models, respectively. Their equivalence ('(i)⇔(ii)') is then shown in Section 5, where the connections to axiomatic measurement theory will become obvious. Generalized random utility models which satisfy noncoincidence ($\Pr[U_a = U_b] = 0$ if $a \neq b$) and those which do not are treated separately and related to isomorphic and homomorphic representations, respectively. In Section 6 it is shown that such models can be characterized by suitable systems of linear inequalities ('(i)⇔(iii)'), and a useful method is outlined which allows one to derive simple necessary inequalities from corresponding universal axioms (as considered in axiomatic measurement theory). Finally, Section 7 applies the concepts and results of the foregoing sections to the more complex examples mentioned above. In Sections 2 to 4 the notation needed for the formulation of our general results will be illustrated with some simple examples. Further examples are discussed in Sections 5 to 7 to give an impression of the range of potential applications of the equivalence theorems just mentioned.

2. PROBABILITY ASSIGNMENTS

   Typically, the 'raw material' or 'data base' of the examples discussed in the following are the relative frequencies with which certain observable elementary events have occurred in some experiment. These relative frequencies can be conceived as estimates of corresponding probabilities. Such probabilities then give rise to the notion of a probability assignment to be introduced and illustrated in this section. Let us consider some examples.

   Binary choice. A finite set A of objects of a certain kind is considered and for each pair $(a, b) \in A \times A$ a subject is repeatedly asked to choose one of the two according to some specific subjective criterion (e.g., utility, brightness). The event that a is chosen over b will be denoted by the 'protocol statement' Bab (while the event that this is not the case could be expressed by the statement $\neg Bab$). In repeated judgments concerning fixed objects a, b, the object a will in some instances be chosen over b whereas in other instances b might be chosen over a. For each pair (a, b) of distinct objects we are then interested in the conditional probability that a is chosen over b given that the objects a, b were presented for comparison. The corresponding (conditional) probability will be denoted by $\mathbb{P}[Bab]$. If Φ denotes the set of all statements of the kind Bab, $a \neq b$, the mapping $\mathbb{P} : \Phi \to [0, 1]$ which assigns the probability $\mathbb{P}[Bab]$ to each statement Bab is an example of what we will call a *probability assignment*. In binary choice theory it is customary to write more briefly p_{ab} or $p(a, b)$ for $\mathbb{P}[Bab]$. Under the assumption that

$$p(a, b) + p(b, a) = 1 \qquad \text{for} \quad a \neq b, \tag{1}$$

which is obviously satisfied in the experimental paradigm just mentioned, such a probability assignment is called a *binary choice system*. Notice that, from a mathematical viewpoint, the elements of Φ are to be understood as formal, syntactical entities (i.e., strings of symbols) which by themselves do not carry any meaning.[3] So in different experimental settings they can be interpreted differently. For example, instead of considering forced-choice experiments one could also study choice experiments where the subjects are allowed to make a neutral decision of indifference between a and b. Such weaker choice experiments lead to different probability assignments on Φ, which need not satisfy (1). (For each such $\mathbb{P}$ on Φ there might in turn be *different* mixture models, or none, which are apt to explain it.)

Notice in passing that in this and the following examples instead of considering repeated judgments of a single subject (individual choice behavior) we could also refer to judgments of different members of a group (social choice) and *vice versa*.

Comparison of pairs. As mentioned in the introduction, instead of comparing single elements as in the previous example, subjects could be asked to compare pairs of objects from a finite set A. For instance, A may be a set of goods and the subjects are asked whether they prefer the combination (commodity bundle) (a, b) over (c, d). If this is recorded by the statement $Qabcd$ and if the set of all such protocol statements is again denoted by Φ, a probability assignment $\mathbb{P} : \Phi \to [0, 1]$ is now given by the corresponding conditional probabilities $\mathbb{P}[Qabcd] = p_{ab;cd}$. A psychophysical example of this type would be an experiment where a subject is asked to compare the binaurally induced subjective loudness of successively presented pairs (a, b), (c, d) of tones, with a and c being presented to the left ear and b and d to the right ear.

Approval voting. A set $A = \{a_1, \ldots, a_n\}$ of politicians is considered. Subjects have to specify a nonempty subset of A of arbitrary size which contains those politicians they favor ('approve of'). If the statement Sa stands for 'politician a belongs to the subset selected', the event that for instance the subset $\{a_1, a_2\}$ is specified by a subject can be recorded by $Sa_1 \wedge Sa_2 \wedge \neg Sa_3 \wedge \cdots \wedge \neg Sa_n$ (as customary in sentential logic, the symbol '$\wedge$' denotes conjunction, i.e., 'and', and the symbol '$\neg$' denotes negation). Obviously each subset $X \subseteq A$ is associated with a corresponding protocol statement of that kind. These statements make up a set Φ and one then studies the probabilities $\mathbb{P}[\phi]$ for all members ϕ of Φ. Sometimes it is useful to consider redundant extensions of Φ; one could for instance add all basic statements of the kind Sa_i themselves to the set just considered (see, e.g., Section 7).[4]

---

[3]More precisely, one would have to refer to formal statements in a suitable formal language as customary in mathematical logic. For instance, if Bab is conceived as a formal statement, 'B' is a relation *symbol* and 'a' and 'b' are *names* for the corresponding objects; see e.g., Shoenfield (1967). To simplify notation, we will identify objects in A and their names.

[4]Throughout the paper statements which involve sentential connectives are usually understood as referring to *single* experimental trials and thus to single persons (social choice) or to single states of a person (individual choice). Hence a statement of the kind $Sa_1 \wedge Sa_2 \wedge \neg Sa_3 \wedge \cdots \wedge \neg Sa_n$ should *not* be understood here as a summary of the results of *different* independent experimental trials as e.g., in Iverson and Falmagne (1985). This means that in general the probability assigned to a conjunction is *not* equal to the product of the probabilities assigned to its components.

The general case. In all of the above examples we referred to a finite set A and to *basic (relational) statements* of the form $Ra_1 \ldots a_k$, where $a_1, \ldots, a_k \in A$. Sometimes the elementary observations considered correspond to these basic statements themselves; in other cases they correspond to a conjunction of such statements and their negations. On the resulting set Φ a probability assignment $\mathbb{P}$ was assumed to be determined by the experimental situation. In general, if Φ is a finite nonempty set of basic statements of the form $Ra_1 \ldots a_k$ and/or of certain statements which can be composed of such basic statements by means of conjunction, disjunction ('$\vee$') and negation, and if $\mathbb{P}$ maps Φ into $[0, 1]$, then $\mathbb{P}$ is called a *probability assignment for A of type $\langle k \rangle$* (hence in the above examples the probability assignments were of type $\langle 2 \rangle$, $\langle 4 \rangle$, and $\langle 1 \rangle$, respectively). Later on we discuss examples where various observable k_j-ary relations R^j, $j = 1, \ldots, m$, simultaneously play a role. Elements of Φ may then be composed of basic statements of the kind $R^j a_1 \ldots a_{k_j}$. Any such nonempty finite set Φ will be called *a set of formal statements about A of type $\langle k_1, \ldots, k_m \rangle$* and any mapping $\mathbb{P} : \Phi \to [0, 1]$ will be called a *probability assignment for A of type $\langle k_1, \ldots, k_m \rangle$*. This concept generalizes the concept of a *probabilistic relational structure* as introduced in Heyer and Niederée (1992) (see Appendix A in Section 9).

As in the above examples the standard application of the concept that we have in mind is that the values $\mathbb{P}[\phi]$, $\phi \in \Phi$, capture the conditional probabilities of specific experimental results, recorded by ϕ, given that a certain experimental condition (associated with ϕ) is realized. For example, in binary choice, the experimental condition associated with Bab was that the objects a, b are presented to the subject in a certain experimental setting.[5] One could of course easily introduce formal event spaces to capture the corresponding 'empirical' conditional probabilities. However, as with the concept of a binary choice system in binary choice theory, such an explicit account is not needed here. So, from a purely mathematical point of view, the following general account formally applies to *arbitrary mappings $\mathbb{P} : \Phi \to [0, 1]$*. (The mixture and generalized random utility models discussed hereafter do however impose certain restrictions on the $\mathbb{P}$'s which yield an independent justification of the term 'probability assignment'.)

The concepts and results presented in the following are always formulated for the general case and illustrated by the examples of binary choice and the comparison of pairs. We will come back to the example of approval voting in Section 7.

3. MIXTURE MODELS

Again, we begin with two examples.

Binary choice. In the theory of binary social choice one often considers the following model. Let $\mathcal{O}$ be the set of all strict linear orders on a set A of objects of cardinality n under investigation. It is assumed that each person (who belongs to the population considered) has an 'internal' strict linear ordering according to

---

[5]If different experimental settings are associated with a single protocol statement ϕ (as e.g. in binary choice different spatial or temporal configurations of the presented stimuli a, b), one simple way to insure that $\mathbb{P}[\phi]$ is still well-defined is to assume that the resulting conditional probabilities are the same (as is often tacitly assumed in the binary choice literature).

which she acts when asked to choose between the objects a, b. For each ordering $\succ \in \mathcal{O}$ there is then a probability, $p_\succ$, that a person randomly drawn out of the population 'possesses' the strict linear order $\succ$. The probability mass $\langle p_\succ \mid \succ \in \mathcal{O} \rangle$ then induces a probability measure P on the powerset $\mathcal{S}(\mathcal{O})$ of the set $\mathcal{O}$, which is defined by $P(W) := \sum_{\succ \in W} p_\succ$ (for all $W \subseteq \mathcal{O}$). This means that $P(W)$ denotes the probability that a person drawn out of the population possesses an ordering $\succ$ belonging to W. It follows that

$$\mathbb{P}[Bab] = P(\{\succ \in \mathcal{O} \mid a \succ b\}) = \sum_{\substack{\succ \in \mathcal{O} \\ a \succ b}} p_\succ. \tag{2}$$

Obviously *mutatis mutandis* the same model can be applied to individual binary choice. Here the model assumes that the orderings are associated with certain 'mental states' which determine the subject's disposition to react to the experimental task if she is in that state; these states may then vary from trial to trial. Of course, such a variability of states within subjects could also be allowed for in the social choice context.

Such a model attempts to explain the probabilities $\mathbb{P}[Bab]$ that correspond to elementary observable ('manifest') events in terms of theoretical entities which usually are themselves unobservable ('latent'), namely the assumed orderings associated with each person (or with the states of the subject considered, respectively), along with the probabilities $p_\succ$ associated with these orderings. This 'latent' character of the assumed orderings is particularly obvious in the case of individual choice; for in one experimental trial the subject is only asked to compare a single pair of objects (a, b). In such a situation it is a natural question to ask whether or not a given binary choice system *can be explained* by such a model, i.e., *whether there is* a probability mass $p_\succ$ ($\succ \in \mathcal{O}$) such that (2) holds. In binary choice theory a binary choice system with this property is called a binary choice system *induced by rankings*. The question as to which testable properties a binary choice system must satisfy for it to be induced by rankings (i.e., for it to be explainable by the above model) is addressed in Section 6. (Recall that the values $\mathbb{P}[Bab]$ correspond here to conditional probabilities; if this aspect is made explicit in terms of a suitable probability space, it is readily seen that an independence assumption is tacitly made here; see Appendix B in Section 9.)

Later on we need a more flexible notation which allows us to develop a general and unifying conceptual framework in which we can state our results in a way that also captures probability assignments on *conjunctions* of basic statements and their negations. The notation needed therefore has to be slightly more complex. So we will explain and illustrate it with two simple examples (probabilistic mixtures of strict linear orders and additive conjoint structures, respectively). Needless to say, it would be unnecessary to introduce such a notation just for these simple cases.

Instead of referring to the strict linear orderings $\succ$ on A, we may likewise consider the corresponding relational structures $\mathcal{A} = \langle A, \succ \rangle$. The set of all these structures will be called $\mathcal{M}_{ord}(A)$. Instead of saying that a binary choice system $\mathbb{P}$ is induced by rankings we will henceforth say that $\mathbb{P}$ *is explainable by an $\mathcal{M}_{ord}(A)$-mixture model* (or more briefly, that it is an $\mathcal{M}_{ord}(A)$-mixture). We briefly speak of $\mathcal{M}_{ord}$-mixtures and write $\mathcal{M}_{ord}$ for $\mathcal{M}_{ord}(A)$, if A is clear from the context.

The next piece of notation to be introduced here refers to a basic concept of mathematical logic, namely the notion of the *validity* of a formal statement in a structure. (This notion is pretty elementary, so no prior knowledge of formal logic will be presupposed.)

Up to now, formal statements (such as *Bab* etc.) have been referred to in connection with probability assignments, where they were used to denote certain experimental outcomes. In what follows we also make use of formal statements of that kind in a different way which will be explained now. Given a relational structure $\mathcal{D} = \langle D, \mathfrak{B} \rangle$, where $\mathfrak{B}$ is a binary relation on D, and two elements $c, d \in D$, one says that *the formal statement Bcd is valid in* $\mathcal{D}$ if $(c, d) \in \mathfrak{B}$. Writing the emphasized phrase more compactly as $\mathcal{D} \models Bcd$, we thus have that by definition, for all $c, d \in D$,

$$\langle D, \mathfrak{B} \rangle \models Bcd \quad \Leftrightarrow \quad (c, d) \in \mathfrak{B}. \tag{3}$$

(Note that the symbol B is 'interpreted' here by the deterministic relation $\mathfrak{B}$.) If one applies this to the above example, that is, to the structures $\mathcal{A} = \langle A, \succ \rangle$, one gets as a special case that

$$\langle A, \succ \rangle \models Bab \quad \Leftrightarrow \quad a \succ b \tag{4}$$

(where B is now interpreted by the 'theoretical' relation $\succ$). In the same vein we could consider the set of reals with its natural ordering, i.e., the structure $\langle \mathbb{R}, > \rangle$. For any pair of real numbers r, s we then have that

$$\langle \mathbb{R}, > \rangle \models Brs \quad \Leftrightarrow \quad r > s. \tag{5}$$

This notation will prove useful in Sections 4 and 5. Note that the definition of validity straightforwardly generalizes to arbitrary relational structures and to more complex formal expressions; the latter may, for instance, involve conjunctions and negations. As an example of the latter consider the expression $Bab \wedge \neg Bbc$. By definition, then,

$$\langle A, \succ \rangle \models Bab \wedge \neg Bbc \quad \Leftrightarrow \quad a \succ b \text{ and not } b \succ c.$$

In the context of first-order predicate logic, a general definition of the validity of a formal statement in a structure is for instance given in Shoenfield (1967). (Note that Footnote 3 applies here as well.)

Clearly, then, a probability assignment $\mathbb{P}$ is explainable by an $\mathcal{M}_{ord}$-mixture if and only if there is a probability measure P on the power set of $\mathcal{M}_{ord}$ (or equivalently, a probability mass $p_{\mathcal{A}}$, $\mathcal{A} \in \mathcal{M}_{ord}$) such that (for all $a \neq b$)

$$\mathbb{P}[Bab] = P(\{\mathcal{A} \in \mathcal{M}_{ord} \mid \mathcal{A} \models Bab\}) = \sum_{\mathcal{A} \in W} p_{\mathcal{A}} \tag{6}$$

where $W = \{\mathcal{A} \mid \mathcal{A} \models Bab\}$.[6] This naturally is nothing but a simple restatement of the original definition given above in terms of the more general 'model-theoretic' notation to be employed in the following. We hope that this and the following example demonstrate how one can easily move from a more customary notation such

---

[6]It should be observed that in the equation $\mathbb{P}[Bab] = P(\{\mathcal{A} \in \mathcal{M}_{ord} \mid \mathcal{A} \models Bab\})$ the formal statement *Bab* on the left-hand side refers to an experimental event, whereas on the right-hand side it refers to the theoretically hypothesized order relations of the structures $\mathcal{A} = \langle A, \succ \rangle$.

as that in Equation 2 to the new notation and *vice versa*. As already mentioned, this model-theoretic notation is *not* introduced here for its own sake, but as a notational tool that allows us to formulate and prove the representation theorem in Section 5 and the characterization theorem in Section 6 in a general manner that covers a wide class of potential applications, which otherwise would have to be proven anew from case to case. Each individual case can of course be treated without using model-theoretic notation, but for the general results some such unifying notation is useful and, in fact, needed.

Comparison of pairs. We now turn to our second example, which concerns comparisons of pairs, that is, probability assignments $\mathbb{P}$ on a set Φ which consists of formal statements of the kind $Qabcd$. Just as the previous model assumed that the choice probabilities were induced by rankings (that is, by strict linear orders) we consider now a model which assumes that the observed choice probabilities $\mathbb{P}[Qabcd]$ are induced by symmetric additive conjoint structures of the form $\mathcal{A} = \langle A \times A, \succsim \rangle$. Such a structure is called a *symmetric additive conjoint structure* if there is a mapping $f : A \to \mathbb{R}$ such that

$$(a, b) \succsim (c, d) \quad \text{if and only if} \quad f(a) + f(b) \geq f(c) + f(d) \tag{7}$$

for all $a, b, c, d \in A$. This is a special case of the well-known measurement-theoretic concept of an additive conjoint structure $\langle A_1 \times A_2, \succsim \rangle$ (see Krantz et al., 1971, Chapter 6, whose notion of a symmetric additive conjoint structure on p. 256 is more general as well). We restrict attention here to this special case only for the sake of notational convenience; all of our concepts and results concerning this example extend straightforwardly to the general case.

Given some finite set A, the set of all symmetric additive conjoint structures on $A \times A$ will be denoted by $\mathcal{M}_{conj}(A)$, or more briefly by $\mathcal{M}_{conj}$ if A is clear from the context. We will then say that *a probability assignment $\mathbb{P}$ is explainable by an $\mathcal{M}_{conj}(A)$-mixture model* if there is a probability measure P on the power set of $\mathcal{M}_{conj}$ (or equivalently, a probability mass $p_{\mathcal{A}}$, $\mathcal{A} \in \mathcal{M}_{conj}$) such that for all $a, b, c, d \in A$

$$\mathbb{P}[Qabcd] = P(\{\langle A, \succsim \rangle \in \mathcal{M}_{conj} \mid (a, b) \succsim (c, d)\}) = \sum_{\mathcal{A} \in W} p_{\mathcal{A}} \tag{8}$$

where $W = \{\langle A, \succsim \rangle \in \mathcal{M}_{conj} \mid (a, b) \succsim (c, d)\}$.

It is obvious how to restate this condition in terms of the general notation used in this paper. To this end, conceive of the binary relations $\succsim$ on $A \times A$ as four-placed relations on A (and interpret, at the theoretical level, Q by these relations). Equation 8 then takes the form

$$\mathbb{P}[Qabcd] = P(\{\mathcal{A} \in \mathcal{M}_{conj} \mid \mathcal{A} \models Qabcd\}) = \sum_{\mathcal{A} \in W} p_{\mathcal{A}} \tag{9}$$

where $W = \{\mathcal{A} \mid \mathcal{A} \models Qabcd\}$.

Empirically testable conditions which are necessary and/or sufficient for a probability assignment $\mathbb{P}$ to be explainable by an $\mathcal{M}_{conj}$-mixture model are discussed in Section 6.

The general case. The notion of a probability assignment explainable by an $\mathcal{M}_{ord}$- or $\mathcal{M}_{conj}$-mixture model, respectively, readily generalizes to other situations. Assume a probability assignment $\mathbb{P}$ on a set Φ of formal statements to be given as described at the end of Section 2, and consider some set, $\mathcal{M}$, of suitable relational structures. We will then say that $\mathbb{P}$ is explainable by an $\mathcal{M}$-mixture model if there is a probability P on the power set $\mathcal{S}(\mathcal{M})$ of $\mathcal{M}$ such that for all $\phi \in \Phi$ the probability $\mathbb{P}[\phi]$ is identical to the probability of the set of relational structures in $\mathcal{M}$ in which ϕ is valid. As above, the structures in $\mathcal{M}$ can be conceived of as 'states' (say, of persons); the state realized in a certain experimental situation determines whether or not ϕ holds in this situation. To make this definition precise, we have to make use of the notation introduced above.

To be more specific, assume now that $\mathbb{P}$ is a probability assignment of type $\langle k_1, \ldots, k_m \rangle$ on Φ for some finite set A (compare Section 2). This means that the elements of Φ may either be of the form $R^j a_1, \ldots, a_{k_j}$ (for $a_1, \ldots, a_{k_j} \in A$ and $j = 1, \ldots, m$) or they may be composed of such basic statements by means of conjunction, disjunction and negation (as in the example of approval voting). Statements of that kind which involve only certain objects $a_1, \ldots, a_q$ will in the following be abstractly referred to by the expression $\phi(a_1, \ldots, a_q)$.

A nonempty set $\mathcal{M}$ of relational structures will be called *admissible for Φ* if they have an appropriate type and domain, i.e., if all structures in $\mathcal{M}$ are of the form

$$\mathcal{A} = \langle A, \mathfrak{R}^1, \ldots, \mathfrak{R}^m \rangle,$$

where $\mathfrak{R}^j$ is some k_j-ary relation on A ($j = 1, \ldots, n$) (such structures are called structures of type $\langle k_1, \ldots, k_m \rangle$ with domain A). As in the above examples, in most applications the $\mathcal{M}$-mixture model considered encapsulates some substantive theoretical ideas which relate the observable events addressed by the statements in Φ to certain state-dependent theoretical relations $\mathfrak{R}^j$. With these conceptual tools at hand we can now state the announced definition.

Definition 1. Let $\mathbb{P}$, A and Φ be as above and consider a set, $\mathcal{M}$, of relational structures admissible for Φ. The probability assignment $\mathbb{P}$ is called *explainable by an $\mathcal{M}$-mixture model* (or briefly, an *$\mathcal{M}$-mixture*) if there is a probability measure P on $\mathcal{S}(\mathcal{M})$ such that for all statements $\phi(a_1, \ldots, a_q)$ in Φ the following equation holds

$$\mathbb{P}\left[\phi(a_1, \ldots, a_q)\right] = P\left(\{\mathcal{A} \in \mathcal{M} \mid \mathcal{A} \models \phi(a_1, \ldots, a_q)\}\right). \tag{10}$$

We will then say that the probability measure P *explains* the probability assignment $\mathbb{P}$.

Note that Equations 6 and 9 are special cases of Equation 10. As in these examples, given some probability assignment $\mathbb{P}$, the question here is whether *there is* a probability measure P that explains $\mathbb{P}$ (i.e., which satisfies Equation 10). If so, there can be more than one such probability measure. (In this paper we do not aim at characterizing the set of all probability measures that explain a given probability assignment, which itself is a convex set that corresponds to a convex polytope in $\mathbb{R}^M$ where M is the cardinality of $\mathcal{M}$.)

Conversely, given some probability measure P on $S(\mathcal{M})$, Equation 10 mathematically defines a probability assignment $\mathbb{P}$ on Φ, the *probability assignment induced by P*.[7] (In Section 6 we will introduce the related concept of a probability assignment induced by a single structure $\mathcal{A}$, which is induced by a measure P with $P(\{\mathcal{A}\}) = 1$.)

4. Generalized Random Utility Models

From an abstract measurement-theoretic perspective, the concept of a probability assignment of type $\langle k_1, \ldots, k_m \rangle$ can be conceived as a probabilistic generalization of the concept of a (deterministic) relational structure of the same type. A statement of the form "$\mathbb{P}$ is an $\mathcal{M}_{conj}$-mixture", say, can then be viewed as a probabilistic counterpart to "$\mathcal{A}$ is a symmetric additive conjoint structure." In this section we discuss distribution-free generalized random utility models, which can be conceived of as concepts of 'probabilistic measurement' in the sense of one possible probabilistic generalization of measurement-theoretic concepts of numerical representation. As before, we start with the discussion of the two examples mentioned in the previous section and proceed then to the general case.

Binary choice. As already mentioned in the introduction, random utility models play an important role in binary choice theory. Given a binary choice system $p_{ab} = \mathbb{P}[Bab]$ on a finite set A, one asks whether there is a family of jointly distributed real random variables $\langle U_a \,|\, a \in A \rangle$ such that

$$p_{ab} = \Pr[U_a > U_b] \tag{11}$$

for all $a \neq b$. It is a well-known mathematical fact (Block & Marschak, 1960) that a binary choice system is induced by rankings if and only if there is a family of jointly distributed real random variables $\langle U_a \,|\, a \in A \rangle$ that satisfies Equation 11 as well as

$$\Pr[U_a \neq U_b] = 1 \tag{12}$$

for all $a \neq b$. Notice in passing that by definition binary choice systems satisfy (1), i.e., $p_{ab} + p_{ba} = 1$, for $a \neq b$, whence for a binary choice system every family of random variables which satisfies property (11) automatically satisfies property (12). In line with Falmagne (1983) a family of random variables which satisfies property (12) will be called *noncoincident*.

Again, we first illustrate our general notation by rewriting the just-mentioned concepts accordingly. First, note that the notion of a jointly distributed family of real random variables $\langle U_a \,|\, a \in A \rangle$ implicitly refers to an underlying probability

---

[7]The fact that Equation 10 can be employed 'both ways' allows the introduction of certain 'measure extensions', which can be used to characterize those probability assignments $\mathbb{P}$ that are explainable by an $\mathcal{M}$-mixture model (as will be shown in Heyer & Niederée, 1997). To get an impression of what is meant by such an extension, consider the set $\Phi^* \supset \Phi$ that contains all statements of the corresponding formal language in the sense of first-order predicate logic (in the example of binary choice, Φ^* would e.g. include the axiom $\forall x \forall y \forall z (Bxy \land Byz \rightarrow Bxz)$). If there exists a probability measure P on $S(\mathcal{M})$ that explains $\mathbb{P}$, then $\mathbb{P}$ can be extended to a measure $\mathbb{P}^*$ on Φ^* by applying Equation 10 to the elements of Φ^* (of course different P's may induce different extensions $\mathbb{P}^*$). A crucial property of such an extension is that for axioms $\phi \in \Phi^*$ which are valid in all structures in $\mathcal{M}$ it holds that $\mathbb{P}^*[\phi] = 1$.

space $\langle \Omega, \mathcal{F}, P \rangle$, where $\mathcal{F}$ is a σ-field on Ω and P is a probability measure on $\mathcal{F}$. Consequently Equation 11 is a shorthand for

$$p_{ab} = P\left(\{\omega \in \Omega \mid U_a(\omega) > U_b(\omega)\}\right). \tag{13}$$

Next, recall that according to Equation 5 the inequality $U_a(\omega) > U_b(\omega)$ can be written as $\langle \mathbb{R}, > \rangle \models Brs$, where $r = U_a(\omega), s = U_b(\omega)$. Since binary choice systems are special probability assignments $\mathbb{P}$ with $p_{ab} = \mathbb{P}[Bab]$, Equation 11 thus finally takes on the form

$$\mathbb{P}[Bab] = P\left(\{\omega \in \Omega \mid \langle \mathbb{R}, > \rangle \models Brs, \text{ where } r = U_a(\omega), s = U_b(\omega)\}\right). \tag{14}$$

We will then say that a probability assignment $\mathbb{P}$ on the set Φ of all statements of the form Bab $(a \neq b)$ is *explainable by a [noncoincident] $\langle \mathbb{R}, > \rangle$-random utility model* if and only if there is a probability space $\langle \Omega, \mathcal{F}, P \rangle$ and a [noncoincident] family $\langle U_a \mid a \in A \rangle$ of real random variables on $\langle \Omega, \mathcal{F}, P \rangle$ such that Equation 14 is satisfied.

Using this notation, Block and Marschak's (1960) theorem just cited can now be restated as follows.

Proposition 1. *Let $\mathbb{P}$ be a binary choice system on A. Then the following are equivalent.*

(a) *$\mathbb{P}$ is explainable by an $\mathcal{M}_{ord}$-mixture model.*
(b) *$\mathbb{P}$ is explainable by a noncoincident $\langle \mathbb{R}, > \rangle$-random utility model.*

Remark 1. The equivalence between (a) and (b) holds for arbitrary probability assignments on Φ, since both (a) and (b) independently imply Equation 1. This equivalence and the role of Equation 1 is discussed in more detail later on.

Remark 2. By means of a straightforward factorization technique one can easily show that the probability space underlying a [noncoincident] $\langle \mathbb{R}, > \rangle$-random utility model can always be chosen to be finite with $\mathcal{F} = \mathcal{S}(\Omega)$, i.e., the powerset of Ω. That is, if there is *some* family of [noncoincident] real random variables that satisfies Equation 14, then there is also some such family whose underlying probability space is finite (for a proof see Appendix C in Section 9, *Claim 1*). Conversely, starting out from such a [noncoincident] family of random variables on a finite probability space, one can for any measurable space $\langle \Omega, \mathcal{F} \rangle$ with an infinite (or sufficiently rich finite) σ-field $\mathcal{F}$ straightforwardly construct a probability space and a [noncoincident] family of real random variables on that space which satisfy Equation 14 as well (for a proof see Appendix C in Section 9, *Claim 2*). Both directions together imply that the underlying measurable space $\langle \Omega, \mathcal{F} \rangle$ can nearly be chosen arbitrarily (compare also Regenwetter, 1996; Regenwetter & Marley, 1996). In setting up such models one typically has some event space in mind, which often is not explicitly specified; as with mixture models, the elements of Ω might for instance be associated with certain 'states' of the subject under consideration (individual choice) or with different subjects (social choice), the U_a's representing certain aspects of these states or subjects, respectively. However, in our theorems and in most of the applications considered below all that counts is the *existence* of a probability space and a family of random variables which satisfy certain requirements such as (11) and, possibly, (12).

Comparison of pairs. Consider again a probability assignment on a set Φ which consists of formal statements of the kind $Qa_1a_2a_3a_4$ $(a_1, a_2, a_3, a_4 \in A)$. Having in mind the right hand side of Equation 7 one might raise the question whether there is a family of jointly distributed real random variables such that

$$\mathbb{P}[Qa_1a_2a_3a_4] = \Pr[U_{a_1} + U_{a_2} \geq U_{a_3} + U_{a_4}] \tag{15}$$

for all $a_1, a_2, a_3, a_4 \in A$. In this equation we implicitly refer to a numerical structure $\langle \mathbb{R}, \mathfrak{N} \rangle$ where $\mathfrak{N}$ denotes the 4-placed relation on $\mathbb{R}$ defined by

$$(r_1, r_2, r_3, r_4) \in \mathfrak{N} \quad \Leftrightarrow \quad r_1 + r_2 \geq r_3 + r_4. \tag{16}$$

Using our formal notation introduced above, we can then rewrite Equation 15 as

$$\mathbb{P}[Qa_1a_2a_3a_4] = P\left(\{\omega \mid \langle \mathbb{R}, \mathfrak{N} \rangle \models Qr_1r_2r_3r_4, \text{ where } r_i = U_{a_i}(\omega)\}\right). \tag{17}$$

If this condition is fulfilled for *some* [noncoincident] family of jointly distributed real random variables, we shall say that $\mathbb{P}$ is *explainable by a [noncoincident]* $\langle \mathbb{R}, \mathfrak{N} \rangle$-*random utility model*. Remark 2 *mutatis mutandis* applies here as well.

In Section 5 it is shown that there is a close relation, analogous to that in Proposition 1, between this random-utility-based concept and the notion of $\mathbb{P}$ being explained by an $\mathcal{M}_{conj}$-mixture model, i.e. by a mixture of symmetric additive conjoint structures.

The general case. The two cases just considered can be subsumed under a general definition that is given now. In this definition the following notation is used: Given a formal statement $\phi(a_1, \ldots, a_q) \in \Phi$, the formal statement that results by replacing each a_i with (a name for) the real number r_i is denoted by $\phi(r_1, \ldots, r_q)$. For instance, if $\phi(a_1, a_2, a_3)$ is $Ba_1a_2 \wedge \neg Ba_2a_3$, then $\phi(U_{a_1}(\omega), U_{a_2}(\omega), U_{a_3}(\omega))$ is the statement $Br_1r_2 \wedge \neg Br_2r_3$ where $r_i = U_{a_i}(\omega)$.

Definition 2. Let $\mathbb{P} : \Phi \to [0, 1]$ be a probability assignment of type $\langle k_1, \ldots, k_m \rangle$ for a finite set A. Let $\mathcal{C} = \langle C, \mathfrak{N}^1, \ldots, \mathfrak{N}^m \rangle$ be a relational structure of the same type (e.g., a numerical structure). We will say that $\mathbb{P}$ is *explainable by a $\mathcal{C}$-random utility model* if there is a probability space $\langle \Omega, \mathfrak{F}, P \rangle$ and a family $\langle U_a \mid a \in A \rangle$ of mappings $U_a : \Omega \to C$ such that for all statements $\phi(a_1, \ldots, a_q) \in \Phi$ the following equation holds

$$\mathbb{P}[\phi(a_1, \ldots, a_q)] =$$
$$P\left(\{\omega \in \Omega \mid \langle C, \mathfrak{N}^1, \ldots, \mathfrak{N}^m \rangle \models \phi(U_{a_1}(\omega), \ldots, U_{a_q}(\omega))\}\right). \tag{18}$$

The family $\langle U_a \mid a \in A \rangle$ is then called a *$\mathcal{C}$-random representation for* $\mathbb{P}$ w.r.t. P. If there is a noncoincident such family (i.e., a family that additionally satisfies $P[U_a = U_b] = 0$ whenever $a \neq b$), we say that $\mathbb{P}$ *is explainable by a noncoincident $\mathcal{C}$-random utility model* and the family itself is called a *noncoincident $\mathcal{C}$-random representation for* $\mathbb{P}$ w.r.t. P.

Remark 3. Obviously Equations 14 and 17 are instances of Equation 18. Such equations (as well as simplified notational variants thereof such as (11) and (15)) will be called the *characteristic conditions* of the corresponding random utility models. It should be observed that Equation 18 implicitly presupposes that the probabilities considered are defined, which means that the subsets of Ω referred to have to belong to $\mathcal{F}$. (This measurability requirement is part of the definition, and in what follows it is assumed to be satisfied whenever characteristic conditions are referred to.) When noncoincident random representations are considered, the same goes for the measurability of the sets $\{\omega \mid U_a(\omega) = U_b(\omega)\}$ (which is trivially satisfied if the U_a's are jointly distributed real random variables).

Remark 4. The underlying probability space $\langle \Omega, \mathcal{F}, P \rangle$ can always be chosen in such a way that Ω is finite and $\mathcal{F} = \mathcal{S}(\Omega)$ (in which case the measurability requirements mentioned in Remark 3 are trivially met). For it is easy to see that Remark 2 straightforwardly extends to the general case considered here (cf. Appendix C in Section 9). Notice that in the above general definition the U_a's can be arbitrary mappings, i.e., they are not required to be measurable w.r.t. to some specified σ-field on C. However, if $\mathcal{F}$ is a powerset of a finite set Ω, then these mappings are trivially measurable w.r.t. any such σ-field. In consequence, if C is a nonempty subset of $\mathbb{R}$, the U_a's can always be chosen to be Borel-measurable mappings, i.e., real random variables.

In view of the obvious facts just mentioned, one could in the present context simplify the discussion by restricting attention, with no loss of generality, to finite sample spaces Ω (as was done in Heyer & Niederée, 1992).[8]

Remark 5. It is easily seen that if there is a noncoincident family $\langle U_a \mid a \in A \rangle$ with the above properties, then there is a family $\langle U_a' \mid a \in A \rangle$ on the same probability space which also satisfies condition (18) and which has the property that $U_a(\omega) \neq U_b(\omega)$ holds for all distinct $a, b \in A$ and all $\omega \in \Omega$. The latter property will be called *strong noncoincidence* (for a proof see Appendix C in Section 9, *Claim 3*).

5. THE RELATION BETWEEN MIXTURE AND GENERALIZED RANDOM UTILITY MODELS

For the case of binary choices, Proposition 1 has already shown that for suitable choices of $\mathcal{M}$ and $\mathcal{C}$ the concepts of 'being explainable by an $\mathcal{M}$-mixture model' and 'being explainable by a $\mathcal{C}$-random utility model' are closely related. The central theorem of this section – whose key ingredients are already contained in Heyer and Niederée (1989, 1992) – shows that this extends to a wide class of cases. The key idea is to construct $\mathcal{C}$-random representations out of representations of the elements of $\mathcal{M}$ in $\mathcal{C}$ in the sense of measurement theory. The corresponding measurement-theoretic concepts are summarized in the following definition.

Definition 3. Assume $\mathcal{D} = \langle D, R^1, \ldots, R^q \rangle$ and $\mathcal{E} = \langle E, S^1, \ldots, S^q \rangle$ to be structures of type $\langle k_1, \ldots, k_q \rangle$. $\mathcal{D}$ is *homomorphically representable* (or *homomorphically embeddable*) in $\mathcal{E}$ if there is a mapping $h : D \to E$ such that for $j = 1, \ldots, q$ and all $d_1, \ldots, d_{k_j} \in D$ we have

$$(d_1, \ldots, d_{k_j}) \in R^j \quad \Leftrightarrow \quad (h(d_1), \ldots, h(d_{k_j})) \in S^j.$$

---

[8]Regenwetter (1996) focuses attention on real random variables on arbitrary, i.e. finite as well as infinite, sample spaces. If one takes into account Remarks 2 and 4, one easily sees that the constructions underlying Theorems 2 and 3 of Regenwetter (1996) (which involve a generalization of noncoincidence) can be reduced to the corresponding simpler constructions for finite sets Ω used e.g., in Sec. 4 of Heyer and Niederée (1992) and in the proof of Theorem 1 below.

The mapping h is then called a *homomorphic representation* of $\mathcal{D}$ in $\mathcal{E}$. If there is such a mapping h which is one-to-one, then $\mathcal{D}$ is *isomorphically representable* (or *isomorphically embeddable*) in $\mathcal{E}$ and this function h is called an *isomorphic representation*.

Given a structure $\mathcal{C}$ of type $\langle k_1, \ldots, k_m \rangle$ and a nonempty set A, the set of all structures of type $\langle k_1, \ldots, k_m \rangle$ with domain A which are homomorphically representable in $\mathcal{C}$ will be denoted by $\mathcal{M}_H(A, \mathcal{C})$ (or briefly, $\mathcal{M}_H$), and the corresponding set of all isomorphically representable structures will be denoted by $\mathcal{M}_I(A, \mathcal{C})$ (or briefly, $\mathcal{M}_I$). For instance, it is a well-known fact that a structure $\mathcal{A}$ belongs to $\mathcal{M}_I(A, \langle \mathbb{R}, < \rangle)$ if and only if $\mathcal{A} \in \mathcal{M}_{ord}(A)$ (compare Section 5 below). Keeping this in mind, one easily sees that Proposition 1 (in the general formulation mentioned in Remark 1) is an immediate corollary to part (b) of the following general theorem.

Theorem 1. (General Representation Theorem) *Let $\mathbb{P} : \Phi \to [0,1]$ be a probability assignment of type $\langle k_1, \ldots, k_m \rangle$ for a finite set A of cardinality n, and let $\mathcal{C} = \langle C, \mathfrak{N}^1, \ldots, \mathfrak{N}^m \rangle$ be some relational structure of the same type. Then the following holds.*

  (a) *$\mathcal{M}_H$ is admissible for Φ and the following are equivalent.*
    (i) *$\mathbb{P}$ is explainable by an $\mathcal{M}_H$-mixture model.*
    (ii) *$\mathbb{P}$ is explainable by a $\mathcal{C}$-random utility model.*
  (b) *Assume further that C has at least n elements. Then $\mathcal{M}_I$ is admissible for Φ and the following are equivalent.*
    (i) *$\mathbb{P}$ is explainable by an $\mathcal{M}_I$-mixture model.*
    (ii) *$\mathbb{P}$ is explainable by a noncoincident $\mathcal{C}$-random utility model.*

Proof of part (a). To show the admissibility of $\mathcal{M}_H$, one only has to verify that $\mathcal{M}_H \neq \emptyset$. To see this, consider an arbitrary mapping $f : A \to C$ and let (for $j = 1, \ldots, m$) $\mathfrak{R}^j := \{ (a_1, \ldots, a_{k_j}) \mid (f(a_1), \ldots, f(a_{k_j})) \in \mathfrak{N}^j \}$. The resulting structure $f^{-1}[\mathcal{C}] := \langle A, \mathfrak{R}^1, \ldots \mathfrak{R}^m \rangle$ is called the *structure induced by f from $\mathcal{C}$*. Obviously f is a homomorphic representation of $f^{-1}[\mathcal{C}]$ in $\mathcal{C}$.

"(i) $\Rightarrow$ (ii)": By assumption there is a probability measure P on the powerset $\mathcal{F}$ of $\mathcal{M}_H$ such that Equation 10 holds for all $\phi(a_1, \ldots, a_q) \in \Phi$. To show (ii), let $\Omega = \mathcal{M}_H$ and consider the probability space $\langle \Omega, \mathcal{F}, P \rangle$. A family of mappings $U_a : \mathcal{M}_H \to C$, $a \in A$, can then be defined by letting

$$U_a(\mathcal{A}) := f_{\mathcal{A}}(a)$$

where $f_{\mathcal{A}}$ is some homomorphic representation of $\mathcal{A}$ in $\mathcal{C}$ (which must exist by definition of $\mathcal{M}_H$). It remains to be shown that (18) is satisfied. First observe that since Φ consists of Boolean combinations of basic statements, and since $f_{\mathcal{A}}$ is a homomorphic representation of $\mathcal{A}$ in $\mathcal{C}$, it follows that for all $\phi \in \Phi$,

$$\mathcal{A} \models \phi(a_1, \ldots, a_q) \Leftrightarrow \mathcal{C} \models \phi(f_{\mathcal{A}}(a_1), \ldots, f_{\mathcal{A}}(a_q)). \tag{19}$$

This implies that

$$
\begin{aligned}
\mathbb{P}\left[\phi(a_1, \ldots, a_q)\right] &= P\left(\{\mathcal{A} \mid \mathcal{A} \models \phi(a_1, \ldots, a_q)\}\right) \\
&= P\left(\{\mathcal{A} \mid \mathcal{C} \models \phi(f_{\mathcal{A}}(a_1), \ldots, f_{\mathcal{A}}(a_q))\}\right) \\
&= P\left(\{\mathcal{A} \mid \mathcal{C} \models \phi(U_{a_1}(\mathcal{A}), \ldots, U_{a_q}(\mathcal{A}))\}\right).
\end{aligned}
$$

Hence $\mathbb{P}$ is explainable by a C-random utility model.

"(ii) $\Rightarrow$ (i)": By assumption, there is a probability space $\langle \Omega, \mathcal{F}, P \rangle$ and a family of mappings $\langle U_a \,|\, a \in A \rangle$ which fulfills condition (18). By Remark 4 we can with no loss of generality assume that Ω is finite, $\mathcal{F}$ being its powerset. For each $\omega \in \Omega$ consider the mapping $f_\omega : A \to C$ that is defined by

$$f_\omega(a) := U_a(\omega).$$

Clearly, then, the mappings f_ω homomorphically represent the corresponding induced structures $\mathcal{A}_\omega := f_\omega^{-1}[C]$ in C. Hence the structures $\mathcal{A}_\omega$ belong to $\mathcal{M}_H$ and (19) applies in this situation, too (where $\mathcal{A}$ and f_A have to be replaced by $\mathcal{A}_\omega$ and f_ω, respectively). Let $g : \Omega \to \mathcal{M}_H$ be the mapping defined by $g(\omega) = \mathcal{A}_\omega$.

Next, let $P' = P_g$, where P_g is the probability measure on the powerset of $\mathcal{M}_H$ that is induced from P by g (which by definition means that for all $W \subseteq \mathcal{M}_H$ we have that $P'(W) = P(g^{-1}[W])$). Condition (10) can then be derived from (18) as follows:

$$\begin{aligned}
P'(\{\mathcal{A} \,|\, \mathcal{A} \models \phi(a_1, \ldots, a_q)\}) &= P\left(g^{-1}\left(\{\mathcal{A} \,|\, \mathcal{A} \models \phi(a_1, \ldots, a_q)\}\right)\right) \\
&= P(\{\omega \,|\, \mathcal{A}_\omega \models \phi(a_1, \ldots, a_q)\}) \\
&= P(\{\omega \,|\, C \models \phi(f_\omega(a_1), \ldots, f_\omega(a_q))\}) \\
&= P(\{\omega \,|\, C \models \phi(U_{a_1}(\omega), \ldots, U_{a_q}(\omega))\}) \\
&= \mathbb{P}[\phi(a_1, \ldots, a_q)].
\end{aligned}$$

Proof of part (b). To show that $\mathcal{M}_I$ is nonempty, pick an arbitrary one-to-one function $f : A \to C$, which exists because C has at least n elements. Clearly, then, $f^{-1}[C]$ is an element of $\mathcal{M}_I$.

"(i) $\Rightarrow$ (ii)": The proof is the same as the one for the corresponding part of (a). Just consider isomorphic representations instead of homomorphic representations. The resulting family $\langle U_a \,|\, a \in A \rangle$ trivially is noncoincident, because for all $\mathcal{A}$ we have that $f_A(a) \neq f_A(b)$ for $a \neq b$ and hence $U_a(\mathcal{A}) \neq U_b(\mathcal{A})$.

"(ii) $\Rightarrow$ (i)": Again, the proof is analogous to the corresponding argument in Part (a). Because of Remark 5, the family of mappings $\langle U_a \,|\, a \in A \rangle$ can with no loss of generality be assumed to be strongly noncoincident. This implies then that the f_ω's constructed are one-to-one and hence isomorphic representations. $\square$

Remark 6. The proof of "(ii)$\Rightarrow$ (i)" shows that, for each family $\langle U_a \,|\, a \in A \rangle$ of mappings $U_a : \Omega \to C$ on a probability space $\langle \Omega, \mathcal{F}, P \rangle$, one can construct an 'associated' induced probability measure $P' = P_g$ on the power set of $\mathcal{M}$ which satisfies

$$P'(\{\mathcal{A} \,|\, \mathcal{A} \models \phi(a_1, \ldots, a_q)\}) = P(\{\omega \,|\, C \models \phi(U_{a_1}(\omega), \ldots, U_{a_q}(\omega))\}) \qquad (20)$$

for all $\phi \in \Phi$, the basic idea being to consider for each $\omega \in \Omega$ an induced structure $g(\omega) = \mathcal{A}_\omega$. Conversely, the proof of "(i) $\Rightarrow$ (ii)" shows that, given a measure P' on the power set of $\mathcal{M}$, there is always a family of U_a's which is associated with P' (where the underlying probability space can be chosen to be $\langle \Omega, \mathcal{S}(\Omega), P' \rangle$, with $\Omega = \mathcal{M}$.) Note that usually there will be many such families $\langle U_a \,|\, a \in A \rangle$, for the construction of the U_a's in the proof, based on the equation $U_a(\mathcal{A}) = f_A(a)$, relies on the choice of an *arbitrary* representation f_A of $\mathcal{A}$ in C for each $\mathcal{A} \in \mathcal{M}$. This imposes only quite weak constraints on the resulting C-random representations for a given $\mathbb{P}$ (as is true for most *distribution-free* models of that kind). To base an account of probabilistic measurement proper on the present approach, one would have to invoke further restrictions.[9]

We now turn to possible applications of Theorem 1. As a first illustration we consider a corollary to Part (a) of the theorem. It concerns the example of comparison of pairs and situations where one wants to explain corresponding probabilities in terms of a mixture model based on symmetric additive conjoint structures or by a $\langle \mathbb{R}, \mathfrak{N} \rangle$-random utility model. Recall that the characteristic condition of the latter (in the sense of Remark 3) is $\mathbb{P}[Qa_1 a_2 a_3 a_4] = P[U_{a_1} + U_{a_2} \geq U_{a_3} + U_{a_4}]$ (for all a_1, a_2, a_3, a_4 in the domain A under consideration) if Φ consists of all formal statements of the form $Qa_1 a_2 a_3 a_4$.

Corollary 1. *Let A be a finite set, Φ the set of formal statements of the form $Qabcd$ for all $a, b, c, d \in A$, and $\mathbb{P}$ a probability assignment on Φ. Let $\mathfrak{N}$ be the relation on $\mathbb{R}$ that is defined by (16). Then the following are equivalent.*

(a) $\mathbb{P}$ *is explainable by an $\mathcal{M}_{conj}(A)$-mixture model.*
(b) $\mathbb{P}$ *is explainable by an $\langle \mathbb{R}, \mathfrak{N} \rangle$-random utility model.*

Proof. This follows directly from the fact that by definition the set $\mathcal{M}_{conj}(A)$ is identical to $\mathcal{M}_H(A, \langle \mathbb{R}, \mathfrak{N} \rangle)$. □

Remark 7. The above theorem is also relevant for some classes $\mathcal{M}$ other than $\mathcal{M}_H$ and $\mathcal{M}_I$. If $\mathcal{M}$ is a nonempty subset of $\mathcal{M}_H$, then "(i) $\Rightarrow$ (ii)" of Part (a) is valid with respect to $\mathcal{M}$-mixture models; conversely, if $\mathcal{M}$ is admissible and includes $\mathcal{M}_H$, then "(ii) $\Rightarrow$ (i)" of Part (a) holds for $\mathcal{M}$-mixture models. A corresponding statement is true for Part (b) of the theorem. This trivially follows from the general fact that if $\mathcal{M}_1 \subseteq \mathcal{M}_2$, then each $\mathbb{P}$ explainable by an $\mathcal{M}_1$-mixture model is explainable by an $\mathcal{M}_2$-mixture model.

Axiom systems and the role of noncoincidence. Assume that we are given some set $\mathcal{M}$ of structures of type $\langle k_1, \ldots, k_m \rangle$ with finite domain A as well as some (e.g., numerical) structure C of the same type. How can we find out whether, say, Part (b) of the theorem is applicable, that is, whether $\mathcal{M} \subseteq \mathcal{M}_I(A, C)$ and/or $\mathcal{M} \supseteq \mathcal{M}_I(A, C)$? Usually the class $\mathcal{M}$ one is interested in consists of structures of a certain kind. More specifically, there is often an axiom system Σ (i.e., a set of formal statements) such that $\mathcal{M}$ consists of all structures with domain A which satisfy all axioms in Σ; this specific set $\mathcal{M}$ will be denoted by $\mathcal{M}_\Sigma(A)$. For the sake of illustration we consider here once more the example of strict linear orders. Here

---

[9] An inspection of the role that the representations f_A (and f_ω) play in the proof shows that one could consider a third, equivalent, type of probabilistic modeling, which is based on such mappings (as was first observed by Regenwetter & Marley, 1996). In the context of Theorem 1 this means the following. Let $\mathcal{H}$ be the set of all mappings $f : A \to C$, and $\mathcal{I}$ its restriction to one-to-one mappings. Then in Part (a) one could add the following equivalent condition:
(iii) There is a σ-field $\mathcal{F}$ on $\mathcal{H}$ and a probability measure P on $\langle \mathcal{H}, \mathcal{F} \rangle$ which explains $\mathbb{P}$ in the sense that for all $\phi(a_1, \ldots, a_q) \in \Phi$ the set $V := \{f \in \mathcal{H} \mid C \models \phi(f(a_1), \ldots, f(a_q))\}$ belongs to $\mathcal{F}$ and $\mathbb{P}[\phi(a_1, \ldots, a_q)] = P(V)$. The same goes for Part (b), where $\mathcal{H}$ has to be replaced by $\mathcal{I}$.

we have $\mathcal{M}_{ord}(A) = \mathcal{M}_{\Sigma_0}(A)$ where Σ_0 consists of the axioms

$$\forall x \forall y \forall z \, (Bxy \wedge Byz \rightarrow Bxz) \qquad \text{(transitivity)}$$
$$\forall x \forall y \, (Bxy \vee Byx \vee x = y) \qquad \text{(connectedness)}$$
$$\forall x \forall y \, (Bxy \rightarrow \neg Byx) \qquad \text{(asymmetry)}$$

(where we use our formal notation Bxy introduced above instead of the more usual one, $x > y$). From the viewpoint of axiomatic measurement theory, to prove that $\mathcal{M}_\Sigma(A) \subseteq \mathcal{M}_I(A, \mathcal{C})$ for arbitrary *finite* A is to prove a representation theorem to the effect that all finite structures that satisfy Σ are isomorphically representable in $\mathcal{C}$. (In the case of strict linear orders this representability is a well-known fact for $\mathcal{C} = \langle \mathbb{R}, > \rangle$). While this means that Σ is *sufficient* for isomorphic representability, the converse claim $\mathcal{M}_I(A, \mathcal{C}) \subseteq \mathcal{M}_\Sigma(A)$ means that Σ is a *necessary* condition for it. Often the latter can be directly seen by means of the following useful model-theoretic lemma (which is easy to prove by elementary methods of mathematical logic, see Footnote 10):

Lemma 1. *If Σ is a set of universal axioms and if $\mathcal{C}$ satisfies all axioms in Σ, then $\mathcal{M}_I(A, \mathcal{C}) \subseteq \mathcal{M}_\Sigma(A)$.*[10]

In our example the lemma clearly applies, since $\langle \mathbb{R}, > \rangle$ is itself a strict linear order and hence satisfies Σ_0.

Note that axiom systems studied in measurement theory often contain axioms other than universal ones, since usually infinite structures are considered as well. For finite structures it is sufficient to consider universal axiom systems. (However, such axiom systems may be infinite; see for example Scott, 1964, where such an infinite axiom system for finite additive conjoint structures is specified. We return to this example later.)

Mutatis mutandis, the same considerations apply to Part (a) of the theorem. However, Lemma 1 has to be replaced by the following one (which is easy to prove by the same method).

Lemma 2. *If Σ is a set of universal axioms which do not contain the identity symbol ('$=$', '$\neq$') and if $\mathcal{C}$ satisfies all axioms in Σ, then $\mathcal{M}_H(A, \mathcal{C}) \subseteq \mathcal{M}_\Sigma(A)$.*

The above axiom system Σ_0 is no candidate for the application of this lemma because it contains the identity symbol. However, the lemma does for example apply to $\mathcal{C} = \langle \mathbb{R}, > \rangle$ together with the axiom system Σ_1 for *strict weak orders*, which consists of the following axioms:

$$\forall x \forall y \, (Bxy \rightarrow \neg Byx) \qquad \text{(asymmetry)}$$
$$\forall x \forall y \forall z \, (Bxy \rightarrow Bxz \vee Bzy) \qquad \text{(negative transitivity)}.$$

Since conversely each finite strict weak order is homomorphically representable in $\langle \mathbb{R}, > \rangle$ (compare Roberts, 1979, p. 101), it follows that $\mathcal{M}_H(A, \langle \mathbb{R}, > \rangle) = \mathcal{M}_{\Sigma_1}(A)$.

---

[10] A universal axiom is an axiom (in the sense of first-order predicate logic) of the form $\forall x_1 \ldots \forall x_m \phi(x_1, \ldots, x_m)$ where $\phi(x_1, \ldots, x_m)$ does not contain quantifiers itself. All the axioms considered here are universal axioms. The lemma follows from the elementary model-theoretic fact that whenever a structure $\mathcal{A}$ is isomorphically embeddable in a structure $\mathcal{B}$ then each universal axiom valid in $\mathcal{B}$ is also valid in $\mathcal{A}$.

As a corollary to Part (a) of Theorem 1 we thus obtain that a probability assignment $\mathbb{P}$ is explainable by an $\mathcal{M}_{\Sigma_1}(A)$-model if and only if it is explainable by an $\langle \mathbb{R}, > \rangle$-random utility model.

The two examples just discussed highlight the crucial role of the noncoincidence condition. For, $\mathbb{P}$ is explainable by an $\mathcal{M}$-mixture model based on strict *linear* orders only if it is explainable by a *noncoincident* $\langle \mathbb{R}, > \rangle$-random utility model. The weaker assumption that $\mathbb{P}$ is explainable by an (unrestricted) $\langle \mathbb{R}, > \rangle$-random utility model only yields the weaker conclusion that $\mathbb{P}$ is explainable by an $\mathcal{M}$-mixture model based on strict *weak* orders. This distinction always has to be kept in mind when $\mathcal{M}_I(A, \mathcal{C}) \neq \mathcal{M}_H(A, \mathcal{C})$.

A Few Applications of the General Representation Theorem. In the straightforward manner just outlined the applicability of Theorem 1 immediately follows for a number of standard classes of relational structures as considered in measurement theory. In Table 1 we list a few examples which refer to probability assignments of type $\langle 2 \rangle$ for some set Φ that consists of formal statements of the form Bab. Other examples for probability assignments of various types could easily be added (see, for instance, the example of additive conjoint measurement, covered by Corollary 1). The first column of the table specifies some universal axiom system Σ and the second a suitable structure $\mathcal{C}$. The characteristic condition of the corresponding $\mathcal{C}$-random utility model is listed in the third column. The fourth column indicates whether Part (a) or Part (b) of the theorem applies. "No" means that $\mathbb{P}$ is explainable by an $\mathcal{M}_\Sigma$-mixture model if and only if $\mathbb{P}$ is explainable by a $\mathcal{C}$-random utility model; "yes" means that this holds with respect to a *noncoincident* $\mathcal{C}$-random utility model. Corresponding observations concerning strict weak orders and semiorders are also to be found in Regenwetter (1996); Suck (1995a, 1995b), too, deals with the "(i)$\Rightarrow$ (ii)" implication for semiorders and also discusses the corresponding results for equivalence relations, partial orders and interval orders. Suitable representation theorems are found in Roberts (1979).[11]

In principle all of the cases listed in Table 1 are already covered by the corresponding theorems in Heyer and Niederée (1989, 1992). One of the advantages of the present account is that it applies to a wider range of possible sets Φ. First, note that the set Φ presupposed in Table 1 need not contain all statements of the form Bab, $a, b \in A$. This makes sense because for empirical or theoretical reasons one sometimes wants to exclude certain statements from consideration. For instance, Φ may or may not include statements of the form Baa. If a statement Baa *is* included, then in all of the cases listed in the table it is either implied that $\mathbb{P}(Baa) = 1$ (linear orders, weak orders, equivalence relations, partial orders)

---

[11] The measurement-theoretic account of semiorders goes back to Luce (1956) and Scott and Suppes (1958); that of interval orders is due to Fishburn (1970). The results for semiorders listed in Table 1 and Table 2 below were presented in our talk "Probabilistic measurement structures and axioms as generalizations of deterministic measurement structures and axioms" at the Workshop on Mathematical Systems Underlying Axiomatic Measurement Theories, University of California at Irvine, 27–31 July, 1992.

System of universal axioms Σ:	Representing structure $\mathcal{C}$	Characteristic condition: $\mathbb{P}[Bab] =$	Noncoincidence yes/no?
Strict linear orders: $\forall x \forall y \forall z (Bxy \wedge Byz \rightarrow Bxz)$ $\forall x \forall y (Bxy \rightarrow \neg Byx)$ $\forall x \forall y (Bxy \vee Byx \vee x = y)$	$\langle \mathbb{R}, > \rangle$	$P[U_a > U_b]$	yes
Strict weak orders: [a] $Bxy \rightarrow \neg Byx$ $\neg Bxy \wedge \neg Byz \rightarrow \neg Bxz$	$\langle \mathbb{R}, > \rangle$	$P[U_a > U_b]$	no
Linear orders: $Bxy \wedge Byz \rightarrow Bxz$ $Bxy \wedge Byx \rightarrow x = y$ $Bxy \vee Byx \vee x = y$	$\langle \mathbb{R}, \geq \rangle$	$P[U_a \geq U_b]$	yes
Weak orders: $Bxy \wedge Byz \rightarrow Bxz$ $Bxy \vee Byx$	$\langle \mathbb{R}, \geq \rangle$	$P[U_a \geq U_b]$	no
Semiorders: $\neg Bxx$ $Bxy \wedge Buv \rightarrow Bxv \vee Buy$ $Bxy \wedge Byu \rightarrow Bxv \vee Bvu$	$\langle \mathbb{R}, >_\delta \rangle$ [b]	$P[U_a > U_b + \delta]$	no
Equivalence relations: $Bxy \wedge Byz \rightarrow Bxz$ Bxx $Bxy \rightarrow Byx$	$\langle \mathbb{R}, = \rangle$	$P[U_a = U_b]$	no
Partial orders: $Bxy \wedge Byz \rightarrow Bxz$ Bxx $Bxy \vee Byx \vee x = y$	$\langle \mathcal{S}(\mathbb{R}), \supseteq \rangle$	$P[U_a \supseteq U_b]$	yes
Interval orders: $\neg Bxx$ $Bxy \wedge Buv \rightarrow Bxv \vee Buy$	$\langle \mathcal{I}(\mathbb{R}), \sqsupset \rangle$ [c]	$P[U_a \sqsupset U_b]$	no

[a] For brevity, the universal quantifiers $\forall x \, \forall y$ etc. have been omitted here and in the following examples.
[b] For all $r, s \in \mathbb{R}, r >_\delta s :\Leftrightarrow r > s + \delta$ (δ being an arbitrarily fixed positive real).
[c] $\mathcal{I}(\mathbb{R}) = \{[r, s] \mid r, s \in \mathbb{R}, r < s\}; [r, s] \sqsupset [r', s'] :\Leftrightarrow s > r'$.

TABLE 1. Some straightforward corollaries to Theorem 1 for situations of type $\langle 2 \rangle$. Each row says that probability assignments $\mathbb{P}$ are explainable by an $\mathcal{M}_\Sigma(A)$-mixture model if and only if they are explainable by the corresponding $\mathcal{C}$-random utility model (for details see text).

or that $\mathbb{P}(Baa) = 0$ (strict linear orders, strict weak orders, semiorders, interval orders).[12]

---

[12] No restriction for the values of $\mathbb{P}(Baa)$ is implied by the following model. Simply consider $\mathcal{C} = \langle \mathbb{R}, >^* \rangle$ where $>^* := \{(i, i) \mid i \text{ is an integer}\} \cup \{(r, s) \mid r > s\}$. The corresponding set

Second, since Theorem 1 also applies to sets Φ that involve conjunctions or other sentential connectives, Table 1 immediately extends to sets Φ that contain conjunctions, say, of basic statements Bab. For example, consider the set Φ_1 that is composed of statements of the form $Bab \wedge Bbc$ for distinct objects $a, b, c \in A$. It then holds that a probability assignment $\mathbb{P}$ for Φ_1 is explainable by an $\mathcal{M}_{ord}$-mixture model if and only if it is explainable by an $\langle \mathbb{R}, > \rangle$-random utility model, the characteristic condition of the latter being

$$\mathbb{P}[Bab \wedge Bbc] = P[U_a > U_b \ \& \ U_b > U_c]. \tag{21}$$

The other lines of the table extend to such cases analogously. An experimental situation where such a set Φ_1 might be considered appropriate could be a ranking experiment in which subjects have to rank the elements of triplets $\{a, b, c\}$ according to some criterion, with $\mathbb{P}[Bab \wedge Bbc]$ being the conditional probability that the subject, when presented with these stimuli, produces the ranking abc, that is, that she chooses a over b and b over c.

An interesting situation emerges if two experiments are to be compared. Consider, for instance, a probability assignment $\mathbb{P}_1 : \Phi_1 \to [0, 1]$ of the kind just described and a probability assignment $\mathbb{P}_0 : \Phi_0 \to [0, 1]$ that relies on binary choices for the same set A (i.e., Φ_0 consists of all formal statements of the form Bab, $a \neq b$). For each of the two probability assignments one can independently ask whether or not it is explainable by an $\mathcal{M}_{ord}$-mixture model. Assume both answers are positive. Then a third question could be raised, namely, whether they are *jointly* explainable by a common $\mathcal{M}_{ord}$-mixture model, that is, whether the joint probability assignment $\mathbb{P}_0 \cup \mathbb{P}_1 : \Phi_0 \cup \Phi_1 \to [0, 1]$ is explainable by an $\mathcal{M}_{ord}$-mixture model.[13] This amounts to the question whether there is some probability measure P on the power set of $\mathcal{M}_{ord}$ that explains *both* $\mathbb{P}_0$ *and* $\mathbb{P}_1$. (Some necessary testable conditions are mentioned in Section 6.) Needless to say, Theorem 1 also applies to such a joint probability assignment.

Further applications of Theorem 1 to $\mathbb{P}$'s that involve conjunctions are to be found in Section 7.

In sum, the previous considerations show that explainability by a (noncoincident or unrestricted) $\mathcal{C}$-random utility model is equivalent to explainability by an $\mathcal{M}$-mixture model for a suitable $\mathcal{M}$; i.e., given $\mathcal{C}$, a corresponding set $\mathcal{M}$ always exists for each finite domain A (unless the cardinality of A exceeds that of $\mathcal{C}$). One simply has to choose $\mathcal{M} = \mathcal{M}_I(A, \mathcal{C})$ or $\mathcal{M} = \mathcal{M}_H(A, \mathcal{C})$, respectively. It is worth noting that the converse is not generally true, that is, given some $\mathcal{M}$ on a domain A, there need not necessarily exist a structure $\mathcal{C}$ such that explainability by an $\mathcal{M}$-mixture model and by a (noncoincident or unrestricted) $\mathcal{C}$-random model are equivalent. These are the cases where there is no suitable representing structure $\mathcal{C}$

$\mathcal{M}_I(A, \mathcal{C})$ coincides with $\mathcal{M}_\Sigma(A)$ where Σ consists of the axioms of transitivity, connectedness and antisymmetry. The corresponding relations $\succ^*$ essentially behave like linear orders except that $a \succ^* a$ may or may not hold for each individual object $a \in A$. The set $\mathcal{M}_H(A, \mathcal{C})$ can be described similarly by modifying the concept of a weak order. Of course, in many situations comparisons of the kind "Baa" should more appropriately be described as comparisons between two 'copies' of a, i.e. between two objects rather than one.

[13]Notice that $\mathbb{P}$ is well-defined, since the intersection of Φ_0 and Φ_1 is empty. Otherwise $\mathbb{P}_0$ and $\mathbb{P}_1$ would have to coincide on the intersection.

for which $\mathcal{M}$ coincides with $\mathcal{M}_I(A,\mathcal{C})$ or $\mathcal{M}_H(A,\mathcal{C})$, respectively. Indeed, $\mathcal{M}$ may be an *arbitrary* collection of structures of a suitable type with domain A. It could, for instance, consist of all semiorders *and* all equivalence relations on A or, at the other extreme, only of two specified individual linear orders on A. (Another case in point are knowledge spaces; see Section 7.) In this sense mixture models are more general than $\mathcal{C}$-random utility models, so in the next section we will restrict attention to the former.

6. LINEAR INEQUALITIES CHARACTERIZING $\mathcal{M}$-MIXTURE MODELS

Let us now turn to the problem of specifying necessary and sufficient *testable conditions* for a probability assignment $\mathbb{P}$ to be explainable by an $\mathcal{M}$-mixture model for some fixed $\mathcal{M}$. Adopting a term coined by Marley (1990) in his discussion of the special case of binary choice, we call this the *characterization problem* for $\mathcal{M}$-mixture models. The preceding section showed that the corresponding characterization problem for $\mathcal{C}$-random utility models reduces to the characterization problem for $\mathcal{M}$-mixture models, so it need not be discussed separately. In the following subsection we show that (for finite domains A as considered here) there is always a finite set of testable necessary conditions which are jointly sufficient.

A General Characterization Theorem. In the binary choice literature there has been a long-standing discussion of the characterization problem for the special case $\mathcal{M} = \mathcal{M}_{ord}(A)$, A finite (for a survey see e.g., Marley, 1990; Fishburn, 1992). For instance, a well-known *necessary* condition for a binary choice system $\mathbb{P}$ to be explainable by an $\mathcal{M}_{ord}$-mixture model is the so-called *triangle inequality*

$$\mathbb{P}[Bca] \leq \mathbb{P}[Bcb] + \mathbb{P}[Bba]$$

or equivalently (under the assumption of (1)),

$$\mathbb{P}[Bab] + \mathbb{P}[Bbc] - \mathbb{P}[Bac] \leq 1, \tag{22}$$

for all distinct $a, b, c \in A$. This is a prototypical example of what we just called a "testable condition" (ignoring for now the problems concerning statistical tests of such probabilistic inequalities on the basis of frequency data). Since it is known that the triangle inequality is *sufficient* only for cardinalities of A up to $n < 6$, the question arose whether for each n there exists a finite set of such linear inequalities which are necessary *and* sufficient for a binary choice system $\mathbb{P}$ for a set A of that cardinality to be explainable by an $\mathcal{M}_{ord}$-mixture model. It turns out that by means of methods of the theory of convex polytopes it can easily be shown that for each n such a finite set of conditions exists (Grötschel, Jünger, & Reinelt, 1985). In the following theorem – which extends Theorem 3.2 in Heyer and Niederée (1992) to the more general framework developed here – we use the same approach to show that an analogous result obtains for arbitrary sets $\mathcal{M}$ and Φ for finite domains A.

Theorem 2. (General Characterization Theorem) *Let $\Phi = \{\phi_1, \ldots, \phi_N\}$ be a set of formal statements about some finite set A of type $\langle k_1, \ldots, k_m \rangle$, and $\mathcal{M}$ a set of structures admissible for Φ. Then for some integer K there exists a $K \times N$-matrix $\Gamma = (c_{ij})_{ij}$ and a vector $\mathbf{d} = (d_1, \ldots, d_K)$ of real coefficients such that for all probability assignments $\mathbb{P} : \Phi \to [0,1]$ the following are equivalent:*

(a) $\mathbb{P}$ *is explainable by an* $\mathcal{M}$*-mixture model,*
(b) $\mathbb{P}$ *satisfies the linear inequalities*

$$c_{i1}\mathbb{P}[\phi_1] + \cdots + c_{iN}\mathbb{P}[\phi_N] \leq d_i \qquad (i = 1, \ldots, K),$$

or equivalently,

$$\mathbf{\Gamma} \cdot \begin{pmatrix} \mathbb{P}[\phi_1] \\ \vdots \\ \mathbb{P}[\phi_N] \end{pmatrix} \leq \mathbf{d}.$$

Before we turn to the proof of the theorem, we insert a useful definition and lemma.

Definition 4. Let $\mathcal{M}$ be a finite set of structures of a fixed type with finite domain A and let Φ be a set of formal statements about A of the same type.

(i) For all $\mathcal{A} \in \mathcal{M}$ the *probability assignment on* Φ *induced by* $\mathcal{A}$ is the mapping $\mathbb{P}_{\mathcal{A}} : \Phi \to [0,1]$ defined by

$$\mathbb{P}_{\mathcal{A}}[\phi] := \begin{cases} 1, & \text{if } \mathcal{A} \models \phi \\ 0 & \text{otherwise} \end{cases}$$

for all $\phi \in \Phi$.

(ii) Given a probability mass $\langle p_{\mathcal{A}} \mid \mathcal{A} \in \mathcal{M} \rangle$ (i.e. $p_{\mathcal{A}} \geq 0$ and $\sum_{\mathcal{A}} p_{\mathcal{A}} = 1$), the probability assignment $\sum_{\mathcal{A} \in \mathcal{M}} p_{\mathcal{A}} \mathbb{P}_{\mathcal{A}} : \Phi \to [0,1]$ is defined by

$$\left(\sum_{\mathcal{A} \in \mathcal{M}} p_{\mathcal{A}} \mathbb{P}_{\mathcal{A}} \right)[\phi] := \sum_{\mathcal{A} \in \mathcal{M}} p_{\mathcal{A}} \mathbb{P}_{\mathcal{A}}[\phi].$$

Lemma 3. *Consider a probability assignment* $\mathbb{P} : \Phi \to [0,1]$ *for some finite set A and some set, $\mathcal{M}$, of structures which is admissible for $\mathbb{P}$. Then the following are equivalent:*

(a) $\mathbb{P}$ *is explainable by an* $\mathcal{M}$*-mixture model,*
(b) *there is a probability mass* $\langle p_{\mathcal{A}} \mid \mathcal{A} \in \mathcal{M} \rangle$ *such that* $\mathbb{P} = \sum_{\mathcal{A} \in \mathcal{M}} p_{\mathcal{A}} \mathbb{P}_{\mathcal{A}}$.

Proof. This follows immediately from Definitions 1 and 4. $\qquad\qquad\square$

Proof of Theorem 2. To begin with, we assign to each probability assignment $\mathbb{P} : \Phi \to [0,1]$ a vector $\xi(\mathbb{P}) \in \mathbb{R}^N$ that is defined by

$$\xi(\mathbb{P}) := (\mathbb{P}[\phi_1], \ldots, \mathbb{P}[\phi_N]).$$

Clearly, then, $\xi(\sum_{\mathcal{A}} p_{\mathcal{A}} \mathbb{P}_{\mathcal{A}}) = \sum_{\mathcal{A}} p_{\mathcal{A}} \xi(\mathbb{P}_{\mathcal{A}})$ (for arbitrary probability masses $p_{\mathcal{A}}$), whence for the subset

$$\Pi := \{ \xi(\mathbb{P}) \mid \mathbb{P} : \Phi \to [0,1] \text{ is an } \mathcal{M}\text{-mixture} \}$$

of $\mathbb{R}^N$ we obtain by Lemma 3 that

$$\Pi = \left\{ \xi\left(\sum_{\mathcal{A}} p_{\mathcal{A}} \mathbb{P}_{\mathcal{A}} \right) \mid \langle p_{\mathcal{A}} \rangle_{\mathcal{A} \in \mathcal{M}} \text{ is a probability mass} \right\}$$

$$= \left\{ \sum_{\mathcal{A}} p_{\mathcal{A}} \xi(\mathbb{P}_{\mathcal{A}}) \mid \langle p_{\mathcal{A}} \rangle_{\mathcal{A} \in \mathcal{M}} \text{ is a probability mass} \right\}.$$

This means that Π is a polytope, namely the convex hull of $\{\xi(\mathbb{P}_A) \mid A \in \mathcal{M}\}$. Hence, by a well-known result of convex analysis (see for example Rockafellar, 1970, Theorem 19.1) Π is a polyhedron, i.e., the intersection of finitely many closed half-spaces H_i, $i = 1, \ldots, K$. By definition each of these half-spaces is the set of all solutions $\mathbf{x} \in \mathbb{R}^N$ of a linear inequality of the form

$$c_{i1}x_1 + \cdots + c_{iN}x_N \leq d_i .$$

Let $\boldsymbol{\Gamma}$ be the resulting matrix of coefficients c_{ij}. Clearly then, $\mathbb{P}$ is explainable by an $\mathcal{M}$-mixture if and only if $\xi(\mathbb{P}) \in \Pi$, which in turn holds if and only if $\boldsymbol{\Gamma} \cdot \xi(\mathbb{P})^t \leq \mathbf{d}$.

$\square$

Remark 8. As pointed out in the proof, the set of all probability assignments on Φ explainable by an $\mathcal{M}$-mixture model is associated with a polytope $\Pi = \Pi(\mathcal{M}, \Phi) \subset \mathbb{R}^N$ (where N is the cardinality of Φ). Notice that this polytope depends both on $\mathcal{M}$ and the set Φ considered (and hence in particular on the size of the underlying set A). The vertices of this polytope form a subset of the set $\{0, 1\}^N$, each vertex corresponding to a structure $A \in \mathcal{M}$ (in the proof: $\xi(\mathbb{P}_A)$). This polytope is then described by the resulting inequalities, which from the geometrical viewpoint underlying convex analysis means the following. The polytope is located in a uniquely determined affine subspace of $\mathbb{R}^N$ of minimal dimensionality M (which is called the dimensionality of the polytope). Given this subspace, one has to describe the facets of the polytope, that is, loosely speaking, the finite number of $(M - 1)$-dimensional surfaces bounding it. The affine subspace is characterized by a minimal system of equations (each of which corresponds to two inequalities of the above kind), and each of the facets can be described by some linear inequality (see e.g., Ziegler, 1994). A detailed discussion of these matters is beyond the scope of this paper. Suffice it to say that (for fixed sets A, $\mathcal{M}$ and Φ) such equations and inequalities can in principle be determined *algorithmically*, and that the coefficients c_{ij} can always be chosen to be *integers*. For the case of $\mathcal{M}_{ord}$ see Suck (1992) and Fishburn (1992); there also exists corresponding software applicable to arbitrary polytopes.[14] So one might say that in principle the characterization problem is solved.

However, what one would like to have is, for each axiom system Σ of interest, a "closed-form" scheme (or a transparent collection of such schemes) that provides, for arbitrary finite sets A, a necessary and sufficient set of inequalities for $\mathcal{M}_\Sigma(A)$ (see Falmagne, 1978, for a prototypical example of such a scheme). In this – less clearly specified – sense the characterization problem has not even completely been solved for the much-discussed binary choice case where $\mathcal{M} = \mathcal{M}_{ord}(A)$ and $\Phi = \{Bab \mid a \neq b\}$ (see e.g., Grötschel et al., 1985; Fishburn, 1992; Suck, 1992; Koppen, 1995). Some results concerning the polytopes associated with equivalence relations, semiorders, interval orders, and partial orders are found in Suck (1995a, 1995b). These investigations show that some of the inequalities listed below in Table 2 define the corresponding affine subspaces or facets.

---

[14] A program that determines, for given vertices of a polytope, the corresponding inequalities (and the other way round) is PORTA by Christof (see References).

Some Simple Methods for Checking and Generating Necessary Inequalities. A test of maximal strength of a hypothesis of the form "$\mathbb{P}$ is explainable by an $\mathcal{M}$-mixture model" would be to check whether a minimal set of facet-defining inequalities (including the equations defining the affine subspace) which completely specifies the corresponding polytope is satisfied empirically. However, even without a complete geometrical understanding of the polytope the above hypothesis can be subjected to a (weaker, but possibly more feasible) empirical test based only on some necessary inequalities.

In the remainder of the section we turn to the question of how to find, in a straightforward manner, certain basic linear inequalities which are necessary for probability assignments to be explainable by an $\mathcal{M}$-mixture model. In the following, such inequalities are briefly called *necessary inequalities for $\mathcal{M}$*. To begin with, we state a lemma which provides a general criterion and simple finite procedure for deciding whether or not, for a given $\mathcal{M}$, some linear inequality put forward for consideration is a necessary inequality for $\mathcal{M}$.

Lemma 4. *Let $\Phi = \{\phi_1, \ldots, \phi_N\}$ be a set of formal statements about some finite set A and assume that $\mathcal{M}$ is admissible for Φ. Then for all real numbers $c_1, \ldots, c_N, d$ the following are equivalent.*

(a) *The inequality*

$$c_1 \mathbb{P}[\phi_1] + \cdots + c_N \mathbb{P}[\phi_N] \leq d \tag{23}$$

is necessary for $\mathcal{M}$, i.e. it is satisfied by all $\mathbb{P} : \Phi \to [0, 1]$ which are explainable by an $\mathcal{M}$-mixture model.

(b) *Inequality (23) is satisfied by all induced probability assignments $\mathbb{P}_{\mathcal{A}}$ with $\mathcal{A} \in \mathcal{M}$.*

Proof. "(a) $\Rightarrow$ (b)": This follows immediately from the obvious fact that each induced probability assignment $\mathbb{P}_{\mathcal{A}}$ is explainable by an $\mathcal{M}$-mixture model.

"(b) $\Rightarrow$ (a)": Under the assumption of (b) it is easy to verify that (for all probability masses $\langle p_{\mathcal{A}} \mid \mathcal{A} \in \mathcal{M} \rangle$) Inequality (23) is satisfied by the probability assignment $\sum_{\mathcal{A}} p_{\mathcal{A}} \mathbb{P}_{\mathcal{A}}$. Now (a) follows by Lemma 3. $\square$

Starting with some set Σ of universal axioms and a finite domain A, we now describe a procedure which assigns to each axiom in Σ a set of 'associated' inequalities. These are *necessary* inequalities for $\mathcal{M} = \mathcal{M}_{\Sigma}(A)$. Note that in many situations these associated inequalities are *not* (jointly) *sufficient*, however, for probability assignments on Φ to be explainable by an $\mathcal{M}$-mixture model. Table 2 lists some basic necessary inequalities that can be generated by this method. An essential component of this procedure is the following corollary to Lemma 4.

Corollary 2. *Let Φ be a set of statements about a finite set A of type $\langle k_1, \ldots, k_m \rangle$ and let $\mathcal{M}$ be a set of relational structures which is admissible for Φ. Consider formal statements $\phi_1, \ldots, \phi_{n_1}, \psi_1, \ldots, \psi_{n_2} \in \Phi$ (where either n_1 or n_2 may be 0). Then the following holds.*

(a) *For all structures $\mathcal{A}$ of type $\langle k_1, \ldots, k_m \rangle$ with domain A the following are equivalent:*

   (i) $\mathcal{A} \models \phi_1 \vee \cdots \vee \phi_{n_1} \vee \neg\psi_1 \vee \cdots \vee \neg\psi_{n_2}$

   (ii) $\sum_{i=1}^{n_2} \mathbb{P}_\mathcal{A}[\psi_i] - \sum_{j=1}^{n_1} \mathbb{P}_\mathcal{A}[\phi_j] \leq n_2 - 1.$

(b) *If (i) holds for all $\mathcal{A} \in \mathcal{M}$, then the inequality*

$$\sum_{i=1}^{n_2} \mathbb{P}[\psi_i] - \sum_{j=1}^{n_1} \mathbb{P}[\phi_j] \leq n_2 - 1 \tag{24}$$

holds for all probability assignments $\mathbb{P} : \Phi \to [0,1]$ which are explainable by an $\mathcal{M}$-mixture model, that is, Equation 24 is necessary for $\mathcal{M}$ (w.r.t. the set Φ considered).

Proof. Part (a). Clearly, (i) is equivalent to $\sum_{j=1}^{n_1} \mathbb{P}_\mathcal{A}[\phi_j] + \sum_{i=1}^{n_2} (1 - \mathbb{P}_\mathcal{A}[\psi_i]) \geq 1$, which in turn is equivalent to (ii).

Part (b). By Lemma 4, (b) follows immediately from (a). □

To get an impression of how Corollary 2 can be applied, consider the class $\mathcal{M}$ of all interval orders on some finite set A. Recall that all interval orders satisfy the axiom $\forall x \forall y \forall u \forall v (Bxy \wedge Buv \to Bxv \vee Buy)$ (compare Table 1). This means that for all $\mathcal{A} \in \mathcal{M}$ and for all $a, b, c, d \in A$, the statement $Bab \wedge Bcd \to Bad \vee Bcb$ is valid in $\mathcal{A}$. An easy transformation shows that this statement is logically equivalent to $\neg Bab \vee \neg Bcd \vee Bad \vee Bcb$. Hence by Corollary 2 the inequality

$$\mathbb{P}[Bab] + \mathbb{P}[Bcd] - \mathbb{P}[Bad] - \mathbb{P}[Bcb] \leq 1 \,.$$

is necessary for $\mathcal{M}$ for all $a, b, c, d \in A$ (provided, of course, that the respective statements Bab, Bcd, etc. belong to the set Φ under consideration).

Remark 9. By means of a generalization of this strategy, Corollary 2 can be brought to bear on arbitrary universal axioms that do not contain the identity symbol. Consider sets A, Φ, and $\mathcal{M}$ (as in the Corollary) and some universal axiom $\forall x_1 \ldots \forall x_q \chi(x_1, \ldots x_q)$ that is valid in all structures $\mathcal{A} \in \mathcal{M}$. Then, for all $a_1, \ldots, a_q \in A$, the statement $\chi(a_1, \ldots a_q)$ is valid in all structures $\mathcal{A} \in \mathcal{M}$. Assume further that $\chi(a_1, \ldots, a_q)$ is composed, in the sense of sentential logic, of elements of Φ. By a standard result of sentential logic (see e.g., Mendelson, 1964), $\chi(a_1, \ldots, a_q)$ is then logically equivalent to a conjunction $\chi_1 \wedge \cdots \wedge \chi_k$ where each of the χ_i in turn is a disjunction of elements of Φ or their negations (*conjunctive normal form*). Corollary 2 can then be applied to each of these disjunctions χ_i, yielding a set of linear inequalities associated with the universal axiom considered. With a minor modification these considerations extend to axioms which contain the identity symbol. This is illustrated by the following example (we refrain from describing the general 'recipe').

Consider the set $\mathcal{M}$ of all linear orders on a finite set A, and the axiom of antisymmetry, $\forall x \forall y (Bxy \wedge Byx \to x = y)$, which is valid in all $\mathcal{A} \in \mathcal{M}$. This means that for all $a, b, c, d \in A$, the formal statement $Bab \wedge Bba \to a = b$ is valid in these structures. Since this statement is logically equivalent to $a \neq b \to \neg Bab \vee \neg Bba$, this is to say that for all *distinct* elements $a, b \in A$ and all $\mathcal{A} \in \mathcal{M}$ it holds that $\mathcal{A} \models \neg Bab \vee \neg Bba$, yielding the associated necessary inequality

$$\mathbb{P}[Bab] + \mathbb{P}[Bba] \leq 1 \,.$$

Universal axioms Σ	Testable inequalities
Strict linear orders [a]	
$\forall x \forall y \forall z (Bxy \wedge Byz \to Bxz)$	$p(a,b) + p(b,c) - p(a,c) \leq 1$
$\forall x \forall y (Bxy \to \neg Byx)$	$p(a,b) + p(b,a) \leq 1$
$\forall x \forall y (Bxy \vee Byx \vee x = y)$	$p(a,b) + p(b,a) \geq 1$ *for* $a \neq b$
Weak orders	
$Bxy \wedge Byz \to Bxz$ [b]	$p(a,b) + p(b,c) - p(a,c) \leq 1$
$Bxy \vee Byx$	$p(a,b) + p(b,a) \geq 1$
Semiorders	
$\neg Bxx$	$p(a,a) = 0$
$Bxy \wedge Buv \to Bxv \vee Buy$	$p(a,b) + p(c,d) - p(a,d) - p(c,b) \leq 1$
$Bxy \wedge Byu \to Bxv \vee Bvu$	$p(a,b) + p(b,c) - p(a,d) - p(d,c) \leq 1$
Equivalence relations	
$Bxy \wedge Byz \to Bxz$	$p(a,b) + p(b,c) - p(a,c) \leq 1$
Bxx	$p(a,a) = 1$
$Bxy \to Byx$	$p(a,b) \leq p(b,a)$
Partial orders	
$Bxy \wedge Byz \to Bxz$	$p(a,b) + p(b,c) - p(a,c) \leq 1$
Bxx	$p(a,a) = 1$
$Bxy \vee Byx \vee x = y$	$p(a,b) + p(b,a) \geq 1$ *for* $a \neq b$
Symmetric additive conjoint structures [c] [d]	
$Qxyuv \leftrightarrow Qyxvu$	$p(a,b;c,d) = p(b,a;d,c)$
$Qxyuv \vee Quvxy$	$p(a,b;c,d) + p(c,d;a,b) \geq 1$
$\displaystyle \bigwedge_{i=0}^{k-1} Qx_i y_i x_{\pi(i)} y_{\sigma(i)}$ $\to Qx_{\pi(k)} y_{\sigma(k)} x_k y_k$	$\displaystyle \sum_{i=0}^{k-1} p(a_i, b_i; a_{\pi(i)} b_{\sigma(i)})$ $- p(a_{\pi(k)}, b_{\sigma(k)}; a_k, b_k) \leq k-1$
for all permutations π, σ *of* $\{1,\ldots,k\}$	*for all permutations* π, σ *of* $\{1,\ldots,k\}$

[a] $p(a,b)$ is short for $\mathbb{P}[Bab]$ (provided that Bab belongs to Φ).
[b] For brevity, universal quantifiers $\forall x$, $\forall y$, etc. have been omitted here and in the following axioms.
[c] An additive conjoint structure $\langle A \times A, \succsim \rangle$ is a *symmetric* additive conjoint structure if and only if it satisfies the axiom $\forall x \forall y \forall u \forall v (Qxyuv \leftrightarrow Qyxvu)$. The remaining axioms are an axiom scheme for *finite* additive conjoint structures (Scott, 1964).
[d] $p(a,b;c,d)$ is short for $\mathbb{P}[Qabcd]$.

TABLE 2. Some examples of associated linear inequalities which are necessary for mixture models based on $\mathcal{M}_\Sigma(A)$.

(Notice that we now have to restrict attention to situations where $a \neq b$; of course, in many applications the excluded statements Baa do not belong to the set Φ under consideration, anyway.)

By way of illustration, Table 2 lists some associated necessary inequalities that can be easily derived in this manner. Further examples could be added at will. It is worth noting that Equation 1, i.e., the equation $p_{ab} + p_{ba} = 1$, $a \neq b$, which is commonly used to define the concept of a binary choice system, corresponds to two inequalities associated with the axioms of connectedness and antisymmetry, and that the triangle inequality as specified in Equation 22 is associated with transitivity. In many applications the validity of Equation 1 (or some other inequality) is already implied by the experimental paradigm used (e.g., forced choice), in which case it cannot, of course, play the role of a critical testable condition for the $\mathcal{M}$-mixture model under investigation.

We add a final simple example which illustrates how (by the same method) Corollary 2 can be applied to situations where Φ contains statements that involve sentential connectives. Recall that at the end of Section 5 we considered two sets of statements, Φ_0 and Φ_1, containing all statements of the form Bab and $Bab \wedge Bbc$, respectively, for distinct elements a, b, c from some finite set A. Furthermore, we assumed two probability assignments $\mathbb{P}_i : \Phi_i \rightarrow [0, 1]$ ($i = 0, 1$), based on two different experiments, to be given. One may then ask whether the union $\mathbb{P} := \mathbb{P}_0 \cup \mathbb{P}_1$ is explainable by an $\mathcal{M}$-mixture model where $\mathcal{M} = \mathcal{M}_{ord}(A)$. In this case we are also interested in necessary inequalities for $\mathcal{M}$ that involve statements in Φ_1. Consider, for example, the axiom of transitivity which is valid in all structures in $\mathcal{M}$. This means that, for all $a, b, c \in A$, the formal statement $Bab \wedge Bbc \rightarrow Bac$ is valid in all structures in $\mathcal{M}$. The same goes for the logically equivalent statement $\neg \psi_1 \vee \phi_1$ where ψ_1 and ϕ_1 are the statements $Bab \wedge Bbc$ and Bac, respectively. If a, b, c are distinct, ϕ_1 and ψ_1 belong to Φ, whence by Corollary 2 the inequality

$$\mathbb{P}[Bab \wedge Bbc] - \mathbb{P}[Bac] \leq 0 \tag{25}$$

is necessary for $\mathcal{M}$ (w.r.t. to the extended set Φ considered). Inequalities of that kind relate the two experiments to each other, for, by definition, Equation 25 simply says that $\mathbb{P}_1[Bab \wedge Bbc] \leq \mathbb{P}_0[Bac]$.[15] Notice in passing that Equation 25 is implied by the stronger necessary inequality

$$\mathbb{P}[Bab] = \mathbb{P}[Bca \wedge Bab] + \mathbb{P}[Bac \wedge Bcb] + \mathbb{P}[Bab \wedge Bbc], \tag{26}$$

whose necessity can easily be verified by means of Lemma 4.

7. FURTHER EXAMPLES

As we have seen, the results of Sections 5 in conjunction with those of Section 6 provide a unifying framework for $\mathcal{M}$-mixture and $\mathcal{C}$-random utility models based on various types of structures (see e.g., Table 1 and Corollary 1, on the one hand, and Table 2, on the other). In this section we briefly outline some examples based on probability assignments which involve conjunctions, so as to convey an impression of how this approach could be brought to bear on more complex situations.

Choices out of a set of alternatives. Consider an experiment in which a subject is presented with subsets of a finite set A of cardinality n. The subject is then asked to choose the one object she prefers to all the other objects in the presented subset. The conditional probability that the object a is the one selected given that the subset D was presented, is denoted by p_{aD}. In accordance with the example concerning joint explainability of binary choices and rankings at the end of Section 5, we denote this conditional probability by

$$\mathbb{P}[Bab_1 \wedge \cdots \wedge Bab_k]$$

where $b_1, \ldots, b_k$ is an enumeration of the set $D \setminus \{a\}$. Note that this defines a probability assignment $\mathbb{P}$ on the set of protocol statements of the form $Bab_1 \wedge \cdots \wedge Bab_k$ where $a, b_1, \ldots, b_k$ are pairwise distinct elements of A and $k = 1, \ldots, n - 1$.

---

[15]It is sometimes useful to apply the same procedure to formal universal statements that are logical consequences of Σ (including tautologies). The tautology '$\forall x \forall y \forall z ([Bxy \wedge Byz] \rightarrow Bxy)$', for instance, yields for all distinct $a, b, c \in A$ the consistency condition '$\mathbb{P}_1[Bab \wedge Bbc] \leq \mathbb{P}_0[Bab]$'.

By the General Representation Theorem (Theorem 1) the resulting probability assignment $\mathbb{P}$ is explainable by an $\mathcal{M}_{ord}$-mixture model if and only if $\mathbb{P}$ is explainable by a noncoincident $\langle \mathbb{R}, > \rangle$-random utility model, the characteristic condition of the latter being

$$\mathbb{P}[Bab_1 \wedge \cdots \wedge Bab_k] = P[U_a > U_{b_1} \& \ldots \& U_a > U_{b_k}]. \tag{27}$$

Observing that for noncoincident families of U_a's the right-hand side of Equation 27 is equal to $P[U_a = \max \{U_c \mid c \in D\}]$, it is readily seen that $\mathbb{P}$ is explainable by a noncoincident $\langle \mathbb{R}, > \rangle$-random utility model if and only if the corresponding system of choice probabilities p_{aD} is a random scale system as introduced in Falmagne (1978). By the General Characterization Theorem (Theorem 2) there exists a finite set of linear inequalities that are necessary and sufficient for $\mathbb{P}$ to be explainable by an $\mathcal{M}_{ord}$-mixture model. Such a sufficient system of necessary inequalities was specified by Falmagne (1978).

Approval voting. In experiments on approval voting subjects are presented with a nonempty subset D of a finite set A of stimuli (for example politicians; see e.g., Brams & Fishburn, 1983). Their task is to specify a nonempty subset X of D which contains those elements they "approve of" (according to some criterion). The conditional probability that subjects (randomly drawn from a specified population) select the subset X when presented with the set D will be denoted by p_{XD}. For the sake of simplicity, we first restrict our attention to a toy example where $A = \{a_1, a_2, a_3\}$; the formulation of the general case would be basically the same, but more tedious. Extending the notation introduced in Section 2, the possible outcomes of such an experiment may be recorded by protocol statements of the following form. The outcome that $\{a_2\}$ is selected out of $\{a_2, a_3\}$ will be recorded by

$$S^2(a_2; a_2, a_3) \wedge \neg S^2(a_3; a_2, a_3),$$

the outcome that $\{a_1, a_2\}$ is selected out of A will be denoted by

$$S^3(a_1; a_1, a_2, a_3) \wedge S^3(a_2; a_1, a_2, a_3) \wedge \neg S^3(a_3; a_1, a_2, a_3),$$

and the other cases treated similarly. Note that these protocol statements involve two relation symbols, S^2, S^3, the indices referring to the cardinality of the set presented. The resulting set Φ is of type $\langle 3, 4 \rangle$. The probabilities p_{XD} then define a probability assignment $\mathbb{P}$ on Φ.

Regenwetter (1996) discusses (for the special case $D = A$) the so-called *topset voting* model in the context of his account of generalized random utility models. Regenwetter's model is a mixture model that assumes that each subject possesses a semiorder $\succ$ and that she selects exactly those elements out of the set D presented for which there is no bigger element in D with respect to this semiorder. In our framework this amounts to an $\mathcal{M}_{top}$-mixture model where $\mathcal{M}_{top} = \mathcal{M}_{top}(A)$ consists of relational structures of the form $\langle A, \mathfrak{S}^2, \mathfrak{S}^3, \succ \rangle$ with the following properties. The relation $\succ$ is a semiorder, and $\mathfrak{S}^2$, $\mathfrak{S}^3$ are 3-placed and 4-placed relations on A (by which, at this theoretical level, the symbols S^2 and S^3 are interpreted);

they are related to $\succ$ as follows

$$(a, b, c) \in \mathfrak{S}^2 \iff b \not\succ a \ \& \ c \not\succ a \tag{28}$$

$$(a, b, c, d) \in \mathfrak{S}^3 \iff b \not\succ a \ \& \ c \not\succ a \ \& \ d \not\succ a. \tag{29}$$

It is obvious how to set up a system Σ of universal axioms which characterizes these structures (and does not contain the identity symbol). Clearly, then, the probabilities p_{XD} considered are explainable by the topset voting model if and only if $\mathbb{P}$ is explainable by an $\mathcal{M}_{top}$-mixture model.[16]

Next, consider the numerical structure $\mathcal{C} := \langle \mathbb{R}, \mathfrak{N}^2, \mathfrak{N}^3, >_\delta \rangle$ where $>_\delta$ is defined by $r >_\delta s :\Leftrightarrow r > s + \delta$ ($\delta > 0$ fixed); the definitions of $\mathfrak{N}^2$, $\mathfrak{N}^3$ correspond to those in (28) and (29) with $\succ$ being replaced by $>_\delta$. It is routine to show that $\mathcal{M}_{top}(A) = \mathcal{M}_H(A, \mathcal{C})$; the inclusion "$\subseteq$" follows from the representation theorem for semiorders and "$\supseteq$" from Lemma 2. Hence by Theorem 1 $\mathbb{P}$ is explainable by an $\mathcal{M}_{top}(A)$-mixture model if and only if it is explainable by a $\mathcal{C}$-random utility model. An example of a typical characteristic condition involving S^2 is

$$\mathbb{P}\Big[S^2(a; a, b) \wedge \neg S^2(b; a, b)\Big] =$$
$$= P\Big(\Big\{\omega \ \Big| \ (U_a(\omega), U_a(\omega), U_b(\omega)) \in \mathfrak{N}^2 \ \& \ (U_b(\omega), U_a(\omega), U_b(\omega)) \notin \mathfrak{N}^2\Big\}\Big)$$
$$= P\Big[U_b \leq U_a + \delta \ \& \ U_a > U_b + \delta\Big].$$

As with the other cases considered before, by Theorem 2 there exists a finite set of linear inequalities characterizing the probability assignments so explainable.

Some necessary inequalities can be easily derived by means of Corollary 2. Let us consider a few examples (where A may be an arbitrary finite set). For simplicity, we will assume that Φ also includes basic statements of the form $S^2(a; b, c)$ and $S^3(a; b, c, d)$ themselves, where $a \in \{b, c\} \subseteq A$ and $a \in \{b, c, d\} \subseteq A$, respectively (compare Section 2; $\mathbb{P}[S^2(a; b, c)]$ and $\mathbb{P}[S^3(a; b, c, d)]$ denote the conditional probability that a belongs to the subset X selected by the subject when she is presented with $D = \{b, c\}$ or $D = \{b, c, d\}$, respectively). Now, since the universal statement $\forall x \forall y (\neg S^2(x; x, y) \leftrightarrow Byx)$ is valid in all $\mathcal{A} \in \mathcal{M}_{top}$, one immediately sees that each necessary inequality for semiorders directly leads to a corresponding inequality for the present situation. For example, substituting $1 - \mathbb{P}[S^2(b; b, a)]$ for $p(a, b)$ etc. in the inequality $p(a, b) + p(c, d) - p(a, d) - p(c, b) \leq 1$ that was listed for semiorders

---

[16]The set Φ was introduced above of being of type $\langle 3, 4 \rangle$. Although the structures in $\mathcal{M}_{top}$ are of type $\langle 3, 4, 2 \rangle$, $\mathcal{M}_{top}(A)$ is nevertheless admissible for Φ because, by definition, Φ may also be conceived as an (incomplete) set of type $\langle 3, 4, 2 \rangle$.

This example shows the flexibility of the approach presented. It allows one to choose sets $\mathcal{M}$ of theoretically well-behaved structures whose relations need not directly correspond to a possible outcome of the experiment considered. This applies not only to $\succ$, but also to the other relations involved. For example, a relation $\mathfrak{S}^2$ satisfying (28) may contain elements of the form (a, b, c) where a, b, c are pairwise distinct, whereas $S^2(a; b, c)$ does not occur in any protocol statement in Φ. Note, however, that condition (10) in Definition 1 is only required to hold for statements that belong to Φ. Concerning the distinction between theoretically defined and empirical events compare also Appendix B in Section 9.

in Table 2 yields

$$\mathbb{P}[S^2(d;d,a)] + \mathbb{P}[S^2(b;b,c)] - \mathbb{P}[S^2(b;b,a)] - \mathbb{P}[S^2(d;d,c)] \leq 1.$$

Another example is the inequality

$$\mathbb{P}[S^3(a;a,b,c)] \leq \mathbb{P}[S^2(a;a,b)],$$

By the method outlined in Section 6 this inequality can be derived from the statement $\forall x \forall y \forall z (S^3(x;x,y,z) \rightarrow S^2(x;x,y))$, which clearly is valid in all $\mathcal{A} \in \mathcal{M}_{top}$.

A notable feature of the approval voting example is that it shows how additional theoretical relations (such as the semiorders $\succ$) can be profitably brought into play in the framework discussed here.

Knowledge spaces. The range of potential applications of the present approach is surprisingly rich and includes diverse areas of mathematical psychology. Let us consider a final elementary example. Being based on *unary* relations, it is quite different in nature.

Consider a system of probabilities $\mathbb{P}[(\neg)Ta_1 \wedge \cdots \wedge (\neg)Ta_k]$ denoting the probability that subjects solve (or do not solve, respectively) items $a_1, \ldots, a_k$ out of some test which contains a finite set A of items.[17] This defines a probability assignment for A of type $\langle 1 \rangle$. In the theory of knowledge spaces (see e.g., Falmagne, Koppen, Villano, Doignon, & Johannesen, 1990) one assumes (a) that the answer given by a subject at a certain time depends on her underlying *knowledge state* (which in the present context may be conceived as a relational structure $\langle A, \mathfrak{T} \rangle$, where $\mathfrak{T} \subseteq A$ is the set of all items the subject is able to solve at that time), and (b) that only knowledge states are possible which belong to a specific *knowledge space* $\mathcal{M}$. It could, for instance, be the case that whenever a subject is able to solve a_1 and a_2, she is also able to solve a_3 (where a_1, a_2 and a_3 are specific elements of A). This is tantamount to saying that all knowledge states that belong to $\mathcal{M}$ satisfy the condition $Ta_1 \wedge Ta_2 \rightarrow Ta_3$. For each knowledge space $\mathcal{M}$, there is in fact a characteristic set Σ of conditions of that kind such that $\mathcal{M} = \mathcal{M}_\Sigma(A)$, which is to say that a knowledge state belongs to $\mathcal{M}$ if and only if it satisfies all these conditions (notice that these conditions refer to specific elements of A, i.e., they do not correspond to universal axioms as in the examples before). Clearly, if assumptions (a) and (b) are satisfied for a specific knowledge space $\mathcal{M} = \mathcal{M}_\Sigma(A)$, the resulting probability assignment $\mathbb{P}$ must be a probabilistic mixture of possible knowledge states, i.e., an $\mathcal{M}$-mixture.

By Theorem 2, probability assignments with this property are characterized by a corresponding system of linear inequalities. Again, some necessary inequalities can be routinely derived by the method described in Section 6, which is particularly easy if Φ is chosen in such a way that it includes all basic statements (i.e., all statements Ta, $a \in A$, with $\mathbb{P}[Ta]$ denoting the probability that subjects solve item a). Then, if Σ includes the condition $Ta_1 \wedge Ta_2 \rightarrow Ta_3$, say, Corollary 2 implies

---

[17]As before (e.g., individual vs social choice) this could either refer to a single subject across time (varying states) or to a population of subjects with fixed solution patterns (with varying states as well, as the case may be). The present considerations are applicable to any of these interpretations.

that (for these very items a_1, a_2, a_3) $\mathbb{P}[Ta_1] + \mathbb{P}[Ta_2] - \mathbb{P}[Ta_3] \leq 1$ is a necessary inequality for $\mathcal{M}$.

Such inequalities could be of interest in situations where only data sets based on different subtests (subsets of A) are available and where one would like to test empirically whether these data are jointly explainable by the same set of assumptions Σ, i.e. by the same knowledge space.

8. SUMMARY AND OPEN PROBLEMS

As illustrated by the various examples discussed in the chapter, for a variety of experimental situations the experimental outcome can be captured by a probability assignment $\mathbb{P} : \Phi \rightarrow [0,1]$ (on a finite set Φ of formal statements) which captures the probability with which elements of a (finite) domain A stand in certain observable relations to each other. Usually, the corresponding probabilities can be explained by an $\mathcal{M}$-mixture model if and only if they can be explained by a $\mathcal{C}$-random utility model (General Representation Theorem). Here $\mathcal{M}$ is an 'urn' of relational structures on A of the appropriate type, $\mathcal{C}$ being a suitable 'representing structure' for the structures in $\mathcal{M}$ in the sense of the representational theory of measurement. Noncoincident random utility models correspond to cases where all the representations are isomorphic embeddings, whereas unrestricted random utility models correspond to cases where the representations are homomorphic embeddings. While every $\mathcal{C}$-random utility model is equivalent to some $\mathcal{M}$-mixture model, the converse need not always be true.

It was further shown that (for fixed sets A and Φ) the empirical content of each such model is described by a finite set of linear inequalities which the values $\mathbb{P}[\phi]$, $\phi \in \Phi$, must satisfy, and that *some* of the linear inequalities implied by such a model can be derived by an easy general method.

The great number of potential applications of these comparatively simple results was illustrated by various examples (see in particular Corollary 1, Table 1, Table 2, Section 7). In these and other cases the determination of an optimal system of linear inequalities that captures the empirical content of the model under consideration, amounts (for fixed Φ and $\mathcal{M}$) to the task of characterizing an associated polytope. While the General Characterization Theorem in Section 6 guaranteed the *existence* of such finite systems of linear inequalities, the *concrete specification* of such facet-defining inequalities for individual cases has been outside the scope of this paper.

An important feature of the probabilistic models considered here is that they are *distribution-free*. In many substantive applications of such models additional distributional assumptions will play an important role. Of course, the results described before *mutatis mutandis* also apply to such restricted $\mathcal{M}$-mixture and $\mathcal{C}$-random utility models. From a geometrical perspective, the introduction of distributional constraints amounts to cutting away parts of the original polytope associated with the corresponding distribution-free model (where the result may or may not be a polytope itself). The necessary inequalities for the distribution-free model, which characterize the original polytope, naturally remain *necessary* testable conditions for such stronger models, whereas the sufficiency of the set of inequalities considered in the General Characterization Theorem is lost. Note in passing that many probabilistic conditions discussed in the literature are in fact *not* implied by the distribution-free models considered here. An example is the condition $\mathbb{P}[Baa] = 1/2$ which follows from Equation 1 when the restriction $a \neq b$ is dropped; in the context of $\mathcal{M}$-mixture models this equation amounts to an additional *distributional assumption* (see Heyer & Niederée, 1989). The same goes for other *observable properties* in the sense of Luce and Suppes (1965), such as product rules and various forms of stochastic transitivity. As with most 'observable' properties considered in probabilistic measurement theory, the problem of developing rigorous *statistical tests*, based on frequency data, which allow one to test systems of linear inequalities associated with $\mathcal{M}$-mixture models is, to our knowledge, still an important open problem.

Let us return to the topics discussed in this paper for a final remark. Our present account referred to *finite* sets A of objects. From a theoretical perspective – e.g. from a measurement-theoretic viewpoint – infinite situations should be considered, too. In fact, similar results can be obtained for *infinite* sets A with the help of methods of probabilistic logic. In this connection measure extensions (of the kind mentioned in Footnote 7) play a central role. An account of probabilistic measurement for the infinite case based on such methods will be provided in a separate paper (Heyer & Niederée, 1997).

9. APPENDICES

Appendix A. *Relation between the present approach and Heyer and Niederée (1992).* The concept of a probability assignment introduced in Section 2 generalizes the concept of a *probabilistic relational structure of type* $\langle k_1, \ldots, k_m \rangle$ as introduced in Heyer and Niederée (1992). If Φ is the set of all basic statements of the form $R^j a_1 \ldots a_{k_j}$ $(j = 1, \ldots, m)$, and if $\mathbb{P}$ is a probability assignment on Φ, then for each j a k_j-ary probabilistic relation on A in the sense of Heyer and Niederée (1992) is defined by $\mathcal{R}^j(a_1, \ldots, a_{k_j}) := \mathbb{P}[R^j a_1 \ldots a_{k_j}]$, the resulting system $\langle A; R^1, \ldots, R^m \rangle$ being a probabilistic structure. Conversely, the latter defines a probability assignment on Φ. In this sense, the basic concepts and key results of Heyer and Niederée (1989, 1992) are included as special cases of those presented here.

However, the present approach is more general. First, it allows one to consider 'incomplete' sets Φ, which correspond to partially defined probabilistic structures. Second, and more importantly, the present approach includes cases where probabilities are also assigned to conjunctions of basic statements, or more generally, to Boolean combinations thereof, whereas probabilistic relations refer only to basic statements, as it were.

It is worth noting that cases involving conjunctions and other sentential connectives could in principle also be subsumed under the approach of Heyer and Niederée (1992). (The conjectures to the contrary found at the end of Section 8 of Regenwetter, 1996, rely on a misconception of how this could be accomplished.) To this end, one would have to introduce suitable additional probabilistic relations on A. One generally applicable, though often somewhat cumbersome, method is to expand the probabilistic structure considered by including for each type of statement $\phi(a_1, \ldots, a_q)$ one is interested in (with $a_1, \ldots, a_q$ varying over A) a new q-ary probabilistic relation R_ϕ on A (with $R_\phi(a_1, \ldots, a_p) := \mathbb{P}[\phi(a_1, \ldots, a_q)]$). In the approval voting example in Section 2, this would for instance mean that one probabilistic relation is introduced for statements of the form $Sa_1 \wedge \cdots \wedge Sa_n$, another one for statements of the form $\neg Sa_1 \wedge Sa_2 \wedge \ldots Sa_3$, and so on and so forth.

Notice further that in Heyer and Niederée (1992), noncoincident $\mathcal{C}$-random representations were called 'strict', and that the concept of an $\mathcal{M}$-mixture was defined in such a way that the classes $\mathcal{M}$ are allowed to include structures with arbitrary domains (e.g.: class of all orders; since only structures with domain A are actually taken into account, this is merely a notational variant, though).

Appendix B. *An implicit independence assumption involved in mixture models.* As pointed out in Section 2, in most applications the values $\mathbb{P}[\phi]$ correspond to conditional probabilities. If this is made explicit in terms of a corresponding probability space, it turns out that a hidden independence assumption comes into play. Let us illustrate this with the concept of a binary choice system induced by rankings (see Section 3). A 'sample space' Ω would have to be introduced here which corresponds to possible 'states of the world' relevant to the experiment and which, for each pair (a, b) of elements out of A ($a \neq b$), allows one to distinguish the following events: O_{ab} (the set of all $\omega \in \Omega$ with the 'outcome' Bab), E_{ab} (the set of all $\omega \in \Omega$ where the objects a, b are presented) and T_{ab} (the set of all $\omega \in \Omega$ where the subject possesses an ordering $\succ$ with $a \succ b$). The theoretical considerations underlying Equation 2 imply that $\omega \in E_{ab} \Rightarrow (\omega \in O_{ab} \Leftrightarrow \omega \in T_{ab})$ for all $\omega \in \Omega$, i.e. $O_{ab} \cap E_{ab} = T_{ab} \cap E_{ab}$. This implies that $\mathbb{P}[Bab] := \Pr(O_{ab}|E_{ab}) = \Pr(T_{ab}|E_{ab})$. Equation 2, in contrast, is tantamount to $\mathbb{P}[Bab] = \Pr(T_{ab})$. To reconcile these two equations, one has to assume that $\Pr(T_{ab}|E_{ab}) = \Pr(T_{ab})$, i.e., that the events T_{ab} and E_{ab} are independent. Loosely speaking, this means that the experiment does not change the underlying state (ordering) of the subject. These considerations directly extend to arbitrary $\mathcal{M}$-mixture models as introduced in this paper.

Appendix C. *Proofs for Claims 1–3 in Remarks 2, 4 and 5.*

Proof of Claim 1 (Remark 2). Assume a family $\langle U_a \mid a \in A \rangle$, A finite, on some probability space $\langle \Omega, \mathcal{F}, P \rangle$ to be given that satisfies Equation 14. Let $\mathcal{G}$ be the finite subset of $\mathcal{F}$ that contains all sets of the form $\{\omega \mid U_a(\omega) > U_b(\omega)\}$. An equivalence relation $\approx$ on Ω can then be defined by letting $\omega_1 \approx \omega_2$ if and only if ω_1 and ω_2 belong to the same sets in $\mathcal{G}$. Let $[\omega]$ denote the equivalence class of ω w.r.t. $\approx$. Clearly, for each $\omega \in \Omega$ the equivalence class $[\omega]$ is the intersection of all elements of $\mathcal{G}$ which contain ω; hence all of these equivalence classes belong to $\mathcal{F}$ and there is only a finite number of such classes. We can now consider the finite probability space $\langle \Omega', \mathcal{F}', P' \rangle$ where Ω' is the set of all equivalence classes, $\mathcal{F}' = \mathcal{S}(\Omega')$, and P' is the probability measure on $\mathcal{F}'$ determined by $P'(\{[\omega]\}) := P([\omega])$. To define the new random variables, choose one element $\rho_{[\omega]}$ out of each class $[\omega]$ and let $U_a'([\omega]) := U_a(\rho_{[\omega]})$ for all $\omega \in \Omega$ and all $a \in A$. It is routine to show that this family is a family of real random variables on the probability space $\langle \Omega', \mathcal{F}', P' \rangle$ and that Equation 14 is satisfied. Furthermore, noncoincidence is satisfied by the U_a''s if it is fulfilled by the U_a's.

To extend this proof to the more general situation considered in *Remark 4*, one just has to replace the sets $\{\omega \mid U_a(\omega) > U_b(\omega)\}$ with the subsets of Ω referred to in Equation 18, along with the sets $\{\omega \mid U_a(\omega) \neq U_b(\omega)\}$ ($a \neq b$) if noncoincident families are considered. (Here Remark 3 becomes relevant.)

Proof of Claim 2 (Remark 2). Assume a finite probability space $\langle \Omega', \mathcal{F}', P' \rangle$ and a family $\langle U_a' \,|\, a \in A \rangle$ with the desired properties to be given. With no loss of generality we may assume that $\mathcal{F}' = \mathcal{S}(\Omega')$. Consider now an arbitrary measurable space $\langle \Omega, \mathcal{F} \rangle$ with an infinite $\mathcal{F}$. By a standard argument one can assign to each $\omega' \in \Omega'$ an element $F_{\omega'}$ of $\mathcal{F}$ such that the family $\langle F_{\omega'} \,|\, \omega' \in \Omega' \rangle$ is a partition of Ω. Select for each ω' an element $\kappa_{\omega'}$ of $F_{\omega'}$ and let $P(F) := P'(\{\omega' \in \Omega' \,|\, \kappa_{\omega'} \in F\})$ for each $F \in \mathcal{F}$. Clearly, then, P is a probability measure on $\mathcal{F}$. Finally define for each $a \in A$ a mapping $U_a : \Omega \to \mathbb{R}$ by setting $U_a(\omega) := U_a'(\omega')$ whenever $\omega \in F_{\omega'}$. Again it is routine to show that the U_a''s are measurable and thus real random variables, and that they satisfy Equation 14. Noncoincidence is satisfied by the U_a's if it is fulfilled by the U_a''s.

This proof, too, straightforwardly extends to the general case considered in *Remark 4.*

Proof of Claim 3 (Remark 5). Assume $\langle U_a \,|\, a \in A \rangle$ is a noncoincident $\mathcal{C}$-random representation of $\mathbb{P}$ w.r.t. the probability measure P. To show the existence of a strongly noncoincident random representation, consider the set $\Omega' := \bigcap_{a \neq b} \{\omega \in \Omega \,|\, U_a(\omega) \neq U_b(\omega)\} \in \mathcal{F}$. By noncoincidence it follows that $P(\Omega') = 1$. Choose an arbitrary element ω_0 out of Ω' and define $U_a'(\omega) = U_a(\omega)$ if $\omega \in \Omega'$, and $U_a'(\omega) = U_a(\omega_0)$ otherwise. It is routine to show that the family $\langle U_a' \,|\, a \in A \rangle$ has the desired properties.

Choice, Decision, and Measurement
A. A. J. Marley (Ed.),
©Lawrence Erlbaum Associates, NJ, 1997.

ON SUBJECTIVE INTENSITY AND ITS MEASUREMENT

LOUIS NARENS

University of California, Irvine

ABSTRACT. Threshold functions and subjective estimations of ratios and differences are a few examples from a class of psychological functions that can be conceptualized as functions from a set of stimuli onto itself. This paper analyzes axiomatically the structural properties of a broad subset of such functions, with an emphasis on general properties of their psychological processing. Measurement-theoretic representation and uniqueness results are derived for Weber's Law, ratio magnitude estimation, and a version of Luce's Possible Psychophysical Laws. An explanation is also provided for the experimental findings of W. Torgerson and others that indicates a *qualitative* identity between subjective estimation of ratios and subjective estimation of differences.

1. INTRODUCTION

In many paradigms in psychophysics and other areas of psychology, a subject's behavior can often be idealized as sets of functions from a set of stimuli onto itself. Two examples from psychophysics are (i) threshold functions F_p on X, where $1 > p > .5$ and for each x in X, $F_p(x)$ is the stimulus such that if y has more of the physical attribute than $F_p(x)$, then the proportion of time y is judged subjectively more intense than x is $> p$; and (ii) ratio estimation functions G_r on X such that for each x and y in X, $y = G_r(x)$ if and only if the subject judges y as being r times as intense as x. Functions from X onto itself that result from subjects' responses to instructions are called *behavioral,* and this chapter presents an axiomatic treatment of behavioral functions that result from responses involving a subject's evaluation of subjective intensities of stimuli. One main result is a characterization of situations where for a nonempty set $\mathcal{B}$ of behavioral functions there exists a mapping of the stimuli into the positive reals such that each element of $\mathcal{B}$ is represented as a multiplication by a positive real. This result is used to characterize axiomatically a generalization of the psychophysical power law. Another result provides a new perspective for Luce's (1959b) seminal research on possible psychophysical laws.

As a motivation for the kind of modeling and theory developed in this chapter, consider the following important and puzzling empirical finding of Torgerson (1961).

Key words and phrases. Psychophysics, subjective intensity, ratio estimation, difference estimation, Weber's law, power law, psychophysical law.

Acknowledgments. Research for this chapter was supported by the NSF grant SBR-9520107 to the Department of Cognitive Sciences, University of California, Irvine.

Address for correspondence: Louis Narens, Department of Cognitive Sciences, University of California Irvine, Irvine, CA 92697. Email: lnarens@vmsa.oac.uci.edu

The situation turns out to be much the same in the quantitative judgment domain. Again, we have both distance methods,
where the subject is instructed to judge subjective differences between stimuli, and ratio methods, where the subject is instructed to
judge subjective ratios. Equisection and equal appearing intervals
are examples of distance methods. Fractionation and magnitude
estimation are examples of ratio methods.

In both classes of methods, the subject is supposed to tell us
directly what the differences and ratios are. We thus have the possibility of settling things once and for all. Judgments of differences
take care of the requirements of the addition commutative group.
Judgments of ratios take care of the multiplication commutative
group. All we need to show is that the two scales combine in the
manner required by the number system. This amounts to showing
that scales based on direct judgments of subjective differences are
linearly related to those based on subjective ratios.

Unfortunately, they are not. While both procedures are subject to internal consistency checks, and both often fit their own
data, the two scales are not linearly related. But when we plot
the logarithm of the ratio scale against the difference scale spaced
off in arithmetic units, we usually do get something very close to
a straight line. Thus, according to the subject's own judgments,
stimuli separated by equal subjective intervals are also separated
by approximately equal subjective ratios.

This result suggests that the subject perceives or appreciates
but a single quantitative relation between a pair of stimuli. This
relation to begin with is neither a quantitative ratio or difference,
of course – ratios and differences belong only to the formal number
system. It appears that the subject simply interprets this single
relation in whatever way the experimenter requires. When the
experimenter tells him to equate differences or to rate on an equal
interval scale, he interprets the relation as a distance. When he is
told to assign numbers according to subjective ratios, he interprets
the same relation as a ratio. Experiments on context and anchoring
show that he is also able to compromise between the two. (*pp.
202–203*)

For the purposes of this chapter, Torgerson's conclusion may be restated as
follows: There is a function Ψ that maps stimuli in X into sensations of a subject.
When asked for kinds of difference judgments the subject responds in accordance
with a subjective difference function on the set of sensations $\Psi(X)$; and when asked
for kinds of ratio judgments the subject responds in accordance with a subjective
ratio function on the same set of sensations $\Psi(X)$. Torgerson's empirical studies
indicate that each difference function is a ratio function and visa versa. But, why
should this be the case? That is, under what kinds of general conditions about
subjective processing of stimuli should we expect a result like this?

By "general conditions" I mean conditions or principles that apply to many different kinds of phenomena, and not conditions specific to particular experimental paradigms or the data they generate. They should be construed as conditions or principles like the laws of physics. Einstein's Principle of Relativity is a particularly good example of what I call a "general condition."

A general condition that drives many of the mathematical results of this paper is that the sensations in $\Psi(X)$ are processed "homogeneously": that is, the sensations in $\Psi(X)$ are processed in a manner that does not distinguish *individual* elements of $\Psi(X)$. A precise statement of "homogeneity" is given later in the chapter. It is often a consequence of concepts used routinely in science. For example, whenever one is in a situation where there is a set of isomorphisms from an underlying qualitative structure into a numerical one that forms a ratio, interval, or ordinal scale, the underlying qualitative structure is homogeneous.

The axiomatizations presented in this chapter are designed to explain why we observe what we observe; they are not constructed to be slick descriptions of what is observed. Because of this, when there are axioms about both observables and mental phenomena, the axioms about observables are by design very weak. Great care is taken throughout the chapter to separate what is being assumed to be observed about the stimulus, what is being assumed to be observed about the subject's responses, and what is theoretically taking place in the mental processing of the subject in producing his or her responses to instructions and stimuli.

The intent of the chapter is to show how fairly simple and plausible assumptions about the production of psychophysical functions combine to produce powerful results about observable relationships. Discussions of these results in terms of the empirical literature are brief and generally limited to issues raised by the above quotation of Torgerson.

2. PRELIMINARIES

The following definitions and conventions are observed throughout this chapter:

Definition 1. $\mathfrak{Y} = \langle Y, U_1, U_2, \ldots \rangle$ is said to be a *structure* if and only if Y is a nonempty set, called the *domain* of $\mathfrak{Y}$, and each U_i is either an element of Y, a set of elements of Y, a relation on Y, a set of relations on Y, a set of sets of relations on Y, etc. $Y, U_1, U_2, \ldots$ are called the *primitives* of $\mathfrak{Y}$.

$\mathbb{R}$ denotes the set of reals and $\mathbb{R}^+$ the set of positive reals.

A *scale* on a nonempty set Y is a nonempty set of functions $\mathcal{F}$ onto a subset R of $\mathbb{R}$.

$\mathcal{F}$ is said to be a *ratio scale* if and only if (1) $\mathcal{F}$ is a scale and the range of each element of $\mathcal{F}$ is a subset of $\mathbb{R}^+$, and (2) for any f in $\mathcal{F}$,

$$\mathcal{F} = \{rf | r \in \mathbb{R}^+\}.$$

$\mathcal{F}$ is said to be an *interval scale* if and only if (1) $\mathcal{F}$ is a scale, and (2) for any f in $\mathcal{F}$,

$$\mathcal{F} = \{rf + s | r \in \mathbb{R}^+ \text{ and } s \in \mathbb{R}\}.$$

$\mathcal{F}$ is said to be an *ordinal scale* if and only if (1) $\mathcal{F}$ is a scale and the range of each element of $\mathcal{F}$ is a subset of $\mathbb{R}^+$, and (2) for any f in $\mathcal{F}$,

$$\mathcal{F} = \{g * f | g \text{ is a strictly increasing function from } \mathbb{R}^+ \text{ onto } \mathbb{R}^+\},$$

where $*$ is the operation of function composition.

Note that the definitions of ratio and ordinal scales in Definition 1 are more restrictive than usually given in the literature; in particular, the ranges of the elements of ratio and ordinal scales are required to be subsets of $\mathbb{R}^+$.

Definition 2. A *theory of measurement* consists of a precise specification of how a scale $\mathcal{F}$ of functions is formed. The theory of measurement used throughout this chapter is a variant of the *representational theory of measurement*. This variant says that a scale $\mathcal{F}$ on a set Y results by providing a structure of primitives $\mathfrak{Y}$ with domain Y and a numerical structure $\mathfrak{N}$ with domain either $\mathbb{R}^+$ or $\mathbb{R}$ such that $\mathcal{F}$ is a set of isomorphisms of $\mathfrak{Y}$ onto $\mathfrak{N}$.

In the representational theory, elements of a scale $\mathcal{F}$ are often called *representations*.

Note that the variant of the "representational theory" given in Definition 2 is more restricted than the theory of measurement presented in Krantz, Luce, Suppes, & Tversky (1971) in that it requires (1) elements of $\mathcal{F}$ to be isomorphisms (instead of homomorphisms), and (2) the range of elements of $\mathcal{F}$ to be *onto* (instead of *into*) either $\mathbb{R}^+$ or $\mathbb{R}$.

Definition 3. A structure $\mathfrak{Y}$ is said to be *ratio* (respectively, *interval, ordinal*) *scalable* if and only if it has a ratio (respectively, interval, ordinal) scale of isomorphisms onto some numerical structure.

Definition 4. A structure $\langle X, \succsim \rangle$ is said to be a *continuum* if and only if it is isomorphic to $\langle \mathbb{R}^+, \geq \rangle$.

The definition of "continuum" given in Definition 4 is not qualitative. A famous qualitative characterization of "continuum" was given by Cantor (1895). (See pp. 31–35 of Narens, 1985).

Definition 5. $\langle X, \succsim, \oplus \rangle$ is said to be a *continuous extensive structure* if and only if $\langle X, \succsim, \oplus \rangle$ is isomorphic to $\langle \mathbb{R}^+, \geq, + \rangle$.

The definition of "continuous extensive structure" given in Definition 4 is not qualitative. Qualitative axiomatizations of it can be given (e.g., combining qualitative axiomatization of "continuum" with an axiomatization of "extensive structure," for example, the axiomatization of "closed extensive structure" given in Chapter 3 of Krantz et al., 1971).

Definition 6. Isomorphisms of a continuous extensive structure $\langle X, \succsim, \oplus \rangle$ onto $\langle \mathbb{R}^+, \geq, + \rangle$ are often called *additive representations*.

The following is a well-known theorem of representational measurement theory:

Theorem 1. *The set of additive representations of a continuous extensive structure forms a ratio scale.*

3. Basic Axioms

The primitives for the basic axioms consist of *physical primitives* and *behavioral primitives*. The physical primitives capture some of the physical relationships inherent in the stimuli used in the experiment. The behavioral primitives capture, in terms of the stimuli, some of the important psychological structure inherent in the subject's responses to instructions and stimuli. Both the physical and behavioral primitives are assumed to be observable.

The physical primitives in this chapter will consist of a nonempty set of stimuli, X, a total ordering $\succsim$ on this set of stimuli, and occasionally a binary operation $\oplus$ on X called a *concatenation* operation. Most of the results of the chapter rely on the primitives X and $\succsim$. (Because many sets of stimuli considered in psychology have natural behaviorally induced total orderings on them, the results of this paper that do not use the concatenation operation $\oplus$ often extend to behavioral situations based on stimulus sets with such orderings.)

The *behavioral primitives* in this chapter consist of the set of stimuli, X, and one or more functions, $B_1, B_2, \ldots$, on X. (Cases of infinitely many B_i are allowed.)

Note that the set of stimuli X is considered both a physical and a behavioral entity.

The physical and behavioral primitives are assumed to be observable. They make up the *behavioral-physical structure,* which has the form

$$\langle X, \succsim, B_1, B_2, \ldots \rangle$$

or if the physical concatenation operation $\oplus$ is relevant, the form

$$\langle X, \succsim, \oplus, B_1, B_2, \ldots \rangle .$$

The following are two examples of behavioral functions:

(1) *Direct Ratio Estimation:* The subject is given stimuli from X and is asked for each such stimulus x to select a stimulus y from X such that "y is s times as intense as x." A function $y = R_s(x)$ on X results.

(2) *Direct Difference Estimation:* The subject is given stimuli from X and is asked for each such stimulus to select a stimulus y from X such that "the difference of y and x in intensity is s." A function $y = D_s(x)$ on X results.

The usual numerical representation of the behavioral function R_s is the function that is multiplication by the number s. I find this practice strange, unfounded, and non-rigorous. Unfortunately, it is a widely used practice in the behavioral and social sciences, and many important findings depend on it. In this chapter, a much weaker version of representing R_s by a multiplication (not necessarily multiplication by s) is pursued. (This issue is also discussed in Narens, 1996a.)

Definition 7. Let $\mathfrak{X}$ be the behavioral physical structure

$$\langle X, \succsim, B_1, B_2, \ldots \rangle .$$

Then a function β from $\mathfrak{X}$ onto $\mathbb{R}^+$ is said to be a *multiplicative representation* for $\mathfrak{X}$ if and only if the following two statements are true:

(a) For each x and y in X,

$$x \succsim y \text{ iff } \beta(x) \geq \beta(y) .$$

(b) For each B_i there exists a positive real r_i such that for all x and y in X,

$$y = B_i(x) \text{ iff } \beta(y) = r_i \cdot \beta(x).$$

Note that in Definition 7, no mention is made about how the behavioral primitives were obtained; in particular, the real number r_i in Statement 2 does not depend on whether B_i was obtained through direct ratio estimation or direct difference estimation.

Definition 8. Let $\mathfrak{X}$ be the behavioral-physical structure

$$\langle X, \succsim, B_1, B_2, \ldots \rangle .$$

Then two multiplicative representations β and γ for $\mathfrak{X}$ are said to be *equivalent* if and only if for each B_i there exists a positive real r_i such that for all x and y in X,

$$y = B(x) \text{ iff } \beta(y) = r_i \cdot \beta(x) \text{ iff } \gamma(y) = r_i \cdot \gamma(x).$$

In particular, note that by Definition 8, if β is a multiplicative representation of $\mathfrak{X}$, then $r\beta$ is an equivalent multiplicative representation of $\mathfrak{X}$ for each positive real r. As is indicated in the discussion following Theorem 2 below, there are examples of behavioral-structures that have equivalent multiplicative representations β and γ such that for all positive reals r, $\beta \neq r\gamma$.

Similar definitions hold for a *difference representation* for $\mathfrak{X}$ and *equivalent difference representations* for $\mathfrak{X}$.

The *Basic Axioms*, which are about the behavioral-physical structure

$$\langle X, \succsim, B_1, B_2, \ldots \rangle ,$$

consist of the following three axioms:

Axiom 1 (Physical Axiom). $\langle X, \succsim \rangle$ *is a continuum (Definition 4).*

Axiom 2 (Behavioral Axiom). *Each B_i is a function from X onto X.*

Axiom 3 (Behavioral-Physical Axiom). *For each B_i and each x and y in X,*

$$x \succsim y \text{ iff } B_i(x) \succsim B_i(y).$$

Axioms 1 to 3 are indeed very basic, saying very little of mathematical or psychological substance.

4. WEBER'S LAW AND THE GENERALIZED POWER LAW

The Basic Axioms are not sufficient for establishing the existence of a multiplicative representation for the behavioral-physical structure. This section considers a particularly simple, observable, behavioral-physical condition that together with the Basic Axioms implies the existence of multiplicative representations. The additional behavioral-physical condition uses the physical concatenation operation $\oplus$. (Narens, 1996a, provides observable behavioral conditions that implies the existence of multiplicative representations without using any physical structure beyond the ordering $\succsim$.)

Definition 9. Assume $\langle X, \succsim \rangle$ is a continuum (Definition 4). A function B from X onto X is said to be a *threshold function* on X if and only if (1) for all x and y in X,

$$x \succsim y \text{ iff } B(x) \succsim B(y),$$

and (2) for all x in X,

$$B(x) \succ x.$$

The "threshold interpretation" of B in Definition 9 is that for each x in X, $B(x)$ is the element of X such that for all elements y of X, if $y \succ B(x)$, then the subject according to some behavioral criteria is able to discriminate y as being more intense than x, and for all elements z of X, if $B(x) \succ z$, then the subject is not able according to the behavioral criteria to discriminate z as being more intense than x.

Threshold functions are often represented by Weber representations:

Definition 10. Assume B is a threshold function on the continuum $\langle X, \succsim \rangle$ and c is a positive real number. Then φ is said to be a *Weber representation* for $\langle X, \succsim, B \rangle$ with *Weber constant* c if and only if φ is an isomorphism of $\langle X, \succsim \rangle$ onto $\langle \mathbb{R}^+, \geq \rangle$ such that for all x and y in X,

$$y \succ B(x) \text{ iff } \frac{\varphi(y) - \varphi(x)}{\varphi(x)} > c.$$

Suppose φ is a Weber representation for $\langle X, \succsim, B \rangle$ with Weber constant c. Then it easily follows that $1 + c$ is a multiplicative representation for $\langle X, \succsim, B \rangle$. Conversely suppose $\langle X, \succsim, F \rangle$ has a multiplicative representation as a multiplication $k > 1$. Then it easily follows that $\langle X, \succsim, F \rangle$ has a Weber representation with Weber constant $k - 1$.

The following theorem shows that each threshold function has a Weber representation, and therefore by the above observation, each threshold function has a multiplicative representation.

Theorem 2. (Existence Theorem). *Suppose B is a threshold function on the continuum$\langle X, \succsim, \rangle$. Then for some $c > 0$, $\langle X, \succsim, B \rangle$ has a Weber representation with Weber constant c.*

Proof. Theorem 5.3 of Narens (1994). □

The corresponding uniqueness theorem for Theorem 2 is a consequence of Theorem 4.1 of Narens (1994). The latter also shows that $\langle X, \succsim, B \rangle$ has Weber representations γ and θ with the same Weber constant c such that for all $r \in \mathbb{R}^+$, $\gamma \neq r\theta$. Thus $\langle X, \succsim, B \rangle$ also has multiplicative representations β and δ such that $\beta \neq r\delta$ for all $r \in \mathbb{R}^+$.

Weber's Law consists of much more than having a Weber representation: Weber's Law results when the stimuli have been measured priory in terms of a standard physical representation φ, and then *with respect to* φ, a Weber representation results. Thus for Weber's Law to hold for a threshold function B, a particular kind of compatibility between B and the physical structure is needed for φ to also be a multiplicative representation of the behavioral-physical structure. Theorem 4 below is one method of formulating the needed compatibility in terms of observables.

Note that Theorem 4 also provides for simultaneous Weber Law representations for several threshold functions.

Theorem 3. (Generalized Power Law Theorem). *Assume Axioms 1 to 3. Suppose $\oplus$ is a physical operation and φ is an additive representation for $\langle X, \succsim, \oplus \rangle$. Suppose the following (observable) psychophysical axiom: For all B_i and all x and y in X,*

$$B_i(x \oplus y) = B_i(x) \oplus B_i(y).$$

Then the following two statements are true:

(a) *(Existence) φ is a multiplicative representation for behavioral-physical structure*

$$\langle X, \succsim, B_1, B_2, \ldots \rangle.$$

(b) *(Uniqueness) Let β be a multiplicative representation for*

$$\mathfrak{X} = \langle X, \succsim, B_1, B_2, \ldots \rangle.$$

Then there exists a multiplicative representation γ of $\mathfrak{X}$ that is equivalent to β and a positive real number t such that for each x in X,

$$\gamma(x) = \varphi(x)^t. \tag{1}$$

Furthermore, if $\mathfrak{X}$ is ratio scalable, then γ in Equation 1 is $r\beta$ for some positive real r.

The following is an immediate consequence of Theorem 3 and the above discussion about the relationship of multiplicative representations and Weber representations:

Theorem 4. (Existence Theorem). *Assume the hypotheses of Theorem 3. Suppose that for each B_i and each x in X, $B_i(x) \succ x$. Then for each B_i, there exists a positive real c_i such that φ is a Weber representation for B_i with Weber constant c_i.*

5. COGNITIVE AXIOMS

The *cognitive primitives* consist of a subset S of sensations, a binary relation $\succsim'$ on S, and additional primitives, $T_1, T_2, \ldots$, which may be first-order (e.g., subsets of S, relations on S) or higher-order (sets of relations on S, relations between relations on S and elements of S, etc.) The cognitive primitives are theoretical in nature and presumed to be unobservable to the experimenter. Also, it is not assumed that all these primitives are observable to the subject in the sense that he or she is capable of becoming aware of each of them. $\mathfrak{S} = \langle S, \succsim', T_1, T_2, \ldots \rangle$ is called the *structure of cognitive primitives*. Axioms about $\mathfrak{S}$ will provide a theory that is used to relate the observable behavioral functions B_i to non-observable processing of instructions presented to the subject.

Definition 11. Throughout this paper Ψ will denote a primitive relation. Axiom 4 below will establish that Ψ is a function from X onto S. Since X is both physical and behavioral, Ψ is considered to be both a *cognitive-physical* and a *cognitive-behavioral* primitive.

Axiom 4 (Cognitive-Physical Axiom). Ψ *is a function from X onto S.*

Axiom 5 (Cognitive-Physical Axiom). *For all x and y in X,*

$$x \succsim y \text{ iff } \Psi(x) \succsim' \Psi(y).$$

It is an immediate consequence of Axioms 1, 4, and 5 that the function Ψ^{-1} exists.

$\succsim'$ is intended to be an ordering consistent with subjective intensity. It is not assumed that for all x and y in X with $x \succ y$, $\Psi(x) \succ' \Psi(y)$ is phenomenologically observable by the subject. Indeed, for different x and y sufficiently close in terms of the $\succsim$ ordering, one might want as a theoretical axiom that they are not distinguished phenomenologically in terms of subjective intensity.[1]

The following cognitive-behavioral axiom describes how a stimulus item is processed in terms of an instruction to the subject and the structure $\mathfrak{S}$. For purposes of exposition, the instruction is specialized to a form of a direct ratio or difference estimation. The axiom and the results that depend on it extend to a wide variety of instructions.

Axiom 6 (Cognitive-Behavioral Axiom). *Let I be an instruction given to the subject. It is assumed that I is of one of the following two forms: (1) the ratio instruction, "Find y in X such that y is p times as intense as the stimulus presented;" or (2) the difference instruction, "Find y in X such that the difference in intensity between y and the presented stimulus is p." Then there exists a cognitive function F_I that is produced by an algorithmic procedure using only S and primitives of $\mathfrak{S}$ such that for each stimulus x in X, if x is presented to the subject, then the subject responds by selecting y in X, where*

$$y = \Psi^{-1}[F_I(\Psi(x))].$$

Furthermore, it is assumed that each primitive behavioral function B of behavioral-physical structure results from such a cognitive function, i.e., there exists an instruction J such that for all x and y in X,

$$y = B(x) \text{ iff } \Psi(y) = F_J(\Psi(x)).$$

The intuition for Axiom 6 is as follows: When given instruction I and presented with stimulus x, the subject responds with y. The subject does this by implementing I as a function F_I on S, which he or she applies to $\Psi(x)$ to yield $F_I(\Psi(x))$, which happens to be $\Psi(y)$. The implementation of I as F_I is carried out by an algorithmic procedure that involves some of the primitives $\{S, \succsim', T_1, T_2, \dots\}$. Different instructions J may give rise to different algorithmic procedures, which may involve different primitives of $\{S, \succsim', T_1, T_2, \dots\}$. It is explicitly assumed that each such implemented function is algorithmic in terms of primitives of $\mathfrak{S}$.

The notion of "algorithm" intended here is much more general than the ones ordinarily encountered in computer science – the latter being usually a form of Turing computability or some equivalent. (Turing computability is too restrictive,

---

[1] An example of this is to have one of the cognitive primitives, say T_1, a semiorder (Luce, 1956) that is phenomenologically observable by the subject, and have $\succsim'$ be the total ordering that is induced by T_1.

since it can only apply to situations that are encodable into arithmetic, and $\Psi(X)$ cannot be appropriately so encoded, because $\Psi(X)$ has greater cardinality than that of the set of natural numbers.)

It should be noted that the proofs of results employing Axiom 6 use much weaker conditions than those needed for this general concept of "algorithm"–namely, that the functions F_I in Axiom 6 have precise mathematical descriptions in terms of the primitives of $\mathfrak{S}$. Thus, in particular, the results of this chapter that depend on Axiom 6 are valid for any *formal* concept of "algorithm" appropriate to the situation described in Axiom 6.

Definition 12. Let $\mathfrak{Y} = \langle Y, W_1, \ldots, W_n \rangle$ be a structure. Isomorphisms of $\mathfrak{Y}$ onto itself are called *automorphisms.* $\mathfrak{Y}$ is said to be *homogeneous* if and only if for each x and y in Y there exists an automorphism α of $\mathfrak{Y}$ such that $\alpha(x) = y$.

Axiom 7. $\mathfrak{S}$ *is homogeneous.*

I admit that because of the abstract nature of the above definition of "homogeneity," Axiom 7 looks more like arcane mathematics than substantive psychology. However, homogeneity is a logical consequence of concepts and hypotheses used routinely throughout psychophysics, and more generally throughout science. For example, many important cases in science involve ratio, interval, or ordinal scales. When such scales can be justified through the representational theory of measurement, homogeneity is a consequence:

Suppose $\mathfrak{Y}$ is a qualitative structure with domain Y, $\mathfrak{N}$ is a numerical structure with domain N, and $\mathcal{M}$ is the scale of isomorphisms of $\mathfrak{Y}$ onto $\mathfrak{N}$ (Definition 2). The following is a necessary condition for $\mathcal{M}$ to be a ratio, interval, or ordinal scale:

For each x in Y and r in N there exists β in $\mathcal{M}$ such that $\beta(x) = r$.   (2)

Assume Equation 2. It immediately follows from the definition of "automorphism" that for all γ and δ in $\mathcal{M}$, $\delta^{-1} * \gamma$ is an automorphism of $\mathfrak{Y}$. Let x and y be arbitrary elements of Y, and let γ be an element of $\mathcal{M}$. By Equation 2, let δ in $\mathcal{M}$ be such that

$$\delta(y) = \gamma(x).$$

Then $y = \delta^{-1} * \gamma(x)$, where $\delta^{-1} * \gamma$ is an automorphism of $\mathfrak{Y}$. Since x and y are arbitrary elements of Y, it has been shown that $\mathfrak{Y}$ is homogeneous.

By arguments similar to the above, it is easy to establish that $\mathfrak{Y}$ is homogeneous if and only if Equation 2 holds. In most scientific applications, the primitives of $\mathfrak{Y}$ would correspond to observable relations and Equation 2 would be a consequence of generalizations and idealizations of observed facts about the primitives. However, because of principled lack of knowledge about the cognitive relations $T_1, T_2 \ldots$, a corresponding strategy cannot be adopted for the cognitive structure $\mathfrak{S}$. Instead, general assumptions about $\mathfrak{S}$ are needed. In psychology this is often done by making scale type assumptions about numerical interpretations of subjects' responses without direct reference to the structure $\mathfrak{S}$. For example, a subject's ratings of intensities of items are often assumed to be a portion of a function from a ratio scale (or interval scale) without giving any indication of what is being assumed about the psychological system and how that is related to the numerical interpretations of responses that justifies this feat of measurement.

Intuitively, the condition of homogeneity is saying that from the point of view of the primitives of a structure, *individually* each element of the domain looks like each other element. This does not mean that for a pair of elements (or triple, etc.) that one element of the *pair* (triple, etc.) must look like the other element of the *pair,* (triple, etc.); for example, for the pair $\{\Psi(x), \Psi(y)\}$ of $\mathfrak{S}$, $\Psi(x)$ may be $\succ' \Psi(y)$, but if this is the case, then certainly $\Psi(y)$ is not $\succ' \Psi(x)$. In Chapter 4 of Narens (1996b), the following result is shown: If $\mathfrak{Y}$ is homogeneous, then for each predicate $P(x)$ that is defined in terms of the primitives of $\mathfrak{Y}$ and pure mathematics, if $P(a)$ holds for some element a in the domain of $\mathfrak{Y}$, then $P(b)$ holds for all elements b in the domain of $\mathfrak{Y}$. This result shows that clearly in terms of "predicates defined in terms of the primitives of $\mathfrak{Y}$ and pure mathematics" that each element of the domain looks like each other element. Narens (1996b) also shows that when the primitives of $\mathfrak{Y}$ are finite in number, this condition of all elements of the domain looking like each other for predicates defined in terms of the primitives of $\mathfrak{Y}$ and pure mathematics is logically equivalent to $\mathfrak{Y}$ being homogeneous.

Axioms 1 to 7 yield the following existence theorem:

Theorem 5. *Assume Axioms 1 to 7. Then there exists a multiplicative representation for* $\langle X, \succsim, B_1, B_2, \ldots \rangle$.

6. EMPIRICAL CONSIDERATIONS

Assume Axioms 1 to 7. Suppose $\{B_1, B_2, \ldots\} = \{R_1, R_2, \ldots\} \cup \{D_1, D_2, \ldots\}$, where $R_1, R_2, \ldots$ are direct ratio judgments and $D_1, D_2, \ldots$ are direct difference judgments. Then by Theorem 5, a multiplicative representation ρ for

$$\langle X, \succsim, R_1, R_2, \ldots \rangle$$

exists that is also a multiplicative representation for

$$\langle X, \succsim, D_1, D_2, \ldots \rangle .$$

This is consistent with the empirical findings of Torgerson (1961) discussed earlier.

Recall that Torgerson (1961) made the following observation about his findings:

> This result suggests that the subject perceives or appreciates but a single quantitative relation between a pair of stimuli. ... It appears that the subject simply interprets this single relation in whatever way the experimenter requires. (*p. 203*)

It appears to me that this observation is little more than a restatement of the empirical findings in cognitive terms, and therefore it should not be taken as an "explanation," because it lacks reason as to why "the subject simply interprets this single relation in whatever way the experimenter requires." In contrast Axioms 1 to 7 supply a reason: The subject uses a single homogeneous structure for forming his or her responses to instruction and stimulus inputs. The singleness of the structure is always achievable, e.g., if the subject employed $\langle \Psi(X), \succsim', U_1, U_2, \ldots \rangle$ for direct ratio estimations and $\langle \Psi(X), \succsim', V_1, V_2, \ldots \rangle$ for direct difference estimations, then he or she could employ the single structure

$$\langle \Psi(X), \succsim', U_1, U_2, \ldots, V_1, V_2, \ldots \rangle$$

for both. Thus it is the homogeneity of the (resulting) single structure that is the important consideration.

It is worthwhile to note that Torgerson's findings and his "observation" are also consistent with Axioms 1 to 6 and the assumption that the subject is employing a non-homogeneous structure for forming his or her responses to instruction and stimulus inputs. Because of these considerations, I take Axioms 1 to 7 to be substantively different from his "observation." Also, Axioms 1 to 7 are consistent with a wider range of direct estimation results than are obtainable by the kinds of analysis employed by Torgerson: Torgerson's method of representing direct estimation functions rely on representing them numerically in terms of the numbers and the kinds of estimation referred to in the instructions; e.g., the behavioral function that results from the instruction, "Estimate twice the stimulus presented," as the numerical function that is multiplication by 2. Theorem 5 does not require a strict relationship between numerical representations and the instructions that generated them; e.g., the above behavioral function that is multiplication by 2 may equally well be represented by the numerical function that is multiplication by 3.

Torgerson's empirically based conclusion that "The subject perceives or appreciates but a single quantitative relation between a pair of stimuli," is consistent with a number of empirical studies. In a review of the topic, Birnbaum (1982) writes,

> In summary, for a number of social and psychophysical continua, judgments of "ratios" and "differences" can be represented by the same comparison operation. If it is assumed that this operation is subtraction, the J_R function (for magnitude estimation of "ratios") can be approximated by the exponential, and the J_D function (for ratings of "differences") is approximately linear. ... In other words, judgments of "ratios" and "differences" are consistent with the proposition that the *same* operation underlies both tasks, but they do not permit specification of what that operation might be. (*p. 413*)

An important consideration in Axiom 6 is that the algorithms can be mathematically specified entirely in terms of primitives of $\mathfrak{S}$ and instructions. Thus if the mathematical specification of an algorithm depends in an essential way on individual elements of $\Psi(X)$, then, by the way Axiom 6 is formulated, these elements must be primitives of $\mathfrak{S}$. Axiom 7 keeps this from happening, for if an element a of $\Psi(X)$ is a primitive of $\mathfrak{S}$, then for each automorphism γ of $\mathfrak{S}$, $\gamma(a) = a$, and therefore $\mathfrak{S}$ cannot be homogeneous. Thus keeping the above relationship between Axioms 6 and 7 intact, it could happen that for paradigms that produce behavioral functions (of one input variable), Axioms 1 to 7 are valid, but for more complicated paradigms producing behavioral functions of several input variables, Axioms 1 to 5 and the appropriate modification of Axiom 6 to functions of several variables may be valid, but Axiom 7 fails because some of the algorithms in the modified version of Axiom 6 use inputed stimuli in essential ways in their mathematical specifications, i.e., the cognitive system uses "context" (the imputed stimuli) as well as the structure $\mathfrak{S}$ to produce algorithms for the more complicated behavioral functions of several variables.

Although Axioms 4 to 7 cannot be tested directly, the axiom system consisting of Axioms 1 to 7 is potentially falsifiable through tests of its consequence, the conclusion of Theorem 5. Because one would ordinarily be involved in situations where one believed Axioms 1 to 3 to be reasonable generalizations and idealizations, the empirical failure of the conclusion of Theorem 5 could be taken as a refutation of the conjunction of Axioms 4 to 7. The conclusion of Theorem 5 is testable by both quantitative and qualitative means: quantitatively by testing whether there is a multiplicative representation for $\mathfrak{X}$, and qualitatively by testing one of the following two qualitative consequences of it:

(1) For all primitive behavioral functions B_i and B_j of $\mathfrak{X}$ and all stimuli x in X,

$$B_i * B_j(x) = B_j * B_i(x),$$

where $*$ denotes function composition.

(2) For all primitive behavioral functions B_i and B_j of $\mathfrak{X}$ if $B_i(x) \succ B_j(x)$ for some x in X, then $B_i(y) \succ B_j(y)$ for all y in X.

7. THE POSSIBLE PSYCHOPHYSICAL POWER LAW

Luce (1959b) presented a theory that related hypotheses involving the scale types of the independent and dependent variables of a quantitative psychophysical function with its the mathematical form. The following is an application of one of his results:

Theorem 6. *Assume Axioms 1 to 6. Suppose the physical structure $\langle X, \succsim, \oplus \rangle$ has a ratio scale $\mathcal{U}$ of isomorphisms onto $\langle \mathbb{R}^+, \geq, + \rangle$ and the cognitive structure $\mathfrak{S}$ has a ratio scale of isomorphisms $\mathcal{V}$ onto a numerical structure with domain $\mathbb{R}^+$. Suppose for each φ in $\mathcal{U}$ there exists θ in $\mathcal{V}$ such that for all x in X,*

$$\Psi(\varphi(x)) = \theta(\Psi(x)). \tag{3}$$

Then there exists $r \in \mathbb{R}^+$ such that for all $\varphi \in \mathcal{U}$ and $\theta \in \mathcal{V}$ there exists $s \in \mathbb{R}^+$ such that for all x in X,

$$\theta(\Psi(x)) = s\varphi(x)^r. \tag{4}$$

The conclusion of Theorem 6 describes a power relation between an observable representation φ of the physical dimension of stimuli and a non-observable representation θ of a psychological dimension of sensations. The representation θ and the scale $\mathcal{U}$ are theoretical in nature; they are not assumed to be cognitive constructs of the subject.

In performing a direct estimation task, say estimating ratios of subjective intensities, one might theorize that the subject is using some cognitively constructed numerical function ξ from a ratio scale on $\Psi(X)$ as a basis for his or her responses, e.g., the subject selects stimulus $\Psi(y)$ as twice as intense as $\Psi(x)$ if and only if $\xi(\Psi(y)) = 2\xi(\Psi(x))$. Foundationally, there are grave difficulties with this account, because ξ, a cognitively constructed function assigns entities of pure mathematics – numbers – to sensations, which means that the mind mentally represents parts of pure mathematics as *pure mathematics,* a view that is metaphysically at odds with most current psychological theorizing. This kind of difficulty is avoided by saying that ξ is a function from $\Psi(X)$ onto an algebraic system of mental entities that is isomorphic to a fragment of the real number system. But even with this modification the problem still persists about the nature of the construction of the function ξ.

Axiom 6 provides an alternative to the use of cognitively constructed numerical-like functions like ξ: In Axiom 6, the instruction I causes the subject to relate a response sensation $\Psi(y)$ to the sensation $\Psi(x)$ of each stimulus x by an algorithmic process describable in terms of primitives of $\mathfrak{S}$. This process is viewed as a function C_I on $\Psi(X)$. An important contrast between the functions ξ of the previous paragraph and C_I is that C_I is the description in terms of sensations all possible results of a *single* instruction I, whereas ξ is used to describe in terms of sensations all possible results of *all* instructions. Axiom 6 does not assume that the *set* C of all cognitive functions resulting from all instructions given to the subject is cognitively accessible or cognitively organized in a manner such that it can be employed to mimic the uses of the function ξ in the previous paragraph. Because of these considerations, the process described in Axiom 6 appear to me to be a fundamentally weaker cognitive process than one that uses a numerical-like measurement function like ξ in carrying out instructions.

Axiom 8. *The physical structure* $\mathfrak{P} = \langle X, \succsim, \oplus \rangle$ *is a continuous extensive structure (Definition 5), and for each automorphism α of $\mathfrak{P}$ there exists an automorphism γ of $\mathfrak{S}$ such that for each x in X,*

$$\Psi(\alpha(x)) = \gamma(\Psi(x)).$$

Axiom 8 states a form of harmony between physics and psychology. It is similar to the principle of the "invariance of the substantive theory" of Luce (1959b) for a psychophysical functions with independent and dependent variables from ratio scales, except that it is qualitative and makes no reference to the scale type of the dependent variable (i.e., the scale type of $\mathfrak{S}$). Luce (1990b) revised his 1959 theory of possible psychophysical functions. The revised theory is formulated qualitatively in terms of automorphisms of structures that measure the independent and dependent variables of a function of a single variable. Axiom 8 is very close in spirit to principles employed by Luce (1990b), but is technically different in that the dependent variable may assume scale types not covered in Luce (1990b).

Assume Axiom 8. Then by Theorem 1, $\mathfrak{P} = \langle X, \succsim, \oplus \rangle$ has a ratio scale of isomorphisms onto $\langle \mathbb{R}^+, \geq, + \rangle$. From this it is an easy consequence that $\mathfrak{P}$ is homogeneous. The following lemma is an easy consequence of the homogeneity of $\mathfrak{P}$:

Lemma 1. *Assume Axioms 4 and 5. Then Axiom 8 implies Axiom 7.*

Theorem 7. *Assume Axioms 1 to 6 and Axiom 8. Then the Generalized Power Law holds, i.e., the following three statements are true:*

(a) (Qualitative Formulation) *For all behavioral primitives B_i of $\mathfrak{X}$ and all x and y in X,*

$$B_i(x \oplus y) = B_i(x) \oplus B_i(y).$$

(b) (Existence: Quantitative Formulation) *By Axiom 8 let φ be an additive representation of $\langle X, \succsim, \oplus \rangle$. Then φ is a multiplicative representation for the behavioral structure*

$$\mathfrak{X} = \langle X, \succsim, B_1, B_2, \ldots \rangle.$$

(c) (Uniqueness: Quantitative Formulation) *Suppose γ is a multiplicative representation for the behavioral structure*

$$\mathfrak{X} = \langle X, \succsim, B_1, B_2, \ldots \rangle.$$

By Axiom 8 let φ be an additive representation of $\langle X, \succsim, \oplus \rangle$. Then there exist a multiplicative representation β for $\mathfrak{X}$ that is equivalent to γ and there exists a positive real number t such that for all x in X,

$$\beta(x) = \varphi(x)^t.$$

Furthermore, if $\mathfrak{S}$ is ratio scalable, then for some positive real r, $\beta = r\gamma$.

8. EMPIRICAL CONSIDERATIONS

Because of the non-observable nature of Axioms 4, 5, 6, and 8, they cannot be tested directly. However, the axiom system consisting of Axioms 1 to 6 and Axiom 8 is potentially falsifiable through tests of various of its consequences. Because one ordinarily would be involved in situations where one believed Axioms 1 to 3 to be reasonable generalizations and idealizations, the falsification of a conclusion of Axioms 1 to 6 and Axiom 8 could be taken as a refutation of the conjunction of Axioms 4, 5, 6, and 8. Thus, in particular, by Lemma 1 the conjunction of Axioms 4, 5, 6 and 8 is potentially falsifiable through the tests discussed earlier of the axiom system consisting of Axioms 1 to 7. The following lemma provides a basis for additional ways of potentially falsifying the conjunction of Axioms 4, 5, 6, and 8:

Lemma 2. *Assume Axioms 1 to 6 and Axiom 8. Then each automorphism of the physical structure $\langle X, \succsim, \oplus \rangle$ is an automorphism of the behavioral-physical structure*

$$\langle X, \succsim, \oplus, B_1, B_2, \ldots \rangle.$$

Let φ be an additive representation of $\langle \mathfrak{X}, \succsim, \oplus \rangle$. It is assumed that the experimenter has access to a highly accurate empirical rendering of φ. Let B_i be one of the behavioral primitives $B_1, B_2, \ldots$, and let a and b be distinct elements of X such that it is observed that $b = B_i(a)$. Let

$$r = \frac{\varphi(a)}{\varphi(b)}.$$

Then it is a an easy consequence of Lemma 2 that for each x and y in X,

$$\text{If } \frac{\varphi(x)}{\varphi(y)} = r, \text{ then } y = B_i(x). \tag{5}$$

Equation 5 is testable. By the discussion preceding Lemma 2, tests of Equation 5 are also tests of the conjunction of Axioms 4, 5, 6, and 8.

9. CONCLUSIONS

The observable Axioms 1 to 3 about behavioral functions are very weak mathematically, and from the perspectives of behavioral psychophysics, they can be considered as minimal. The non-observable cognitive-physical Axioms 4 and 5 linking the observable ordered structure of stimuli $\langle X, \succsim \rangle$ to an unobservable structure of sensations $\langle \Psi(X), \succsim' \rangle$ are also very weak mathematically. On the surface, Axiom 4, which says a stimulus x from X presented to the subject produces within him or her a sensation $\Psi(x)$, appears to be obvious and have minimal psychological content. However, implicit in the axiom is that *each time* x is presented the *same* sensation $\Psi(x)$ is produced within this subject. This is clearly an assumption that has more than minimal psychological content. For example, for the paradigms discussed in this chapter, it is implicit in Axiom 4 that the sensation produced in the subject by stimulus x when the subject is presented x and instruction $\boldsymbol{I}$ is the same sensation produced when the subject is presented x and instruction $\boldsymbol{J}$. Thus as an idealization, Axiom 5 is more than "minimal" in psychological content.

The cognitive Axioms 6 and 7 provide considerable mathematical content. Axiom 6 is a general theory about the cognitive processing of instructions, and Axiom 7 is a theoretical hypothesis about the non-observable cognitive structure of sensations $\mathfrak{S}$ that the subject uses in his or her responses to instructions. Axiom 7 may be viewed as a cognitive version of a consequence of many prominent quantitative psychophysical models.

The ideas behind the axiomatization, Axioms 1 to 7, as well as the ideas behind the proof of its consequence, Theorem 5, are flexible, and are applicable to a wide range of psychophysical phenomena. Because other applications may involve different primitives, appropriate changes in the physical, behavioral, and behavioral-physical axioms may have to be made. Also the cognitive Axiom 6 may have to be changed to reflect the new behavioral primitives. This could be accomplished by an appropriate instantiation of the following principle inherent in Axiom 6: "The cognitive correlates of the behavioral primitives can be viewed as relations that are algorithmic in terms of the cognitive structure of primitives." However, the cognitive-behavioral Axioms 4 and 5 and the cognitive Axiom 7 could remain the same.

The power of the theorems presented in this chapter is largely due to the behavioral primitives being limited to functions of a single variable. Such functions, if required to remain invariant under rich sets of transformations, necessarily have highly restricted mathematical forms. As discussed in the following section, Axiom 6 requires a cognitive correlate C of a primitive behavioral function B to be invariant under the automorphisms of $\mathfrak{S}$, and thus, because by Axiom 7 $\mathfrak{S}$ has a rich set of automorphisms, it follows (from Axioms 4 and 5) that B must also be invariant under a rich set of transformations. In settings with primitives that are functions of more than two variables, this line of argument is greatly weakened. For the case of functions of two variables, it still yields interesting results (see, for example, the discussion of homogeneous concatenation structures in Luce & Narens, 1985).

10. METHODS OF PROOF

Details of proofs are not presented in this chapter. There are three main theorems: Theorems 3, 5 and 7. Theorem 3 follows by applying the remarks just after Theorem 5.5 of Narens (1994) to several threshold functions. The proof of Theorem 7 relies on Theorem 5 and the method of proof of Theorem 3. Thus what is both mathematically and conceptually the most important theorem, and from the point of view of the proof the most novel, is Theorem 5. The following are the key ideas of its proof:

Let I be an instruction given to the subject. By Axiom 6, I produces a cognitive function C_I from $\Psi(X)$ onto itself that is algorithmic in terms of primitives of $\mathfrak{S}$. Assume C_I is different from the identity function on $\Psi(X)$. By Axiom 7, $\mathfrak{S}$ is homogeneous. Because C_I is algorithmic in terms of the primitives of $\mathfrak{S}$, it follows from results of Chapter 4 of Narens (1996b) that C_I is invariant under the set $\mathcal{A}$ of automorphisms of $\mathfrak{S}$; that is, for all α in $\mathcal{A}$ and all u and v in $\Psi(X)$,

$$v = C_I(u) \text{ iff } \alpha(v) = C_I(\alpha(u)). \tag{6}$$

That Equation 6 holds for all elements of $\mathcal{A}$ is used to derive additional algebraic conditions on $\mathcal{A}$. (These are described in Chapter 7 of Narens, 1996b). In terms of the "homogeneity-uniqueness classification" of Narens (1981a, 1981b), $\mathfrak{S}$ is homogeneous and either is 1-point unique or satisfies a special variety of ∞-point uniqueness. The algebraic conditions on $\mathcal{A}$ are then used to produce a scale of isomorphisms S of $\mathfrak{S}$, and Equation 6 is used to derive the numerical form of the representation of C_I for each element of S. Because the instruction I also produces a behavioral function B (related to C_I by $y = B(x)$ iff $\Psi(y) = C_I(\Psi(x))$), φ and the numerical characterization of C_I by elements of S can be used to represent and characterize B numerically. Theorem 5 results by repeating the process for each instruction, using the same scale of isomorphisms S.

Choice, Decision, and Measurement
A. A. J. Marley (Ed.),
©Lawrence Erlbaum Associates, NJ, 1997.

A GEOMETRIC APPROACH TO TWO DIMENSIONAL MEASUREMENT

MICHAEL V. LEVINE AND SHERMAN TSIEN

University of Illinois and ADAMS (Algorithm Design and Measurement Services)

ABSTRACT. Some recent measurement results and basic concepts from differential geometry are applied herein to two dimensional probabilistic latent variable models. The purpose of the chapter is to introduce a strategy for using unidimensional methods to study two and higher dimensional data sets.

Each latent variable model is associated with a manifold. Curves in a model's manifold are approximated by fitting one dimensional models to data. This paper shows how fitted one dimensional curves can be used to select an appropriate multidimensional model.

The data sets motivating this work are formed by sampling people. Each sampled person is asked a standard set of questions. The answers to each question are dichotomous, or can be easily made dichotomous.

Vocational interest inventory data exemplify the data we seek to understand. Each year 4,200,000 young adults answer a standard set of questions about their vocational interests when they complete ACT's UNIACT interest inventory (Swaney, 1995, p. 1). Each inventory question or item describes an activity. Each response is one of "like", "dislike", or "indifferent."

Our approach is intended to be broadly applicable. Instead of vocational interest data, other data formed by eliciting a vector of qualitative responses from a large number of sampled individuals might have been used. Examples include ability or achievement measurement data, cognitive, attitudinal or personality survey data, census data, and reliability testing data.

1. OVERVIEW

Latent variable models are used to define manifolds. Linear (vector) models and quadratic (ideal point) models are treated in detail. The submodel theorem (Levine, 1995) provides the mathematical rationale for our reduction of multidimensional models to unidimensional models. Section 2, which is best skipped on first reading, states the submodel theorem and relates it to similar measurement results.

Key words and phrases. Item response theory, dimensionality, manifold, latent variable modeling, vocational interests, vector model, ideal point model, unfolding.

Acknowledgments. The work reported here is part of a continuing team effort. J. Douglas Carroll, George Henly, Michael Levine, Sherman Tsien, Bruce Williams, and Michael Zickar are making fundamental contributions to this project. Except where noted the results reported here were obtained primarily by Levine and Tsien. We gratefully acknowledge support from National Science Foundation grant SBR-9515038.

Address for correspondence. M. V. Levine, 905 Shurts St, Urbana, IL 61801. Email: m-levine@ux1.cso.uiuc.edu

In Section 3, vector and ideal point models are defined by functional equations and related to contemporary models for vocational interests. Section 4 contrasts the geometry of vector models and ideal point models.

Section 5 introduces tangents. Tangents are needed to translate the geometric statements about unobserved latent variables (Section 4) into objective statements referring only to observed quantities and quantities that can be accurately estimated.

Section 6 contains pilot, proof-of-concept calculations with simulation data. The calculations in Section 6 illustrate basic concepts and demonstrate that our multidimensional nonparametric methods may be practical, even with the sample sizes ordinarily used for unidimensional measurement.

The analysis in this paper is nonparametric and "item-level." The alternative (referenced in Section 3) analyses of vocational choice group related items into separately scored scales. Item-level modeling is the limiting case of scale level modeling in which each "scale" consists of exactly one item. Our reasons for pursuing an item-level, nonparametric analysis are discussed in the Section 7.

2. SMOOTHNESS AND THE SUBMODEL THEOREM

The results in all of the other sections of this paper can be understood without reading this brief outline of related latent variable theory technical results.

The submodel theorem (Levine, 1995) asserts that smooth multidimensional latent variable models are indistinguishable from some of their unidimensional submodels. Thus, even if data have been generated by a computer simulation of a smooth multidimensional model, at least one smooth unidimensional submodel can be found that will fit the data just as well as the multidimensional simulation model.

Concrete examples of smooth multidimensional latent variable models are the ideal point and vector models described in Sections 3 and 6. Latent variable models are used to account for complex dependencies between observed random variables. Rigorous definitions and a literature review are in Holland and Rosenbaum (1986).

A latent variable model is a probability model specifying the joint distribution of several observed random variables and one hypothetical or constructed "latent" variable. In this paper, the observed random variables assume only finitely many different values ("like" and "either indifferent or dislike"). The latent variable is a number-valued or vector-valued random variable.

If the latent variable is a d-vector, the latent variable model is called d-dimensional. The set of possible values of the latent variable is called the latent space. When latent trait models are used to measure scholastic ability or achievement the latent space is usually the set of real numbers. These models are one dimensional. When latent variable models are used to measure vocational interests, the latent space usually is a subset of the real plane. These models are two dimensional.

In this paper a real-valued function defined on numbers or vectors will be called *smooth* if it has a continuous derivative. A d-dimensional latent variable model is smooth if the conditional probability of each observable outcome (i.e., value of the vector of observed random variables) is a smooth function of the latent variable.

A latent variable model is *proper* (or satisfies *propriety*) if the conditional probability of each observable outcome given the latent variable is strictly between zero and one. This implies that every logically possible observable outcome has positive probability of occurring.

Most psychometric applications of latent variable models implicitly assume propriety. The assumption of propriety enters psychometric applications via parametric assumptions. The parametric formulas for conditional probabilities used by most psychometricians have values strictly between zero and one.

In the terminology to be developed in this paper, a latent variable model is a *submodel* of a second latent variable model if its "measurement manifold" (Section 3, below) is a submanifold (Boothby, 1986, p. 75, Section 5) of the second model's manifold.

In more familiar terms, a latent variable model M is a submodel of latent variable model N if the latent space of M is a subset of the latent space of N and if for every observable outcome X and every number or vector t in the latent space of M, the conditional probability of X given t calculated using model M is the same as the conditional probability of X calculated using model N. In psychometric terms, "the item response functions of M are restrictions of the item response functions of N."

The main assumption of latent variable modeling is local independence. Local independence asserts that the observed random variables of a latent variable model are conditionally independent given the value of the latent variable.

Suppes and Zanotti (1981) (see also Holland & Rosenbaum, 1986) proved that any probability model – smooth or not, proper or not – for an experiment with finitely many possible outcomes can be reformulated as a one dimensional latent variable model. The submodel theorem has a less general hypothesis and more specific conclusion. It applies only to smooth, proper models. But it concludes that the one dimensional latent variable model will be smooth and proper. The submodel theorem asserts that a probability model for an experiment with finitely many outcomes that can be defined with a smooth, proper, d-dimensional latent variable model can also be defined with a smooth, proper, one dimensional latent variable model. Indeed, the one dimensional model can be taken to be one of the d-dimensional model's submodels.

Smoothness and propriety are important for scientific applications. Conventional numerical optimization techniques incorporated in well-tested, frequently used computer packages (e.g., MULTILOG, Thissen, 1988, or ForScore, Section 6, below) are regularly used to fit smooth, proper models to the sort of data we wish to model. We know of no practical way to fit the 2^{100} parameters of the Suppes and Zanotti models to item response data for a hundred item, vocational interest inventory.

The submodel theorem is the starting point for our strategy for understanding data that may have been generated by a multidimensional process. Put briefly, our strategy is to fit several one dimensional models to a data set that may conform to a multidimensional latent variable model. The fitted one dimensional models are then used to make inferences about the generating multidimensional model.

The submodel theorem implies that this strategy will succeed under admittedly complicated, difficult to verify circumstances. The submodel theorem implies that the strategy will succeed if enough data are available, if the data can be fit by a smooth, proper, low dimensional model, if the one dimensional model-fitting algorithm is statistically consistent, and if the one dimensional model-fitting algorithm has in its "repertoire" of models to fit to data at least one of the equivalent submodels but no equivalent models that are not submodels.

3. TWO BASIC MEASUREMENT MODELS AND THEIR MANIFOLDS

Much of latent variable modeling can be organized under two headings: vector models and ideal point models. Vector models evolved from factor analysis. Ideal point model assumptions play a central role in multidimensional scaling. Carroll (1980) reviews the history and basic results for both models from a scaling point of view. Carroll's paper also considers the relationship between vector and ideal point models.

Ideal Point Models and the RIASEC model. In an ideal point model, choices and people making choices are both represented as points in a common Euclidean space. In an ideal point model, the probability of a person choosing an object depends only on the distance between the person's point and the object's point.

The RIASEC (Realistic, Investigative, Artistic, Social, Enterprising or Conventional type) model (Holland, 1985) for vocational interests can be formulated as either an ideal point model or a vector model. This subsection presents an ideal point, item-level version of RIASEC. (Previous quantifications of RIASEC were scale-level.) Table 1 contrasts our item-level quantification with our understanding of the various scale-level versions of RIASEC (Rounds, 1995; Rounds, Tracey, & Hubert, 1992, p. 241).

Many publishing counseling psychologists consider vocations to differ along two dimensions: a Person/Thing dimension (in this paragraph referred to as α) and an Idea/Data dimension (here referred to as β). In a continuous, ideal point version of the RIASEC model such as that of Prediger and Vansickle (1992), each person completing a vocational interest questionnaire has a personal vocational ideal, represented by a pair of numbers $x = \alpha$, $y = \beta$. Each profession or professional activity referenced by an item on one of these questionnaires is represented by a pair of numbers $\langle a, b \rangle$. The probability that a person sampled from all those with $\langle \alpha, \beta \rangle = \langle x, y \rangle$ responds that s/he would like to participate in an activity referencing a vocation perceived as having $\langle \alpha, \beta \rangle = \langle a, b \rangle$ is assumed to be a function of the distance $((x - a)^2 - (y - b)^2)^{\frac{1}{2}}$ between $\langle x, y \rangle$ and $\langle a, b \rangle$. Thus the conditional probabilities of the model satisfy the following equation:

$$P_i(x, y) = \text{Probability of an affirmative response to the } i\text{th item}$$
$$\text{or question from a person randomly sampled from all}$$
$$\text{those with vocational ideal } \langle x, y \rangle$$
$$= F_i[(x - a_i)^2 + (y - b_i)^2]$$

where F_i is a smooth function. This equation is later referred to as the *ideal point functional equation*.

Contrast	Current Quantification	Proposed Quantification
Unit of analysis	Six sets of items are analyzed separately to obtain six scores for a person. Six separate scores are then combined to obtain a two dimensional geometric representation of a person.	The items for all six types – realistic, investigative, artistic, social, enterprising and conventional – are modeled simultaneously to locate persons and items in a two dimensional, person/thing, idea/data space.
Type/subtype	The scale with highest score defines type. The second and third highest scores define the subtype. Thus, there are 720 possible subtypes.	A point estimate of the location of a person's vocational ideal in the person/thing, idea/data space is computed. The point estimate $\langle \hat{\alpha}, \hat{\beta} \rangle$ is expressed in polar coordinates. "Type" is the angle component of a person's estimated vocational ideal, i.e., $\arctan(\hat{\alpha}/\hat{\beta})$. Currently we plan to use the mode of the posterior distribution of the person's vocational ideal as the point estimate. The posterior density itself defines subtype. Thus there are infinitely many possible subtypes.
Differentiation	"Differentiation means the magnitude of the difference between highest and lowest scores on the six variables [RIASEC] ... . The greater the difference between the highest and lowest of the six scores, the greater the differentiation. Graphically, the profile of a differentiated person will have high peaks and low valleys; the profile of an undifferentiated pattern will appear relatively flat." (Holland, 1973, p. 39).	Differentiation is interpreted as the modulus $(\hat{\alpha}^2 + \hat{\beta}^2)^{\frac{1}{2}}$ of a point estimate $\langle \hat{\alpha}, \hat{\beta} \rangle$ of a person's vocational ideal expressed in polar coordinates. Thus the proportional profiles in Holland's Figure 2 (Holland, 1973, p. 2) represent vocational ideals of equal type but unequal differentiation.

TABLE 1. Current and proposed RIASEC model quantifications contrasted (continued on next page).

Whereas parametric formulations of ideal point models specify the F_i functions explicitly, we do not. We are currently developing numerical algorithms for using data to approximate the F_i functions. (See Section 7 for our reasons for avoiding parametric assumptions.)

Contrast	Current Quantification	Proposed Quantification
Consistency	Holland provides a verbal description and adjective list to describe each of the six basic types. (Holland, 1973, pp. 13-18). Some pairs of types have similar descriptions; some pairs of types have conflicting descriptions. Holland specifies three levels of consistency by sorting pairs of types into a high, middle and low consistency level [Table 3, p. 22]. A set of six scores for a person is consistent if the highest scores have a high level of consistency.	The posterior distribution of the person's vocational ideal may be concentrated about a single mode, a pair of well separated modes, or diffusely distributed over a large region of the person/thing, idea/data space. Holland's notion of consistency seems to correspond to the dispersion of the posterior distribution of the counselee's vocational ideal. One measure of dispersion is the diameter of the smallest circle containing 1/3 of the posterior density.
Calculus	Persons and environments are represented in a common, two dimensional space. Angles and distances in the space lead to testable hypotheses.	Same

TABLE 1. (continued from previous page). Current and proposed RIASEC model quantifications contrasted.

Measurement Manifolds. A differentiable manifold consists of a point set and a "differential structure" formed by vectors called "tangents" (Lauritzen, 1987, Section 2, p. 167). The point set of the manifold of a measurement model is a set of vectors of conditional probabilities. The point set of the measurement manifold of a measurement model for n responses is the set of all n-vectors of probabilities $\langle \ldots, P_i(x, y), \ldots \rangle$ that can be obtained by choosing numbers x and y and substituting them in formulas for conditional probabilities. Thus the point set for an ideal point model of 30 UNIACT items satisfying the above equations with specified F_i's, a_i's and b_i's is the set of all 30-vectors $\langle \ldots, F_i[(x-a_i)^2+(y-b_i)^2], \ldots \rangle$ that can be obtained by replacing x and y by a pair of numbers in 30 formulas.

The tangents of a measurement manifold are defined after a motivating discussion (Section 4) on the geometry of ideal point and vector models.

Vector Models. Vector models have been used for choice data, including vocational choice data. In a two dimensional vector model for an n item questionnaire each counselee is represented by a pair of numbers $\langle x, y \rangle = \langle \alpha, \beta \rangle$, as in the ideal point models. As in ideal point models, each item is characterized by a pair of numbers $\langle a_i, b_i \rangle$ and a smooth function F_i. The vector model functional equation for the probability of an affirmative response to each item is given by

$P_i(x, y) =$ Probability of an affirmative response to the ith

question from a person randomly sampled from all

those with $\langle \alpha, \beta \rangle = \langle x, y \rangle$

$= F_i[a_i x + b_i y]$

where F_i is a smooth function.

The point set of the manifold of a vector model for n inventory questions is also a set of n vectors. The manifold consists of all the n vectors $\langle \ldots, P_i(x, y), \ldots \rangle$ that can be obtained by substituting numbers x and y in the above formula. The tangents of a vector model and other measurement manifold are discussed in Sections 5 and 6.

4. THE GEOMETRY OF IDEAL POINT AND VECTOR MODELS CONTRASTED

If $P_i(x, y) = F_i[(x - a_i)^2 + (y - b_i)^2]$ and the derivative F_i' is not zero at $(x_0 - a_i)^2 + (y_0 - b_i)^2$ then the greatest rate of change in P_i is obtained when one moves away from $\langle x_0, y_0 \rangle$ along the line connecting the points $\langle x_0, y_0 \rangle$ and $\langle a_i, b_i \rangle$. (The directional derivative of P_i is maximized in this direction.) Thus if $P_i(x, y)$ could somehow be evaluated in a neighborhood of $\langle x_0, y_0 \rangle$, it would be possible to find a ray pointing toward the ideal point $\langle a_i, b_i \rangle$.

The expression "ray at $\langle x_0, y_0 \rangle$" is reserved throughout this paper for line segments in R^2 of the form $\{ \langle x_0, y_0 \rangle + t \langle s_1, s_2 \rangle : 0 \leq t < 1 \}$.

Triangulation. Now consider a second and third point in the latent variable space, say $\langle x_1, y_1 \rangle$ and $\langle x_2, y_2 \rangle$. For a two dimensional ideal point model the slope of a ray of maximum increase at $\langle x_2, y_2 \rangle$ can be calculated from rays at $\langle x_0, y_0 \rangle$ and $\langle x_1, y_1 \rangle$. This follows from the fact that if $\langle x_0, y_0 \rangle$, $\langle x_1, y_1 \rangle$, and $\langle a_i, b_i \rangle$ do not lie on a line, the location of the ideal point $\langle a_i, b_i \rangle$ can be obtained as the intersection of the lines containing the maximizing rays at $\langle x_0, y_0 \rangle$ and $\langle x_1, y_1 \rangle$. A maximizing ray at $\langle x_2, y_2 \rangle$ must lie on the line connecting $\langle a_i, b_i \rangle$ and $\langle x_2, y_2 \rangle$. This relationship is summarized in Figure 1.

A Qualitative Difference between Ideal Point and Vector Models. An essential geometric difference between ideal point models and vector models concerns the angles formed by maximizing rays at different points in the latent space. In Figure 2 it is shown how the angle between the maximizing ray for item i and the maximizing ray for item j depends upon the point in the latent variable space at which the maximizing directions are computed. Thus the angle is obtuse for $\langle x_0, y_0 \rangle$ but acute for $\langle x_1, y_1 \rangle$ in Figure 2.

Constant Angles in Vector Models. The geometry of vector models is simpler than the geometry of ideal point models. If the functional equation defining a vector model is correct and if the function F_i is strictly increasing then a small motion away from $\langle x, y \rangle$ will give the largest rate of increase if it has slope $-a_i / b_i$. The rate of change will be zero if the ray has slope b_i / a_i. (These assertions can be

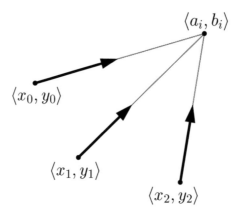

FIGURE 1. Triangulation in ideal point models.

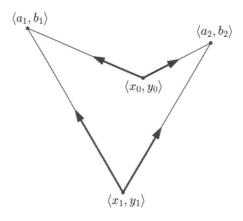

FIGURE 2. Changing angles in an ideal point model

verified by computing the partial derivatives of $P_i(x, y)$ using the vector model's functional equation.) Thus the direction of a maximizing ray at $\langle x, y \rangle$ for an item i is independent of the which point $\langle x, y \rangle$ is being considered in the latent space. Implications for data of this invariance are developed in Section 6.

5. APPROXIMATING TANGENTS WITH FITTED SUBMODELS

Tangents are used to translate the geometric statements about unobserved latent variables into statements referring only to observed quantities and quantities that can be accurately estimated. This section defines the tangents of a measurement manifold and introduces our method for using data to approximate tangents.

Tangents Defined. At each point p, say $p = \langle P_1(x_0, y_0), \ldots, P_n(x_0, y_0) \rangle$, of a measurement model manifold there is a two dimensional vector space of vectors called *tangents at p*. To introduce a notation for tangents, let $D_1 P_i(x_0, y_0)$ denote the partial derivative of P_i with respect to its first variable evaluated at $\langle x_0, y_0 \rangle$ and let $D_2 P_i(x_0, y_0) = \partial/\partial\beta P_i(x_0, y_0)$. The n-vectors $\langle \ldots, D_1 P_i(x_0, y_0), \ldots \rangle$ and $\langle \ldots, D_2 P_i(x_0, y_0), \ldots \rangle$ are tangents at p. Any linear combination of these vectors is a tangent at p. No other vector is a tangent at p.

A two dimensional model manifold has infinitely many tangents at each point p. However, if any two linearly independent tangents at p are known, then any third tangent at p can be expressed uniquely as a linear combination of these two.

Approximating Tangents with Fitted Unidimensional Models. Our strategy for approximating tangents begins with fitting a unidimensional model to data. The submodel theorem (in the context of the additional assumptions listed at the end of Section 2) implies that unidimensional model fitting computer programs can be used to estimate some differentiable real valued functions G_i $(i = 1, \ldots, n)$. The G_i will all be defined on a common interval. Furthermore, there will be a pair of differentiable real valued functions x, y defined on the same interval such that

$$G_i(t) = P_i[x(t), y(t)] \qquad (i = 1, \ldots, n)$$

for all t in the interval. Thus for any number t in the interval,

$$G_i'(t) = D_1 P_i[x(t), y(t)]x'(t) + D_2 P_i[x(t), y(t)]y'(t).$$

Thus the vector of derivatives

$$\langle \ldots, G_i'(t), \ldots \rangle = x'(t)\langle \ldots, D_1 P_i, \ldots \rangle + y'(t)\langle \ldots, D_2 P_i, \ldots \rangle$$

will be a tangent at some point $p = \langle \ldots, P_i[x(t), y(t)], \ldots \rangle$ on the manifold. Therefore, if ε is small, then the vector of difference ratios $\langle \ldots, [G_i(t + \varepsilon) - G_i(t)]/\varepsilon, \ldots \rangle$ will approximate a tangent at $p = \langle \ldots, G_i(t), \ldots \rangle$.

In sum, we approximate tangents by numerically differentiating fitted unidimensional models. The approximation is illustrated and evaluated with simulation data in Section 6. Section 6 also shows how a second, linearly independent tangent can be approximated at some points.

Null-i and max-i tangents. Two types of tangents are especially important: Tangents indicating directions of maximum rate of change and tangents indicating directions of no change of one of the n conditional probability functions P_i.

If $A = \langle A^{(1)}, \ldots, A^{(n)} \rangle$ and $B = \langle B^{(1)}, \ldots, B^{(n)} \rangle$ are tangents at p, then the tangent $C = B^{(1)}A - A^{(1)}B = \langle C^{(1)}, \ldots, C^{(n)} \rangle$ must have $C^{(1)} = B^{(1)}A^{(1)} - A^{(1)}B^{(1)} = 0$. Geometrically this means that it will be possible to move away from p in direction C without changing the first conditional probability. This assertion is made precise by Boothby (1986, Chapter IV); see also Murray and Rice (1993, Section 2.2.2) .

A non-zero tangent at p is *null-i* if its i-th component is zero. Since for two dimensional models the tangent space at p is a two dimensional vector space, if non-zero C and D are both null-i at p then for some constant k, $C = kD$. Put simply, C and D are proportional vectors.

A non-zero tangent at p is *max-i* if it is orthogonal to a null-i tangent at p. If D is a max-i tangent vector at p, then the rate of change of P_i is greatest along a curve with gradient vector D at p. For two dimensional models any two max-i tangents at p are proportional.

The geometric properties in Section 4 can be expressed as conditions on max-i and null-i tangents. This is a step forward because max-i and null-i vectors can be approximated by fitting unidimensional submodels.

6. A DEMONSTRATION EXPERIMENT

The second author has completed a series of pilot studies to evaluate the following hypotheses:

(a) One dimensional model fitting software now on hand can be applied to data generated by a two dimensional mechanism to estimate one dimensional submodels.

(b) The sample sizes generally used for one dimensional nonparametric latent variable modeling are large enough for the purposes of this project.

(c) Even with crude numerical differentiation techniques, the angle constancy of the vector model can be demonstrated in data generated by a two dimensional vector model.

Tsien's Simulation Data. Tsien simulated a vector model by sampling pairs of numbers $\langle x, y \rangle$ uniformly distributed over the disk in R^2 centered at the origin and having radius one. Three thousand $\langle x, y \rangle$ pairs were sampled. For each $\langle x, y \rangle$ pair, thirty zeros and ones were generated. The first of these thirty was one with probability $P_1(x, y)$; the second was one with probability $P_2(x, y)$; the third, with probability $P_3(x, y)$; etc.

In Tsien's vector model studies, $P_i(x, y) = F_i[a_i x + b_i y]$. Each F_i was linear (in one set of studies) or logistic (in a replication of the linear studies). In Tsien's ideal point model studies $P_i(x, y) = F_i[(x - a_i)^2 + (y - b_i)^2]$ with $F_i(t)$ proportional to $\exp\{-t^2/2\}$.

ForScore. ForScore is a suite of unidimensional model fitting programs that has been in continuous development for fifteen years. ForScore constructs a unidimensional latent trait model to fit sampled item responses. ForScore has been successfully applied hundreds of times to simulation and actual data sets (Drasgow, Levine, Tsien, Williams, & Mead, 1995; Drasgow, Levine, Williams, McLaughlin, & Candell, 1989; Levine, Drasgow, Williams, McCusker, & Thomasson, 1992). Bruce Williams has written the code for the current version of ForScore. Williams and Levine have collaborated on the design and development of the ForScore's numerical optimizations. James O. Ramsay (1991, 1993) and Fumiko Samejima (1984) have proposed alternative strategies for fitting nonmonotonic latent variable models. We prefer ForScore because it is easily adapted to large, complicated data sets. A general description of ForScore's computation follows.

ForScore first uses heuristics to select a set of continuous differentiable functions on the interval $[-3, +3]$. ForScore represents one dimensional conditional probability functions as linear combinations of 12 (± 5, depending on the application) of these differentiable functions. For any specification of 30×12 numbers and unidimensional latent variable distribution, the probability of sampling the sample of 3,000 30-vectors can be calculated by a numerical integration. The conditional probability of sampling a particular vector of zeros and ones $\langle u_1, \ldots, u_{30} \rangle$ given unidimensional latent variable value t is

$$\prod_{1 \leq i \leq n} G_i(t)^{u_i} [1 - G_i(t)]^{1 - u_i},$$

where $G_i(t)$ is the conditional probability of an affirmative response to item i. The unconditional probability of the vector $\langle u_1, \ldots u_{30} \rangle$ is

$$\int_{[-3,3]} \prod_{1 \leq i \leq n} G_i(t)^{u_i} [1 - G_i(t)]^{1 - u_i} d\mu(t),$$

where μ is a probability distribution on $[-3, 3]$, which in one dimensional nonparametric latent trait theories is arbitrary. (The distribution of the latent variable is arbitrary and unidentifiable because

$$\int_{[-3,3]} \prod_{1 \leq i \leq n} G_i(t)^{u_i} [1 - G_i(t)]^{1 - u_i} d\mu(t) =$$

$$\int_{[-3,3]} \prod_{1 \leq i \leq n} G_i[\vartheta(t)]^{u_i} \{1 - G_i[\vartheta(t)]\}^{1 - u_i} d\mu[\vartheta(t)]$$

for any continuous, invertible transformation ϑ of $[-3, 3]$ onto $[-3, 3]$.) The *sample likelihood function* for a particular sample of 3,000 30-vectors is the product of the 3,000 individual probabilities, each of which is a function of 30×12 parameters.

ForScore searches for 30×12 numbers that make the probability of the data (i.e., the sample likelihood function) as large as possible. Thus ForScore maximizes a bounded, continuous non-negative function over a subset of $R^{30 \times 12}$.

ForScore's optimization is constrained to a convex, compact subset of $R^{30 \times 12}$ by a set of linear inequalities. The linear inequalities express conditions on the conditional probability functions. Some a priori conditions (e.g., conditional probabilities are non-negative) are always used. Optional linear inequalities and equations can be used to further restrict ForScore's search space. In earlier applications of ForScore, linear equations and inequalities have been used to force ForScore to find the best fitting monotonic, S-shaped, smooth, unimodal, concave or convex functions.

Tsien used constraints to find alternative, equally well-fitting unidimensional models for each of his data sets. On half of his ForScore runs Tsien imposed the constraints $G_i(-3) = G_i(+3)$ for $i = 1, \ldots, n$. On the other half of his ForScore runs he did not set these constraints.

In sum, ForScore accepts as input vectors of zeros and ones. ForScore returns conditional probability functions G_i for a unidimensional latent variable model for the zeros and ones. The conditional probability functions maximize the probability of the sample. The maximization is done over a large space of continuous functions. Constraints are used to force ForScore to fit different unidimensional models to the same data set on successive runs. For research applications of ForScore, contact Levine at m-levine@ux1.cso.uiuc.edu

Tests of Key Components of the Strategy with Simulation Data. The submodel theorem implies that under a complex set of conditions that will be only approximated in actual data, ForScore's estimated models will approximate a unidimensional submodel of a multidimensional model. To get an idea of how ForScore would behave with the sample sizes and data structures we anticipate, Tsien applied ForScore to the 2-dimensional vector model data described above. If 3,000 is a sufficiently large sample then there will be a continuous function θ defined on ForScore's latent variable continuum $[-3, +3]$ and taking values in R^2 and satisfying the following conditions:

Smoothness condition: $\theta(t) = \langle x(t), y(t) \rangle$ for some continuous, differentiable functions x and y.

Submodel condition: The functions $x(t)$ and $y(t)$ can be chosen so that for $i = 1, \ldots, 30$ each of ForScore's fitted one dimensional conditional probability functions G_i satisfy

$$G_i(t) = P_i[x(t), y(t)] \text{ for } -3 \leq t \leq 3.$$

Equivalence condition: The theoretical probability of each of the 2^{30} vectors of zeros and ones should be the same whether it is calculated using ForScore's one dimensional model or the simulation 2 dimensional model.

Empirical tangents condition: For each latent variable value t in each of ForScore's fitted one dimensional models, the vector of derivatives of fitted unidimensional conditional probability functions $G_i(t)$ should be a tangent at some point p of the two dimensional simulation model's manifold.

Constant angle prediction: Tangents computed with ForScore should satisfy any algebraic identities that are consequences of the constant angle property of vector models described in Section 4.

Smoothness and Submodel Condition Test. 61 equally spaced points t_j between -3 and +3 on ForScore's continuum were studied. For each t_j value a pair of numbers x_j, y_j were selected to minimize the distance in R^{30} between ForScore's vector of 30 conditional probabilities and the simulation model's conditional probabilities. The points $\langle x_j, y_j \rangle$ traced a smooth curve in the plane. The root mean square between a ForScore's vector $\langle \ldots, G_i(t), \ldots \rangle$ and the closest 2d simulation model vector of probabilities was generally less than .04.

Equivalence Condition Test. If the 2^{30} theoretical probabilities are equal for ForScore's fitted model and the simulation model, then an objective rule for deciding whether a 30-vector was obtained with the simulation model or with ForScore's model should be correct only 50% of the time in a Two Alternative Forced Choice experiment (Green & Swets, 1966, p. 44) . Conversely (Levine et al., 1992), if every statistical classification procedure has only a probability of .5 of being correct, then each of ForScore's 2^{30} probabilities are equal to its corresponding simulation model probability.

Tsien found that an optimal statistical classification rule (Levine et al., 1992), made correct classifications only about 60% of the time. Thus it is possible but hard to distinguish data generated by ForScore's model from the simulation model data.

Empirical Tangents Test. To determine whether ForScore's fitted model fits well enough to allow recovering tangents by numerical differentiation of fitted functions, Tsien used pairs of ForScore runs. The first run computed a maximum likelihood estimated unidimensional model with only the default (non-negative probabilities) constraints. The second run was additionally constrained to fit a model with conditional probability functions satisfying $G_i(-3) = G_i(3)$ $(i = 1, \ldots, 30)$.

As expected, both models passed the 3 preceding tests (Smoothness, Submodel, Equivalence). However, the $\theta: [-3, +3] \rightarrow R^2$ curves were different for the two models. The θ curve for the constrained run was a closed curve, typically with an hourglass shape. The graph of the θ curve for the unconstrained run typically had a doubled S shape. The two curves appeared to intersect transversely (i.e., with linearly independent tangents; Guillemin & Pollack, 1974, p. 30) in at least two points.

If the fitted G_i functions define a submodel of the simulation model, then for any t_j, the vector of derivatives $\langle \ldots, G_i'(t_j), \ldots \rangle$ will be a tangent at some point p on the simulation model's measurement manifold (Section 4, second subsection). Thus for small $\varepsilon > 0$ the vector of difference ratios $\varepsilon^{-1}\langle \ldots, G_i(t_j + \varepsilon) - G_i(t_j), \ldots \rangle$ should approximate a tangent at some point p.

Tsien took $\varepsilon = 0.1$. Near one of the intersections he computed

$$A = \varepsilon^{-1}\langle \ldots, G_i(t_j + \varepsilon) - G_i(t_j), \ldots \rangle.$$

The G_i functions used in the calculation were from one of the fitted ForScore estimated models. The index j was selected so that t_j was in the set $\{\langle \ldots, G_i(t), \ldots \rangle : t_j \leq t < t_j + \varepsilon\}$. Using the other set of ForScore fitted curves at the same intersection a second approximated tangent B was computed.

To evaluate ForScore's ability to recover tangents, a unit length null-1 vector at the intersection was computed using the simulation model parameters. If A and B are linearly independent tangents, then $A^{(1)}B - B^{(1)}A$ will also be null-1 (Section 5, third subsection). Since any two null-1 tangents at the intersection must be proportional, the vector computed with simulation parameters must equal $\pm(A^{(1)}B - B^{(1)}A)/|A^{(1)}B - B^{(1)}A|$.

The approximated null-1 vector and the null-1 vector computed with simulation parameters were close in R^{30}. The root mean squared difference between corresponding coordinates was typically smaller than .05. This calculation was repeated for null-i vectors $(i = 2, \ldots, 30)$ for several intersections and several simulation data sets. Theoretical tangents were generally well approximated for both vector (logistic and linear) and ideal point models. Exceptions were observed near the end points of the estimated curves.

Constant Angles Test. The geometry of vector models (Section 4) implies that the tangent spaces of a vector model will have an unusual property. If ForScore can adequately estimate tangents, then data consistent with a vector model should be recognizable from its fitted one dimensional submodels.

The angle constancy of vector models (Section 4, last subsection) implies that for each point p on the measurement manifold it will be possible to define an inner product in the tangent space at p such that relative to this inner product the angle between null-i and null-j vectors at p will be independent of p. Ideal point models do not have this property.

Tsien proceeded as follows to test for the invariance. At one of the intersections described above, he chose a pair A, B of linearly independent tangents. Each tangent X at the intersection could then be uniquely represented by a pair of numbers, $\sigma_A(X)$, $\sigma_B(X)$. The relation

$$X = \sigma_A(X)A + \sigma_B(X)B$$

defines a pair of functions on the tangent space at the intersection because A, B form a basis for the tangents at the intersection.

Tsien defined the angle of a tangent X relative to a basis A, B with the formula

$$\text{Angle}(X; A, B) = \arctan[\sigma_A(X)/\sigma_B(X)].$$

At the intersection at p Tsien chose $A = A_p$ and $B = B_p$ so that for X_i $(i = 1, 2, 3)$ null-i at p,

$$\text{Angle}(X_1; A, B) = 0°, \ \ \text{Angle}(X_2; A, B) = 90°, \ \ \text{Angle}(X_3; A, B) = 45°.$$

Such a basis choice is generally possible for 2 dimensional manifolds. Two dimensional *vector* model manifolds are special in that the three conditions – Angle(X_1; A_p, B_p) = 0°, Angle(X_2; A_p, B_p) = 90°, Angle(X_3; A_p, B_p) = 45° – imply that for each null-i X_i $(i > 3)$, Angle(X_i; A_p, B_p) will be independent of p. In other words, the tangent spaces at various points p for a vector model can be portrayed graphically so that the angle that each null-i tangent makes with the x-axis is independent of p.

Table 2 shows typical results for a test of the ability of fitted unidimensional models to detect this invariance in data. The first of the six columns is i. The second column is the null-i item's angle computed from the simulation parameters. No estimation or approximation is involved. The third column is the angle computed from an intersection of ForScore θ-curves. The submodel conditional probability functions G_i are estimated, and their derivatives are approximated. The fourth column is the angle computed from a second intersection of ForScore θ-curves. (The roles of items 3 and 5 have been interchanged to avoid forcing most angles to be less than 45°.) The 2 remaining columns are angles computed from ideal point simulation data intersections. Note the high degree of agreement in the third and fourth columns. Note that both of these empirical angles are quite close to their theoretical value in column two. This high degree of agreement was typical of Tsien's linear and logistic vector model simulations.

The fifth and sixth columns are analyses of ideal point data at two intersections. Ideal point models, unlike vector models, do not have constant angles (Section 4, second subsection). Bases were chosen in both tangent spaces to force angle equality for items 1, 5 and 10. The invariance is not expected and it is not observed. Thus this analysis may be useful for choosing between a vector model and ideal an point model representation of data.

Item	Theoretical	Vector Model 1 & 2		Ideal point 1 & 2	
1	90.0	90.0	90.0	90.0	90.0
2	0.0	0.0	0.0	95.0	107.1
3	-151.2	-156.6	-149.7	100.6	66.8
4	38.6	36.5	35.2	90.3	67.5
5	45.0	45.0	45.0	45.0	45.0
6	51.5	53.0	50.8	17.3	31.1
7	-118.1	-120.9	-121.8	-6.2	18.8
8	95.3	74.1	75.8	-16.5	17.8
9	4.4	-23.8	6.9	-16.5	2.6
10	-150.1	-151.4	-151.1	0.0	0.0
11	39.2	36.9	37.8	-4.0	-8.6
12	-134.5	-134.9	-135.1	-7.2	-12.6
13	52.1	51.7	50.5	2.7	-19.9
14	-116.8	-118.3	-121.4	-6.4	-29.1
15	101.2	74.1	101.8	12.3	-33.5
16	8.0	6.5	12.1	53.1	-35.3
17	-149.2	-150.5	-152.4	73.3	-46.3
18	39.7	38.2	38.2	97.7	-38.4
19	-134.1	-135.0	-135.2	114.9	-40.1
20	52.7	54.7	52.7	123.0	-41.2
21	-115.4	-116.7	-116.7	114.9	-39.5
22	106.3	93.4	100.5	133.0	-48.3
23	10.7	8.7	5.5	137.3	-58.3
24	-148.2	-149.4	-147.0	100.7	-25.6
25	40.1	38.5	38.8	127.4	161.7
26	-133.6	-134.0	-134.1	105.5	147.7
27	53.4	54.4	53.1	112.3	131.5
28	-114.1	-115.8	-113.8	86.4	119.4
29	114.7	128.8	119.0	94.7	107.7
30	13.9	15.2	21.6	86.2	119.4

TABLE 2. Vector model angle invariance.

Angle constancy seems to be a fundamental property of vector models, including factor analytic models. It asserts that the relative importance of each of the factors for each item is the same at every location in the latent space. Table 3 summarizes the computation involved in the verification of angle constancy.

7. WHY ITEM-LEVEL, NONPARAMETRIC MEASUREMENT

Item-level modeling takes as its unit of analysis each individual question. Scale-level modeling, by contrast, aggregates related questions into groups of items called "scales." A score is computed for each scale, usually by counting the number of affirmative or correct responses. Scale-level modeling (with factor analysis and

Subgoal	Computation
Unidimensional Model Estimation	Fit a unidimensional model to a sample of 3,000 examines. Using weak constraints fit the sample again to get a second unidimensional model.
Locate at least two intersections	Each fitted unidimensional model gives a point set in R^n $\{\langle \ldots, G_i(t), \ldots \rangle : -3 \leq t \leq 3\}$. The G_i functions are estimated with ForScore. A point in R^n is an intersection if it is in both of these sets.
Check each intersection angle	Numerically differentiate estimated G_i functions from one ForScore run to obtain an estimated tangent A. Repeat with a second set of estimated G_i to obtain a second tangent B. Compute the angle between A and B in R^n. If the intersection angle is small (less than $15°$) conditioning will be poor, and the run will give equivocal results.
Approximate null tangents at each intersection	Approximate null-i direction for a vector of estimated derivatives by the formula (ith entry of B)A-(ith entry of A)B.
Reorder the items, if necessary	Renumber the items at one of the intersections so that no two of the first three items form a small angle in R^{30}. Use the same item numbering at each intersection.
Select a convenient basis at each intersection	Choose a basis A, B at each intersection so that at each intersection Angle(null-1; A, B) = $0°$, Angle(null-2; A, B) = $90°$, Angle(null-3; A, B) = $45°$.
Interpret results	$2d$ vector model formulas imply that for $i > 3$, Angle(null-i; A, B) depends on i but not on the intersection. If for some i Angle(null-i) clearly is different at different intersections, then there is no $2d$ vector model containing item i. However, the subtest obtained by deleting item i may be $2d$ vector.

TABLE 3. Synopsis of angle constancy check calculation

multidimensional scaling) attempts to account for the statistical structure of a score-by-people data matrix. Item level modeling is the limiting case of scale level modeling in which every scale has exactly one item.

Item level analysis eliminates the need for subjective decisions about which items are related. Furthermore, as demonstrated in Section 6, item level analyses can be used to support or reject structural hypotheses without correlating discrete variables. The angle constancy test can be completed without parametric assumptions and without assuming the existence of normally distributed latent variables.

The main disadvantage of item level analysis is that it currently requires much more data and computation than scale level analyses.

Most item level modeling is parametric in the sense that the data are assumed to conform to a model that is fully specified except for a small number of numerical parameters. The parameters are estimated by fitting data.

Parametric models implicitly incorporate consequential commitments to disputed substantive issues. These include issues that counseling psychologist dispute. For example, parametric ideal point models (Section 3) implicitly assume that choices depend on Euclidean psychological distances. Gati's (1986, 1991) hierarchical models show that distance assumptions may in fact be incorrect for counseling data. (See also Fouad & Dancer, 1992, pp. 221-222, on alternative models).

Parametric vector models (Sections 3, 4) provide a second example of implicit disputed substantive assumptions. Vector models imply additivity assumptions. Ideal point and hierarchical models do not imply additivity.

The implicit inclusion of substantive assumptions complicates data analysis. A parametric model's failure to fit data well may be due to an infelicitous parameterization or due to an incorrect substantive assumption. By contrast, our nonparametric approach explicitly directs data analysis towards properties that are common to all vector models (specifically, angle invariance, Sections 4 and 6) and towards properties of all ideal point models (specifically, triangulation, Section 4).

Choice, Decision, and Measurement
A. A. J. Marley (Ed.),
©Lawrence Erlbaum Associates, NJ, 1997.

BISYMMETRY AND CONSISTENT AGGREGATION: HISTORICAL REVIEW AND RECENT RESULTS

JÁNOS ACZÉL

University of Waterloo

ABSTRACT. The problem of consistent aggregation asks, for example, whether the aggregate of maximal outputs of several producers in an industry may be determined by the aggregates of their (microeconomical) inputs through a macroeconomical production function. This turns out to be equivalent to a functional equation, that of rectangular generalized bisymmetry. Nevertheless, the two topics evolved from 1946 till now with rather little contact. We present this history and the solution of the relevant functional equation on general sets and apply the results to intervals of real numbers. Interpretation, representativity considerations, and compatibility and incompatibility examples follow.

1. INTRODUCTION

In this paper we point out that two notions, one from mathematics and statistics (though with some economics overtone), the other in (mathematical) economics and psychology, largely overlap and this helps dealing with the latter in very general (and also in quite specific) setups.

Consistency is of importance, for instance, when *aggregating* inputs and outputs of production, employment, investment, consumption, etc. in economics, responses to stimuli over subject and/or repetition, among others in psychology (to be consistent, in this paper we will always use the production model). *Bisymmetry* was originally introduced for characterization of quasiarithmetic and of quasilinear means (transforms of the symmetric or weighted arithmetic means, respectively). By a fortunate quest of mathematicians for generalization, bisymmetry eventually led to *generalized bisymmetry*, equivalent to consistent aggregation. In Sections 2 and 3 we present a short history of bisymmetry, its generalizations and of consistent aggregation, respectively.

Key words and phrases. Aggregation, consistency, incompatibility, representativity. Production, employment, investment, responses to stimuli, inputs and outputs. Cobb-Douglas and CES functions, extension, continuity. Generalized bisymmetry. Quasiarithmetic and quasilinear means. Replication invariance, population substitution, choice aggregation consistency.

Acknowledgments. This research has been supported in part by the Natural Sciences and Engineering Research Council of Canada, Grant No. CPL0169211. The author is also grateful for two referees' thoughtful reports.

Address for correspondence. János Aczél, Faculty of Mathematics, University of Waterloo, Ontario, Canada N2L 3G1. Email: jdaczel@math.uwaterloo.ca

Section 4 gives the exact announcement of results, followed in Section 5 by comments. In particular, it is shown, on examples of the most frequently used production functions, that, if the conditions appear to be too restrictive, the situation can often be remedied by extension.

Section 6 contains a generalization of the "big surprise" of consistent aggregation, namely that aggregation by addition is *inconsistent* with the usual production functions (we give also examples of *consistency*). Then the question is answered whether the aggregates can be considered as some (fictive) "*representative's*" inputs and outputs. A final section comments on the meaning, in particular for applications, of some of the results.

2. Bisymmetry and its generalizations

In this paper we discuss two concepts, *generalized bisymmetry* and *consistent aggregation*, that are in a certain sense equivalent. It is remarkable that both bisymmetry and consistent aggregation appeared (independently) for the first time in 1946, and, in the half century since, the two topics evolved on different paths and the two almost never met or knew about each other (for exceptions see Gorman, 1968; von Stengel, 1991, 1993; Aczél & Maksa, 1996; Aczél, Maksa, & Taylor, 1997).

Bisymmetry had its origin in characterizations of quasiarithmetic and quasilinear means

$$A_n(x_1, \ldots, x_n) = \varphi^{-1}((\varphi(x_1) + \ldots + \varphi(x_n)) / n) \tag{1}$$

and

$$L_n(x_1, \ldots, x_n) = \varphi^{-1}(q_1\varphi(x_1) + \ldots + q_n\varphi(x_n)) \quad (n = 2, 3, \ldots) \tag{2}$$

$(x_1, \ldots, x_n$ are in a nondegenerate real interval I; φ is a continuous and strictly monotonic function on I, φ^{-1} is its inverse; $q_1, \ldots, q_n$ are positive, $q_1 + \ldots + q_n = 1$).

The quasiarithmetic means (1) have been characterized (Kolmogorov, 1930; Nagumo, 1930) by symmetry, continuity, strict monotonicity (in each variable), "unanimity"

$$A_n(x, \ldots, x) = x \tag{3}$$

and "replicative invariance"

$$A_n(A_k(x_1, \ldots, x_k), \ldots, A_k(x_1, \ldots, x_k), x_{k+1}, \ldots, x_n) =$$
$$A_n(x_1, \ldots, x_n) \quad (k \leq n = 2, 3, \ldots). \tag{4}$$

The mathematical-statistical meaning of these properties is clear. Moreover, the condition (4) has also interpretations in economics; it has been called "population substitution" (Blackorby & Donaldson, 1984) or even "choice aggregation consistency" (Diewert, 1993).

The characterization by the (continuity, strict monotonicity and) unanimity, symmetry and replication invariance properties has, however, drawbacks also. First, (4) is a sequence of functional equations involving not one but a *sequence* $A_2, A_3, \ldots$ *of unknown functions*. Second, *it is not satisfied by the quasilinear means* L_n (see

(2)). The *bisymmetry* equation (Aczél, 1946, 1948)

$$F(F(x_{11},\dots,x_{1n}),\dots,F(x_{n1},\dots,x_{nn}))$$
$$= F(F(x_{11},\dots,x_{n1}),\dots,F(x_{1n},\dots,x_{nn})) \quad (5)$$

has neither of these flaws. We wrote here F rather than A_n exactly because it contains only one unknown function and because it is satisfied also by L_n.

Actually, the general continuous strictly monotonic solution of (5) is even more general:

$$F(x_1,\dots,x_n) = \varphi^{-1}(a_1\varphi(x_1) + \dots + a_n\varphi(x_n) + b),$$

where $a_1,\dots,a_n$ are arbitrary nonzero constants and b is an arbitrary constant (some restrictions apply to the intervals in which $x_1,\dots,x_n$ can be, compare Aczél, 1966). If the unanimity property $F(x,\dots,x) = x$ also holds and F is strictly *increasing* in each variable then $F = L_n$ with some positive $q_1,\dots,q_n$ satisfying $q_1 + \dots + q_n = 1$ and, if F is also symmetric, then $F = A_n$.

While these results have been announced and proof in the symmetric case with unanimity was given in Aczél (1946) in this generality, the details of proof for the cases without symmetry, and/or unanimity were given in Aczél (1948) just in the case $n = 2$, for the sake of simplicity. A shortcut in Fuchs (1950) and Aczél (1966) seems more difficult to apply for $n > 2$. Independently, the above statements in the case with unanimity were proved in Münnich, Maksa, and Mokken (1997) for all $n \geq 2$ by induction on n. Thus the first complete proof for $n > 2$ in the nonsymmetric unanimous case was published in Münnich et al. (1997).

Staying with $n = 2$ for the time being, a generalization, the single functional equation

$$G(F_1(x_{11},x_{12}), F_2(x_{21},x_{22})) = F(G_1(x_{11},x_{21}), G_2(x_{12},x_{22})), \quad (6)$$

containing six unknown functions (not a sequence of equations or a sequence of unknown functions as in (4)) has been solved for differentiable functions on real intervals by Hosszú (1953) and even on quite general algebraic systems under certain solvability conditions which were rather restrictive but have been gradually weakened (Aczél, Belousov, & Hosszú, 1960; Taylor, 1973, 1978). Equation (6) has been called the generalized bisymmetryequation. In view of what follows, we will refer to (6) as *the 2×2 generalized bisymmetry equation.*

Finally, and this time not independently of the consistent aggregation problem, the "ultimate generalization"

$$G(F_1(x_{11},\dots,x_{1n}),\dots F_m(x_{m1},\dots,x_{mn}))$$
$$= F(G_1(x_{11},\dots,x_{m1}),\dots,G_n(x_{1n},\dots,x_{mn})), \quad (7)$$

called $m \times n$ (or *rectangular*) *generalized bisymmetry*, has been solved under rather weak solvability suppositions in Aczél and Maksa (1996) and Aczél et al. (1997), both on general sets and, under weak continuity conditions, on real intervals (cf. Section 4).

Pro- ducers	Inputs (goods and services)					(Maximal) outputs (production functions)
	1	$\cdots$	k	$\cdots$	n	
1	x_{11}	$\cdots$	x_{1k}	$\cdots$	x_{1n}	$y_1 = F_1(x_{11},\ldots,x_{1n})$
$\vdots$	$\vdots$		$\vdots$		$\vdots$	$\vdots$
j	x_{j1}	$\cdots$	x_{jk}	$\cdots$	x_{jn}	$y_j = F_j(x_{j1},\ldots,x_{jn})$
$\vdots$	$\vdots$		$\vdots$		$\vdots$	$\vdots$
m	x_{m1}	$\cdots$	x_{mk}	$\cdots$	x_{mn}	$y_m = F_m(x_{m1},\ldots,x_{mn})$
aggre- gates	$z_1 =$ $G_1(x_{11},$ $\ldots,x_{m1})$	$\cdots$ $\cdots$	$z_k =$ $G_k(x_{1k},$ $\ldots,x_{mk}$	$\cdots$ $\cdots$	$z_n =$ $G_n(x_{1n},$ $\ldots,x_{mn})$	$z = G(y_1,\ldots,y_m)$ $= y = F(z_1,\ldots,z_n)$

TABLE 1. Consistent aggregation of inputs and outputs.

3. CONSISTENT AGGREGATION

Consistent aggregation (for instance of inputs and of outputs) means that aggregates of microeconomical outputs, or of maximal outputs by some measure, depend only upon aggregates of microeconomical inputs through a macroeconomical production function. This, see Table 1, is equivalent to the $m \times n$ generalized bisymmetry equation (7). The first serious attempt to deal with this question (see Table 2) was made during what came to be known as "Econometrica debate" (1946-48, see van Daal & Merkies, 1987), though (7) appeared then just implicitly. The solution proposed in Klein (1946a) and Nataf (1948) brought immediate vehement reaction. Such reaction was caused by their surprising result that the most popular production functions, the *Cobb-Douglas* (CD) functions

$$F(z_1,\ldots,z_n) = az_1^{c_1} z_2^{c_2} \cdots z_n^{c_n}$$

and the *Constant Elasticity of Substitution* (CES) functions

$$F(z_1,\ldots,z_n) = (c_1 z_1^b + \ldots + c_n z_n^b)^{1/b}$$

$(c_1,\ldots,c_n, a > 0, b \neq 0$ constants), are (except in the trivial case $b = 1$) *incompatible with* what seemed to be the natural way of aggregation, namely *addition* (of the monetary values of outputs or inputs), but *are compatible* among others with

$$G(z_1,\ldots,z_n) = z_1 z_2 \cdots z_n$$

or

$$G(z_1,\ldots,z_n) = (z_1^b + \ldots + z_n^b)^{1/b},$$

respectively. (For a generalization of this result see Section 6 and for extension considerations see Section 5.) A typical reaction was that of Pu (1946): who stated that the CD-aggregates in Klein (1946a) are "monsters, completely void of economic significance ... They certainly have no connection whatsoever with the economic variables which we are actually interested in, such as total volume of employment, or total quantity of capital". To which Klein answered in Klein (1946b): "There is no reason to assume, as Pu does, that there is something sacred about a sum." Our first task is not "to look for things familiar to the layman. Any macroeconomic theory which will enable us to make people happier through an analysis of the

Years	Bisymmetry	Consistent aggregation
1946-48	Characterization of quasiarithmetic means and quasilinear functions by ordinary 2×2 bisymmetry (Aczél)	The Econometrica debate (Klein, Pu, Nataf): Aggregation need not, often cannot be done by addition
1952-54	2×2 generalized bisymmetry for differentiable functions (Hosszú)	
1958-66	2×2 generalized bisymmetry on quasi-groups: solvability but no regularity conditions (Hosszú, Belousov, Aczél)	Consistent aggregation ($m \times n$ generalized bisymmetry) for differentiable functions (Green)
1968		Consistent aggregation for continuous functions using $$F(G(x,y),z) = H(x,K(y,z))$$ (Gorman)
1972-78	2×2 generalized bisymmetry on more general sets (Taylor)	Consistent aggregation for monotonic functions on ordered sets, particular conditions (Pokropp)
1991-93		Consistent aggregation on more general sets (von Stengel)
1996-97	$m \times n$ generalized bisymmetry = consistent aggregation on quite general sets; no topology, no ordering supposed; inputs, outputs need not be measurable by real numbers or on ordinal scales (Aczél, Maksa, Taylor)	

TABLE 2. Sketch of the parallel development of bisymmetry and of consistent aggregation, 1946-97.

interrelationships between aggregates of income, employment, output, etc., is a good theory, regardless of the specific form of the aggregates."

From then on, till about 1964, consistent aggregation was discussed and it was solved under supposition of differentiability of the involved functions, at the level of exactness appropriate to that time (Klein, 1946a; Pu, 1946; Nataf, 1948; Green, 1964, and others). Nataf (1948) and, more explicitly, Green (1964), seem to have been the first to recognize the problem's equivalence to (7), which they reduced to partial differential equations, whose local solutions they determined and considered these solutions to be global solutions of the problem (as was the case also in Hosszú, 1953).

We now arrive at a significant milestone in form of the seminal paper by Gorman (1968). This was the first time the two lines of research met – almost. Gorman was familiar with Aczél (1966) and chose from it the "generalized associativity"

$$F(G(x,y),z) = H(x,K(y,z))$$

for finding the continuous and monotonic solutions of the consistent aggregation problem, rather than choosing the 2×2 generalized bisymmetry equation (6) which was discussed a few pages later (this is the "almost" part).

Finally, the results of Aczél and Maksa (1996) concerning (7), on which we report in Section 3, have been proved from (6) by (double) induction. We also mention some corrections to Gorman (1968) in von Stengel (1991, 1993). In these papers similar results were also proved on more general sets, while in Pokropp (1972, 1978) the monotonic solutions on ordered sets were determined under somewhat involved conditions.

Table 2 illustrates the timelines of the two lines of research, bisymmetry and consistent aggregation; the reader may find the coincidences (or lack of them) amusing.

We finish this historical part by pointing out why results on general, even non-ordered sets are of interest. In that setup *anything* could be in the domains and ranges, even whole collections of possible inputs and outputs. (The conditions in Section 4 may restrict the behavior of the input and output sets but not their nature.) We will also determine the continuous real solutions in Section 4.

4. DEFINITIONS, RESULTS

Let X and Y be arbitrary sets. For a *function* $f: X \to Y$ (mapping X *into* Y), the set of values which f attains on X, the *image* of X under f, is denoted by $f(X)$. If $Y = f(X)$ then f is a *surjection* of X *onto* Y. If $f(x_1) \neq f(x_2)$ for $x_1 \neq x_2$ ($f(X) = Y$ not required) then f is an *injection*. A *bijection* is both an injection and a surjection.

If in a multiplace function $F : Z_1 \times \ldots \times Z_n \to S$ (the variable z_k goes through Z_k, $k = 1, \ldots, n$, the values of F lie in S) we keep all variables but z_ℓ constant, we get a *partial function* $F^\ell : Z_\ell \to S$ (really one for each choice of the constants of $z_1, \ldots, z_{\ell-1}, z_{\ell+1}, \ldots, z_n$). For details of what follows, see Aczél and Maksa (1996).

Theorem 1. *Let* X_{jk}, Y_j, Z_k, S *be nonempty sets,* $F_j : X_{j1} \times \ldots \times X_{jn} \to Y_j$, $G_k : X_{1k} \times \ldots \times X_{mk} \to Z_k$ ($j = 1, \ldots, m$; $k = 1, \ldots, n$), $F : Z_1 \times \ldots \times Z_n \to S$, $G : Y_1 \times \ldots \times Y_m \to S$ *be functions. Then the partial functions* F_j^k, G_k^j *are surjections,* F^k, G^j *injections* ($j = 1, \ldots, m$; $k = 1, \ldots, n$) *and (7) holds for all* $x_{jk} \in X_{jk}$ ($j = 1, \ldots, m$; $k = 1, \ldots, n$) *if, and only if, there exist a set* $T \subseteq S$, *an operation* $\circ$ *on* T *with* $(T, \circ)$ *a commutative group, surjections* $f_{jk} : X_{jk} \to T$ *and bijections* $g_j : Y_j \to T$, $h_k : Z_k \to T$ *such that*

$$F(z_1, \ldots, z_n) = h_1(z_1) \circ \ldots \circ h_n(z_n), \qquad G(y_1, \ldots, y_m) = g_1(y_1) \circ \ldots \circ g_m(y_m),$$

$$F_j(x_{j1}, \ldots, x_{jn}) = g_j^{-1}(f_{j1}(x_{j1}) \circ \cdots \circ f_{jn}(x_{jn})),$$

$$G_k(x_{1k}, \ldots, x_{mk}) = h_k^{-1}(f_{1k}(x_{1k}) \circ \ldots \circ f_{mk}(x_{mk})) \ (j = 1, \ldots, m; \ k = 1, \ldots, n).$$

Corollary 1. *Let* X_{jk}, Y_j, Z_k *be proper real intervals. The functions*

$$G_k : X_{1k} \times \ldots \times X_{mk} \to Z_k$$

*are continuous, $F: Z_1 \times \ldots \times Z_n \to \mathbb{R}$ is continuous nonconstant, $G: Y_1 \times \ldots \times Y_m \to \mathbb{R}$
continuous, F_j^k, G_k^j surjections, F^k, G^j injections $(j = 1, \ldots, m; \ k = 1, \ldots, n)$ and
(7) holds if, and only if, Y_j, Z_k, and $T = F(Z_1, \ldots, Z_n) = G(Y_1, \ldots, Y_m)$ are open
real intervals and there exist continuous surjections $\beta_{jk}: X_{jk} \to \mathbb{R}$ and continuous
bijections $\alpha_k: Z_k \to \mathbb{R}, \gamma_j: Y_j \to \mathbb{R} \quad (j = 1, \ldots, m; \ k = 1, \ldots, n)$, and $\varphi: T \to \mathbb{R}$
such that*

$$
\begin{aligned}
F(z_1, \ldots, z_n) &= \varphi^{-1}(\alpha_1(z_1) + \ldots + \alpha_n(z_n)), \\
F_j(x_{j1}, \ldots, x_{jn}) &= \gamma_j^{-1}(\beta_{j1}(x_{j1}) + \ldots + \beta_{jn}(x_{jn})) \qquad (j = 1, \ldots, m),
\end{aligned}
\tag{8}
$$

$$
\begin{aligned}
G(y_1, \ldots, y_m) &= \varphi^{-1}(\gamma_1(y_1) + \ldots + \gamma_m(y_m)), \\
G_k(x_{1k}, \ldots, x_{mk}) &= \alpha_k^{-1}(\beta_{1k}(x_{1k}) + \ldots + \beta_{mk}(x_{mk})) \qquad (k = 1, \ldots, n).
\end{aligned}
\tag{9}
$$

5. INTREPRETATION, EXAMPLES, EXTENSION

A possible interpretation of the formulas (8)-(9) in Corollary 1 is that the inputs and outputs should "rightly" be measured by $\beta_{jk}(x_{jk})$ and $\gamma_j(y_j)$, respectively. Then the *aggregation* is done by *addition*, the "right" measures of the aggregated inputs and output being $\alpha_k(z_k)$ and $\varphi(t)$, respectively. In the next section we will see that aggregation of the "raw" inputs and outputs by straightforward addition is *incompatible* with production functions important in economics.

The CD (Cobb-Douglas) and CES (Constant Elasticity of Substitution) functions

CD
$$
F(z_1, \ldots, z_n) = a z_1^{c_1} z_2^{c_2} \ldots z_n^{c_n}
$$

CES
$$
F(z_1, \ldots, z_n) = (c_1 z_1^b + \ldots + c_n z_n^b)^{1/b}
$$

are important examples of production functions $(a > 0, c_1, \ldots, c_n > 0, b \neq 0$ are constants). They are of the form (8). Moreover, CD satisfies the conditions of Corollary 1 right away when Z_k, X_{jk} are the set of positive numbers. If CES is *extended* to

$$
\bar{F}(z_1, \ldots, z_n) = \varphi_b^{-1}(c_1 \varphi_b(z_1) + \ldots + c_n \varphi_b(z_n)) \ \text{with} \ \varphi_b(z) = \begin{cases} z^b & \text{if } z > 0, \\ 0 & \text{if } z = 0, \\ -|z|^b & \text{if } z < 0, \end{cases}
$$

on $\mathbb{R}^n$ then, for $b > 0$, it also satisfies the conditions of Corollary 1. For $b < 0$, φ_b (and thus $\bar{F}$) is not continuous at 0 but the conditions of Theorem 1 still hold. In Aczél et al. (1997) the above Corollary 1 has been extended to apply to such situations. A further extension, eliminating restrictive surjectivity conditions, has recently been established by Gy. Maksa.

6. COMPATIBILITY, REPRESENTATIVITY

Surprisingly, it is incompatible that even one production function (8) be CD or CES with $b \neq 1$ if even one aggregating function (9) is simple addition (cf. Aczél

& Maksa, 1996). However, the CD production functions

$$F_j(x_1,\dots,x_n) = a_j x_1^{c_1} x_2^{c_2} \cdots x_n^{c_n}, \quad F(z_1,\dots,z_n) = a_1 a_2 \cdots a_m z_1^{c_1} z_2^{c_2} \cdots z_m^{c_m}$$

are compatible with the simple products

$$G(y_1,\dots,y_m) = y_1 y_2 \cdots y_m, \quad G_k(x_1,\dots,x_m) = x_1 x_2 \cdots x_m,$$

and the CES production functions

$$F(z_1,\dots,z_n) = F_j(z_1,\dots,z_n) = (c_1 z_1^b + \dots + c_n z_n^b)^{1/b} \quad (j=1,\dots,m)$$

are compatible with

$$G(y_1,\dots,y_m) = G_k(y_1,\dots,y_m) = (y_1^b + \dots + y_m^b)^{1/b} \quad (k=1,\dots,n).$$

A possible interpretation (cf. Section 5) is that

$$\beta_{jk}(x_{jk}) = c_k \ln(x_{jk}) \quad (\beta_{jk}(x_{jk}) = c_k x_{jk}^b),$$
$$\gamma_j(y_j) = \ln(y_j/a_j) \quad (\gamma_j(y_j) = y_j^b)$$

and

$$\alpha_k(z_k) = c_k \ln z_k \quad (\alpha_k(z_k) = c_k z_k^b)$$

$(j=1,\dots,m; \ k=1,\dots,n)$

$$\varphi(t) = \ln(t/(a_1 a_2 \dots a_m)) \quad (\varphi(t) = t^b)$$

could be the "right" measures of inputs, outputs and their aggregates by addition for CD functions (CES functions, respectively).

Finally, the question of *representativity* (cf. van Daal & Merkies, 1987) asks whether the aggregates can be considered as some (fictive) representative "producer's" inputs and outputs, connected by a macroeconomical production function F of the same form as the microeconomical production functions $F_1,\dots,F_m$. The answer depends on what we mean by "same form." The similarity of the two formulas in (8) suggests that under the conditions of the Corollary or of the Theorem the answer is positive *in general*. But *if*, in particular, $F_1,\dots,F_m$ are CD or CES *functions* then we have in (8) $\gamma_j(y) = \ln(y/a_j)$, $\beta_{jk}(x) = c_k \ln x$ or $\gamma_j(y) = y_j^b, \beta_{jk}(x) = c_k x^b$, respectively, which does not restrict φ and α_k at all $(j=1,\dots,m; \ k=1,\dots,n)$. So *we may choose F to be CD (CES) or not*.

7. DISCUSSION

In this paper we explored, historically and in their present state, several aspects of consistent aggregation in relation to bisymmetry and its generalizations.

In a recent result, the outputs and inputs can be elements of quite arbitrary sets, in particular they can themselves be sets of items which can be produced or the sets of goods and services which are available for production. While the domains and ranges are arbitrary and the regularity conditions are light (continuity) or non-existent, there are surjectivity conditions on some (production, aggregation) functions (and injectivity on others).

The assumptions about the behavior of the functions (that the partial production functions be surjective) may appear restrictive. As shown in Section 5, however, straightforward extension may *create* surjectivity even if it was not there originally. Moreover, recently surjectivity conditions have been weakened, then eliminated.

We also examined compatibility and incompatibility, noting the strange fact that CD and CES functions are incompatible with aggregation by addition. A popular interpretation (Wolfgang Eichhorn, personal communication in 1994) is that "in these cases consistent aggregation is not possible." Aggregate economic production models, however, are not grounded upon concrete economic activities unless consistent aggregation is possible. So our interpretation in Sections 5 and 6 may be more appropriate.

Our representativity result was qualified: the aggregates follow a production function "of the same form" as the producers, but if the production function of the producers are, for instance, CD (or CES) then that of the aggregates may but need not be CD (or CES).

The general result is that *consistent (and even representative) aggregation is possible but it might not be if the aggregating functions are predetermined ("the wrong way").*

PART 4

PSYCHOPHYSICS AND RESPONSE TIME

Choice, Decision, and Measurement
A. A. J. Marley (Ed.),
©Lawrence Erlbaum Associates, NJ, 1997.

THE WRITER IS INDEBTED TO A REFEREE...

WILLIAM J. McGILL

President Emeritus, Columbia University

ABSTRACT. The smooth surface of a published paper often masks a struggle between author and referee to bring the manuscript into its final form. Here we describe an unreported case in which a referee stunned the author by giving an entirely new look to a problem the author thought he had solved. The referee was Duncan Luce.

1. COLUMBIA – SUMMER OF 1959

The idea came as Connie Mueller and I were sitting in his drab laboratory room on the 3rd floor of Schermerhorn-Extension staring at an oscilloscope. It was August, 1959, hot and steamy in New York, but we had planned to work together that summer, and there we were.

No part of Columbia's Schermerhorn Hall could ever be described as suitable for science. The building was old and misshapen. Portions of it were truly forbidding. Yet over the years remarkable work had been done there by a succession of notable residents: C. Wright Mills, Margaret Mead, Clarence Graham, Theodosius Dobzhansky, and Enrico Fermi.

As a new Assistant Professor, I was given temporary laboratory space in the Extension basement when I moved to Columbia in 1956. Clarence Graham, our chair, told me that J.T. Poffenberger had worked down there in the 1930s and that some of Poff's artifacts might still be on the shelves. It turned out to be true. They were old and battered but many were still functional. Among the heirlooms was an ingenious pendulum timer made in Germany in the mid-19th Century. Clarence said I could do what I wished with the stuff.

One day Nat Schoenfeld came downstairs to visit. He mentioned that during World War II, Fermi made his first attempts to build a reactor in these very same rooms. This really alarmed me. It seemed possible that the walls and floors might still be hot. Schoenfeld doubted that the Columbia administration would release space for general use unless radiation levels were back to normal. He tried to reassure me, but his story left me very uneasy.

In those days a junior faculty member did not quarrel with the decisions of the department chair. Clarence Graham told me to work in the basement and I did, although I wondered what scourges might be oozing out of the walls and ceilings.

Key words and phrases. Excitation, harmonic distribution, reaction time.

Acknowledgments. We thank the Psychometric Society for permission to reproduce adaptations of Figures 1, 3 of McGill (1962).

Address for correspondence. William J. McGill is currently Adjunct Professor of Psychology, University of California, San Diego, La Jolla, CA 92093-0109. Email: wjmcgill@psy.ucsd.edu

I never did summon up courage to measure the background level with a Geiger counter.

Instead, I got out of there as soon as new space opened up on the 3rd floor. My new quarters were in a room just across the hall from Connie Mueller's laboratory. The basement rooms were passed on to the next junior member of the department.

2. SCHERMERHORN-EXTENSION

Schermerhorn was part of a grand scheme for Columbia devised by New York's finest architects: McKim, Mead, and White. Today, their plan for the Morningside Heights campus is regarded as a masterpiece. It provided an eight-building complex to house the main activities of the university following Columbia's move to the Upper West Side of Manhattan in 1895. For the previous 38 years Columbia had tried and failed to make a home in an old asylum on what was then the northern edge of the city at 49th St. close by Saint Patrick's Cathedral. Although larger than Columbia's original campus near City Hall, the asylum had a name marking it forever in the annals of political incorrectness: "The New York Deaf and Dumb Institution." Columbia bought the property hoping to transform it into a college campus, but encountered formidable problems. The flavor of the old place is best conveyed by a nickname students bestowed on its principal instructional facility: *maison de punk.*

Schermerhorn Hall was constructed on Morningside Heights in 1896 by then president Seth Low, later Mayor of New York, for the departments of Geology and Botany.

Schermerhorn-Extension is an annex added on the older structure in 1929 to provide permanent quarters for Psychology and Anthropology, and to meet other needs of the original tenants. The annex faces Amsterdam Avenue behind Schermerhorn at a point where the street begins to run sharply down hill from its summit at 116th St. This fact of nature, together with modified building codes, decreed that adjacent floors of Schermerhorn and its annex did not quite match. To get from the main building to the Extension on the same floor required detouring down a three or four-step staircase. Moving equipment from one building to the other on the same floor was always an adventure. It still is.

Connie Mueller's laboratory was typical of the rooms in Schermerhorn-Extension. Both the lab and the building had seen better days. Slides were scattered over all the table tops, reprints lay piled on the floor, and glossy prints of scope traces were scotch-taped at crazy angles on every wall. To the right of the entry, on a beat-up table, an old Dumont oscilloscope glowed green in the dark. Its input came from a reel-to-reel tape machine mounted on a rack next to the scope. Connie was showing me data recorded in his guest-research cubicle in H. K. Hartline's laboratory across town at Rockefeller University. The tape was a run of action potentials acquired that morning from the optic nerve of Limulus, the horseshoe crab.

3. NERVE FIBERS THAT TICK

Mueller and I were trying to develop a rationale for the latency of the first nerve impulse generated by the crab's visual receptor when light enters the eye. First-impulse latencies were different for continuous light and brief flashes at the same power level. We were trying to deduce the two latency distributions on the basis of the flow of energy into the eye. But as I sat staring at nerve impulses marching across the scope display, I found myself more impressed by the way the optic nerve, stimulated by a steady light, seemed to be ticking away like a watch. Impulses were spaced so regularly as to suggest some kind of periodic excitation. What if the creature were producing regular excitations, and nerve impulses were triggered by each excitation after a brief random delay? What would be the distribution of time intervals between successive impulses in that case?

I tried to interest Connie in the ticking problem, but he was fixed firmly on finishing the work we had started. He relented to the extent of agreeing to make a special tape with a run of at least 500 nerve impulses and a 1000 Hz time signal recorded simultaneously on a second channel. We could then use the time signal to remove variations in the speed of the tape-drive when measuring interresponse times.

Connie's tape was delivered within a week. It was the first of several he made for us with his nerve recording instrumentation in Hartline's laboratory at Rockefeller.

4. HOMEBREW ELECTRONICS

Michael Studdert Kennedy was a graduate student at Columbia in 1959. He was assigned as my laboratory assistant that year. For a summer project, we had built a four-decade counter out of electronic counting units bought from the surplus stores on Canal Street. Our homemade counter proved to be quite accurate. The chief requirement for analyzing Limulus data was to get accurate measurements on time intervals of about 200 milliseconds. This was what the Limulus was putting out, and our counter could handle it easily.

We played Connie Mueller's tape into our apparatus. The first impulse triggered a flip-flop allowing milliseconds to flow from the recorded 1000 Hz time signal. The next nerve impulse turned it off. The next turned it on again, and the next off, and so on until the entire tape was read.

This gave us time intervals between alternate pairs of nerve impulses. By running the tape a second time, now offset by a single impulse, we could recover the entire distribution. Our little machine was primitive, but it worked and we understood it. That counts for a great deal.

At first we did not own a printing counter. We needed some way to hold an interresponse time long enough to record it. One solution was to count successive impulses up to a preset number n. The timer would display a new inter-impulse time only at this index number. Thus we displayed every nth interval, holding each display until the next index n was reached. Bob Berryman in the animal behavior laboratory on the floor below us had built just such a device. Michael and I persuaded him to lend it to us until we could make a duplicate. A modest index count was chosen so that times could be spoken into a tape recorder comfortably before the next interval was displayed.

Starting on different impulses permitted us to get the entire distribution by rerunning the tape and piecing a complete record together. Later we substituted a printing counter with memory. It enabled us to avoid all this labor. Both methods should have produced the same result. It was a relief when comparison runs showed they did.

5. LAPLACE DISTRIBUTION

The idea that came as I studied Connie's limulus data tries to account for the near-constancy of intervals between successive nerve impulses. Responses must be driven by a periodic excitatory process as shown in Figure 1.

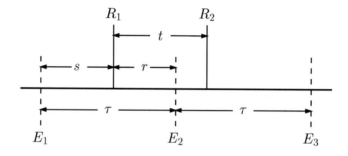

FIGURE 1. Stochastic latency mechanism yielding variable inter-response times with a periodic component. Excitations (not observable) come at regular intervals τ, but are subject to random delays before producing responses. Heavy line is the time axis. Adapted from Figure 1 of McGill (1962). Used by permission of the Psychometric Society.

E and R denote excitation and response respectively. Times between successive responses constitute a random variable t, whereas intervals between excitations are fixed and identified as τ. Responses are observable. Excitations and their locations are not. Thus the exact value of τ cannot be known. It can be estimated from t if the distribution of interresponse times is known. Excitation and response will coincide only when the response delay is zero. Hence, each response is located between a pair of excitations. The distance from either excitation is given by location coordinates r and s. They add up to τ.

The first coordinate, s in Figure 1, is the interval between a response and the excitation immediately preceding it. We assume it to be an exponential random delay. Our problem is to find the distribution of t when the distribution of s is known.

If (random) delays between excitation and response can be guaranteed small relative to the (fixed) intervals between excitations, the problem is easy. Figure 1 shows that the difference $t - \tau$ should be distributed as the difference between two exponentials, each having the same delay constant. This is the famous LaPlace distribution:

$$f(t - \tau) = \frac{\lambda}{2} e^{-\lambda|t-\tau|}, \qquad -\infty \leq \tau - t \leq \infty. \tag{1}$$

The LaPlace is much more sharply peaked than a normal curve. Chiefly for that reason, it offers an excellent description of interresponse times that "tick" like a watch or pulse like a heartbeat. Our limulus optic nerve data, as recorded by Connie Mueller and measured by Michael Kennedy with the writer, are shown in Figure 2.

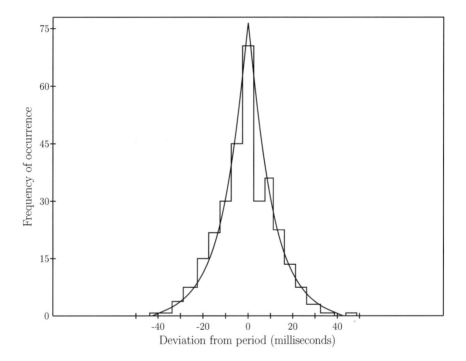

FIGURE 2. Frequency distribution of 303 interresponse times observed in a single fiber of the optic nerve of *limulus* when the eye was illuminated by a steady light. The nerve fiber adapted continuously to the illumination, resulting in a slow linear increase in period from 261 to 291 milliseconds. Measured intervals are deviations from the linear drift. Smooth curve is a LaPlace distribution. Adapted from Figure 3 of McGill (1962). Used by permission of the Psychometric Society.

We had to make one further adjustment to produce Figure 2. The crab's eye adapted slowly to continuous light. Intervals between nerve impulses increased in nearly linear fashion from an average of 261 milliseconds to 291 milliseconds over the duration of our data recording. We plotted each successive pulse interval and fitted the trend line. Interresponse times in Figure 2 are deviates from this line.

6. PAPER DRAFTED

All of us were happy with the outcome. We began looking for other examples of responses driven by periodic excitations. I sat down to draft a paper. I got no further than the form of Equation 1 when I realized there was a big problem. Suppose a new excitation arrives before a response occurs. If the latter is timed from this second excitation, nothing really changes except that the period is doubled. Moreover, any number of excitations might intervene. The probability of these longer periods should fall off geometrically. Hence, our LaPlace distribution is an approximation occurring when the probability of two or more excitations between responses proves negligible.

Suppose it is not. If the interval between excitations is zero (i.e., excitation is continuous), interresponse times should be exponential. A trigger is always there to call the next response. The distribution of interresponse times, whatever it turns out to be, should limit on the LaPlace when excitations are widely spaced, and on the exponential when they are continuous.

Evidently a key component of the distribution of interresponse times spans a single excitation period. This same component, now weighted by the lower probability of an added excitation, reappears as a harmonic at double the period; and so on for three, four, and more excitation periods. The complete distribution of interresponse times is formed by adding the corresponding densities contributed by each of these harmonic components.

The idea of harmonic distributions of interresponse times excited me greatly. I worked out an expression for the single period distribution, and also for the probabilities of successive harmonic components. It was neat and clean. By this time I also had data on paced responding in rats and pigeons, and could show periodic excitation in nerve impulse records taken from the spinal cord of the cat. We found examples of harmonic pulse interval distributions all over the neuroscience literature.

I finished the paper in a burst of activity during the fall of 1959, and mailed it off to *Psychometrika* just before the Christmas holidays. I felt very good about it. Rarely do things work out so smoothly from an original idea to the confirming data.

The electronics that Michael Kennedy and I had put together were all home-made. We spent less than $200 on the entire project, although later we invested in an expensive printing counter. Of course, Connie Mueller picked up the cost of data recording out of the goodness of his heart, and had lent us his two-channel tape machine. Everything worked surprisingly well. And we did it all without federal grant money or special help from Columbia; just old-fashioned science. The harmonic distribution of periodically excited interresponse times struck me as particularly interesting.

7. THE REVIEW

My manuscript was reviewed and returned during the autumn of 1960. It had been accepted subject to a number of revisions. Along with the original draft came a thorough, exceptionally perceptive review that took me some time to digest. The reviewer liked the paper and recommended its acceptance, but said there were easier ways to prove the interresponse time distribution. He provided clean proofs of recommended alterations.

The big shocker was his proof that after a sharp peak at the period τ, the harmonic components piece themselves together neatly into a simple exponential tail. They just disappear! By going over to a generating function, he showed how to break up the components and put them back together so that each harmonic contribution can be traced. These points are all included in the paper as finally published (McGill, 1962). Interested readers are referred to the proof of Equation 2 in the published paper, and to the footnote acknowledging indebtedness to a referee.

It was a tour de force. I was astonished by the referee's analysis. Using my own notation and what I thought was my idea, the reviewer had shown how I should have developed the argument in the first place. There was nothing really wrong with what I had done. It was just incomplete, and in referring to harmonic components, somewhat misleading.

8. DUNCAN LUCE UNMASKED

Despite *Psychometrika's* attempts to preserve their referee's anonymity, this review had Duncan Luce's name written all over it. Anyone who has corresponded with Duncan more than once on any technical matter comes to recognize his writing style: precise, elegant, lucid, and a teeny bit formal. I did not need the FBI to uncover Duncan's role in the review.

So I called him at the University of Pennsylvania. He and I had been good friends since we first met at MIT in 1952. There was no need for preliminary fencing on the phone. I told him that only he could have written that review. He admitted that indeed he was my referee. I then confessed that the review was extremely helpful but left me with an ethical problem. I would certainly adopt every recommendation he made for improving the paper, but could not think of a way to do it without making him a co-author.

Duncan laughed and said something like: "No Bill, it is your paper. It is good. I like it a lot. All I did was add a few extra touches to the proof." He would not budge on becoming a co-author. In the end I managed to get his agreement to a footnote thanking a referee for services beyond the call of duty.

9. FINAL CONFESSION

Any of Duncan's students or co-workers can testify to similar episodes. It is very elevating to have such high standards applied to one's work, but it is also a little embarrassing. Duncan's scrutiny is never routine. Sloppy work never gets by. At the time of this incident I was young and not altogether sure of myself. I did not go around advertising what Duncan had done for my paper. I simply accepted and basked in the attention that it brought. It certainly provided a big boost to my reputation. So I kept the refereeing incident to myself hoping that no one else would put two and two together. Anyone comparing my original draft with the paper as finally published would know what happened.

There is no need for a cover-up or a Nixonian limited, partial hang-out now. It is time for full disclosure – or confession – or whatever you want to call it. I owe Duncan a lot.

Choice, Decision, and Measurement
A. A. J. Marley (Ed.),
©Lawrence Erlbaum Associates, NJ, 1997.

ACTIVATION-STATE REPRESENTATION OF MODELS FOR THE REDUNDANT-SIGNALS-EFFECT

HANS COLONIUS

Universität Oldenburg

JAMES T. TOWNSEND

Indiana University

ABSTRACT. The redundant signals effect (RSE) refers to the fact that subjects generally respond faster to simultaneously presented redundant targets than to single targets in a detection task where they are required to monitor two or more information sources. Based on the notion of an activation state representation, a unifying formal framework for the various response time models developed for the RSE is presented. Prospects for testing between different model classes are discussed and illustrated by some first results.

1. INTRODUCTION: THE REDUNDANT SIGNALS EFFECT

Consider a task requiring people to monitor two (or more) information sources ("channels") for the presence of a target signal requiring a particular speeded response. A common finding is that people respond faster (or more accurately) when signals are presented simultaneously on both channels than when a signal is presented on a single channel alone. This has been referred to as the *redundant signals effect* (RSE), or the *redundant targets effect*. For example, when signals are presented on two modalities, visual and auditory, say, responses to such bimodal stimuli tend to be faster than responses to unimodal stimuli (an effect also known as *intersensory facilitation*). The experimental literature on the RSE is voluminous and the results depend on whether or not the stimuli are presented within the same modality, the nature of the stimulus materials, and other contextual factors. Many different explanations of the RSE have been suggested over the years, some of them in terms of formalized quantitative models, others more informal (for a recent review, see Townsend & Nozawa, 1995).

The purpose of this paper is to provide a unifying formal framework within which most theoretical approaches to the RSE can be embedded. Apart from yielding a common language to describe the various theoretical approaches, such

Key words and phrases. Redundant signals effect, separate activation model, coactivation model, channel interaction, race model.

Acknowledgment. The authors are grateful to Ehtibar Dzhafarov and an anonymous reviewer for comments and suggestions. This research was supported by a German-American Collaborative Research Award sponsored by the American Council of Learned Societies (ACLS) and by Deutscher Akademischer Austauschdienst (DAAD). Support was also provided by U.S. National Science Foundation Grant BNS 9112813 to the second author.

Address for correspondence. Hans Colonius, Institut für Kognitionsforschung, Universität Oldenburg, D-26111 Oldenburg, Germany. Email: colonius@psychologie.uni-oldenburg.de

a framework may help point to techniques required to differentiate among various models and to make evident where model mimicking or excessive generality, relative to certain experimental domains, makes hypothesis testing difficult or impossible (cf. Townsend & Ashby, 1983; Dzhafarov, 1993).

The central concept of our framework is the notion of a *time-dependent activation state* representing the momentary effect of a signal within one or several channels. The motivation for this notion relates to a basic distinction between models of *separate activation* and models of *coactivation* as introduced by Miller (1982). In the former, presentation of the stimuli triggers the buildup of activation in each sensory channel separately. A response is initiated as soon as activation reaches a criterion level of activation in either channel. These models are commonly called "race models," because the response to a redundant signal is produced by the winner of the race between two (or more) stochastic response activation processes (Meijers & Eijkman, 1977; Raab, 1962). The RSE is explained by statistical facilitation, i.e., the mean of the winner's time is at most as large as the mean of either of the racers. Alternatively, *coactivation* models allow activation from different channels to combine over time in satisfying a *single* criterion for response initiation. Responses to redundant signals will be especially fast, because two sources feed activation into satisfying a single criterion level of activation.

While the distinction between separate and coactivation models makes sense at an intuitive level, the above characterization of the separate activation and the coactivation models allows for rather broad realizations of specific stochastic mechanisms within both classes of models. As in certain other fundamental distinctions, such as parallel vs. serial processing (see, e.g., Townsend, 1990), our analyses below will show that any attempt at empirically distinguishing between the two hypotheses hinges upon specific additional assumptions being made in either case, and experimental manipulations based on those assumptions.

The next section introduces some notation and gives a more explicit definition of separate activation and coactivation models for the RSE. In Section 3, the formal framework of an activation state representation is developed. Section 4 discusses some special cases within this framework, while Section 5 considers prospects for testability of these model classes and presents some first results. Finally, Section 6 reviews evidence for the localization of the RSE from some psychophysiological studies.

2. BASIC ASPECTS OF SEPARATE ACTIVATION AND COACTIVATION

Let $\mathcal{X}, \mathcal{Y}$ be two different sets of stimuli, e.g., from two different modalities, visual and auditory, say. The elements of $\mathcal{X}$ (respectively, $\mathcal{Y}$) can be defined in a given experimental condition either as target or as non-target (distractor) stimuli. For brevity, in this section we will only consider the case without distractors, i.e., where non-target stimuli will not be presented. For target stimuli $X \in \mathcal{X}$ and $Y \in \mathcal{Y}$, let T_X and T_Y denote (random) trigger times for response initiation by the sensory channels corresponding to $\mathcal{X}$ and $\mathcal{Y}$, respectively[1]. According to the

---

[1] By an abuse of language, we will often refer to $\mathcal{X}$ and $\mathcal{Y}$ as channels.

separate activation point of view, response time in the redundant target condition is defined by

$$RT_{XY} = \min(T_X, T_Y). \tag{1}$$

For simplicity, we disregard any residual components of the response time here. Note that (1) implies the existence of a bivariate distribution function $P[T_X \leq s, T_Y \leq t]$ with $s, t \geq 0$. Thus, in separate activation models, the observable RT distribution in the redundant target condition is

$$P[RT_{XY} \leq t] = P[\min(T_X, T_Y) \leq t]$$
$$= 1 - P[T_X > t, T_Y > t]. \tag{2}$$

This equation implies that the underlying bivariate distribution $P[T_X \leq s, T_Y \leq t]$ is unobservable under the given experimental conditions except at the points (t, t). Thus, it is impossible to test for stochastic independence of the trigger times T_X and T_Y without adding further assumptions. One assumption commonly made in separate activation models is referred to as *context independence* by Colonius (1990) or as *perceptual separability* by Ashby and Townsend (1986) (see also Luce, 1986b, p. 128ff). In a context independent separate activation model, the distribution of the trigger time T_X (resp., T_Y) is the same in the single target condition and in the redundant target condition. Technically, context independence equates the single target distribution $F_X(t) = P[T_X \leq t]$ with the redundant target marginal distribution $P[T_X \leq t, T_Y \leq \infty]$ (analogously, for T_Y). Under this condition, separate activation models predict the following inequality, as first observed by Miller (1982):

$$\max(F_X(t), F_Y(t)) \leq P[RT_{XY} \leq t] \leq F_X(t) + F_Y(t). \tag{3}$$

It should be emphasized that, under context independence, this inequality is valid no matter whether the trigger times are stochastically independent or not. In fact, stochastic independence occurs when $P[RT_{XY} \leq t]$ equals $F_X(t) + F_Y(t) - F_X(t)F_Y(t)$, while the upper and the lower bound in (3) represent the cases of maximal positive and maximal negative stochastic dependence between the trigger times T_X and T_Y with fixed given marginals, also known as Fréchet bounds (see Colonius, 1990). Ulrich and Giray (1986) and Colonius (1986, 1990) studied the influence of stochastic dependence on the RSE. The predicted RSE is greater if the trigger times are negatively correlated, because in this case a large latency in one channel tends to be compensated by a small latency in the other channel.

Inequality (3) has been found violated in many empirical studies. In particular, response times in the redundant target condition often are faster than allowed by the upper bound (e.g., Miller, 1982, 1986; Diederich & Colonius, 1987; Westendorf & Blake, 1988; Mordkoff & Yantis, 1993). This prompted the development of so-called coactivation models. As Miller (1991) notes, coactivation models have so far been defined primarily by default, i.e., as models that produce faster detection of redundant targets than race models or, more specifically, than race models under context independence. As mentioned in the introductory section, one way to conceive of coactivation is in terms of a combination of activations across channels with a single criterion to be satisfied for response initiation.

A prominent example of a mathematical coactivation model is the *Poisson superposition* model (cf., Diederich & Colonius, 1991; Schwarz, 1989). Let $X(t)$ and $Y(t)$ denote the number of Poisson counts that occur by time t in the channel processing X and Y, respectively. The RT distribution in the redundant target condition is defined by the first-passage time associated with the superposition of the Poisson counters, that is,

$$RT_{XY} = \inf\{t : X(t) + Y(t) > c\}, \tag{4}$$

where c is the shape parameter of the gamma distribution associated with the superposed Poisson processes. Thus, by definition, the response time is the *greatest lower bound* (infimum) of the set of all time points t where the summed counters exceed the criterion c. Townsend and Nozawa (1995) have developed general coactivation models that include the Poisson model as special case. Other types of coactivation models are based on the concept of random walk (e.g., Smith, 1990) or on the superposition of certain diffusion processes (Diederich, 1992, 1995; Schwarz, 1994). Superposition models have fared much better in accounting for RSE data than separate activation models, both at the level of central tendencies (means, medians) and at the level of variance of the RT distributions.

3. ACTIVATION STATE REPRESENTATIONS

The counters in the Poisson superposition model presented in Equation 4 provide a simple example of an activation state representation for a coactivation type model where the momentary effect of a signal within a sensory channel is captured by time-dependent random variables, $X(t)$ and $Y(t)$. However, the concept of a time-dependent state of activation initiates a much more general approach that will be outlined in this section. In particular, it encompasses separate activation type models. For example, a slight modification of the first-passage time of Equation 4 yields an activation state representation for a separate activation type of model. Defining

$$RT_{XY} = \inf\{t : \max\{X(t), Y(t)\} > c\} \tag{5}$$

provides an activation state formulation for the redundant target response time defined in Equation 1 with, in the Poisson case, gamma-distributed trigger times racing against each other.

A more elaborate view of how sensory information in the channels develops over time involves the idea of interactions occurring among the channels. For example, in the *interactive race model* recently proposed by Mordkoff and Yantis (1991), separate sensory channels begin exchanging information about the identity of the element being processed in either channel (e.g., whether it is a target or a non-target) as soon as any channel has partially identified its signal. Given specific experimenter-determined signal contingencies, processing time in a given channel may be speeded up either by increasing the level of activation or by lowering the response initiation criterion in the redundant target conditions. Of course, inhibitory interactions across channels could also occur in such models.

It is interesting to note that the occurrence of channel interactions implies the existence of at least two functionally and, most likely, also morphologically distinct

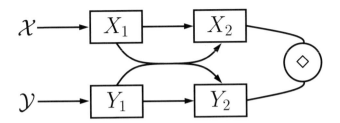

FIGURE 1. Flow chart sketch of general activation state model

stages of processing. The first stage refers to the state of activation at an early, peripheral stage of processing where no interaction among channels can occur. The second stage refers to a later, central state of activation where interaction among different channels is possible. For the $\mathcal{X}$-channel, let $X_1(t)$ and $X_2(t)$ denote the activation state for the first and second stage, respectively. For the $\mathcal{Y}$-channel, $Y_1(t)$ and $Y_2(t)$ are defined analoguously. It should be stressed here that these two stages are not limited to be discrete, serial subprocesses in the sense of Donders (1868). Rather, at any point in time t the peripheral activation state may continuously "feed" into the second, more central stage. Moreover, $X_2(t)$ may also get "cross-talk" from $Y_1(t)$ and, simultaneously, $Y_2(t)$ from $X_1(t)$. However, the two processes do not interact directly. Formally, this can be captured by introducing two *functionals* G_x and G_y as follows:

$$X_2(t) = G_x[(X_1(t'), Y_1(t')) : t' \in [0, t]]$$
$$Y_2(t) = G_y[(Y_1(t'), X_1(t')) : t' \in [0, t]]. \qquad (6)$$

Thus, the level of activation at time t in the second stage in the $\mathcal{X}$-channel, $X_2(t)$, ($Y_2(t)$ in the $\mathcal{Y}$-channel, respectively) is a function of the entire "history" of the activation in the first stage up to t both of the $\mathcal{X}$- and the $\mathcal{Y}$-channel (see Townsend & Fikes, 1995, for a detailed treatment of the "functional" concept in sequential but continuous flow types of models). Adding a first passage time assumption then leads to the following general representation:

$$RT_{XY} = \inf\{t : X_2(t) \diamond Y_2(t) > C\} \qquad (7)$$

where $\diamond$ refers to some binary operation on the pairs $(X_2(t), Y_2(t))$ and C is a constant criterion level of activation.

It turns out that Equation 7 encompasses the classes of models considered above. Assuming $\diamond$ to be the *max* operation defines the class of *separate activation* or *race models* with possibly interactive channels; replacing $\diamond$ by the *min* operation yields a class of *(parallel) exhaustive models* where activation in both channels must meet a criterion value to trigger the response (see, for example, Colonius & Vorberg, 1994; Townsend & Colonius, in press). Finally, the class of *coactivation models* can be defined by considering $\diamond$ to be a *generalized addition operation* $\oplus$, say, an operation possessing all principal properties of addition[2]. The rationale for choosing

---

[2]The operation is defined as follows: Let g be an arbitrary real-valued, strictly monotonic (increasing or decreasing) and continuous function with some open interval of the reals as its domain.

an addition-like operation, rather than simple addition, for the combination of channel activations in the definition of coactivation models is that the inequality in (7) for "$\oplus$" can always be reduced to an equivalent inequality for "+" by a monotonic transformation of the channel activations and the criterion C without changing the response time predictions.

While Equation 7 is a compact description of an activation state model of a rather general kind, there are at least two further possible directions in which to extend this representation. The first concerns the criterion. Rather than assuming a constant criterion level of activation, the criterion may be time-dependent as suggested by refractory phenomena (cf., Tuckwell, 1989). Moreover, the criterion itself may vary randomly over time, possibly as a function of the activations states in the two channels $X_2(t)$ and $Y_2(t)$ (e.g., Pike, 1973). Depending on how this functional dependence of C occurs, it is possible to rewrite the inequality in (7) in terms of a constant criterion.

The second extension of representation (7) is more fundamental. It is conceivable that in some cases, information concerning the activation in the separate channels is retained until a very late stage of processing. Thus, final detection in this *hybrid model* may depend on both the combined activation $X_2(t) \diamond Y_2(t)$ as well as the separate channel activations $X_2(t)$ and $Y_2(t)$. Obviously, there are different ways how these three activations could combine to determine the final output. The hybrid model will be considered in Section 4.

Finally, it should be mentioned that representation (7) does not include the *serial exhaustive model* for the RSE recently discussed in Townsend and Nozawa (1995).

4. SOME SPECIAL CASES

The simplicity of Equation 7 is deceptive since the occurrence of the functionals G_x and G_y permits very complex relations between the X_1 and Y_1 trajectories and X_2 (or Y_2, respectively). In the following, a few special cases illustrate some of the possibilities. While some of these model classes have been pursued in the literature, others, to our knowledge, have not yet been developed in any detail, let alone tested empirically.

Markovian Models. A considerable simplification of the two-process activation model (Equation 7) is obtained if the Markov property is introduced. For simplicity, and to avoid writing differential equations, only the discrete time case is considered here:

$$X_2(t+1) = G_x[X_1(t), Y_1(t), X_1(t-1), Y_1(t-1), \ldots, X_1(0), Y_1(0)]$$
$$Y_2(t+1) = G_y[Y_1(t), X_1(t), Y_1(t-1), X_1(t-1), \ldots, Y_1(0), X_1(0)].$$

In a *Markovian activation state model*, the level of activation in the second stage at time $t+1$ only depends on the most recent history of the activations in the first

---

Then $a \oplus b = g^{-1}[g(a) + g(b)]$ defines a new binary operation that is associative, commutative, increasing in both arguments, and continuous in both arguments (cf., Aczél, 1966; Dzhafarov & Schweickert, 1995).

stage and on its own state at time t. Specifically,

$$X_2(t+1) = g_x(X_1(t), Y_1(t), X_2(t))$$
$$Y_2(t+1) = g_y(Y_1(t), X_1(t), Y_2(t)). \tag{8}$$

The specific form of g_x, g_y determines whether the system is linear or nonlinear.

Activation Without Channel Interaction. Assuming that no channel interaction occurs up until the activation process crosses a critical criterion level C makes the two-process formulation introduced in Section 3 dispensable. In fact, consider the representation in (6) without the "cross-talk" terms:

$$X_2(t) = G_x[X_1(t') : t' \in [0, t]]$$
$$Y_2(t) = G_y[Y_1(t') : t' \in [0, t]]. \tag{9}$$

Since there is no restriction on the definition of X_2 we may, without loss of generality, set $X_2(t)$ equal to $X_1(t)$ for any t. Then, Equation 9 simply states that $X_1(t)$ is a function of t that depends on all its values $t' < t$. The same argument holds for channel $\mathcal{Y}$. Nonetheless, it may still be plausible to distinguish between a peripheral and a more central stage of processing. However, any exploitation of this calls for additional assumptions and/or experimental manipulations, for example applying some kind of systems factorial technology (Sternberg, 1969; Townsend & Nozawa, 1995). Without channel interaction, the general representation (7) thus reduces to

$$RT_{XY} = \inf\{t : X_1(t) \diamond Y_1(t) > C\}. \tag{10}$$

Choosing an appropriate interpretation of $\diamond$, this representation encompasses all separate activation and coactivation models mentioned in Section 2.

Hybrid Models. One way to conceive of the hybrid model type is to postulate the existence of an additional channel $\mathcal{Z}$, say, integrating convergent input from the other channels. For example, the Markov version from Section 4 would be

$$X_2(t+1) = g_x(X_1(t), Y_1(t), X_2(t))$$
$$Y_2(t+1) = g_y(Y_1(t), X_1(t), Y_2(t))$$
$$Z(t+1) = g_z(X_2(t), Y_2(t), Z(t)). \tag{11}$$

Final detection, i.e., the first-passage time determining the response time, could then be some function of the activation in both the $\mathcal{Z}$-channel and the $\mathcal{X}$, $\mathcal{Y}$-channels. This hypothesis ties in with a recent observation by Miller (1991). In a bimodal experiment with auditory signals varying in pitch and visual signals varying in location ("high" vs. "low"), he found responses to redundant targets were faster when both were high or low than when they were incongruent. Preserving the activation information from both the $\mathcal{X}-$ and the $\mathcal{Y}-$channel up to the final stage, in parallel with the integrating channel $\mathcal{Z}$, could then account for these congruence effects. Obviously, alternative hypotheses locating the congruence effects at an earlier stage are conceivable. In our view, further empirical work is needed to decide this issue.

5. DISCUSSION: PROSPECTS FOR TESTABILITY

The distinction between separate activation and coactivation has been the starting point of our investigation. As pointed out in Section 2, violation of Inequality (3) allows rejection of all separate activation (race) models as long as context independence is assumed. On the other hand, non-violation of the inequality presents only weak support for the race model since other models may also be consistent with the inequality. Moreover, context independence is the key assumption for the inequality to be of any diagnostic value (cf., Ashby & Townsend, 1986; Colonius, 1986). As noted by Luce (1986b), one possibility for a race model to violate the inequality would be the following form of context *dependence*: The presence of a (nontarget) signal speeds up the detection of the other (target) signal. Interestingly, this is exactly an example of one type of *interchannel cross talk* effect that Mordkoff and Yantis (1991) hypothesized from their empirical studies and that led them to propose their "interactive race model" (mentioned in Section 3). Although this model has not been presented in a formal way, it seems obvious that it can be subsumed under the general class of (two-process) separate activation models with possibly interactive channels defined from Equation 7 in Section 3 by:

$$RT_{XY} = \inf\{t : max\{X_2(t), Y_2(t)\} > C\}. \tag{12}$$

The upshot of this is that the general class of separate activation models defined by Equations 6 and 12 is not constrained by Inequality 3 because context independence may no longer hold.

Next, one may ask whether this model class can be tested against the general class of coactivation models defined in Section 3 by Equation 6 and by

$$RT_{XY} = \inf\{t : X_2(t) \oplus Y_2(t) > C\}. \tag{13}$$

Not surprisingly, the answer to this is in the negative since these two general classes are not disjoint. This is illustrated by the following example, where a separate activation model with channel interaction degenerates into a coactivation model.

Example. Consider a separate activation model of a simplified Markov type (12) with the following representation:

$$X_2(t+1) = g_x(X_1(t), Y_1(t))$$
$$Y_2(t+1) = g_y(Y_1(t), X_1(t)). \tag{14}$$

Assume that, due to some inhibitory effect, activation in the $\mathcal{Y}$-channel converges to an upper bound lying below the criterion C. A plausible example for this situation is the *focused-attention task*, where subjects are instructed to make a speeded response as soon as they detect a visual signal or a visual signal accompanied by an accessory auditory signal, and to withhold their response if the auditory signal occurs alone. Although the auditory signal is irrelevant for performing this task, shorter RTs result under bisensory stimulation than if the visual signal is presented alone (e.g., Bernstein, Clark, & Edelstein, 1969). Thus, while the auditory signal adds to the sensory activity generated by the visual signal, the activity level in the auditory channel by itself is not sufficient to cross the criterion and to trigger the response (see also Giray & Ulrich, 1993). Then Equation 12 reduces to

$$RT_{XY} = \inf\{t : X_2(t) > C\}. \tag{15}$$

This, however, is the first-passage time of a coactivation model as long as

$$g_x(X_1(t), Y_1(t)) = X_1(t) \oplus Y_1(t),$$

where $\oplus$ is an addition-like operation.

Note that examples like this one do not preclude the possibility of testing specific separate activation models against specific coactivation models, even under context dependence. However, such a test will always be a test of the model and, simultaneously, some auxiliary conditions added to the model (see also Dzhafarov, 1993). This will be illustrated here by the following result. The class of coactivation models includes the general idea of superposition (as exemplified by the Poisson superposition model). While the falsifiability of the general superposition idea is still an open question, Townsend and Nozawa (1995) present some first results under auxiliary conditions. The following is a slightly stronger version of their result (Townsend & Nozawa, 1995, Theorem 7):

Proposition 1. *Let X_t and Y_t denote the number of counts (not necessarily Poisson distributed) that occur by time t in the $\mathcal{X}$- and in the $\mathcal{Y}$-channel, respectively. Assuming the (constant) criterion c for the first-passage times to be identical in both the superposition and in the race model,*

$$F_{superposition}(t) = P[RT_{XY} \leq t] = P[X_t + Y_t > c],$$
$$F_{race}(t) = P[RT_{XY} \leq t] = P[max\{X_t, Y_t\}] > c],$$

implies

$$F_{race}(t) \leq F_{superposition}(t)$$

for all t.

Proof. For a proof, consider the following subsets of the sample space: $S(t) = \{\omega | X_t(\omega) + Y_t(\omega) > c\}$ and $R(t) = \{\omega | \max\{X_t(\omega), Y_t(\omega)\} > c\}$. Obviously, because X_t and Y_t are nonnegative, $R(t) \subseteq S(t)$ for all t, implying the distribution ordering. Note that X_t, Y_t are not assumed to be independent.   □

6. LOCALIZING THE REDUNDANT SIGNALS EFFECT

As the previous section indicates, there appear to be some severe limits on the testability of the most general models for the RSE, within single experimental conditions of an RT experiment. However, the development of meta-modeling strategies that help to test and discriminate large classes of architectures and process issues suggests that careful development of model-oriented methodology offers hope for the future (see, in this regard, Dzhafarov & Schweickert, 1995; Townsend & Nozawa, 1995). Nonetheless, it is natural to ask whether there are other dependent variables, behavioral or physiological, that could yield useful information on the nature of the RSE. Given the significant difference in the level of functional descriptions between neurophysiology and psychology, it would be presumptuous to expect physiological data to delineate psychological models for the RSE in any detail. On the other hand, there is a multitude of data on the RSE collected to date, both neurophysiological and other non-RT data like response force, in particular in the area of multisensory integration (e.g., visual-auditory-somatosensory), and the neurophysiological-behavioral parallels prove to be striking (cf. Stein & Meredith, 1993). No attempt is made here to review these findings. Rather, the aim of this section is to see whether some broad aspects of the activation state approach are supported by evidence from data beyond measures of response speed.

Early on, a speed-up of response time for redundant signals beyond that predicted by probability summation was taken as evidence for the existence of "neural summation" performed by some specific neural correlate. For example, from their comparison of monocular and binocular response times, Blake, Martens, Garrett, and Westendorf (1980) hypothesized the existence of binocular neurons activated only by binocular stimulation. Notably, a multitude of electrophysiological studies have shown that there exist multimodal cells in the deep layers of the superior colliculus (DLSC) (of anaesthetized cats) that respond with a firing rate more than 10 times the optimal unimodal stimulus response (see Stein & Meredith, 1993, for a review). Moreover, spatial and temporal disparities of the visual-auditory stimulation caused a gradual decrease of these bimodal interactions similar to those found in the latencies of human saccadic eye movements (Frens, van Opstal, & van der Willigen, 1995; Hughes, Reuter-Lorenz, Nozawa, & Fendrich, 1994). Most interestingly, more recent electrophysiological studies suggest the existence of multisensory cortical neurons that do not project to the superior colliculus and that may be involved in higher order cognitive functions (Wallace, Meredith, & Stein, 1993).

In our view, the existence of multiple sites of multisensory integration renders models of separate activation without any channel interactions quite implausible. While, as hypothesized in Hughes et al. (1994), these different sites may be involved depending on the pathways used by a particular task (directed gaze vs. simple manual responses), the existence of at least two stages of signal processing as postulated in our general representation (6) and (7) appears tenable.

Finally, there is some evidence on the issue of separate activation models (with channel interaction) vs. coactivation models from a study of *response force* by Giray and Ulrich (1993). Besides producing the usual RSE in their response times, subjects also gave more forceful responses under bimodal than under unimodal stimulation. As noted by these authors, this evidence for a (at least) partial localization of the effect at a motoric level is not easy to reconcile with a separate activation model, even under channel interaction. The reason is that while race models assume separate response activations ("trigger times"), response execution should not depend on whether the signal was unimodal or bimodal. A coactivation model where activation is summed over possibly different sites of neural convergence, may be more appropriate for this situation.

Choice, Decision, and Measurement
A. A. J. Marley (Ed.),
©Lawrence Erlbaum Associates, NJ, 1997.

PROCESS REPRESENTATIONS AND DECOMPOSITIONS OF RESPONSE TIMES

EHTIBAR N. DZHAFAROV

University of Illinois at Urbana-Champaign

ABSTRACT. Response times (in a very general meaning of the term, including physiological latencies and durations of theoretically assumed mental actions) can be subjected to two basic forms of analysis: (a) the representation of response times by durations of unobservable processes identified by their final outcomes and developing until they meet certain termination conditions; and (b) the decomposition of response times into component durations identified by observable external factors that influence them selectively. This chapter overviews and elaborates theoretical concepts and mathematical results related to these two analyses. It begins with a general theory of process representations for arbitrary response arrangements (i.e., the rules determining which responses may co-occur within a trial). This theory extends the Grice-representability and McGill-representability analysis proposed previously for mutually exclusive responses. Then the notion of selectively influenced but (generally) interacting processes is introduced and related to that of selectively influenced but (generally) stochastically interdependent component durations: the two notions turn out to be related in an indirect and complex way. Finally, an overview is given of the available mathematical facts related to (a) the recovery of the algebraic operation connecting the response time components that are identified by the factors selectively influencing them and by the form of stochastic relationship among them (independence or perfect positive interdependence); and (b) the choice between the independence and perfect positive interdependence of signal-dependent and signal-independent components identified by the algebraic operation connecting them.

1. INTRODUCTION

This chapter is about two basic forms of the theoretical analysis of response times: the representation of response times by abstract processes with certain termination rules, and the decomposition of response times into component durations selectively influenced by different external factors. The chapter is not meant to serve as a survey of the extensive and diverse literature that bears upon these issues. Rather it relates to and somewhat extends one particular line of research, in whose development I have participated myself. The primary focus is on the logic of theoretical constructs rather than empirical facts and generalizations. In particular, the analysis is not predicated on specific assumptions concerning the form

---

Key words and phrases. Response time, selective influence, decomposition into components, decomposition rule, stochastic relationship.
Address for correspondence. E. N. Dzhafarov, Beckman Institute, University of Illinois, 405 North Mathews Urbana, IL 61801. Email: edzhafar@s.psych.uiuc.edu

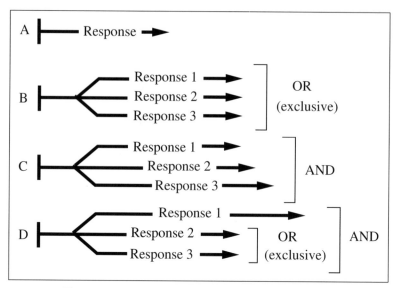

FIGURE 1. Examples of response arrangements.

of the response time distributions, except for occasionally needed constraints of a technical nature.

The term "response" refers primarily to an observable physical event, such as a key press or a certain activity level in a neuronal structure. However, to incorporate some of the traditional "information processing" issues, it is convenient to allow the term to also refer to hypothetical mental events, such as a visual representation of an object's shape or a retrieval of an item from a memory storage. In all cases the use of the term implies that responses occur within well-defined trials, that they belong to well-defined finite sets of possible responses, and that the moments when responses occur within a trial (even if theoretically derived or assumed) are viewed as (if they were) observable empirical data, subject to further analysis. In a typical experiment only one of possible responses may occur within a trial. Mutually non-exclusive responses, however, are also conceivable, such as activity bursts in several distinct neuronal structures or mental representations of different aspects of a stimulus. Figure 1 shows some of the variety of *response arrangements* to which the present discussion applies (i.e., the rules determining which responses may or may not co-occur within a trial; note that arrangements A and B correspond to the conventional simple and choice response time paradigms). Arrangements in which all responses may be withheld within a trial are also possible (e.g., a conventional disjunctive response time paradigm).

Response times, measured from some zero moment within a trial, are generally random variables. For a response arrangement like C in Figure 1, denoting the times of all possible responses by $\mathbf{T}_1$, ..., $\mathbf{T}_n$ (boldface letters indicate random variables), all empirical information about these response times is contained in their joint distribution function,

$$\mathcal{T}(t_1, ..., t_n; \Xi) = \mathrm{Prob}\{\mathbf{T}_1(\Xi) \leq t_1, ..., \mathbf{T}_n(\Xi) \leq t_n\}. \tag{1}$$

Here, Ξ stands for a description of those aspects of the external situation (such as target stimulus intensity, speed-accuracy emphasis, etc.) that may vary from trial to trial, deterministically or randomly, inducing changes in the joint distribution of $\mathbf{T}_1(\Xi), ..., \mathbf{T}_n(\Xi)$. Strictly speaking, therefore, one deals here with a *family* of random vectors (and the corresponding family of distribution functions), one vector (and distribution) for every possible value of Ξ.

The joint distribution function in (1) can be made applicable to response arrangements other than C in Figure 1, with the following proviso: If a response i does not occur within a trial, then the value of $\mathbf{T}_i$ is considered indefinite (or infinitely large): in other words, $\mathbf{T}_i(\Xi) \leq t$ is then false for any t. Thus understood (1) is the universal object of response time analysis. Since response times are observable (or treated as if they were such), the joint probability distributions are (assumed to be) known, at least on a sample level.

To construct a *process representation* for a vector of response times $\mathbf{T}_1(\Xi)$, ..., $\mathbf{T}_n(\Xi)$ means to theoretically derive certain n processes (neutrally referred to as *response processes*, i.e., processes preparing a response) and postulate certain *critical conditions*, so that the response i occurs if and as soon as the i-th process meets these conditions. Obviously, either the processes or the critical conditions (or both) should have stochasticity built in them to account for the randomness of response times. Figures 2 and 3 show two different process representations for a single-response arrangement (as in the simple response time paradigm). In both cases the parameters of the process change with changing values of the situation Ξ, and in both cases the critical condition is that the level of the process exceed a *preset criterion*. In Figure 2, the "McGill modeling scheme" (after McGill, 1963), the criterion is fixed whereas the process is stochastic. In Figure 3, the "Grice modeling scheme" (after Grice, 1968, 1972), the process is deterministic whereas the criterion is randomly chosen on every trial from a distribution. (Figure 3 consists of two concatenated graphs, the "response level" serving as the ordinate for the process graph and the abscissa for the criterion distribution function graph. Note that the external situation Ξ, as indicated in Figures 2 and 3, is generally a function of time within a trial.)

Contrary to tradition, *decompositions* of response times can be introduced as an issue logically unrelated to their process representations or even to response arrangements. The object of analysis here is not the joint distribution of $\mathbf{T}_1(\Xi)$, ..., $\mathbf{T}_n(\Xi)$ but rather the distribution of a single random duration $\mathbf{T}(\Xi)$ derived from this joint distribution. $\mathbf{T}(\Xi)$ may be the response time for a particular response i conditioned upon its occurrence, or the time when *some* response occurs in a choice paradigm, or one of many similar constructs. Decompositions of $\mathbf{T}(\Xi)$ are contingent on the decompositions of the external situation Ξ into a list of factors, α, β, γ, ..., with crossable levels. Once these factors are listed, one can define *time components* of $\mathbf{T}(\Xi)$ as "a component $\mathbf{A}(\alpha)$, influenced exclusively by α," "a component $\mathbf{B}(\beta)$, influenced exclusively by β," etc. To decompose $\mathbf{T}(\Xi)$ means to present it as

$$\mathbf{T}(\alpha, \beta, \gamma, \dots) \stackrel{d}{=} H\{\mathbf{A}(\alpha), \mathbf{B}(\beta), \mathbf{C}(\gamma), \dots\}, \tag{2}$$

where H is some function (the *decomposition rule*), and the symbol $\stackrel{d}{=}$ stands for "is distributed as."

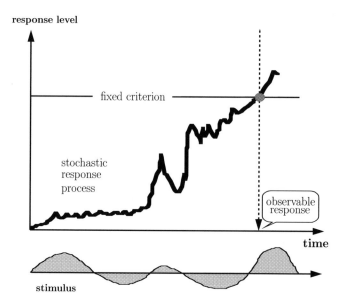

FIGURE 2. The McGill modeling scheme for a single response
(explanations in text).

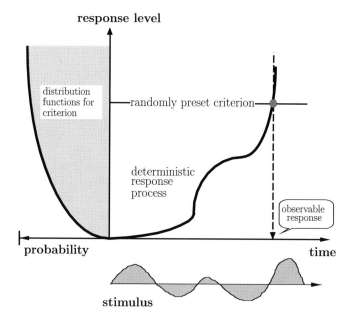

FIGURE 3. The Grice modeling scheme for a single response
(explanations in text).

Note an important logical difference between process representations and decompositions of response times. Response processes are identified by their *potential effects*, the responses to which they lead if certain critical conditions are met. Any change in the external situation Ξ generally influences the course of all these processes. By contrast, time components $\mathbf{A}(\alpha)$, $\mathbf{B}(\beta)$, $\mathbf{C}(\gamma)$, etc., are identified by the changes in the external situation that *influence them selectively*. Thus $\mathbf{A}$ is *defined* as a component influenced by α, and only by α – irrespective of whether such a component exists or whether it is uniquely determinable. The time components may be interpreted as corresponding to specific (unobservable) effects, but such an interpretation is inconsequential for recovering the decomposition rule H or the distributions of the time components. The precise meaning of selective influence in its relationship with possible joint distributions of time components is a rather subtle issue, discussed later.

Another significant difference between the two issues is that on a principal level the problem of process representations lends itself to a complete solution: unless one imposes additional constraints, such as selective influence, process representations can be constructed by a universal algorithm, for any response arrangement and any family of response time vectors. By contrast, only rudimentary knowledge is available on response time decompositions; this knowledge only applies to limited choices of the decomposition rule H in Equation 2 and the simplest forms of the stochastic relationships among the time components.

2. PROCESS REPRESENTATIONS

The problem of constructing process representations for single-response arrangements is quite simple, and the logical and operational meaning of the concepts involved is especially transparent in this case. Consider first the Grice-representation scheme (Figure 3), according to which the Ξ-dependent process $R(t; \Xi)$ representing a response time $\mathbf{T}(\Xi)$ is deterministic, and $\mathbf{T}(\Xi)$ is the time when $R(t; \Xi)$ exceeds for the first time a Ξ-independent randomly preset criterion $\mathbf{C}$. It is easy to show (Dzhafarov, 1993) that whatever the distribution function $\mathcal{T}(t; \Xi)$ for $\mathbf{T}(\Xi)$, the latter can be Grice-represented by choosing some distribution function $\mathcal{C}(c)$ for the criterion $\mathbf{C}$ and putting

$$R(t; \Xi) = \mathcal{C}^{-1}\{\mathcal{T}(t; \Xi)\}. \tag{3}$$

The choice of the criterion distribution function $\mathcal{C}(c)$ is arbitrary, except for minor technicalities.[1] Indeed, by a monotonic transformation of the "response level" axis in Figure 3 one can change $\mathcal{C}(c)$ into any other distribution function. Such a transformation, however, simultaneously changes the representing process $R(t; \Xi)$, so that its times of crossing the criterion, the only observables in the scheme, do not change. The sole role of the criterion distribution, therefore, is to calibrate the otherwise "rubber-band" axis on which both the criterion and the process assume their values. The "assumptions" that the criterion distribution has a particular form and that it is Ξ-independent are totally void of empirical content.

---

[1] The criterion distribution should be continuous. For technical convenience, it is preferable also to make it strictly increasing and non-negative (as in Figure 3).

The same conclusion applies to the "assumption" that the response time $\mathbf{T}(\Xi)$ can be represented by a deterministic Ξ-dependent process. It is clear from (3) that the deterministic process $R(t; \Xi)$ is just one of many possible descriptions for the distribution of $\mathbf{T}(\Xi)$, on a par with its distribution function $\mathcal{T}(t; \Xi)$, whose monotonic transformation $R(t; \Xi)$ is. In fact, with a specific choice of the criterion (namely, choosing it uniformly distributed between 0 and 1), $R(t; \Xi)$ and $\mathcal{T}(t; \Xi)$ can be made to formally coincide. At the same time, the use of the term "process" is not a misnomer here, because for any choice of the criterion the process $R(t; \Xi)$ is *physically realizable*, in the sense of causal consistency: If the external situation Ξ develops within a trial, the value of $R(t; \Xi)$ at any time t (given its initial value) only depends on the values of Ξ previous to the moment t:

$$R(t; \Xi) = R[\Xi(u) \mid_{u < t}].^2$$

Although quite elementary mathematically, the analysis above may appear surprising. It turns out that the principal idea of modeling response times by deterministic Ξ-dependent processes developing until they reach randomly present Ξ-independent criteria is not an empirically falsifiable model, but rather a theoretical language that applies to all conceivable response time distribution families. The term used in Dzhafarov (1993) is the "modeling scheme," a conceptual system that is not a model itself but that allows one to formulate all falsifiable models within its framework. Grice's (1968, 1972) original formulation of this modeling scheme was even weaker, as it allowed (unnecessarily) the criterion to depend on the external situation Ξ – and even in this weakened form the idea was widely considered too simplistic to be empirically applicable.

Any falsifiable model for response times (having been translated into the Grice scheme's language) can be of one of two kinds. It may state that the processes $R(t; \Xi)$, for one or more values of Ξ, have a particular shape when the "rubber-band" axis for their values is calibrated by the distribution of a particular form. For instance, the falsifiable part of Grice's original proposal is that the process $R(t; \Xi)$ is linear (Grice, 1968) or negative-exponential (Grice, 1972; Grice, Nullmeyer, & Spiker, 1982) when the response level axis is calibrated by a normal distribution.[3] A falsifiable model of another kind states that the processes $R(t; \Xi)$ for different values of Ξ have a particular mathematical relationship among them – without specifying the criterion distribution. For instance, in a visual motion detection model proposed in Dzhafarov and Allik (1984) and Dzhafarov, Sekuler, and Allik (1993) a moving stimulus initiates a "kinematic energy" process uniquely determined by

---

[2]Note that $\Xi(u) \mid_{u < t}$ is a function, that is, its values are taken with the moments at which they occur. In particular, the truncation point t is part of the function's identity, because of which t need not be included as a separate argument. A different though equivalent way of presenting the deterministic process $R(t; \Xi)$ is by a differential equation $\dot{R}(t; \Xi) = r[\Xi(u) \mid_{u \leq t}, R(u; \Xi) \mid_{u \leq t}]$, where the time derivative $\dot{R}(t; \Xi)$ may have to be expressed through Dirac's delta function. This representation is more readily generalizable to a vector of deterministic processes, as discussed later.

[3]An attempt to substantiate the choice of a normal distribution by such arguments as the central limit theorem is meaningless. This choice is arbitrary. At the same time, as shown in Dzhafarov (1993), the choice of a negative-exponential process on a normally calibrated axis is logically flawed.

the position-versus-time function. In such a model the question is whether one can find a single criterion distribution for all different processes.

The analysis of the McGill-representability (Figure 2) yields analogous results. According to this scheme, $\mathbf{T}(\Xi)$ is the time when a Ξ-dependent stochastic process $\mathbf{R}(t; \Xi)$ exceeds for the first time a fixed level (say, unity). Even the simplest and most restrictive versions of this scheme turn out to be mathematically equivalent to the Grice modeling scheme. They too, therefore, are merely descriptive theoretical languages. One can always McGill-represent $\mathbf{T}(\Xi)$ by computing $\mathbf{R}(t; \Xi)$ as a mathematical composition of a deterministic Ξ-dependent part $R(t; \Xi)$ and a Ξ-independent stationary noise $\mathbf{C}(t)$:

$$\mathbf{R}(t; \Xi) = G\{R(t; \Xi), \mathbf{C}(t)\}. \tag{4}$$

Except for technicalities, one is free to choose any composition function G and any stationary process $\mathbf{C}(t)$ (Ξ-independent). These two facts may appear even more surprising than the arbitrariness of the criterion distribution in the Grice modeling scheme. Nevertheless they are straightforward consequences of the equivalence between the two modeling schemes.[4] Using different composition functions (additive, multiplicative, etc.) one can construct a variety of generalizations for the stochastic processes commonly used in response time modeling (such as the diffusion processes with drift). The role of $\mathbf{C}(t)$ in (4) is precisely the same as that of the criterion in the Grice scheme: in fact, if the momentary distribution function of $G^{-1}\{1, \mathbf{C}(t)\}$ is matched with that of the criterion $\mathbf{C}$, then $R(t; \Xi)$ is the same in the two modeling schemes, in both cases computed by (3). Note that stochastic relationships among the distributions of $\mathbf{C}(t)$ at different moments of time are inconsequential: any two stochastic processes $\mathbf{R}(t; \Xi)$ with the same deterministic part $R(t; \Xi)$ and the same momentary distribution of $\mathbf{C}(t)$ represent the same response time $\mathbf{T}(\Xi)$. This shows that the McGill modeling scheme is conceptually more redundant than the Grice one.

The mathematical theory of the Grice-representability is considerably more sophisticated for multiple-response arrangements (Dzhafarov, 1993). The family of response time vectors $\mathbf{T}_1(\Xi), ..., \mathbf{T}_n(\Xi)$ is said to be Grice-represented by deterministic processes $R_1(t; \Xi), ..., R_n(t; \Xi)$ if there is a Ξ-independent vector of randomly preset criteria $\mathbf{C}_1, ..., \mathbf{C}_n$ (not necessarily stochastically independent) such that $\mathbf{T}_1(\Xi), ..., \mathbf{T}_n(\Xi)$ are the times when the respective processes exceed, each for the first time, their respective criteria.

The key issue here is how one understands the concept of a *vector of deterministic processes*. A single process $R(t; \Xi)$ is deterministic if its initial value is fixed and its value at time $t > 0$ only depends on the external situation Ξ (up to the moment t, if it develops in time). In the case of a vector $R_1(t; \Xi), ..., R_n(t; \Xi)$, however, one cannot just use the same definition componentwise, because the external situation Ξ here may not be the sole determinant of the processes. In addition, the

---

[4]G should be chosen increasing in the first argument and continuous in the second. The critical condition in the McGill scheme, $G\{R(t; \Xi), \mathbf{C}(t)\} \geq 1$, is then equivalent to $R(t; \Xi) \geq G^{-1}\{1, \mathbf{C}(t)\}$, which is the critical condition in the Grice scheme, provided the criterion distribution is matched with that of $G^{-1}\{1, \mathbf{C}(t)\}$. ($G^{-1}$ denotes the inverse of G with respect to the first argument.)

processes themselves form an "internal environment" for each other, or "interact" with each other, using the term descriptively. The definition, therefore, should be modified: processes $R_1(t; \Xi), ..., R_n(t; \Xi)$ are deterministic if their initial values are fixed and if

$$\dot{R}_i(t; \Xi) = r_i[\Xi(u) \mid_{u \leq t}, R_1(u; \Xi) \mid_{u \leq t}, ..., R_n(u; \Xi) \mid_{u \leq t}],$$

where the meaning of the time derivative $\dot{R}_i$ is the same as in Footnote 2.

Superficially the definition just given may seem unnecessarily complicated, because there may seem to be no way of changing one of the processes, say $R_1(t; \Xi)$, in order to observe the effect of this change on, say, $R_2(t; \Xi)$, while keeping the external situation Ξ unchanged. One cannot, for example, evaluate the impact of $R_1(t; \Xi)$ on other processes by either including or not including the first response in the response arrangement, because this would mean a manipulation of the external situation whose part the response arrangement is (provided it varies, as in this example, from trial to trial). This general argument, however, overlooks the mechanism of *process termination* built in the Grice modeling scheme. According to this scheme, the i-th response is generated if and when $R_i(t; \Xi)$ crosses its respective criterion, $\mathbf{C}_i$, at which moment the process is terminated. The terminated process can be thought of as not being defined or being set equal to infinity after the termination moment – whatever the formalization, we have here a change in the course of the process that is not determined by changes in the external situation. By the definition of deterministic processes, as soon as this happens (i.e., the i-th response occurs) the remaining processes generally change their course as compared to how they would have proceeded if the response did not occur.

A simple contemplation reveals that this is the only mechanism by which deterministic processes may develop differently in different trials with one and the same external situation. Because of this, the definition of deterministic processes can be made more specific: the value of $R_i(t; \Xi)$ at time $t > 0$ only depends on $i, \Xi(u) \mid_{u < t}$ and the list of response times (identified by responses) previous to the moment t. The way the occurrence of a response affects the remaining processes is different for different response arrangements. In the case when all responses are mutually exclusive (like in arrangement B in Figure 1) the occurrence of a response should "freeze" the upward development in all other processes – they must not increase beyond their achieved values till the end of the trial, in order to be prevented from crossing their criteria, however close these criteria might be to the achieved positions.

For an arrangement like C in Figure 1 the pattern of interactions among the processes may be more complex. Figure 4 provides an illustration involving three processes, $R_1(t; \Xi)$, $R_2(t; \Xi)$, and $R_3(t; \Xi)$, whose development is shown for a particular Ξ and a particular triad of preset criteria. The graphs in this figure have the same structure as Figure 3 (the axes are not labeled to avoid clutter). Small circles, vertically aligned, indicate moments when one of the processes terminates. The solid lines stemming from the origins show the development of the three processes until $R_1(t; \Xi)$ crosses its criterion; if this did not occur, the processes would have continued as shown by the dashed lines. The process $R_1(t; \Xi)$ does terminate, however, and this causes $R_2(t; \Xi)$, and $R_3(t; \Xi)$ to change their course (solid lines stemming from the first circle). The continuation after $R_2(t; \Xi)$ crosses its criterion is considered analogously.

Having established the meaning of the Grice-representability for multiple-response arrangements, it turns out that the main result here is essentially a straightforward multivariate analogue of that for single-response arrangements. Whatever the family of response time vectors $\mathbf{T}_1(\Xi)$, ..., $\mathbf{T}_n(\Xi)$, it can be Grice-represented by a vector of deterministic processes $R_1(t; \Xi), \dots, R_n(t; \Xi)$ coupled with a Ξ-independent vector of criteria $\mathbf{C}_1$, ..., $\mathbf{C}_n$. Moreover, the joint distribution function for the criteria can be chosen arbitrarily, except for some weak technical constraints that I will not discuss here. Analogous to the single-response case, the sole role of the criteria is to establish an n-dimensional system of coordinates for the vector $R_1(t; \Xi), ..., R_n(t; \Xi)$. For instance, choosing the criteria $\mathbf{C}_1$, ..., $\mathbf{C}_n$ stochastically independent (which is always an option) corresponds to making these coordinates orthogonal.

In Dzhafarov (1993), the Grice-representability is only proved for mutually exclusive responses (like in arrangement B in Figure 1), that is, it is established there for the situation where the only observable response time is associated with the process that reaches its criterion first. The way to generalize this result to arbitrary response arrangements is simple: it consists in successively applying the Grice-representability analysis to intervals between responses (the intercompletion times, in Townsend's terminology; Townsend, 1974) while considering the list of previously given responses and response times as part of the external situation. Let $[\mathbf{I}_{(1)}(\Xi), \mathbf{T}_{(1)}(\Xi)]$ be the identity and time of the response given first, $[\mathbf{I}_{(2)}(\Xi), \mathbf{T}_{(2)}(\Xi)], ..., [\mathbf{I}_{(n)}(\Xi), \mathbf{T}_{(n)}(\Xi)]$ being defined analogously. Consider the following sequence:

$$[\mathbf{I}_{(1)}(\Xi), \mathbf{T}_{(1)}(\Xi)]$$
$$\{\mathbf{I}_{(2)}(\Xi), \mathbf{T}_{(2)}(\Xi) \mid [\mathbf{I}_{(1)}(\Xi), \mathbf{T}_{(1)}(\Xi)] = (i_1, t_1)\}$$
$$\cdots$$
$$\{\mathbf{I}_{(n)}(\Xi), \mathbf{T}_{(n)}(\Xi)] \mid [\mathbf{I}_{(1)}(\Xi), \mathbf{T}_{(1)}(\Xi)] = (i_1, t_1), \dots, [\mathbf{I}_{(n-1)}(\Xi), \mathbf{T}_{(n-1)}(\Xi)] = (i_{n-1}, t_{n-1})\}.$$

The bivariate distribution of these "label and time" variables is uniquely computable from the joint distribution of $\mathbf{T}_1(\Xi)$, ..., $\mathbf{T}_n(\Xi)$. Let a Ξ-independent vector of criteria $\mathbf{C}_1$, ..., $\mathbf{C}_n$ be chosen. The theory presented in Dzhafarov (1993) allows one to compute processes $R_1(t; \Xi), ..., R_n(t; \Xi)$ such that $[\mathbf{I}_{(1)}(\Xi), \mathbf{T}_{(1)}(\Xi)] = (i, t)$ if and only if the process $R_i(t; \Xi)$ crosses its criterion at time t while the other processes are still below their criteria.[5] In other words, knowing $[\mathbf{I}_{(1)}(\Xi), \mathbf{T}_{(1)}(\Xi)]$ one can reconstruct the processes up to the first circle in Figure 4.

---

[5] The actual computation of the processes involves differential equations that may or may not be solvable analytically. If the criteria are chosen stochastically independent, however, a closed form solution exists. The potential crossing times for these processes (i.e., the crossing times for each of the processes conditioned upon its finishing first) are then stochastically independent random variables whose distributions, save for technical details, are derived by different means in Townsend (1976) and Marley and Colonius (1992).

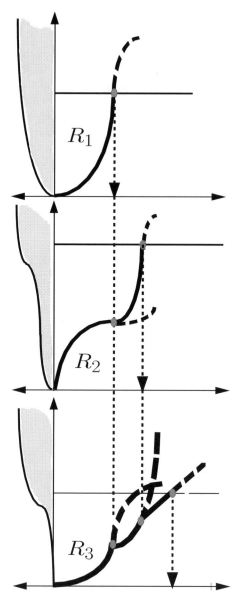

FIGURE 4. A Grice model for three non-exclusive responses (explanations in text).

Assuming now that $[\mathbf{I}_{(1)}(\Xi), \mathbf{T}_{(1)}(\Xi)] = (i_1, t_1)$, redefine the criteria as the $(n-1)$-component vector

$$\mathbf{C}_1 - R_1(t_1; \Xi), ..., \mathbf{C}_{i_1-1} - R_{i_1-1}(t_1; \Xi), \mathbf{C}_{i_1+1} - R_{i_1+1}(t_1; \Xi), ..., \mathbf{C}_n - R_n(t_1; \Xi),$$

and take as a new multidimensional origin the moment t_1 and the positions

$$R_1(t_1; \Xi), ..., R_{i_1-1}(t_1; \Xi), R_{i_1+1}(t_1; \Xi), ..., R_n(t_1; \Xi).$$

Now applying Dzhafarov's (1993) theory to the conditional "label and time" variable $\{\mathbf{I}_{(2)}(\Xi), \mathbf{T}_{(2)}(\Xi) \mid [\mathbf{I}_{(1)}(\Xi), \mathbf{T}_{(1)}(\Xi)] = (i_1, t_1)\}$, one reconstructs the continuations for the $n-1$ processes remaining after the first response, until one of them crosses its criterion (as between the first and second circles in Figure 4). The following steps are made analogously, leading from one process termination to another, until one exhausts all the processes. Obviously, a complete Grice-representation of the family of response time vectors $\mathbf{T}_1(\Xi)$, ..., $\mathbf{T}_n(\Xi)$ requires that the entire procedure is replicated across all possible sequences $(i_1, t_1), ..., (i_{n-1}, t_{n-1})$ and for all possible values of Ξ.

Note that the stochastic relationship among the criteria does not determine the stochastic relationship among observable response times – in addition one has to know the pattern of interactions among the deterministic processes. For instance, if the criteria are chosen stochastically independent, the times of different responses are stochastically independent if and only if the processes representing them do not interact (i.e., if the solid and dashed lines in Figure 4 coincide).[6]

The equivalence between the Grice and McGill modeling schemes for multiple-response arrangements is established in the same way as it is for single-response arrangements. Having chosen (essentially arbitrarily) some composition functions G_1, ..., G_n, one can always McGill-represent response times $\mathbf{T}_1(\Xi)$, ..., $\mathbf{T}_n(\Xi)$ by stochastic processes $\mathbf{R}_1(t; \Xi)$, ..., $\mathbf{R}_n(t; \Xi)$ computed as

$$\mathbf{R}_i(t; \Xi) = G_i\{R_i(t; \Xi), \mathbf{C}_i(t)\}, \qquad i = 1, ..., n,$$

so that the i-th response occurs when $\mathbf{R}_i(t; \Xi)$ crosses a unity level. Here, $\mathbf{C}_1(t)$, ..., $\mathbf{C}_n(t)$ is a stationary Ξ-independent vector of noise processes that, save for technicalities, can be chosen arbitrarily. The deterministic parts $R_1(t; \Xi), ..., R_n(t; \Xi)$ can be made to coincide with the deterministic processes in the Grice modeling scheme if the joint distribution of $\mathbf{C}_1$, ..., $\mathbf{C}_n$ in that scheme is chosen to be identical with the momentary joint distribution of $G_1^{-1}\{1, \mathbf{C}_1(t)\}$, ..., $G_n^{-1}\{1, \mathbf{C}_n(t)\}$ (see Footnote 4).

Once again we come to the conclusion, this time with no restrictions on response arrangements, that the most principal ideas underlying the construction of process representations for response times (such ideas as "deterministic processes cross random criteria," "stochastic processes cross a fixed criterion," "criteria are stimulus-independent," "processes horse-race for their individual criteria," etc.) are not empirically testable. In a sense one could say that they are testable in conjunction with other assumptions, but even this would not be satisfactory: Indeed, one would not say, for example, that the non-falsifiable idea of representing a random variable by its distribution function is testable in conjunction with the assumption that the distribution is normal. The Grice and McGill representations, as defined in this section, form universally applicable theoretical languages allowing one to formulate within their frameworks all conceivable testable propositions. One

---

[6]If the criteria are chosen stochastically independent but the processes do interact, then the potential crossing times for the processes are stochastically independent random variables *if counted from the moment of the last response.* Townsend and Ashby (1983) call this "within-stage independence," and Vorberg (1990) derives the distribution of the potential crossing times using a combination of the step-by-step reconstruction just presented with the technique mentioned in Footnote 5.

may decide, of course, to formulate one's models in other, equally non-falsifiable languages (involving, e.g., processes interacting with criteria, criteria that are non-stationary stochastic processes, criteria coupled with deadlines, etc.) but such a decision cannot be construed as aimed at overcoming limitations of the Grice modeling scheme or the simplest versions of the McGill modeling scheme – because no such limitations exist.

3. SELECTIVE INFLUENCE

Although most of the concepts discussed in this section are quite general, the primary focus is on a special case of (2), involving just two time components selectively influenced by two factors:

$$\mathbf{T}(\alpha,\beta) \stackrel{d}{=} \mathbf{A}(\alpha) \diamond \mathbf{B}(\beta). \tag{5}$$

The decomposition rule here is, for convenience, presented as an algebraic operation $\diamond$. The decomposed duration $\mathbf{T}(\alpha,\beta)$ is the only observable in this formulation; for this reason I will refer to $\mathbf{T}(\alpha,\beta)$ as the "response time," even though it is generally computed from a joint distribution of response times as explained in the introduction. A precise definition of selectively influenced time components is given below. The meaning, however, is obvious when $\mathbf{A}(\alpha)$ and $\mathbf{B}(\beta)$ are stochastically independent (for any given values of α, β).

The traditional approach consists in treating the time components $\mathbf{A}(\alpha)$ and $\mathbf{B}(\beta)$ as durations of separate processes whose developments are selectively influenced by the factors α and β. It is often assumed, based on this interpretation, that the decomposition rule in (5) can only be one of three operations: *plus* (the two processes are serially concatenated), *maximum*, or *minimum* (the two processes develop in parallel until the termination of both of them, in the case of *maximum*, or either one of them, in the case of *minimum*).[7] To understand the merits of this approach, one has to begin with clarifying the notion of *processes selectively influenced by different factors*. Using, for simplicity, the language of the Grice modeling scheme, the most general definition involving two such processes would be

$$\dot{R}_1(t;\alpha,\beta) = r_1[\alpha, R_1(u;\alpha,\beta)\mid_{u \leq t}, R_2(u;\alpha,\beta)\mid_{u \leq t}],$$
$$\dot{R}_2(t;\alpha,\beta) = r_2[\beta, R_1(u;\alpha,\beta)\mid_{u \leq t}, R_2(u;\alpha,\beta)\mid_{u \leq t}], \tag{6}$$

where I write α and β instead of more rigorous $\alpha(u)\mid_{u \leq t}$ and $\beta(u)\mid_{u \leq t}$. For the present purposes it is sufficient to only consider two special cases of this definition.

In the most restrictive case,

$$R_1(t;\alpha,\beta) = R_1[t;\alpha, I_2(t)],$$
$$R_2(t;\alpha,\beta) = R_2[t;\beta, I_1(t)],$$

where $I_i(t)$ is an indicator variable whose value is, say, 0 or 1 depending on whether or not the i-th process has terminated by the moment t. A pair of such processes is shown in Figure 5, whose structure is essentially the same as that of Figure 4. Suppose that the two processes are linear on axes calibrated by some choice of the criteria $\mathbf{C}_1$, $\mathbf{C}_2$ (for now they may be thought to be stochastically independent). R_1

---

[7]In the case of *minimum* the longer of the two durations is, of course, only "potential," the duration the process would have had had it finished first.

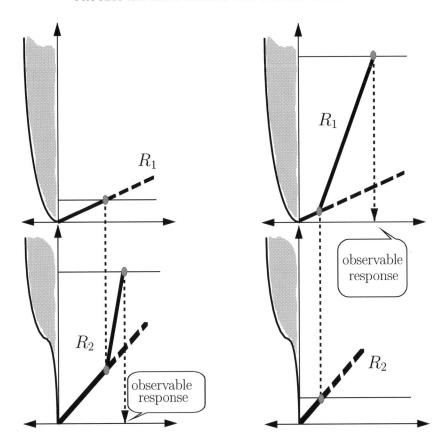

FIGURE 5. Deterministic selectively influenced parallel processes (explanations in text).

develops with the rate v_α (that only depends on α) if R_2 is still in progress, but as soon as R_2 terminates (right panel) R_1 increments its rate to hv_α; if R_1 terminates first (left panel), then R_2 whose rate before that was v_β (only depending on β) increments it to hv_β. The observable response time $\mathbf{T}(\alpha,\beta)$ is the time when all processing ends, that is, $\mathbf{T}(\alpha,\beta)$ is the maximum of two durations: of the process R_1 and of the process R_2 (a "parallel-AND" connection, in traditional terms).

The second special case of the definition of selectively influenced interacting processes, (6), is slightly less restrictive:

$$R_1(t; \alpha,\beta) = R_1[t; \alpha, J_2(t)],$$
$$R_2(t; \alpha,\beta) = R_2[t; \beta, J_1(t)],$$

where $J_i(t)$ equals the termination time for the i-th process if it has terminated by the moment t, and $J_i(t)$ is undefined (or equal to infinity) otherwise. A pair of such processes is shown in Figure 6 (a "fixed-order serial" connection). Here, the process R_1, while in progress, completely "inhibits" the process R_2 (i.e., keeps it below the minimum level of its criterion); after R_1 has terminated, R_2 begins developing and

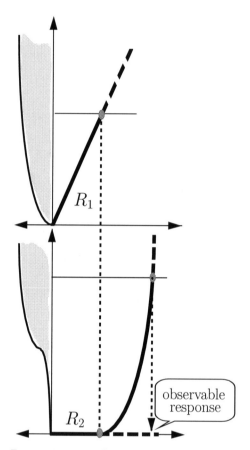

FIGURE 6. Deterministic selectively influenced fixed-order serial
processes (explanations in text).

the moment at which it reaches its criterion coincides with the observable response
time $\mathbf{T}(\alpha,\beta)$. Suppose that with some choice of the criteria $\mathbf{C}_1$, $\mathbf{C}_2$ (again, for now
they may be considered stochastically independent), R_1 develops linearly with the
rate v_α (that only depends on α); after it terminates, R_2 develops as

$$R_2[t; \beta, J_1(t)] = v_\beta \left[t^p - J_1(t)^p\right]^{1/p}, p \geq 1.$$

It is easy to derive that for the parallel-AND connection in Figure 5,

$$\mathbf{T}(\alpha,\beta) \overset{d}{=} \min\{\mathbf{C}_1/v_\alpha, \mathbf{C}_2/v_\beta\}(1 - h^{-1}) + \max\{\mathbf{C}_1/v_\alpha, \mathbf{C}_2/v_\beta\}h^{-1},$$

whereas for the serial connection in Figure 6,

$$\mathbf{T}(\alpha,\beta) \overset{d}{=} \left[(\mathbf{C}_1/v_\alpha)^p + (\mathbf{C}_2/v_\beta)^p\right]^{1/p}.$$

Varying the values of h or p, one can relate the results to decomposition formula
(5) by renaming the terms depending only on v_α and $\mathbf{C}_1$ into $\mathbf{A}(\alpha)$ and the terms

depending only on v_β and $\mathbf{C}_2$ into $\mathbf{B}(\beta)$. One can observe then that the parallel-AND and fixed-order serial connections shown in Figures 5 and 6 yield a wide variety of different decomposition rules ◇, including the familiar

$$\mathbf{T}(\alpha,\beta) \overset{d}{=} max\{\mathbf{C}_1/v_\alpha, \mathbf{C}_2/v_\beta\} = max\{\mathbf{A}(\alpha), \mathbf{B}(\beta)\}, \qquad \text{when } h = 1,$$

$$\mathbf{T}(\alpha,\beta) \overset{d}{=} \{\mathbf{C}_1/2v_\alpha + \mathbf{C}_2/2v_\beta\} = \mathbf{A}(\alpha) + \mathbf{B}(\beta), \qquad \text{when } h = 2,$$

$$\mathbf{T}(\alpha,\beta) \overset{d}{=} min\{\mathbf{C}_1/v_\alpha, \mathbf{C}_2/v_\beta\} = min\{\mathbf{A}(\alpha), \mathbf{B}(\beta)\}, \qquad \text{when } h = \infty,$$

for the parallel-AND connection, and

$$\mathbf{T}(\alpha,\beta) \overset{d}{=} \{\mathbf{C}_1/v_\alpha + \mathbf{C}_2/v_\beta\} = \mathbf{A}(\alpha) + \mathbf{B}(\beta), \qquad \text{when } p = 1,$$

$$\mathbf{T}(\alpha,\beta) \overset{d}{=} max\{\mathbf{C}_1/v_\alpha, \mathbf{C}_2/v_\beta\} = max\{\mathbf{A}(\alpha), \mathbf{B}(\beta)\}, \qquad \text{when } p = \infty,$$

for the serial connection.

These simple examples demonstrate several things. First, they show that the operations *plus, minimum,* and *maximum* in the domain of time components need not correspond to, respectively, serial, parallel-OR, and parallel-AND arrangements in the domain of hypothetical processes, *even if the selective influence by the factors α and β holds both for the time components and for the processes.* Second, by setting h and p equal to values different from those above, one can see that the *plus, minimum,* and *maximum* do not have a privileged status among a variety of possible decomposition rules. Such decomposition rules as, say, the "Minkowski-norm" operations $[\mathbf{A}(\alpha)^p + \mathbf{A}(\beta)^p]^{1/p}$ are as realizable physically at the unconventional values of $p = 2$ or 3 as they are for the conventional $p = 1$ or ∞. Third, the examples show that the time components in (5) can *characterize* certain processes *without being their durations*: for instance, neither of the two additive time components in the case $h = 2$ of the parallel-AND connection is the duration of either of the two processes. Finally, the examples show that selectively influenced (interacting) processes need not have selectively influenced durations. It is easy to check that the durations $\mathbf{T}_1(\alpha,\beta)$ and $\mathbf{T}_2(\alpha,\beta)$ of (the non-zero portions of) R_1 and R_2 are not selectively influenced by α and β, because of which it is not surprising that, say, for $h = 2$ in the parallel-AND connection

$$max\{\mathbf{T}_1(\alpha,\beta), \mathbf{T}_2(\alpha,\beta)\} \overset{d}{=} \mathbf{A}(\alpha) + \mathbf{B}(\beta),$$

or that for $p = \infty$ in the serial connection

$$\mathbf{T}_1(\alpha,\beta) + \mathbf{T}_2(\alpha,\beta) \overset{d}{=} max\{\mathbf{A}(\alpha), \mathbf{B}(\beta)\}.$$

Having established that the relationship between selectively influenced processes and selectively influenced time components is both indirect and complex, it seems reasonable to dissociate these two issues. The approach suggested in Dzhafarov and Schweickert (1995) consists in treating decomposition (5) as a structural property of the observable response time, $\mathbf{T}(\alpha,\beta)$, rather than evidence for a particular processing architecture. A time component, say $\mathbf{A}(\alpha)$, of $\mathbf{T}(\alpha,\beta)$ can be viewed as a "would-be" version of $\mathbf{T}(\alpha,\beta)$: The response time that would be observed if it were only affected by one factor (in this case, α). The problem of decomposing $\mathbf{T}(\alpha,\beta)$ according to (5) becomes, therefore, the one of determining the algebraic operation by which the factual response time $\mathbf{T}(\alpha,\beta)$ can be computed from its two "would-be" forms. The first step in dealing with this problem is to define the very notion of the time components being selectively influenced by different factors; so far, I only used this notion for the case of stochastically independent components. The account below is a systematic version of those given in Dzhafarov (1992) and Dzhafarov and Schweickert (1995).

Any two random variables (A, B) whose joint distribution depends on some set of variables Ξ can be presented as

$$(\mathbf{A},\mathbf{B}) = \{A(\Xi, \mathbf{P}_1, \mathbf{P}_2), B(\Xi, \mathbf{P}_1, \mathbf{P}_2)\},$$

where $\mathbf{P}_1, \mathbf{P}_2$ are stochastically independent random variables uniformly distributed between 0 and 1, and A, B are some functions.[8] (This simple mathematical fact has interesting philosophical implications: *all stochasticity in the dependence of some random variables on external factors can be relegated to random variables that do not depend on these factors.*)

When Ξ is (α, β), it is natural to adopt the following definition: **A** and **B** are selectively influenced by factors α and β, respectively, if (and only if) they can be presented as

$$(\mathbf{A},\mathbf{B}) = \{A(\alpha, \mathbf{P}_1, \mathbf{P}_2), B(\beta, \mathbf{P}_1, \mathbf{P}_2)\}. \tag{7}$$

A special case of this representation is obtained when the function A depends on $\mathbf{P}_1, \mathbf{P}_2$ only through some transformation $\mathbf{C}_1 = C_1(\mathbf{P}_1, \mathbf{P}_2)$, and the function B only through some transformation $\mathbf{C}_2 = C_2(\mathbf{P}_1, \mathbf{P}_2)$:

$$(\mathbf{A},\mathbf{B}) = \{A^\star(\alpha, \mathbf{C}_1), B^\star(\beta, \mathbf{C}_2)\}, \tag{8}$$

where the joint distribution of $\mathbf{C}_1, \mathbf{C}_2$ does not depend on either α or β. Thus in all examples discussed earlier in connection with Figures 5 and 6 one can drop the requirement that $\mathbf{C}_1$ and $\mathbf{C}_2$ (the criteria) be stochastically independent: The components $\mathbf{C}_1/v_\alpha$ and $\mathbf{C}_2/v_\beta$, for instance, are selectively influenced by α and β irrespective of the joint distribution of $\mathbf{C}_1$ and $\mathbf{C}_2$. The essence of this definition is that the selectivity in the time components' dependence on external factors and the components' stochastic interdependence are logically orthogonal.

It is useful to relate this definition to two other concepts proposed in the literature with the intent of capturing the same relationship. The first is the *marginal selectivity* (Townsend & Schweickert, 1989), a weak requirement that the marginal distributions of the components **A** and **B** in (5) only depend on α and β, respectively. This is obviously implied by the above definition of selective influence. The second notion is that of *indirect nonselective influence* (Townsend, 1984; Townsend & Ashby, 1983; Townsend & Thomas, 1994) which takes place when **A** and **B** are stochastically interdependent but either the conditional distribution of **A**|**B** only depends on α or the conditional distribution of **B**|**A** only depends on β. The example associated with Figure 6 provides an illustration: If the criteria $\mathbf{C}_1$

---

[8]This proposition is a multivariate version of Smirnov's fundamental representation used in Monte-Carlo simulations (e.g., Yermalov, 1971). Let, for example, B be the inverse of the marginal distribution function for **B** (depending on Ξ). Then $\mathbf{B} = B(\Xi, \mathbf{P}_2)$. Let $\mathcal{Q}$ be the inverse of the conditional distribution function for **A** given a value of **B** (also depending on Ξ). Then $\mathbf{A} = \mathcal{Q}[\Xi, \mathbf{P}_1 \mid B(\Xi, \mathbf{P}_2)]$, which can be written as $A(\Xi, \mathbf{P}_1, \mathbf{P}_2)$. In the text I use a symmetrical version of this representation. Observe that by this construction A and B can always be made increasing in, respectively, $\mathbf{P}_1$ and $\mathbf{P}_2$. The generalization to more than two components is trivial.

and $\mathbf{C}_2$ are stochastically independent, then the duration of the second process, $[(\mathbf{C}_1/v_\alpha)^p + (\mathbf{C}_2/v_\beta)^p]^{1/p}$, does not depend on α other than through the duration of the first process, $\mathbf{C}_1/v_\alpha$. (This is not true, however, for interdependent $\mathbf{C}_1$ and $\mathbf{C}_2$.) It is easy to see that the indirect nonselective influence and the selective influence in the sense of (7) or (8) are mutually exclusive concepts. The components $\mathbf{C}_1/v_\alpha$ and $\mathbf{C}_2/v_\beta$, to use this example again, are selectively influenced by α and β but for interdependent $\mathbf{C}_1$ and $\mathbf{C}_2$ the conditional distribution of $\mathbf{C}_1/v_\alpha$ given $\mathbf{C}_2/v_\beta = const$ will depend on both α and β. The indirect nonselective influence, therefore, must not be treated as a generalization or even analogue of selective influence.

4. Decompositions

For any given decomposition rule $\diamond$, decomposition (5) is not well-defined unless one specifies the stochastic relationship between the selectively influenced response time components $\mathbf{A}(\alpha) = A(\alpha, \mathbf{P}_1, \mathbf{P}_2)$ and $\mathbf{B}(\beta) = B(\beta, \mathbf{P}_1, \mathbf{P}_2)$, as defined in (7). This stochastic relationship is determined by the functions A and B since the joint distribution of $\mathbf{P}_1$, $\mathbf{P}_2$ is fixed. A general formulation of the decomposition problem, therefore, is as follows: given (a family of) observable response times $\mathbf{T}(\alpha, \beta)$, determine all $(A, B, \diamond)$ such that decomposition (5) holds. There is no known way of solving this problem without either severely restricting the class of possible response time distributions (which is not an option as the present work only deals with distribution-free considerations), or severely restricting the class of possible triads $(A, B, \diamond)$. The following is an account of results established for two special versions of the decomposition problem. In one of them, the decomposition rule $\diamond$ is being sought within a wide class of operations under the assumption that the functions A and B induce a known (and very simple) stochastic relationship between $\mathbf{A}(\alpha)$ and $\mathbf{B}(\beta)$. In another, the choice is being made between two such simple forms of stochastic relationship under the assumption[9] that the decomposition rule is known.

The two simple forms of stochastic relationship just mentioned are (*stochastic*) *independence* and *perfect positive (stochastic) interdependence*, formally obtained as special cases of representation (8). If $\mathbf{C}_1$ and $\mathbf{C}_2$, that can be referred to as the "sources of random variability," are stochastically independent (in symbols, $\mathbf{C}_1 \perp \mathbf{C}_2$), then so are the time components, $\mathbf{A}(\alpha) \perp \mathbf{B}(\beta)$. If $\mathbf{C}_1 = \mathbf{C}_2$ (i.e., the time components have a common source of random variability) and if the functions $A^\star$ and $B^\star$ are increasing transformations of each other (for any given α, β), then we have the case of perfect positive interdependence, in symbols, $\mathbf{A}(\alpha) \| \mathbf{B}(\beta)$. In this case the time components vary randomly but always "increase and decrease together."

The theory presented in Dzhafarov and Schweickert (1995) is aimed at the recovery of the decomposition rules for which

$$\mathbf{T}(\alpha, \beta) \overset{d}{=} \mathbf{A}(\alpha) \diamond \mathbf{B}(\beta), \mathbf{A}(\alpha) \overset{s}{-\!\!-} \mathbf{B}(\beta), \tag{9}$$

---

[9]Here and in the previous sentence, the "assumptions" should be understood as part of the definition of the components for which one wishes to determine the unknown connecting operation or unknown stochastic relationship.

where $\overset{s}{-}$ stands either for $\perp$ (decomposition into independent components) or for $\parallel$ (decomposition into perfectly positively interdependent components). The theory requires that the distribution of $\mathbf{T}(\alpha,\beta)$ be known at the four treatments of a 2×2 factorial design, $(\alpha_1,\alpha_2)\times(\beta_1,\beta_2)$, and that both factor manipulations be *effective*. Denoting $\mathbf{T}_{ij}=\mathbf{T}(\alpha_i,\beta_j)$, $i=1,2,j=l,2$, the effectiveness means that the unordered pair of the random variables $(\mathbf{T}_{11},\mathbf{T}_{22})$ differs from the pair $(\mathbf{T}_{12},\mathbf{T}_{21})$.[10]

The following proposition is referred to as the ($\diamond$)-test under the stochastic relationship $\overset{s}{-}$:

$$\mathbf{T}_{11}\diamond\mathbf{T}_{22}\overset{d}{=}\mathbf{T}_{12}\diamond\mathbf{T}_{21}\ (\mathbf{T}_{11}\overset{s}{-}\mathbf{T}_{22},\mathbf{T}_{12}\overset{s}{-}\mathbf{T}_{21}).\tag{10}$$

If this proposition holds, then the ($\diamond$)-test is called *successful* under the stochastic relationship $\overset{s}{-}$.

It is convenient to explain the meaning of (10) on a sample level, as this simultaneously provides a lead to a statistical realization of the decomposition tests (Cortese & Dzhafarov, 1996; Dzhafarov & Cortese, 1996). Let $\{\mathbf{T}_{ij}^1,...,\mathbf{T}_{ij}^n\}$ be a random sample from $\mathbf{T}_{ij}$ ($i=1,2,j=1,2$). Pairing the sampled values for $\mathbf{T}_{11}$ with those for $\mathbf{T}_{22}$ (in no particular order) and doing the same with $\mathbf{T}_{12}$ and $\mathbf{T}_{21}$, one forms two sequences,

$$\{\mathbf{T}_{11}^1\diamond\mathbf{T}_{22}^1,...,\mathbf{T}_{11}^n\diamond\mathbf{T}_{22}^n\}\text{ and }\{\mathbf{T}_{12}^1\diamond\mathbf{T}_{21}^1,...,\mathbf{T}_{12}^n\diamond\mathbf{T}_{21}^n\}.\tag{11}$$

The ($\diamond$)-test is successful under independence, if and only if the empirical distribution functions based on these two sequences converge to one and the same population distribution function as $n\to\infty$. The limit distribution is, obviously, that of $\mathbf{T}_{11}\diamond\mathbf{T}_{22}$ ($\mathbf{T}_{11}\perp\mathbf{T}_{22}$) and $\mathbf{T}_{12}\diamond\mathbf{T}_{21}$ ($\mathbf{T}_{12}\perp\mathbf{T}_{21}$). For perfect positive interdependence the sample-level account is essentially the same, except that the samples have to be ordered first, $\{\mathbf{T}_{ij}^{(1)}\le...\le\mathbf{T}_{ij}^{(n)}\}$, and the paired values should have identical quantile ranks. The ($\diamond$)-test is successful under perfect positive interdependence if and only if the empirical distribution functions based on thus formed sequences

$$\{\mathbf{T}_{11}^{(1)}\diamond\mathbf{T}_{22}^{(1)}\le...\le\mathbf{T}_{11}^{(n)}\diamond\mathbf{T}_{22}^{(n)}\}\text{ and }\{\mathbf{T}_{12}^{(1)}\diamond\mathbf{T}_{21}^{(1)}\le...\le\mathbf{T}_{12}^{(n)}\diamond\mathbf{T}_{21}^{(n)}\}\tag{12}$$

converge to one and the same population distribution function as $n\to\infty$. The limit distribution here is that of $\mathbf{T}_{11}\diamond\mathbf{T}_{22}$ ($\mathbf{T}_{11}\parallel\mathbf{T}_{22}$) and $\mathbf{T}_{12}\diamond\mathbf{T}_{21}$ ($\mathbf{T}_{12}\parallel\mathbf{T}_{21}$).

Assume now that $a\diamond b$ is an associative and commutative operation, such as $min\{a,b\}, max\{a,b\}, a+b, a\times b, (a^k+b^k)^{1/k}$, etc. It is easy to establish that if $\mathbf{T}(\alpha,\beta)$ is ($\diamond$)-decomposable under a stochastic relationship $\overset{s}{-}$, then for any 2×2 design the ($\diamond$)-test is successful under the same $\overset{s}{-}$. For the case when $\diamond$ is addition and $\overset{s}{-}$ is $\perp$ (additive decomposition into independent components) this statement has been long since known (Ashby & Townsend, 1980; Roberts & Sternberg, 1992), but even for *maximum* and *minimum*, the "classical" alternatives to addition, the precise analogy has been overlooked.

---

[10]In fact the requirement is stronger: one of the identities $max\{F_{12}(t),F_{21}(t)\}\equiv max\{F_{11}(t),F_{22}(t)\}$ and $min\{F_{12}(t),F_{21}(t)\}\equiv min\{F_{11}(t),F_{22}(t)\}$ must not be satisfied (F_{ij} being the distribution function for $\mathbf{T}_{ij}$). For all practical purposes, however, all one has to be concerned with is the effectiveness of the factor manipulations.

The just formulated necessary condition for ($\diamond$)-decomposability can, in fact, be generalized beyond the associative and commutative operations. Let us call an operation $\star$ *renderable* by an operation $\diamond$ if for some functions f and g, both increasing or both decreasing,

$$a \star b \equiv f(a) \diamond g(b).$$

For example, the non-associative and non-commutative operations $pa + qb$ and $a^p + b^q$, where p and q are constants of the same sign, are both renderable by addition. It is easy to verify now that the following generalization holds: If $\mathbf{T}(\alpha,\beta)$ is ($\star$)-decomposable under a stochastic relationship $\overset{s}{-}$, and if $\star$ is renderable by an associative and commutative operation $\diamond$, then for any 2×2 design the ($\diamond$)-test is successful under the same $\overset{s}{-}$. The verification is based on observing that $f[\mathbf{A}(\alpha)]$ and $g[\mathbf{B}(\beta)]$) are selectively influenced by α and β under the same stochastic relationship ($\perp$ or $\parallel$) as $\mathbf{A}(\alpha)$ and $\mathbf{B}(\beta)$ themselves.

Since a single associative and commutative operation can render many different operations, it is clear that in this trivial sense decomposability (9) is not unique. It is more interesting, however, to find out whether a response time $\mathbf{T}(\alpha,\beta)$ can be simultaneously ($\diamond$)-decomposed and ($\Diamond$)-decomposed (under one and the same stochastic relationship $\overset{s}{-}$) when $\diamond$ and $\Diamond$ are associative, commutative, and mutually nonrenderable. The answer to this question turns out to be negative, provided that the two operations are "well-behaved." Dzhafarov and Schweickert (1995) give the following sufficient (but not necessary) conditions for the "well-behavedness." First, $\diamond$ and $\Diamond$ belong to the class of *simple operations*, that consists of all *addition-like operations* $a \oplus b$ (i.e., those continuous in both arguments, strictly increasing in both arguments, and mapping onto their domains) and appended to them $min\{a,b\}$ and $max\{a,b\}$.[11] Second, the operations $\diamond$ and $\Diamond$ are *algebraically distinct*, which means that for any u and v, there is at most one unordered pair (x, y) such that $x \diamond y = u$ and $x \Diamond y = v$. These conditions are not very stringent: theoretically interesting competing decomposition rules are likely to be algebraically distinct simple operations. Under these conditions the decomposition rule uniqueness holds: the ($\diamond$)-decomposability excludes the ($\Diamond$)-decomposability, under the same $\overset{s}{-}$. In fact, this result follows from a yet stronger one according to which the ($\diamond$)-test and ($\Diamond$)-test for any two operations with postulated properties cannot be successful simultaneously under the same $\overset{s}{-}$.

The decomposition rule uniqueness does not imply any form of uniqueness for the time components. Generally, if a response time $\mathbf{T}(\alpha,\beta)$ is ($\diamond$)-decomposable under $\overset{s}{-}$, then one can find an infinity of the component times $\mathbf{A}(\alpha)$, $\mathbf{B}(\beta)$, into which this decomposition can be made. Nor does the decomposition rule uniqueness imply a form of uniqueness for the stochastic relationship. The latter should be treated as part of the time components' definition, and one can construct examples when $\mathbf{T}(\alpha,\beta)$ is both ($\diamond$)-decomposable under independence and ($\Diamond$)-decomposable under perfect positive interdependence (including the possibility that $\diamond$ and $\Diamond$ coincide).

---

[11] *Minimum* and *maximum* can be construed as limiting cases of addition-like operations. The results of Dzhafarov and Schweickert (1995) can be generalized to other limiting operations, but the extent of such a generalization is not quite clear.

An obvious but important consequence of the decomposition rule uniqueness is that decomposition (9) is an empirically falsifiable proposition rather than a descriptive characterization. If the four distributions of $\mathbf{T}(\alpha,\beta)$ in a 2×2 design are known precisely, and if the factor manipulations are found to be effective, then the decomposability can be verified or falsified for any decomposition rule and under either of the two forms of stochastic relationship. Moreover, in a list of simple operations that are pairwise algebraically distinct, all but at most one of them have to be rejected as true decomposition rules under a given form of stochastic relationship. When the distributions of $\mathbf{T}(\alpha,\beta)$ in a 2×2 design are only known on a sample level, one should expect that the difference between the two sequences in (11) or (12), depending on the form of $\overset{s}{=}$, will be small if $\diamond$ is the true decomposition rule and large if it is not. A sampling distribution theory for this difference (specifically, the Smirnov maximum distance between the empirical distribution functions) developed in Dzhafarov and Cortese (1996) allows one to formally test the hypothesis that a given operation is the true decomposition rule. In a Monte-Carlo simulation study Cortese and Dzhafarov (1996) evaluate the minimum size of the samples $\{\mathbf{T}_{ij}^1,..,\mathbf{T}_{ij}^n\}$ $(i=1,2,j=1,2)$ at which the true decomposition rule chosen from the "classical" list $\{+,min,max\}$ yields a reliably smaller difference between the two sequences in (11) or (12) than the remaining two operations. The results indicate that this minimum sample size is realistically achievable provided the effectiveness of the factor manipulations is sufficiently high[12]: the minimum sample size required is on the order of 10^3 under independence and on the order of 10^2 under perfect positive interdependence.

Returning to population-level considerations, a successful $(\diamond)$-test being a necessary condition for $(\diamond)$-decomposability (under the same form of $\overset{s}{=}$), a natural question arises as to whether this condition is also sufficient. Dzhafarov and Schweickert (1995) show that the answer to this question is affirmative for all simple operations under perfect positive interdependence: Under this stochastic relationship, if a $(\diamond)$-test is successful, then $\mathbf{T}(\alpha,\beta)$ is $(\diamond)$-decomposable (under the same relationship). With some technical qualifications, the same is true under independence for the operations *minimum* and *maximum*: If $\diamond$ is one of these two operations, then a successful $(\diamond)$-test under independence implies $(\diamond)$-decomposability under independence. For addition-like operations, however, this result does not hold. For instance, it is possible that the $(+)$-test under independence (i.e., the Ashby-Townsend-Roberts-Sternberg "summation test") is successful but that the response time cannot be additively decomposed into stochastically independent time components. Observe that due to the decomposition rule uniqueness, when this happens, the response time cannot be decomposed under independence by any other (algebraically distinct) operation either – in a sense, this response time is absolutely indecomposable into selectively influenced components.

---

[12]The construction of an effectiveness measure, that is, a measure of difference between $\{F_{12}(t),F_{21}(t)\}$ and $\{F_{11}(t),F_{22}(t)\}$ taken as unordered pairs (see Footnote 10), is a difficult and rather subtle issue that I will not discuss here. Obviously, if the factor manipulations are not effective at all, then the true decomposition rule cannot be distinguished from any other operation.

This concludes the discussion of the main results related to the problem of determining the decomposition rule under a known form of stochastic relationship. The reverse of this problem, determining the form of stochastic relationship under a known decomposition rule, appears substantially less tractable, even with as limited a choice as that between independence and perfect positive interdependence. Dzhafarov (1992) and Dzhafarov and Rouder (1996) propose a solution for a special case of this problem, based on an experimental design and theoretical assumptions very different from those discussed above. Suppose that α is the only factor in an experiment, and that it forms a "unidimensional strength continuum" with respect to some response time $\mathbf{T}(\alpha)$; that is, α is or can be transformed into a real-valued variable whose increase causes $\mathbf{T}(\alpha)$ to decrease in all quantiles. Consider an additive decomposition of $\mathbf{T}(\alpha)$ into an α-dependent and α-independent components (a unifactorial version of selective influence):

$$\mathbf{T}(\alpha) \overset{d}{=} \mathbf{A}(\alpha) + \mathbf{B}.$$

The results described below also apply to other addition-like operations because they can be transformed into addition by a monotonic transformation of the components (which would preserve both selectivity and stochastic relationship).

Using the asymmetric representation mentioned in Footnote 8, which here is more convenient than (7),

$$\{\mathbf{A}(\alpha),\mathbf{B}\} = \{A(\alpha, \mathbf{P}_1, \mathbf{P}_2), B(\mathbf{P}_2)\},$$

one can see that independence and perfect positive interdependence correspond to

$$A(\alpha)\perp\mathbf{B} \Leftrightarrow A(\alpha, \mathbf{P}_1, \mathbf{P}_2) = A^\star(\alpha,\mathbf{P}_1),$$
$$A(\alpha)\|\mathbf{B} \Leftrightarrow A(\alpha, \mathbf{P}_1, \mathbf{P}_2) = A^\star(\alpha,\mathbf{P}_2)$$

(in the latter case $A^\star$ is assumed to be increasing in the second argument).

It turns out that one can distinguish between these two possibilities if the following requirements are satisfied: as α increases, $A(\alpha,p_1,p_2)$ decreases and vanishes for any pair of values p_1,p_2 of $\mathbf{P}_1,\mathbf{P}_2$, and it vanishes with asymptotically proportional rates for any two such pairs (p_1,p_2) and $(p_1^\star,p_2^\star)$. It can be proved then that

$$T_p(\alpha) = B_p + \Gamma(p)s(\alpha) + o\{s(\alpha)\}, \tag{13}$$

where $T_p(\alpha)$ and B_p are the rank-p quantiles ($0 < p < 1$) of $\mathbf{T}(\alpha)$ and $\mathbf{B}$, respectively, $s(\alpha)$ is a strictly decreasing and vanishing positive function, and $\Gamma(p)$ is a coefficient such that

$$\mathbf{A}(\alpha)\perp\mathbf{B} \Leftrightarrow \Gamma(p) \equiv const$$
$$\mathbf{A}(\alpha)\|\mathbf{B} \Leftrightarrow \Gamma(p) \text{ increases in } p.$$

The transformation $s(\alpha)$ can be evaluated in several ways (Dzhafarov, 1992), but one can circumvent this problem altogether by observing that $s(\alpha)$ in (13) can be replaced with any asymptotically linear transformation thereof, and that $T_p(\alpha)$ for a fixed rank p or some average $T_\bullet(\alpha)$ of $T_p(\alpha)$ across a certain interval of ranks present observable examples of such linear transformations. Thus plotting $T_p(\alpha)$ against $T_\bullet(\alpha)$ one gets

$$T_p(\alpha) = \left[B_p - \frac{\Gamma_{(p)}}{\Gamma_\bullet}B_\bullet\right] + \frac{\Gamma(p)}{\Gamma_\bullet}T_\bullet(\alpha) + o\{s(\alpha)\},$$

where the subscript dots indicate averaging across some interval of quantile ranks. The result is that the tangent lines drawn to several $T_p(\alpha)$-versus-$T_\bullet(\alpha)$ curves at progressively smaller values of $s(\alpha)$ (i.e., progressively higher values of α) tend to a parallel pattern of unit-slope lines under independence and to a diverging fan pattern, with slopes changing from below unity to above unity, under perfect positive interdependence. Dzhafarov and Rouder (1996) show how this prediction can be converted to a practical test, when $\mathbf{T}(\alpha)$ are only known on a sample level and only for several distinct values of α.

5. POSSIBLE DEVELOPMENTS

Here, I mention a few directions of research that seem to stem naturally from the discussion above.

(A) *A physicalist account of selectively influenced interacting processes.* Representation (6) is obviously too flexible, and it is desirable to have a systematic way of subjecting it to restrictions that could lead to general but falsifiable theories. One possible approach consists in treating all interactions between processes as local in time, so that changes in the levels of the processes at a given moment only depend on the characteristics of these processes (levels, velocities, accelerations, etc.) at the same moment. This approach leads to differential equations of the form

$$\dot{R}_1(t) = r_1[\alpha, R_1(t), R_2(t), \dot{R}_2(t), \ddot{R}_1(t), \ddot{R}_2(t), ...]$$
$$\dot{R}_2(t) = r_2[\beta, R_2(t), R_1(t), \dot{R}_1(t), \ddot{R}_2(t), \ddot{R}_1(t), ...]$$

subject to certain initial conditions. The levels of the processes in such a representation may be defined in terms of their quantile ranks in relation to their respective criteria, or on scales calibrated by a specific choice of the criteria.

(B) *Decompositions into more than two components.* Even with only two factors involved, the general form of the response time decomposition into selectively influenced components is not (5) but rather

$$\mathbf{T}(\alpha,\beta) \stackrel{d}{=} \mathbf{A}(\alpha) \diamond \mathbf{B}(\beta) \lozenge \mathbf{C} = A(\alpha,\mathbf{P}_1,\mathbf{P}_2,\mathbf{P}_3) \diamond B(\beta,\mathbf{P}_1,\mathbf{P}_2,\mathbf{P}_3) \lozenge C(\mathbf{P}_1,\mathbf{P}_2,\mathbf{P}_3),$$

with some order of the operations implied. The Dzhafarov-Schweickert decomposition tests allow one to recover some such decompositions under perfect positive interdependence of all three components. For instance, in the decomposition

$$\mathbf{T}(\alpha,\beta) \stackrel{d}{=} max\{\mathbf{A}(\alpha),\mathbf{B}(\beta)\} + \mathbf{C},$$

if $\mathbf{A}\|\mathbf{B}\|\mathbf{C}$, then the operation *max* can be recovered by the (*max*)-test under perfect positive interdependence, because the right-hand expression is $max\{\mathbf{A}(\alpha)+\mathbf{C}, \mathbf{B}(\beta)+\mathbf{C}\}$ and $\mathbf{A}(\alpha)+\mathbf{C}\|\mathbf{B}(\beta)+\mathbf{C}$. Such a recovery is not possible, however, if $\mathbf{A}\perp\mathbf{B}\perp\mathbf{C}$, because then $\mathbf{A}(\alpha)+\mathbf{C}$ and $\mathbf{B}(\beta)+\mathbf{C}$ are interdependent in a complex way. Although partial results in dealing with this and similar problems are available (Colonius & Vorberg, 1994; Townsend & Nozawa, 1995), it is yet to be seen whether some generalizations of the Dzhafarov-Schweickert tests can be developed for at least three-component decompositions $\mathbf{A}(\alpha)\diamond\mathbf{B}(\beta)\lozenge\mathbf{C}$ or $\mathbf{A}(\alpha)\diamond\mathbf{B}(\beta)\lozenge\mathbf{C}(\gamma)$ under stochastic independence.

(C) *Decompositions under other forms of stochastic relationship.* Dealing with stochastic relationships other than independence and perfect positive interdependence is arguably the most challenging problem in the context of time decompositions. Existence and uniqueness properties of decompositions such as

$$\mathbf{T}(\alpha,\beta) \overset{d}{=} A(\mathbf{P}_1, \mathbf{P}_2) \diamond B(\beta, \mathbf{P}_1, \mathbf{P}_2)$$

remain unknown if one imposes no or only mild constraints on the form of the functions A and B and on the decomposition rule $\diamond$. It is possible that not very much can be achieved in this direction, and the abstract algebraic approach of Dzhafarov and Schweickert (1995) will have to be eventually abandoned in favor of recovering architectures of selectively influenced interacting processes, perhaps along the "physicalist" lines suggested earlier in this section. It is also possible that the two simplest forms of stochastic relationship considered in this chapter will prove to be sufficient for describing a good deal of empirical data, perhaps in conjunction with strict limitations imposed on the shape of response time distributions. It would be highly beneficial, therefore, to develop powerful techniques for determining, at least in very simple situations, whether independence or perfect positive interdependence is truly present, as opposed to choosing between them under the assumption that one of them holds.

Choice, Decision, and Measurement
A. A. J. Marley (Ed.),
©Lawrence Erlbaum Associates, NJ, 1997.

A LIMITED CAPACITY, WAVE EQUALITY, RANDOM WALK MODEL OF ABSOLUTE IDENTIFICATION

PETER KARPIUK, JR.
OPTUM Software

YVES LACOUTURE
Université Laval

A. A. J. MARLEY
McGill University

ABSTRACT. Identification of a particular stimulus selected from a set of easily discriminable stimuli, with these stimuli varying along some unidimensional physical dimension, produces consistent patterns of accuracy and response time performance. Some of the most robust features are the so-called bow effects : accuracy is highest for stimuli at the ends of the physical range and lowest for stimuli in the middle of the range; (mean) response times are fastest for stimuli at the ends of the range and slowest for stimuli in the middle of the range. Marley and Cook (1984) have demonstrated that the magnitude of the bow effect for accuracy, which is dependent upon set size and range, can be accounted for by postulating that subjects rely on a fixed rehearsal capacity that must be allocated over the stimulus range. The present paper extends their model to response time predictions by postulating a decision mechanism based upon the accumulation of discrete units of the memory information, X, proposed by the Marley and Cook model. A separate random walk process is postulated for each of the N possible responses in a N stimulus absolute identification task. The general form of the random variable accumulated in each of these processes equals the value of $|(U_j - X)(X - L_j)|$, where U_j and L_j are the upper and lower boundaries of response category j, $j = 1, 2, 3, \ldots, N$. Link (1992) proposed a similar form to account for similarity and equality judgments. The correspondence between experimental and simulation measures of accuracy, response time, information transmitted and d' for various set sizes are examined.

1. INTRODUCTION

Hipparchus (circa 150 B.C.) developed a classification system for stars based upon their apparent brightness. His method produced a six point psychological scale associated with the digits one through six, whereby each increment was apparently equal and larger integers were associated with brighter stars. Jastrow

Key words and phrases. Absolute identification, response times, probabilistic models, random walk models, bow effects.

Acknowledgments. This work was supported by Research and Equipment grants to each of Lacouture and Marley from the Natural Science and Engineering Research Council of Canada (NSERC); an Equipment Grant to Lacouture and Marley from the Fond pour la Formation de Chercheurs et l'Aide à la Recherche (FCAR); an FCAR Young Researcher Grant to Lacouture; and funds to Karpiuk from the Faculty of Science at McGill University and from the Faculté des Sciences Sociales de l'Université Laval. We are very appreciative of Rob Nosofsky's detailed evaluation of an earlier version of this chapter.

Address for correspondence. Peter Karpiuk, Jr., OPTUM Software, 3330 Harbor Blvd., Costa Mesa, CA 92626. Email: pkarpiuk@atkc.com

(1887) showed that this equal interval psychological scale was a logarithmic function of light intensity as measured by photometer readings. Suppose there were only six stars, one for each unit on Hipparchus' scale, and you were asked to identify, one at a time and randomly, which of these six stars you were seeing. The greatest difficulty in identifying these stars would arise whenever the third or fourth star was presented. If Hipparchus' scale was expanded to a ten point scale by including two brighter and two duller stars, an unusual change in one's identification performance would result. The fifth and sixth stars, originally the third and fourth, would become even more difficult to accurately identify. This result illustrates the fact that as the size of the stimulus set increases greater confusion occurs in stimulus identification. In addition to creating more confusion among the stimuli, increasing set size is accompanied by corresponding increases in response times.

The task just described is known as *unidimensional absolute identification*. In general the task involves a set of N stimuli which vary along a unidimensional physical scale, such as sound pressure or length. The stimuli are randomly presented one at a time and the subject is asked to identify, typically with a key press, the identity of the current stimulus. The stimulus often remains available for examination until the subject produces one of N possible responses. Most attempts to explain and model absolute identification performance have focused on the effects of the number, arrangement and range of stimuli within and across sets of various size. The performance or dependent measure most commonly used in these models is accuracy. In the hypothetical example above of the absolute identification of the apparent brightness of celestial bodies, the suggested pattern of accuracy and response time performance illustrates the so-called *bow effect*. That is, subjects identify very quickly and accurately stimuli at the ends of the continuum. On the other hand, subjects have greater difficulty correctly identifying stimuli from the middle of the range, taking both a greater amount of time and committing more errors. Although it could be that this effect is due to a response bias or to the limited number of response alternatives towards the ends of the range, much data when appropriately analyzed confirm that this is a true sensitivity effect (e.g., Braida & Durlach, 1972; Berliner, Durlach, & Braida, 1977; Luce, Nosofsky, Green, & Smith, 1982).

In general, the size of the bow effect, measured by the relative difference in performance between the middle and ends of the stimulus range, becomes increasingly more pronounced as the number of possible stimuli increases. Even when any given pair of stimuli are perfectly discriminable, a subject generally cannot maintain perfect performance if the experiment involves more than seven stimuli (Shiffrin & Nosofsky, 1994). Furthermore, despite extensive practice, perfect performance appears elusive, and in terms of accuracy, does not normally exceed 2.5 to 3.0 bits of transmitted information (Pollack, 1952; Braida & Durlach, 1972; Shiffrin & Nosofsky, 1994). Also, when the stimuli are perfectly discriminable, that is when stimulus separation is well above Weber's constant, increasing the range while keeping adjacent stimuli equidistant has little or no effect on performance (Lacouture, in press).

The bow effect is often described as a contextual effect because performance depends on the relative position of the stimuli within the set. There are also other consistent effects due to the range and arrangement of the stimuli which point to context as the chief source of influence in absolute identification. Gravetter and Lockhead (1973), for example, convincingly demonstrated that identification performance for two fixed stimuli can be affected simply by adjusting the range of the whole stimulus set. In two of their experimental conditions the fixed pair of stimuli were embedded in either a narrow or a wide range of surrounding stimuli. Perhaps surprisingly, subjects identified the fixed pair of stimuli with greater accuracy in the narrow range condition.

In a somewhat more complex experimental design, Weber, Green, and Luce (1977) studied accuracy in absolute identification, using among others, stimulus sets with various gaps in the center of the set of stimuli. The results show that the discriminability of the stimuli located on each side of the gap depends on the whole stimulus range. This would lead us to suspect that the width of the range plays a determining role in absolute identification. However, as mentioned earlier, increasing stimulus range while keeping the relative distance between stimuli fixed has little or no effect on accuracy. Thus, it is probable that accuracy in absolute identification is affected by the *relative* spacing among the stimuli in the stimulus set.

Only a few reports have addressed the effects of experimental manipulations on response times in absolute identification. Nevertheless, the obtained connection between response time and accuracy is robust and consistent in absolute identification: within and across stimulus sets, greater accuracy is coupled with faster response time. While the association between accuracy and response time is strong, Lacouture (in press) has shown that stimulus separation can affect accuracy more than it affects (mean) response time.

2. MODELS OF ABSOLUTE IDENTIFICATION

Trying to account simultaneously for set size, range, and other context effects in absolute identification has proved to be challenging for classical psychophysical models. Following a Thurstonian view, some authors have concluded that stimulus noise and criterial noise are not independent of experimental context; for instance, Durlach and Braida (1969) and Gravetter and Lockhead (1973) propose contextual models of absolute identification in which the variance of the assumed distribution of the stimulus representation is proportional to the square of the range covered by the possible stimuli.

An alternative view espoused by Weber et al. (1977) proposes a selective attention mechanism called the *attention band*. The idea behind the attention band is that subjects tend to focus their attention in the area of psychological space "near" the psychological location of the most recently presented stimulus. This attention mechanism would produce strong sequential dependencies that could possibly explain the bow effect.

Luce et al. (1982) support their attention band hypothesis with results showing that the bow effect in response probabilities is essentially eliminated when a "small step" stimulus selection method is used. This procedure involves, at a given trial, the presentation of a stimulus in the immediate (ordinal) neighborhood of the stimulus presented on the previous trial. Luce et al. (1982) also implemented a "large step" condition where the stimulus at any given trial is several steps away (in ordinal position) from the stimulus of the previous trial. In this condition identification performance (measured by probability correct) is poorer than that observed with the usual "random" selection procedure. According to Luce et al. (1982) and Luce and Nosofsky (1984) such results show that advance knowledge alone regarding the possible values of a stimulus is not sufficient to improve identification performance. Nevertheless, the presentation of a series of stimuli clustered together in a sub-region of the stimulus range enables performance to be enhanced. Although their data support the attention band hypothesis in a qualitative manner, Luce et al. did not use this hypothesis to make quantitative fits to their data nor did they explain in other than general terms how the bow effect follows from the attention band hypothesis.

Arguing that range alone is not sufficient to explain performance limitations in absolute identification, Berliner and Durlach (1973) developed a theory in which the end stimuli are used as anchors or comparison points and, as a direct consequence of their theoretical assumptions, stimuli further away from the anchors are associated with higher scaling variance and hence poorer resolution. Thus, overall performance limitations are attributed to the number of stimuli represented in the psychological space and the bow effect to the relative distance of each stimulus representation from the anchor points. The anchor hypothesis was later formalized by Marley and Cook (1984, 1986) and Braida, Lim, Berliner, Durlach, Rabinowitz, and Purks (1984). For Marley and Cook, fixed processing capacity, which they call rehearsal, explains performance limitations, while distance in the psychological space between the representation of the stimulus and the anchor points (in conjunction with the fixed processing capacity and appropriate decision rules) explains the bow effect. This model predicts accuracy for individual stimuli according to set size and ordinal position but like Braida et al. (1984) does not provide an account of response times.

Lacouture and Marley (1991, 1995) have developed a rather different approach to modeling absolute identification performance. In their 1991 paper they proposed a connectionist implementation to model several aspects of the task. The model is based on a connectionist three-layered feed-forward network with a single hidden unit. The associated learning process is a variant of back propagation (Rumelhart, Hinton, & Williams, 1986). Input to the network is noisy and a simple recurrent network added to the output layer performs response selection. In this model, the sensorial input is mapped, following a noisy process, to an internal scalar representation along a limited range. Another mapping then provides an output that is decoded through a dynamic process that provides the response. A similar connectionist dual mapping process applied to word recognition is described by Lacouture (1989) and Hinton and Shallice (1991). The idea of dual mapping applied to psychophysical judgments was initially developed by Atkinson, Bower, and Crothers (1965) in their matrix model. The main new contribution of Lacouture and Marley (1991) is to provide a framework to model response times in absolute identification. In the later version of the model (Lacouture & Marley, 1995), and following empirical work supporting the idea of a limited response process (Ward & Lockhead, 1970; Mori, 1989), it was proposed that the bow effect is a direct consequence of both the *mapping* and the *response selection* process.

In our view, a model of absolute identification performance must first account for the bow effect in accuracy and response times both within and across stimulus sets of various sizes. Following a successful account of these fundamental and consistent results, there are numerous empirical manipulations and results on which to further test one's model, such as the effects of various stimulus spacings and sequential response patterns. Our aim in this chapter is to present a model together with empirical and simulation results which address the most robust features of absolute identification performance.

The current model builds upon the work of Marley and Cook (1984) who developed a fixed capacity rehearsal model to account for the accuracy of absolute identification judgments. That model assumes that for each stimulus the subject possesses a corresponding psychological and memory representation. Assuming Fechner's law, for a set of logarithmically spaced stimuli, such as the stars discussed above, the physical intensities would be mapped onto an equal interval psychological scale. These psychological representations are assumed to be normally distributed with equal variances along the continuum formed by the psychological representation, and cut points and a decision rule determine which response is made on a given trial. An example of the assumed memory distributions arising from 10 stimuli, logarithmically spaced on a physical dimension, is shown in Figure 1. While each pair of adjacent means of these memory distributions are equally spaced, the variance is clearly largest for the middle stimuli and smallest for the end stimuli.

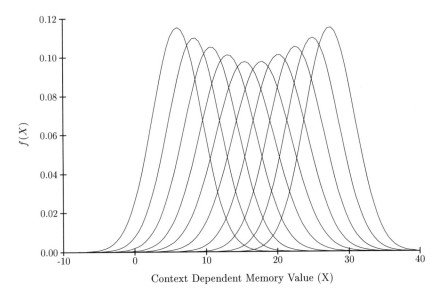

FIGURE 1. Marley and Cook (1984) context-dependent, memory representations for an absolute identification experiment with 10 stimuli.

Marley and Cook's model assumes that a subject decides which stimulus is present by categorizing a single sample from the memory representation of the current stimulus. The weakness of this approach is that all judgments take equal amounts of time, which does not find support in data. Our model extends Marley and Cook (1984) by assuming that one sample does not provide sufficient evidence for an identification judgment. Instead, the subject sets a criterion which requires an accumulation of supportive evidence to produce a response. In general, when a stimulus is presented, information is accumulated simultaneously for all possible responses. The overt response occurs as soon as the amount of information for one of the responses reaches the criterion referred to as the *decision boundary* (alternatively, *response criterion*). Each information accrual process can be considered as a random walk with a single absorbing barrier.

The key components of the model, shown in Figure 2, illustrate the nature of the information that is accumulated. The normal distribution shown here is the memory representation distribution for stimulus 5 in a 10 stimulus identification task. For each of the 10 possible responses there exists a category interval (U_j, L_j), $j = 1, 2, 3 \ldots, 10$. The two arrows in the figure point to the category boundaries for response 5 while the remaining intervals, marked by vertical bars, are numbered according to their respective accumulator processes. Upon presentation of stimulus i, a sequence of random variates, $X_i(n)$, indexed by time epoch n within the presentation, $n = 1, 2, 3, \ldots$, is generated from the "memory representation" distribution, with mean μ_i and variance σ_i, where the values of the means and variances follow from Marley and Cook's (1984) model. Again, for each of the N possible responses there exists a separate accumulation process. If the sampled value $X_i(n)$ lies within the jth category interval, $j = 1, \ldots, N$, then an amount equal to $|(U_j - X_i(n))(X_i(n) - L_j)|$ is accumulated for response R_j. This quantity achieves its maximum value when the sampled value is at the midpoint of the relevant category; hence, the amount of information accumulated for each of the responses depends upon how near the sampled information is to its category center. If the sampled value lies outside a category interval, then zero information is accumulated for the associated response. Provided the intervals (U_j, L_j), $j = 1, 2, 3, \ldots, N$, are not overlapping, this ensures that information is accrued for only one process for each random variate generated. The subject makes response R_j, $j = 1, \ldots, N$, when the amount of information equals or exceeds the value R of the decision boundary. The idea for the accumulation of a random variable with the above cross product structure comes from Link's wave theory (Link, 1992). However, the random variables X_i, $i = 1, 2, 3, \ldots, N$, in our model are normally distributed, whereas Link (1992) constructs his model from Poisson distributed random variables.

We now expand upon the assumptions of the memory rehearsal model (see Marley & Cook, 1984, for full details). Each stimulus has a psychological representation with mean I^* and variance β^2, and a corresponding context dependent "memory storage representation" which is normally distributed with mean and variance dependent upon: $M_u^* - M_l^*$, the rehearsal range, where M_u^* (respectively, M_l^*) is the upper (respectively, lower) end of the rehearsal range; η, the ratio of the memory decay rate, α, to the rehearsal rate, λ; and β^2, the constant variance of the psychological values of each stimulus.

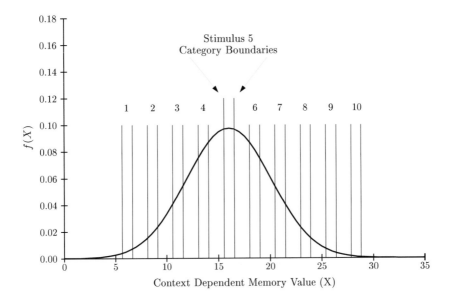

FIGURE 2. Category boundaries for a 10 stimulus absolute identification task superimposed on the memory representation distribution of stimulus 5.

The rehearsal range, $M_u^* - M_l^*$, is assumed to be adjusted by the subject to sub-
sume the psychological range of the stimulus representations. For logarithmically
spaced stimuli, the psychological range of stimuli increases as stimuli are added to
a set, and consequently the rehearsal range also increases.

In Marley and Cook's application of their model to absolute identification of
sound intensity, η, the ratio of the memory decay rate α to the rehearsal rate
λ, was assumed to be constant. In our application, this parameter is allowed to
vary. Our suggestion is that subjects may rehearse at a lower rate for easy tasks
compared to more difficult tasks. Assuming that absolute identification becomes
inherently easier as the number of stimuli are reduced, we might therefore expect a
correspondence between the rehearsal rate and number of stimuli in the presentation
set, especially for "simple" tasks such as those with 2 or 4 widely spaced stimuli.

It is also assumed that subjects are able to control the width of the category
ranges, in order to enhance or diminish the accuracy of their responses. However, we
assume that this difference, $(U_j - L_j)$, $i = 1, 2, 3, \ldots, N$, is constant for all categories
within a particular set. Subjects can theoretically produce faster response times by
increasing the width of these categories, but as a consequence will normally be less
accurate.

Subjects can also control the value R of the decision boundary (response criterion). A subject is able to decrease response time by lowering the response criterion,
but not usually without a loss in accuracy. This speed-accuracy tradeoff and the
accompanying change in the response criterion is demonstrated convincingly by
Link and Tindal (1971) in a two alternative forced choice experiment using line
length.

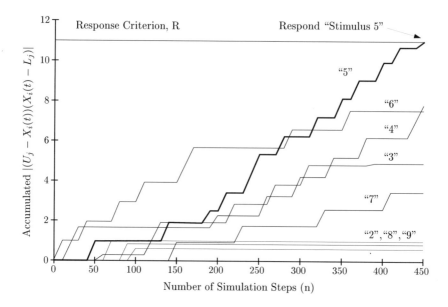

FIGURE 3. Sequence of information accumulation for 10 response categories during presentation of stimulus 5.

An example of the information accrual process for a set of 10 stimuli is depicted in Figure 3. The distribution parameters for the sequence of random variates equal those of stimulus 5. In this figure, the first accrual process to reach the response criterion value of 11 units corresponds to that associated with response (stimulus) 5 and is traced by the thickest line. This would result in the subject identifying the present stimulus as stimulus "5." Figure 3 also indicates that the simulation "time" for the response "5" is approximately 450 simulation steps. Information accumulated for responses "3," "4," "6," and "7" at the "time" of the response are shown to range from approximately 3.8 to 7.9 units. Three of the remaining processes show slightly less than one unit of information accumulation. Only eight processes appear on this figure because no information was accumulated for responses "1" and "10."

We now describe how the experimental data was collected followed by a description of the simulation method and a comparison of the data and simulation results.

3. EXPERIMENT

We collected behavioral data in an absolute identification task using line segments of various lengths. Three participants were recruited and each one performed the task for several sessions using stimulus sets varying in size.

Participants. Three undergraduate students performed the task and each received $25 (Canadian) for their participation in one training and five experimental sessions. All participants reported having normal or corrected-to-normal vision and no one reported having a motor handicap.

Apparatus. The experiment was conducted in a dimly lit and sound attenuated chamber. An MS-DOS-286 micro-computer running Micro Experimental
Laboratory software (MEL©; Schneider, 1988) was used for presentation of the
stimuli and recording of the responses. Stimuli were presented within an angular
distance of 10° on a VGA screen (Fujikama, Modulux III with 640 × 480 pixels and
28 pixels/cm) located approximately 120 cm away from the participant. Stimulus
presentation was synchronized with the vertical retrace of the screen.

Responses were collected using a custom made keyboard with 11 buttons. One
button, labeled "START," is located at the center of the keyboard while the ten
other buttons are positioned in a semi-circle such that each one is located at the
same distance from the START button. Each square button is approximately one
cm by one cm. The distance between the START button and each response button
is 101 mm. Some details of the technical implementation for this keyboard are
described in Lacouture (1995). The keyboard was placed such that participants
were able to use their dominant hand. The response buttons were numbered from
one to ten beginning with the leftmost button. In all experimental sessions a single
response key was associated with each stimulus.

Response time – the time elapsed between onset of the stimulus on the screen
and response selection – was recorded and timed in milliseconds through MEL©
timing routines. Previous experimental results obtained with the same apparatus
and reported by Lacouture and Lacerte (in press) and Lacouture (in press) demonstrated that the configuration of the keyboard allows for adequate measurement of
response time for all response keys. In particular, the above equipment has been
used to study the (absolute) identification of visually presented digits. The data
from this task show minimal bow effects in response time, and no bow effect in
probability correct. However, subjects are correct 100% of the time in this experiment. Nonetheless, the minimal bow effect in response times in this experiment
is suggestive that the position of the response keys is not the major determining
factor of the bow effect in response times. Also, Marley and Lacouture (1996) have
collected data in an interesting categorization design that gives further support to
the belief that the bow effects in response time that are found in absolute identification tasks with "unidimensional" stimuli are not simply artifacts associated with
the location of response keys on the response keyboard.

The stimulus sets are such that the set of 10 stimuli has the largest range and
the other stimulus sets are central subsets of this set. The participants performed
a training session with the set containing 10 stimuli. Subjects were then tested
during 5 different sessions with sets of 2, 4, 6, 8, and 10 stimuli, with the order of
presentation of the sets randomized across subjects.

Stimuli. The stimuli were line segments of different lengths presented horizon-
tally in the center of the screen. The stimulus set size (the number of line segments)
varied from session to session. Set sizes were 2, 4, 6, 8 and 10. The line segments
were three pixels thick and appeared in white on a black background. From the
participant's viewpoint the stimuli appeared like continuous lines. For set size 10,
the length of each segment, measured in pixel units (screen dots), was 92, 106, 120,
138, 160, 184, 212, 242, 278, and 320, and thus each successive stimulus was 15%

longer than the previous one; consequently, each adjacent pair of stimuli are well above Weber's fraction for line length (0.029 according to Teghtsoonian, 1971). The stimuli were given "correct" response labels of one to ten according to increasing length. Five subsets were created from the set of 10 stimuli. Set size ten contained stimuli "1" through "10"; set size eight contained stimuli "2" through "9"; set size six contained stimuli "3" through "8"; set size four contained stimuli "4" through "7"; and set size two contained stimuli "5" and "6." For each subset the appropriate set of centrally located keys on the keyboard were used as the response keys for that subset - for instance, the experiment involving stimuli "5" and "6" used keys "5" and "6."

Procedure. The experiment involved five sessions run over a two day period. Each session was performed with a stimulus set of fixed size. The five sets of stimuli were randomized across these sessions. A session consisted of 60 presentations of each stimulus. Thus there were 120 trials in the session where set size two was used, 240 trials in the session where set size four was used, and so on. The longest session involved 600 trials with set size ten. Instructions regarding the task were presented on the screen prior to each session. The participants were instructed to respond as fast and accurately as possible. Each stimulus in the set used in a session was presented to each participant, with its respective correct response label, once before each session.

In each session the participant initiated each trial by pressing the START button. One of the possible stimuli, randomly selected from the relevant stimulus set, was shown on the screen 100 ms later. The participant had to identify the stimulus by pressing the corresponding response button. After onset, the stimulus remained on the screen until the participant pressed a response button.

Five hundred ms after recording the participant's response, feedback was provided for one second, in the form of a numeral between 1 and 10, corresponding to the correct response. When the participant made an incorrect response, a low frequency (500 Hz) tone was simultaneously generated for 500 ms. The trial ended with the presentation of a blank screen. If the participant waited more than 30 seconds before pressing the START button to begin the next trial, a short sequence of three tones was generated to regain the participant's attention.

4. SIMULATIONS

A Sun Sparc 10 computer running MATLAB© software was used for developing the programs for simulations of the model[1]. The simulation first calculates the means and standard deviations of the memory distributions as follows. For an absolute identification experiment with N (line) stimuli, the line lengths are logarithmically transformed into values representing the psychological mean magnitudes I_i^*, $i = 1, 2, 3, \ldots, N$. With M_u^* (respectively, M_l^*) the upper (respectively, lower) anchor, η the ratio of the memory decay rate, α, to the rehearsal rate, λ, and β^2 the common variance of the psychological representations of each stimulus,

---

[1]The simulation programs are available from the first author.

then the mean and variance of stimulus i, $i = 1, \ldots, N$, computed from the single end anchor version of the Marley and Cook (1984) model are given by:

$$
E[X_i] = \begin{cases} \dfrac{I_i^* - M_l^*}{\eta(M_u^* - M_l^*)} & \text{when } I_i^* \leq \dfrac{M_u^* + M_l^*}{2}, \\[2ex] \dfrac{M_u^* - I_i^*}{\eta(M_u^* - M_l^*)} & \text{when } I_i^* > \dfrac{M_u^* + M_l^*}{2}, \end{cases}
$$

$$
Var[X_i] = \begin{cases} \dfrac{I_i^* - M_l^*}{2\eta(M_u^* - M_l^*)} + \left(\dfrac{\beta}{\eta(M_u^* - M_l^*)}\right)^2 & \text{when } I_i^* \leq \dfrac{M_u^* + M_l^*}{2}, \\[2ex] \dfrac{M_u^* - I_i^*}{2\eta(M_u^* - M_l^*)} + \left(\dfrac{\beta}{\eta(M_u^* - M_l^*)}\right)^2 & \text{when } I_i^* > \dfrac{M_u^* + M_l^*}{2}. \end{cases}
$$

As did Marley and Cook (1984), we assume that $M_l^* = I_l^* - z\beta$, $M_u^* = I_N^* + z\beta$, where z is a further parameter of the model. This extension of the rehearsal range beyond the psychological means of the smallest and largest possible stimuli is conceptually necessary to prevent psychological stimulus values occurring outside the rehearsed range.

Next the random walk component of the model is simulated. The parameters introduced at this stage are $(U_j - L_j)$, $j = 1, 2, 3, \ldots, N$, the category widths, and R, the value of the response criterion. For each stimulus in each set the program is iterated 180 times, the same number of trials per stimulus as the grouped participant data. Within each iteration a loop counts the number of iterations of the simulation necessary for the first of the N processes to reach or exceed the value R of the response criterion.

The search for a satisfactory ('best') fit of the simulation to the data was performed as follows. An extensive set of simulations was run with the parameter values differing by small amounts over the whole of the relevant range (here "differing by small amounts" means relative to the resultant changes in the simulation output of response proportion and number of simulation steps to reach criterion.) As discussed below, in the first simulations certain parameter values were fixed across set size; some of these constraints had to be weakened later in order to obtain satisfactory fits to the data. For each set of parameter values, the simulated probability correct was compared with the corresponding data values (averaged over three subjects), with the overall fit evaluated by a mean-square deviation criterion. Independently, the mean number of iterations of the simulation to reach or exceed the response criterion for each stimulus in each experiment was compared to the corresponding mean response times (averaged over the three subjects), with the fit being evaluated by the correlation (linear regression) between the simulated and the real results. The 'best' fit ('best' set of parameter values) in the relevant search region was then selected by first determining a range of parameter values that yielded good fits to the probability correct data, then selecting a single set of parameter values within this region that yielded the best linear regression between the mean number of iterations of the simulations to reach or exceed the response criterion for each stimulus in each experiment and the corresponding mean response time values. The mean response time values predicted by this best linear regression are the values plotted in the relevant figures as the response time predictions of the

Parameter

s

		β^2	η	$(U - L)$	z	R
	4	0.0025	0.150	1.0	0.01	11.0
Set Size	6	0.0025	0.045	1.0	2.00	11.0
	8	0.0025	0.035	1.0	2.00	11.0
	10	0.0025	0.030	1.0	2.25	12.0

TABLE 1. Parameter values used in simulation of response proportions and response times for the four sets of stimuli.

simulations. Thus, in addition to the model parameters already discussed, we have two additional parameters (the mean and intercept) from this regression.

The initial search of the of the parameter space constrained each of β_k, $U_k - L_k$, η_k, $k = 4, 6, 8, 10$, to be independent of k. (In our later fits of the simulation to data we omit the results for set size 2 as we believe this task may be more accurately described as a discrimination, or relative judgment, task). However, the obtained fits were quite inadequate, both quantitatively and qualitatively. For instance, we could not obtain predicted mean response times that increased with set size. We then attempted to fit the data with $\beta_k, \eta_k, U_k - L_k, k = 4, 6, 8, 10$, independent of k, but with z_k and R_k being allowed to depend on k. The fits were significantly better but still quantitatively inadequate. For instance, with η_k independent of k, if an adequate fit was obtained for the probability correct values for, say, set size 6, then the predicted probability correct values for set sizes 8, 10 were too small. Thus, the final constraints on the parameter space search were as follows. For each set size k, $k = 4, 6, 8, 10$, there are potentially five parameters: $\beta_k, \eta_k, (U_k - L_k), z_k, R_k$. We fixed β_k and $U_k - L_k$ across set sizes, and allowed η_k, z_k, R_k to vary across set sizes, but with the restriction that η_k be monotonically decreasing in k. The latter constraint is a direct consequence of our earlier suggestion that as the set size increases (and concomitantly the task becomes more difficult), subjects might allocate more rehearsal capacity (up to some limit) to the task. Since η is inversely related to rehearsal rate, λ, this would result in η decreasing with set size (up to some limit). Thus the total number of free parameters so far (with a monotonicity constraint on η) is 14. We also have available the two (free) parameters of the regression between response time and simulation 'time', for a total of 16 parameters. The data contains at least 56 independent values: the 28 probability correct values (thus ignoring the off diagonal elements in the stimulus/response matrix) and the 28 mean response times. The simulation results reported in this paper are based on the average of 1000 runs of the simulation using the parameters values listed in Table 1.

5. RESULTS OF COMPARISIONS OF SIMULATIONS WITH DATA

The response proportions and response times of all three participants were averaged together to yield 180 observations for each stimulus in each set. For the empirical data, trials with extreme response time (less than 300 ms or more than 5000 ms) were excluded from the analysis. This represents less than 3% of the trials. The parameters of the model were selected to fit the performance of this averaged data for the experiments with 4, 6, 8, and 10 stimuli. The results of the set containing 2 stimuli were excluded because we believe this task may be more properly modeled as relative judgment.

Figure 4 shows the observed mean response times and the mean number of iterations of the simulation to reach the response criterion for the four set sizes. As set size increases, mean response times (number of iterations) in the data (simulation) increase almost linearly. Mean response time for the 4 stimulus set is 824 ms, and increases up to 1170 ms for the 10 stimulus set, or approximately 115 ms for each additional pair of stimuli in the set. The mean number of iterations of the simulation to reach the response criterion follow the same pattern - the number of steps ranges from 478 for a set of 4 stimuli up to 655 for a set of 10 stimuli.

The similarity between the observed data and the simulation results for the proportion of correct responses is also quite good. The well-documented loss in accuracy as the number of stimuli in a set increases is clearly evident in Figure 5. Performance accuracy of both data (open squares) and simulation (solid squares) is greater than 90% when only four stimuli are possible. As stimuli are added performance declines, reaching approximately 74% for the participant data and 76% for the simulation when ten stimuli are possible.

An index of perceptual sensitivity taken from engineering and often used in psychophysics is information transmitted. While accuracy decreases as set size increases, the amount of information transmitted increases. Figure 6 plots information transmitted for both observed and simulation data as a function of the stimulus set size. The agreement between participant performance and our model is near perfect. Information transmitted increases from approximately 1.50 to 2.30 as the size of the stimulus set is increased from 4 to 10 elements.

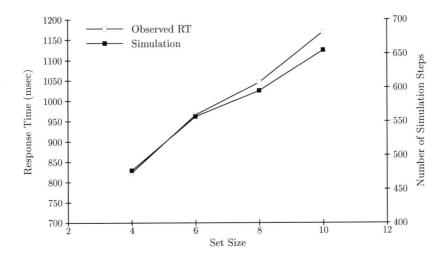

FIGURE 4. Observed mean response times and mean number of iterations of simulation to reach the response criterion as a function of stimulus set size.

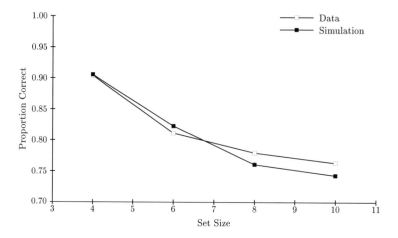

FIGURE 5. Observed and simulation proportion correct as a function of stimulus set size.

The overall relationship between observed mean response times and mean number of iterations of the simulation to reach the response criterion is shown in Figure 7. The mean response time for each stimulus in each set is plotted against the corresponding mean number of iterations of the simulation to reach the response criterion. The 28 points in the figure arise from the mean response times of the four sets comprising 4, 6, 8, and 10 stimuli. The two outliers in Figure 7 are from the discrepancy between observed and simulation times for the largest and smallest stimuli in the 10 stimulus set (see Figure 8).

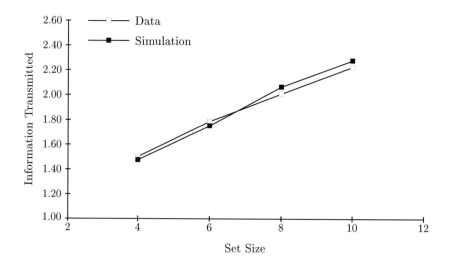

FIGURE 6. Observed and simulated information transmitted as a function of stimulus set size.

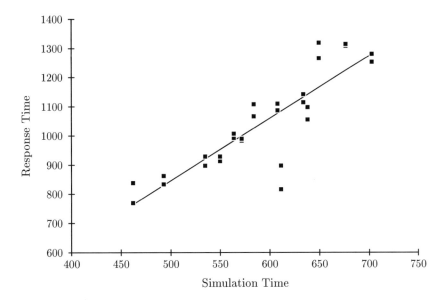

FIGURE 7. Observed mean response times versus mean number of iterations of the simulation to reach the response criterion (solid line is least squares linear fit).

The near linear relationship between mean response times and the mean number of iterations of the simulation to reach the response criterion allows us to convert mean number of iterations of the simulation to the response criterion to real time by linear regression. This linear regression has a slope of 1.95, and an intercept of -113.22. We caution against interpreting the negative value of the intercept as the predicted response time when the number of simulation steps is zero because of the spurious conclusions often reached when projecting beyond the range of data values in a regression result.

The predicted mean response times are plotted for each stimulus for all four set sizes in Figure 8. Also shown are the mean observed response times for each stimulus set. The predicted and observed response times share the typical features of absolute identification performance. Response time increases with the addition of stimuli to a set; and within a set, response time is greatest for the middle stimuli. The overall shape of the response time function for the simulation is somewhat different from the observed data. In the simulation, response time increases in an approximately linear fashion from the ends to the middle of the stimulus range. The observed response times, however, increase sharply as one moves away from the ends of the range, and then remain relatively constant for the remaining stimuli.

The proportion of correct responses for participant and simulation results for each of the four set sizes are shown in Figure 9. The participant data while some-what irregular exhibits the common pattern of absolute identification performance. The smallest stimulus in each set is correctly identified approximately 85% of the time. Then, for sets of 6, 8, and 10 stimuli, performance declines, reaching a

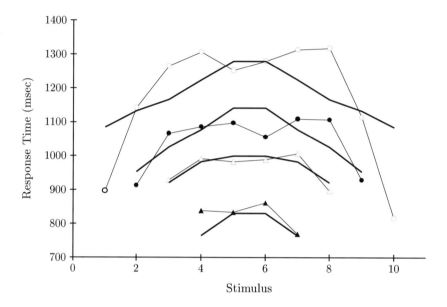

FIGURE 8. Observed (connected points) and simulated (solid lines) mean response times for sets containing 4, 6, 8, and 10 stimuli.

minimum at the 6th stimulus. When only four stimuli are present accuracy is approximately 91% for all stimuli. The simulated results, for set sizes of 6, 8, and 10 stimuli, mimic the general features of human performance: accuracy is poorest away from the end stimuli, yielding the so-called bow effect, and overall accuracy on individual stimuli diminishes as set size increases. The simulation results for set size four are also slightly different from the observed data in that the simulation results exhibit a clear bow effect that is not evident in the data. Nevertheless, the mean proportion correct for set size 4 for the simulation is 90%, one percent less than that of the subject data.

The agreement between the observed and simulation response proportion data is shown in Figure 10 where the observed response proportions are plotted against their corresponding simulation proportions. Except for the grouping of points into two clusters the relationship follows the diagonal line of perfect agreement, indicating that the observed and simulation results mirror each other. The upper cluster of points reveals an important subset of the response set. These 10 points correspond to the ends of the stimulus ranges for the three largest sets together with the four responses from the 4 stimulus set. This upper cluster of points, separated from the lower cluster in the vertical direction, would also be separated from the lower cluster in the horizontal direction if the subject data exhibited more uniform bowing. The clearest example of the subject data departing from the prototypical bow function occurs in the response proportions for stimulus "7" in the set containing 8 stimuli. Accuracy for this stimulus is above 85%, which is a substantial jump of over 15% from the accuracy for stimulus "6." A change in performance of this magnitude, particularly for a stimulus not at the end of the range, is not consistent

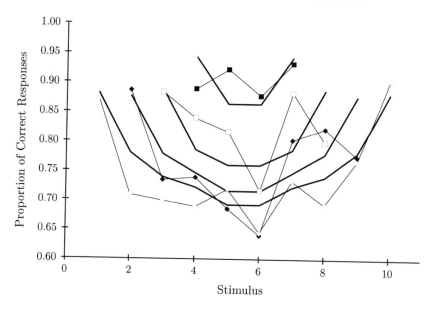

FIGURE 9. Observed (connected points) and simulated (solid lines) proportion of correct responses for sets containing 4, 6, 8, and 10 stimuli.

with typical data sets. This abrupt change in performance is observed in only one of the three subjects, but nevertheless is large enough to influence the average data. Unfortunately, the smoothing techniques that can be applied to minimize the influence of inconsistent response patterns and/or outliers in response time data are not readily applicable to response proportion data.

A pattern similar to that of the response proportion data shown in Figure 9 also appears in the d' values. This is shown in Figure 11, which plots the observed and simulation d's for adjacent pairs of stimuli for the four set sizes. This d' measure (suggested by Luce et al., 1982) appears to manifest a bow effect in two ways. First, d' increases as the set size decreases and second, within each set, the minimum value of d' corresponds to the middle stimulus pair. There is some disagreement between the observed and simulation results, specifically for the 10 stimulus set. The simulation d' curve does not exhibit as great a change over the stimulus set as does the observed data. However, Lacouture and Marley (1995) have noted that the calculation of d' from absolute identification data is sensitive to small variations in the response frequency matrix and therefore some of this discrepancy may be due to variability in the subject data.

The correspondence between the observed and simulation d' measures is shown in Figure 12 which plots these measures against each other. The upper cluster of three points are from the set containing four stimuli, where the 90% accuracy performance in this set produces d' measures of approximately 3. The departure of the remaining points from the diagonal line of perfect agreement is due mainly to the difference that we have already discussed between the observed and simulation results for the 10 stimulus set.

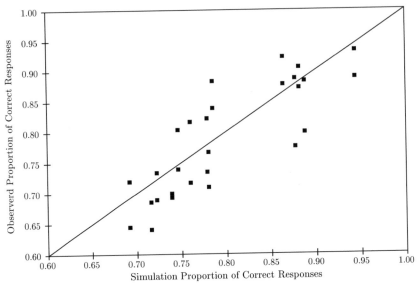

FIGURE 10. Observed versus simulation proportion of correct responses.

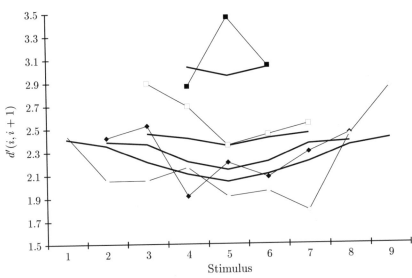

FIGURE 11. Observed and simulated d' for adjacent pairs of stimuli for sets containing 4, 6, 8, and 10 stimuli.

6. DISCUSSION

Our model testing was directed at the average performance of three individuals. This approach was necessitated by the substantial variability of the individual data sets. Nevertheless, we are confident that more reliable individual subject data, obtained by increasing the number of trials for each individual subject, would evidence

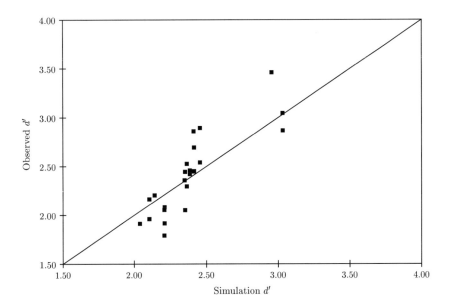

FIGURE 12. Observed versus simulation d' for sets containing 4, 6, 8, and 10 stimuli.

the same distinctive performance effects as the average data. The general features of absolute identification performance, both within and across stimulus sets, are well captured by our model. Specifically, as set size increases, the simulations accurately reproduce the response time increments and the accuracy decrements. Similarly, within stimulus sets, the simulation results duplicate the distinctive concave downward (concave upward) shapes of the response times (response proportions) of subject performance. However, there is one marked difference between the data and simulation results in the overall shape of the response times across stimuli, particularly in the set containing ten stimuli. The data exhibit a very sharp decrement near the ends of the stimulus range, while in our model response time declines gradually as one moves in either direction from the middle of the range.

The simulation results are achieved using a total of 16 parameters: 14 appear in Table 1, and the remaining two are the coefficients from the linear regression of mean response times on mean simulation times across the four sets of stimuli (of size 4, 6, 8, 10). The data contain at least 56 independent observations; this number derives from considering the 28 diagonal elements in the stimulus by response matrices and the 28 (mean) response time matrices.

Two opposite trends, interpretable within the framework of our model, are evident in the parameters η and z. First, the parameter η decreases from 0.15 to 0.030 as the number of stimuli in the test set increases from 4 to 10. The change in this parameter, the ratio of the decay rate to the rehearsal rate, is interpreted by us to be a consequence of subjects increasing their rehearsal rate as the number of stimuli, and hence the inherent difficulty of the task, increases. We assume, however, that there is a limit to the rehearsal rate, a limit that may or may not have been reached by subjects in the 10 stimulus task. Perhaps by stressing accuracy we could force subjects to perform to the limit of their ability and thereby provide an accurate measure of the rehearsal rate limit. The approximately 10% error rate for the four stimulus task suggests that our subjects were performing below their optimal ability. The magnitude of η supports this interpretation. While less intuitively plausible, an alternative explanation is that the change in η is due to a decreasing decay rate as the size of the stimulus set increases. However, it is difficult to conceive of a plausible psychological mechanism which would lead to a reduction in the decay rate in memory as the size of the stimulus set increases.

The second trend in the parameter set occurs in the values of z. The increase in z which accompanies increases in the size of the stimulus set is interpreted simply as an increase in the memory rehearsal range. For the largest stimulus set size, the z value of 2.25 indicates that subjects rehearse a psychological space ranging from 2.25 standard deviations below the mean of the representation of the smallest stimulus to 2.25 standard deviations above the mean of the representation of the largest stimulus. Our model also suggests that for the smallest stimulus set subjects rehearse barely enough of the psychological continuum to contain the means of the representations of all the stimuli.

The two trends for η and z both show a sharp change from four to six stimuli. Subject performance also shows a distinctive change from four to six stimuli. When only four stimuli are possible the response proportions and response times are relatively constant across stimuli. However, when the size of the stimulus set is increased to six, the response proportions show a significant decline for the middle of the stimulus range. Further, the response times show the signature of absolute identification performance: the greatest amount of time is spent attempting to identify stimuli in the middle of the range.

There are two tendencies in subject performance, revealed only by inspection of the response frequency matrix, that the current model cannot mimic. First, subjects will sometimes identify stimulus 5, for example, as stimulus 3 or even 2, "missing" the mark by two or three response categories. Our simulation results, on the other hand, do not miss the mark by more than one response category. We do not think these errors arise from subjects becoming inattentive and introducing guesses into the data because the errors cluster around the correct response. This pattern, however, is due mainly to subject number one. Subject number two performs exactly like our simulation and for subject three an error of greater than one stimulus rank occurs approximately once every 300 trials. Second, there is a pattern of asymmetry in the errors made by the subjects that is not captured by the model. Subjects identify stimuli from the lower portion of the stimulus range as larger than they actually are, more often than they identify them as smaller than they actually are. The exact opposite response pattern occurs for stimuli from the upper portion of the stimulus range. Again, this bias or response strategy occurs in subject one and not in the other two subjects.

In conclusion, we believe that the addition of a random walk component to the Marley and Cook (1984) absolute identification model provides another step towards a comprehensive account of human performance in the intriguing task of absolute identification of unidimensional stimuli. The ability of the extended model to account for response times, both within and across different stimulus set sizes, is encouraging for our approach. The next important step is to apply the model to individual subject data, with a sufficient number of trials for each subject that we can also study complete response time distributions.

THE GENERALIZED AREA THEOREM IN SIGNAL DETECTION THEORY

GEOFFREY IVERSON
University of California, Irvine

DONALD BAMBER
Naval Command, Control and Ocean Surveillance Center

ABSTRACT. In the context of standard signal detection theory, the data from the infinite sequence of forced-choice tasks that involve a single realization of a signal and k independent realizations of a noise source, $k = 1, 2, \ldots$, are shown to be sufficient to reconstruct the receiver operating characteristic (ROC) for the corresponding yes-no detection task. This follows from a novel interpretation of forced-choice probabilities as the moments of a random variable whose distribution function determines the yes-no ROC; the first moment is just the area subtended by the ROC. We further develop the standard theory of the forced-choice paradigm, and obtain conditions allowing that theory to be verified in empirical data.

1. INTRODUCTION

The "Area Theorem" of signal detection theory (Bamber, 1975; Green & Moses, 1966) relates performance in the basic yes-no (YN) detection task to that obtained in the two-interval forced-choice (2IFC) task, employing the same stimuli: the area subtended by the YN *receiver operating characteristic* (ROC) equals the probability of a correct response in the corresponding 2IFC task. Largely for this reason, the area subtended by a YN ROC has long been regarded as a useful index of detectability. Consider the sequence of forced-choice tasks involving a single instance of the signal and k independent realizations of the noise source, $k = 1, 2, \ldots$. Each member of the sequence $p_c^{(1)}, p_c^{(2)}, \ldots, p_c^{(k+1)}, \ldots$ of correct-response probabilities

Key words and phrases. Signal detection theory, area theorem, moments, ranking, random utility theory.

Dedication. Each of the authors independently established a version of the generalized area theorem over a decade ago. It seemed to us appropriate to publish our work in this volume as a tribute to our dear colleague R. Duncan Luce, whose own contributions to the theory of signal detectability are legion.

Acknowledgments. The authors are most grateful to Jean-Claude Falmagne and Jack Yellott for their comments on an earlier version of this chapter and to Ms. Stefania Za for converting this manuscript to LaTeX format.

Address for correspondence. Geoffrey J. Iverson, Department of Cognitive Sciences and the Institute for Mathematical Behavioral Sciences, University of California, Irvine, CA 92717; E-mail: giverson@.aris.ss.uci.edu Donald Bamber, Naval Command, Control & Ocean Surveillance Center, Research, Development, Test & Evaluation Division, NCCOSC RDTE DIV 44215, 53355 Ryne Road, Rm. 222, San Diego, CA 92152-7252; E-mail: bamber@nosc.mil

provides an independent numerical characteristic of the underlying ROC. In fact, according to standard signal detection theory

$$p_c^{(k+1)} = k \int_0^1 (1 - t)^{k-1} \rho(t)dt, \quad k = 1, 2, \ldots \tag{1}$$

where the function $t \mapsto \rho(t), t \in [0, 1]$ appearing in the right hand term of (1) is the YN ROC. While the above formula is well known (Green & Swets, 1966) we shall interpret it afresh via a simple integration by parts:

$$p_c^{(k+1)} = \int_0^1 t^k d(1 - \rho(1 - t)), \quad k = 1, 2, \ldots \tag{2}$$

We recognize the function $t \mapsto 1 - \rho(1 - t)$ as the distribution function of a random variable V concentrated on the closed interval $[0, 1]$. Equation (2) thus reads

$$p_c^{(k+1)} = E(V^k), \quad k = 1, 2, \ldots \tag{3}$$

In the following Section 2 we show in detail that the *infinite* sequence $p_c^{(2)}, p_c^{(3)}$, ... of forced-choice probabilities is sufficient to reconstruct the distribution function of V and hence the ROC ρ. This fact is the Generalized Area Theorem referred to in the title of this paper. We give a couple of examples showing that ROCs can often be reconstructed with good accuracy from the first few terms of the moment sequence (3). The method of reconstruction that we use is sketched in Section 3. Another task that is closely related to the $k + 1$ interval forced-choice ($(k + 1)$IFC) task asks an observer to rank order the $k + 1$ intervals from most likely (rank=1) to least likely (rank=$k + 1$) to contain the signal. In Section 4 we note the equivalence between the data provided by the ranking task, and the sequence of the first k forced-choice probabilities. The theory of the $(k + 1)$IFC task and that of the ranking task fits naturally into the framework of *random utility theory* (Block & Marschak, 1960; Luce & Suppes, 1965; Falmagne, 1978). In Section 5 we reinterpret matters in that framework, and obtain an observable criterion providing necessary and sufficient conditions for the validity of the system of equations (1). In Section 6 we address a few miscellaneous topics, including a discussion of statistical issues that arise when dealing with realistic, fallible data.

2. THE GENERALIZED AREA THEOREM

Let us begin by establishing some more or less standard nomenclature and notation. Performance in the basic YN detection task is idealized in the form of a receiver operating characteristic (ROC) which expresses "hits" (correctly identifying a signal as such) as a function of "false alarms" (incorrectly identifying an instance of noise as signal). In the context of Bamber's (1979) analysis of cause and effect, an ROC is a type of state-trace.

A wealth of empirical evidence is compatible with the assumption that an ROC is a function $t \mapsto \rho(t)$ from the closed interval $[0, 1]$ into itself, increasing and continuous on $(0, 1)$ with $\rho(0) = 0$. Standard theory for the YN task (Green & Swets, 1966; Falmagne, 1985) involves a pair (U_s, U_n) of independent random variables, such that each point (p_{FA}, p_H) on an ROC satisfies

$$p_{FA}(\lambda) = \Pr(U_n > \lambda),$$
$$p_H(\lambda) = \Pr(U_s > \lambda)$$

for some real *criterion* λ. We say that the pair (U_s, U_n) provides a *random representation* for the ROC.

Proposition 1. *Every ROC ρ admits a random representation.*

Proof. With V_n a random variable uniformly distributed on $[0, 1]$, write

$$p_{FA}(t) = \Pr(V_n > t) = 1 - t, \tag{4}$$

and define the (independent) random variable V_s on $[0, 1]$ via

$$p_H(t) = \Pr(V_s > t) = \rho(1 - t). \tag{5}$$

It is clear by construction that the pair (V_s, V_n) provides a random representation for ρ. □

There are of course many random representations for a given ROC. Suppose (U_s, U_n) provides such a representation, with U_n continuous on an interval of the reals (since by assumption an ROC is defined at every point of $[0, 1]$). If F_n is the distribution function of U_n, then $F_n(U_n)$ is uniform on $[0, 1]$ (Quesenberry, 1986) and is identified with the random variable V_n appearing in the proof of Proposition 1; likewise V_s is distributed as the random variable $F_n(U_s)$. Most applications of signal detection theory involve decision variables concentrated on the whole real line, or on the non-negative reals; but in this paper we shall find it especially useful to focus on the special random representation provided by the pair (V_s, V_n) defined jointly on the closed unit interval $[0, 1]$.

If (U_s, U_n) is a random representation for a YN ROC, standard theory for the 2IFC task asserts that $p_c^{(2)}$, the probability of a correct response, is given as

$$p_c^{(2)} = \Pr(U_s > U_n)$$

and since F_n is increasing we have

$$
\begin{aligned}
p_c^{(2)} &= \Pr(F_n(U_s) \geq F_n(U_n)) \\
&= \Pr(V_s \geq V_n) \\
&= \int_0^1 \Pr(V_n \leq t) dF_{V_s}(t) \\
&= \int_0^1 t\, dF_{V_s}(t) \\
&= E(V_s).
\end{aligned}
$$

There are thus two useful interpretations of the area theorem. On the one hand the probability $p_c^{(2)}$ is the area subtended by the ROC ρ; on the other hand the same probability is the expected value of the signal random variable V_s. The latter interpretation suggests looking for additional choice probabilities that provide information on the higher moments of V_s; and fortunately such probabilities are not hard to unearth. In terms of the random representation (V_s, V_n) defined above, standard theory for the $(k+1)$IFC task gives the probability of a correct response as

$$p_c^{(k+1)} = \Pr(V_s > \max_{1 \le i \le k} V_n^{(i)})$$

where the random variables $V_n^{(1)}, V_n^{(2)}, \ldots, V_n^{(k)}$ are independent and uniformly distributed on $[0,1]$ and are independent of V_s. It follows that for $k = 1, 2, \ldots,$

$$
\begin{aligned}
p_c^{(k+1)} &= \int_0^1 \Pr(\max_{1 \le i \le k} V_n^{(i)} < t) dF_{V_s}(t) \\
&= \int_0^1 t^k dF_{V_s}(t)
\end{aligned}
$$

and thus

$$p_c^{(k+1)} = E(V_s^k) \tag{6}$$

as anticipated in our introductory remarks (cf. Equation 3). A famous theorem of Hausdorff (Shohat & Tamarkin, 1943; Feller, 1966) asserts that the collection of all moments of a random variable concentrated on a *finite* interval serves to characterize that variable. In the present context this means that the infinite sequence $p_c^{(2)}, p_c^{(3)}, \ldots$ of forced-choice probabilities contains sufficient information to reconstruct the corresponding YN ROC. Conversely the ROC ρ determines the random variable V_s (via Equation 5) and the sequence of choice probabilities $p_c^{(2)}, p_c^{(3)}, \ldots$ via Equations (1) or (2). We summarize this discussion as follows:

Theorem 1. (Generalized Area Theorem)[1] *In the context of standard signal detection theory the YN detection task and the sequence of $(k+1)$IFC tasks, $k = 1, 2, \ldots$, provide equivalent information as to the ability of an observer to detect a given signal source from a given noise source.*

We now illustrate this theorem in a couple of special cases. To do so we employ knowledge of successive moments to build a sequence of polynomial approximations to an ROC. There are many ways to do this, and following Shohat and Tamarkin (1943) we use Legendre polynomials. In section 3 we outline the method.

Example 1. The ROC has the analytic form $\rho(t) = \sqrt{t}$ on $[0,1]$. The corresponding random variable V_s has distribution function $F_{V_s}(t) = 1 - \sqrt{1-t}$, and

$$E(V_s^k) = \frac{\Gamma(k+1)\Gamma(1/2)}{2\Gamma(k+3/2)}, \quad k = 1, 2, \ldots.$$

Numerically the moment sequence is $2/3, 8/15, 16/35, \ldots$. This example is a well known signal detection model with random variables (U_s, U_n) concentrated on the positive reals and distributed as members of the exponential family.

---

[1] Recently, Scurfield (1996) has given a very interesting and quite different generalization of the Area Theorem. His work involves identification (more than two stimulus categories) rather than detection, which is our concern in this paper.

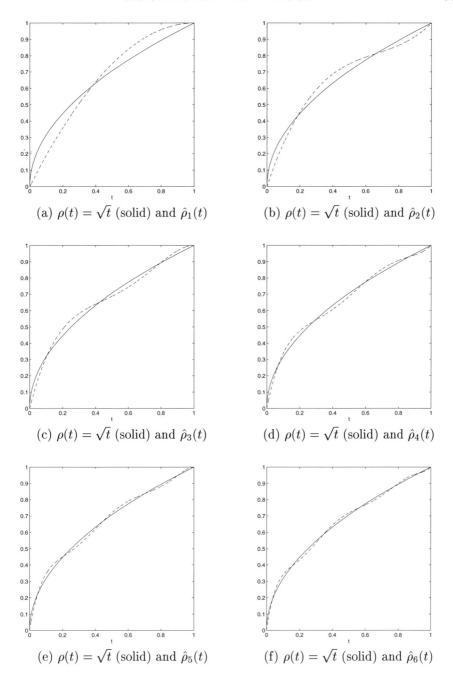

(a) $\rho(t) = \sqrt{t}$ (solid) and $\hat{\rho}_1(t)$

(b) $\rho(t) = \sqrt{t}$ (solid) and $\hat{\rho}_2(t)$

(c) $\rho(t) = \sqrt{t}$ (solid) and $\hat{\rho}_3(t)$

(d) $\rho(t) = \sqrt{t}$ (solid) and $\hat{\rho}_4(t)$

(e) $\rho(t) = \sqrt{t}$ (solid) and $\hat{\rho}_5(t)$

(f) $\rho(t) = \sqrt{t}$ (solid) and $\hat{\rho}_6(t)$

FIGURE 1. The ROC $\rho(t) = \sqrt{t}$, and the successive approximants $\hat{\rho}_1, \hat{\rho}_2, \ldots, \hat{\rho}_6$.

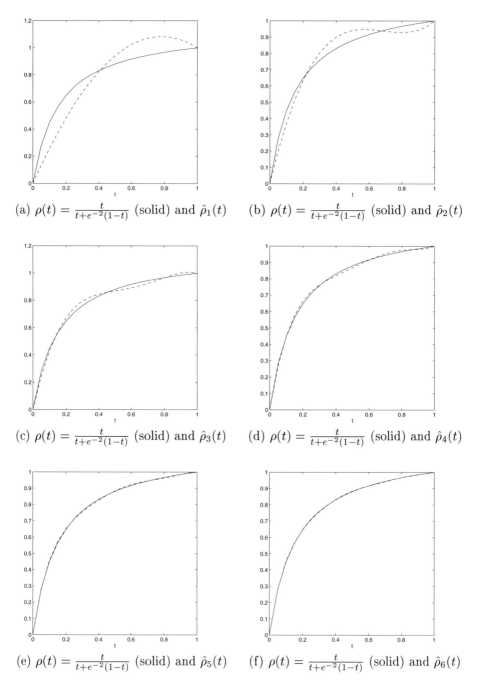

FIGURE 2. The ROC $\rho(t) = \frac{t}{t+e^{-2}(1-t)}$, and the successive approximants $\hat{\rho}_1, \hat{\rho}_2, \ldots, \hat{\rho}_6$.

In Figures 1a-1f, we have used the first through sixth moments to provide successive approximations to $\rho(t)$. As can be seen from the sequence of graphs, four moments are sufficient to approximate $\rho(t)$ uniformly within an error of 0.05. For future reference to Examples 3, 6 we note here that the first approximant to $\rho(t) = \sqrt{t}$ is $\hat{\rho}_1(t) = 2t - t^2$. These two functions are plotted in Figure 1a; $\hat{\rho}_1$ is *dual* to ρ (see Section 6).

Example 2. In this example we employ a "symmetric" ROC with a random representation involving logistic variables concentrated on $\mathbb{R}$: $\rho(t) = \frac{t}{t + e^{-2}(1-t)}$. The logistic and equal-variance normal ROCs are practically indistinguishable, although the former model is more tractable analytically. Again we estimate $\rho(t)$ on the basis of the first moment, the first two moments, ..., the first six moments. The results are shown in the sequence of Figures 2a-2f. Convergence of the approximating polynomials to the ROC is effectively achieved in Figure 2f; again knowledge of four moments is sufficient to determine the ROC to within 0.05 everywhere on $[0, 1]$.

Remark 1. The polynomial approximations shown in Figures 1 and 2 are not necessarily bona-fide ROCs. This is particularly evident in Figure 2a, and to a lesser extent in Figure 2c. The interesting problem of building approximations that stay within the function space of ROCs is one issue that we do not pursue in this work; the discussion surrounding Example 6, Section 6 should be read with this remark in mind.

3. RECONSTRUCTING ROCS FROM FORCED-CHOICE PROBABILITIES

Define the polynomials $L_n(t)$ on $[0, 1]$:

$$L_n(t) = \frac{(-1)^n}{n!} \frac{d^n}{dt^n} (t(1-t))^n, \quad n = 0, 1, 2, \dots .$$

These polynomials are orthogonal; in particular

$$\int_0^1 L_n(t) L_m(t) dt = \begin{cases} \frac{1}{2n+1} & n = m, \\ 0 & \text{otherwise.} \end{cases}$$

We remark that the $L_n(t)$ are variants of the classical Legendre polynomials $P_n(x)$ on the interval $[-1, 1]$. In fact $L_n(t) = P_n(2t - 1)$, $0 \leq t \leq 1$.

Let $F(t)$ be the distribution function of a random variable concentrated on $[0, 1]$. Form the sequence of numerical indices

$$\begin{aligned} \gamma_n &= \int_0^1 L_n(t) dF(t) \\ &= \sum_{m=0}^n l_m^n \mu_m \end{aligned}$$

where $\mu_m = \int_0^1 t^m dF(t)$ are the moments of $F(t)$, and $L_n(t) = \sum_{m=0}^n l_m^n t^m$. Then it is known (Shohat & Tamarkin, 1943) that the sequence of polynomials

$$F_n(t) = \sum_{m=0}^n (2m + 1) \gamma_m \mathcal{L}_m(t)$$

converges as $n \to \infty$ to $F(t)$ at each point of continuity of the latter function; here $\mathcal{L}_m(t) = \int_0^t L_m(t')dt'$.

The application of this fact (which provides a constructive proof of the Hausdorff moment theorem) to the reconstruction of a YN ROC $\rho(t)$ from knowledge of the forced-choice probabilities $p_c^{(1)} = 1, p_c^{(2)}, p_c^{(3)}, \ldots$ is immediate. The sequence of functions

$$\hat{\rho}_n(t) = \sum_{m=0}^{n} (2m+1)(-1)^m \gamma_m \mathcal{L}_m(t)$$

converges pointwise, as $n \to \infty$, to the ROC $\rho(t)$. The constants γ_m are determined by the forced-choice probabilities $p_c^{(k+1)}$ via

$$\gamma_m = \sum_{k=0}^{m} l_k^m p_c^{(k+1)}.$$

In Figures 1a-1f, and Figures 2a-2f, we have depicted the functions $\hat{\rho}_n(t)$ for $n = 1, 2, \ldots, 6$ corresponding to the ROCs $\rho(t) = \sqrt{t}$ and $\rho(t) = \frac{t}{t+e^{-2}(1-t)}$. For easy reference we give the explicit expansion of the constants γ_m in terms of $p_c^{(k+1)}$, for $m = 0, 1, \ldots, 6$:

$$
\begin{aligned}
\gamma_0 &= p_c^{(1)} = 1 \\
\gamma_1 &= 2p_c^{(2)} - 1 \\
\gamma_2 &= 6p_c^{(3)} - 6p_c^{(2)} + 1 \\
\gamma_3 &= 20p_c^{(4)} - 30p_c(3) + 12p_c^{(2)} - 1 \\
\gamma_4 &= 70p_c^{(5)} - 140p_c^{(4)} + 90p_c^{(3)} - 20p_c^{(2)} + 1 \\
\gamma_5 &= 252p_c^{(6)} - 630p_c^{(5)} + 560p_c^{(4)} - 210p_c^{(3)} + 30p_c^{(2)} - 1 \\
\gamma_6 &= 924p_c^{(7)} - 2772p_c^{(6)} + 3150p_c^{(5)} - 1680p_c^{(4)} + 420p_c^{(3)} - 42p_c^{(2)} + 1.
\end{aligned}
$$

4. THE RANKING TASK

As an alternative to the information provided by the sequence of forced-choice tasks, one can garner equivalent information in a *single* ranking task. In this latter task an observer is required to rank $k + 1$ intervals from most likely to contain the signal (rank=1) to least likely (rank=$k + 1$) to contain the signal. The data from the ranking task are summarized in terms of ranking probabilities Π_{j+1}^{k+1}, i.e. the probability of giving the interval containing the signal a rank of $j + 1, j = 0, 1, \ldots, k$. The labeling of the random variables $V_n^{(1)}, V_n^{(2)}, \ldots, V_n^{(k)}$ being arbitrary (i.e. $V_n^{(1)}, V_n^{(2)}, \ldots, V_n^{(k)}$ are *exchangeable*), an easy combinatorial argument gives

$$
\begin{aligned}
\Pi_{j+1}^{k+1} &= \binom{k}{j} \Pr(\min_{i \leq j}\{V_n^{(i)}\} > V_s > \max_{j+2 \leq i \leq k+1}\{V_n^{(i)}\}) \\
&= \binom{k}{j} \int_0^1 t^{k-j}(1-t)^j \, dF_{V_s}(t) \qquad (7) \\
&= \binom{k}{j} E(V_s^{k-j}(1 - V_s)^j), \quad j = 0, 1, \ldots, k
\end{aligned}
$$

where we have used the independence of all random variables appearing in the above expressions, and the fact that the $V_n^{(i)}$ are uniform on $[0, 1]$. The binomial theorem applied to the term $(1 - t)^j$ in (7) makes it clear that Π_{j+1}^{k+1} can be expressed as a linear combination of the forced-choice probabilities. There is a compact way to do this: introduce the finite difference operator Δ defined on a real sequence α_r via $\Delta(\alpha_r) = \alpha_{r+1} - \alpha_r$, together with its iterates $\Delta^2(\alpha_r) = \Delta(\Delta(\alpha_r)), \ldots, \Delta^p(\alpha_r) = \Delta(\Delta^{p-1}(\alpha_r))$. In these terms Equation 7 can be written

$$\Pi_{j+1}^{k+1} = \binom{k}{j}(-1)^j \Delta^j p_c^{(k-j+1)}, \quad j = 0, 1, \ldots, k. \tag{8}$$

Equation 8 can be inverted so as to express the forced-choice probabilities in terms of the ranking probabilities:

$$\binom{k}{j} p_c^{(j+1)} = \sum_{i=0}^{k-j} \binom{k-i}{j} \Pi_{i+1}^{k+1}, \quad j = 0, 1, \ldots, k. \tag{9}$$

The pair of Equations 8, 9 make it clear that the $(k + 1)$-interval ranking task generates data equivalent to those obtained from the finite sequence 2IFC, 3IFC,..., $(k + 1)$IFC, of forced-choice tasks. In the same vein these equations show that the $(k + 1)$-interval ranking task determines the data from all ranking tasks involving fewer intervals. In fact

$$\Pi_{i+1}^{m+1} = \binom{m}{i} \sum_{j=i}^{k-m+i} \frac{\binom{k-m}{j-i}}{\binom{k}{j}} \Pi_{j+1}^{k+1}, \quad 0 \le i \le m \le k. \tag{10}$$

Example 3. Suppose U_s, U_n are independent, double-exponential random variables, with respective means $\mu(s), \mu(n)$ satisfying $\mu(s) \ge \mu(n)$, and common variance $\pi^2/6$. Let $\delta = exp(\mu(s) - \mu(n))$. Then the ROC with random representation (U_s, U_n) has the analytic expression

$$\rho_\delta(t) = 1 - (1 - t)^\delta.$$

This one-parameter family of ROCs is *dual* to the family

$$\rho_\delta^*(t) = 1 - \rho_\delta^{-1}(1 - t) = t^{1/\delta}.$$

The special cases $\rho_2^*(t) = \sqrt{t}$ and $\rho_2(t) = 1 - (1 - t)^2$ arose already in connection with Example 1 above.

As is well known (Yellott, 1977) the double-exponential distribution plays a decisive role in rendering Luce's Choice model (Luce, 1959a) as a random utility theory. For the $(k + 1)$-interval forced-choice task the prediction of the double exponential model is

$$p_c^{(k+1)} = \frac{\delta}{\delta + k}$$

$$= \frac{v(s)}{v(s) + kv(n)}$$

with $v(s) = e^{\mu(s)}, v(n) = e^{\mu(n)}$. This expression for the choice probabilities is exactly that given by Luce's Choice Axiom applied to $k + 1$ choice objects, k of which have identical scale values $v(n)$.

The corresponding ranking probabilities are readily computed from Equation 8. We have

$$\Pi_1^{k+1} = p_c^{(k+1)} = \frac{\delta}{\delta + k},$$

$$\Pi_2^{k+1} = k\left(p_c^{(k)} - p_c^{(k+1)}\right)$$

$$= k\left(\frac{\delta}{\delta + k - 1} - \frac{\delta}{\delta + k}\right)$$

$$= \left(\frac{k}{\delta + k}\right)\left(\frac{\delta}{\delta + k - 1}\right)$$

and for $1 \leq j \leq k$

$$\Pi_{j+1}^{k+1} = \left(\frac{k}{\delta + k}\right)\left(\frac{k - 1}{\delta + k - 1}\right) \cdots \left(\frac{k - j + 1}{\delta + k - j + 1}\right)\left(\frac{\delta}{\delta + k - j}\right).$$

This expression for the ranking probabilities admits the following interpretation, in agreement with Luce's Choice model: in the $(k + 1)$ interval ranking task, an observer selects (gives rank 1 to) the signal interval with probability $\frac{\delta}{\delta + k}$. If the signal interval is not selected (with probability $\frac{k}{\delta + k}$) the process continues in the same way on a set of one fewer intervals (one of which contains the signal) until the signal interval is selected at the $(j + 1)$st stage. In other words, ranking is achieved by successively eliminating intervals, one at a time.

The quantity on the right hand side of Equation 8 is evidently non-negative. In particular, $(-1)^j \Delta^j p_c^{k-j+1} \geq 0$ for $j = 0, 1, \ldots, k$ and all $k = 1, 2, \ldots$. This (infinite) sequence of inequalities provides an empirically testable system of predictions for the validity of standard theory for the $(k+1)$-interval forced-choice and ranking tasks. We now take up this fact, placing it in the more general context of random utility theory.

5. RANDOM UTILITY THEORY

A common choice task requires a subject to select the most preferred object from a finite set A of offerings. To account for a subject's unreliability over repeated choices, each choice object a is associated with a random variable U_a such that if $a \in B$, where $B \subseteq A$, and $P_{a,B}$ denotes the probability of choosing a from the set B,

$$P_{a,B} = \Pr(U_a = \max_{b \in B}\{U_b\}), \qquad (11)$$

for all non-empty subsets B of A.

The theory embodied in Equation 11 is known as random utility theory, and has been the subject of numerous theoretical investigations (Block & Marschak, 1960; Luce & Suppes, 1965; Falmagne, 1978; each give manifold references). The fundamental problem of random utility theory, to establish conditions on the choice probabilities $P_{a,B}$ which guarantee the existence of a collection of random variables $\{U_a | a \in A\}$ satisfying Equation 11, was solved by Falmagne (1978) following earlier

analysis of Block and Marschak (1960). The crucial conditions on the choice probabilities can be described in the following way. For any choice objects $a, b, c, d, \ldots$
in $B, B \subseteq A$ consider the sequence

$$P_{a,B},$$
$$P_{a,B-\{b\}} - P_{a,B},$$
$$P_{a,B-\{b,c\}} - P_{a,B-\{b\}} - P_{a,B-\{c\}} + P_{a,B},$$
$$P_{a,B-\{b,c,d\}} - (P_{a,B-\{b,c\}} + P_{a,B-\{b,d\}} + P_{a,B-\{c,d\}}) +$$
$$(P_{a,B-\{b\}} + P_{a,B-\{c\}} + P_{a,B-\{d\}}) - P_{a,B},$$
$$\text{etc.,}$$

(12)

of expressions linear in the choice probabilities. If the random utility formula (11)
holds for the choice probabilities, Block and Marschak (1960) showed that each of
the above terms in (12) (the so-called Block-Marschak functions or "polynomials")
must be non-negative. In a *tour de force* of combinatorial analysis, Falmagne (1978)
established the converse i.e. the non-negativity of the Block-Marschak functions is
both necessary and sufficient for the existence of a random utility representation
(11) governing a finite system of choice probabilities.

Formally, the $(k + 1)$IFC paradigm is a special case of the general choice paradigm applied to a situation in which k of the choice objects are, so so to speak,
"copies" of one another. If we identify the choice object a in (12) with the signal in
a $(k + 1)$-interval task, and likewise identify each of the choice objects $b, c, d, \ldots$ in
(12) with a noise stimulus, we obtain for each $j = 0, 1, \ldots, k$ the following sequence
of expressions linear in the forced-choice probabilities:

$$p_c^{(j+1)},$$
$$p_c^{(j)} - p_c^{(j+1)},$$
$$p_c^{(j-1)} - 2p_c^{(j)} + p_c^{(j+1)},$$
$$p_c^{(j-2)} - 3p_c^{(j-1)} + 3p_c^{(j)} - p_c^{(j+1)},$$
$$\text{etc.}$$

(13)

Note that the sequence of expressions (13) can be written in terms of the finite
difference operator introduced above in Section 4:

$$p_c^{(j+1)},$$
$$- \Delta p_c^{(j)},$$
$$(-1)^2 \Delta^2 p_c^{(j-1)},$$
$$(-1)^3 \Delta^3 p_c^{(j-2)},$$
$$\text{etc.,}$$

and for each of these terms to be non-negative requires

$$(-1)^r \Delta^r p_c^{(j-r+1)} \geq 0, \quad r = 0, 1, \ldots, j.$$

(14)

In (14) and in the following we invoke the conventions $\Delta^{(0)}(p_c^{(k+1)}) = p_c^{(k+1)}$ for all
k and $p_c^{(1)} = 1$. We summarize our discussion in the form of a

Criterion 1 (Falmagne). *A finite sequence $p_c^{(2)}, p_c^{(3)}, \ldots, p_c^{(k+1)}$ of forced-choice detection probabilities admits a random representation*

$$p_c^{(k+1)} = \Pr(V_s > \max_{1 \le i \le k} \{V_n^{(i)}\}) \tag{15}$$

iff the system of inequalities (14) obtains for each $j = 0, 1, \ldots, k$.

The random variables $V_s, V_n^{(i)}$ appearing in Equation 15 can be chosen as concentrated on $[0, 1]$ and moreover the variables $V_n^{(1)}, V_n^{(2)}, \ldots, V_n^{(k)}$ are identically distributed. However these variables are not necessarily independent and the $V_n^{(i)}$ need not be uniformly distributed. We thus seek to strengthen the above criterion so as to obtain the representation (15) in terms of *independent* random variables. As is made evident in Equation 6, standard theory for the forced-choice paradigm allows the probabilities $p_c^{(k+1)}$ to be interpreted as moments of a signal random variable V_s concentrated on the unit interval $[0, 1]$. As mentioned earlier in connection with Equation 6 and elaborated on in Section 3 a classical result of Hausdorff (Feller, 1966) asserts that the moments of a random variable concentrated on a finite interval determine that variable. With that in mind, we have the desired

Criterion 2. *An infinite sequence $p_c^{(2)}, p_c^{(3)}, \ldots$ of forced-choice detection probabilities admits a random representation (15) involving mutually independent random variables $V_s, V_n^{(1)}, V_n^{(2)}, \ldots$ iff the system of inequalities (14) holds for all integers $j = 0, 1, \ldots$. All random variables can be chosen so as to be concentrated on $[0, 1]$ with $V_n^{(1)}, V_n^{(2)}, \ldots$ identically and uniformly distributed.*

We clarify the distinction between the two criteria 1, 2 in the following examples.

Example 4. The finite sequence $p_c^{(j+1)} = \frac{2}{(j+2)}, j = 0, 1, \ldots, k$ satisfies

$$(-\Delta)^j p_c^{(k-j+1)} = \frac{2 \cdot j!}{(k-j+2)(k-j+3)\ldots(k+2)} > 0$$

and by Criterion 1 we are guaranteed a random representation of the random utility form (15). However since the criterion applies for *every* $k = 1, 2, \ldots$, Criterion 2 also applies and we have the representation

$$p_c^{(k+1)} = \int_0^1 t^k dF_{V_s}(t) \tag{16}$$

for some random variable V_s concentrated on $[0, 1]$. In fact in this example V_s has the distribution function $F_{V_s}(t) = t^2$; the corresponding YN ROC is $\rho(t) = 2t - t^2$.

Example 5. Suppose one observes $p_c^{(2)} = 0.8$ and $p_c^{(3)} = 0.6$. It is easy to check that Criterion 1 applies. However Criterion 2 cannot apply; for if it did, $p_c^{(2)}$ and $p_c^{(3)}$ would be the first and second moments of a random variable on $[0, 1]$. The variance of that random variable would thus have to be $0.6 - 0.64 = -0.04 < 0$ which is impossible. It is nevertheless instructive to exhibit an explicit random representation for these data. Take $U_s, U_n^{(1)}, U_n^{(2)}$ concentrated on the set $\{1, 2, 3\}$ of ranks, with joint distribution

$$\Pr(U_s = 3, U_n^{(1)} = 2, U_n^{(2)} = 1) = \Pr(U_s = 3, U_n^{(1)} = 1, U_n^{(2)} = 2) = 0.3$$

and

$$\Pr(U_s = 2, U_n^{(1)} = 3, U_n^{(2)} = 1) = \Pr(U_s = 2, U_n^{(1)} = 1, U_n^{(2)} = 3) = 0.2$$

with all other joint probabilities equal to zero. We check that

$$
\begin{aligned}
p_c^{(3)} &= \Pr(U_s > U_n^{(1)} > U_n^{(2)}) + \Pr(U_s > U_n^{(2)} > U_n^{(1)}) \\
&= 0.3 + 0.3 = 0.6
\end{aligned}
$$

and

$$
\begin{aligned}
p_c^{(2)} &= \Pr(U_s > U_n^{(1)}) \\
&= \Pr(U_s > U_n^{(1)} > U_n^{(2)}) + \Pr(U_s > U_n^{(2)} > U_n^{(1)}) + \\
&\quad \Pr(U_n^{(2)} > U_s > U_n^{(1)}) \\
&= 0.3 + 0.3 + 0.2 = 0.8
\end{aligned}
$$

as required. To relate this representation to one concentrated on $[0, 1]$ (as mentioned in Criterion 1) define $V_s = (U_s - 1)/2$ and define $V_n^{(1)}, V_n^{(2)}$ similarly. However this random representation is not of the desired form (16).

It is straightforward to generalize the method of constructing a random representation that was used in Example 5. Define random variables $U_s, U_n^{(1)}, U_n^{(2)}, ..., U_n^{(k)}$ on the set $\{1, 2, ..., k+1\}$ of ranks with joint distribution as follows: if $(\zeta_1, \zeta_2, ..., \zeta_{k+1})$ is a permutation of $(1, 2, ..., k+1)$ and $\zeta_1 = j + 1$, set

$$\Pr(U_s = \zeta_1, U_n^{(1)} = \zeta_2, ..., U_n^{(k)} = \zeta_{k+1}) = \frac{1}{k!} \Pi_{k-j+1}^{k+1}, \quad j = 0, 1, ..., k;$$

otherwise all joint probabilities are zero. The marginal probabilities are readily computed as $\Pr(U_s = j + 1) = \Pi_{k-j+1}^{k+1}$, and $\Pr(U_n^{(i)} = j + 1) = \frac{1}{k}(1 - \Pi_{k-j+1}^{k+1})$ independent of the index i. To concentrate these variables on $[0, 1]$ define $V_s^* = \frac{1}{k}(U_s - 1)$ and $V_n^{*(i)} = \frac{1}{k}(U_n^{(i)} - 1)$ for all $i = 1, 2, ..., k$. Then the random representation (15) obtains in terms of the variables $V_s^*, V_n^{*(1)}, ..., V_n^{*(k)}$; however the variables are not independent and the representation is not of the desired form (16). On the other hand, if the inequalities (14) hold for all $k = 1, 2, ...$ we know from Criterion 2 that the alternative representation (16) exists, suggesting that there must be a connection between the two representations, and indeed this is so. Consider the respective distribution functions $F_k(t) = \sum_{j \le kt} \Pi_{k-j+1}^{k+1}$ and $G_k(t) = \frac{1}{k} \sum_{j \le kt}(1 - \Pi_{k-j+1}^{k+1})$ of the random variables V_s^*, V_n^*. It follows from a theorem of Feller (1966) that as $k \to \infty$, $F_k(t) \to F(t)$ at points of continuity of the limit function F; and from this fact we see that as $k \to \infty$, $G_k(t) \to t$, the distribution function of a uniform variate on $[0, 1]$. The limit $F(t)$ provides the distribution function of the random variable V_s appearing in the random utility representation (16).

As a final remark we note that the sequence of distribution functions F_k provides a sequence of approximations to an ROC via $\rho_k(t) = 1 - F_k(1 - t)$. Such staircase approximations are rather crude in comparison to the polynomial approx-imations used above in Sections 2 and 3, and we discuss them no further.

6. MISCELLANEOUS TOPICS

(1) Symmetric ROCs. The literature is replete with decision models pre-dicting symmetric ROCs; witness e.g. the ubiquitous equal-variance normal model. For this reason it is useful to explore the properties of such models. If an ROC is invariant under reflection about the line $p_H + p_{FA} = 1$ i.e. if $(p_{FA}, p_H) \in \rho \Rightarrow (1 - p_H, 1 - p_{FA}) \in \rho$, it is said to be *symmetric*. The *dual* ρ^* of a YN ROC ρ is defined by plotting "correct rejections" (responding correctly to the presentation of a noise stimulus) against "misses" (responding incorrectly on a signal trial); thus an ROC is symmetric iff it coincides with its dual. Note that an ROC and its dual subtend the same area, whether or not the ROC is symmetric.

The following remarks are restricted to symmetric ROCs which are strictly increasing from $[0, 1]$ onto $[0, 1]$. Such ROCs have inverses, and symmetry is equiv-alently written

$$\rho(t) + \rho^{-1}(1 - t) = 1. \tag{17}$$

In terms of the distribution function of V_s, equation (17) translates as

$$F_{V_s}(t) + F_{V_s}^{-1}(1 - t) = 1. \tag{18}$$

To any $(k + 1)$IFC task there corresponds a dual task involving k independent realizations of the signal together with a single instance of noise. In the dual task an observer is asked to select the interval most likely to contain the noise stimulus. We shall write $p_c^{*(k+1)}$ for the probability of a correct response in this task. Standard theory applies, and we have

$$
\begin{aligned}
p_c^{*(k+1)} &= \Pr(\min\{V_s^{(1)}, V_s^{(2)}, \ldots, V_s^{(k)}\} > V_n) \\
&= \int_0^1 (1 - F_{V_s}(t))^k \, dt \\
&= \int_0^1 (1 - t)^k \, dF_{V_s}^{-1}(t) \\
&= \int_0^1 t^k \, d(1 - F_{V_s}^{-1}(1 - t)).
\end{aligned}
$$

If an ROC is symmetric, it follows from Equation 18 applied to the last line and Equation 16 that $p_c^{*(k+1)} = p_c^{(k+1)}$. Conversely, if $p_c^{*(k+1)} = p_c^{(k+1)}$, the sequence of moments of the measure $d(1 - F_{V_s}^{-1}(1 - t))$ matches that of the measure $dF_{V_s}(t)$ and it follows that the two distribution functions $F_{V_s}(t)$ and $1 - F_{V_s}^{-1}(1 - t)$ are one and the same. From Equations 17, 18 it follows that the corresponding ROCs satisfy $\rho = \rho^*$. We have thus proved the

Theorem 2 (Symmetry). *In the context of standard signal detection theory a YN ROC is symmetric iff performance in the infinite sequence of 2-interval, 3-interval,... forced-choice tasks matches, term by term, performance in the sequence of dual tasks.*

(2) Non-linear moment inequalities. The linear inequalities (14) can be supplemented by familiar non-linear inequalities that govern moments of a random variable. We mention two such non-linear inequalities here.

(a) Because $t \mapsto t^k$ is a convex function for each $k = 1, 2, \ldots$ Jensen's inequality applies i.e. $E(V_s^k) \geq (E(V_s))^k$ and by equation (6) we see that

$$p_c^{(k+1)} \geq (p_c^{(2)})^k. \tag{19}$$

(b) By Schwarz' inequality

$$(p_c^{(k+1)})^2 \leq p_c^{k+j+1} \cdot p_c^{k-j+1} \tag{20}$$

for all integers $k \geq j \geq 0$. Note that these and other such inequalities are, in a sense, subordinate to the system of linear inequalities (14), provided of course the latter apply. Nevertheless they remain useful, as in Example 4 of the prior section.

(3) Statistical Issues. As we have repeatedly emphasized, the system of linear inequalities (14) for $j = 1, 2, \ldots$ is key to verifying standard (random utility) theory for the forced-choice tasks. Of course it is impossible to test an infinite chain of constraints on any realistic system of data; but one can test the system (14) truncated at some finite value of j by methods of inference developed to handle ordinal hypotheses (Barlow, Bartholomew, Bremmer, & Brunk, 1972; Iverson & Harp, 1985; Robertson, Wright, & Dykstra, 1988). Still, as we have seen above in connection with Falmagne's Criterion 1, no *finite* system is strong enough in general to guarantee the existence of a random representation involving independent random variables.

Two other sorts of tests remain to be explored. These examine the assumption of standard theory that calls for the same random variables (up to a monotone increasing transformation) to be used by an observer across the YN and forced-choice tasks. New methods of fitting ROCs to YN data involving concave splines have been recently developed by Harp (1995). It seem plausible to estimate the forced-choice probabilities from a fitted ROC by numerical integration, and to compare the estimates obtained therein with estimates obtained in actual forced-choice experiments. On the other hand we have seen in Examples 1, 2 that it is possible to use a few well estimated forced-choice probabilities to estimate the corresponding YN ROC quite satisfactorily. The estimated ROC allows one to generate via integration further estimates of forced-choice probabilities that can be compared to empirical frequencies from the corresponding forced-choice tasks. We illustrate this by way of a simple example.

Example 6. In Example 1 of Section 2 we built a sequence of polynomial approximations to the ROC $\rho(t) = \sqrt{t}$. Each approximant can be written as a linear form in the choice probabilities $1, p_c^{(2)}, p_c^{(3)}, \ldots, p_c^{(k)}$ with polynomial coefficients. We now consider the realistic situation in which the choice probabilities are not known exactly but are empirical frequencies. Using these frequencies in place of the actual probabilities provides estimators for the approximants obtained earlier; these estimators are unbiased for the approximants (not the ROC $\rho(t) = \sqrt{t}$ itself). For example, suppose the data from the $2IFC$ task has been summarized as a proportion $\hat{p}_c^{(2)}$ based on N trials. The corresponding estimator for the first approximant to the ROC is given by

$$\tilde{\rho}_1 = (3t^2 - 2t) + 6\hat{p}_c^{(2)}(t - t^2)$$

and since $E(\hat{p}_c^{(2)}) = p_c^{(2)} = 2/3$, we have $E(\tilde{\rho}_1(t)) = 2t - t^2$ which is the first polynomial approximant to $\rho(t) = \sqrt{t}$ (depicted in Figure 1a). Let us use the estimator $\tilde{\rho}_1(t)$ to provide predictions of the further choice probabilities $p_c^{(3)}, p_c^{(4)}, \ldots$ via

$$\tilde{p}_c^{(k+1)} = k \int_0^1 (1-t)^{k-1} \tilde{\rho}_1(t) dt, \quad k = 2, 3, \ldots .$$

These estimates are not particularly good, being based on the single empirical frequency $\hat{p}_c^{(2)}$; as estimators for $p_c^{(3)}, p_c^{(4)}, \ldots$ they are of course systematically biased, regardless of the sample size N. Still, it is instructive to compute them. We obtain

$$\tilde{p}_c^{(k+1)} = \frac{6k\hat{p}_c^{(2)} - 2k + 2}{(k+1)(k+2)}, \quad k = 1, 2, \ldots .$$

Since $E(\hat{p}_c^{(2)}) = 2/3$, we have $E(\tilde{p}_c^{(k+1)}) = \frac{2}{2+k}$, and $Var(\tilde{p}_c^{(k+1)}) = \frac{8k^2}{N[(k+1)(k+2)]^2}$. A few numerical values are shown in Table 1. Note the systematic bias (which arises mainly from the difference in behavior of $\tilde{\rho}_1(t)$ and $\rho(t)$ near zero). There is a tradeoff between variance and bias, with the bias dominating rms error for large sample sizes. The successive estimates $\tilde{p}_c^{(k+1)}$ are of course correlated.

This example points to a generalization in which independent estimators $\hat{p}_c^{(2)}$, $\hat{p}_c^{(3)}, \ldots, \hat{p}_c^{(k+1)}$ are used to predict the $(k+2)$IFC and subsequent tasks, but we do not pursue the matter any further here.

(4) **A Remark on detectability.** The long history of signal detection in psychology has been accompanied by a plethora of numerical indices purporting to measure the "detectability" of an observer. We have little desire to add to the confusion of claim and counter-claim concerning the advantage of using one such measure over a rival. We do point out however that each successive forced-choice task adds to the evidence on which *any* measure of detectability must be based. This suggests that observers be (partially) ordered by their performance in the sequence of forced-choice tasks using the same signal and noise sources. For example, if two observers O and $\tilde{O}$ yield respective forced choice probabilities $p_c^{(k+1)}$ and $\tilde{p}_c^{(k+1)}$ with $p_c^{(k+1)} \geq \tilde{p}_c^{(k+1)}$ for $k = 1, 2, \ldots$ then it is reasonable to say that O's performance as a detector is (in the sequence of forced-choice tasks) at least as good as that of $\tilde{O}$. Another way to partially order observers $O, \tilde{O}$ is via their respective ROCs $\rho, \tilde{\rho}$: if $\rho(t) \geq \tilde{\rho}(t)$, for all $t \in [0, 1]$, O's performance as a detector is at least as good as that of $\tilde{O}$ for the YN task. This latter way of ordering observers is stronger than that of the former; for if $\rho \geq \tilde{\rho}$ one has, by Equation 1,

$$p_c^{(k+1)} - \tilde{p}_c^{(k+1)} = k \int_0^1 (1-t)^{k-1}(\rho(t) - \tilde{\rho}(t)) dt$$
$$\geq 0.$$

k	$p_c^{(k+1)}$	$E(\tilde{p}_c^{(k+1)})$	$N.Var(\tilde{p}_c^{(k+1)})$
1	$2/3=0.67$	$2/3=0.67$	0.222
2	$8/15=0.53$	$2/4=0.50$	0.222
3	$16/35=0.46$	$2/5=0.40$	0.180
4	$128/315=0.41$	$2/6=0.33$	0.142
5	$256/693=0.37$	$2/7=0.29$	0.113

TABLE 1. Means and variances of the estimators $\hat{p}_c^{(k+1)}$.

On the other hand the ROCs $\rho(t) = \sqrt{t}$ and $\tilde{\rho}(t) = 2t - t^2$ intersect at $t = \frac{3-\sqrt{5}}{2}$ (see Figure 1a) but $p_c^{(k+1)} = \frac{k!\Gamma(1/2)}{2\Gamma(k+3/2)}$, and $\tilde{p}_c^{(k+1)} = \frac{2}{2+k}$ satisfy $p_c^{(k+1)} \geq \tilde{p}_c^{(k+1)}$ for all $k = 1, 2, \ldots$ with strict inequality for $k \geq 2$.

Neither of the above orderings is connected, i.e., there exist pairs of observers who cannot be compared under either one. In view of this fact, we suggest adopting a *lexicographic* ordering of observers by their performance in the sequence of forced-choice detection tasks, beginning of course with the $2IFC$ task. Thus for example we would say that a detector characterized by the ROC $\sqrt{t}$ dominates one with ROC $2t - t^2$, despite the fact that they subtend the same area. This is consistent with the ordering of the ROCs in a neighborhood of 0, i.e., if one detector has a higher hit rate than another for small false-alarm rates, we consider it superior regardless of their respective behaviors for large false-alarm rates. This viewpoint seems to us to be relatively uncontroversial, typical airport security protocol notwithstanding.

7. CONCLUDING REMARKS

The theory of signal detection offers numerous predictions relating the data of one empirical task to those of another. However, such predictions are typically obtained only within the scope of specific distributional assumptions on the decision random variables; see Noreen (1981) for an extensive collection of results based on the constant-variance normal model. In contrast, the theoretical results obtained above rely on no strong distributional assumptions, i.e. they are "non-parametric". Should any one of the theoretical predictions embodied in Equations 1, 8, 9, 10, 14 fail in practice, it is because the commonly accepted "standard" theory given in Green and Swets (1966) has broken down. For this reason, it is important to review existing empirical evidence that pertains to our theoretical results; such evidence is, unfortunately, rather fragmentary and scattered throughout the literature.

Like the fundamental area theorem of Green and Moses (1966), the generalized area theorem involves idealized data – ROCs and forced-choice probabilities are never known exactly, but rather are estimated on the basis of noisy data. Non-trivial and interesting problems of statistical estimation thus confront any serious attempt to asses the empirical validity of the generalized area theorem; the remarks of Section 6 serve to point out some of the statistical issues involved.

Green and Swets (1966) summarize early attempts to verify the predictions of Equation 1, for small values of k. Those early studies were conducted in ignorance of the system of inequalities (14) which must be obeyed if Equations 1 or 2 obtain. If raw relative frequencies obtained in forced-choice experiments do not satisfy the inequalities (14) they should be refined so that they do, eg. using algorithms given in

Barlow et al. (1972) or Robertson et al. (1988). To our knowledge, no systematic empirical study of the inequalities (14) has appeared in the literature. As was emphasized in Section 5, those inequalities are critical for the standard theory of forced-choice data.

Surprisingly perhaps, it is the theory of Section 4 on ranking data that has received most attention in the literature. The British theorists Brown (1965), Dalrymple-Alford (1970), and Wilcox (1982) have developed an "answer-until-correct" procedure which is a variant of the ranking task. In the context of the $(k + 1)$-interval forced-choice paradigm, the "answer-until-correct" paradigm can be described as follows: an observer initially selects one of the $k + 1$ intervals as most likely to contain the single instance of the signal. If this selection is correct, the trial ends; if the initial selection is a realization of noise, the selected interval is deleted and the remaining k intervals are subjected to a similar elimination process, which continues until the signal interval is located. Provided one ignores the differential load on short-term memory that accompanies the ranking task, and its "answer-until-correct" variation, the two tasks should yield the same data; indeed, Brown (1965) and Dalrymple-Alford (1970) obtain predictions for their method that amount to those contained in our Equation 10. Thus, the empirical support offered by those authors for their theory of the "answer-until-correct" procedure warrants further empirical exploration of the ranking task, and the theory contained above in Section 4.

PART 5

CHOICE AND CATEGORIZATION

Choice, Decision, and Measurement
A. A. J. Marley (Ed.),
©Lawrence Erlbaum Associates, NJ, 1997.

SOME REFLECTIONS ON THE ROLE OF THE CHOICE MODEL IN THEORIES OF CATEGORIZATION, IDENTIFICATION, AND LEARNING

W. K. ESTES

Harvard University

ABSTRACT. Performance in a wide variety of cognitive tasks – classification, identification, psychophysical judgment, preference – takes the form of choice from a set of alternatives. Prior to the appearance of Luce's choice model in 1959, it was standard for choice behavior to be interpreted by means of domain-specific, data-based models. Luce's approach, in contrast, was to start with a very general, rationally based axiom and derive theorems and functions that constrain the forms of performance measures and relationships among them in the various task domains. Further, an extension of the 1959 formulation termed the similarity choice model has become the most influential complement to signal detection theory as a basis for distinguishing the effects of stimulus discriminability and response bias in psychophysical and preferential choice data. Following a review of the role of the similarity choice model in cognitive research, I address the central theoretical question of whether choice behavior is basically probabilistic or deterministic – concretely, do predictions of choice probability derived from the model apply to the choices made by individuals on particular experimental trials or only to data obtained by averaging over groups of individuals or blocks of trials? The theoretical work of several investigators taken together with some relevant empirical results of my own research lead to a provisional resolution of the issue.

1. INTRODUCTION

"For the most part our knowledge and understanding of nature come from observation and experiment. But perhaps not entirely. The last century has seen a number of notable instances in which assumptions dictated, not by empirical considerations, but by the mathematician's sense of form, simplicity, and elegance have turned out to provide strikingly accurate descriptions and predictions of events in the physical world. The present volume reports the first extended effort to achieve comparable triumphs of rational (in the author's terminology, "axiomatic") analysis in psychology." (Estes, 1960, *p. 113*)

Key words and phrases. Categorization, choice, decision algorithms, probabilistic/deterministic distinction.

Acknowledgments. Preparation of this chapter was supported by grant SBR 93-17256 from the National Science Foundation.

Address for correspondence. W. K. Estes, Department of Psychology, William James Hall Harvard University, 33 Kirkland St. Cambridge, MA 02138. Email: wke@wjh.harvard.edu

The passage above opened and set the theme for my review of *Individual Choice Behavior* (Luce, 1959a) in *Contemporary Psychology* three and a half decades ago. Though the book itself was of modest dimensions, the task the author had undertaken staggered the imagination of his contemporaries, and it is hard to overestimate the extent to which the theory he presented has influenced the development of mathematical psychology, broadly defined, from then to the present.

2. THE WAKE OF THE "RED MENACE"

My first brush with Luce's approach had occurred a couple of years earlier when he distributed a forerunner of his book, in the form of a mimeographed pamphlet with a crimson cover, to a summer conference of mathematical psychologists at Stanford. The immediate effect was to divert the conferees from the anticipated agenda to intense discussions of the "red menace," which unsettled the assembled investigators of learning, decision, and cognitive theory by challenging the rules of the game, that is, the basic working assumptions on which they habitually relied. Foremost among these was the presumption that progress in constructing models in the psychological domain must proceed from the ground up – starting with the accumulation of data appropriate for quantification, then proceeding to the formulation of limited models capable of representing the data, and finally to more general theories arising from combinations or generalizations of the limited models. Luce's approach was, in contrast, to start, in the manner of theoretical physics, by employing intuition and rational analysis to arrive at a set of general assumptions that, if they hold for the domain, will enable the formulation of a coherent body of theory for interpreting particular phenomena. As a start on this route, Luce had noted a characteristic common to all situations in which people discriminate, identify, or categorize objects, exhibit preferences, or modify their decision making on the basis of experience – namely that an individual must, in order to accomplish whatever task is required, make a choice from a set of alternatives. Proceeding, evidently, on the basis of general observations coupled with intuition, he arrived at what he termed an axiom, expressing a simple but powerful constraint on how choices are made regardless of the particular setting. This axiom together with the standard axioms of probability theory constituted the choice model of Luce (1959a).

The gist of the choice model is that, regardless of the characteristics of a particular task, an individual confronted by a choice among a set of K alternatives is assumed to have some tendency to choose each alternative, this tendency being measurable on a ratio scale and having the critically important property that the ratio of strengths of any two members of a set of alternatives is constant over all subsets containing those two members.[1] If, for example, a student were offered a choice between courses in French and History and the ratio of strengths was 2:1, the ratio of strengths of French versus History would still be 2:1 if the selection offered were Arabic, French, and History, or if it were Arabic, French, History, and Mathematics. A second important property of the choice axiom is that choice probabilities are determined by ratios of strengths. Specifically, an individual's

---

[1] A qualification is that the axiom, as stated here, holds only if pairwise preferences for all members of the set of alternatives are imperfect.

probability, p_i, of choosing alternative i from a set of K alternatives is given by the expression

$$p_i = \frac{1}{\left(1 + \frac{v_2}{v_1} + \frac{v_3}{v_1} + \cdots + \frac{v_K}{v_1}\right)} \tag{1}$$
$$= \frac{v_i}{(v_1 + v_2 + \cdots + v_K)},$$

where v_i denotes the strength associated with alternative i.[2] These two properties, taken together, imply that choice behavior should conform to a principal of "independence of irrelevant alternatives," well-known in treatments of social choice before the advent of the individual choice model (Arrow, 1951). Another general implication is transitivity of choice: If alternatives x, y, and z are members of a set that satisfies the conditions of the choice axiom, and if x is always chosen over y and y is always chosen over z, then x is always chosen over z.[3]

With differing definitions for the v_i, Equation 1 has been the standard expression for choice probability in behavioral and cognitive models since the early 1950's, though its generality was not recognized prior to the work of Luce (1959a). In stimulus sampling theory, v_i is the number of elements or aspects of a stimulating situation that are associated with response i (Estes, 1950). In the stochastic learning models of Bush and Mosteller (1951, 1955), v_i is simply the probability of choosing alternative i. In current models of categorization deriving from Medin and Schaffer (1978), and in related models of identification and recognition (Nosofsky, 1986, 1988), v_i is the global similarity of a perceived stimulus pattern to all pattern representations stored in memory as members of category i. In a number of connectionist network models for processes ranging from simple learning to speech production, v_{ij} is the output of the network to the output node corresponding to choice response j when stimulus i is the input to the network (Gluck & Bower, 1988; Kruschke, 1992; McClelland & Elman, 1986).

Several reasons for the wide-ranging application of the choice axiom are easy to discern: (1) Regardless of the particular empirical domain of a model that incorporates the choice axiom, behavior is predicted to conform to the general principles that flow from the axiom – transitivity and independence of irrelevant alternatives, among others. And this feature of the model is well appreciated. Statements like the following have become almost routine, "For now, we wish only to capture basic properties any actual response selection mechanism must have: It must be sensitive to the input pattern, and it must approximate other basic aspects of response selection behavior captured by the Luce ... choice model" (McClelland & Rumelhart, 1986, *p. 195*). This kind of generality has rarely been achieved in behavioral science. (2) For models that incorporate the choice axiom, empirical tests are greatly

---

[2]More than one road leads to Equation 1. For example, it is implied by a random utility model for choice probabilities and reaction times under the condition that choices and choice times are independent (Marley & Colonius, 1992), and, within the framework of comparative judgment theory (Thurstone, 1927), it is implied by an assumption related to but weaker than the choice axiom (Yellott, 1977).

[3]For a more general, probabilistic, characterization of transitivity, termed "strong stochastic transitivity," see Luce and Suppes (1965), *p. 340*.

facilitated because differences in goodness of fit of predictions to data can be taken to reflect differences in the aspects of the models that are usually of prime interest (assumptions about representational structures, learning processes, and the like) rather than differences in output mechanisms. (3) The choice axiom as originally formulated for a single dimension of strength of preference is readily extendable to more complex cases involving multiple dimensions.

3. THE SIMILARITY CHOICE MODEL

Perhaps the best-known extension of the choice model, and the one that has adduced the most diverse empirical support, was put forward by Luce (1963) as a means of interpreting the burgeoning body of research in psychophysics and perception associated with applications of signal detection theory (Tanner & Swets, 1954). The prime contribution of signal detection theory (SDT) to psychology had been to provide a simple and convenient means of addressing the longstanding problem of distinguishing the effects of stimulus discriminability and response bias on performance in psychophysical or cognitive tasks. In spite of an early burst of successes in applying SDT for this purpose, there was room for reservations about some strong, and in practice rarely verifiable, assumptions of the model concerning such matters as the form of distributions of sensory states of an observer produced by repeated presentation of a stimulus. Luce's approach to the problem was to measure discriminability (or stimulus similarity) and response bias in terms of values on two scales of the kind defined by the choice axiom. An individual's tendency, v_{ij}, to respond to a stimulus i by choosing response j from a set of alternatives was assumed to equal the product of η_{ij}, the similarity of stimulus i to the stimulus identified by response j, and b_j, the individual's a priori bias for choosing response j regardless of the stimulus. The quantity v_{ij} could then be substituted for v_i in Equation 1 to generate predicted response probability.

This extension of the choice axiom, termed the similarity choice model[4] (or, alternatively, the biased choice model) met a pressing need for an alternative to SDT that would be more conveniently applicable to the situations involving large sets of stimulus and response alternatives that were commonly encountered in research on visual and auditory information processing.

Beyond the model's notable ease of application, several factors have been implicated in its extremely widespread use by investigators of perception and cognition during the years since its initial publication. One is the impressive goodness of fit of the model to many bodies of data arising in studies of letter and word recognition (Marley, 1991; Townsend, 1971a; Townsend & Ashby, 1982). This factor, at first surprising but ultimately taken for granted, was a necessary precondition of the usefulness of the model for assessing the roles of stimulus discriminability and response bias (Estes & Brunn, 1987). A second factor, flowing from the first, has been the value of the model in providing a base line against which one could assess

---

[4]The similarity choice model includes also a set of axioms ensuring, in a manner suggested by Shepard (1957), that the parameter η has the properties of a measure of similarity in a psychological space.

progress in constructing new models of greater scope, as in numerous efforts to construct models of letter identification and recognition that would take account of the featural structures of letter representations (Estes, 1982; Smith, 1992; Townsend, 1971a, 1971b; Townsend & Ashby, 1982).

4. HOW CAN A MODEL OF INDIVIDUAL CHOICE BEHAVIOR BE TESTED?

Even as the record of useful applications and extensions of the choice model has continued to accumulate, it has not been possible to ignore a persistently nagging question – does the model actually describe and predict *individual* choice behavior? The importance of this question was recognized by Luce (1959a), but no way of answering it was at hand; and no clear answer has emerged during ensuing decades. Of necessity, testing a model whose theoretical dependent variable is choice probability requires the estimation of choice probabilities from empirical data, and the estimation requires some form of aggregation. In practice, the only alternatives are to estimate choice probabilities from response proportions based either on repeated observations on the same individual or on observations from each of a group of individuals; and each tactic confronts difficulties of interpretation. Estimating a choice probability for an individual decision maker in a given situation depends on assumptions of stationarity and independence – that the true probability is constant and responses on successive trials are independent over the series of trials that provides the data – assumptions that can rarely be justified. If the situation arises in a learning experiment, choice probabilities must necessarily be expected to change progressively over trials. If the situation arises in a psychophysical experiment, choice responses are likely to exhibit sequential effects, that is, nonindependence of responses on successive trials and thus not to yield valid probability estimates when aggregated (Laming, 1973; Senders & Sowards, 1952). In theory, a model for sequential effects can be coupled with the choice model under investigation(Atkinson, Carterette, & Kinchla, 1962) but this procedure entails a regression in that development and testing of the sequential effect model depends on use of the same data that raise the problem of estimation for the choice model.

Owing to the conceptual difficulties, not to speak of time and expense, involved in estimating choice probabilities from individual subject data, the much more common practice has been to base estimates on data aggregated for groups of subjects tested under the same conditions. However, this path is also rocky. The hazards of using group data as a basis for inferences about theoretical variables assumed to characterize individuals have long been recognized (Estes, 1956), but some recent work suggests that theories employing the similarity choice model may be especially vulnerable (Ashby, Maddox, & Lee, 1994; Maddox, 1995). In the study of Maddox (1995), for example, categorization data were generated by computer-simulated subjects who responded on the basis of a decision rule of the kind familiar in signal detection theory, yet the group data were better fit by a model of the similarity choice family than by the model that produced the data. Clearly, much more work of this kind will be needed to clarify the conditions under which group data can yield useful assessments of models for individual behavior.

5. Is Choice Behavior Probabilistic or Deterministic?

In his original formulation of the choice model, Luce introduced as its basic conceptual machinery a universal set $\mathcal{U}$ of choice alternatives potentially available to an individual and probabilities $P_T(x)$ that an alternative x, belonging to a subset T of $\mathcal{U}$, will be chosen from T. "These probabilities are the basic ingredients of the following theory" (Luce, 1959a, p. 4). Thus, choice behavior is assumed to be *probabilistic* in the sense that, given full knowledge of the state of an individual's cognitive system at any time, we can only assign probabilities to his or her alternative choice responses. In contrast, we would speak of *deterministic* behavior if, given the same knowledge, we could predict with certainty the response that would be made.

Throughout the history of research on learning and classification related to the choice model, the probabilistic conception seems to have been generally assumed, usually without discussion, because it has not been obvious how the distinction between probabilistic and deterministic choice behavior could be tested empirically. With the advance in sophistication of models in this domain, however, it has become feasible to obtain reasonably compelling, though indirect, evidence bearing on this distinction, and concern with the issue has increased sharply. Thus, Marley (1992, p. 304) remarks on much current debate as to whether the decision rule connecting memory to response is deterministic; and Ashby and Maddox (1993, p. 373) characterize this issue as "the major point of contention between the current models [of categorization]."

The few studies that have yielded empirical evidence on the probabilistic/deterministic distinction are not entirely in agreement. Ashby and his associates have obtained results that suggest deterministic responding (Ashby, 1992; Ashby & Lee, 1991; Maddox & Ashby, 1993). However, those studies were limited to categorization of very simple stimuli that varied on only two sensory dimensions, the categories being describable by simple rules.

To obtain evidence from a task employing the more complex, multidimensional stimuli characteristic of most current research on categorization, I used data from a study in which subjects learned to classify symptom charts of hypothetical patients into disease categories.[5] The experimental conditions seem intuitively to be favorable for deterministic responding, if that mode is available to the subjects, because there were only four distinct stimulus patterns, constructed from independent, binary-valued attributes. To prepare for a test bearing on response mode, I modified an instance-based categorization model (the "exemplar-similarity model" described in Estes (1994, pp. 239–240) to include two alternative response-generation processes – the standard process based on the choice model ("probabilistic responding") and a process in which on each trial the response with the higher value of the quantity p_i in Equation 1 is always chosen (deterministic responding). These processes were combined by means of a "mixture parameter" ρ, whose value prescribed the proportion of trials in a series on which the response was chosen probabilistically. In two replications of the experiment, with different stimulus sets and category structures, the mean estimates of ρ were .74 and .77,

---

[5]W. Todd Maddox collaborated in this analysis, more fully described by Estes (1995).

signifying preponderantly probabilistic responding. Six of twenty-four subjects in the first replication and eleven in the second yielded ρ estimates of 1.0, indicating uniform probabilistic responding, and none in either replication yielded an estimate of 0, which would have signified uniform deterministic responding. In the total of 48 analyses for individual subjects, 38 yielded ρ estimates signifying probabilistic responding on a majority of trials. A quite different type of analysis of an experiment in which a series of no-feedback test trials was given following categorization training (also described in Estes, 1995) yielded very similar conclusions.

Although more work on this problem is needed, my provisional conclusion is that when the structure of a task permits near optimal responding on the basis of a simple rule, responding is likely to be deterministic but otherwise responding is predominantly probabilistic. Thus, it seems that for many types of research designs, application of decision algorithms based on the choice model may be quite well justified.

6. Postscript

In closing, I would like to comment on my rewarding association and interactions with R. Duncan Luce, the individual honored in this volume, over nearly four decades. We have had many occasions for collaboration, among them being our parts in the founding of the Society for Mathematical Psychology and the *Journal of Mathematical Psychology*, the organizing and leading of the American delegation to a U.S.-Soviet conference on decision making and mathematical psychology held in Tblisi in 1979, our co-terms as president and vice president of the Federation of Behavioral, Psychological, and Cognitive Sciences, and our joint teaching of a course on mathematical models in psychology at Harvard.

It is interesting to note that, although Duncan and I came to psychology, and mathematical psychology, from very different backgrounds, and started with quite different outlooks, our views have converged somewhat over the years. Duncan entered our joint field as a mathematician interested in developing rational, axiomatic foundations for theory in behavioral and social science. I started as an experimental psychologist with some proclivity for cautiously exploring the potential uses of mathematics in the analysis of behavioral data and construction of models. In recent years, Duncan has become increasingly involved in empirical investigations, and has expressed some disillusionment, or at least ambivalence, about prospects for major contributions of mathematical modeling to psychology in our time (Luce, 1995a). For my part, though still strongly identified with experimental psychology, I feel increasingly that its contributions to science are measurable largely in terms of its role in the evolution of the formal models that become indispensable to the fruitful interpretation of research and to significant linkages between disciplines.

Thus, I have been increasingly convinced that theoretical progress in much of psychology, especially the cognitive domain, which I know best, depends on ever better exploitation of the tools of mathematics and computation. And the forebodings, sometimes amounting to pessimism, that I feel concerning prospects for the future of behavioral and cognitive science are due, not to the difficulty of applying mathematics in these fields, but to the failure of present-day society to supply enough young people with adequate backgrounds and interest in mathematics and other formal sciences to give us a chance of coming up with the Duncan Luces we will need to lead our efforts into the next century.

Choice, Decision, and Measurement
A. A. J. Marley (Ed.),
©Lawrence Erlbaum Associates, NJ, 1997.

A NETWORK MODEL FOR MULTIPLE CHOICE: ACCURACY AND RESPONSE TIMES

RICHARD M. SHIFFRIN

Indiana University

ABSTRACT. Suppose a choice must be made among N alternatives. A network model is proposed in which the decision process is represented as a serial movement along the paths of the network, from node to node, along links connecting the nodes. The process along any link between two nodes may be thought of as a two choice process embedded within the larger network. Some of the nodes are choice nodes, corresponding to the N choices; choice j is selected at the time when the decision process reaches the choice node corresponding to choice j. Suppose that the probabilities of setting out from a node along the possible links are specified, and suppose that the subsequent probabilities of reaching either end of the link (and the times to do so) are derivable or assumed. This chapter gives simple analytic methods for deriving the choice probabilities and all the moments of the conditional and unconditional response time distributions.

1. INTRODUCTION

This article presents a network model for decision making. Suppose one is interested in both the probability that a subject will make one of n responses (i.e., make a choice or a decision), and the first m moments of the response time distribution associated with that response. The case of two responses has been explored fairly thoroughly, and in particular the use of random walk or diffusion theory has proved useful in the two choice setting. The present work can be viewed in part as providing a generalization of random walk and diffusion models to multiple responses. However, the model applies much more generally.

Consider first the two choice setting, with a particularly simple discrete random walk model, as illustrated in Figure 1A. The idea is that there are discrete positions on a unique path. The subject starts a trial at decision position N_0 (termed the start node), and takes steps at discrete times, with a probability $p(0,2)$ of moving one position to the right, and probability $p(0,1) = 1 - p(0,2)$ of moving one position to the left (these steps usually are interpreted as representing accumulation of evidence in favor of one or the other alternative, and $p(0,1)$ is often termed the drift rate of the walk). If the random walk reaches the position labeled N_1 (termed the choice-1

Key words and phrases. Choice, multiple-choice, network model, response times.

Acknowledgments. This research was supported by NIMH Grant 12717, a Cattell Fellowship, and a grant from EPOS, a graduate research institute sponsored by the University of Amsterdam, the Free University of of Amsterdam, and the University of Leiden.

Address for correspondence. Richard M. Shiffrin, Psychology Dept., Indiana University, Bloomington, IN 47405. Email: shiffrin@indiana.edu

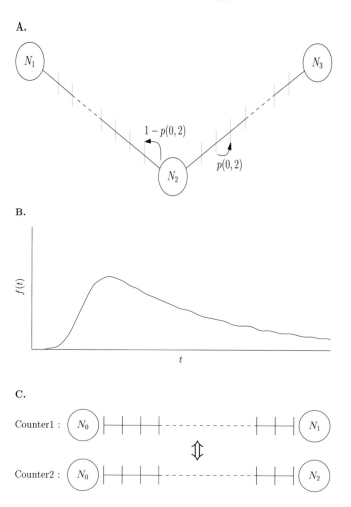

FIGURE 1. Panel A: A two-barrier random walk with start position N_0, and a drift rate $p(0,1) = 1 - p(0,2) =$ probability of a single step in the direction of barrier N_1. Panel B: Typical response time distribution produced by a random walk process. Panel C: Alternate characterization of the random walk in panel A, with two counters that are linked so that a count in one causes subtraction of a count in the other.

node), which is at a distance d_{01} from N_0, then choice 1 is made; if the random walk reaches position N_2 (termed the choice-2 node), which is at a distance d_{02} from N_0, then choice 2 is given. It is typical to generalize this process to one in which the number of steps taken in either direction may be greater than one. A summary of derivations for this case is given in Luce (1986b, Chapter 8); see also Townsend and Ashby (1983). A closely related generalization of the random walk process is a diffusion process in which there is a distribution of the distance and direction taken at a given moment of the process, and the distance is a continuous variable. A summary of results for this case is given in Luce (1986b, Chapter 9). For either version, the probabilities of making the choices, and the conditional response times for the two choices, are derivable.

In one guise or another variants of this two choice decision model have appeared many times in the literature (e.g., Link, 1992; Ratcliff, 1978). Figure 1B illustrates the typical shape of a conditional response time distribution that results from a random walk process, with a skewing toward long response times. In some models, such predicted response time distributions are mapped directly onto the observed data, while in other models, observed response times are assumed to consist of a time produced by the random walk added to a base time usually assumed to have a Gaussian distribution. The successes of such models are due in part to the fact that the observed response time distributions are indeed skewed toward long response times (e.g., Hohle, 1965; Ratcliff, 1978; Ratcliff & Murdock, 1976).

Random walk and diffusion models are of course not the only models explored for two choice response time settings. A brief review of others is given in Luce (1986b, Chapters 8 and 9).

A question that has arisen on many occasions concerns the proper way to extend such models to more than two responses. One approach is rooted in the following characterization of the random walk: Let there be two counters, each accumulating counts; one counter causes emission of Response 1, when d_{01} counts have been accumulated, and the other counter causes emission of response 2, when d_{02} counts have been accumulated. The probability of a positive count in Counter 1 is $p(0,1)$, and the probability of a positive count in Counter 2 is $p(0,2) = 1 - p(0,1)$, and the two counters are linked: When a positive count occurs in either, a count is subtracted from the other (Figure 1C). This model is of course a restatement of the model in Figure 1A (see LaBerge, 1994). To generalize, one can increase the number of counters to n, and choose a suitable rule by which the counters are linked. For example, a positive step in any counter could cause all other counters to lose a count (see Palmeri, in press). One obvious problem with this system is the distinct possibility that no response would ever be made, since negative counts generally accumulate more rapidly than positive counts (Nosofsky, this volume, discusses a variant system in which counters accumulating large negative values drop out).

Alternatively, if one were willing to generalize to non-integral or continuous counters, a positive count of size 1 in a given counter could be associated with a negative count of size $1/(n-1)$ in all other counters (e.g., Palmeri, in press). As n becomes larger, however, this systems loses the dependence between the different responses that is characteristic of a two dimensional random walk – since almost nothing is lost from most counters when a given counter accumulates a step, the process approaches an accumulator model of the type explored by LaBerge (1962) and Audley and Pike (1965). In such models each response is associated with a criterion count in an accumulator assigned to that response; counts added to one accumulator don't cause a change in the counts of any other, and the first accumulator to reach its criterion triggers a response (see Karpiuk, Lacouture & Marley, this volume). Many other variants of this type could be imagined, including models with stopping rules based on maximum likelihood or number of successive counts in a given response counter (see Chapters 8 and 9 Luce, 1986b).[1] Recently, models have been studied in which one counter is chosen when its counts exceed the maximum of all the other counters by a criterion amount (see Ratcliff & McKoon, in press).

The network model[2] introduced in this chapter is motivated mathematically by the following observation: models for two choices have been explored fairly systematically, and for quite a few such models, analytical solutions for accuracy and response time have been derived. On the other hand, analytical solutions for paradigms with more than two choices are rare, except for one or two special cases with particular distributional assumptions (see Audley & Pike, 1965; Marley & Colonius, 1992, for examples). The network model therefore posits a system for multiple choices that is comprised of an interconnected series of two-choice subsystems (as described shortly, each such two-choice subsystem is identified with a pair of nodes connected directly by a link containing intermediate positions). It turns out that whenever analytic derivations are available for the two choice subsystems, analytical derivations are easily available for the entire network. Further, it turns out that network derivations are available without specifying a particular model for each two-choice sub-system, but only specifying the accuracy and moments of the response times for each two-choice sub-system.

It is useful to introduce the network model in a severely restricted form, as illustrated in Figure 2, which generalizes Figure 1A by adding additional spokes emanating from the start node, each spoke terminating in a different choice. It is easiest to describe such a system by introducing 'dummy nodes' N_{d0i}. N_{d0i} is at a distance of one unit from the start node, N_0, along the spoke leading to choice node N_i. Such a system would be defined by the probabilities $p_0(i)$ of taking a unit step along spoke i to N_{d0i}, by the drift rates along each spoke, $p(0, i)$, and the lengths of the spokes, d_{0i}.

One interpretation of such a decision system would equate the probability of leaving the start node along spoke i with the probability of considering choice i; then the subsequent normal random walk along a spoke reflects the accumulation of evidence about that choice; whenever a return to the start node occurs, the whole decision process begins anew. The introduction of dummy nodes allows an easy separation of the choice of responses to consider (i.e., the spoke chosen) and the subsequent random walk that begins at the dummy node. This system (i.e., the spoke network depicted in Figure 2) will be analyzed in detail later in this chapter. It is a special case of the more general network model that is presented next.

---

[1]A different approach to generalization would add additional dimensions to the random walk, but the number of possible models, and the ways of defining choice boundaries, leads to complexities that cannot be addressed in this chapter.

[2]Note that 'network' in the present context does not refer to 'neural network' and does not imply any parallel architecture. The present network consists of nodes and links that are traversed serially until a decision node is reached.

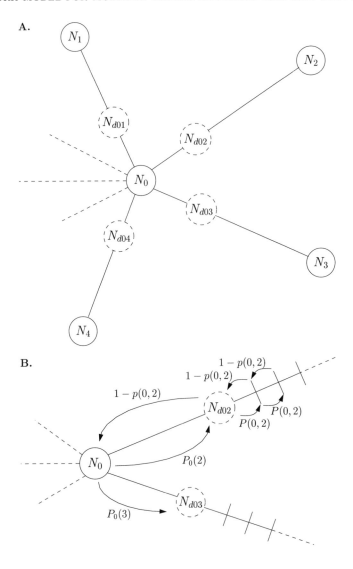

FIGURE 2. Panel A: Generalization of the two-choice process in Figure 1A to n choices. The dashed circles represent 'dummy' nodes at a distance of one step from the start node. Panel B: A detailed picture of part of the network in Panel A. A single step is taken from the start node along a link toward choice j with probability $P_0(j)$. Once at the dummy node, a random walk commences with drift rate $P(0, j)$.

2. A NETWORK MODEL FOR CHOICES AND RESPONSE TIMES

Figure 3A depicts a decision network with *hidden* nodes (single circles) and *choice* nodes (doubled circles) connected by links. Not all pairs of nodes are directly

A.

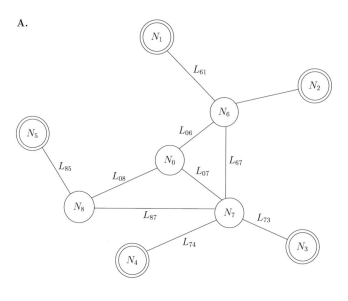

B.

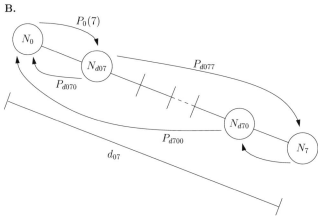

FIGURE 3. Panel A: An example of a generalized network with
choice nodes (doubled circles) and hidden nodes (single circles).
Panel B: A detailed illustration of the link L_{07}, which has length
d_{07}. From dummy node N_{d07}, for example, the probability of reaching N_0 before N_7 is P_{d070}, and $P_{d077} = 1 - P_{d070}$.

connected. Without significant loss of generality, assume a decision process that
takes place as a discrete process in both time and space. In particular, assume
that a link L_{ij} connecting node N_i to node N_j consists of a series of d_{ij} steps (i.e.,
having $d_{ij} - 1$ intermediate positions on the link), and assume a given decision
process starts at a start node N_0, and moves sequentially through the network in
evenly timed steps, until a choice node is reached. One of the hidden nodes in
each network is designated as a *starting* node. It is sometimes convenient to label

nodes in the following way: the start node is labeled N_0; the n choice (or response) nodes are labeled N_i for $i = 1, \ldots, n$; the $k - 1$ remaining hidden nodes are labeled N_i for $i = n + 1, \ldots, n + k - 1$. In almost all applications that are useful, there will be at least one connected path, but not necessarily a direct link, from the start node to each choice node.

As illustrated in the portion of the network shown in Figure 3B, it is useful to designate some of the intermediate positions along links as *dummy* nodes: whenever there is at least one intermediate position on a link (i.e., $d_{ij} > 1$), there will be a dummy node N_{dij} one unit of distance from node N_i, and a dummy node N_{dji} one unit of distance from node N_j, except when the only adjacent node is a choice node. (When there is just one intermediate position, N_{ij} and N_{ji} will be the same node, of course.) These dummy nodes play the same role as discussed for the spoke network in Figure 2. They allow convenient separation of the probabilities of leaving a start or hidden node from the subsequent (two choice) random process that operates within a link. To eliminate the possibility of confusion in the following, it should be noted that a *link* is defined so that it only connects a hidden or choice node to another hidden or choice node; dummy nodes lie within links.

Let the times at which choice, hidden, or dummy nodes are reached be termed epochs (as distinct from the times at which the decision process reaches other intermediate positions along the links). When a choice node is reached, the corresponding response is chosen or initiated. The movement along a link will typically go forward and backward stochastically, and in general a step need not be restricted to single units of distance (however no step can go any further than the ends of the current link). For all nodes, including dummy nodes, let p_{ij} denote to the probability of moving from node N_i to node N_j over two successive epochs (although awkward, p_{dijj} will denote the probability of moving from dummy node N_{dij} to node N_j, and p_{diji} the probability of moving from dummy node N_{dij} to node N_i).

Whenever a hidden node is reached, there must be probabilities assigned to the chances of setting out along any of the links emanating from that node: assume that the decision process has reached hidden node N_j at some epoch. It is convenient to assume that the first step away from any hidden node is one unit of distance in length (usually to a dummy node). Then let $p_i(j)$ be the probability of setting out along link L_{ij}, where $S_{jpi}(j) = 1$. (In this version of the model, the decision process cannot 'idle' at a given start or hidden node, but the techniques apply equally well if the probability of remaining at a given start or hidden node is allowed to be greater than zero.) Note that the $p_i(j)$ probabilities are just a subset of the p_{ij} probabilities that are singled out for special designation whenever N_i is a hidden node (because the next state is one unit of distance and is reached in one unit of time). It is important to note the following convention adopted for simplicity in this chapter: once a dummy node is reached, the next epoch is defined by the next choice or hidden node that is reached, not another dummy node (including itself). Thus when the process is at a dummy node, i, the $p_i(j)$ probabilities are defined only for choice or hidden nodes, j. (The equations given below will work fine, and give the same answers, if instead probabilities and times of movements from one dummy node to itself or other dummy nodes are allowed, but this increases the number of equations, and for most purposes is not needed.)

Epoch $K + 1$

	N_0	N_{d01}		N_{djk}		N_j	N_k
N_0	0	$F(0, d01, t)$	$\cdots$	0	$\cdots$	0	0
N_{d01}	$F(d01, 0, t)$	0	$\cdots$	0	$\cdots$	0	0
$\vdots$	$\vdots$	$\vdots$	$\vdots$	$\vdots$	$\vdots$	$\vdots$	$\vdots$
N_{djk}	0	0	$\cdots$	0	$\cdots$	$F(djk, j, t)$	$F(djk, k, t)$
$\vdots$	$\vdots$	$\vdots$	$\vdots$	$\vdots$	$\vdots$	$\vdots$	$\vdots$
N_j	0	0	$\cdots$	$F(j, djk, t)$	$\cdots$	0	0
N_k	0	0	$\cdots$	0	$\cdots$	0	0

(Left vertical label: Epoch K)

TABLE 1. Part of the matrix formulation of the semi-Markov process representing a choice network. Entries give the probability that the process starting in state i at epoch k will move to state j at epoch $k + 1$ in a time less than or equal to t.

Once the decision process starts along a link (i.e., reaches a dummy node), the subsequent behavior until one of the nodes at the end of the link is reached can be modeled by any convenient stochastic process. For example the movement along a link L_{ij} might consist of a simple random walk with probability $p(i, j)$ of a step toward node N_j, and probability $1 - p(i, j)$ of a step toward node N_i.

Most important, the networks under consideration in this chapter are recurrent in terms of node position at different epochs: the probabilities and time course of the decision process depend only on the node at which the process resides at a given epoch, and not the past history of the process.[3]

A semi-markov representation of the network. Knowledge concerning the intermediate positions along links is unnecessary for the derivations and predictions concerning choice probabilities and response times, as long as one can derive or stipulate both the probabilities of reaching either end of a link given a start at a dummy node, and the moments of the time needed to reach a given end of a link. Thus the essential elements of the network can be represented as a semi-Markov process as indicated in Table 1. The states along the vertical side of the matrix in Table 1 represent the potential nodes the process is in at epoch k, and the states along the horizontal side of the matrix represent the potential nodes reached at epoch $k + 1$. The entries give the conditional probabilities that the decision process moves from node N_i at epoch k to node N_j at epoch $k + 1$, in an amount of time less than or equal to t. Thus these entries are non-proper cumulative distribution functions, $F(i, j, t)$. The value $F(i, j, \infty)$, termed p_{ij} for convenience, is the conditional probability that the decision process arrives at node N_j at epoch $k + 1$ given that it had been at node N_i at epoch k. The sum of the p_{ij} across a row (across the values of j) must equal 1.0 since we only consider systems where the decision process must eventually reach another node. It should be noted that the model described in this way need make no assumption about the nature of the stochastic process along a given link, as long as the process eventually reaches one end or the

---

[3]Thus, for example, the present system would not be suited for analysis of a network in which a link is explored, not terminated, and ruled out from further consideration.

other; in particular, the process on a link could be a random walk or a diffusion process.

As stated earlier, in almost all applications it makes derivations and descriptions easiest to disallow the possibility of a direct move from a dummy node to itself or another dummy node on two successive epochs (which is why they are termed dummy nodes; if other assumptions would be desirable, then one would just add the node in question to the set of hidden nodes). The resultant matrix representation then has a characteristic form: for each dummy state on the left hand axis of the matrix, there will be two non-zero entries in the row, corresponding to the two ends of the link on which the dummy node resides.[4] For each choice node (none are illustrated in the table) there would be no entries in the row, since the process ends when a choice node is reached. For each hidden node there are as many entries as there are links emanating from that node.

An equivalent semi-markov representation. An equivalent formulation of the semi-Markov process representing the network decision process is given in the matrices of Table 2. Table 2A gives the values of p_{ij} and Table 2B gives matrices v_{ij}^r with indices r. Each such matrix gives the rth (raw) moments of the time from epoch k to epoch $k+1$ given that the decision process did move from node N_i at epoch k to node N_j at epoch $k+1$. The matrices in Table 2 can be calculated from the matrix given in Table 1. Furthermore, it is in principle possible to generate the entries in Table 1 given all the matrices in Table 2. It turns out that the p_{ij} matrix and the v_{ij}^r matrices for $r = 1$ through m are necessary and sufficient to calculate both the choice probabilities, and the first m moments of the time to make a given choice. Furthermore, the methods of calculation are simple and easy to implement.

The matrices in Tables 1 and 2 of course have the same placement of non-zero entries. The entries in Matrix 2A for rows corresponding to hidden nodes are the $p_i(j)$ values. The corresponding entries in Matrix 2B are all 1.0, because it is our convention that the first step from such nodes will always be one unit of distance and take one unit of time.

An example with random walks along the links. Suppose the processes along all links are simple random walks. The first step from a hidden node will place the decision process at a point one unit of distance along a link, usually at a dummy node, N_{dij}. The process now undergoes a standard random walk where one boundary is at a distance of one and the other boundary is at a distance $d_{ij} - 1$. Random walk theory provides established methods to determine both p_{dijj} (the probability of reaching node N_j before node N_i, assuming a start one unit from Node N_i) and v_{dijj}^r (the rth moment of the time taken).

There is of course nothing essential about the use of a random walk process along the links. Any process that will always reach one of the ends of the link, and for which the probabilities and moments can be calculated or prescribed, will work

---

[4]It seems strange to write the probabilities and times to reach the node adjacent to a hidden node, ignoring the fact that the random process on a link may well pass through the hidden node one or more times before the end of the link is reached. However, the solutions are identical to the alternate form in which the decision process is allowed to return to a dummy node over successive epochs, when one writes the matrix representations correctly in both cases.

A.   Epoch $K + 1$

Epoch K		N_0	N_{d01}		N_{djk}		N_j	N_k
	N_0	0	P_{0d01}	$\cdots$	0	$\cdots$	0	0
	N_{d01}	P_{d010}	0	$\cdots$	0	$\cdots$	0	0
		$\vdots$	$\vdots$	$\vdots$	$\vdots$	$\vdots$	$\vdots$	$\vdots$
	N_{djk}	0	0	$\cdots$	0	$\cdots$	P_{djkj}	P_{djkk}
		$\vdots$	$\vdots$	$\vdots$	$\vdots$	$\vdots$	$\vdots$	$\vdots$
	N_j	0	0	$\cdots$	P_{jdjk}	$\cdots$	0	0
	N_k	0	0	$\cdots$	0	$\cdots$	0	0

B.   Epoch $K + 1$

Epoch K		N_0	N_{d01}		N_{djk}		N_j	N_k
	N_0	0	$V^r_{0d01} = 1$	$\cdots$	0	$\cdots$	0	0
	N_{d01}	V^r_{d010}	0	$\cdots$	0	$\cdots$	0	0
		$\vdots$	$\vdots$	$\vdots$	$\vdots$	$\vdots$	$\vdots$	$\vdots$
	N_{djk}	0	0	$\cdots$	0	$\cdots$	V^r_{djkj}	V^r_{djkk}
		$\vdots$	$\vdots$	$\vdots$	$\vdots$	$\vdots$	$\vdots$	$\vdots$
	N_j	0	0	$\cdots$	$V^r_{jdjk} = 1$	$\cdots$	0	0
	N_k	0	0	$\cdots$	0	$\cdots$	0	0

TABLE 2. Alternate representation of the semi-Markov process of Table 1. Panel A: The probabilities of moving from one state to another over successive epochs. Panel B: This matrix represents a series of matrices with index r; each matrix gives the rth raw moments of the time taken to move from one state to another over successive epochs, conditional upon the fact that a move between those states took place.

as well, and allow calculation of the choice probabilities and the moments of the choice times. These assertions are easy to verify, and the methods of calculation are straightforward, based on results by Shiffrin and Thompson (1988). We shall return to such details later. First, I shall describe some of the qualitative general properties of different types of such networks.

3. NETWORK PROPERTIES

As stated, the present framework in no way requires that the movement along links be based on a simple random walk. However, it is convenient for discussion to assume this to be the case, and this assumption is adopted in this section.

A network without structural representation of similarity. Probably the simplest network is that illustrated in Figure 2, in which a start node is connected by spokes to n choice nodes. The parameters are the probabilities of setting out along any of the spokes, $p_0(j)$, the length of the spokes, d_{0j}, and the drift rates of the random walks toward the end of the spokes, $p(0, j)$. The model has some relation to the model by Palmeri (in press) in that a step toward one response is a step away from all the other responses. On the other hand, in the present system a step away from a response, while on the link leading to that response, is a step toward all the others, which is not the case in the above mentioned models. It should be evident that the system is critically dependent on the positioning of the central node in the network. As we will show later, this system has some interesting properties. For example, let w_j represent the probability that the decision process will leave the start node along Link L_{0j} and then reach choice node N_j before returning to the start node. The probability that choice N_j is selected, overall, will be shown below (Equation 7) to equal $w_j / \sum w_i$, a simple ratio rule (e.g., see Luce, 1959a; Shepard, 1957).

Bias and sensitivity can be modeled in this system in various ways. In a two dimensional random walk, bias for one alternative versus the other is usually instantiated as the placement of the starting node relative to the ends that remain a fixed distance apart, overall bias to change response speed (at the cost of accuracy) is usually modeled by changing the distance between the boundaries, and sensitivity is usually modeled as the drift rate, and is not changed unless the conditions of the study change. These ideas can be extended to the present situation. Sensitivity can be identified with the drift rates along the spokes, justified, for example, if one thinks of the drift rate as representing the accumulation of small bits of evidence. Bias shifts in favor of some alternatives at the expense of others can be modeled by changing the lengths of the different spokes, while keeping the sum of all lengths constant. An overall bias to respond more quickly or more slowly can be modeled by increasing or decreasing all lengths by some constant factor. A bias to consider a particular set of alternatives with a higher priority than others can be modeled by adjusting the probabilities of setting forth along the various links from the start node; such an interpretation would be consistent, for example, with a conception in which alternatives are considered in succession, and the choice of path from the start node is considered a decision concerning which alternative to consider next. Finally, it is worth noting that there is nothing in the system requiring this particular identification of parameters with sensitivity and bias. Other interpretations of the parameters of the network would also be possible.

Whatever the interpretations of the parameters, it is clear that the similarity between alternatives is not embedded structurally in the network. Although one might suppose that similar alternatives accumulate evidence at similar rates, or have similar distances from the start node, equating these quantities does not capture the essence of similarity, since a movement along a link toward one of a set of similar alternatives does not move the decision process any closer to a choice of one of the other alternatives in the same similarity class. In the next section we consider network structures in which similarity has a natural interpretation.

Even in such a simple system there are a number of interesting sub-models, depending on parameter choices. For example, one might want to distinguish psychologically between processes on links emanating from the start node that tend to drift toward the response at the end of the link (i.e., with $p(i, j) > .5$), in contrast to those that tend to return to the start node. One could identify the former as 'approach' links, and the latter as 'avoidance' links (e.g., Busemeyer & Townsend, 1993). Note that the process on a link starts from a position only one unit from the start node, so even for an 'approach' link there may be a higher probability of returning to the start node than reaching the response node (when the distance to the response node is high, and $p(i, j)$ close to .5).

Networks with representation of similarity. One problem with the very simple network model of Figure 2A is that it really has no very compelling way of handling similarity among different subsets of choices. However, similarity may be incorporated structurally in expanded networks. Consider for example the simple four choice network in Figure 4A (in this figure, the dummy nodes are not shown, to reduce clutter in the diagrams, and to make it easier to extract the essentials of the network structure). Figure 4A has two subsets of two choices. The subsets are not too similar and are therefore separated by a link (L_{12}); the choices within the subsets are fairly similar and therefore close to their common nodes (N_1 and N_2). When the decision process is on the central link a movement toward node N_1 represents a tendency toward responding with one of the choices A or B, and a tendency away from responding with choices C and D (and vice versa). This is the simplest non trivial example of a kind of network called a *free tree* (Cunningham, 1978); it is structurally defined as a network in which any two nodes are connected by a unique set of links. The concept can of course be generalized (as shown by Cunningham, 1978) to larger sets of nodes, as in the 'linear' tree of Figure 4B, thereby incorporating more complex similarity relations.

In general, similarity can be represented in networks in two ways, one quantitative, depending on the values of the parameters of the network (e.g., the $p_i(j)$ values, the lengths of the links and the drift rates on the links), and one structural, depending on the topological properties of the network. In most cases, the quantitative and structural properties of the network interact to represent similarity. For example, the networks in Figure 4A and 4C are structurally identical, but quantitatively different, assuming that the $p_i(j)$ and the drift rates on links are the same, but the distances along the links differ, as illustrated. The network in Figure 4C has a longer central link, and shorter choice links, than the network in Figure 4A, most easily interpreted as a greater dissimilarity of cluster (A,B) to cluster (C,D), and greater within cluster similarities.

If one moves to more complex structural networks, as in Figure 4D, then the ability to represent similarity by structure alone is generally lost (except for any sub-free-trees within the network; for example in Figure 4D, choices A and B remain similar to each other and dissimilar from the remaining choices). In these more complex networks there are internal cycles and multiple paths linking two nodes. In such cases, the lengths of and drift rates on the links will generally be a critical component of any representation of similarity. For example, in Figure 4D, if the

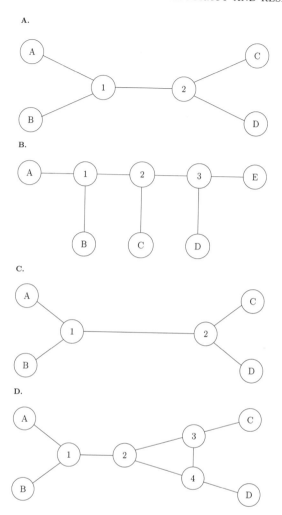

FIGURE 4. Examples of networks incorporating various forms of similarity. Panel A: Choices A and B are similar and differ from choices C and D. Panel B: A linear structure with similarity clusters consisting of (A,B) and (D,E), and choice C of intermediate similarity. Panel C: Network with identical topological structure to Panel A, but with quantitative differences represented by links of different lengths. Panel D: Network with a loop among the internal nodes, complicating structural interpretations of similarity.

decision process is moving to the right on link L_{23}, it is not possible to state without reference to the parameter values whether the decision process is moving closer to C, closer to D, closer to C than to D, closer to C than to cluster (A,B), or closer to D than to cluster (A,B). This is evident when one notices, for example, that for some values of the parameters (distances, drift rates and probabilities), it might be shorter and/or more probable for a decision process on link L_{23} to reach node

N_3 by returning to node N_2, and traversing links L_{24} and L_{43}, than by continuing directly toward node N_3.

Given that it is the case that quantitative elements of a network will generally interact with structure to represent similarity, it is appropriate to ask what quantitative elements are assigned to such a role. One view, for example, would represent similarity only by distances, ignoring the probabilities $p_i(j)$ of choosing links at a node, and ignoring the drift rates (and drift directions). It is by no means obvious that this choice is necessary or desirable, and other ways of representing similarity could also be entertained.

4. GENERALITY AND PARAMETERIZATION

Although a virtue of the present framework is its generality, this generality comes at a cost: the enormous (infinite) number of structures that can be represented, and the large number of free parameters associated with any one structure. In practice, it will often be necessary to assume constraints and restrictions that specify the subclass of allowable models, and specify the number and use of free parameters. Suppose for example that one decides to limit modeling to networks of the type shown in Figure 2 (a network set up as a central node with spokes), and further decides to assume simple random walks on the links. Even under this severe restriction, there are many free parameters in the general model: for n choices, there would be $n-1$ free $p_0(j)$ parameters (governing choices of spokes emanating from the start node), n free $p(i,j)$ parameters (drift rates on the spokes), and n free d_{ij} parameters (lengths of the spokes). To estimate these would at the minimum require the $n-1$ choice probabilities, and for the individual choices, the n mean response times and the n variances of the response times. Although such an enterprise may be feasible according to current empirical practice, more complicated models would certainly require simplifying restrictions. For example, the addition of hidden nodes in addition to the start node would increase the number of free parameters to the point where reliable estimation would not be practical. In such cases, further restrictive assumptions would be necessary, such as assuming $p_i(j)$ all equal, or d_{ij} all equal.

The need in general for such restrictive assumptions and constraints means that the present network approach is to be considered a framework for generating and testing models, rather than an argument in favor of any particular model. Nonetheless, despite the generality of the approach, it is possible to derive all the necessary predictions that would allow testing of any model that fits the framework. I turn next to the rather simple methods of derivation.

5. DERIVATIONS OF PREDICTIONS FOR THE NETWORK MODEL

The methods of derivation are borrowed from Shiffrin and Thompson (1988, that article also presents all necessary proofs). The method given there applies to a completely general class of semi-Markov processes, and arbitrary random variables associated with such processes, and is considerably more general than needed for present applications. Thus I give the results here in a much simpler form, sufficient for all derivations for the class of network models under consideration. For convenience, assume that the model is represented in the form of the matrices given in Table 2.

Let $g_i(k)$ be the probability that a decision process currently at node N_i will eventually settle on choice N_k, and define $g_i(i) = 1$. For convenience, and to simplify terminology, the indicator of the choice response will usually be deleted in what follows, so $g_i(k)$ will be denoted g_i, and it will be understood that some particular choice is being discussed. Then we can write

$$g_i = \sum_j p_{ij} g_j \tag{1}$$

where there is an equation like this for each possible starting node (i.e., hidden nodes).

These are a set of linear simultaneous equations that may always be solved simultaneously for the probabilities g_i. The idea is simple: for each node that the process may be in at a given epoch, one writes the probability of eventually reaching a given choice as a sum over the nodes to which the process can move at the next epoch, each element of the sum being the probability of moving to that node times the probability of eventually reaching the given choice from that node.

A rather similar approach works to calculate the moments of the time to reach a given choice starting from node i. Consider the mean time as an illustration. Let μ_i be the mean time to make a given choice given a start in node N_i and define $\mu_i(i) = 0$. Also for convenience, let v_{ij} (without the explicit designation v_{ij}^1) denote the mean time to move from node N_i to node N_j, given that such a move occurs in successive epochs. Then

$$\mu_i = \frac{1}{g_i} \sum_j p_{ij} g_j (v_{ij} + \mu_j). \tag{2}$$

This again is a set of linear simultaneous equations that can always be solved for the μ_i as long as equations 1 have already been solved for the g_i. The idea is again to sum over the nodes to which the process can move at the next epoch, assigning to the move the mean time taken for the current step (v_{ij}) plus the expected time to continue the process after the current step until the choice is eventually made (μ_j) weighted by the probability of moving to that node (p_{ij}). The only complication is that one must include g_i and g_j terms to adjust for the possibility that a move to a given node might result in some other choice being reached.

The equations are similar but slightly more complex for higher order moments, μ_i^r, where r denotes the rth raw moment, and N is the number of nodes:

$$\mu_i^r = \frac{1}{g_i} \sum_{j=1}^{N} p_{ij} g_j \sum_{s=0}^{r} \binom{r}{s} v_{ij}^s \mu_j^{r-s}. \tag{3}$$

Once again, for a given value of r these are a set of linear simultaneous equations that may be solved for the μ_i^r, as long as these moments have already been solved for all lower values of r.

6. AN EXAMPLE WITH DERIVATIONS

Consider the network of Figure 2 again. Let us assume there are $n + 1$ nodes: a start node N_0, and n choice nodes. To obtain the probabilities of the different choices (say, choice k), Equation 1 is used, conveniently broken down as the following $n + 1$ equations (in the third line j ranges over the $n - 1$ spokes leading to choices other than i):

$$g_0 = p_0(k)g_{d0k} + \sum_{j \neq k} p_0(j)g_{d0j}, \tag{4}$$

$$g_{d0k} = p_{d0kk} + [1 - p_{d0kk}]g_0, \tag{5}$$

$$g_{d0j} = [1 - p_{d0jj}]g_0, \qquad j \neq k, \qquad j \neq 0. \tag{6}$$

Substituting Equations 5 and 6 into Equation 4 and rearranging gives

$$g_0 = \frac{p_0(k)p_{d0kk}}{\sum_{j=1}^{n} p_0(j)p_{d0jj}}. \tag{7}$$

Note that the term p_{d0jj} is the solution of the random walk process on the jth spoke, and it depends on the drift rate, and the spoke length. This answer is a form of the Luce ratio rule for multiple choices (e.g. Luce, 1959a, 1963)

For the moments of the response times, Equations 2 and/or 3 are used. As an illustration, the mean times are calculated for the present example. Suppose we want to know the mean time to make choice k, given a start in node N_i, $\mu_i(k)$. As usual, the notation k for the choice is suppressed (but assumed to be present) in the following equations. Equation 2 takes the form of the following $n + 1$ equations (Equation 10 represents $n - 1$ equations, for the spokes other than that leading to N_k):

$$\mu_0 = \frac{1}{g_0} \sum_{j=1}^{n} p_0(j)g_{d0j}[1 + \mu_{d0j}], \tag{8}$$

$$\mu_{d0k} = \frac{1}{g_{d0k}}[p_{d0kk}v_{d0kk} + (1 - p_{d0kk})g_0(v_{d0k0} + \mu_0)], \tag{9}$$

$$\mu_{d0j} = \frac{1}{d_{d0j}}(1 - p_{d0jj})g_0(v_{d0j0} + \mu_0) \tag{10}$$

for $j \neq 0$ and $j \neq k$. To solve, first use Equation 7 with Equation 5 to calculate g_{d0k}, and Equation 7 with Equation 6 to calculate g_{d0j}. Then substitute Equations 9 and 10 into Equation 8:

$$\mu_0 = v_{d0kk} + \frac{\alpha}{\gamma} + \frac{1}{\gamma} \sum_{j=1}^{n} \beta_j v_{d0j0} \tag{11}$$

where $\alpha = 1 + [1 - p_0(k)][1 - p_{d0kk}]$, $\beta_j = p_0(j)[1 - p_{d0jj}]$, and $\gamma = \sum_j p_0(j)p_{d0jj}$. Note that the v terms are solutions of the random walk on each link, and are derived by standard methods. The first term of the solution (11) is the expected time to move from the dummy node to choice k; it appears alone because this move is made once and only once in any process that ends at choice k. The second term is the expected number of steps made from the start node to dummy nodes (which take one unit of time each), and the third term is the expected time spent in returning from dummy nodes to the start node.

Several special cases of this solution might be of interest. One such case allows an easy cross check of the validity of the solution. If $p_0(k) = 1$ then choice k will always be made, and the time to make this choice will be the result of a random walk with a reflecting barrier at the start node. In this case

$$\mu_0 = v_{d0kk} + \frac{1}{p_{d0kk}} + \frac{(1 - p_{d0kk})}{p_{d0kk}} v_{d0k0}.$$

The second term is the expected number of times a step is made from the start node to the dummy node. The factor in front of the third term is the expected number of returns from the dummy node to the start node; this is one less than the second term, as should be the case.

7. EXTENSIONS AND GENERALIZATIONS

The network model outlined in Section 3 is far from the most general model that can be handled within the present framework. In fact, predictions are derivable for any model that can be represented in the semi-Markov representations of Tables 1 and 2 (and some generalizations of these as well). This means, for example, that direct returns from a node to itself over successive epochs is perfectly acceptable (perhaps interpretable as the decision process 'treading water').

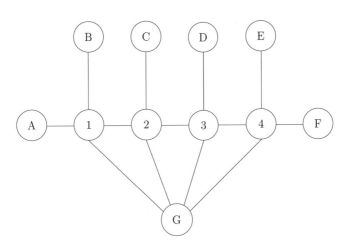

FIGURE 5. Network with multiple links to a given choice.

Interesting models can be imagined in which direct links exist from several hidden nodes to a given choice node (essentially equivalent to allowing several different nodes to be assigned the same choice). Using this option broadens the way in which similarity can be incorporated in the network. For example, the linear structure in the lower part of the network depicted in Figure 5 induces a structural similarity ordering among choices A through F, but choice G has a different relation

(One could say that choice G is always a feasible option, regardless of the ongoing decision making that differentiates among the other alternatives).

Actually, the article by Shiffrin and Thompson (1988) allows considerably more freedom than has yet been discussed, because it is possible to assign arbitrary random variables to the transits between nodes, not just transit time. In practice this option is likely to prove most useful through the setting of some of the values assigned to inter-node transitions to zero (rather than t). This approach would correspond to the assumption that some of the transitions between nodes occur in zero time. This option would allow a greater dissociation of the choice probabilities and choice times than is usually the case.

8. CONCLUSIONS

This purely theoretical rendition of network models for choice probabilities and choice times provides simple methods by which derivations can be made, and thereby opens up a potential class of useful theories. It can be thought of as a natural generalization of certain classes of two-choice models, including random walk models. The class of models can be conceptualized as one in which the choice process is thought of as a journey through a psychological space, with the momentary state of the decision process identified with the momentary position of a single point in this space, and with that position being the only determinant of the future (stochastic) progress of the journey. One value of the approach lies in the fact that the network consists of a series of two-choice stochastic processes. Derivations of predictions for the network are easy to obtain whenever derivations of predictions for the two-choice subprocesses are available, and many such cases exist in the literature.

Choice, Decision, and Measurement
A. A. J. Marley (Ed.),
©Lawrence Erlbaum Associates, NJ, 1997.

AN EXEMPLAR-BASED RANDOM-WALK MODEL OF SPEEDED CATEGORIZATION AND ABSOLUTE JUDGMENT

ROBERT M. NOSOFSKY

Indiana University

ABSTRACT. Nosofsky and Palmeri (in press) proposed and tested an exemplar-based random walk model for predicting response times in tasks of speeded multidimensional perceptual classification. According to the model, test items serve as retrieval cues for category exemplars stored in memory. The exemplars race to be retrieved with rates determined by their similarity to the presented items. The retrieved exemplars then provide information that enters into a random walk process. In this chapter, after first reviewing the model, I present tests of its ability to fit categorization response-time distributions. I also explore extensions of the model designed to account for unidimensional absolute judgment and category same-different judgment.

1. INTRODUCTION

Models of multidimensional perceptual classification have grown increasingly sophisticated in recent years, providing detailed quantitative accounts of patterns of classification learning, transfer, and generalization (e.g., Anderson, 1991; Ashby, 1992; Estes, 1994; Kruschke, 1992; Nosofsky, 1992a). However, a fundamental limitation of most competing models in the field today is that they offer no processing account of the time course of categorization. As suggested by Luce (1986b, p. *vii*), "... we surely do not understand a choice process very thoroughly until we can account for the time required for it to be carried out." Thus, a critical goal is to extend current models to account for classification response times. In this chapter I present an overview of a newly proposed process-oriented model for predicting response times in tasks of speeded multidimensional perceptual classification (Nosofsky & Palmeri, in press). I then present some preliminary tests of the model's ability to fit highly structured response-time distributions obtained for individual subjects in such tasks. Finally, I consider extensions of the model designed to account for response times in tasks of speeded unidimensional absolute judgment and same-different judgment. I refer to the model as an *exemplar-based random walk* (EBRW) model. The EBRW integrates and extends two well known

Key words and phrases. Categorization, absolute judgment, response time, exemplar-based random walk.

Acknowledgments. This work was supported by Grant PHS R01 MH48494-05 from the National Institute of Mental Health to Robert M. Nosofsky. The author would like to thank Yves Lacouture and two anonymous reviewers for their helpful comments.

Address for correspondence. Robert M. Nosofsky, Department of Psychology, Indiana University, Bloomington, IN 47405. Email: nosofsky@indiana.edu

exemplar models of cognitive processes: Nosofsky's (1984, 1986) *generalized context model* (GCM) of perceptual classification, and Logan's (1988) *instance-based model* of automaticity. For brevity, in this chapter I bypass a history of each component model and simply present the integrated product. More details regarding how the EBRW integrates and extends each component model are provided by Nosofsky and Palmeri (in press).

2. OVERVIEW OF THE FORMAL MODEL

In the EBRW, exemplars of categories are represented as points in a multi-dimensional psychological space. Similarities between objects are determined by their distances in the space. When an item is presented to be classified, it acts as a retrieval cue for all category exemplars stored in memory. These category exemplars race to be retrieved with rates determined by their similarity to the test item. The exemplar that wins the race is retrieved and provides information that enters into a random walk process. The classification choice and response time are determined by the outcome of this exemplar-based random walk. Specifically, let x_{im} denote the psychological value of exemplar i on dimension m. The distance between exemplars i and j is given by

$$d_{ij} = (\sum_{m=1}^{M} w_m(x_{im} - x_{jm})^2)^{1/2}, \tag{1}$$

where M is the number of dimensions that compose the objects, and w_m is the "attention weight" given to dimension m when judging psychological distance (Carroll & Wish, 1974; Nosofsky, 1986). Following Shepard (1987), the similarity between item i and exemplar j is an exponential decay function of their distance,

$$s_{ij} = e^{-cd_{ij}}, \tag{2}$$

where c is an overall sensitivity parameter for scaling distances in the space. Because of factors such as recency of presentation, exemplars may reside in memory with differing strengths. Let M_j denote the memory strength for exemplar j. The degree to which exemplar j is activated when item i is presented is given by

$$a_{ij} = M_j s_{ij}. \tag{3}$$

When item i is presented, all exemplars race to be retrieved. The race times are independently exponentially distributed with rate parameters determined by the activations a_{ij}. Thus, the probability density that exemplar j completes its race at time t is given by

$$f(t) = a_{ij}e^{-a_{ij}t}. \tag{4}$$

Note from Equations 3 and 4 that the exemplars that are most likely to be retrieved are those with the greatest memory strengths and that are highly similar to the test item. Marley (1992) used this type of exponential race process as a means of characterizing a wide variety of modern models of identification and classification.

In the EBRW, the random-walk process works as follows (see Figure 1). First, a random-walk counter is established with a starting value of zero. In an experiment with two categories, A and B, a positive criterion $(+A)$ and a negative criterion

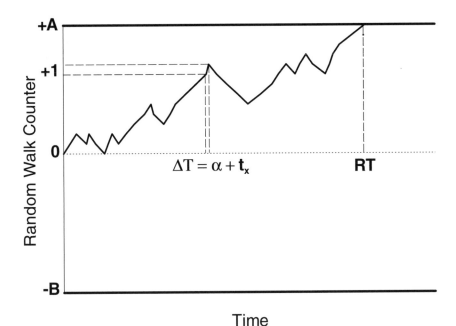

FIGURE 1. Schematic illustration of the random-walk process in the EBRW. Adapted with permission from Figure 1 of Nosofsky and Palmeri (in press). Copyright© 1997 by the American Psychological Association.

$(-B)$ are established. (As I describe later in this chapter, multiple criteria can be established in situations involving multiple categories.) If the first exemplar that is retrieved belongs to Category A, then the random-walk counter is increased by unit value, whereas if the retrieved exemplar belongs instead to Category B, then the counter is decreased by unit value. If the counter reaches either the $+A$ criterion or the $-B$ criterion, then the appropriate categorization response is made. Else, a new race is initiated, a second exemplar is retrieved, and the process continues.

The time to take each individual step in the random walk is given by

$$T = \alpha + t_w, \tag{5}$$

where α is a constant and t_w is the time to retrieve the "winning" exemplar. This aspect of the EBRW, in which the time to take each individual step is itself a random variable, represents a departure of the EBRW from standard random walk models.

To account for increases in response accuracy as a function of classification training, I imagine that "background noise elements" also participate in the race (Estes, 1994; Nosofsky, Kruschke, & McKinley, 1992). I assume that an equal proportion of the background elements point to each respective category. The race time of each background element follows an exponential distribution with rate parameter b, independent of the test item that the experimenter presents to be classified. Early in learning, when few exemplars are stored in memory, there is a relatively high probability of the background elements winning the races and entering into the random walk, so classification performance will hover around chance. As an increased number of category exemplars come to be stored in memory, however, the probability of the background elements winning each race declines, so classification accuracy improves.

The random-walk process just described is intended to model the time course of the classification decision-making stage. A complete model of response times also requires specification of other stages, such as encoding and response execution. For simplicity, I assume that the time course for these other stages is independent of the decision-making stage and, for all stimuli, follows a normal distribution with mean μ and variance σ_R^2.

Some conceptual predictions associated with the EBRW can now be discussed. Note that, according to the EBRW, classification response time is determined jointly by the number of steps required to complete the random walk and by the speed with which each individual step is made. The first main prediction is that classification response time should be shortest (and accuracy greatest) for objects that are highly similar to the exemplars of one category and dissimilar to exemplars of alternative categories. Under such circumstances, each exemplar that is retrieved belongs to the same category, and the random walk marches consistently to the appropriate category criterion. By contrast, items that are similar to the exemplars of multiple categories result in slow classification response times. The reason is that the random walk will tend to wander back and forth, sometimes retrieving exemplars from one category and other times retrieving exemplars from alternative categories.

A second prediction is that increases in classification training will facilitate performance. As category training increases, more exemplars come to be stored in memory. The greater the number of exemplars that race to enter the random walk, the faster the winning retrieval times will be (Logan, 1988; Townsend & Ashby, 1983). These faster retrieval times result in faster individual steps in the random walk process (Equation 5). As explained previously, by incorporating the assumption of background-noise elements, increased training is also predicted to result in improved classification accuracy.

A third prediction is that, all other things being equal, increased "familiarity" with individual exemplars should also facilitate speeded classification. An exemplar is highly familiar if it has been presented frequently or recently, or if it is highly similar to numerous training exemplars. Familiarity should increase classification response speed because numerous exemplars will race with high activation rates, resulting in fast individual steps in the random walk process.

The random-walk mechanism is an important processing aspect of the EBRW. A model that bases decisions instead on only the *first* exemplar retrieved [such as Logan's (1988) single-instance race model] will often yield implausible predictions of classification response times. For example, suppose that one added an exemplar to Category B that was highly similar to an exemplar from Category A. This manipulation, which increases classification difficulty, would undoubtedly lead to slower response times. A pure single-exemplar race model predicts the opposite, however. Adding a highly similar exemplar to the race, even from a contrast category, could only speed the winning retrieval times, albeit at the cost of more errors in performance. The random-walk mechanism leads the system to accumulate more evidence for difficult-to-discriminate items, thereby trading speed for accuracy.

Fitting the EBRW to speeded classification response-time data requires a multidimensional scaling (MDS) solution for the exemplars (i.e., the x_{im} coordinate values in Equation 1). Typically, some form of similarity-scaling study is needed to derive this MDS solution (e.g., Nosofsky, 1992a). Once the solution is derived, the free parameters in the EBRW include: the overall sensitivity parameter (c) for scaling distances in the space (Equation 2); the attention weights (w_m) in the distance function (Equation 1); the step-time constant (α) in the random walk (Equation 5); the $+A$ and $-B$ response criteria; the activation-rate of the background noise elements (b); and the mean (μ) and variance (σ_R^2) of the duration of the residual processing stages. Furthermore, because the duration of the random walk is in arbitrary units, a scaling constant (k) needs to be estimated for transforming the predictions of the EBRW into milliseconds. Finally, in situations in which exemplar memory-strengths are expected to vary, free parameters may be required for predicting these differential strengths. Although the model has a large number of free parameters, many of them can often be set at default values. Furthermore, there is a large number of degrees of freedom in the data of the response-time distributions to be fitted, so the tests of the model are more than challenging.

3. TESTS OF THE EBRW IN A SPEEDED CLASSIFICATION TASK

In an initial experiment designed to test the EBRW, Nosofsky and Palmeri (in press) ran three subjects in an extended task of speeded perceptual classification. The stimuli were a set of 12 computer-generated colors of a roughly constant red hue (according to the Munsell system) but varying in their brightness and saturation. The configuration of stimuli that was used is illustrated in Figure 2. All stimuli enclosed by squares were members of Category A, whereas stimuli enclosed by circles were members of Category B. The goal in designing the experiment was to create a structure in which: i) more than one dimension was relevant for performing the classification; ii) the categories could be separated by a single continuous boundary; and iii) the exemplars varied in their distance from this boundary.

Each subject participated for a period of five days of testing, with a total of 360 stimulus presentations per day. On each trial, one of the colors was randomly selected, and the subject was instructed to classify it into Category A or B as rapidly as possible without making errors. Feedback was provided on each trial. The subjects quickly learned the category assignments and rarely made errors, so the key dependent variable was classification response time. In addition to the speeded classification task, extensive similarity-scaling work was performed to derive individual-subject MDS solutions for the colors. The goal was to use these MDS solutions in conjunction with the EBRW to predict the response-time data for each individual subject. Further details regarding the experimental method are provided by Nosofsky and Palmeri (in press).

The main pattern of results is illustrated for a representative subject in Figure 3. The center of each circle gives the MDS coordinates obtained for each color based on an analysis of the individual subject's similarity ratings. (These MDS solutions accounted for an average of 94.5% of the variance in the similarity ratings

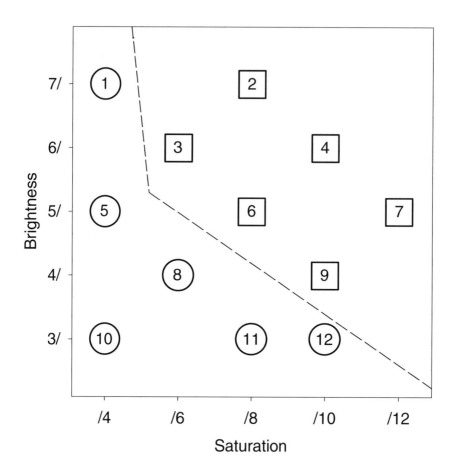

FIGURE 2. Schematic illustration of the category structure tested
in Nosofsky and Palmeri's (in press) experiment.

of the three subjects.) The diameter of each circle is linearly related to the mean
response time with which the subject classified each color. (The first day's data
were considered practice and were not included in computing these means.) The
dashed boundary represents the set of points that have equal summed similarity to
the exemplars of Category A and Category B (as computed in Equations 1 and 2).
This boundary is illustrated simply for descriptive convenience and does not enter
into the formal modeling of the data. It is obvious from inspection that the mean
response times follow a systematic pattern: in general, the further the distance of a
color from the exemplar-based category boundary, the shorter is the mean response
time.

Nosofsky and Palmeri (in press) demonstrated previously that, with relatively
few free parameters, the EBRW yielded predictions that correlated highly with the
observed mean response times. The model predicts these results because colors
far from the category boundary tend to retrieve exemplars only from their own

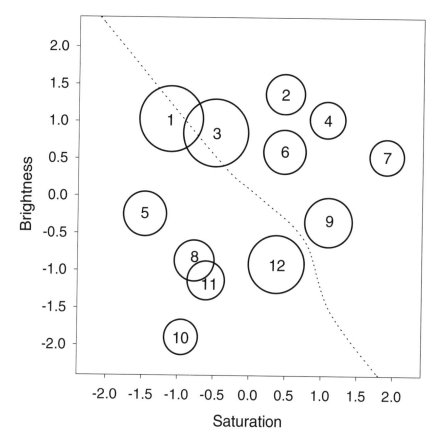

FIGURE 3. Summary of mean response-time results for Subject 2 of Nosofsky and Palmeri's (in press) experiment. Adapted with permission from Figure 4B of Nosofsky and Palmeri (in press). Copyright© 1997 by the American Psychological Association.

category and not from the contrast category. Thus, the random walk marches in consistent fashion to the appropriate response criterion. Colors that lie close to the boundary yield slow response times because the random walk wanders back and forth, sometimes retrieving exemplars from the correct category and other times retrieving exemplars from the incorrect category.

Another important result was that, for all three subjects, mean response time for the colors declined systematically as a function of blocks of training. The EBRW yielded good quantitative predictions of this facilitation in response speed. The EBRW predicts this facilitation because, as training proceeds, more and more exemplars are stored in memory. The greater the number of exemplars that race to be retrieved, the faster the winning retrieval times tend to be, so the steps in the random walk are taken more quickly.

My first new goal in this chapter is to begin to develop more detailed tests of the EBRW by fitting it to the entire distribution of response times obtained for each color rather than simply to the mean response times. The cumulative response-time distributions for each of the three subjects are given in Tables 2-4 at the end of the chapter. The distributions are organized into bins of 100 msec. So, for example, for each subject and color, the entry in bin 600 gives the probability that the subject classified the color with a response time of less than or equal to 600 msec. Because errors were rare, there are insufficient data to separately model the distributions corresponding to correct and incorrect responses, so only correct responses are included in the data summaries. Also, the first day's data are considered practice and are not included.

Although Nosofsky and Palmeri (in press) derived analytic predictions from the EBRW for the mean response times and accuracies for any given stimulus, at this stage of development I need to rely on computer simulation for predicting the response-time distributions. I fitted the EBRW to the response-time distributions of the individual subjects by conducting 1200 simulations for each color presentation and searching for the parameters that minimized the sum of squared deviations between predicted and observed probabilities of each response-time bin[1]. The free parameters were c, w_1, α, $+A$, $-B$, k, μ, and σ_R^2. The background-noise constant b was set at 0 and did not enter into the response-time predictions. I arbitrarily assumed there was a total of 20 tokens of each color exemplar stored in memory, and that all exemplars had equal strength. Note that the set of response-time distributions for each subject contains 252 data points (12 stimuli by 21 response-time bins), while the EBRW has 8 free parameters[2].

The EBRW accounted for 94.9, 97.4, and 98.0% of the variance in the response-time distributions of Subjects 1, 2, and 3, respectively. Inspection of the model-fitting results for Subject 1 revealed that the EBRW predicted response times for Stimuli 1 and 12 that were too large. A post hoc explanation is that Subject 1 may have devoted extra "attention" or "rehearsal" to these difficult-to-classify items (see Figure 2). One way of improving the fit is to add stimulus-specific sensitivity parameters to the model (Kruschke, 1992; Nosofsky, 1991). In this elaborated

---

[1] A more appropriate measure of fit would involve computing some form of weighted sum of squared deviations (SSD) between predicted and observed values, where the weights are determined by the error variance of each data entry. However, as will be acknowledged later in this section, the EBRW fails to account for some very large response times observed in the extreme tails of the distributions. In these initial stages of model development, my judgment is that giving large weight to these infrequent but extreme data entries would unduly influence the parameter estimates for the model. The unweighted SSD measure is intended to provide a first approximation as to the ability of the model to characterize the main body of the response-time distributions. Finally, I note that although computer simulation is a stochastic process, because of the large number of simulations that were used, changes in SSD from one run of the model to the next were negligible.

[2] Furthermore, I should note that the precise values of $+A$ and $-B$ have very little effect on the model fit, as long as they are sufficiently large to account for the extremely accurate performance that was observed in the experiment. Only their relative values are important. Because the best-fitting values of $+A$ and $-B$ turn out to be essentially equal in magnitude for all three subjects (see Table 1), there are actually fewer than 8 "effective" free parameters in the model.

		Subject	
Parameter	1	2	3
c	1.713	1.518	2.764
w_1	0.588	0.572	0.300
α	0.216	0.102	0.120
$+A$	15.000	15.000	14.000
$-B$	-16.000	-14.000	-15.000
μ_R	271.081	339.700	359.900
σ_R	101.875	64.375	93.850
k	94.944	92.600	90.156
c_1	1.904	—	—
c_{12}	1.511	—	—
Fits			
% Var	98.480	97.440	98.010
SSD	0.433	0.583	0.484
RMSD	0.041	0.048	0.044

TABLE 1. % Var = Percentage of variance accounted for; SSD = sum of squared deviations between predicted and observed bin probabilities; RMSD = root mean squared deviation.

model, the similarity of stimulus i to stimulus j is given by

$$s_{ij} = e^{-c_i d_{ij}}, \tag{6}$$

where c_i is the sensitivity parameter associated with Stimulus i. Devoting extra attention to these individual stimuli improves a subject's sensitivity in discriminating them from the remaining exemplars in the set. This elaboration requires adding two free parameters to the model for Subject 1, namely c_1 and c_{12}. The elaborated model accounts for 98.5% of the variance in Subject 1's response-time distributions data. The best-fitting parameters and summary fits for all three subjects are reported in Table 1.

A plot of the predicted response-time (RT) distributions against the observed RT distributions is illustrated in Figures 4A-4C. Because each individual stimulus RT distribution is based on only 120 observations, the results need to be interpreted with some caution. Nevertheless, the EBRW seems to provide a reasonably good account of the general pattern of results. Although no attempt was made to fit the mean response times directly, the correlations between predicted and observed values for the 12 stimuli were $r = .982$, $r = .974$, and $r = .955$, for Subjects 1-3, respectively. Some clear shortcomings of the model are also apparent, however. First, there are various cases in which the observed distribution of response times has an extra "hump" that is discontinuous with the main body of the distribution. The EBRW does not predict this result. Indeed, the model greatly underpredicts the standard deviation for these discontinuous distributions. I suspect that it will

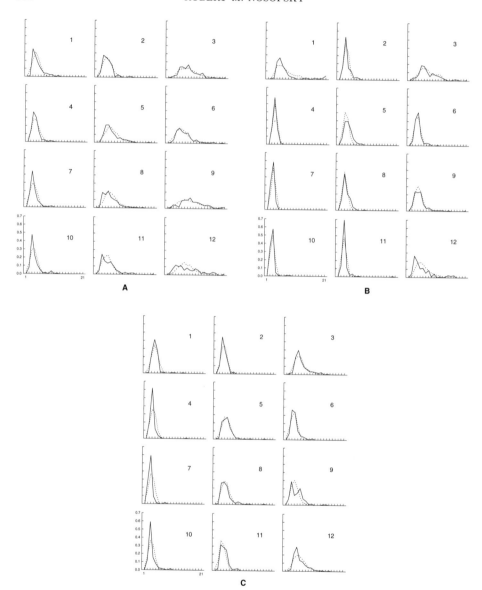

FIGURE 4. Plot of predicted response-time distributions (dashed lines) against observed response-time distributions (solid lines) for each subject in Nosofsky and Palmeri's (in press) experiment. Panel A = Subject 1, Panel B = Subject 2, Panel C = Subject 3.

be difficult for any single-process model to fit distributions with this form. Second, there are various cases in which the observed response-time distributions for easy-to-classify stimuli have a sharper peak than is predicted by the EBRW. It may be that the present parameter settings are attempting to achieve a compromise between fitting the discontinuous response clusters and the peaks of the distributions. It seems likely that providing a complete account of these response-time distributions will require some dual-process model.

4. COMPARISONS WITH A BILINEAR DECISION-BOUND MODEL

As an initial source of comparison for the EBRW, I fit a version of an alternative model of classification response time to these distributions. According to the *RT-distance hypothesis* of Ashby, Boynton, and Lee (1994, *p. 11*), "... RT decreases with the distance in psychological space from the stimulus representation to the decision bound that separates the exemplars of the contrasting categories." Although not a process-based model, the RT-distance hypothesis is the main current proposal in the field for predicting multidimensional classification response times. Versions of the hypothesis have been applied successfully by Ashby and his colleagues to a variety of speeded classification data (Ashby & Maddox, 1991, 1994; Ashby et al., 1994; Maddox & Ashby, 1996). The hypothesis also has a long history of success in unidimensional tasks, and process-oriented versions of the hypothesis have been developed by Link (1992) and Karpiuk, Lacouture & Marley (this volume) in these domains.

To apply the RT-distance hypothesis, a multidimensional decision boundary for separating the categories needs to be defined. Because boundaries of any degree of complexity can be defined, it is not possible to test the hypothesis in its general form. Previous tests conducted by Ashby et al. (1994) and Maddox and Ashby (1996) used category structures in which it was plausible to assume linear decision boundaries. In the present case, I extend this linear version by testing a bilinear model with a form illustrated by the dashed boundary in Figure 2. Furthermore, following Murdock (1985) and Maddox and Ashby (1996), I assume that the classification decision-making time decreases exponentially with distance (D) from the bound,

$$T = ke^{-\beta D}, \tag{7}$$

where k and β are scaling constants. Note that for this exponential function, k is the decision time for a percept that falls exactly on the decision bound, and β determines the rate at which decision time decreases with distance from the bound. Although Maddox and Ashby (1996) noted some limitations of the exponential model, it provided the best overall quantitative fits to their data among the alternative models they proposed.

According to the RT-distance hypothesis, variability in decision time is the result of fluctuations in the perceptual representations yielded by each stimulus. As a first approximation to modeling this variability, I assume that each stimulus gives rise to a bivariate normal distribution of points, with mean given by the MDS coordinates for the color, variability σ_P^2 along each dimension, and zero covariance between the dimensions. (A more sophisticated approach to testing the model would involve estimating the parameters of each individual stimulus distribution in separate similarity-scaling work, but this more ambitious approach goes beyond the scope of the present chapter.) Finally, just as is the case in the EBRW, I assume that the duration of the residual stages of processing, such as encoding and response-execution, follows a normal distribution with mean μ and variance σ_R^2.

The bilinear distance-from-boundary model has 9 free parameters: a slope (m) and y-intercept (b) for each limb of the bilinear boundary; the scaling parameters k and β in the decision-time function (Equation 7); the perceptual variance parameter σ_P^2; and the mean μ and variance σ_R^2 of the residual processing stages. Using the same simulation procedures as I described previously for the EBRW, I found that the bilinear model accounted for 98.4, 97.0, and 96.6% of the variance in the response-time distributions of Subjects 1-3, respectively. Note that the (unelaborated) EBRW fitted the data worse than the bilinear distance-from-boundary model for Subject 1, was essentially the same for Subject 2, and fitted slightly better for Subject 3. Undoubtedly, improved fits of the distance-from-boundary model could be achieved by estimating more complex decision boundaries. Also, by estimating separate perceptual distributions for each individual stimulus, improved fits might also be achieved. Nevertheless, the present analysis suggests that the EBRW is at least competitive with an alternative descriptive model of classification response time that has a good record of success and that has roughly the same number of free parameters.

It is also worth noting here that previous tests have demonstrated some advantages for the EBRW over the pure distance-from-boundary model. For example, Nosofsky and Palmeri (in press) found that the EBRW accounted for the roughly power-law decreases in mean response times that were observed as a function of practice, as well as for familiarity effects associated with individual stimuli. Current versions of the RT-distance model provide no account of these effects.

5. EXTENSIONS OF THE EBRW TO UNIDIMENSIONAL ABSOLUTE JUDGMENT

Although the EBRW was developed to model multidimensional perceptual classification, extended versions of the model can also be applied in other domains. One domain of interest is unidimensional absolute judgment. In this task, there is a set of n stimuli lying along a unidimensional continuum (such as length, brightness, or loudness), and each stimulus is assigned a unique identifying label varying from 1 to n. On each trial, a stimulus is randomly selected, the subject attempts to identify it, and feedback is then provided. A variety of robust phenomena emerge in this task (for reviews, see Luce & Nosofsky, 1984; Miller, 1956). First, as one increases the number of equally spaced stimuli lying along the continuum (and therefore their total range), people's ability to identify individual stimuli within the set declines systematically. This effect is termed a *range effect*. However, performance on the stimuli near each edge of the range is always quite accurate, which produces a strong "bow" in the plot of accuracy against serial position of each stimulus (e.g., Braida & Durlach, 1972; Luce et al., 1982). This effect is termed a *bow* or *edge* effect. In addition, research by Karpiuk et al. (this volume) reveals that similar range and edge effects emerge for identification response times. Subjects are faster to identify stimuli lying near the edges of the range, and overall response time gets faster as the range decreases. Important sequential and clustering effects also arise in unidimensional absolute judgment (Luce et al., 1982; Luce & Green, 1978; Lockhead, 1984; Purks, Callahan, Braida, & Durlach, 1980), but consideration of these effects goes beyond the scope of the present chapter.

Note that to fit the EBRW to identification or classification data, a psychological scaling solution is required for the exemplars. The EBRW does not by itself explain the psychological spacings or perceptual/memory variances associated with individual objects. Rather, psychophysical theories are needed to accomplish this task. A variety of such theories have been proposed in the domain of unidimensional absolute judgment (e.g., Braida et al., 1984; Durlach & Braida, 1969; Luce, Green, & Weber, 1976; Marley & Cook, 1984). Although these theories differ in important details, they have in common the idea that the means of the stimulus representations are equally spaced along the unidimensional continuum, but the variances associated with the stimulus representations increase systematically with the distance of the stimulus from the edge of the range.

In this section I consider an integration in which the EBRW is combined with a simple descriptive model of stimulus representation. Karpiuk et al. (this volume) have taken a similar approach by combining the limited-capacity rehearsal model of Marley and Cook (1984) with ideas from Link's (1992) wave-equality random-walk model. In Karpiuk et al.'s model, however, absolute identification is based on the distance of objects from response criteria or decision boundaries established along the range, whereas in the EBRW identification is assumed to be based on the retrieval of exemplar memories. The integration I propose should be considered a simple representative from a large class of possible models. In particular, I adopt a highly simplified descriptive model of stimulus representation. My limited goal in this chapter is only to provide initial demonstrations of the potential viability of combining the EBRW with a rich, psychophysical theory in the domain of unidimensional absolute judgment.

I imagine that associated with each stimulus is a normally distributed memory representation. The means of the memory representations are equally spaced along the continuum. However, the variances of the memory representations are linearly related to the distance of the stimulus from the nearest edge of the range. (The edges are defined as being one unit below and one unit above the lowest and highest stimulus magnitudes, respectively.) As suggested by Braida et al. (1984), it may be that subjects form "perceptual anchors" at the edges of the range, and memory variance for the exemplars is influenced by their distance from these anchors. For simplicity, I assume that the psychological scale value assigned to a presented stimulus is exactly equal to the mean of the normally distributed memory representation with which it is associated, i.e., there is zero sensory noise.

To represent observers' fallible memory for the exemplar locations on the psychological scale, I assume that, on each trial, a single exemplar trace from each of the n individual, normally distributed memory representations is currently active. The exemplar traces that are active on each trial do not depend on the presented stimulus but are selected at random from their respective memory distributions. Now, suppose that stimulus i is presented to be identified. The n exemplars that are currently active race to be retrieved in accord with how similar they are to the presented stimulus (as formalized earlier in Equations 1-5). (Note that because the memory variance for edge stimuli is small, a presented edge stimulus is likely to be highly similar to its active memory trace, whereas presented interior stimuli may be quite dissimilar to their active memory traces. Thus, the memory-retrieval process will tend to be more efficient for the edge stimuli.) If exemplar j wins the race, then a counter associated with response j is incremented by 1. Counters associated with all the remaining responses are decreased by 1. If the j-counter exceeds its criterion, then the subject identifies the stimulus with response j. Otherwise, a new race (involving the same n traces) is initiated, another exemplar is retrieved, and the process continues. A problem with this model is that, in situations involving a large number of highly confusable stimuli, all counters will move towards negative infinity and no identification response will ever be made. To avoid this problem, I assume that once any counter falls below a given negative criterion, the stimulus associated with that counter no longer participates in the races that contribute to the random walk. Thus, eventually, a given counter will exceed its positive criterion, or will be associated with the only remaining object in the retrieval process.[3]

Figure 5 illustrates in schematic fashion the predictions of the model based on 1000 simulations for each stimulus. Following the design of Karpiuk et al. (this volume) there are stimulus sets of size 4, 6, 8, and 10, with all sets centered around the same values and with the stimuli equally spaced. The parameters were set at default values of $c = 1$, $\alpha = 1$, and positive criteria of +10 and negative criteria of -10 for all counters. As discussed previously, the variances of the memory representations were linearly related to the distance of a stimulus from the edges of the range. Based on preliminary explorations with the model, I used a proportionality constant of .075.

As shown in the figure, the EBRW reproduces the main qualitative phenomena of interest. The overall probabilities of correct identification responses increase as the size of the set decreases, but there is a strong bow effect wherein the stimuli towards the edge of the range are always identified quite accurately. Furthermore, overall response times are fastest for the smaller sets, there is an inverse bow effect in the plot of response time against serial position of each stimulus, and the edge signals are identified particularly rapidly. A limitation of the model is that it predicts virtually identical performance for the edge stimuli across the different set sizes, whereas Karpiuk et al.'s (this volume) data show some variations, especially for set-size 4.

There are various approaches to extending the model to provide a more complete account of unidimensional absolute judgment. In the present simulation, only a single randomly selected exemplar from each memory representation participated in the races on each trial. An alternative idea is that multiple exemplars from each memory representation participate. Furthermore, by allowing memory strengths for these individual exemplars to vary as a function of factors such as recency, the model might be able to account for the robust sequential effects that exist in unidimensional absolute judgment. Also, in the present simulations I assumed that all noise in the stimulus representations was due to memory noise. However, there is

---

[3]For a discussion of alternative approaches to extending the random-walk model to designs involving multiple category responses, see, for example, Palmeri (in press) and Shiffrin (this volume).

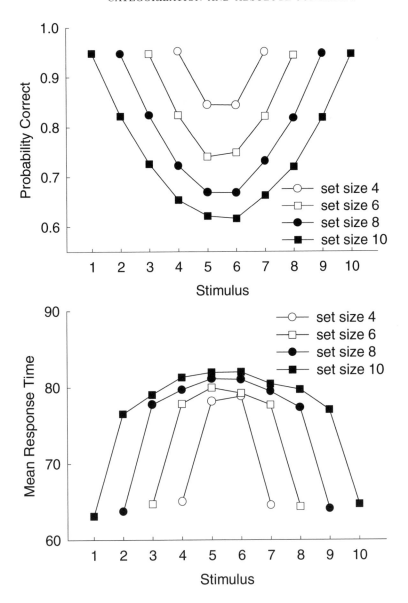

FIGURE 5. Schematic predictions from the EBRW of accuracies and mean response times in absolute identification experiments that vary set size. Response time predictions are in arbitrary units.

evidence that noise in the sensory or perceptual representations also plays an important role in unidimensional absolute judgment (Luce et al., 1976; Luce, 1977b, 1994; Luce & Nosofsky, 1984; Nosofsky, 1983), so the model needs to be extended in this direction as well.

In a nutshell, based on this preliminary investigation, I believe that the core ideas involved in applying the EBRW to unidimensional absolute judgment are quite promising, but a good deal more work is needed in developing a fully specified model. Most critically, a more sophisticated psychophysical theory of stimulus representation needs to be incorporated, as Karpiuk et al. (this volume) have done with their model. Comparisons with alternative modeling approaches, such as the noisy mapping and accumulation process formalized in Lacouture and Marley's (1995) connectionist model of unidimensional absolute judgment, are also needed.

6. Applications the EBRW to Same-Different Category Judgment

In this final section, I consider applications of the EBRW to category same-different judgment on a unidimensional continuum. An example of the paradigm of interest was an experiment conducted by Cartwright (1941), which was quite influential in the development of Link's (1992) wave similarity theory and other response-time theories in which distance-from-boundary is a fundamental construct (e.g., Ashby & Maddox, 1991). In Cartwright's (1941) experiment, subjects first learned to recognize stimuli with angles ranging from 60° to 100° in steps of 10°. Following this study phase, subjects were presented with a series of comparison stimuli ranging from 10° to 160°. Subjects were instructed to judge whether a given pattern was the same as one of those presented during the learning series. Not surprisingly, the general pattern of results was that the highest probabilities of "same" judgments were associated with the original training stimuli. These "same" probabilities decreased precipitously with the distance of the new comparison stimuli from the edges of the category. More important, response times for the new comparison stimuli decreased systematically with their distance from each edge. Finally, response times for the original training stimuli also decreased with their distance from the edges. That is, the fastest "same" response times were associated with those training stimuli in the center of the category range.

Extending the EBRW to this "same-different" category judgment task is straightforward. As before, a stimulus is assumed to act as a retrieval cue for the exemplars stored in memory, and the exemplars race with rates determined by their similarity to the test item. At the same time, background elements race with a fixed rate b independent of the test item that is presented. If one of the training exemplars wins the race, then the random-walk counter is incremented in the "same" direction, whereas if a background element wins the race, the counter is decreased in the "different" direction. The process continues until the counter reaches either the "same" or "different" criterion.

I simulated the EBRW process with arbitrary parameter settings of $c = 1$, $\alpha = 1$, $b = 1$, $+A = 5$, and $-B = -5$. I assumed that the stimuli were equally spaced along the range with adjacent stimuli separated by unit distance. As was the case in simulating the unidimensional absolute judgment data, I assumed that a single randomly selected exemplar from each of the five training stimulus distributions participated in the retrieval process on each trial. The memory variance for all five distributions was held constant at .50. The results, based on 10,000 simulations of

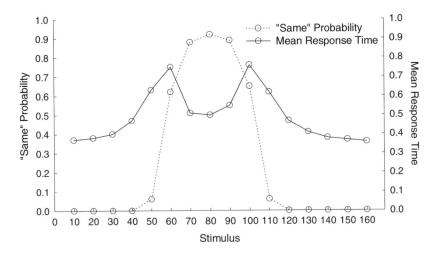

FIGURE 6. Schematic predictions of "same" probabilities and mean response times in the category "same-different" experiment conducted by Cartwright (1941). Response times prediction are in arbitrary units.

each stimulus, are shown in Figure 6. Both the response-probability curve and the mean response-time curve exhibit the central characteristics seen in Cartwright's (1941) data.[4] Response times for the new comparison stimuli decrease with their distance from the edges because the less similar an object is to the original training stimuli, the less likely it is for a training exemplar to be retrieved. Thus, the random walk marches quickly to the "different" response criterion. The training stimuli near the center of the category are most likely to result in fast retrievals of exemplars, so the fastest "same" responses occur for these objects.

7. SUMMARY

In summary, in this chapter I reviewed the exemplar-based random-walk model of speeded multidimensional perceptual classification proposed by Nosofsky and Palmeri (in press). I then tested the model on its ability to fit response-time distributions observed for individual subjects in an extended task of color classification. The model did a reasonably good job of fitting the main body of the distributions, and was competitive with an alternative bilinear decision-bound model in its overall

---

[4]I have not attempted to quantitatively fit the EBRW to Cartwright's (1941) data, as accounting for various idiosyncrasies in each individual subject's data would require the addition of post hoc assumptions. For example, Cartwright's Subject 1 apparently "shifted" the category, producing a much higher "same" probability for the new 110° stimulus than for the original 60° stimulus (see Cartwright, 1941, Figure 2). One way to account for this result in terms of the EBRW would be to introduce the assumption of a systematic distortion in the subjects' memory for the exemplars. Likewise, distance-from- boundary models could introduce the assumption of a systematic shift in the subject's category boundaries. In this chapter I focus instead on the global pattern of results that was common across the individual subjects.

fits. However, the model failed to account for some infrequent response times observed at the extreme tails of the distributions. I also suggested some preliminary extensions of the model designed to handle unidimensional absolute judgment and category same-different judgment. Although still in its early stages of development, the exemplar-based random walk model seems to offer promise as a process-oriented model capable of explaining the time course of decision making in categorization, identification, and same-different judgment.

					Stimulus							
RT Bin	1	2	3	4	5	6	7	8	9	10	11	12
500	0.00	0.00	0.01	0.00	0.00	0.00	0.00	0.00	0.01	0.00	0.00	0.00
600	0.01	0.06	0.02	0.13	0.00	0.01	0.17	0.01	0.02	0.08	0.04	0.03
700	0.35	0.33	0.05	0.50	0.09	0.05	0.61	0.20	0.06	0.55	0.29	0.10
800	0.60	0.58	0.08	0.80	0.31	0.20	70.82	0.36	0.10	0.78	0.45	0.22
900	0.76	0.78	0.22	0.93	0.53	0.39	0.91	0.56	0.11	0.88	0.58	0.33
1000	0.85	0.93	0.35	0.95	0.67	0.54	0.96	0.69	0.21	0.93	0.73	0.44
1100	0.89	0.93	0.47	0.97	0.77	0.66	0.97	0.80	0.32	0.94	0.83	0.50
1200	0.93	0.97	0.64	0.97	0.82	0.79	0.97	0.88	0.42	0.96	0.88	0.59
1300	0.96	0.97	0.73	0.99	0.88	0.85	0.98	0.92	0.55	0.96	0.92	0.65
1400	0.98	0.97	0.79	1.00	0.91	0.87	1.00	0.94	0.63	0.99	0.92	0.70
1500	0.98	0.97	0.84	1.00	0.94	0.92	1.00	0.95	0.71	0.99	0.95	0.78
1600	1.00	0.99	0.89	1.00	0.97	0.93	1.00	0.97	0.78	1.00	0.96	0.84
1700	1.00	1.00	0.95	1.00	0.98	0.95	1.00	0.97	0.83	1.00	0.97	0.85
1800	1.00	1.00	0.96	1.00	0.99	0.96	1.00	0.98	0.87	1.00	0.99	0.89
1900	1.00	1.00	0.96	1.00	0.99	0.97	1.00	0.99	0.91	1.00	0.99	0.91
2000	1.00	1.00	0.97	1.00	0.99	0.97	1.00	0.99	0.95	1.00	0.99	0.92
2100	1.00	1.00	0.98	1.00	0.99	0.99	1.00	1.00	0.96	1.00	0.99	0.96
2200	1.00	1.00	0.98	1.00	0.99	0.99	1.00	1.00	0.96	1.00	0.99	0.98
2300	1.00	1.00	0.99	1.00	1.00	0.99	1.00	1.00	0.96	1.00	0.99	0.98
2400	1.00	1.00	0.99	1.00	1.00	1.00	1.00	1.00	0.98	1.00	0.99	0.98
2500	1.00	1.00	1.00	1.00	1.00	1.00	1.00	1.00	1.00	1.00	1.00	1.00

TABLE 2. Cumulative response-time distributions for subject 1.

Stimulus

RT Bin	1	2	3	4	5	6	7	8	9	10	11	12
400	0.00	0.00	0.00	0.00	0.00	0.00	0.00	0.00	0.00	0.00	0.00	0.00
500	0.00	0.15	0.03	0.22	0.08	0.06	0.33	0.13	0.07	0.36	0.13	0.04
600	0.02	0.68	0.07	0.79	0.38	0.38	0.91	0.58	0.30	0.93	0.82	0.31
700	0.24	0.82	0.14	0.97	0.67	0.79	1.00	0.78	0.53	0.97	0.93	0.50
800	0.50	0.93	0.33	1.00	0.86	0.91	1.00	0.93	0.77	0.98	0.95	0.60
900	0.66	0.95	0.50	1.00	0.93	0.93	1.00	0.97	0.86	0.98	0.98	0.72
1000	0.77	0.98	0.61	1.00	0.97	0.97	1.00	0.99	0.89	0.98	0.98	0.77
1100	0.82	1.00	0.66	1.00	0.98	0.99	1.00	0.99	0.93	0.99	0.99	0.86
1200	0.84	1.00	0.76	1.00	1.00	0.99	1.00	0.99	0.95	1.00	0.99	0.87
1300	0.86	1.00	0.82	1.00	1.00	0.99	1.00	1.00	0.96	1.00	0.99	0.91
1400	0.86	1.00	0.88	1.00	1.00	1.00	1.00	1.00	0.97	1.00	0.99	0.91
1500	0.86	1.00	0.92	1.00	1.00	1.00	1.00	1.00	0.97	1.00	0.99	0.92
1600	0.87	1.00	0.95	1.00	1.00	1.00	1.00	1.00	0.98	1.00	0.99	0.92
1700	0.89	1.00	0.96	1.00	1.00	1.00	1.00	1.00	0.98	1.00	0.99	0.93
1800	0.90	1.00	0.96	1.00	1.00	1.00	1.00	1.00	0.99	1.00	0.99	0.96
1900	0.90	1.00	0.97	1.00	1.00	1.00	1.00	1.00	0.99	1.00	0.99	0.97
2000	0.92	1.00	0.98	1.00	1.00	1.00	1.00	1.00	0.99	1.00	0.99	1.00
2100	0.93	1.00	0.99	1.00	1.00	1.00	1.00	1.00	0.99	1.00	0.99	1.00
2200	0.94	1.00	0.99	1.00	1.00	1.00	1.00	1.00	0.99	1.00	0.99	1.00
2300	0.95	1.00	0.99	1.00	1.00	1.00	1.00	1.00	0.99	1.00	1.00	1.00
2400	1.00	1.00	1.00	1.00	1.00	1.00	1.00	1.00	1.00	1.00	1.00	1.00

TABLE 3. Cumulative response-time distributions for subject 2.

Stimulus

RT Bin	1	2	3	4	5	6	7	8	9	10	11	12
500	0.00	0.00	0.00	0.00	0.00	0.00	0.00	0.00	0.00	0.00	0.00	0.00
600	0.01	0.10	0.01	0.21	0.02	0.08	0.28	0.02	0.08	0.12	0.03	0.00
700	0.27	0.55	0.04	0.82	0.23	0.44	0.88	0.28	0.36	0.71	0.34	0.03
800	0.68	0.82	0.24	0.94	0.47	0.78	0.97	0.55	0.48	0.86	0.63	0.24
900	0.95	0.97	0.54	0.98	0.74	0.88	0.98	0.78	0.63	0.93	0.88	0.54
1000	0.97	0.97	0.70	0.99	0.88	0.93	0.98	0.86	0.83	0.96	0.94	0.67
1100	0.97	1.00	0.79	0.99	0.94	0.97	0.98	0.91	0.91	0.97	0.96	0.79
1200	0.97	1.00	0.85	0.99	0.96	0.98	1.00	0.92	0.96	0.98	0.97	0.86
1300	0.97	1.00	0.89	0.99	0.97	0.98	1.00	0.96	0.97	0.98	1.00	0.90
1400	0.98	1.00	0.92	0.99	0.97	1.00	1.00	0.97	0.98	1.00	1.00	0.95
1500	0.99	1.00	0.95	0.99	0.98	1.00	1.00	0.97	0.98	1.00	1.00	0.96
1600	0.99	1.00	0.96	0.99	0.98	1.00	1.00	0.98	0.98	1.00	1.00	0.97
1700	0.99	1.00	0.99	0.99	0.99	1.00	1.00	0.99	0.98	1.00	1.00	0.98
1800	1.00	1.00	0.99	0.99	0.99	1.00	1.00	0.99	0.99	1.00	1.00	0.99
1900	1.00	1.00	1.00	1.00	0.99	1.00	1.00	0.99	1.00	1.00	1.00	0.99
2000	1.00	1.00	1.00	1.00	0.99	1.00	1.00	0.99	1.00	1.00	1.00	1.00
2100	1.00	1.00	1.00	1.00	0.99	1.00	1.00	0.99	1.00	1.00	1.00	1.00
2200	1.00	1.00	1.00	1.00	1.00	1.00	1.00	1.00	1.00	1.00	1.00	1.00
2300	1.00	1.00	1.00	1.00	1.00	1.00	1.00	1.00	1.00	1.00	1.00	1.00
2400	1.00	1.00	1.00	1.00	1.00	1.00	1.00	1.00	1.00	1.00	1.00	1.00
2500	1.00	1.00	1.00	1.00	1.00	1.00	1.00	1.00	1.00	1.00	1.00	1.00

TABLE 4. Cumulative response-time distributions for subject 3.

CATEGORIZATION AS A SPECIAL CASE OF DECISION-MAKING OR CHOICE

F. GREGORY ASHBY AND PATRICIA M. BERRETTY

University of California, Santa Barbara

ABSTRACT. Categorization is a special kind of choice or decision-making task. Yet the categorization literature seems to contradict the choice and decision-making literature. One literature argues that human categorization is optimal, or nearly optimal, whereas the other literature argues that humans are often irrational, or at least sub-optimal, decision-makers. We show that most popular categorization models are constrained by some properties that are considered empirically invalid in the choice literature (e.g., strong stochastic transitivity, simple scalability, Luce's choice axiom), but only if an assumption is added that the parameter values of each model do not depend on context. We also examine the representativeness heuristic, which is generally regarded as one of the heuristics that frequently lead to irrational decision-making. We argue that representativeness is not generally valid in categorization tasks. We also argue that at least some of the decision-making irrationalities that are attributed to representativeness are consistent with optimal responding when interpreted within a categorization context. These conclusions indicate there is less discrepancy between the categorization and decision-making and choice literatures than at first appears.

1. INTRODUCTION

In a categorization task, subjects divide objects and events in the environment into separate classes or categories. All animals categorize. If they did not, they would be unable to distinguish between nutrients and toxins or between predators and prey. Certainly categorization is among the most important tasks performed by humans.

Categorization can be viewed as a special kind of decision-making or choice task. To categorize a stimulus, the subject must choose among a set of alternative category responses, each of which is correct or incorrect with some (typically unknown) probability. In the natural world, correct category assignments are frequently rewarded (an unfamiliar plant is nutritive) and incorrect assignments are punished (an unfamiliar plant is poisonous). Viewed this way, a categorization task

Key words and phrases. Categorization, choice, decision-making.

Acknowledgments. This research was supported in part by National Science Foundation Grant DBS92-09411. We thank A. A. J. Marley, Robert Nosofsky, and Michael Wich for their helpful comments.

Address for correspondence. F. Gregory Ashby, Department of Psychology, University of California, Santa Barbara, CA 93106. Email: ashby@psych.ucsb.edu

is a sort of gamble. The subject chooses from a set of alternatives, where each choice is associated with some probability of winning and losing.

Given this close correspondence between categorization and decision-making in general, one would expect to find categorization theorists making frequent reference to the decision-making and choice literatures. Yet despite a huge literature on decision-making and choice (e.g., Krantz et al., 1971; Luce, 1959a; Luce & Suppes, 1965; Suppes, Krantz, Luce, & Tversky, 1989) and an equally huge literature on categorization (e.g., Ashby & Maddox, in press; Estes, 1994; Smith & Medin, 1981), we know of no articles that attempt to bridge the two areas (but see Medin, Goldstone, & Markman, 1995).

Surprisingly, an examination of the two literatures leads to very different conclusions about the nature of human decision processes. The decision-making and choice literature is replete with evidence and arguments that humans are often irrational, or at least sub-optimal, decision-makers. For example, the limitations of Luce's (1959a) choice axiom have long been known (e.g., Luce, 1977a) and a number of irrational biases and heuristics have been identified that seem to characterize human decision-making (e.g., Tversky & Kahneman, 1974, 1983). In contrast, the loudest voice in the categorization literature is shouting optimality. Currently, the most popular theory of categorization is exemplar theory, which assumes subjects compute the similarity between the stimulus and each category member (or exemplar) of every relevant category. A response is then selected on the basis of these similarity computations (Brooks, 1978; Estes, 1986, 1994; Hintzman, 1986; Medin & Schaffer, 1978; Nosofsky, 1986). Ashby and Alfonso-Reese (1995) showed that, as usually formulated, exemplar models predict that asymptotic performance is essentially optimal in virtually all tasks and all reasonable parameter settings[1].

How can these two views of human decision processes be reconciled? There are several possibilities. For example, categorization may be a special kind of decision process that is not subject to the limitations of more general kinds of decision-making behaviors. This chapter views categorization as a special case of decision-making and choice. First, we briefly review a number of popular categorization models. Second, we choose some well known results and/or conditions from the decision-making and choice literature and then translate them into the language of the categorization task (e.g., strong stochastic transitivity). The third step is to examine the relation of these results to the current categorization models (i.e., which categorization models are constrained by strong stochastic transitivity?). Finally, we speculate on the empirical validity of these translated conditions (i.e., is human categorization behavior likely to be constrained by strong stochastic transitivity?).

Although the literature relating categorization to decision-making and choice is sparse, a number of elegant papers have studied the relation between identification and choice (e.g., Luce, 1963; Townsend & Landon, 1982; van Santen & Bamber, 1981). Identification is a special case of categorization in which each category contains a single exemplar. As such, many of the results derived by considering identification as a special case of choice are directly relevant to this chapter. In

---

[1]For example, in the case of Nosofsky's (1986) generalized context model, the only requirements are that the subject not completely ignore any relevant stimulus dimension and that overall discriminability gradually increases with experience.

some cases, however, the complications caused by categories that contain multiple exemplars are significant. It is in these latter situations where this chapter will make its greatest contribution.

2. CATEGORIZATION MODELS

This chapter focuses on three different types of categorization models: prototype models, exemplar models, and decision bound models. Each model type will be introduced within the context of a generic categorization experiment. Let $T = \{A_1, A_2, ..., A_m\}$ denote the set of m alternative category responses and let X denote the presented stimulus. On each trial, an exemplar is drawn randomly from one of the categories in the set T. The subject's task is to name the category to which the stimulus X belongs. The performance of the subject is summarized by the conditional response probabilities $P_T(A_j|X)$ where $A_j \in T$.

Prototype models assume the category representation is dominated by the category prototype (Posner & Keele, 1968, 1970; Reed, 1972; Rosch, 1973a, 1977), which is usually defined as some central tendency of the category. A common choice is to define the prototype as the most typical or representative category exemplar, but the prototype is not necessarily even a category member. For this reason, prototype theory is not a special case of exemplar theory. Let $\mathcal{P}(A_j)$ denote the prototype of category A_j. On each trial, the subject is assumed to compute the similarity $\eta_{X,\mathcal{P}(A_j)}$ between the presented stimulus X and the prototype of each relevant category (i.e., for $j = 1, \dots, m$). Two versions of the model are popular. The versions differ on whether response selection is deterministic or probabilistic. In the deterministic version, the subject responds with the category associated with the most similar prototype (Reed, 1972). To account for variability in observed performance, computation of the similarities is assumed to be noisy. As as result, deterministic prototype models assume

$$P_T(A_j|X) = P[\eta_{X,\mathcal{P}(A_j)} + \epsilon_j + \beta_j = \max(\eta_{X,\mathcal{P}(A_1)} + \epsilon_1 + \beta_1, \dots ,$$
$$\eta_{X,\mathcal{P}(A_m)} + \epsilon_m + \beta_m)], \quad (1)$$

where $\epsilon_1, \epsilon_2,...,\epsilon_m$ are all mutually independent and identically distributed random variables with mean 0 and variance σ^2 and β_j is the bias in favor of category A_j. Without loss of generality, one can assume $\sum_{j=1}^m \beta_j = 0$. In contrast, probabilistic prototype models (Nosofsky, 1987) assume a response is selected by guessing with probability proportional to the various similarities; that is, with probability

$$P_T(A_j|X) = \frac{\beta_j \eta_{X,\mathcal{P}(A_j)}}{\beta_1 \eta_{X,\mathcal{P}(A_1)} + \beta_2 \eta_{X,\mathcal{P}(A_2)} + \cdots + \beta_m \eta_{X,\mathcal{P}(A_m)}}. \quad (2)$$

In this model, β_j is again the bias in favor of category A_j, but now without loss of generality, one can assume $\sum_{j=1}^m \beta_j = 1$. It is well known that the probabilistic version is equivalent to a deterministic prototype model in which the noise ϵ_j has a double exponential distribution (e.g., Townsend & Landon, 1982; van Santen & Bamber, 1981; Yellott, 1977).

As mentioned above, exemplar models assume that the subject computes the similarity of the stimulus to each exemplar in every relevant category (e.g., Brooks,

1978; Estes, 1986, 1994; Hintzman, 1986; Medin & Schaffer, 1978; Nosofsky, 1986).
As in the probabilistic prototype model, the subject selects a response by guessing
according to the relative magnitudes of the summed similarities. Let Y denote an
arbitrary exemplar in one of the categories in the set T and let η_{XY} denote the
similarity between the stimulus X and the stored exemplar Y. Then, most popular
exemplar models assume the probabilistic response selection rule of Equation 2.
Therefore,

$$P_T(A_j|X) = \frac{\beta_j \sum_{Y \in A_j} \eta_{XY}}{\beta_1 \sum_{Y \in A_1} \eta_{XY} + \beta_2 \sum_{Y \in A_2} \eta_{XY} + \cdots + \beta_m \sum_{Y \in A_m} \eta_{XY}}. \tag{3}$$

Exemplar models that assume a deterministic response selection rule were proposed
by Nosofsky (1992b) and Ashby and Maddox (1993).

Decision bound models assume the subject constructs a set of decision bounds
that partition the perceptual space into m response regions, one for each relevant
category. On each trial, the subject determines the region in which the stimulus
representation falls and then emits the associated response (Ashby, 1992; Ashby &
Gott, 1988; Ashby & Lee, 1991, 1992; Ashby & Townsend, 1986; Maddox & Ashby,
1993).

To illustrate the model, consider the special case where there are only two
possible category responses, A_1 and A_2. Let the vector $\mathbf{x}$ denote the coordinates of
the stimulus X in the (multidimensional) perceptual space. In most applications
of decision bound theory, because of perceptual noise, $\mathbf{x}$ is assumed to be random
with some multivariate normal distribution. However, in this chapter, we only
consider versions of decision bound theory with no perceptual noise. Let $h(\mathbf{x})$ be
some function of $\mathbf{x}$ with the property that $h(\mathbf{x}) = 0$ for all points on the decision
bound between the two category response regions, $h(\mathbf{x}) > 0$ for all points in the
category A_1 response region, and $h(\mathbf{x}) < 0$ for all points in the category A_2 region.
All decision bound models assume

$$P_T(A_1|X) = P[h(\mathbf{x}) > \epsilon_c|X], \tag{4}$$

where ϵ_c is a random variable representing criterial noise, with mean 0 and variance
σ_c^2. By varying the restrictions on the discriminant function h, different versions
of the model can be created. The *optimal classifier* assumes h is selected so as to
maximize response accuracy (thus, when the category base rates are equal, $h(\mathbf{x}) =$
$\log[f_1(\mathbf{x})/f_2(\mathbf{x})]$, where $f_j(\mathbf{x})$ is the likelihood that $\mathbf{x}$ is a percept resulting from
presentation of an exemplar from category A_j). The *minimum distance classifier*
assumes the subject responds with the category associated with the nearest mean.
This strategy guarantees a linear decision bound that bisects the chord connecting
the two category means. The *general linear classifier* assumes only that h is some
linear function of $\mathbf{x}$ and the *general quadratic classifier* assumes that h is a quadratic
function of $\mathbf{x}$. Clearly, the minimum distance classifier is a special case of the
general linear classifier and the general linear classifier is a special case of the
general quadratic classifier.

Marley (1992) developed a very general model, based on multidimensional Poisson processes, that contains all of the above categorization models as special cases.

Thus, whereas the exemplar and decision bound models are conceptually distinct, mathematically they are related.

3. CHOICE THEORY

This section reviews a number of well known results from choice theory. In the generic choice experiment, a subject is presented on every trial with a set of alternatives, and is asked to choose one on the basis of some criterion (e.g., preference, length, etc.). Let $W = \{a_1, a_2, \ldots, a_m\}$ denote the set of choice alternatives. The subject's behavior is summarized by the choice probabilities $P_W(a_j)$, for all $a_j \in W$. A special case of this experiment requires the subject to make paired comparisons. In this paradigm, two alternatives are selected from W on each trial and the subject is required to choose between these two alternatives. Let $P(a_i, a_j)$ denote the probability that the subject chooses alternative a_i when given a choice between a_i and a_j.

One popular question that arises in paired comparison experiments is whether choice is transitive. When behavior is described by choice probabilities, a number of different forms of transitivity can be defined. The most important of these are defined in the following way.

Definition 1. Suppose that $P(a_i, a_j) \geq \frac{1}{2}$ and $P(a_j, a_k) \geq \frac{1}{2}$ (for any $a_i, a_j, a_k \in W$). Then
  i) *weak stochastic transitivity* holds if $P(a_i, a_k) \geq \frac{1}{2}$.
  ii) *moderate stochastic transitivity* holds if $P(a_i, a_k) \geq \min[P(a_i, a_j), P(a_j, a_k)]$.
  iii) *strong stochastic transitivity* holds if $P(a_i, a_k) \geq \max[P(a_i, a_j), P(a_j, a_k)]$.

A large class of models of choice, called *constant utility models*, assume each choice alternative is associated with a constant utility or scale-value, and that the choice probabilities are some function of these utilities. Many constant utility models satisfy a property called *simple scalability*, which holds if there exists some real-valued function ϕ on W, and functions G^j, $j = 1, \ldots, m$, that are strictly increasing in the jth argument and strictly decreasing in the others, such that the predicted choice probabilities can be written in the form (Krantz, 1964; Suppes et al., 1989; Tversky, 1972b)

$$P_W(a_j) = G_W^j[\phi(a_1), \phi(a_2), \ldots, \phi(a_m)]. \tag{5}$$

Simple scalability, which embodies a form of independence, has a number of strong consequences. For example, suppose alternative a_k is replaced by some new alternative $a_{k'}$ with the same utility [i.e., so that $\phi(a_k) = \phi(a_{k'})$]. Call the new choice set W'. Then it is easy to see, for example, that according to simple scalability $P_W(a_j) = P_{W'}(a_j)$. In other words, there can be no unique interaction effect between a_j and a_k.

Tversky and Russo (1969) showed that strong stochastic transitivity is equivalent to the binary form of simple scalability (i.e., where $W = \{a_1, a_2\}$). It is well known that human choice does not always satisfy these conditions. In particular, strong stochastic transitivity, and therefore also simple scalability, will often be violated in a choice experiment in which two of the alternatives are similar and a third is dissimilar to the first two (Becker, DeGroot, & Marschak, 1963; Debreu,

1960), and especially if one of the two similar alternatives dominates the other along some attractive dimension (Luce & Suppes, 1965; Tversky & Russo, 1969). For example, a well known counterexample to strong stochastic transitivity involves a boy choosing a birthday present from among a pony, a bike, and a second bike that is identical to the first except that it also has a shiny new bell. It is easy to imagine that the boy is indifferent between the pony and the first bike, and that when given a choice between the two bikes, he always chooses the one with the extra bell. Strong stochastic transitivity predicts that when given a choice between the pony and the bike with the bell, the boy should always choose the bike. However, if the boy is indifferent between the first bike and the pony, then adding a bell to the bike should not greatly affect his choice. Thus, in contradiction to strong stochastic transitivity, we expect $\frac{1}{2} \leq P(bike + bell, pony) < 1$.

A well known special case of simple scalability occurs in the *strict utility model* (Luce, 1959a), which assumes that

$$P_W(a_j) = \frac{\phi(a_j)}{\phi(a_1) + \phi(a_2) + \cdots + \phi(a_m)}. \tag{6}$$

Because Equation 6 is a special case of simple scalability, the strict utility model implies strong stochastic transitivity but strong stochastic transitivity does not imply the paired comparison version of the strict utility model.

Luce (1959a) provided an axiomatic justification of the strict utility model. Let $R \subseteq S \subseteq W$ and let $P_W(S) = \sum_{a_s \in S} P_W(a_s)$ denote the probability that the subject chooses an element in the set S when given a choice among all alternatives in the set W. Suppose $P_W(a_j) \neq 0, 1$ for all $a_j \in W$. Luce's (1959a) well known choice axiom holds if and only if

$$P_W(R) = P_W(S)P_S(R). \tag{7}$$

Among many other important results, Luce (1959a) showed that if all choice probabilities are imperfect (i.e., if $P_W(a_j) \neq 0, 1$ for all $a_j \in W$) then the choice axiom is equivalent to the strict utility model. The choice axiom is often interpreted as an expression of rationality in human choice, because if the choice probabilities in Equation 7 are interpreted as conditional probabilities (which, of course, is not necessary), then Equation 7 follows immediately from Bayes Theorem.

Note that if simple scalability holds, the function ϕ does not depend on which elements are in the choice set W. Thus, the scale value, or utility, of alternative a_j, namely $\phi(a_j)$, is the same for any experiment in which a_j is a member of the choice set (i.e., $a_j \in W$). In fact, Luce (1963) noted that the strict utility model satisfies the choice axiom if and only if ϕ satisfies this context insensitive property. Equation 5 will always fit the data from any single choice experiment perfectly (e.g., Marley & Colonius, 1992), but to fit data from several different experiments simultaneously may require that the $\phi(a_j)$ change when the alternatives in the choice set change. This context sensitive version of simple scalability assumes

$$P_W(a_j) = G_W^j[\phi_W(a_1), \phi_W(a_2), ..., \phi_W(a_m)].$$

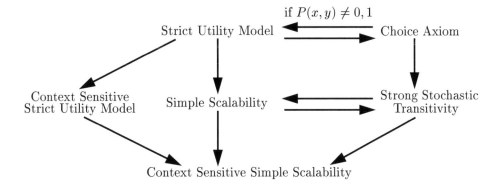

FIGURE 1. Relations between various choice conditions and models. Arrows point in the direction of the implied conditions or models.

Similarly, the context sensitive strict utility model is in the form

$$P_W(a_j) = \frac{\phi_W(a_j)}{\phi_W(a_1) + \phi_W(a_2) + \cdots + \phi_W(a_m)}. \tag{8}$$

It is straightforward to show that the context sensitive version of simple scalability is not constrained by strong stochastic transitivity, nor is the context sensitive strict utility model. In fact, without additional constraints on ϕ_W, either of these models can never be falsified. Nevertheless, we introduce them here because they help clarify the relations between models of choice and categorization. The relations between the various conditions and models introduced in this section are illustrated in Figure 3.

4. CATEGORIZATION AS A CHOICE EXPERIMENT

In the Introduction, we argued that categorization is a special kind of choice experiment. If so, then two questions become immediately important: 1) do any of the current categorization models assume simple scalability (or equivalently, strong stochastic transitivity)? and 2) is human categorization data constrained by simple scalability? Before answering either question, we must translate simple scalability and the other choice theory conditions into the language of categorization.

In a categorization experiment, the set of choice alternatives is the set of alternative category responses (i.e., so that the set T equals the set W). However, the categorization analogue of the choice probability, $P_W(a_j)$, is stimulus dependent. Specifically, a categorization experiment where the subject must choose a response on each trial from the set of alternative categories T, is equivalent to a set of separate choice experiments – one for each stimulus in the categorization experiment. Each stimulus the subject must categorize provides the context for the choice task, because as the stimulus changes, the choice (i.e., categorization) response probabilities change. Thus, the set of conditional response probabilities $P_T(A_j|X)$ for

Term	Choice Experiment	Categorization Experiment
Choice Set	W	T
Choice Probability: Single Item	$P_W(a_i)$	$P_T(A_i\|X)$
Choice Probability: Set	$P_W(S) = \sum_{a_s \in S} P_W(a_s)$	$P_T(S\|X) = \sum_{A_s \in S} P_T(A_s\|X)$
Paired Comparison Probability	$P(a_i, a_j)$	$P_{\{A_i,A_j\|T\}}(A_i\|X)$

TABLE 1. Notation used in this chapter.

$j = 1, 2, \ldots, m$ define a complete set of choice probabilities for each fixed stimulus X.

The definition of the various forms of stochastic transitivity requires comparing performance across various paired comparison conditions in which the choice set is systematically varied. Such a manipulation is not typically encountered in the categorization literature. Even so, it is straightforward to design a categorization experiment in which stochastic transitivity can be tested. The complete set of alternative category responses is the set $T = \{A_1, A_2, \ldots, A_m\}$. On each trial, the experimenter selects two category labels at random from the set T. Call these A_i and A_j. The subject is then informed to respond A_i or A_j on that trial, even if he or she believes the stimulus belongs to some other category. Given this design, the analogue to the choice probability $P(a_i, a_j)$ is $P_{\{A_i,A_j\|T\}}(A_i\|X)$. The dependence on T allows for the possibility that the probability the subject chooses category A_i over category A_j depends on the other alternatives in the choice set T. The notation used to describe results from choice experiments and their categorization analogues is summarized in Table 1.

Using these interpretations of the choice probabilities, it is simple to define the various forms of stochastic transitivity for categorization. Simple scalability becomes

$$P_T(A_j|X) = G^j_{T,X}[\phi_X(A_1), \phi_X(A_2), ..., \phi_X(A_m)] \qquad (9)$$

where ϕ_X is a real-valued function depending on X, whose arguments are all the alternative category responses A_i, $i = 1, \ldots, m$. The function G^j, which is increasing in the first argument and decreasing in the others, may depend on both T and

X. The categorization version of the strict utility model follows directly from the categorization form of simple scalability.

$$P_T(A_j|X) = \frac{\phi_X(A_j)}{\phi_X(A_1) + \phi_X(A_2) + \cdots + \phi_X(A_m)}. \tag{10}$$

Luce's (1959a) choice axiom also has a straightforward categorization interpretation. It requires comparing categorization response probabilities to a fixed stimulus (i.e., stimulus X) across two separate experiments. The experiments differ only in the set of possible response alternatives. In one experiment, the subject may respond with any category label in the set T, whereas in the other experiment, choices are restricted to the set $S \subseteq T$. The choice axiom holds if and only if

$$P_T(R|X) = P_T(S|X)P_S(R|X). \tag{11}$$

As in the general case, if all categorization response probabilities are imperfect (i.e., $P_T(A_j|X) \neq 0, 1$, for all $A_j \in T$), then Equations 10 and 11 are equivalent.

As with the traditional versions of simple scalability and the strict utility model, the categorization analogues are context insensitive. Context sensitive versions are created by replacing $\phi_X(A_j)$ with $\phi_{X,T}(A_j)$ for each $A_j \in T$. The distinction between context insensitive and sensitive models becomes important when we ask which categorization models are constrained by the various choice theory conditions. Current categorization models make assumptions about the events that occur within a single categorization experiment. They also define parameters that they assume are related to certain special aspects of the experiment (e.g., the stimuli, the category responses, the experimenter's instructions to the subject). As a result, if one of these special aspects changes, then the models often predict systematic changes in their analogous parameter. Even so, if some other aspect of the experiment changes, current categorization models have little or nothing to say about how, or if, their parameters should change.

For example, consider Nosofsky's (1986) *generalized context model* (GCM), which is an exemplar model in which the conditional response probabilities are specified by Equation 3 and similarity is defined as a decreasing function (either exponential or Gaussian) of the weighted distance (either Euclidean or city-block) between point representations of the stimuli. The GCM predicts that an attention weight parameter should be zero only in experiments where the associated stimulus dimension is irrelevant. Thus, the model predicts systematic changes in its attention weight parameters when switching from an experiment where all stimulus dimensions are relevant to an experiment where only one dimension is relevant (or vice versa). Even so, the GCM makes no specific predictions about how the attention weights should change if all stimulus dimensions are relevant in both experiments. It also says nothing about how its overall discriminability parameter or its response bias parameters will change across any pair of experiments. The same is true of the background noise parameter, the memory decay parameter, and the response consistency parameter, which were added to later versions of the model (Ashby & Maddox, 1993; Nosofsky et al., 1992).

To formalize this discussion, consider a model that assigns one or more free parameters to describe the psychological representation of the exemplars of category

A_j. Suppose $A_j \in S \subset T$ and that the experiment is run with S as the choice set. Should the parameters describing the exemplars of category A_j change if the experiment is rerun with T as the choice set? Following Townsend and Landon (1982), we call models in which the relevant parameters are invariant across changes in the choice set, *strong categorization models*, and models in which at least some of the relevant parameters change when the choice set changes, *weak categorization models*.

Although the categorization versions of the various choice theory conditions and models are slightly more complex than the usual definitions, it is straightforward to show that the relations among the categorization analogues are exactly the same as the relations illustrated in Figure 3. We are now ready for our first major result.

Theorem 1. *The strong versions of the probabilistic exemplar model, the probabilistic prototype model, the deterministic exemplar model, the deterministic prototype model, the minimum distance decision bound model, and the optimal decision bound model all satisfy simple scalability. The strong versions of the general linear classifier and the general quadratic classifier (from decision bound theory) are not constrained by simple scalability. In fact, neither model is even constrained by weak stochastic transitivity.*

Proof. Throughout the proof, when referring to a particular categorization model, we mean the strong version of that model. It is obvious from Equations 2 and 3 that the probabilistic prototype and exemplar models, satisfy simple scalability. To show that the other models satisfy simple scalability, we use a result due to Tversky (1972b). Before stating the result, a definition is needed. Let T and R denote sets of alternative categorization responses. Then a set of categorization probabilities satisfies *order-independence* if and only if for all $A_i, A_j \in T - R$ and $A_k \in R$

$$P_T(A_i|X) \geq P_T(A_j|X) \text{ if and only if } P_{R \cup \{A_i\}}(A_k|X) \leq P_{R \cup \{A_j\}}(A_k|X). \quad (12)$$

Tversky (1972b) showed that simple scalability is satisfied if and only if order-independence holds. As a consequence, we show that the deterministic exemplar and prototype models and the minimum distance and optimal decision bound models satisfy simple scalability by showing that they satisfy order-independence. To begin, note that all four models can be written in the form

$$P_T(A_j|X) = P\left\{g_j(X) + \epsilon_j = \max_{A_i \in T}[g_i(X) + \epsilon_i]\right\} \quad (13)$$

for some function $g_j(X)$ and some set of mutually independent and identically distributed random variables ϵ_j (for all $A_i \in T$). In the deterministic prototype model $g_j(X) = \eta_{X, \mathcal{P}(A_j)}$, in the deterministic exemplar model $g_j(X) = \sum_{Y \in A_j} \eta_{XY}$, in the optimal decision bound model $g_j(X) = \log[f_j(\mathbf{x})]$, and in the minimum distance decision bound model $g_j(X) = -d_{XJ}$, where d_{XJ} is the distance between the psychological representation of stimulus X and the mean of category A_j.

We now show that for any model satisfying Equation 13, $P_T(A_i|X) \geq P_T(A_j|X)$ if and only if $P_{R \cup \{A_i\}}(A_k|X) \leq P_{R \cup \{A_j\}}(A_k|X)$. To begin, note that for any model of the Equation 13 type, $P_T(A_i|X) \geq P_T(A_j|X)$ if and only if $g_i(X) \geq g_j(X)$. This latter inequality holds if and only if

$$P\left[g_k(X) + \epsilon_k > g_i(X) + \epsilon_i\right] \leq P\left[g_k(X) + \epsilon_k > g_j(X) + \epsilon_j\right]. \tag{14}$$

Equation 14 is equivalent to

$$P\left\{g_k(X) + \epsilon_k = \max\left[g_k(X) + \epsilon_k, g_i(X) + \epsilon_i\right]\right\}$$
$$\leq P\left\{g_k(X) + \epsilon_k = \max\left[g_k(X) + \epsilon_k, g_j(X) + \epsilon_j\right]\right\},$$

which holds if and only if

$$P\left\{g_k(X) + \epsilon_k = \max_{A_q \in R \cup \{A_i\}}\left[g_q(X) + \epsilon_q\right]\right\}$$
$$\leq P\left\{g_k(X) + \epsilon_k = \max_{A_q \in R \cup \{A_j\}}\left[g_q(X) + \epsilon_q\right]\right\},$$

or equivalently if and only if

$$P_{R \cup \{A_i\}}(A_k|X) \leq P_{R \cup \{A_j\}}(A_k|X).$$

Therefore, any model of the Equation 13 type satisfies order-independence.

Finally, we consider the general linear and general quadratic decision bound models. In both of these models, no constraints are placed on the location of any decision bounds, only on their form. As a consequence, the location of the bound in experimental conditions with categories $\{A_i, A_j\}$ and categories $\{A_j, A_k\}$, place no restrictions on the location of the bound in the condition with categories $\{A_i, A_k\}$. This is true even if the set of all bounds used in the categorization analogue of the paired comparison experiment is the same as the bounds used in a categorization experiment using the full choice set T. Because of this, strong or even weak stochastic transitivity need not hold. □

This result immediately raises two questions. First, is human categorization behavior likely to be constrained by simple scalability? Second, how serious is the restriction that only *strong* versions of the exemplar, prototype, minimum distance, and optimal models satisfy simple scalability? We consider each question in turn.

The well known counterexamples to the traditional form of simple scalability are readily adapted to the categorization arena. For example, consider an experiment where subjects are asked to taste a food dish and then assign it to one of two categories. Suppose the food (i.e., the stimulus X) is sweet and sour chicken and the choice set T contains the three categories: A_1 – moderately sour chicken dishes, A_2 – moderately sweet chicken dishes, and A_3 – sweet chicken dishes. It is easy to imagine that subjects would be indifferent between category responses A_1 and A_2 (so that $P_{\{A_1, A_2|T\}}(A_1|X) = \frac{1}{2}$) but that, when forced to choose between categories A_2 and A_3, they always choose A_2 (so that $P_{\{A_2, A_3|T\}}(A_2|X) = 1$). According to strong stochastic transitivity, and therefore also simple scalability, when forced to choose between categories A_1 and A_3, subjects should now always choose category A_1. It seems much more likely, however, that $\frac{1}{2} < P_{\{A_1, A_3|T\}}(A_1|X) < 1$, in violation of simple scalability. Thus, simple scalability seems as empirically dubious for categorization as for other forms of choice.

Simple scalability is implied by the strict utility model and Luce's choice axiom and the binary form of simple scalability is equivalent to strong stochastic transitivity. To test Luce's choice axiom, two separate experiments must be run – one with S as the choice set and one with T (where $S \subseteq T$) as the choice set. In contrast, strong stochastic transitivity can be tested with data from a single experiment. On each trial, the subject chooses between two category responses that are selected randomly from the set T. Despite these differences in experimental design, however, in both cases data are compared across conditions in which the effective choice set differs. This makes it difficult to determine why simple scalability failed. There are two important possibilities. First, it could be that the form of Equation 9 is in error. For example, G^j might not be strictly increasing in its jth argument and strictly decreasing in its others, or ϕ may depend simultaneously on the exemplars from more than one category. The second possibility is that the form of Equation 9 is correct, but ϕ depends on T as well as X, or in other words that there are context effects on ϕ. Failures of simple scalability of the first type would falsify many current categorization models, or at least require them to be revised substantially, whereas failures of the second type cause hardly a concern.

Theorem 1 states that many strong categorization models can be written in the Equation 9 form. Specifically, the strong models assume that response probabilities from any particular categorization experiment can be written in the Equation 9 form. Thus, if the form of 9 is incorrect, the models are incorrect. On the other hand, if the form of 9 is correct, but ϕ depends on T as well as X, the models could, potentially, provide excellent fits to any single set of categorization data. Therefore, since the models have little or nothing to say about the effects on the previously existing parameters of adding new categories, this type of failure of simple scalability would not trouble most categorization theorists.

In fact, as mentioned earlier, virtually all categorization models have a structure that makes it easy to account for certain types of context effects. For example, the generalized context model (an exemplar model proposed by Nosofsky, 1986) assumes a multidimensional scaling psychological representation of the stimuli and category exemplars. Attention weights separately stretch or shrink each psychological dimension (as in the INDSCAL model of Carroll & Chang, 1970) when the stimulus set or the form of the contrasting categories is changed. For example, in the hypothetical counterexample described above, subjects might allocate equal amounts of attention to sweet and sour dimensions, except when deciding between categories A_2 (moderately sweet chicken dishes) and A_3 (sweet chicken dishes), in which case all attention is allocated to the sweet dimension. Focusing attention on sweetness magnifies the difference between categories A_2 and A_3, and thereby allows the model to predict $P_{\{A_2, A_3 | T\}}(A_2 | X) = 1$.

Therefore, many categorization theorists (e.g., most exemplar theorists) would argue that the form of Equation 9 is correct and that violations of simple scalability are due to context effects[2] on ϕ. If so, then it is reasonable to argue that such violations do not signal a suboptimality or an irrationality. In fact, weak exemplar

---

[2]For example, in Nosofsky's (1984) Ph.D. dissertation, he argued that Luce's (1959a) choice axiom would fail in categorization experiments because of systematic changes in the similarity parameters across experimental conditions.

models, which violate simple scalability but which can be written in the form of Equation 9 for any single experiment, virtually always predict optimal performance (Ashby & Alfonso-Reese, 1995).

Figure 3 illustrates that the strict utility model and Luce's choice axiom are stronger than simple scalability and strong stochastic transitivity. Thus, for example, a categorization model may satisfy simple scalability but not the choice axiom. It is of interest, then, to ask whether any of the categorization models satisfying simple scalability also satisfy the choice axiom. Theorem 2 addresses this issue.

Theorem 2. *The strong versions of the probabilistic exemplar model and the probabilistic prototype model satisfy Luce's (1959a) choice axiom. The deterministic prototype and exemplar models and all decision bound models satisfy Luce's choice axiom if and only if the distribution of the independent and identically distributed noise terms is double exponential.*

Proof. The first part of the theorem is obvious since Equations 2 and 3 are clearly special cases of the strict utility model. The general linear and general quadratic decision bound models do not satisfy the choice axiom since they do not satisfy simple scalability. To investigate the conditions under which the deterministic prototype and exemplar models, and the optimal decision bound and minimum distance decision bound models satisfy the choice axiom, recall that all four models can be written in the form of Equation 13. Equation 13 is a special case of Thurstone's (1927) law of comparative judgment, and it is well known that Thurstone's model is equivalent to the strict utility model if and only if the distribution of each ϵ_i is double exponential (assuming that there are more than two alternative categories; e.g., Yellott, 1977). $\square$

The categorization models considered here all assume that in the categorization analogue of the paired comparison experiment the subject ignores all elements in the choice set T except the two categories relevant to that trial. Other models are possible. For example, one prominent alternative[3] is that the subject chooses response A_1 on trials when the choice set is $\{A_1, A_2|T\}$ with probability

$$P_{\{A_1, A_2|T\}}(A_1|X) = \frac{P_T(A_1|X)}{P_T(A_1|X) + P_T(A_2|X)}. \tag{15}$$

Now, since $P_{\{A_1, A_2|T\}}(A_1|X) + P_{\{A_1, A_2|T\}}(A_2|X) = 1$, this model assumes

$$\frac{P_{\{A_1, A_2|T\}}(A_1|X)}{P_{\{A_1, A_2|T\}}(A_1|X) + P_{\{A_1, A_2|T\}}(A_2|X)} = \frac{P_T(A_1|X)}{P_T(A_1|X) + P_T(A_2|X)},$$

or equivalently,

$$\frac{P_{\{A_1, A_2|T\}}(A_1|X)}{P_{\{A_1, A_2|T\}}(A_2|X)} = \frac{P_T(A_1|X)}{P_T(A_2|X)}. \tag{16}$$

In other words, the relative preference for a category A_1 response over a category A_2 response is the same whether the choice set is $\{A_1, A_2\}$ or T. Equation 16 is known as the constant ratio rule (Clarke, 1957; Townsend & Landon, 1982) and it is well known to be equivalent to Luce's (1959a) choice axiom when $P_{\{A_i, A_j|T\}}(A_i|X) \neq$

---

[3]We thank A. A. J. Marley for suggesting this interesting alternative.

$0, 1$, for all $A_i, A_j \in T$ (Luce, 1959a). Thus, for example, the strong versions of the probabilistic prototype and exemplar models satisfy Equation 15, even though they assume the subject ignores all elements in the choice set T except the two categories relevant on that trial.

Suppose a categorization model that satisfies Luce's (1959a) choice axiom fails to account for data collected across a number of different categorization experiments. There are two prominent possibilities. The first is that some version of the strict utility model holds for each separate experiment but the scale values $\phi_X(A_j)$ change from one experiment to the next. The second possibility is that the strict utility model is of the wrong functional form, and so it fails on the data from each separate experiment. Ideally, one would like a method for testing between these two possibilities (i.e., whether violations are due to context effects or to the fact that Equation 10 is of the wrong functional form). Such a test exists for traditional choice experiments. Suppose, that for all a_i, a_j, and $a_k \in W$,

$$P(a_i, a_j)P(a_j, a_k)P(a_k, a_i) = P(a_k, a_j)P(a_j, a_i)P(a_i, a_k) \qquad (17)$$

This condition, known as the product rule, holds if and only if the strict utility model holds (e.g., Luce & Suppes, 1965). A similar condition was developed for the identification task, which is a special case of categorization in which each stimulus forms its own category (so the subject's task is to identify the stimulus uniquely). When generalized to the identification task, the product rule becomes

$$P(a_i|a_j)P(a_j|a_k)P(a_k|a_i) = P(a_i|a_k)P(a_k|a_j)P(a_j|a_i). \qquad (18)$$

This version of the product rule holds if and only if some form of the context sensitive strict utility model holds for each separate identification experiment (Townsend & Landon, 1982). Thus, the identification version of the product rule tests whether the form of the strict utility model (i.e., Equation 10) is correct, regardless of whether there are context effects on ϕ.

Thus, to decide why the strict utility model fails in categorization tasks, one could check the validity of a categorization version of the product rule. Unfortunately, constructing such a version is problematic. In Equation 18, note that each stimulus also appears as a response on the same side of the equality. This symmetrical structure is the defining aspect of the product rule. In categorization experiments, however, a stimulus is not an admissible response (i.e., $X \notin T$) and a response is not an admissible stimulus (i.e., category A_j is not a viable stimulus). Thus, the symmetrical structure of Equation 17 is impossible to duplicate with categorization data. As such, we know of no way to test the weak version of the strict utility model on categorization data.

In summary, like the early models of human choice, the strong (i.e., parameter invariant) versions of many of the current categorization models satisfy simple scalability, and therefore, are constrained by strong stochastic transitivity. Although we know of no empirical tests of strong stochastic transitivity on categorization data, it seems likely that the well known counterexamples in the choice literature will generalize to a categorization setting. If so, then the strong versions of most current categorization models are not universally applicable. It is impossible to determine, at this time, whether the failure of these models is due to the strong assumption of parameter invariance (when new categories are added) or to some fundamental flaw in the structure of the models.

5. CATEGORIZATION AND THE MISUSE OF HEURISTICS IN DECISION-MAKING

Although elegant generalizations of decision-making models continue to appear (e.g., Luce & Fishburn, 1991, 1995; Luce & Weber, 1986; Mellers, Ordóñez, & Birnbaum, 1992a), much of the recent focus of the decision-making literature is on irrationality. Tversky and Kahneman (Tversky & Kahneman, 1971, 1974; Kahneman & Tversky, 1972, 1973) proposed that people simplify complex decision-making problems via a limited number of heuristic principles. In most cases, these heuristics work well, but in certain predictable cases, they fail. The study of these heuristics remains popular in the decision-making literature (Carlson, 1990; Wanke, Schwartz, & Bless, 1995; Wallsten, 1983). The three most heavily studied heuristics are availability, anchoring and adjustment, and representativeness.

When applied to categorization, the availability heuristic states that people estimate the base-rate of a category according to how easy it is to recall or imagine an exemplar from that category. The anchoring and adjustment heuristic states that base-rate estimates are made by adjusting an initial estimate, and that usually these adjustments are insufficient, so the final estimate is biased in the direction of the initial estimate. The sensitivity of subjects to category base-rates is a topic of current heated interest in the categorization literature (e.g., Estes, Campbell, Hatsopoulos, & Hurwitz, 1989; Gluck & Bower, 1988; Maddox, 1995; Medin & Edelson, 1988; Nosofsky et al., 1992).

To date, this work has proceeded independently of research on base-rate sensitivity in more general decision-making settings. Our understanding of how subjects deal with base-rate differences in categorization tasks might be improved by a careful study of the decision-making literature on the availability and anchoring and adjustment heuristics.

When applied to categorization, the representativeness heuristic states that a stimulus is categorized by evaluating the degree to which it is representative of, or similar to, each alternative category. Similarity and representativeness are not formally defined, so interpreting the representativeness heuristic from a categorization perspective requires caution. Nevertheless, it appears that this heuristic is essentially equivalent to a minimum distance or prototype rule of categorization. For example, after describing a hypothetical person named Steve, Tversky and Kahneman (1974) say that "In the representativeness heuristic, the probability that Steve is a librarian, for example, is assessed by the degree to which he is representative of, or similar to, the stereotype of a librarian" (*p. 1124*). If the stereotype is interpreted as the category prototype, then this is exactly the categorization rule postulated by prototype theory (or equivalently, the minimum distance classifier of decision bound theory).

Many studies have shown convincingly that humans are not constrained to use prototype or minimum distance rules in categorization (e.g., Ashby & Gott, 1988; Ashby & Maddox, 1990, 1992; Busemeyer, Dewey, & Medin, 1984; Maddox

& Ashby, 1993; Medin & Schaffer, 1978; Medin & Schwanenflugel, 1981; Nosofsky, 1987, 1992b; Shin & Nosofsky, 1992). Some of these studies compared prototype models with exemplar models, other compared prototype models with decision bound models. In every case, the prototype models were rejected in favor of either an exemplar or decision bound model. Thus, the representativeness heuristic does not seem to hold universally for all human decision processes.

One possibility is that the representativeness heuristic holds only when the decision problem exceeds a certain minimum level of complexity. The categorization studies that showed humans do not always use the representativeness heuristic mostly used stimuli that varied on only a few dimensions and only two or three contrasting categories. Perhaps as the number of stimulus dimensions or alternative categories increases, subjects must resort to simpler strategies, such as the representativeness heuristic. Some evidence for this comes from a study by Lee and Ashby (1995), in which subjects were presented with one of nine (two dimensional) stimuli on each trial, and asked to identify the stimulus uniquely. The resulting data were best accounted for by a suboptimal decision bound model that assumed a minimum distance or prototype decision rule. In particular, this prototype model fit better than other models that assumed a more sophisticated decision process (including a model that assumed arbitrary quadratic bounds).

It is also possible that results appearing irrational in a general decision-making context are not irrational in a categorization setting. For example, Kahneman and Tversky (1973) claim that "a major determinant of representativeness ... is the consistency, or coherence, of the input" (p. 249), and that unduly attending to input consistency can lead to certain consistent forms of irrationality. Such errors are said to be due to an 'illusion of validity.' As a demonstration, Kahneman and Tversky (1973) asked subjects to predict the grade point average (GPA) of a hypothetical student from his or her scores on two separate, but equally valid, aptitude tests. Next, subjects were asked to rate the confidence in their predictions. There were two conditions. In one, the scores were uncorrelated and in the other, they were positively correlated. Subjects were told the true correlation in both conditions. As Kahneman and Tversky predicted, subjects were more confident in their predictions when the scores were correlated.

Kahneman and Tversky (1973) interpreted these results as a form of irrationality because "a higher predictive accuracy can be achieved with the uncorrelated than with the correlated pair of tests" (p. 249). To see this claim, let X_1 and X_2 denote the scores on the two aptitude tests, and let X_0 denote the GPA. Since the two aptitude tests are equally valid, they should have the same correlation with GPA. Call this correlation ρ, and denote the correlation between X_1 and X_2 by ρ_{12}. Then it can be shown that the squared multiple correlation, $\rho_{0\cdot12}^2$ between X_0 and the best linear combination of X_1 and X_2 is (e.g., Lord & Novick, 1968)

$$\rho_{0\cdot12}^2 = \frac{2\rho^2(1-\rho_{12})}{1-\rho_{12}^2}. \tag{19}$$

If ρ is held constant, then Equation 19 decreases monotonically with ρ_{12}. Thus, the squared multiple correlation is higher when the scores on the two aptitude tests are uncorrelated than when they are positively correlated (although the correlation is

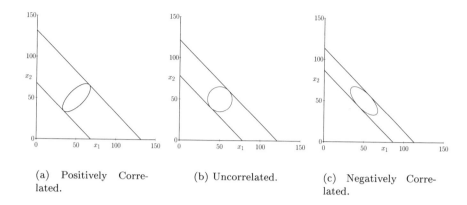

(a) Positively Corre-
lated.

(b) Uncorrelated.

(c) Negatively Corre-
lated.

FIGURE 2. Graphical illustration of Kahneman and Tversky's
(1973) "illusion of validity" task. x_1 and x_2 represent scores on the
aptitude tests. The scores are positively correlated, uncorrelated,
and negatively correlated in parts (a), (b) and (c), respectively.
The diagonal lines indicate the range of GPA's that may be predicted.

highest when ρ_{12} is negative). A graphical illustration of this fact is shown in Figure
2. Because the two aptitude tests are equally valid, the linear combination of X_1
and X_2 that best predicts GPA should weight X_1 and X_2 equally. As a consequence,
every set of X_1 and X_2 scores for which $X_1 + X_2$ is constant should yield the same
predicted GPA. Test scores yielding a constant sum (i.e., $X_1 + X_2 = c$, for some
constant c) are represented in Figure 2 by the diagonal lines. It is easy to see that
the variability in this sum is greatest when the test scores are positively correlated
and least when they are negatively correlated.

Suppose now that this same problem was redesigned as a categorization task.
For example, subjects might be told that there are two populations of students –
students who are members of a national honor society and students who are not. On
each trial, subjects will again be shown a single pair of scores from a hypothetical
student on the two aptitude tests. However, rather than predict GPA, subjects
will now be asked to determine whether the student was a member of the honor
society (e.g., by responding YES or NO). After responding, subjects will rate the
confidence of their categorization judgment. There will again be two conditions
– one in which the aptitude scores are uncorrelated and one in which they are
positively correlated. The mean scores from each population will be adjusted so
that optimal accuracy in the two conditions is equal.

A reasonable model of this task is shown in Figure 3. Now there are two populations of test scores. The students in the national honor society should have a
higher mean on both aptitude tests, since the tests are assumed to be equally valid
predictors of GPA, and since admission into honor societies is usually determined
by GPA. The decision bound for the optimal classifier in this task is shown as the

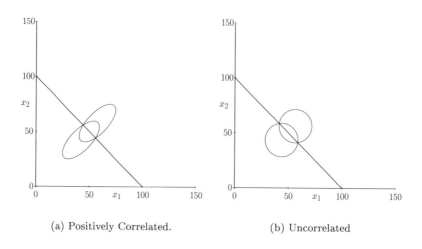

(a) Positively Correlated.   (b) Uncorrelated

FIGURE 3. Categorization version of Kahneman and Tversky's (1973) "illusion of validity" task. The two categories represent students in the national honor society and students not in the national honor society. The optimal decision bound is represented by the diagonal line.

diagonal line in Figure 3 – that is, the optimal classifier responds YES to any student whose test scores lie above the diagonal bound and NO to any student whose scores fall below the bound. Note that the optimal bound in Figure 3 is parallel to the $X_1 + X_2 = c$ contours in Figure 2. This means that the optimal decision rules in the two tasks are similar. In the prediction task, the subject computes the sum $X_1 + X_2 = c$ and then gives a response that is some linear function of c. In the categorization task, the subject computes the same sum and responds YES if c is greater than some criterion value and NO if it is not.

How should the subject's confidence ratings in the uncorrelated and positively correlated conditions be related? There are two popular models of confidence in signal detection theory. Let $f_H(X_1, X_2)$ and $f_G(X_1, X_2)$ denote the probability density functions on the test scores for students in the honor society and in the general student population, respectively. The likelihood ratio model assumes confidence increases monotonically with the absolute value of the log-likelihood ratio; that is, with $|\log[f_H(X_1, X_2)/f_G(X_1, X_2)]|$. In contrast, the distance-from-bound model assumes confidence increases monotonically with the distance between the sample (X_1, X_2) and the decision bound. Balakrishnan and Ratcliff (in press) recently reported evidence favoring the distance-from-bound model over the likelihood ratio model, but in the present application, the two models make identical predictions. The next result can be used to predict the effects of a correlation between X_1 and X_2 on the subject's confidence.

Theorem 3. *Consider a task in which subjects must discriminate between samples from one of two multivariate normal distributions, for which minimum* *distance classification is optimal. Create the marginal distribution along the di-rection (or dimension) orthogonal to the minimum distance bound. Suppose two experimental conditions are created by increasing the variance of these marginal distributions, while holding optimal accuracy constant. Then mean confidence will be greater in the condition with the greater variance, if confidence increases either with distance-from-bound or with the absolute value of the log-likelihood ratio.*

Proof. This theorem follows from a result of Thomas and Myers (1972). They investigated the response time (RT) predictions of a univariate signal detection theory model in which i) the hazard function of the underlying signal and noise distributions is monotonically increasing, and ii) RT decreases monotonically with distance from the response criterion. Thomas and Myers showed that if probability of error is invariant, then an increase in the variance of the signal and noise distributions leads to a decrease in mean RT. Their result is not unique to RT, but holds for any random variable monotonic with distance-from-criterion. Thus, the Thomas and Myers (1972) result implies that, under the same conditions, mean confidence increases with perceptual variance. This result applies to the Figure 3 model in a straightforward fashion. When predicting performance, the only relevant dimension in Figure 3 is the one coincident with the line $X_2 = X_1$. For example, it is straightforward to show that variation in a direction parallel to the decision bound (and so orthogonal to the line $X_2 = X_1$) has no effect on performance. It can also be shown that the marginal distribution of $f_H(X_1, X_2)$ and $f_G(X_1, X_2)$ along the dimension defined by the line $X_2 = X_1$ is normal with variance equal to the eigenvalue of the covariance matrix associated with the eigenvector coincident with the line $X_2 = X_1$. Since the hazard function of the normal distribution is strictly increasing, the result follows directly.   □

In the Figure 3 categorization task, minimum distance classification is opti-mal. The marginal distribution along the dimension orthogonal to the minimum distance bound (i.e., $X_1 + X_2 = c$) is the distribution of summed scores from the two populations (i.e., the distribution of $X_1 + X_2$). Note that the variance along this dimension increases with within-category correlation. As a result, Theorem 3 implies that mean confidence will be greater in the positive correlation condi-tion than in the zero correlation condition. This agrees with the Kahneman and Tversky (1973) results, and yet optimality was assumed throughout. Thus, in this case, a suboptimality or irrationality in a decision-making task is consistent with optimality when placed within a categorization context.

Why should a subject respond with confidence ratings that are rational in a categorization task and irrational in a numerical prediction task, especially since categorization might be viewed as a form of binary (i.e., in this example) numerical prediction? For example, if category G is associated with a numerical value of 0 and category H is associated with a 1, then one interpretation of a categorization trial is that the subject must predict the true numerical value (i.e., either 0 or 1) associated with the current test scores. Despite this formal relationship between numerical prediction and categorization, the subject's feelings of confidence might be very different in the two tasks. In categorization, the evidence indicates that confidence would increase with the distance between the current test scores and the category decision bound (e.g., Balakrishnan & Ratcliff, in press). In numerical prediction, Kahneman and Tversky (1973) assumed that confidence should decrease with the distance between the test scores and the line with slope -1 that passes through the category mean (at least, for a rational decision-maker). The Kahneman and Tversky (1973) data indicate that confidence in numerical prediction is better described by the former model than the latter. One reason for this might be that subjects get much more practice with categorization judgments than with numerical prediction. Every day, a person makes hundreds, and perhaps thousands, of categorization judgments, whereas numerical predictions are rarely, if ever, made. For example, a person might look out the window in the morning, see the sun shining, and predict that the day will be warm. This is a categorization judgment and not numerical prediction. To qualify as a traditional numerical prediction task, the person would have to look out the window, see the sun, and predict that the day's high temperature will be 78° F.

Given that people have far more experience with categorization, how might they respond when placed in an unfamiliar numerical prediction task? One possibility is that subjects respond by using whatever algorithms are available. Since categorization algorithms should be much better developed than numerical prediction algorithms, they respond as if in a categorization task. When categorizing students by intelligence, confidence increases with the correlation between the aptitude test scores, so when asked their confidence following numerical prediction, subjects indicate that their confidence is greater in the positive correlation condition.

Theorem 3 does not require a multidimensional category. For example, suppose the same categorization task was run, except that subjects must decide whether the hypothetical student is a member of the honor society or the general student population on the basis of only a single aptitude test score. Again, there are two conditions. In the first, the variance of the test scores is small and in the second, the variance is large. The category means are adjusted so that optimal accuracy is the same in the two tasks. Theorem 3 holds in this experiment, so a subject responding optimally should have more confidence in the large variance condition than in the small variance condition. An analogous numerical prediction task could also be run. In this case, the subject is given a single aptitude test score and is asked to predict GPA. If confidence ratings in numerical prediction mimic those in categorization, then confidence in the corresponding numerical prediction task should be greater in a large variance condition than in a small variance condition. This result would also be consistent with the two test prediction task illustrated in Figure 2, since Kahneman and Tversky (1973) found that confidence increased with the variance of the predictor variable (i.e., the sum $X_1 + X_2 = c$).

Whereas prediction tasks based on a single test score have been reported (e.g., Birnbaum, 1976; Birnbaum & Stegner, 1981), we know of no such studies that collected confidence ratings. Even so, Kahneman and Tversky (1973) report that "people predict an overall B average with more confidence on the basis of B grades in two separate introductory courses than on the basis of an A and a C" (p. 249). This result seems to contradict the results from the prediction task illustrated in Figure 2. However, although this new task is similar to numerical prediction, it differs in several key ways. The two most important differences, probably, are that the prediction is based on two samples from the distribution of test scores rather than one, and that the confidence judgment is based on a single prediction rather than on many. In a prediction task where the subject is given only a single test score, extreme values are likely to elicit strong feelings of confidence, which, of course, agrees with the results from the two-test Figure 2 prediction task.

6. Summary and Conclusions

Although categorization is a special case of choice or decision-making, the study of human categorization behavior has developed independently from the study of human choice and decision-making. A casual reading of the two separate literatures seems to indicate striking disagreement. To some extent, this reflects an historical difference in the theoretical developments that have occurred in the two areas. Formal theorizing in choice and decision-making predates such efforts in categorization by several decades.[4] As in categorization, early models of choice and decision-making assumed rationality. For example, during the 1950s and '60s, choice theory was dominated by Luce's (1959a) choice axiom, and decision-making was dominated by expected utility theory (e.g., Luce & Krantz, 1971; Savage, 1954; von Neumann & Morgenstern, 1947).

The focus on suboptimality and irrationality developed only after these early rational models were explored and rejected.

One might argue that theories of categorization are evolving in the same general direction. In fact, there are current hints in the categorization literature that the optimality assumption may need revision. For example, McKinley and Nosofsky (1995) recently reported the results of a categorization task with two contrasting categories, and with stimuli varying on only two dimensions, which roughly half of the subjects were unable to learn, even with payoffs for accuracy and extended practice (although all subjects eventually performed better than chance).

Although this historical argument has some validity, it is naive to assume that the categorization literature is simply lagging 10 or 20 years behind the choice and decision-making literatures. For example, although most popular categorization models satisfy context sensitive simple scalability, they are generally mute on the issue of how their parameters change with experimental context. As a result, they do not necessarily satisfy strong stochastic transitivity. Thus, the optimality identified in the categorization literature is not necessarily in conflict with the suboptimality in the choice literature associated with violations of strong stochastic transitivity. The relation to the decision-making literature is more complex. On the one hand, decision processes in categorization frequently violate at least some of the heuristics that have been said to lead to decision-making irrationalities (e.g., representativeness). On the other hand, some of the decision-making data interpreted as irrational is consistent with optimality when interpreted within the context of a categorization task.

Although the relation between the categorization and choice and decision-making literatures is more complex than it might first seem, we believe that each

---

[4]On the other hand, the formal development of identification models occurred at about the same time as formal theorizing in choice and decision-making (e.g., Luce, 1963; Shepard, 1957).

literature could benefit from study of the other. For example, decision-making theorists who study the categorization literature might better understand the limits of the representativeness heuristic as a description of human decision processes. For categorization theorists, whose field is still relatively young, the choice and decision-making literature represents an untapped wealth of theoretical and empirical results.

Choice, Decision, and Measurement
A. A. J. Marley (Ed.),
©Lawrence Erlbaum Associates, NJ, 1997.

TOWARD AN ANALYTIC MODEL OF ATTENTION TO VISUAL SHAPE

DAVID LABERGE, ROBERT L. CARLSON, AND JOHN K. WILLIAMS

University of California, Irvine

ABSTRACT. The expression of attention to an object in the brain is assumed to involve increased activity at the location of that object relative to the activity in the surrounding area. The mechanism that is mainly responsible for this selective enhancement of activity is believed to be the thalamocortical circuit, which directly connects virtually every area of the cortex with a corresponding area within the thalamus. The operation of the thalamocortical circuit has been modeled by a neural network, whose operation shows that the circuit can simultaneously enhance and concentrate activity at a coded target location; in other words, the circuit has the capability of increasing activity at a target location while progressively reducing the amount of activity that is spread to surrounding locations. However, the equations of the neural network model involve a large number of parameters, and the solution of the equations requires numerical integration. We present here a model which contains many fewer parameters and whose equations can be solved analytically. This analytic model is based in part on the metaphor of a tubelight optical device that projects light energy upon a receiving surface, corresponding to the manner in which the thalamic neurons are presumed to project activity onto a cortical area. In particular, the analytic model mimics the neural network's ability to simultaneously enhance and concentrate activity at a coded location. Predicted trajectories of target and distractor activity levels for both the neural network and the analytic model appear highly similar. It is concluded that the analytic model is potentially more suitable for empirical tests than the corresponding neural network model.

1. INTRODUCTION

The purpose of this paper is to propose a relatively simple analytic model of attentional expression in information pathways which is intended to mimic the main properties of a more complex neural network model of attention (LaBerge, Carter, & Brown, 1992), whose structure is based on the relatively well-established properties of the thalamocortical circuit. Both the simple analytic model and the complex network model have output characteristics that allow the attentional process to be

Key words and phrases. Attention models, thalamocortical circuit, attentional emphasis.

Acknowledgments. The authors thank Dr. Eileen Handelman of Simon's Rock College in Great Barrington, Massachusetts, for helpful advice on matters of physical optics, and special appreciation is given to W. K. Estes and R. M. Shiffrin for excellent critiques of an earlier version of this paper.

Address for correspondence. David LaBerge, Cognitive Sciences Department, University of California, Irvine, CA 92717. Email: dlaberge@vmsa.oac.uci.edu

coupled to a response-time model, in the general way that an earlier version of the present attention models were coupled to a class of counter models (LaBerge, 1992, 1994). To illustrate an application of the joint operation of the analytic attention model and a counter model of response time, a prediction is derived for the time required to identify a letter shape displayed with distractors that are separated from it by varying distances.

The expression of attention to an object, attribute, or location can be described as a process located at particular areas of the cerebral cortex, where large groups of neurons increase their firing rates relative to the firing rates in the surrounding groups of neurons. This relative enhancement of neural activity in localized regions of the cortical sheet has been observed in human and monkey brains by means of a variety of physiological measures, including single-cell recordings (e.g., Moran & Desimone, 1985; Motter, 1993), event-related potentials (e.g., Hillyard, Mangun, Woldorff, & Luck, 1995), magnetoencephalography (e.g., Woldorff, Gallen, Hampson, Hillyard, Pantev, Sobel, & Bloom, 1993), positron emission tomography (e.g., Corbetta, Miezin, Dobmeyer, Shulman, & Petersen, 1991; Haxby, Horowitz, Ungerleider, Maison, Pietrini, & Grady, 1994; Liotti, Fox, & LaBerge, 1994), and functional magnetic resonance imaging (e.g., Sereno, Dale, Reppas, Kwang, Belliveau, Brady, Rosen, & Tootell, 1995).

The mechanism that generates the expression of attention in cortical neurons is assumed to be the thalamus, or more exactly, the thalamocortical circuit, through which a particular area of cortex is excited by a particular nucleus of the thalamus. Of interest in the case of visual perception is the pulvinar nucleus, which is the large posterior thalamic volume known to connect directly with the occipitotemporal area of cortex where neurons code letter shapes. A PET experiment of focal attention to letter shapes (LaBerge & Buchsbaum, 1990) showed increased activity in the pulvinar, but because the PET scan had been restricted to brain slices that overlapped the thalamus, there was no opportunity to observe concurrent activity in the lower-lying occipitotemporal region of the cortex. However, a recent PET study (Liotti et al., 1994) observed activity in the entire brain, and found large concurrent increases in blood flow in both the pulvinar nucleus and in the occipitotemporal area of the cortex during focal attention to a letter shape (compared to a neutral control condition). These findings support the hypothesis that the cortical area that processes shape information and the thalamic area that is directly connected to it function together when called upon to concentrate attention on the identification of a letter shape.

It seems reasonable to regard the observed increase in cortical activity as the *expression* of attention, because it is in the cortex that attention works its particular effects on the stimulus information flowing from the primary visual areas to higher areas of processing. The observed increase in thalamic pulvinar activity may be considered the *mechanism* of attention, because it contains the main parts of the thalamocortical circuit that generates the enhanced activity in the cortical neurons. Finally, the controlling input to the mechanism of attention is assumed to arise from voluntary *control* circuits in the anterior cortex, which are associated with task instructions. These three components of attention are indicated in the flow diagram shown in Figure 1.

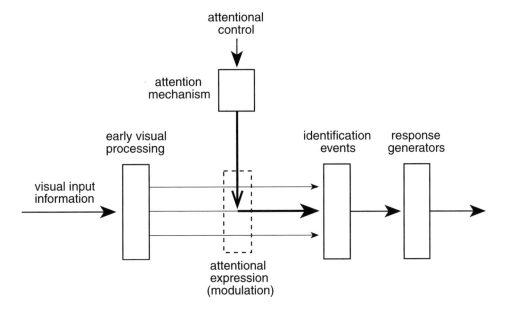

FIGURE 1. A schematic representation of information flow from stimulus input, through modular processing, to overt response. The attention mechanism is assumed to be the thalamocortical circuit, which is modeled in the present paper both by a neural network and by an analytical model based on a tubelight device.

2. A NEURAL NETWORK MODEL OF THE THALAMOCORTICAL CIRCUIT OPERATIONS

Since the circuit that links a thalamic area to its cortical area is well-known and quite simple in structure, it is relatively straightforward to model its operation with a network scheme. The activity of each of each of the five basic neuron-like units, shown in Figure 2, is described by a difference equation which relates the "firing-rate" output to the inputs to that unit (LaBerge et al., 1992). Specifically, the inputs to a neural unit are summed and then passed through a nonlinear threshold function. Because each difference equation is nonlinear, the solution of the set of difference equations is not obtainable by analytic means but requires a numerical integration procedure, typically carried out on a computer. Furthermore, the number of free parameters in the present network simulation of the thalamocortical circuit activity is uncomfortably large (24 parameters).

The attention task represented by the network model is the same task used in the PET studies of pulvinar activity already described. The stimulus display consists of a target letter positioned in the midst of distractor letters that are highly similar to the target letter (e.g., an O surrounded by G's and Q's). The high target-distractor similarity is intended to minimize preattentive selection of the target, sometimes termed "pop-out" (e.g., Julesz & Bergen, 1983; Treisman,

THALAMOCORTICAL CIRCUIT

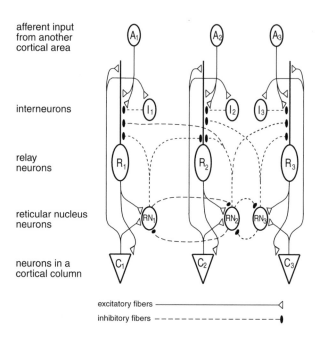

FigurE 2. The structure of the thalamocortical circuit by which every cortical area is reciprocally connected to a thalamic nucleus. Modeled as a neural network, this circuit is believed to contain a mechanism of attention, which increases the contrast between firing rates of neurons in a particular cortical area compared with its surround. The center column of the network represents a target, and the outside columns represent adjacent distractors. The output of the attention mechanism are the neurons in cortical columns, represented in Figure 1 by the area within the rectangle with the dashed-line boundary.

1985). The preattentive processing of a target displayed among dissimilar (but homogeneous) distractors (e.g., an O within V's and X's) is assumed to increase the target-display contrast (saliency) earlier in pathways than the point where the present attentional expression (controlled by spatial location) presumably occurs. Thus, some degree of target-distractor contrast may be induced by lateral inhibitory connections within cortical pathways, but the target-distractor contrast produced by attentive operations are assumed to arise from the connections through the pulvinar nucleus of the thalamus via triangular circuits that connect one cortical area to another (LaBerge, 1995b, 1995a).

The high similarity between target and distractors in the stimulus QOG is produced by their having many features shared in common. If the stimulus were XOV instead, then the curved line features of the center item, O, would presumably result in preattentive contrast, and would be represented in the model as larger values at the target location than in the distractor locations for the cortical input - in Figure 1, the pathways entering the dotted rectangle from the left. The operations which produce the preparatory attention to curved-line features are assumed to involve the same structures as those represented by the present network and analytic models. Since our present purpose is to describe how a specific attentional process may modulate target and distractor information flow, we wish to begin with approximately equal rates of flow for the target and distractors, and this requires selecting stimulus items that are presumed not to be differentially modulated by preattentive or attentive processes that operate prior to the point where the particular attention process of interest operates.

At the onset of the display, the neural units in the thalamocortical columns corresponding to the target letter's location are activated from control circuits in the anterior cortical areas, and this activation continues until the target is identified and signals from the identification circuits (presumed to be located in the inferotemporal area) are sent to the control circuits to terminate activation of the attention mechanism. When a control circuit initiates attentional activity in the thalamocortical circuits, these columns of cells respond by increasing the activities of cortical units that code the target information over the activities of the cortical units that code the adjacent distractor information. A typical graph of the trajectories of the averaged outputs of the cortical target units and the combined distractor units are shown in Figures 3 and 4.

When the activities of the cortical target units are sufficiently greater than the activities in the distractor units, the resulting contrast selects the target information which is then sent forward to the identification circuits, where matching of the target information against stored patterns eventually produces an identification event. The amount of target information needed for identification of the visual target is represented in Figures 3 and 4 by the shaded area between the target and distractor curves; actually, as will be discussed later, a difference between the target and distractor points is divided by the absolute value of the distractor point to compute the contrast value. The accumulation of target information by the identification circuits begins when the difference between the target and distractor reaches a specific value. The accumulation of information at the identification circuits ends when an identification event occurs, which is the time value corresponding to the right side of the shaded area of Figures 3 and 4. The time values a and b define the beginning and end of the identification process, respectively.

Prior to the time that the information flow from the target letter reaches a threshold contrast at time a the information reaching identification circuits is presumed to arise from the entire display of three items. For example, the display of the letter string COG initially sends information from all three letter locations to the identification module, with the result that a match is made with the word "cog"; in contrast, the task of identifying the center letter involves emphasizing the flow of stimulus information from the center letter location of the letter string, COG, which must be increased sufficiently over that from the adjacent letter locations so that the identification module attempts to match only the information from the

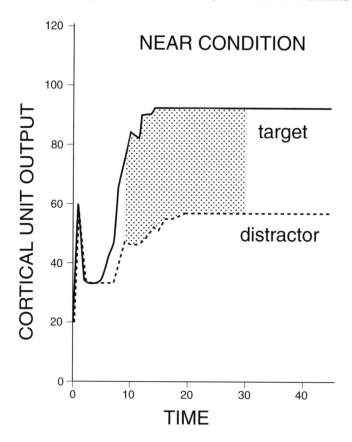

FIGURE 3. Simulated output from the neural network model for target and adjacent (NEAR) distractors (after LaBerge, Carter, & Brown, 1992). Shaded region represents the rate and duration of target information sent to the identification module. The onset of the shaded area occurs at time a, and the end of the shaded area occurs at time b (see text). The time to complete an (elemental) identification event is 30 time units.

center letter location. This selective modulation of information flow at the center letter location is what the mechanism of attention is assumed to provide for the system (as shown in the flow diagram of Figure 1).

3. CRITIQUE OF THE NEURAL NETWORK MODEL

From the viewpoint of a neuroscientist, the present network model of the thalamocortical circuit is incomplete because it ignores the fine structure of each neuron, for example, the ionic current flow in the neural membrane, the influence of ubiquitous neuromodulators upon synaptic events, and the spatial-temporal aspects of integrating inputs at synapses that are distributed across the dendritic tree to

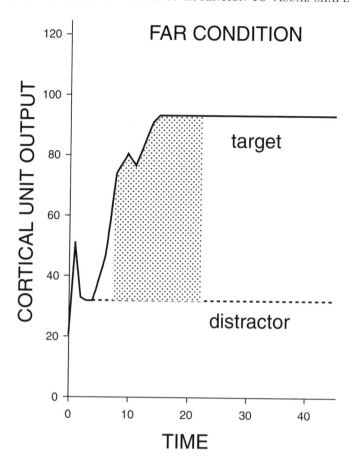

FIGURE 4. Simulated output from the neural network model for target and distant (FAR) distractors. Shaded region represents the rate and duration of target information sent to the identification module. The time to complete an (elemental) identification event is 22 time units.

produce the momentary voltage potential at the cell body which gives rise to the axon firing rate. However, since the number of synapses on a typical cortical neuron numbers in the tens of thousands, the number of parameters in the difference equation representing the input-output relationship of each neuron would increase greatly beyond the approximately 30 parameters of the present network model. An alternative approach would be to look for a summarizing rule at the membrane level by which the bulk of the parameters may be condensed into a few parameters, but thus far this approach has not yielded fruitful results.

In contrast to the neuroscientist's preference for fidelity to the details of the neuron membrane in describing how assemblies of neurons work together, the cognitive psychologist looks to the more global characteristics of brain circuitry which may be mapped in a straightforward way onto measurements of overt behavior, such as response frequency and response time. Given the many formal models of response time in the recent literature (for reviews, see Luce, 1986b; Townsend & Ashby, 1983), the problem would seem to be one of formulating the model of attention in such a way that it can be effectively coupled to a reasonably large subset of the existing response time models. To make progress toward this goal, the number of parameters in the attention model should be minimized, not expanded.

One way to reduce the parameters in the present neural network model of attention is to observe a variety of trajectory plots of the simulation program (of which the plots in Figures 3 and 4 are examples), and observe the characteristics of the trajectories that seem most relevant to the present conceptualization of the expression and mechanism of attention. In this light, the two main aspects of the trajectories are: (1) the large difference between input firing rate and output firing rate of the target unit, and in many cases, of the distractor unit as well, and (2) the widely separated asymptotes of the target and distractor units. These two features of the output appear to correspond to two components of the circuit structure: The increase of output firing rate over input firing rate of the target may be traced to the recurrent excitatory loop between the cortical unit and thalamic relay unit, and the difference in target and distractor unit asymptotes may be traced to the lateral inhibitory links between reticular nucleus units of target columns and relay units of neighboring distractor columns (see Figure 2). The first component corresponds to the enhancement property of attention and the second property to the concentration property of attention. Viewed in this manner, the neural network model may be called a "concentrated-enhancement model of attention."

We now attempt to incorporate these two global characteristics of the thalamocortical operation into a model having fewer parameters. In addition, the equations expressing the trajectories involve simple closed-form exponential solutions to simple linear difference equations, so that the model is analytic, and thus there is no need for numerical integration to solve the basic equations that describe the target and distractor trajectories during the course of attentional development. Ultimately, of course, the analytic model should be linked mathematically with a response-time model. However, the equations describing this bridge between the two models are unwieldy in their present form. It is hoped that future refinements of the link between the present analytic model and some appropriate response-time model will enable effective empirical tests of the attention model.

4. AN ANALYTIC MODEL OF ATTENTION

The present analytic model is based on the analogy of a relatively simple optical device consisting of a light source and a surface upon which light energy is projected, corresponding to the attention mechanism and the pathways in which information flow is modulated by the attention mechanism (see Figure 1). The structural parameters of the optical device are shown in Figure 5. The intensity of the light source is denoted by β, and the received light energy at some point, x, on the receiving surface is denoted by $f(x)$. The distance from the light source to the receiving surface is fixed, but extending from the light source is a tube of varying

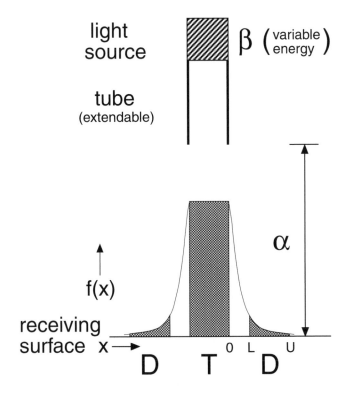

FIGURE 5. The structure and output of the tubelight device. The light-source and tube represent the attention mechanism, and the receiving surface the firing rates of neurons in a cortical pathway (e.g., corresponding to the attention mechanism together with the rectangle with the dashed-line boundary). The target area is labeled as T, and each of the distractor areas labeled as D. The upper and lower boundaries of a distractor area are indicated by U and L.

length which reduces the spread of radiant light given off by the source. The distance between the end of the tube and the receiving surface is denoted by α. When $\alpha = 0$, the tube is completely extended and touches the receiving surface, resulting in the concentration of radiant light on a surface area whose border corresponds to the configuration of the end of the tube (e.g., circular or elliptical, and of varying size). The maximum value of α is the distance between the light source and the receiving surface, which is fixed.

In typical task situations, the area of attentional expression registers activity corresponding to locations of objects prior to the onset of attentional operations, and the pattern of activity across objects is expected to vary as a function of object contrasts previously computed (as discussed in the foregoing section). For simplicity, we assume that the receiving surface of the tubelight device has prior energy levels that are equal across the target and distractor locations. We can approximate this assumption by using similar target-distractor relationships (e.g., in the stimulus QOG, as opposed to XOY).

The tubelight mechanism operates to vary the intensity and spread of light energy at the receiving surface over time, in the same general way that the thalamic mechanism appears to vary the overall intensity and spread of neural activity in a cortical area. Typically, the cortical firing rates produced by stimulus information alone is relative low, and the thalamocortical circuit operates at some stage or stages of the information flow (e.g., in area V4) to increase the firing rate of only a part of the information flow (e.g., of the neurons coding the letter O in the letter string QOG). The tubelight device represents the time course of this selective increase in activity by an exponential increase in the light-source intensity, β, coupled with a gradual extension of the tube toward the receiving surface of light. An illustration of this process is the operation of a flashlight fitted with a movable tube (such as found on some cameras and binoculars) and pointed toward a wall surface; as the thumb depresses the button on the body of the flashlight, the light source increases in intensity and at the same time the tube extends in length. It may be noted that the present tubelight device assumes that the overall intensity (power) varies across a considerable range of values, while in a lens model (e.g., the zoom lens model of Eriksen & Yeh, 1985) the overall intensity, or power, is constant. A lens model also assumes that the source of intensity is within the flow of stimulus information itself, while for the present models, the source of intensity lies outside the flow of stimulus information (see Figure 1).

The two structural components of the tubelight device correspond to the two main components of the thalamocortical circuit believed to generate selective attentional activations (i.e., activity contrasts) in cortical pathways. The increasing-intensity component corresponds to recurrent excitation in the loop connecting a thalamic relay cell with a cortical cell, and the component of tube-to-surface separation corresponds to the lateral inhibition between these loops provided by the reticular nucleus cells (see Figure 2). The positive feedback in the thalamocortical loops generate a growth in neural activity in the cortical stream, and the lateral inhibitory connections between the loops confine most of the increased activity to a selected part of this cortical stream.

We turn now to the formal description of the analytic model of concentrated attentional enhancement.

5. DERIVATION OF THE ANALYTIC MODEL EQUATION

The present analytic model is formulated on the analogy of the optical characteristics of the physical tubelight device, shown in schematic form in Figure 5. The tubelight and receiving surface of the optical device correspond to the attention mechanism and the site of attentional expression represented in the flow diagram of Figure 1, respectively. The intensity of the tubelight projects light energy onto the receiving surface, and the extension of the tube concentrates this activity within a compact area by blocking the spread of light energy. These two effects correspond to the enhancement and lateral inhibition properties of the thalamocortical circuit shown in Figure 2.

To ease the derivation of equations, the terms employed in this section of the paper will mainly use terminology appropriate to the tubelight device that provides the optical analog of the attention process. However, in the interest of clarity, definitions of tubelight-related terms in the following paragraph are accompanied by corresponding attention-related terms within parentheses.

Let x be the coded spatial location of an element at the receiving surface (site of attentional expression), and let $f_t(x)$ be the level of activity of that element at time t. Then

$$f_t(x) = \frac{\beta_t \alpha_t^2}{\alpha_t^2 + x^2} + c_t(x),$$ (1)

where

(i) β_t denotes the tubelight intensity (attentional source activity) at time t, $0 \leq \beta_t \leq \beta_{max}$,

(ii) α_t denotes the distance separating the end of the tube from the receiving surface (lateral inhibition of spreading attentional activity) at time t, $0 \leq \alpha_t \leq \alpha_{max}$, and

(iii) $c_t(x)$ denotes the intensity of an element on the receiving surface produced from other sources (stimulus input activity to the site of attentional expression) at time t, $0 \leq c_t(x) \leq c_{max}$.

Noting that light intensity is intended to correspond with firing rate (and is not to be interpreted as perceived intensity), we assume that the maximum intensity of the light-source intensity is $\beta_{max} = 100$, and the maximum intensity of inputs from other sources to a receiving surface element is $c_{max} = 100$, whose sum represents a reasonable approximation to the upper range of firing rates expected for the kinds of behavioral tasks considered here. For simplicity, we scale the range of α in the unit interval, such that $\alpha_{max} = 1.0$. In general, the value of $c_t(x)$ is allowed to vary with time, but in almost all applications of the model, these other inputs to the surface intensity remain constant while the tubelight parameters, α_t and β_t, operate to modulate surface intensity over time.

The light source within the tubelight is assumed to increase as a function of time, t, by the exponential equation

$$\beta_t = \beta_{max} - (\beta_{max} - \beta_0)e^{-k_\beta t},$$ (2)

where k_β the rate constant, $0 < k_\beta$. This equation is a solution of the linear differential equation

$$\frac{d(\beta_{max} - \beta)}{dt} = k_\beta(\beta_{max} - \beta)$$

in which the rate of increase in intensity of the tubelight source is proportional to the remaining amount of increase possible.

The distance from the light-source within the tube and the receiving surface is fixed; hence the energy at the receiving surface area directly under the tube is simply β_t for all values of t. However, the distance from the end of the tube to the receiving surface increases as a function of t, according to the exponential equation

$$\alpha_t = \alpha_0 e^{-k_a(\beta_t - \beta_0)t},$$ (3)

where k_α is the rate constant, $0 < k_\alpha$. This equation is a solution of the linear differential equation

$$\frac{d\alpha}{dt} = k_\alpha(\beta_t - \beta_0)\alpha\,,$$

in which the rate of decrease in separation between the end of the tube and the receiving surface is proportional to the remaining amount of separation multiplied by the momentary intensity of the light-source. These last two equations express the relationship between the tube length and the light-source intensity.

This change in distance between the end of the tube and the receiving surface determines the spread of light energy away from the area directly under the tube. Strictly speaking, Equation 1 does not precisely describe actual optical intensities (photon probabilities) at a receiving surface, because the absorption characteristics of the tube interior are not specified. For example, if the tube interior were a perfect mirror and absorbed no light, then the location of the light source is, in effect, at the end of the tube. An analog of this case is a device in which the tube is removed from the light source, and the source itself is moved toward the receiving surface over time, like moving a typical flashlight toward a wall. In this case, the illuminance at the receiving surface is determined simply from the inverse square law,

$$f_t(x) = \frac{\beta_t}{\alpha_t^2 + x^2}\,.$$

The resulting spread of light, which is approximated by Equation 1 with α_t^2 removed from the numerator, turns out to be too high near the target area to mimic the corresponding spread of neural activity in the neural network model. On the other hand, if the interior of the tube were black so that light radiating from the light source toward the tube wall is completely absorbed, then the illuminance at the target area of the surface decreases as the length of the tube increases. The resulting intensity of light at the target area would then decrease as the tube extends, a result which does not accord with the corresponding characteristics of the neural network model.

The best approximation to the operations of the neural network model, for present applications, would result from a compromise between making the tube completely reflective (mirrored) and completely absorbent (colored black), while preserving two important properties (exhibited by the neural network model): (1) that the intensity at the light source be the same as the intensity received at the target area independent of the tube length, and (2) that the gradient of intensity away from the target area be capable of exhibiting a wide range of values for each tubelight-source intensity. However, regardless of whether or not an optical device can be envisioned that possesses these two properties in exactly the way described by Equation 1, the present analytic model does possess these two properties in the manner expressed by Equation 1. In this respect, the analytic model differs from the tubelight optical device. Nevertheless, for convenience in exposition, we continue to use the optical terminology, while keeping in mind the correspondences between the optical descriptions and the attention-related descriptions (given previously, following Equation 1).

We now proceed to a description of the changes in the intensities of light energy (the "illuminance values") across the receiving surface as attentional processing develops its concentration at the target location under the tube-end relative to the distractor locations in the surrounding locations. The average intensity over a particular surface sector (corresponding to an object's location) is the area under the function, $f_t(x)$, between the upper and lower boundaries of that sector, designated respectively as X_U and X_L (see Figure 5). The choice of boundaries for the distractor is based on the number of columns representing a stimulus object and the number of columns representing the space between objects in the neural network model of the thalamocortical circuit (LaBerge et al., 1992).

Owing to the symmetry of the right and left distractor locations and their assumed equal intensities at $t = 0$, we need to describe only the changes in the areas beneath the curve corresponding to the distractor on the right of the target, and then multiply the result by two (or a higher number, if more than two distractors are located in the neighborhood of the target). However, it may be well to keep in mind that the precise effect of adding additional distractors to the display, and the effects of where they are positioned around the target, should be arrived at by experiment rather than by the a priori assumption that each additional distractor adds a constant amount of competitive processing between the target location and the distractor locations in the development of dominant attentional activity at the target location. But, given the lack of appropriate data, we assume that we may pool the separate contributions of two distractor objects located on each side of a target object.

Turning to the derivations of the appropriate equations for target and distractor intensities at the receiving surface, we note from Equation 1 that the area under $f_t(x)$ corresponding to the target sector of the receiving surface (the ordinate values corresponding to the interval $-1 \leq x \leq 0$) is obtained very easily and we denote it by the symbol $A_t(T)$, where T denotes x-values corresponding to the target area:

$$A_t(T) = \beta_t + c_t(T). \tag{4}$$

The derivation of the expression for the area under $f_t(x)$ above the adjacent distractor location is denoted by $A_t(D)$, where D denotes the x-values corresponding to the distractor area, which is bounded above by $x = X_U$ and below by $x = X_L$; the expression is obtained by slightly more complicated operations:

$$
\begin{aligned}
A_t(D) &= \int_{x_L}^{x_U} f_t(x)\,dx = \int_{x_L}^{x_U} \frac{\beta_t \alpha_t^2}{\alpha_t^2 + x^2}\,dx + c_t(D) \\
&= \alpha_t \beta_t \int_{x_L}^{x_U} \frac{\alpha}{\alpha_t^2 + x^2}\,dx = \alpha_t \beta_t \left[\tan^{-1}(\frac{x}{2}) \right]_{X_L}^{X_U} + C + c_t(D) \\
&= \alpha_t \beta_t \left[\tan^{-1}\left(\frac{x_U}{\alpha_t} \right) - \tan^{-1}\left(\frac{x_L}{\alpha_t} \right) \right] + c_t(D).
\end{aligned}
\tag{5}
$$

Since

$$\tan^{-1}(a) - \tan^{-1}(b) = \tan^{-1}\left(\frac{a - b}{1 + ab} \right),$$

it follows that

$$A_t(D) = \alpha_t \beta_t \left[\tan^{-1} \left(\frac{\alpha_t(x_U - x_L)}{\alpha_t^2 + x_U x_L} \right) \right] + c_t(D). \tag{6}$$

Having at hand the equations for expressing the light intensities at sectors of the receiving surface corresponding to the target and distractor locations, we can plot the trajectory of the target and the trajectory of the combined distractors.

6. A SAMPLE PREDICTION: SETTING PARAMETER VALUES

The choice of parameters of the analytic model is determined by several considerations:

(a) Sizes of areas on the receiving surface correspond proportionally to the target, distractor, and the spaces between them. The typical widths of a character and an intervening space on our laboratory monitor are 5 and 3 pixels, respectively, or 6 and 2 pixels, respectively. In the present applications of both the analytic and neural network models, we adopt the 6/2 ratio of character-to-space width. Since the 6/2 ratio is equivalent to a 3/1 ratio, the unit on the x-axis of the receiving surface will be 1/3. Thus, the width of a character consists of 3 units @1/3 and the size of a space consists of one unit @1/3. Thus, we can conveniently define the upper and lower boundaries of the target location at x values of -1.0 and 0.0, and we define two different distractor separations as follows: for the Near Distractor case, the distractor location (on the right side of the target) has a lower bound of $x = .33$, and an upper bound of 1.33; for the Far Distractor case, the distractor location has a lower bound at $x = 1.67$ and an upper bound at $x = 2.67$. In each case, a second distractor is located at the same distance to the left of the target.

(b) The analytic model (and the corresponding neural network model to which it will be compared) assumes that the input to the receiving surface from non-attentional sources has a constant energy flow (corresponding to firing rates) of 20 units/sec, i.e., that $c_t(x) = 20$ for the target and distractor sectors, and $c_t(x) = 1$ for the space sectors adjacent to the target and distractor locations, for all values of t. The corresponding "receiving surface" in the cortex is presumed to be at or near V4, and it is known that V4 receives direct connections from visual areas V1, V2, V3, and V5. It is presumed that featural information corresponding to the displayed objects arrives at V4 from these other visual areas, and that location information from other areas of the cortex (e.g., the posterior parietal spatial maps) guides the concentrating of attention on the featural information arising from a particular stimulus object.

(c) The beginning value for β_t of 20 units/sec is a somewhat arbitrary choice in the lower range of values of β_t; the same value is chosen for the corresponding neural network model to represent the initial afferent input to the target columns of cells.

(d) The beginning value for α_t of 1.0 represents the maximum distance between the tube-end and the receiving surface, and using this value allows us to observe the effects of α_t throughout much of its range; it decreases toward zero automatically as the energy in the light-source, β_t increases from its initial value. But the initial value for α_t could be set at any value in its range.

(e) The values for the constants, k_α and k_β of .012 and 1.0, respectively, were chosen, after exploratory calculations, to generate trajectories of the target and distractors that would approximate the corresponding trajectories produced by the neural network model.

(f) The maximum value for α_t was set at 1.0, and the maximum values for β_t and $c_t(x)$ were set set at 100.

Thus, the total number of parameters for the present application of the analytic model is 11, of which 7 are fixed ($\alpha_{\max}, \beta_{\max}, c_{\max}, x_U, x_L, c_0(T), c_0(D)$), and only 4 are free to vary ($\alpha_0, \beta_0, k_\alpha$, and k_β).

7. COMPARING PREDICTIONS OF THE ANALYTIC AND NEURAL NETWORK MODELS

Shown in Figures 6 and 7 are the trajectories of light energies at the receiving surface for the target and distractor object locations, using the parameter values indicated in the foregoing section. Two distractor curves are shown, one representing the behavior of a "near" distractor (the right distractor of the pair having boundaries on the x-axis of .33 and 1.33), and the other representing the behavior of a "far" distractor (the right distractor of the pair having boundaries on the x-axis of 1.67 and 2.67). The corresponding trajectories for the neural network model are shown in Figures 3 and 4.

The parameters of the neural network model were quite close to those used in the published simulation study (LaBerge et al., 1992). Notable changes in parameters were as follows: the number of neural columns representing object width and space width are set at 3 and 1, (instead of at 5 and 3) respectively, the thalamic afferent input value at the target location is set at 20 (instead of 38), the same value as β_0, and the initial cortical firing rate is set at 20 for the target and distractor objects, and 1 for the spaces (instead of 5), the same values corresponding to those set for $c_0(x)$ in the analytic model.

The overall shapes of the trajectories of the analytic and network models shown in Figures 3 and 4, and Figures 6 and 7 are quite similar, particularly with respect to the manner of divergence of activity levels (intensities) at the coded locations of the target and distractor objects. The width and location of the distractor along the x-axis requires values to be set for x_U, and x_L. In the infrequent applications in which the widths of the target and distractors differ, an additional parameter is needed to represent the width of the target independent of the width of the distractor. In the illustrative cases shown in Figures 6 and 7, all parameters are fixed except for the locations of the near and far distractor.

In contrast to the 11 parameters of the analytic model, the number of parameters in the corresponding neural network model (e.g, required in the simulations shown in Figures 3 and 4) is 29. Details of the neural network equations and parameters are given in LaBerge et al. (1992). In that study, there were 23 columns of neural units ordered along a dimension corresponding to the x-axis of the present analytic model. Three columns at the center represented the location of the target item, and three columns for each of two distractors were located at varying (symmetric) distances to the right and left of the target location. Thus, the width of

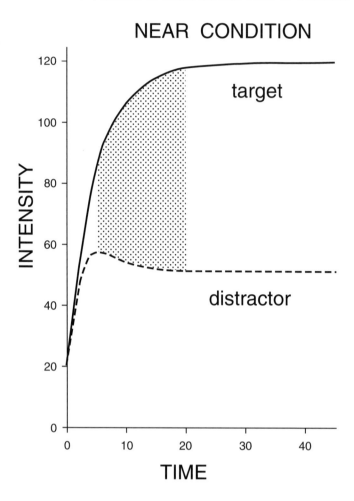

FIGURE 6. Modeled output of the analytic model (based on the tubelight device) for target and adjacent (NEAR) distractors. The shaded region represents the rate and duration of target information sent to the identification module. The time to complete an (elemental) identification event is 20 time units.

a distractor item and its distance from the target item can be represented by two metric parameters defined on the one-dimensional ordering of the columns.

Each column contained 5 neural units: the afferent input unit, the relay unit, the reticular nucleus unit, the interneuron unit, and the cortical unit. The initial values for the afferent input and cortical units were different for the target, distractor, and space columns, amounting to 6 parameters; the initial values of the relay unit, the reticular nucleus unit, and the interneuron unit were each assumed to be constant over the target, distractor and space columns; this simplifying assumption produced only an additional 3 parameters.

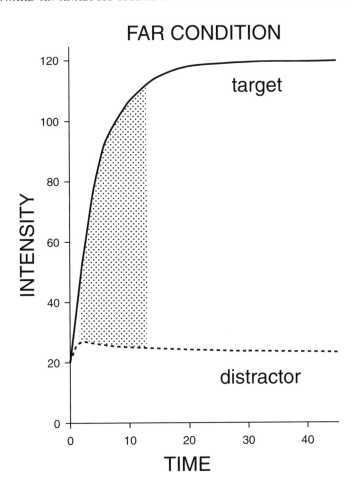

FIGURE 7. Modeled output of the analytic model (based on the tubelight device) for target and distant (FAR) distractors. The shaded region represents the duration and rate of target information sent to the identification module. The time to complete an (elemental) identification event is 12 time units.

The connections between the neural units within and between columns were designated by giving non-zero weights to these connections. There were three slightly different network patterns (corresponding to three slightly different thalamocortical circuit structures) simulated in the LaBerge et al. (1992) study, and the network labeled Model A was simulated here. Thus, the present network contains 9 non-zero connections within a column, so that 9 additional parameters are required for the intra-column connection weights. For the between-column (inter-column) connections, there were only three types, which reflects the relative simplicity of the known structure of the thalamocortical circuit. The first type of connection is an inhibitory connection between reticular nucleus neurons of adjacent and nonadjacent columns. The weight of this connection falls off exponentially with distance between columns and drops to zero at a particular distance termed the radius of inter-column connections. The second type of connection is an inhibitory connection between reticular nucleus neurons of one column and the relay neurons of adjacent and nonadjacent columns. The connection weight of this type of connection also falls off exponentially with distance between columns. However, the fall-off drops to zero at a particular connective distance, which is termed the radius of inter-column connections. The third type of inter-column connection is an excitatory link between adjacent cortical neural units. Thus 3 additional parameters are needed for the three types of inter-column connection weights, 1 parameter for the radius of connections, and 1 parameter for the fall-off rate-constant for two of these types, totaling 5 parameters.

Finally, after the firing-rate inputs for each neural unit are weighted and summed, the sum is transformed by an exponential threshold function that contains three parameters: the initial value, the maximum value, and the rate constant. To simplify computations that are already quite complicated, the same threshold function is assumed for all neural units.

Therefore, the total number of parameters in the present application of the neural network model is 29, of which 5 are fixed (width and distance of the distractor from the target; initial cortical unit values for the target, distractor and space columns), and 24 are free to vary. This contrasts with the 11 parameters of the analytic model for the present application, in which 7 are fixed and 4 are free to vary. The neural network model is further complicated by the nonlinear threshold function which is attached to each difference equation, which represents the output of each type of neural unit. In consequence, the state of the neural network operation at time t is determined by a lengthy process of a numerical solution, while the state of the tubelight operation can be determined directly by analytic methods.

8. RELATING TARGET-DISTRACTOR TRAJECTORIES TO TIME TO IDENTIFY A TARGET

The target and distractor trajectories shown in Figures 3, 4, 6, and 7 are intended to describe the rapid development of selective attention to the location of a target shape in order to segregate the relevant target information from the information arising from the location of distracting objects. An example of a display requiring this kind of selective attention is the letter string QOG, in which the middle letter is designated as the target and the outside letters the distractors. The effect of distance between the target and distractors can be investigated by comparing this display, QOG, with another display, Q O G, in which one character space is interpolated between the items. The time course of attentional intensities to the closely packed items of the QOG display (the NEAR case) is represented by the trajectories in Figures 3 and 6, and the time course of attentional intensities to the more separated items of the Q O G display (the FAR case) is represented by the trajectories in Figures 4 and 7. The development of a difference in the intensities at the coded target and distractor locations represents the development of a partitioning of the total flow of information into that part that arises from the target stimulus and the part that arises from the distractor stimuli. The upward modulation of the information flow arising from the target well beyond the level(s) of flow arising from the distractors enables the identification module (in brain area IT) to match the target information with a remembered code. Without this selective modulation, it is assumed that the identification module simply attempts to identify the three-item string as a whole (which would provide a successful matching event if the display were COG instead of QOG).

Thus, the intensifying of the information arising from the target location may be regarded as a process of "emphasis," which resembles the increased salience of a letter within the physical stimulus display itself, produced by increasing its luminance contrast (COG) or by printing it in a different color from the (single) color of the neighboring distractors. When the contrast is sufficiently large, the emphasized letter may be identified before the word in which it is embedded. This "emphasis" is assumed here to be produced in two ways: (1) by preattentive mechanisms that increase signal intensities in pathways that code the target (which may be embedded in circuits within the cortical sheet and/or in thalamocortical circuits that connect cortical areas; these circuits are termed "triangular circuits" in LaBerge, 1995b, 1995a), (2) by the attentive mechanisms, which increase ("emphasize") information flow under the control of voluntary processes located in the anterior cortex (see Figure 1).

Returning to the trajectories of the target and distractor locations shown in Figures 3, 4, 6, and 7, we ask how long does it take to establish sufficient emphasis (contrast) of the target information to produce an identification event in IT? What induces the featural information at the target location to begin processing a match with the stored shapes in IT? We assume that the beginning of a match to target information alone begins when the trajectories of the target and distractor first reach a criterion of intensity difference, which represents a certain amount of intensity contrast between the target and its surround. However, the intensity difference alone is not adequate for describing contrast, and the absolute level of the intensities must be taken into account. Therefore, the equation expressing the criterion contrast, C^*, that initiates the identification process at time t_a is

$$C^* = \frac{A_T(t_a) - A_D(t_a)}{A_D(t_a)}. \tag{7}$$

An analogy of the attentional operation reaching a contrast criterion is a situation in which the illuminance of a spot of light (whose location and size is initially unknown) gradually increases and thereby its location and size become defined somewhere in a background field of uniform intensity. As the spot increases in intensity, the effect upon an observer is that a corresponding code in a spatial map of the visual system increases its firing rate until a threshold is reached. Similarly, during the unfolding of attentional expression, the flow of information representing the target information is modulated upward, so that eventually the target information begins both to segregate itself from the surround and to dominate the surround, which amounts to a selection process on the basis of intensity contrast.

The segregated target information can then enter into the matching process in the identification module that can result in an identification event.

It is assumed that the identification of an object which results in an overt response or a stored representation in memory systems is not based upon one output signal from the identification module. Rather, it is assumed that a series of read-outs is required from the identification module to trigger an associated overt response or an internal categorization event. The notion that a series of signals may be required to trigger subsequent stages of processing is a basic assumption of accumulator (counter) models of response time (Luce, 1986b; Townsend & Ashby, 1983), where several input signals are assumed necessary to evoke a response. Therefore, we employ the term elemental "identification" to describe the identification event that produces a single readout signal from the identification module, to distinguish it from the usual meaning of the term "identification," which implies that identification of an object has been completed in a form that can be effectively used by other processing modules.

After the target-distractor contrast has reached an intensity contrast criterion, C^*, that initiates matching operations of the target information, the continuation of the criterion trajectory differences allow a series of matching operations to continue until an elementary identification event occurs. The amount of target information needed to complete an elemental identification process is represented by summing Equation 7 over time, t, until a particular criterion amount, C^{**}, is accumulated, where

$$C^{**} = \int_a^b \frac{A_T(t) - A_D(t)}{A_D(t)} dt. \tag{8}$$

When an elemental identification event occurs, two events take place: The coded identification event is read out as one element in a signal string that is sent to associated mechanisms (e.g., response-generating and categorizing mechanisms), and a signal is sent back to the attention mechanism to reset it to its initial state, so that the attentional operation can start over.

The generating of a series of elemental identification events is assumed to be required to trigger an overt response, according to the present model. The repeated attentional sampling of the display involves rapid and automatic fluctuating alignments: This process can generate errors (LaBerge, 1994). In some respects it resembles the rapid and relatively automatic alignment of attention to object locations in search tasks. In the present task, however, the voluntary control of attention is presumed to be initially directed to the location of the target, while in search tasks, attention typically moves about the display in a somewhat involuntary manner. One might conjecture that, for search, the number of elemental identification events needed to control whether attentional alignment remains at a given location or shifts to another location is less than the number of elemental identification events required to produce an overt response, once search has terminated at a target location.

The criteria, C^* and C^{**}, expressed by Equations 7 and 8, are of a complexity that require numerical methods to solve for the time variables $a = G(C^*)$ and $b = H(C^{**})$, where the functions G and H solve for the variables a and b using

Equations 7 and 8. Further development of this linkage between the present analytic model of attention and response models is outside the scope of the present paper, and will be addressed in subsequent papers.

Thus we have two identification criteria; one, C^*, for the initiation of the identification process, and one, C^{**}, for the completion of the identification process. Therefore, the time needed to produce an elemental identification event following the onset of the attention mechanism is simply the time value, $t = b$, that corresponds to the completion of an elemental identification event, which is represented in Figures 3, 4, 6, and 7 by the location of the upper boundary of the shaded area between a pair of curves.

In the present examples of displays containing NEAR and FAR distractors, the time required to produce an identification event is predicted to be greater when the distractors are located near to, compared with far from, the target. Therefore, operations of both the analytic and neural network models of attention can be connected to the operations of the subsequent identification module by an equation that expresses time to an elemental identification event as a function of the existing trajectory variables plus the two criterion variables that corresponding to initiating and completing the elemental identification process. However, to effectively trigger subsequent events such as responses and memory storage, we assume that a series of these outputs must occur in a relatively short interval of time. The next step in the development of the present analytic model is to derive equations that describe the accumulation of the output signals from the elemental identification events.

9. Conclusions

The similarities among the predicted trajectories for activity levels at coded locations of target and distractor objects, shown in Figures 3, 4, 6, and 7, suggest that the present analytic model can serve as a reasonably satisfactory approximation to the neural network model of thalamocortical operations of attention. Specifically, the analytic model appears to mimic quite closely the enhancement (contrast) and concentration (sharpening) properties of the neural network model. Ideally, the frequency and time aspects of overt responses should be linked by closed form equations to the mechanisms of the system that generate them, so that details of the mechanisms can be tested by experiments. Unfortunately, for the present analytic model the integration of the difference ratio of the trajectories, expressed by Equations 7 and 8, does not yield to closed-form solution; the corresponding situation is even more severe in the case of the neural network model. Therefore, it is not possible to express the duration of an identification event directly in terms of the parameters of the attention model. However, numerical methods allow one to describe mathematically the state of the system at time t for any combination of the parameters without resorting to numerical integration from $t = 0$ to the t_1 in question, as is required for the neural network model. This advantage of the analytic model over the neural network model, together with the many fewer free parameters in the case of the tubelight model, allows closer contact between theoretical assumptions about the attention, identification, and response-generating processes. It is hoped that the existing degree of mathematical contact between the analytic model and the response measures of relative frequency and response time is close enough to produce fruitful tests of the underlying attention model, as well as of the identification and response-generating models, and that the present formulation will suggest ways to modify the present component models to allow more detailed contact with data. In the meantime, the capturing of major structural and functional components of the attention process in terms of precise mathematical representations may serve as the clearest way to describe what the authors believe to be the major properties of the visual attention mechanism.

PART 6

SCIENTIFIC PUBLICATIONS OF R. DUNCAN LUCE

SCIENTIFIC PUBLICATIONS OF R. DUNCAN LUCE

1. Books

(1957) (Luce, R. D. & Raiffa, H.) *Games and Decisions: Introduction and Critical Survey.* New York: Wiley. (Reprinted in 1989 by Dover Publications)

(1959) *Individual Choice Behavior: A Theoretical Analysis.* New York: Wiley.

(1971) (Krantz, D. H, Luce, R. D., Suppes, P., & Tversky, A.) *Foundations of Measurement, Vol. I*, Academic Press.

(1986) *Response Times.* New York: Oxford University Press.

(1989) (Suppes, P., Krantz, D. H., Luce, R. D., & Tversky, A) *Foundations of Measurement, Vol. II*, Academic Press.

(1990) (Luce, R. D., Krantz, D. H., Suppes, P., & Tversky, A.) *Foundations of Measurement, Vol. III*, Academic Press.

(1993) *Sound and Hearing*, Hillsdale, NJ: Erlbaum.

2. Edited books

(1959) (Tucker, A. W., & Luce, R. D., Eds.) *Contributions to the Theory of Games, IV*, Annals of Mathematics Study, 40. Princeton, NJ: Princeton University Press.

(1960) (Ed) *Developments in Mathematical Psychology: Information, Learning, Tracking.* Glencoe: Free Press.

(1963) (Luce, R. D., Bush, R. R., & Galanter, E., Eds.) *Handbook of Mathematical Psychology, Vols. 1 & 2.* New York: Wiley.

(1963) (Luce, R. D.,. Bush, R. R., Galanter, E., Eds.) *Readings in Mathematical Psychology, Vol. 1.* New York: Wiley.

(1965) (Luce, R. D., Bush, R. R., & Galanter, E., Eds.) *Handbook of Mathematical Psychology. Vol. 3.* New York: Wiley.

(1965) (Luce, R. D., Bush, R. R., & Galanter, E., Eds.) *Readings in Mathematical Psychology, Vol. 2.* New York: Wiley.

(1974) (Atkinson, R. C., Krantz, D. H., Luce, R. D., & Suppes, P., Eds.) *Contemporary Developments in Mathematical Psychology, Vols. 1 and 2.* San Francisco: Freeman.

(1988) (Gerstein, D., Luce, R. D., Smelser, N. J., & Sperlich, S., Eds.) *The Behavioral and Social Sciences: Achievements and Opportunities.* Washington: National Academy Press.

(1988) (Atkinson, R. C., Herrnstein, R. J., Lindzey, G., & Luce, R. D., Eds.) *Stevens' Handbook of Experimental Psychology. Vols. I and II*, New York: Wiley.

(1989) (Luce, R. D., Smelser, N., & Gerstein, D., Eds.) *Leading Edges in the Behavioral and Social Sciences.* New York: The Russell Sage Foundation.

(1995) (Luce, R. D., D'Zmura, M., Hoffman, D, Iverson, G., & Romney, A. K., Eds.) *Geometric Representations of Perceptual Phenomena: Papers in Honor of Tarow Indow on His 70th birthday.* Hillsdale, NJ: Lawrence Erlbaum Associates.

3. SCIENTIFIC PAPERS

1949

(a) (Luce, R. D., & Perry, A. D.) A method of matrix analysis of group structure. *Psychometrika*, **14**, 95–116. [Reprinted in P. F. Lazarsfeld & N. W. Henry (Eds.), *Readings in Mathematical Social Science.* Chicago: Science Research Association, 1966. Pp. 111–130.]

1950

(a) *On semigroups.* Doctoral dissertation, Massachusetts Institute of Technology.

(b) Connectivity and generalized cliques in sociometric group structure. *Psychometrika*, **15**, 169–190.

1952

(a) A note on Boolean matrix theory. *Proceedings of the American Mathematical Society*, **3**, 382–388.

(b) Two decomposition theorems for a class of finite oriented graphs. *American Journal of Mathematics*, **74**, 701–722.

(c) (Christie, L. S., Luce, R. D., Macy, J., Jr.) *Communication and learning in task-oriented groups.* Technical Report 231, Research Laboratory of Electronics, Massachusetts Institute of Technology.

1953

(a) (Macy, J. Jr., Christie, L. S., & Luce, R. D.) Coding noise in task-oriented groups. *Journal of Abnormal and Social Psychology*, **48**, 401–409.

(b) Networks satisfying minimality conditions. *American Journal of Mathematics*, **75**, 825–838.

(c) (Luce, R. D., Macy, J., Jr, Christie, L. S., & Hay, H.) *Information flow in task-oriented groups.* Technical Report 264, Research Laboratory of Electronics, MIT.

1954

(a) A definition of stability for n-person games. *Annals of Mathematics*, **59**, 357–366.

1955

(a) k-Stability of symmetric and of quota games. *Annals of Mathematics*, **62**, 517–527.

(b) (Luce, R. D., Macy, J., Jr., & Tagiuri, R.) A statistical model for relational analysis. *Psychometrika*, **20**, 319–327. [Reprinted in R. D. Luce, R. R. Bush, & E. Galanter (Eds.), *Readings in Mathematical Psychology, Vol. II.* New York: Wiley, 1965. Pp. 272–280.]

(c) Ψ-Stability: A new equilibrium concept for n-person game theory. In *Mathematical Models of Human Behavior*. Stanford, Conn.: Dunlap and Associates. Pp. 32–44.

1956

(a) (Christie, L. S., & Luce, R. D.) Decision structure and time relations in simple choice behavior. *Bulletin of Mathematical Biophysics*, **18**, 89–112. [Reprinted in R. D. Luce, R. R. Bush, & E. Galanter (Eds.), *Readings in Mathematical Psychology, Vol. I.* New York: Wiley, 1963. Pp. 17–40.]

(b) (Luce, R. D., & Adams, E. W.) The determination of subjective payoff functions. *Econometrica*, **24**, 158–171.

(c) Semiorders and a theory of utility discrimination. *Econometrica*, **24**, 178–191.

(d) Information handling in organized groups, IV. Some aspects of time and decisions. In J. R. McCloskey & J. M. Coppinger (Eds.) *Operations Research for Management, Vol. II.* Baltimore: Johns Hopkins Press. Pp. 489–508.

(e) (Luce, R. D., & Rogow, A. A.) A game theoretic analysis of congressional power distribution for a stable two party system. *Behavioral Science*, **1**, 83–95.

1958

(a) A probabilistic theory of utility. *Econometrica*, **26**, 193–224.

(b) (Luce, R. D., & Edwards, W.) The derivation of subjective scales from just noticeable differences. *Psychological Review* **65**, 222–237.

1959

(a) A note on the article "Some experimental n-person games". In A. W. Tucker & R. D. Luce (Eds.), *Contributions to the Theory of Games, Vol. IV.* (Annals of Mathematics Study 40) Princeton: Princeton University Press. Pp. 279–285.

(b) Analyzing the social process underlying group voting patterns. In E. Burdick & A. J. Brodbeck (Eds.) *American Voting Behavior.* Glencoe: Free Press. Pp. 320–332.

(c) A probabilistic theory of utility and its relationship to Fechnerian scaling. In C. W. Churchman & P. Ratoosh (Eds.) *Measurement: Definitions and Theories.* New York: Wiley. Pp. 144–159.

(d) (Bush, R. R., Galanter, E., & Luce, R. D.) Empirical tests of the beta model. In R. R. Bush & W. K. Estes (Eds.) *Studies in Mathematical Learning Theory.* Stanford: Stanford University Press. Pp. 382–399.

(e) On the possible psychophysical laws. *Psychological Review,* **66**, 81–95. [Reprinted in R. D. Luce, R. R. Bush, & E. Galanter (Eds.) *Readings in Mathematical Psychology, Vol. I.* New York: Wiley 1963. Pp. 69–83. Also in Bobbs-Merril Reprint Series.]

(f) Response latencies and probabilities. In K. J. Arrow, S. Karlin, & P. Suppes (Eds.) *Mathematical Methods in the Social Sciences.* Stanford: Stanford University Press. Pp. 298–311.

1960

(a) A survey of the theory of selective information and some of its behavioral applications. In R. D. Luce (Ed.) *Developments in Mathematical Psychology.* Glencoe: Free Press. Pp. 1–119.

1952

(a) A choice theory analysis of similarity judgments. *Psychometrika,* **26**, 151–163.

(b) (Finnie, B., & Luce, R. D.) *Magnitude-Estimation, Pair-Comparison, and Successive-Intervals Scales of Attitude Items.* University of Pennsylvania, Memorandum MP-9.

1962

(a) (Griswold, B. J., & Luce, R. D.) Choices among uncertain outcomes: A test of a decomposition and two assumptions of transitivity. *American Journal of Psychology,* **75**, 35–44.

(b) (Luce, R. D., & Shipley, E. F.) Preference probability between gambles as a step function of event probability. *Journal of Experimental Psychology,* **63**, 42–49.

(c) An observable property equivalent to a choice model for discrimination experiments. *Psychometrika,* **27**, 163–167.

(d) Psychological studies of risky decision making. In G. B. Strother (Ed.) *Social Sciences Approach to Business Behavior.* Homewood, Ill: Dorsey Press and Richard D. Irwin. Pp. 141–161. [Reprinted in W. Edwards & A. Tversky (Eds.) *Decision Making.* Baltimore: Penguin Books, 1967. Pp. 334–352.]

(e) Comments on Rozeboom's criticisms of "On the possible psychophysical laws." *Psychological Review,* **69**, 548–551.

1963

(a) A threshold theory for simple detection experiments. *Psychological Review,* **70**, 61–79.

(b) (Bush, R. R., Galanter, E., & Luce, R. D.) Characterization and classification of choice experiments. In R. D. Luce, R. R. Bush, & E. Galanter (Eds.) *Handbook of Mathematical Psychology, Vol. 1.* New York: Wiley. Pp. 77–102.

(c) (Luce, R. D., & Galanter, E.) Discrimination. In R. D. Luce, R. R. Bush, & E. Galanter (Eds.) *Handbook of Mathematical Psychology, Vol. 1.* New York: Wiley. Pp. 191–243.

(d) Detection and recognition. In R. D. Luce, R. R. Bush, & E. Galanter (Eds.) *Handbook of Mathematical Psychology, Vol. 1.* New York: Wiley. Pp. 103–189.

(e) (Luce, R. D., & Galanter, E.) Psychophysical scaling. In R. D. Luce, R. R. Bush, & E. Galanter (Eds.) *Handbook of Mathematical Psychology, Vol. 1.* New York: Wiley. Pp. 245–307.

1964

(a) (Bush, R. R., Luce, R. D., & Rose, R. M.) Learning models for psychophysics. In R. C. Atkinson (Ed.) *Studies in Mathematical Psychology.* Stanford University Press. Pp. 201–217.

(b) (Shipley, E. F., & Luce, R. D.) Discrimination among two- and three-element sets of weights. In R. C. Atkinson (Ed.) *Studies in Mathematical Psychology.* Stanford University Press. Pp. 218–232.

(c) Some one-parameter families of commutative learning operators. In R. C. Atkinson (Ed.) *Studies in Mathematical Psychology.* Stanford: Stanford University Press. Pp. 380–398.

(d) Learning and optimal judgments. In M. W. Shelly & G. I. Bryan (Eds.) *Human Judgments and Optimality.* New York: Wiley. Pp. 101–115.

(e) (Luce, R. D., & Tukey, J. W.) Simultaneous conjoint measurement: A new type of fundamental measurement. *Journal of Mathematical Psychology, 1,* 1–27.

(f) A generalization of a theorem of dimensional analysis. *Journal of Mathematical Psychology, 1, 1,* 278–284.

(g) Asymptotic learning in psychophysical theories. *British Journal of Statistical Psychology, 17,* 1–13.

(h) The mathematics used in mathematical psychology. *American Mathematical Monthly, 71,* 364–378.

(i) Discussion. In R. W. Gerard & J. W. Duyff (Eds.) *Information Processing in the Nervous System.* Amsterdam: Excerpta Medica Foundation, pp. 419–429.

1965

(a) (Luce, R. D., & Suppes, P.) Preference, utility, and subjective probability. In R. D. Luce, R. R. Bush, & E. Galanter (Eds.) *Handbook of Mathematical Psychology, Vol. 3.* New York: Wiley. Pp. 249–410.

(b) A "fundamental" axiomatization of multiplicative power relations among three variables. *Philosophy of Science, 32,* 301–309.

(c) (McLaughlin, D. H., & Luce, R. D.) Stochastic transitivity and cancellation of preferences between bitter-sweet solutions. *Psychonomic Science, 2,* 89–90.

(d) (Luce, R. D., & Mo, S. S.) Magnitude estimation of heaviness and loudness by individual subjects. *British Journal of Mathematical and Statistical Psychology, 18,* 159–174.

(e) Utility theory. In S. Sternberg, V. Capecchi, T. Kloek, & C. T. Leenders (Eds.) *Mathematics and Social Sciences*. Paris: Mouton. Pp. 55–71.

(f) Eine theoretische Analyse der Detektion in zeitlich nichtstruktueierten Experimenten. *Zeitschrift für Psychologie*, **171**, 57–68.

1966

(a) A model for detection in temporally unstructured experiments with a Poisson distribution of stimulus presentations. *Journal of Mathematical Psychology*, **3**, 48–64.

(b) Two extensions of conjoint measurement. *Journal of Mathematical Psychology*, **3**, 348–370.

(c) (Lowenton, E., & Luce, R. D.) Measuring equal increments of utility for money without measuring utility itself. *Psychonomic Science*, **6**, 75–76.

(d) Theories of conjoint measurement. In *Proceedings of the XVIII International Congress of Psychology*. Moscow, USSR. Pp. 62–67.

1967

(a) Sufficient conditions for the existence of a finitely additive probability measure. *Annals of Mathematical Statistics*, **38**, 780–786.

(b) Remarks on the theory of measurement and its relation to psychology. In *Les Modèles et la Formalizations du Comportement*. Edition du Centre National de la Recherche Scientifique. Pp. 27–42.

(c) (Green, D. M., & Luce, R. D.) Detection of auditory signals presented at random times. *Perception & Psychophysics*, **2**, 441–450.

(d) (Snodgrass, J. G., Luce, R. D., & Galanter, E.) Some experiments on simple and choice reaction times. *Journal of Experimental Psychology*, **75**, 1–17.

1968

(a) (Bush, R. R., Luce, R. D., & Suppes, P.) Models, mathematical. In D. Sills (Ed.) *International Encyclopedia of the Social Sciences, Vol. 10.* Pp. 379–386. [Reprinted in W. H. Kruskal & J. M. Tamur (Eds.) *International Encyclopedia of Statistics*. New York: MacMillan & Free Press. Pp. 592–601.]

(b) (Luce, R. D., & Suppes, P.) Mathematics. In D. Sills (Ed.) *International Encyclopedia of the Social Sciences, Vol. 10.* Pp. 65–76. [Reprinted in W. H. Kruskal & J. M. Tamur (Eds.) *International Encyclopedia of Statistics*. New York: MacMillan & Free Press. Pp. 580–592.]

(c) On the numerical representation of qualitative conditional probability. *Annals of Mathematical Statistics*, **39**, 481–491.

(d) (Roberts, F. S., & Luce, R. D.) Axiomatic thermodynamics and extensive measurement. *Synthese*, **18**, 311–326.

(e) Algebraic systems of measurement. In C. A. J. Vlek (Ed.) *Algebraic Models in Psychology. Proceedings NUFFIC International Summer Session*, The Hague. Pp. 269–298.

1969

(a) Subjective expected utility. *Proceedings of the 7th Coloquia Brasilero de Matematica*, Pocos Caldos, Brasil, 5–15.

(b) (Luce, R. D., & Marley, A. A. J.) Extensive measurement when concatenation is restricted and maximal elements may exist. In S. Morgenbesser, P. Suppes, & M. G. White (Eds.) *Philosophy, Science, and Method: Essays in Honor of Ernest Nagel.* New York: St. Martin's Press. Pp. 235–249.

1970

(a) What are mathematical models of behavior models of? In R. M. Stogdill (Ed.) *The Process of Model Building.* Columbus: Ohio State University Press. Pp. 115–132.

(b) (Luce, R. D., & Green, D. M.) Detection of auditory signals presented at random times, II. *Perception & Psychophysics*, **7**, 1–14.

1971

(a) (Green, D. M., & Luce, R. D.) Detection of auditory signals presented at random times, III. *Perception & Psychophysics*, **9**, 257–268.

(b) Periodic extensive measurement. *Composito Mathematica*, **23**, 189–198.

(c) (Luce, R. D., & Krantz, D. H.) Conditional expected utility. *Econometrica*, **39**, 253–271.

(d) Similar systems and dimensionally invariant laws. *Philosophy of Science*, **38**, 157–169.

1972

(a) (Luce, R. D., & Green, D. M.) A neural timing theory for response times and the psychophysics of intensity. *Psychological Review*, **79**, 14–57.

(b) What sort of measurement is psychophysical measurement? *American Psychologist*, **27**, 96–106.

(c) Conditional expected, extensive utility. *Theory and Decision*, **3**, 101–106.

1973

(a) (Green, D. M., & Luce, R. D.) Speed-accuracy tradeoff in auditory detection. In S. Kornblum (Ed.) *Attention and Performance, IV.* New York: Academic Press. Pp. 547–659.

(b) Three axiom systems for additive semi-ordered structures. *SIAM Journal of Applied Mathematics*, **25**, 41–53.

(c) Renewal process models for psychophysics. In P. J. Kropp & H. Meyer (Eds.) *Proceedings of a Conference on the Application of Undergraduate Mathematics in the Engineering, Life, Managerial, and Social Sciences.* Atlanta, GA: Georgia Institute of Technology. Pp. 103–137.

(d) Measurement and psychophysics. In H. A. Selby (Ed.) *Notes of Lectures on Mathematics in the Behavioral Sciences.* Mathematical Association of America. Pp. 197–267.

1974

(a) (Luce, R. D., & Green, D. M.) The response ratio hypothesis for magnitude estimation. *Journal of Mathematical Psychology, 11,* 1–14.

(b) (Green, D. M., & Luce, R. D.) Variability of magnitude estimates: A timing theory analysis. *Perception & Psychophysics, 15,* 291–300.

(c) (Green, D. M., & Luce, R. D.) Counting and timing mechanisms in auditory discrimination and reaction time. In D. H. Krantz, R. C. Atkinson, R. D. Luce, & P. Suppes (Eds.) *Contemporary Developments in Mathematical Psychology, Vol. II.* San Francisco: Freeman. Pp. 372–415.

(d) (Luce, R. D., & Green, D. M.) Ratios of magnitude estimates. In H. R. Moskowitz, B. Scharf, & J. C. Stevens (Eds.) *Sensation and Measurement.* Dordrecht, Holland: D. Reidel Pp. 99–111.

(e) (Luce, R. D., & Green, D. M.) Detection, discrimination, and recognition. In E. C. Carterette & M. P. Friedman (Eds.) *Handbook of Perception, Vol. II.* New York: Academic Press. Pp. 299–342.

(f) (Luce, R. D., & Green, D. M.) Neural coding and psychophysical discrimination data. *Journal of the Acoustical Society of America, 56,* 1554–1564. (1975) Erratum: Neural coding and psychophysical discrimination. *Journal of the Acoustical Society of America, 57,* 1552.

(g) (Galanter, E., & Luce, R. D.) Robert R. Bush, Later Career. *Journal of Mathematical Psychology, 11,* 179–189.

(h) (Luce, R. D., & Suppes, P.) Measurement, theory of. *Encyclopedia Britannica, 15th Edition, 11,* 739–745.

1975

(a) (Green, D. M., & Luce, R. D.) Parallel psychometric functions from a set of independent detectors. *Psychological Review, 82,* 483–486. (1976) Correction to "Parallel psychometric functions from a set of independent detectors." *Psychological Review, 83,* 172.

1976

(a) (Luce, R. D., Green, D. M., & Weber, D. L.) Attention bands in absolute identification. *Perception & Psychophysics, 20,* 49–54.

(b) (Narens, L., & Luce, R. D.) The algebra of measurement. *Journal of Pure and Applied Algebra, 8,* 197–233.

(c) (Luce, R. D., & Narens, L.) A qualitative equivalent to the relativistic additive law for velocities. *Synthese, 33,* 483–487.

(d) (Jesteadt, W., Green, D. M., & Luce, R. D.) Sources of variability in magnitude estimation. In H.-G. Geissler & Yu. M. Zabrodin (Eds.) *Advances in Psychophysics.* Berlin: VEB Deutscher Verlag der Wissenschaften. Pp. 239–251.

1977

(a) The choice axiom after twenty years. *Journal of Mathematical Psychology, 15,* 215–233. [Reprinted in R. K. Merton, J. S. Coleman, & P. H. Rossi

(Eds.) *Qualitative and Quantitative Social Research*. New York: The Free Press, Pp. 138–157.]

(b) A note on sums of power functions. *Journal of Mathematical Psychology*, **16**, 91–93.

(c) (Weber, D. L., Green, D. M., & Luce, R. D.) Effects of practice and distribution of auditory signals on absolute identification. *Perception & Psychophysics*, **22**, 223–231.

(d) (Jesteadt, W., Luce, R. D., & Green, D. M.) Sequential effects in judgments of loudness. *Journal of Experimental Psychology: Human Perception and Performance*, **3**, 92–104.

(e) (Green, D. M., Luce, R. D., & Duncan, J. E.) Variability and sequential effects in magnitude production and estimation of auditory intensity. *Perception & Psychophysics*, **22**, 450–456.

(f) Thurstone's discriminal processes fifty years later. *Psychometrika*, **42**, 461–489.

1978

(a) (Luce, R. D., & Green, D. M.) Two tests of a neural attention hypothesis for auditory psychophysics. *Perception & Psychophysics*, **23**, 363–391.

(b) (Luce, R. D., & Narens, L.) Qualitative independence in probability theory. *Theory and Decision*, **9**, 225–239.

(c) Lexicographic tradeoff structures. *Theory and Decision*, **9**, 187–193.

(d) (Wandell, B., & Luce, R. D.) Pooling peripheral information: Averages versus extreme values. *Journal of Mathematical Psychology*, **17**, 220–235.

(e) Dimensionally invariant numerical laws correspond to meaningful qualitative relations. *Philosophy of Science*, **45**, 1–16.

(f) Conjoint measurement: A brief survey. In D. E. Bell, R. L. Keeney, & H. Raiffa (Eds.) *Conflicting Objectives*. New York: Wiley. Pp. 148–171. [Also in C. A. Hooker et al. (Eds.) *Foundations and Applications of Decision Theory, Vol. I*. Dordrecht: D. Reidel. Pp. 311–336.]

(g) A mathematician as psychologist. In T. W. Krawiec (Ed.) *The Psychologists, Vol. 3*, Brandon, VT: Clinical Psychology Publishing Company. Pp. 125–165.

(h) Giving advice on social dynamics. *The National Research Council in 1978*. Washington: The National Academy of Sciences. Pp. 33–44.

1979

(a) Suppes' contributions to the theory of measurement. In R. J. Bogden (Ed.) *Patrick Suppes*. Dordrecht: D. Reidel. Pp. 83–110.

(b) (Heyman, G. M., & Luce, R. D.) Operant matching does not result from maximizing reinforcement rate. *Animal Learning and Behavior*, **7**, 133–140.

(c) (Heyman, G. M., & Luce, R. D.) Reply to Rachlin's comment. *Animal Learning and Behavior*, **7**, 269–270.

1980

(a) (Baird, J. C., Green, D. M., & Luce, R. D.) Variability of sequential effects in cross-modality matching of areas and loudness. *Journal of Experimental Psychology: Human Perception and Performance*, **6**, 227–289.

(b) (Green, D. M., Luce, R. D., & Smith, A. F.) Individual magnitude estimates for various distributions of signal intensity. *Perception & Psychophysics*, **27**, 483–488.

(c) Several possible measures of risk. *Theory and Decision*, *12*, 217–228. (1981) Correction to "Several possible measures of risk." *Theory and Decision*, **13**, 381.

(d) (Luce, R. D., Baird, J. C., Green, D. M., & Smith, A. F.) Two classes of models for magnitude estimation. *Journal of Mathematical Psychology*, **22**, 121–148.

(e) Comments on Chapters by MacCrimmon, Stanbury, and Wehrung; and Schum. In T. S. Wallsten (Ed.) *Cognitive Processes in Choice and Decision Behavior*. Hillsdale, NJ: Erlbaum, 1980. Pp. 155–177.

1981

(a) Axioms for the averaging and adding representations of functional measurement. *Mathematical Social Sciences*, **1**, 139–144.

(b) (Luce, R. D., & Narens, L.) Axiomatic measurement theory. In S. Grossberg (Ed.) *Mathematical Psychology and Psychophysiology*. SIAM-AMS Proceedings, Vol. 13. Providence: American Mathematical Society. Pp. 213–235.

1982

(a) (Burbeck, S. L., & Luce, R. D.) Evidence from auditory simple reaction times for both change and level detectors. *Perception & Psychophysics*, **32**, 117–133.

(b) (Braida, L. D., Cornsweet, T. N., Durlach, N. I., Green, D. M., Leibowitz, H., Liberman, A., Luce, R. D., Pew, R., & Sherrick, C.) Research in psychophysics. In R. McC. Adams, N. J. Smelser, & D. J. Treiman (Eds.) *Behavioral and Social Sciences Research: A National Resource, Part II.* Washington, DC: National Academy Press. Pp. 373–405.

(c) (Luce, R. D., Nosofsky, R., Green, D. M., & Smith, A. F.) The bow and sequential effects in absolute identification. *Perception & Psychophysics*, **32**, 397–408.

1983

(a) (Luce, R. D., & Cohen, M.) Factorizable automorphisms in solvable conjoint structures I. *Journal of Pure and Applied Algebra*, **27**, 225–261.

(b) (Narens, L., & Luce, R. D.) How we may have been misled into believing in the inter-personal comparability of utility. *Theory and Decision*, **15**, 247–260.

(c) (Luce, R. D., & Narens, L.) Symmetry, scale types, and generalizations of classical physical measurement. *Journal of Mathematical Psychology*, **27**, 44–85.

1984

(a) (Luce, R. D., & Nosofsky, R.) Attention, stimulus range, and identification of loudness. In S. Kornblum & J. Requin (Eds.) *Preparatory States and Processes*. Hillsdale, NJ: Erlbaum. Pp. 3–25.

(b) Time perception: Discussion paper. In J. Gibbon & L. Allan (Eds.) *Timing and Time Perception*. Annals of the New York Academy of Sciences, Vol. 423. Pp. 78–81.

(c) (Luce, R. D., & Narens, L.) Classification of real measurement representations by scale type. *Measurement*, **2**, 39–44.

(d) Behavior theory: A contradiction in terms? *Behavioral and Brain Sciences*, **7**, 525–526.

1985

(a) Mathematical modeling of perceptual, learning, and cognitive processes. In S. Koch & D. E. Leary (Eds.) *A Century of Psychology as Science*. New York: McGraw Hill. Pp. 654–677.

(b) (Luce, R. D., & Narens, L.) Classification of concatenation structures according to scale type. *Journal of Mathematical Psychology*, **29**, 1–72.

1986

(a) (Narens, L., & Luce, R. D.) Measurement: The theory of numerical assignments. *Psychological Bulletin*, **99**, 166–180.

(b) (Luce, R. D., & Weber, E. U.) An axiomatic theory of conjoint, expected risk. *Journal of Mathematical Psychology*, **30**, 188–205.

(c) Response time distributions in memory search: A caution. In F. Klix & H. Hagendorf (Eds.) *Human Memory and Cognitive Capabilities: Mechanisms and Performances*. North Holland: Elsevier Science Publishers. Pp. 109–121.

(d) Uniqueness and homogeneity of real relational structures. *Journal of Mathematical Psychology*, **30**, 391–415.

(e) Comments on Plott and on Kahneman, Knetsch, and Thaler. *The Journal of Business*, **59**, S337–S343. [Reprinted in R. M. Hogarth & M. W. Reder (Eds.) *Rational Choice*. Chicago: University of Chicago Press, 1986. Pp. 153–159.]

1987

(a) (Folk, M., & Luce, R. D.) Effects of stimulus complexity on mental rotation rate of polygons. *Journal of Experimental Psychology: Human Perception and Performance*, **13**, 395–404.

(b) (Luce, R. D., & Narens, L.) The mathematics underlying measurement on the continuum. *Science*, **236**, 1527–1532.

(c) Measurement structures with Archimedean ordered translation groups. *Order*, **4**, 165–189.

(d) (Luce, R. D., & Narens, L.) Measurement, theory of. In J. Eatwell, M. Milgate, & P. Newman (Eds.) *The New Palgrave: A Dictionary of Economic Theory and Doctrine, Vol. 3*. New York: The Macmillan Press. Pp. 428–432. [Reprinted in J. Eatwell, M. Milgate, & P. Newman (1990) *Time Series and Statistics*. New York: The Macmillan Press. Pp. 159–170.]

(e) (Narens, L., & Luce, R. D.) Meaningfulness and invariance. In J. Eatwell, M. Milgate, & P. Newman (Eds.) *The New Palgrave: A Dictionary of Economic Theory and Doctrine, Vol. 3*. New York: The Macmillan Press. Pp. 417–421. [Reprinted in J. Eatwell, M. Milgate, & P. Newman (1990) *Time Series and Statistics*. New York: The Macmillan Press. Pp. 140–148.]

1988

(a) (Luce, R. D., & Krumhansl, C.) Measurement, scaling, and psychophysics. In R. C. Atkinson, R. J. Herrnstein, G. Lindzey, & R. D. Luce (Eds.) *Stevens' Handbook of Experimental Psychology*. New York: Wiley. Pp. 1–74.

(b) Goals, achievements, and limitations of modern fundamental measurement theory. In H. H. Bock (Ed.) *Classification and Related Methods of Data Analysis*. Amsterdam: Elsevier Science Publishers. Pp. 15–22.

(c) Measurement representations of ordered, relational structures with Archimedean ordered translations. *Proceedings of a conference on Mathématiques et Sciences Humaines*. Centre International de Rencontres Mathématiques de Marseille-Luminy, June 1987. Pp. 35–47.

(d) Rank-dependent, subjective-utility representations. *Journal of Risk and Uncertainty*, **1**, 305–332.

1989

(a) R. Duncan Luce. In G. Lindzey (Ed.) *Psychology in Autobiography, Vol. VIII*. Stanford, CA: Stanford University Press. Pp. 245–289.

(b) Mathematical psychology and the computer revolution. In J. A. Keats, R. Taft, R. A. Heath, & S. H. Lovibond (Eds.) *Mathematical and Theoretical Systems. Proceedings of the XXIV International Congress of Psychology*. Holland: Elsevier. Pp. 123–137.

1990

(a) "On the possible psychophysical laws" revisited: Remarks on cross-modal matching. *Psychological Review*, **97**, 66–77.

(b) (Bostic, R., Herrnstein, R. J., & Luce, R. D.) The effect on the preference-reversal phenomenon of using choice indifferences. *Journal of Economic Behavior and Organization*, **13**, 193–212.

(c) Rational versus plausible accounting equivalences in preference judgments. *Psychological Science*, **1**, 225–234. [Also in W. Edwards (Ed.) (1992) *Utility Theories: Measurements, and Applications*. Boston: Kluwer Academic Publishers. Pp 187–206.]

(d) (Narens, L., & Luce, R. D.) Three aspects of the effectiveness of mathematics in science. In R. Mickens (Ed.) *Mathematics and Science.* World Scientific Press. Pp. 122–135.

1991

(a) Rank- and sign-dependent linear utility models for binary gambles. *Journal of Economic Theory,* **53**, 75–100.

(b) (Luce, R. D., & Fishburn, P. C.) Rank- and sign-dependent linear utility models for finite first-order gambles. *Journal of Risk and Uncertainty,* **4**, 29–59.

(c) What is a ratio in ratio scaling? In S. J. Bolanowski & G. A. Gescheider (Eds.) *Ratio Scaling of Psychological Magnitudes, In Honor of the Memory of S. S. Stevens.* Hillsdale, NJ: Erlbaum. Pp. 8–17.

1992

(a) Where does subjective expected utility fail descriptively? *Journal of Risk and Uncertainty,* **5**, 5–27.

(b) (Luce, R. D., & Narens, L.) Intrinsic Archimedeanness and the continuum. In C. W. Savage & P. Ehrlich (Eds.) *Philosophical and Foundational Issues in Measurement Theory.* Hillsdale, NJ: Erlbaum. Pp. 15–38.

(c) A theory of certainty equivalents for uncertain alternatives. *Journal of Behavioral Decision Making,* **5**, 201–216.

(d) Generalized concatenation structures that are translation homogeneous between singular points. *Mathematical Social Sciences,* **24**, 79–103.

(e) A path taken: Aspects of modern measurement theory. In A. F. Healy, S. Kosslyn, & R. Shiffrin (Eds.) *Essays in Honor of William K. Estes, Vol. 1.* Hillsdale, NJ: Erlbaum. Pp. 45–64.

(f) (Hunt, E., & Luce, R. D.) SOAR as a world view, not a theory. *Behavior and Brain Science,* **15**, 447–448.

1993

(a) (Luce, R. D., Mellers, B., & Chang, S.-J.) Is choice the correct primitive? On using certainty equivalents and reference levels to predict choices among gambles. *Journal of Risk and Uncertainty,* **6**, 115–143.

(b) (Narens, L., & Luce, R. D.) Further comments on the "non-revolution" arising from axiomatic measurement theory. *Psychological Science,* **4**, 127–130.

(c) Let's not promulgate either Fechner's erroneous algorithm or his unidimensional approach. *Behavior and Brain Sciences,* **16**, 155–156.

(d) Reliability is neither to be expected nor desired in peer review. *Behavioral and Brain Sciences,* **14**, 399–400.

1994

(a) Thurstone and sensory scaling: Then and now. *Psychological Review,* **107**, 271–277.

(b) (Luce, R. D., & von Winterfeldt, D.) What common ground exists for descriptive, prescriptive, and normative utility theories. *Management Science,* **40**, 263–279.

(c) (Luce, R. D., & Narens, L.) Fifteen problems in the representational theory of measurement. In P. Humphreys (Ed.) *Patrick Suppes: Scientific Philosopher, Vol. 2: Philosophy of Physics, Theory Structure, Measurement Theory, Philosophy of Language, and Logic.* Dordrecht: Kluwer Academic Publishers. Pp. 219–245.

(d) (Cho, Y., Luce, R. D., & von Winterfeldt, D.) Tests of assumptions about the joint receipt of gambles in rank- and sign-dependent utility theory. *Journal of Experimental Psychology: Human Perception and Performance,* **20**, 931–943.

(e) (Chung, N.-K., von Winterfeldt, D., & Luce, R. D.) An experimental test of event commutativity in rank-dependent utility theory. *Psychological Science,* **5**, 394–400.

1995

(a) Joint receipt and certainty equivalents of gambles. *Journal of Mathematical Psychology,* **39**, 73–81.

(b) (Fishburn, P. C., & Luce, R. D.) Joint receipt and Thaler's hedonic editing rule. *Mathematical Social Sciences,* **29**, 33–76.

(c) Four tensions concerning mathematical modeling in psychology. *Annual Reviews of Psychology,* **46**, 1–26.

(d) (Luce, R. D., & Fishburn, P. C.) A note on deriving rank-dependent utility using additive joint receipts. *Journal of Risk and Uncertainty,* **11**, 5–16.

(e) (Cho, Y., & Luce, R. D.) Tests of hypotheses about certainty equivalents and joint receipt of gambles. *Organizational Behavior and Human Decision Processes,* **64**, 229–248.

1996

(a) Commentary on aspects of Lola Lopes paper. *Organizational Behavior and Human Decision Processes,* **65**, 190–193.

(b) The ongoing dialogue between empirical science and measurement theory. *Journal of Mathematical Psychology,* **40**, 78–98.

(c) (Aczél, J., Luce, R. D., & Maksa, Gy.) Solutions to three functional equations arising from different ways of measuring utility. *Journal of Mathematical Analysis and Applications,* **204** 451–471.

(d) When four distinct ways to measure utility are the same. *Journal of Mathematical Psychology,* **40**, 297–317.

1997

(a) (von Winterfeldt, D., Chung, N.-K., Luce, R. D., & Cho, Y.) Tests of consequence monotonicity in decision making under uncertainty. *Journal of Experimental Psychology: Learning, Memory and Cognition*, in press.

(b) (Iverson, G., & Luce, R. D.) The measurement approach to psychophysics and judgment. In *Handbook of Perception and Cognition*, in press.

(c) Some unresolved conceptual problems of mathematical psychology. Submitted for publication in the volume from the 1995 meeting of the European Mathematical Psychology Group.

(d) Associative joint receipts. *Mathematical Social Sciences*, in press.

(e) (Luce, R. D. & Alper, T.) Conditions equivalent to unit representations of ordered relational structures. In preparation.

(f) The past seven years: 1988–95. In A. A. J. Marley (Ed.) *Choice, Decision and Measurement: Essays in Honor of R. Duncan Luce.* Mahwah, NJ: Erlbaum. Pp. 3–14.

(g) (Sneddon, R., & Luce, R. D.) Bias in a PEST procedure. In preparation.

(h) Coalescing, event commutativity, and theories of utility. In preparation.

(i) On the interplay of riskless and risky utility. In preparation.

Choice, Decision, and Measurement
A. A. J. Marley (Ed.),
©Lawrence Erlbaum Associates, NJ, 1997.

REFERENCES

Aczél, J. (1946). The notion of mean values. *Norske Videnskabers Selskab Forhandlinger Trondheim,* **19**, 83–86.

Aczél, J. (1948). On mean values. *Bulletin of the American Mathematical Society,* **54**, 392–400.

Aczél, J. (1966). *Lectures on Functional Equations and Their Applications.* New York and London: Academic Press.

Aczél, J., Belousov, V. D., & Hosszú, M. (1960). Generalized associativity and bisymmetry on quasigroups. *Acta Mathematica Academiae Scientiarum Hungaricae,* **11**, 127–136.

Aczél, J., Luce, R. D., & Maksa, Gy. (1996). Solutions to three functional equations arising from different ways of measuring utility. *Journal of Mathematical Analysis and Applications,* **204**, 451–471.

Aczél, J., & Maksa, Gy. (1996). Solution of the rectangular $m \times n$ generalized bisymmetry equation and of the problem of consistent aggregation. *Journal of Mathematical Analysis and Applications,* **203**, 104–126.

Aczél, J., Maksa, Gy., & Taylor, M. A. (1997). Equations of generalized bisymmetry and of consistent aggregation: Weakly surjective solutions which may be discontinuous at places. Manuscript, Faculty of Mathematics, University of Waterloo.

Allais, M. (1953). Le comportement de l'homme rationnel devant le risque: Critque des postulats et axiomes de l'école americaine. *Econometrica,* **21**, 503–546.

Allais, M., & Hagen, O. (Eds.). (1979). *Expected Utility Hypotheses and the Allais Paradox.* Dordrecht: Reidel.

Alper, T. M. (1987). A classification of all order-preserving homeomorphism groups of the reals that satisfy finite uniqueness. *Journal of Mathematical Psychology,* **31**, 135–154.

Anderson, J. R. (1991). The adaptive nature of human categorization. *Psychological Review,* **98**, 409–429.

Anderson, N. H. (1971). Integration theory and attitude change. *Econometrica,* **78**, 171–206.

Anderson, T., & Birnbaum, M. H. (1976). Test of an additive model of social inference. *Journal of Personality and Social Psychology,* **33**, 655–662.

Ansalobehere, S., Iyengar, S., Simon, A., & Valentino, N. (1994). Does attack advertising demobilize the electorate? *American Political Science Review,* **88**, 829–838.

Arrow, K. J. (1951). *Social Choice and Individual Values.* New York: Wiley.

Arrow, K. J. (1965). *Aspects of the Theory of Risk Bearing.* Helsinki: Yrjo Jahnssonis Saatio.

Arrow, K. J. (1971). *Essays in the Theory of Risk Bearing.* Chicago: Markham.

Ashby, F. G. (1992). Multidimensional models of categorization. In F. G. Ashby (Ed.), *Multidimensional Models of Perception and Cognition* (pp. 449–483). Hillsdale, NJ: Erlbaum.

Ashby, F. G., & Alfonso-Reese, L. A. (1995). Categorization as probability density estimation. *Journal of Mathematical Psychology*, **39**, 216–233.

Ashby, F. G., Boynton, G., & Lee, W. W. (1994). Categorization response time with multidimensional stimuli. *Perception and Psychophysics*, **55**, 11–27.

Ashby, F. G., & Gott, R. E. (1988). Decision rules in the perception and categorization of multidimensional stimuli. *Journal of Experimental Psychology: Learning, Memory, and Cognition*, **14**, 33–53.

Ashby, F. G., & Lee, W. W. (1991). Predicting similarity and categorization from identification. *Journal of Experimental Psychology: General*, **120**, 150–172.

Ashby, F. G., & Lee, W. W. (1992). On the relationship among identification, similarity, and categorization: Reply to Nosofsky and Smith. *Journal of Experimental Psychology: General*, **121**, 385–393.

Ashby, F. G., & Maddox, W. T. (1990). Integrating information from separable psychological dimensions. *Journal of Experimental Psychology: Human Perception and Performance*, **16**, 598–612.

Ashby, F. G., & Maddox, W. T. (1991). A response time theory of perceptual independence. In J. P. Doignon & F. C. Falmagne (Eds.), *Mathematical Psychology: Current Developments* (pp. 389–414). New York: Springer Verlag.

Ashby, F. G., & Maddox, W. T. (1992). Complex decision rules in categorization: Contrasting novice and experienced performance. *Journal of Experimental Psychology: Human Perception and Performance*, **18**, 50–71.

Ashby, F. G., & Maddox, W. T. (1993). Relations between prototype, exemplar, and decision bound models of categorization. *Journal of Mathematical Psychology*, **37**, 372–400.

Ashby, F. G., & Maddox, W. T. (1994). A response time theory of separability and integrality in speeded classification. *Journal of Mathematical Psychology*, **38**, 423–466.

Ashby, F. G., & Maddox, W. T. (in press). Stimulus categorization. In M. H. Birnbaum (Ed.), *Handbook of Perception and Cognition: Volume 3.* New York: Academic Press.

Ashby, F. G., Maddox, W. T., & Lee, W. W. (1994). On the dangers of averaging across subjects when using multidimensional scaling or the similarity-choice model. *Psychological Science*, **5**, 144–151.

Ashby, F. G., & Townsend, J. T. (1980). Decomposing the reaction time distribution: Pure insertion and selective influence revisited. *Journal of Mathematical Psychology*, **21**, 93–123.

Ashby, F. G., & Townsend, J. T. (1986). Varieties of perceptual independence. *Psychological Review*, **93**, 154–179.

Atkinson, R. C., Bower, G. H., & Crothers, E. J. (1965). *An Introduction to*

Mathematical Learning Theory. New York: Wiley.

Atkinson, R. C., Carterette, E. C., & Kinchla, R. A. (1962). Sequential phenomena in psychophysical judgments. *Institute of Radio Engineers Transactions on Information Theory,* **IT-8**, 155–162.

Audley, R. J., & Pike, A. R. (1965). Some alternative stochastic models of choice. *British Journal of Mathematical and Statistical Psychology,* **18**, 207–225.

Balakrishnan, J., & Ratcliff, R. (in press). Testing models of decision making using confidence judgments in classification. *Journal of Experimental Psychology: Human Perception and Performance.*

Bamber, D. (1975). The area above the ordinal dominance graph and the area below the receiver operating characteristic graph. *Journal of Mathematical Psychology,* **12**, 387–415.

Bamber, D. (1979). State-trace analysis: A method of testing simple theories of causation.. *Journal of Mathematical Psychology,* **19**, 137–181.

Barlow, R. E., Bartholomew, D. J., Bremner, J. M., & Brunk, H. D. (1972). *Statistical Inference under Order Restrictions.* London: Wiley.

Becker, G. M., DeGroot, M. H., & Marschak, J. (1963). Probabilities of choice among very similar objects. *Behavioral Science,* **8**, 306–311.

Bell, D. E. (1995). Risk, return, and utility. *Management Science,* **41**, 23–30.

Berliner, J. E., & Durlach, N. I. (1973). Intensity perception. IV. Resolution in roving-level discrimination. *Journal of the Acoustical Society of America,* **53**, 1270–1287.

Berliner, J. E., Durlach, N. I., & Braida, L. D. (1977). Intensity perception, VII. Further data on roving-level discrimination and the resolution of bias edge effect. *Journal of the Acoustical Society of America,* **61**, 1577–1585.

Bernstein, I. H., Clark, M. H., & Edelstein, B. A. (1969). Effects of an auditory signal on visual reaction time. *Journal of Experimental Psychology,* **80**, 567–569.

Birnbaum, M. H. (1973). Morality judgment: Test of an averaging model with differential weights. *Journal of Experimental Psychology,* **99**, 395–399.

Birnbaum, M. H. (1974). The nonadditivity of personality impressions. *Journal of Experimental Psychology,* **102**, 543–561. (Monograph).

Birnbaum, M. H. (1976). Intuitive numerical prediction. *American Journal of Psychology,* **89**, 417–430.

Birnbaum, M. H. (1982). Controversies in psychological measurement. In B. Wegener (Ed.), *Social Attitudes and Psychological Measurement* (pp. 401–485). Hillsdale, NJ: Erlbaum.

Birnbaum, M. H. (1987a). *Are people as incoherent when they gamble as I was last night?* Twenty-fifth Annual Bayesian Conference. Los Angeles, CA, February.

Birnbaum, M. H. (1987b). *Searching for coherence in judgment and decision making.* Invited address to Western Psychological Association Meetings. Long Beach, CA, April.

Birnbaum, M. H. (1987c). *Dual bilinear utility: A configural-weight theory of the judge's point of view.* Mathematical Psychology Meetings. Berkeley, CA, August.

Birnbaum, M. H. (1992a). Issues in utility measurement. *Organizational Behavior and Human Decision Processes,* **52**, 319–330.

Birnbaum, M. H. (1992b). Violations of monotonicity and contextual effects in choice-based certainty equivalents. *Psychological Science,* **3**, 310–314.

Birnbaum, M. H., & Beeghley, D. (1997). Violations of branch independence in judgments of the value of gambles. *Psychological Science,* **8**, 87–94.

Birnbaum, M. H., & Chavez, A. (1996). *Tests of branch independence and distribution independence in decision making.* Working paper, Department of Psychology, California State University, Fullerton.

Birnbaum, M. H., Coffey, G., Mellers, B. A., & Weiss, R. (1992). Utility measurement: Configural-weight theory and the judge's point of view. *Journal of Experimental Psychology: Human Perception and Performance,* **18**, 331–346.

Birnbaum, M. H., & McCormick, S. (1991). *Decision weights for equally likely outcomes..* Working paper, Department of Psychology, California State University, Fullerton.

Birnbaum, M. H., & McIntosh, W. R. (1996). Violations of branch independence in choices between gambles. *Organizational Behavior and Human Decision Processes,* **67**, 91–110.

Birnbaum, M. H., & Mellers, B. A. (1989). Mediated models for the analysis of confounded variables and self-selected samples. *Journal of Educational Statistics,* **14**, 146–158.

Birnbaum, M. H., & Rose, B. J. (1973). *Set-size effect in impression formation: Still an albatross for the averaging model.* Paper presented to Western Psychological Association, Anaheim, April.

Birnbaum, M. H., & Sotoodeh, Y. (1991). Measurement of stress: Scaling the magnitudes of life changes. *Psychological Science,* **2**, 236–243.

Birnbaum, M. H., & Stegner, S. E. (1979). Source credibility in social judgment: Bias, expertise, and the judge's point of view. *Journal of Personality and Social Psychology,* **37**, 47–74.

Birnbaum, M. H., & Stegner, S. E. (1981). Measuring the importance of cues in judgment for individuals: Subjective theories of IQ as a function of hereditary and environment. *Journal of Experimental Social Psychology,* **17**, 159–182.

Birnbaum, M. H., & Sutton, S. E. (1992). Scale convergence and utility measurement. *Organizational Behavior and Human Decision Processes,* **52**, 183–215.

Birnbaum, M. H., & Thompson, L. A. (1996). Violations of monotonicity in choices between gambles and certain cash. *American Journal of Psychology,* **109**, 501–523.

Birnbaum, M. H., Thompson, L. A., & Bean, D. J. (in press). Tests of interval independence vs. configural weighting using judgments of strength of preference. *Journal of Experimental Psychology: Human Perception and Performance.*

Blackorby, C., & Donaldson, D. (1984). Social criteria for evaluating population change. *Journal of Public Economics,* **25**, 13–33.

Blake, R., Martens, W., Garrett, A., & Westendorf, D. (1980). Estimating probability summation for binocular reaction time data. *Perception and Psychophysics,* **27**, 375–378.

Block, H. D., & Marschak, J. (1960). Random orderings and stochastic theories of responses. In I. Olkin, S. Ghurye, W. Hoeffding, W. Madow, & H. Mann

(Eds.), *Contributions to Probability and Statistics* (pp. 97–132). Stanford: Stanford University Press.

Bontempo, R. N., Bottom, W. P., & Weber, E. U. (in press). Cross-cultural differences in risk perception: A model-based approach. *Risk Analysis.*

Boothby, W. M. (1986). *An Introduction to Differential Geometry and Riemannian Manifolds* (2nd edition). Orlando: Academic Press.

Bostic, R., Herrnstein, R. J., & Luce, R. D. (1990). The effect on the preference reversal phenomenon of using choice indifferences. *Journal of Economic Behavior and Organization,* **13**, 193–212.

Braida, L. D., & Durlach, N. I. (1972). Intensity perception. II. Resolution in one-interval paradigms. *Journal of the Acoustical Society of America,* **51**, 483–502.

Braida, L. D., Lim, J. S., Berliner, J. E., Durlach, N. I., Rabinowitz, W. M., & Purks, S. R. (1984). Intensity perception. XIII. Perceptual anchor model of context-coding. *Journal of the Acoustical Society of America,* **76**, 722–731.

Brams, S. J., & Fishburn, P. C. (1983). *Approval Voting.* Boston: Birkhäuser.

Brockhaus, R. H. (1982). The psychology of the entrepreneur. In C. A. Ken, D. L. Sexton, & K. G. Vesper (Eds.), *The Encyclopedia of Entrepreneurship* (pp. 321–325). Englewood Cliffs, NJ: Prentice-Hall.

Bromiley, P., & Curley, S. (1992). Individual differences in risk taking. In J. F. Yates (Ed.), *Risk-taking Behavior* (pp. 87–132). New York: Wiley.

Brooks, L. (1978). Nonanalytic concept formation and memory for instances. In E. Rosch & B. B. Lloyd (Eds.), *Cognition and Categorization* (pp. 161–211). Hillsdale, NJ: Erlbaum.

Brothers, A. J. (1990). *An empirical investigation of some properties that are relevant to generalized expected-utility theory.* Ph.D. thesis, University of California, Irvine.

Brown, J. (1965). Multiple response evaluation of discrimination. *British Journal of Mathematical and Statistical Psychology,* **18**, 125–137.

Budescu, D. V., & Weiss, R. (1987). Reflection of transitivity and intransitive preferences: A test of prospect theory. *Organizational Behavior and Human Decision Processes,* **39**, 184–202.

Busemeyer, J. R. (1985). Decision making under uncertainty: Simple scalability, fixed sample, and sequential sampling models. *Journal of Experimental Psychology: Learning, Memory, and Cognition,* **11**, 583–564.

Busemeyer, J. R., Dewey, G., & Medin, D. L. (1984). Evaluation of exemplar-based generalization and the abstraction of categorical information. *Journal of Experimental Psychology: Learning, Memory, and Cognition,* **10**, 638–648.

Busemeyer, J. R., & Townsend, J. T. (1993). Decision field theory: A dynamic-cognitive approach to decision making. *Psychological Review,* **100**, 432–459.

Bush, R. R., & Mosteller, F. (1951). A mathematical model for simple learning. *Psychological Review,* **58**, 313–323.

Bush, R. R., & Mosteller, F. (1955). *Stochastic Models for Learning.* New York: Wiley.

Camerer, C., & Weber, M. (1993). Recent developments in modeling preferences: Uncertainty and ambiguity. *Journal of Risk and Uncertainty,* 325–370.

Cantor, G. (1895). Beiträge zur Begrüundung der transfiniten Mengenlehre. *Mathematische Annalen*, **46**, 481–512.

Carlson, B. W. (1990). Anchoring and adjustment in judgments under risk. *Journal of Experimental Psychology: Learning, Memory, and Cognition*, **16**, 655–676.

Carroll, J. D. (1980). Models and methods for multidimensional analysis of preferential choice (or other dominance) data. In E. D. Lantermann & H. Feger (Eds.), *Similarity and Choice, Papers in Honor of Clyde Coombs* (pp. 234–289). Bern: Hans Huber Publishers.

Carroll, J. D., & Chang, J. J. (1970). Analysis of individual differences in multidimensional scaling via an N-way generalization of Eckart-Young decomposition. *Psychometrika*, **35**, 283–319.

Carroll, J. D., & Wish, M. (1974). Models and methods for three-way multidimensional scaling. In D. H. Krantz, R. C. Atkinson, R. D. Luce, & P. Suppes (Eds.), *Contemporary Developments in Mathematical Psychology, Vol. 2* (pp. 57–105). San Francisco: W. H. Freeman.

Cartwright, D. (1941). Relation of decision-time to the categories of response. *American Journal of Psychology*, **54**, 174–196.

Champeney, D. C. (1987). *A Handbook of Fourier Theorems*. Cambridge: Cambridge University Press.

Chew, S. H., & Wakker, P. P. (1996). The comonotonic sure-thing principle. *Journal of Risk and Uncertainty*, **12**, 5–27.

Cho, Y., & Luce, R. D. (1995). Tests of hypotheses about certainty equivalents and joint receipt of gambles. *Organizational Behavior and Human Decision Processes*, **64**, 229–248.

Cho, Y., Luce, R. D., & von Winterfeldt, D. (1994). Tests of assumptions about the joint receipt of gambles in rank- and sign-dependent utility theory. *Journal of Experimental Psychology: Human Perception and Performance*, **20**, 931–943.

Christof, T. *PORTA: A polyhedron representation transformation algorithm.* Software available from:
ftp://ftp.zib-berlin.de/pub/mathprog/polyth/porta/index.html

Chuaqui, R., & Suppes, P. (1995). Free-variable axiomatic foundations of infinitesimal analysis: A fragment with finitary consistency proof. *Journal of Symbolic Logic*, **60**, 122–159.

Chung, N.-K., von Winterfeldt, D., & Luce, R. D. (1994). An experimental test of event commutativity in decision making under uncertainty. *Psychological Science*, **5**, 394–400.

Churchman, C. W., & Ratoosh, P. (Eds.). (1959). *Measurement: Definitions and Theories*. New York: Wiley.

Clarke, F. R. (1957). Constant-ratio rule for confusion matrices in speech communication. *Journal of the Acoustical Society of America*, **31**, 835.

Cliff, N. (1992). Abstract measurement theory and the revolution that never happened. *Psychological Science*, **3**, 186–190.

Cohen, M., & Jaffray, J.-Y. (1988). Is Savage's independence axiom a universal rationality principle? *Behavioral Science*, **33**, 38–47.

Cohen, M., Jaffray, J.-Y., & Said, T. (1987). Experimental comparison of individual behavior under risk and under uncertainty for gains and losses. *Organizational*

Behavior and Human Decision Processes, **39**, 1–22.

Colonius, H. (1986). Measuring channel dependence in separate activation models. *Perception and Psychophysics*, **40**, 251–255.

Colonius, H. (1990). Possibly dependent probability summation of reaction time. *Journal of Mathematical Psychology*, **34**, 253–275.

Colonius, H., & Vorberg, D. (1994). Distribution inequalities for parallel models with unlimited capacity. *Journal of Mathematical Psychology*, **38**, 35–58.

Converse, P. E. (1964). The nature of belief systems in mass publics. In D. E. Apter (Ed.), *Ideology and Discontent* (pp. 207–261). New York: Free Press.

Converse, P. E. (1975). Public Opinion and Voting Behavior. In F. L. Greenstein & N. Polsby (Eds.), *Handbook of Political Science*, Vol. 4 (pp. 75–169). Reading, MA: Addison-Wesley.

Converse, P. E., & Markus, G. B. (1979). Plus ça change...: The new CPS Election Study Panel. *American Political Science Review*, **73**, 32–49.

Coombs, C. H. (1975). Portfolio theory and the measurement of risk. In M. F. Kaplan & S. Schwartz (Eds.), *Human Judgment and Decision* (pp. 63–68). New York: Academic Press.

Coombs, C. H., & Bowen, J. N. (1971). A test of VE-theories of risk and the effect of the central limit theorem. *Acta Psychologica*, **35**, 15–28.

Coombs, C. H., & Huang, L. (1970). Polynomial psychophysics of risk. *Journal of Mathematical Psychology*, **7**, 317–388.

Coombs, C. H., & Lehner, P. E. (1984). Conjoint design and analysis of the bi-linear model: An application to judgments of risk. *Journal of Mathematical Psychology*, **38**, 1–42.

Cooper, A. C., Woo, C. Y., & Dunkelberg, W. C. (1988). Entrepreneurs' perceived chances for success. *Journal of Business Venturing*, **3**, 97–108.

Corbetta, M., Miezin, F., Dobmeyer, S., Shulman, G., & Petersen, S. (1991). Selective and divided attention during visual discrimination of shape, color, and speed: Functional anatomy by positron emission tomography. *Journal of Neuroscience*, **11**, 2382–2402.

Cortese, J. M., & Dzhafarov, E. N. (1996). Empirical recovery of response time decomposition rules II: Discriminability of serial and parallel architectures. *Journal of Mathematical Psychology*, **40**, 203–218.

Cowley, G. (1995). Silicone: Juries vs. Science. *Newsweek*, **November 13**, 75.

Cunningham, J. P. (1978). Free trees and bidirectional trees as representations of psychological distance. *Journal of Mathematical Psychology*, **17**, 165–188.

Dalrymple-Alford, E. C. (1970). A model for assessing multiple-choice test performance. *British Journal of Mathematical and Statistical Psychology*, **23**, 199–203.

Dawkins, R. (1969). A threshold model of choice behavior. *Animal Behavior*, **17**, 120–133.

Dean, R. A., & Keller, G. (1968). Natural partial orders. *Canadian Journal of Mathematics*, **20**, 535–554.

Debreu, G. (1960). Review of *Individual Choice Behavior: A Theoretical Analysis*. *American Economic Review*, **50**, 186–88.

Diederich, A. (1992). *Intersensory Facilitation with Multiple Stimuli: Race, Superposition, and Diffusion Models for Reaction Time*. Frankfurt: Verlag Peter Lang.

Diederich, A. (1995). Intersensory facilitation of reaction time: Evaluation of counter and diffusion coactivation models. *Journal of Mathematical Psychology*, **39**, 197–215.

Diederich, A., & Colonius, H. (1987). Intersensory facilitation in the motor component? A reaction time analysis. *Psychological Research*, **49**, 23–29.

Diederich, A., & Colonius, H. (1991). A further test of the superposition model for the redundant-signals effect in bimodal detection. *Perception and Psychophysics*, **50**, 83–85.

Diewert, W. E. (1993). Symmetric means and choice under uncertainty. In *Essays on Index Number Theory* (pp. 355–521). Amsterdam and New York: Elsevier.

Doignon, J.-P., & Falmagne, J.-C. (in press). Well graded families of relations. *Discrete Mathematics*.

Donders, F. C. (1868). Over de snelheid von psychische processen. *Onderzoekingen gedaan in het Physiologisch Laboratorium der Utrechtsche Hoogeschool, 1868–1869*, **II**, 92–120.

Drasgow, F., Levine, M. V., Tsien, S., Williams, B., & Mead, A. (1995). Fitting polychotomous item response theory models to multiple-choice tests. *Applied Psychological Measurement*, **19**, 143–165.

Drasgow, F., Levine, M. V., Williams, B., McLaughlin, M. E., & Candell, G. L. (1989). Modeling incorrect responses to multiple-choice items with multilinear formulas score theory. *Applied Psychological Measurement*, **13**, 285–299.

Durlach, N. I., & Braida, L. D. (1969). Intensity perception. I. Preliminary theory of intensity resolution. *Journal of the Acoustical Society of America*, **46**, 372–383.

Dyer, J. S., & Sarin, R. K. (1982). Relative risk aversion. *Management Science*, **28**, 8.

Dzhafarov, E. N. (1992). The structure of simple reaction time to step-function signals. *Journal of Mathematical Psychology*, **36**, 235–268.

Dzhafarov, E. N. (1993). Grice-representability of response time distribution families. *Psychometrika*, **58**, 281–314.

Dzhafarov, E. N., & Allik, J. (1984). A general theory of motion detection. In M. Rauk (Ed.), *Computational Models in Hearing and Vision* (pp. 77–84). Tallin: Estonian Academy of Sciences.

Dzhafarov, E. N., & Cortese, J. M. (1996). Empirical recovery of response time decomposition rules I: Sample-level decomposition tests. *Journal of Mathematical Psychology*, **40**, 185–202.

Dzhafarov, E. N., & Rouder, J. N. (1996). Empirical discriminability of two models for stochastic relationship between additive components of response time. *Journal of Mathematical Psychology*, **40**, 48–63.

Dzhafarov, E. N., & Schweickert, R. (1995). Decompositions of response times: An almost general theory. *Journal of Mathematical Psychology*, **39**, 285–314.

Dzhafarov, E. N., Sekuler, R., & Allik, J. (1993). Detection of changes in speed and direction of motion: Reaction time analysis. *Perception and Psychophysics*,

54, 733–750.

Edwards, W. (1954). The theory of decision making. *Psychological Bulletin*, **51**, 380–417.

Edwards, W. (1962). Subjective probabilities inferred from decisions. *Psychological Review*, **69**, 109–135.

Ellsberg, D. (1961). Risk, ambiguity, and the Savage axioms. *Quarterly Journal of Economic*, **75**, 643–669.

Eriksen, C., & Yeh, Y. (1985). Allocation of attention in the visual field. *Journal of Experimental Psychology: Human Perception and Performance*, **11**, 538–597.

Estes, W. K. (1950). Toward a statistical theory of learning. *Psychological Review*, **57**, 94–107.

Estes, W. K. (1956). On the problem of inference from curves based on group data. *Psychological Bulletin*, **53**, 134–140.

Estes, W. K. (1960). Mathematics and experiment – which first? Review of R. D. Luce, *Individual Choice Behavior. Contemporary Psychology*, **5**, 113–116.

Estes, W. K. (1982). Similarity-related channel interactions in visual processing. *Journal of Experimental Psychology: Human Perception and Performance*, **8**, 353–382.

Estes, W. K. (1986). Array models for category learning. *Cognitive Psychology*, **18**, 500–549.

Estes, W. K. (1994). *Classification and Cognition*. New York: Oxford University Press.

Estes, W. K. (1995). Response processes in cognitive models. In R. F. Lorch Jr. & E. J. O'Brien (Eds.), *Sources of Coherence in Reading* (pp. 51–71). Hillsdale, NJ: Erlbaum.

Estes, W. K., & Brunn, J. L. (1987). Discriminability and bias in the word-superiority effect. *Perception and Psychophysics*, **42**, 411–422.

Estes, W. K., Campbell, J., Hatsopoulos, N., & Hurwitz, J. (1989). Base-rate effects in category learning: A comparison of parallel network and memory storage-retrieval models. *Journal of Experimental Psychology: Learning, Memory, and Cognition*, **15**, 556–571.

Falmagne, J.-C. (1978). A representation theorem for finite random scale systems. *Journal of Mathematical Psychology*, **18**, 52–72.

Falmagne, J.-C. (1983). A random utility model for a belief function. *Synthese*, **57**, 35–48.

Falmagne, J.-C. (1985). *Elements of Psychophysical Theory*. New York: Oxford University Press.

Falmagne, J.-C. (1996). An ergodic theory for the emergence and the evolution of preferences. *Mathematical Social Sciences*, **31**, 63–84.

Falmagne, J.-C. (in press). Stochastic Token Theory. *Journal of Mathematical Psychology*.

Falmagne, J.-C., & Doignon, J.-P. (in press). Stochastic evolution of rationality. *Theory and Decision*.

Falmagne, J.-C., Koppen, M., Villano, M., Doignon, J.-P., & Johannesen, L. (1990). Introduction to knowledge spaces. *Psychological Review*, **97**, 201–224.

Feller, W. (1966). *An Introduction to Probability Theory and its Applications*, Vol. 2.

New York: Wiley.

Fischhoff, B., Lichtenstein, S., Derby, S. L., & Keeney, R. L. (1981). *Acceptable Risk*. Cambridge, UK: Cambridge University Press.

Fishbein, M., & Ajzen, I. (1981). Attitudes and voting behavior. In G. M. Stephenson & J. H. Davis (Eds.), *Progress in Applied Social Psychology*, Vol. 1 (pp. 215–373). New York: Wiley.

Fishburn, P. C. (1970). Intransitive indifference with unequal indifference intervals. *Journal of Mathematical Psychology*, **7**, 144–149.

Fishburn, P. C. (1980). *Utility Theory for Decision Making*. New York: Wiley.

Fishburn, P. C. (1982). Foundations of risk measurement. II. Effects of gains on risk. *Journal of Mathematical Psychology*, **25**, 226–242.

Fishburn, P. C. (1984). Foundations of risk measurement: I. Risk as probable loss. *Management Science*, **30**, 396–406.

Fishburn, P. C. (1992). Induced binary probabilities: A status report. *Mathematical Social Sciences*, **23**, 67–80.

Fishburn, P. C. (1994). On 'choice' probabilities derived from ranking probabilities. *Journal of Mathematical Psychology*, **38**, 274–285.

Fishburn, P. C., & Luce, R. D. (1995). Joint receipt and Thaler's hedonic editing rule. *Mathematical Social Sciences*, **29**, 33–76.

Fishburn, P. C., & Monjardet, B. (1992). Norbert Wiener on the theory of measurement (1914, 1915, 1921). *Journal of Mathematical Psychology*, **36**, 165–184.

Fouad, N. A., & Dancer, L. S. (1992). Comments on the universality of Holland's theory. *Journal of Vocational Behavior*, **40**, 220–228.

Franke, G., & Weber, M. (1996). *Portfolio choice and asset pricing with improved risk measurement*. Working paper, University of Mannheim.

Frens, M. A., van Opstal, A. J., & van der Willigen, R. F. (1995). Spatial and temporal factors determine auditory-visual interactions in human saccadic eye movements. *Perception and Psychophysics*, **57**, 802–816.

Fuchs, L. (1950). On mean systems. *Acta Mathematica Academiae Scientiarum Hungaricae*, **1**, 303–320.

Garramone, G. M. (1985). Effect of negative political advertising: The role of sponsor and rebuttal. *Journal of Broadcasting and Electronic Media*, **29**, 147–159.

Gati, I. (1986). Making career decisions: A sequential elimination approach. *Journal of Counseling Psychology*, **33**, 408–417.

Gati, I. (1991). The structure of vocational interests. *Psychological Bulletin*, **109**, 309–324.

Giray, M., & Ulrich, R. (1993). Motor coactivation revealed by response force in divided and focused attention. *Journal of Experimental Psychology: Human Perception and Performance*, **1993**, 1278–1291.

Gluck, M. A., & Bower, G. H. (1988). From conditioning to category learning: An adaptive network model. *Journal of Experimental Psychology: General*, **117**, 225–244.

Goldstein, W., & Einhorn, H. J. (1987). A theory of preference reversals. *Psychological Review*, **94**, 236–242.

Gorman, W. M. (1968). The structure of utility functions. *Review of Economic*

ircuit operations in selective attention. *Neural Computation*, **4**, 318–331.

re, Y. (1989). From mean square error to response time: a connectionis

odel of word recognition. In T. Sejnowsky (Ed.), *Proceedings of the Secon*

ummer School on Connectionist Models (pp. 371–378). Los Angeles: Morgan

aufman.

re, Y. (1995). Expanding MEL response box to accommodate up to 16

ernal buttons. *Behavioral Methods, Instruments and Computers*, **27**, 506–

re, Y. (in press). Bow, range and sequential effects in absolute identification:

sponse time analysis. *Psychological Research*.

re, Y., & Lacerte, D. (in press). Stimulus-Response compatibility in abso-

identification. *Canadian Journal of Experimental Psychology*.

, Y., & Marley, A. A. J. (1991). A connectionist model of choice and

tion time in absolute identification. *Connection Science*, **3**, 401–433.

Y., & Marley, A. A. J. (1995). A mapping model of bow effects in

ute identification. *Journal of Mathematical Psychology*, **39**, 383–395.

(1973). *Mathematical Psychology*. New York: Academic Press.

, D. J., Payne, J. W., & Crum, R. L. (1980). Managerial risk preferences

low-target returns. *Management Science*, **26**, 1238–1249.

, L. (1987). *Statistical Manifolds in Differential Geometry in Statis-*

ference. Lecture Notes-Monograph Series. Hayward, CA: Institute of

matical Statistics.

(1992). Small worlds and sure things: Consequentialism by the back

W. Edwards (Ed.), *Utility Theories: Measurements and Applications*

–136). Boston: Kluwer.

& Fishburn, P. C. (1995). On the varieties of matrix probabilities in

imedean decision theory. *Journal of Mathematical Economics*, **24**.

er, A., & Thaler, R. H. (1991). Investor sentiment and the closed-end

zle. *Journal of Finance*, **46**, 75–110.

Ashby, F. G. (1995). *Decision processes in stimulus identifica-*

nuscript, Department of Psychology, University of California, Santa

980). A comparison of portfolio theory and weighted utility models

cision making. *Organizational Behavior and Human Performance*,

9.

095). Multidimensional latent variable models have equivalent uni-

l submodels.. Manuscript, Department of Educational Psychology,

f Illinois, Urbana.

rasgow, F., Williams, B., McCusker, C., & Thomasson, G. L.

suring the difference between two models. *Applied Psychological*

t, **16**, 261–278.

witz, H. M. (1979). Approximating expected utility by a function

variance. *American Economic Review*, **69**, 308–317.

Slovic, P. (1971). Reversals of preference between bids and

mbling decisions. *Journal of Experimental Psychology*, **89**, 46–

Studies, **35**, 367–390.

Gravetter, F., & Lockhead, G. R. (1973). Criterial range as a frame of reference for stimulus judgment. *Psychological Review*, **80**, 203–216.

Green, D. M., & Moses, F. L. (1966). On the equivalence of two recognition measures of short-term memory. *Psychological Bulletin*, **66**, 228–234.

Green, D. M., & Swets, J. A. (1966). *Signal Detection Theory and Psychophysics*. New York: Wiley.

Green, H. A. J. (1964). *Aggregation in Economic Analysis*. Princeton, NJ: Princeton University Press.

Grice, G. R. (1968). Stimulus intensity and response evocation. *Psychological Review*, **75**, 359–373.

Grice, G. R. (1972). Application of a variable criterion model to auditory reaction time as a function of the type of catch trial. *Perception and Psychophysics*, **12**, 103–107.

Grice, G. R., Nullmeyer, R., & Spiker, V. A. (1982). Human reaction time: Toward a general theory. *Journal of Experimental Psychology: General*, **111**, 135–153.

Grötschel, M., Jünger, M., & Reinelt, G. (1985). Facets of the linear ordering polytope. *Mathematical Programming*, **33**, 43–60.

Guillemin, V., & Pollack, A. (1974). *Differential Topology*. Englewood Cliffs: Prentice-Hall.

Harp, S. A. (1995). *Convex spline curves for ROC analysis*. Internal Report, Honeywell, Minneapolis.

Hastie, R. (1986). A primer of information processing theory for the political scientist. In R. L. Lau & D. Sears (Eds.), *Political Cognition* (pp. 11–39). Hillsdale: Erlbaum.

Haxby, J., Horowitz, B., Ungerleider, L., Maison, J., Pietrini, P., & Grady, C. (1994). The functional organization of human extrastriate cortex: A PET-rCBF study of selective attention to faces and locations. *Journal of Neuroscience*, **14**, 6336–6353.

Hershey, J. C., & Schoemaker, P. J. H. (1980). Prospect theory's reflection hypothesis: A critical examination. *Organizational Behavior and Human Performance*, **25**, 395–418.

Heyer, D. (1990). *Booleschwertige und probabilistische Meßtheorie*. Frankfurt: Peter Lang.

Heyer, D., & Niederée, R. (1989). Elements of a model-theoretic framework for probabilistic measurement. In E. E. Roskam (Ed.), *Mathematical Psychology in Progress* (pp. 99–112). Berlin: Springer.

Heyer, D., & Niederée, R. (1992). Generalizing the concept of binary choice systems induced by rankings: One way of probabilizing deterministic measurement structures. *Mathematical Social Sciences*, **23**, 31–44.

Heyer, D., & Niederée, R. (1997). *Probabilistic measurement based on probabilistic mixtures of relational structures: The infinite case*. Manuscript in preparation.

Hillyard, S., Mangun, G., Woldorff, M., & Luck, S. (1995). Neural systems mediating selective attention. In M. Gazzaniga (Ed.), *The Cognitive Neurosciences* (pp. 665–681). Cambridge, MA: MIT.

Hinton, G. E., & Shallice, T. (1991). Lesioning an attractor network: Investigations of acquired dyslexia. *Psychological Review*, **98**, 74–95.

Hintzman, D. L. (1986). "Schema abstraction" in a multiple-trace memory model. *Psychological Review*, **93**, 411–428.

Hohle, R. H. (1965). Inferred components of reaction times as functions of foreperiod duration. *Journal of Experimental Psychology*, **69**, 382–386.

Holland, J. L. (1973). *Making Vocational Choices* (2nd edition). Englewood Cliffs: Prentice Hall.

Holland, J. L. (1985). *Making Vocational Choices* (3rd edition). Englewood Cliffs: Prentice Hall.

Holland, P. W., & Rosenbaum, P. R. (1986). Conditional association and unidimensionality in monotone latent variable models. *Annals of Statistics*, **14**, 1523–1543.

Holtgrave, D., & Weber, E. U. (1993). Dimensions of risk perception for financial and health-and-safety risks. *Risk Analysis: An International Journal*, **13**, 553–558.

Hosszú, M. (1953). A generalization of the functional equation of bisymmetry. *Studia Mathematica*, **14**, 100–106.

Hughes, H., Reuter-Lorenz, P. A., Nozawa, G., & Fendrich, R. (1994). Auditory-visual interactions in sensory-motor processing: Saccades versus manual responses. *Journal of Experimental Psychology: Human Perception and Performance*, **20**, 131–153.

Iverson, G. J., & Falmagne, J.-C. (1985). Statistical issues in measurement. *Mathematical Social Sciences*, **10**, 131–153.

Iverson, G. J., & Harp, S. A. (1985). A conditional likelihood ratio test for order restrictions in exponential families. *Mathematical Social Sciences*, **14**, 141–159.

Iyengar, S. (1990). Shortcuts to political knowledge: The role of selective attention and accessibility. In J. Ferejohn & J. Kuklinski (Eds.), *Information and Democratic Process* (pp. 160–185). Urbana-Champaign, Illinois: University of Illinois Press.

Iyengar, S., & Kinder, D. R. (1987). *News that Matters: Television and American Opinion*. Chicago: University of Chicago Press.

Iyengar, S., Peters, M. D., & Kinder, D. R. (1982). Demonstration of the 'Not So Minimal' consequences of television news. *American Political Science Review*, **76**, 848–858.

Jastrow, J. (1887). The psycho-physic law and star magnitude. *American Journal of Psychology*, **1**, 112–127.

Jia, J., & Dyer, J. S. (in press). A standard measure of risk and risk-value models. *Management Science*.

Julesz, B., & Bergen, J. (1983). Textons, the fundamental elements in preattentive vision and perception of textures. *Bell Systems Technical Journal*, **62**, 1619–1645.

Kahneman, D., & Tversky, A. (1972). Subjective probability: A judgment of representativeness. *Cognitive Psychology*, **3**, 430–454.

Kahneman, D., & Tversky, A. (1973). On the psychology of ... ical Review, **80**, 237–251.

Kahneman, D., & Tversky, A. (1979). Prospect theory: A ... under risk. *Econometrica*, **47**, 263–291.

Keller, L. R. (1985a). The effect of problem representatio... substitution principles. *Management Science*, **31**, 73...

Keller, L. R. (1985b). An empirical investigation of rela... *Transactions on Systems, Man, and Cybernetics*, S...

Keller, L. R., Sarin, R. K., & Weber, M. (1986). Empi... properties of the perceived riskiness of gambles. O... *Human Decision Processes*, **38**, 114–130.

Keyes, R. (1985). *Chancing it: Why We Take Risks*. ... and Company.

Klein, L. R. (1946a). Macroeconomics and the theory ... metrica, **14**, 93–108.

Klein, L. R. (1946b). Remarks on the theory of ag... 303–313.

Kolmogorov, A. N. (1930). Sur la notion de la moye... *Nazionale dei Lincei Rendiconti*, **12**, 388–391...

Koppen, M. (1995). Random utility representatio... Critical graphs yielding critical necessary con... *Psychology*, **39**, 21–39.

Krantz, D. H. (1964). *The scaling of small a*... thesis, Department of Psychology, Univers... University Microfilms No. 65-5777.

Krantz, D. H., Luce, R. D., Suppes, P., & T... *Measurement, Volume I*. New York: Aca...

Kruschke, J. K. (1992). ALCOVE: An exempl... egory learning. *Psychological Review*, **9**...

LaBerge, D. (1962). A recruitment theory of ... 375–396.

LaBerge, D. (1992). A mathematical theory ... In A. F. Healy, S. M. Kosslyn, & R. M... *to Connectionist Theory: Essays in* ... 115–132). Hillsdale, NJ: Erlbaum.

LaBerge, D. (1994). Quantitative model ... shape identification tasks. *Journal* ...

LaBerge, D. (1995a). *Attentional Proc*... Cambridge, MA: Harvard Universi...

LaBerge, D. (1995b). Computational a... in object identification. In M. Ga... (pp. 649–663). Cambridge, MA: ...

LaBerge, D., & Buchsbaum, M. (199... ments of pulvinar activity durin... **10**, 613–619.

LaBerge, D., Carter, M., & Brown, ...

Lindman, H. R. (1971). Inconsistent preferences among gambles. *Journal of Experimental Psychology*, **89**, 390–397.

Link, S. W. (1992). *The Wave Theory of Difference and Similarity*. Hillsdale, NJ: Erlbaum.

Link, S. W., & Tindal, A. B. (1971). Speed and accuracy in comparative judgments of line length. *Perception and Psychophysics*, **40**, 77–105.

Linville, P. W., & Fischer, G. W. (1991). Preference for separating or combining events. *Journal of Personality and Social Psychology*, **60**, 5–23.

Liotti, M., Fox, P., & LaBerge, D. (1994). PET measurements of attention to closely spaced visual shapes. *Society for Neurosciences Abstracts*, **20**, 354.

Liu, L. (1995). *A Theory of Coarse Utility and its Application to Portfolio Analysis*. Ph.D. thesis, University of Kansas.

Lockhead, G. R. (1984). Sequential predictors of choice in psychophysical tasks. In S. Kornblum & J. Requin (Eds.), *Preparatory States and Processes* (pp. 27–47). Hillsdale, NJ: Erlbaum.

Logan, G. D. (1988). Toward an instance theory of automatization. *Psychological Review*, **95**, 492–527.

Long, B. L. (1988). Risk communication: Where to from here? In H. Jungermann, R. E. Kasperson, & P. M. Wiedemann (Eds.), *Risk Communication* (pp. 177–182). Julich, Germany: KFA Julich.

Loomis, G. (1990). Preference reversal: Explanations, evidence, and implications. In W. Gehrlein (Ed.), *Intransitive Preference*. Annals of Operations Research.

Lopes, L. L. (1984). Risk and distributional inequality. *Journal of Experimental Psychology: Human Perception and Performance*, **10**, 465–485.

Lopes, L. L. (1987). Between hope and fear: The psychology of risk. *Advances in Experimental Social Psychology*, **20**, 255–295.

Lopes, L. L. (1990). Re-modeling risk aversion: A comparison of Bernoullian and rank dependent value approaches. In G. M. von Furstenberg (Ed.), *Acting Under Uncertainty: Multidisciplinary Conceptions* (pp. 267–299). Boston, MA: Kluwer.

Lord, F., & Novick, M. R. (1968). *Statistical Theories of Mental Test Scores*. Reading, MA: Addison-Wesley.

Los, J. (1967). Semantic representation of the probability of formulas in formalized theories. In M. Przelecki & R. Wojcicki (Eds.), *Twenty-five Years of Logical Methodology in Poland* (pp. 327–340). Dordrecht: Reidel.

Luce, R. D. (1956). Semiorders and a theory of utility discrimination. *Econometrica*, **24**, 178–191.

Luce, R. D. (1959a). *Individual Choice Behavior*. New York: Wiley.

Luce, R. D. (1959b). On the possible psychophysical laws. *Psychological Review*, **66**, 81–95.

Luce, R. D. (1963). Detection and Recognition. In R. D. Luce, R. R. Bush, & E. Galanter (Eds.), *Handbook of Mathematical Psychology* (pp. 103–189). New York: Wiley.

Luce, R. D. (1977a). The choice axiom after twenty years. *Journal of Mathematical Psychology*, **15**, 215–233.

Luce, R. D. (1977b). Thurstone's discriminal processes fifty years later. *Psychometrika*, **42**, 461–489.

Luce, R. D. (1980). Several possible measures of risk. *Theory and Decision*, **12**, 217–228.

Luce, R. D. (1981). Correction to 'Several possible measures of risk'. *Theory and Decision*, **13**, 381.

Luce, R. D. (1986a). Comments on Plott and on Kahneman, Knetsch, and Thaler. *Journal of Business*, **59**, S337–S343.

Luce, R. D. (1986b). *Response Times: Their Role in Inferring Elementary Mental Organization*. New York: Oxford University Press.

Luce, R. D. (1988). Rank-dependent, subjective expected utility representations. *Journal of Risk and Uncertainty*, **1**, 305–332.

Luce, R. D. (1989). R. Duncan Luce. In G. Lindzey (Ed.), *A History of Psychology in Autobiography. Vol. VIII* (pp. 245–289). Stanford, CA: Stanford University Press.

Luce, R. D. (1990a). Rational versus plausible accounting equivalences in preference judgments. *Psychological Science*, **1**, 225–234.

Luce, R. D. (1990b). 'On the possible psychophysical laws' revisited: Remarks on cross-modal matching. *Psychological Review*, **97**, 66–77.

Luce, R. D. (1991). Rank- and sign-dependent linear utility models for binary gambles. *Journal of Economic Theory*, **53**, 75–100.

Luce, R. D. (1992a). Singular points in generalized concatenation structures that otherwise are homogeneous. *Mathematical Social Sciences*, **24**, 79–103.

Luce, R. D. (1992b). A theory of certainty equivalents for uncertain alternatives. *Journal of Behavioral Decision Making*, **5**, 201–216.

Luce, R. D. (1992c). Where does subjective expected utility fail descriptively? *Journal of Risk and Uncertainty*, **5**, 5–27.

Luce, R. D. (1993). *Sound and Hearing*. Hillsdale, NJ: Erlbaum.

Luce, R. D. (1994). Thurstone and sensory scaling: Then and now. *Psychological Review*, **101**, 271–277.

Luce, R. D. (1995a). Four tensions concerning mathematical modeling in psychology. *Annual Review of Psychology*, **46**, 1–26.

Luce, R. D. (1995b). Joint receipt and certainty equivalents of gambles. *Journal of Mathematical Psychology*, **39**, 73–81.

Luce, R. D. (1996). When four distinct ways to measure utility are the same. *Journal of Mathematical Psychology*, **40**, 297–317.

Luce, R. D., & Fishburn, P. C. (1991). Rank- and sign-dependent linear utility models for finite first-order gambles. *Journal of Risk and Uncertainty*, **4**, 29–59.

Luce, R. D., & Fishburn, P. C. (1995). A note on deriving rank-dependent utility using additive joint receipts. *Journal of Risk and Uncertainty*, **11**, 5–16.

Luce, R. D., & Green, D. M. (1978). Two tests of a neural attention hypothesis in auditory psychophysics. *Perception and Psychophysics*, **23**, 363–371.

Luce, R. D., Green, D. M., & Weber, D. L. (1976). Attention bands in absolute identification. *Perception and Psychophysics*, **20**, 49–54.

Luce, R. D., & Krantz, D. H. (1971). Conditional expected utility. *Econometrika*,

39, 253–271.

Luce, R. D., Krantz, D. H., Suppes, P., & Tversky, A. (1990). *Foundations of Measurement, Vol. III.* San Diego: Academic Press.

Luce, R. D., Mellers, B. A., & Chang, S.-J. (1993). Is choice the correct primitive? On using certainty equivalents and reference levels to predict choices among gambles. *Journal of Risk and Uncertainty,* **6**, 115–143.

Luce, R. D., & Narens, L. (1985). Classification of concatenation measurement structures according to scale type. *Journal of Mathematical Psychology,* **29**, 1–72.

Luce, R. D., & Narens, L. (1994). Fifteen problems in the representational theory of measurement. In H. Humphreys (Ed.), *Patrick Suppes: Scientific Philosopher, Vol. 2: Philosophy of Physics, Theory Structure, Measurement Theory, Philosophy of Language, and Logic* (pp. 219–245). Dordrecht: Kluwer.

Luce, R. D., & Nosofsky, R. M. (1984). Attention, stimulus range, and identification of loudness. In S. Kornblum & J. Requin (Eds.), *Preparatory States and Processes* (pp. 3–25). Hillsdale, NJ: Erlbaum.

Luce, R. D., Nosofsky, R. M., Green, D. M., & Smith, A. F. (1982). The bow and sequential effects in absolute identification. *Perception and Psychophysics,* **32**, 397–408.

Luce, R. D., & Raiffa, H. (1957). *Games and Decisions.* New York: Wiley.

Luce, R. D., & Suppes, P. (1965). Preference, utility, and subjective probability. In R. D. Luce, R. R. Bush, & E. Galanter (Eds.), *Handbook of Mathematical Psychology, Volume 3* (pp. 249–410). New York: Wiley.

Luce, R. D., & von Winterfeldt, D. (1994). What common ground exists for descriptive, prescriptive and normative utility theories? *Management Science,* **40**, 263–279.

Luce, R. D., & Weber, E. U. (1986). An axiomatic theory of conjoint, expected risk. *Journal of Mathematical Psychology,* **30**, 188–205.

MacCrimmon, K. R., Stanburg, W. T., & Wehrung, D. A. (1980). Real money lotteries: A study of ideal risk, context effects and simple processes. In T. S. Wallsten (Ed.), *Cognitive Processes in Choice and Decision Behavior* (pp. 155–177). Hillsdale, NJ: Erlbaum.

MacCrimmon, K. R., & Wehrung, D. A. (1986). *Taking Risks: The Management of Uncertainty.* New York: Free Press.

MacCrimmon, K. R., & Wehrung, D. A. (1990). Characteristics of risk taking executives. *Management Science,* **36**, 422–435.

Maddox, W. T. (1995). *On the dangers of averaging across subjects when comparing decision bound and exemplar models of categorization.* Paper given at the 28th Annual Mathematical Psychology Meeting, Irvine, CA.

Maddox, W. T., & Ashby, F. G. (1993). Comparing decision bound and exemplar models of categorization. *Perception and Psychophysics,* **53**, 49–70.

Maddox, W. T., & Ashby, F. G. (1996). Perceptual separability, decisional separability, and the identification-speeded classification relationship. *Journal of Experimental Psychology: Human Perception and Performance,* **22**, 795–817.

Markowitz, H. M. (1952). The utility of wealth. *Journal of Political Economy,* **60**, 151–158.

Markowitz, H. M. (1959). *Portfolio Selection.* New York: Wiley.

Markus, G. B. (1982). Political attitudes during an election year: A report on the 1980 NES Panel Study. *American Political Science Review,* **76**, 538–560.

Marley, A. A. J. (1968). Some probabilistic models of simple choice and ranking. *Journal of Mathematical Psychology,* **5**, 311–332.

Marley, A. A. J. (1982). Random utility models with all choice probabilities expressible as "functions" of the binary choice probabilities. *Mathematical Social Sciences,* **3**, 39–56.

Marley, A. A. J. (1990). A historical and contemporary perspective on random scale representations of choice probabilities and reaction times in the context of Cohen and Falmagne's (1990, Journal of Mathematical Psychology, 34) results. *Journal of Mathematical Psychology,* **34**, 81–87.

Marley, A. A. J. (1991). Context dependent probabilistic choice models based on measures of binary advantage. *Mathematical Social Sciences,* **21**, 201–231.

Marley, A. A. J. (1992). Developing and characterizing multidimensional Thurstone and Luce models for identification and preference. In F. G. Ashby (Ed.), *Multidimensional Models of Perception and Cognition* (pp. 299–333). Hillsdale, NJ: Erlbaum.

Marley, A. A. J., & Colonius, H. (1992). The "horse race" random utility model for choice probabilities and reaction times, and its competing risks interpretation. *Journal of Mathematical Psychology,* **36**, 1–20.

Marley, A. A. J., & Cook, V. T. (1984). A fixed rehearsal capacity interpretation of limits on absolute identification performance. *British Journal of Mathematical and Statistical Psychology,* **37**, 136–151.

Marley, A. A. J., & Cook, V. T. (1986). A limited capacity rehearsal model for psychological judgments applied to magnitude estimation. *Journal of Mathematical Psychology,* **30**, 339–390.

Marley, A. A. J., & Lacouture, Y. (1996). Context effects in absolute identification: Are they "sensory", "cognitive" or "motor". *Proceedings of the Twelfth Annual Meeting of the Society for Psychophysics,* pp. 167–172. Padua.

McClelland, J. L., & Elman, J. L. (1986). Interactive processes in speech perception: the TRACE model. In J. L. McClelland & R. D. Rumelhart (Eds.), *Parallel Distributed Processing: Explorations in the Microstructure of Cognition, Volume 2* (pp. 58–121). Cambridge, MA: MIT Press.

McClelland, J. L., & Rumelhart, D. E. (1986). *Parallel Distributed Processing: Explorations in the Microstructure of Cognition, Volume 2.* Cambridge, MA: MIT Press.

McGill, W. J. (1962). Random fluctuations of response rate. *Psychometrika,* **27**, 3–17.

McGill, W. J. (1963). Stochastic latency mechanisms. In R. D. Luce & E. Galanter (Eds.), *Handbook of Mathematical Psychology* (pp. 309–360). New York: Wiley.

McKelvey, R. D., & Ordeshook, P. C. (1986). Information, electoral equilibria and democratic ideal. *Journal of Politics,* **48**, 909–937.

McKinley, S. C., & Nosofsky, R. M. (1995). Investigations of exemplar and decision bound models in large, ill-defined category structures. *Journal of Experimental Psychology: Human Perception and Performance*, **21**, 128–148.

McPhee, W. N., Andersen, B., & Milholland, H. (1962). Attitude consistency. In W. N. McPhee & W. A. Glaser (Eds.), *Public Opinion and Congressional Elections* (pp. 78–120). New York: Free Press.

Medin, D. L., & Edelson, S. (1988). Problem structure and the use of base-rate information from experience. *Journal of Experimental Psychology: General*, **117**, 65–85.

Medin, D. L., Goldstone, R., & Markman, A. (1995). Comparison and choice: Relations between similarity processes and decision processes. *Psychonomic Bulletin and Review*, **2**, 1–19.

Medin, D. L., & Schaffer, M. M. (1978). Context theory of classification learning. *Psychological Review*, **85**, 207–238.

Medin, D. L., & Schwanenflugel, P. J. (1981). Linear separability in classification learning. *Journal of Experimental Psychology: Human Learning and Memory*, **1**, 335–368.

Meijers, L. M. M., & Eijkman, E. G. J. (1977). Distributions of simple RT with single and double stimuli. *Perception and Psychophysics*, **22**, 41–48.

Mellers, B. A., Berretty, P. M., & Birnbaum, M. H. (1995). Dominance violations in judged prices of two- and three-outcome gambles. *Journal of Behavioral Decision Making*, **8**, 201–216.

Mellers, B. A., & Chang, S.-J. (1994). Representations of risk judgments. *Organizational Behavior and Human Decision Processes*, **57**, 167–184.

Mellers, B. A., Ordóñez, L. D., & Birnbaum, M. H. (1992a). A change-of-process theory for contextual effects and preference reversals in risky decision making. *Organizational Behavior and Human Decision Processes*, **52**, 331–369.

Mellers, B. A., Weiss, R., & Birnbaum, M. H. (1992b). Violations of dominance in pricing judgments. *Journal of Risk and Uncertainty*, **5**, 73–90.

Mendelson, E. (1964). *Introduction to Mathematical Logic*. New York: Van Nostrand Reynhold.

Miller, G. A. (1956). The magical number seven, plus or minus two: Some limits on our capacity for processing information. *Psychological Review*, **63**, 81–97.

Miller, J. O. (1982). Divided attention: Evidence for coactivation with redundant signals. *Cognitive Psychology*, **14**, 247–279.

Miller, J. O. (1986). Time course of coactivation in bimodal divided attention. *Perception and Psychophysics*, **40**, 331–343.

Miller, J. O. (1991). Channel interaction and the redundant-targets effect in bimodal divided attention. *Journal of Experimental Psychology: Human Perception and Performance*, **17**, 160–169.

Miller, K. D., Kets de Vriess, M. F. R., & Toulouse, J. (1982). Top executive locus of control and its relationship to strategy-making, structure, and environment. *Academy of Management Journal*, **25**, 237–253.

Montgomery, H. (1977). A study of intransitive preferences using a think aloud procedure. In H. Jungerman & G. de Zeeuw (Eds.), *Decision Making and Change in Human Affairs* (pp. 347–362). Dordrecht, The Netherlands: Reidel.

Moran, J., & Desimone, R. (1985). Selective attention gates visual processing in the extrastriate cortex. *Science*, **229**, 782–784.

Mordkoff, J. T., & Yantis, S. (1991). An interactive race model of divided attention. *Journal of Experimental Psychology: Human Perception and Performance*, **17**, 520–538.

Mordkoff, J. T., & Yantis, S. (1993). Dividing attention between color and shape: Evidence for coactivation. *Perception and Psychophysics*, **53**, 357–366.

Mori, S. (1989). A limited-capacity response process in absolute identification. *Perception and Psychophysics*, **46**, 167–173.

Motter, B. (1993). Focal attention produces spatially selective processing in visual cortical areas, V1, V2, and V4 in the presence of competing stimuli. *Journal of Neurophysiology*, **70**, 909–919.

Münnich, A., Maksa, Gy., & Mokken, R. J. (1997). *Multi-attribute evaluation and n-component bisection*. Manuscript, Institute of Psychology, Kossuth Lajos University.

Murdock, B. B. (1985). An analysis of the strength-latency relationship. *Memory and Cognition*, **13**, 511–521.

Murray, M. K., & Rice, J. W. (1993). *Differential Geometry and Statistics*. London: Chapman and Hall.

Nagumo, M. (1930). Über eine Klasse der Mittelwerte. *Japanese Journal of Mathematics*, **7**, 71–79.

Narens, L. (1981a). A general theory of ratio scalability with remarks about the measurement-theoretic concept of meaningfulness. *Theory and Decision*, **13**, 1–70.

Narens, L. (1981b). On the scales of measurement. *Journal of Mathematical Psychology*, **24**, 249–275.

Narens, L. (1985). *Abstract Measurement Theory*. Cambridge, MA: The MIT Press.

Narens, L. (1994). The measurement theory of dense threshold structures. *Journal of Mathematical Psychology*, **38**, 301–321.

Narens, L. (1996a). A theory of magnitude estimation. *Journal of Mathematical Psychology*, **40**, 109–129.

Narens, L. (1996b). *Theories of Meaningfulness*. To be published by Springer-Verlag.

Narens, L., & Luce, R. D. (1993). Further comments on the 'nonrevolution' arising from axiomatic measurement theory. *Psychological Science*, **4**, 127–130.

Nataf, A. (1948). Sur la possibilité de construction de certains macromodèles. *Econometrica*, **17**, 232–244.

Noreen, D. L. (1981). Optimal decision rules for some common psychophysical paradigms. In S. Grossberg (Ed.), *Mathematical Psychology and Psychophysiology*, Vol. 13 of *SIAM-AMS Proceedings*, pp. 237–279. Providence, RI: American Mathematical Society.

Norman, F. (1972). *Markov Processes and Learning Models*. New York: Academic Press.

Nosofsky, R. M. (1983). Information integration and the identification of stimulus noise and criterial noise in absolute judgment. *Journal of Experimental Psychology: Human Perception and Performance*, **9**, 299–309.

Nosofsky, R. M. (1984). Choice, similarity, and the context theory of classification.

Journal of Experimental Psychology: Learning, Memory, and Cognition, **10**, 104–114.

Nosofsky, R. M. (1986). Attention, similarity, and the identification-categorization relationship. *Journal of Experimental Psychology: General*, **115**, 39–57.

Nosofsky, R. M. (1987). Attention and learning processes in the identification and categorization of integral stimuli. *Journal of Experimental Psychology: Learning, Memory, and Cognition*, **13**, 87–108.

Nosofsky, R. M. (1988). Exemplar-based accounts of relations between classification, recognition, and typicality. *Journal of Experimental Psychology: Learning, Memory, and Cognition*, **14**, 700–708.

Nosofsky, R. M. (1991). Tests of an exemplar model for relating perceptual classification and recognition memory. *Journal of Experimental Psychology: Human Perception and Performance*, **17**, 3–27.

Nosofsky, R. M. (1992a). Similarity scaling and cognitive process models. *Annual Review of Psychology*, **43**, 25–53.

Nosofsky, R. M. (1992b). Exemplar-based approach to relating categorization, identification, and recognition. In F. G. Ashby (Ed.), *Multidimensional Models of Perception and Cognition* (pp. 363–393). Hillsdale, NJ: Erlbaum.

Nosofsky, R. M., Kruschke, J. K., & McKinley, S. C. (1992). Combining exemplar-based category representations and connectionist learning rules. *Journal of Experimental Psychology: Learning, Memory, and Cognition*, **18**, 211–233.

Nosofsky, R. M., & Palmeri, T. J. (in press). An exemplar-based random walk model of speeded classification. *Psychological Review*.

Paley, R. E. A. C., & Wiener, N. (1934). *Fourier Transforms in the Complex Domain*. New York: American Mathematical Society.

Palmer, C. G. S. (1994). *Dimensions of risk perception for a genetics-based reproductive decision problem*. Working Paper, Division of Human Genetics, University of California-Irvine Medical Center.

Palmer, C. G. S., & Sainfort, F. (1993). Towards a new conceptualization and operationalization of risk perception within the genetic counseling domain. *Journal of Genetic Counseling*, **2**, 275–294.

Palmeri, T. J. (in press). Exemplar similarity and the development of automaticity. *Journal of Experimental Psychology: Learning, Memory, and Cognition*.

Parzen, E. (1962). *Stochastic Processes*. San Francisco: Holden-Day.

Payne, J. W., Laughhunn, D. J., & Crum, R. L. (1980). Translations of gambles and aspiration effects in risky choice behavior. *Management Science*, **26**, 1039–1060.

Petty, R. E., & Cacioppo, J. T. (1981). *Attitudes and Persuasion: Classic and Contemporary Approaches*. Dubuque, Iowa: W. C. Brown.

Pfanzagl, J. (1959). A general theory of measurement – applications to utility. *Naval Research Logistics Quarterly*, **6**, 283–294.

Pike, A. R. (1973). Response latency models for signal detection. *Psychological Review*, **80**, 53–68.

Pokropp, F. (1972). *Aggregation von Produktionsfunktionen*. Berlin, Heidelberg and New York: Springer.

Pokropp, F. (1978). The functional equation of aggregation. In W. Eichhorn,

Functional Equations in Economics (pp. 122–139). Reading, MA: Addison-Wesley.

Pollack, I. (1952). The information of elementary auditory displays. *Journal of the Acoustical Society of America*, **24**, 745–749.

Pollatsek, A., & Tversky, A. (1970). A theory of risk. *Journal of Mathematical Psychology*, **7**, 540–553.

Pommerehne, W. W., Schneider, F., & Zweifel, P. (1982). Economic theory of choice and the preference reversal phenomenon: A re-examination. *American Economic Review*, **72**, 569–574.

Posner, M. I., & Keele, S. W. (1968). On the genesis of abstract ideas. *Journal of Experimental Psychology*, **77**, 353–363.

Posner, M. I., & Keele, S. W. (1970). Retention of abstract ideas. *Journal of Experimental Psychology*, **83**, 304–308.

Pratt, J. W. (1964). Risk aversion in the small and in the large. *Econometrica*, **32**, 122–136.

Prediger, D. J., & Vansickle, T. R. (1992). Location occupations on Holland's hexagon: Beyond RIASEC. *Journal of Vocational Behavior*, **40**, 111–128.

Pu, S. S. (1946). A note on macroeconomics. *Econometrica*, **14**, 299–302.

Purks, S. R., Callahan, D. J., Braida, L. D., & Durlach, N. I. (1980). Intensity perception. X. Effect of preceding stimulus on identification performance. *Journal of the Acoustical Society of America*, **67**, 634–637.

Quesenberry, C. P. (1986). Probability integral transformations. In S. Kotz & N. L. Johnson (Eds.), *Encyclopedia of Statistical Sciences*, Vol. 7 (pp. 225–231). New York: Wiley.

Quiggin, J. (1982). A theory of anticipated utility. *Journal of Economic Behavior and Organization*, **3**, 323–343.

Quiggin, J. (1993). *Generalized Expected Utility Theory: The Rank-Dependent Model*. Boston: Kluwer.

Raab, D. (1962). Statistical facilitation of simple reaction time. *Transactions of the New York Academy of Sciences*, **43**, 574–590.

Ramsay, J. O. (1991). Kernel smoothing approaches to nonparametric item characteristic curve estimation. *Psychometrika*, **56**, 611–630.

Ramsay, J. O. (1993). *TESTGRAF: A computer program for nonparametric analysis of testing data*. Manuscript, Department of Psychology, McGill University.

Ratcliff, R. (1978). A theory of memory retrieval. *Psychological Review*, **85**, 59–108.

Ratcliff, R., & McKoon, G. (in press). A counter model for implicit priming in perceptual word identification. *Psychological Review*.

Ratcliff, R., & Murdock, Jr., B. B. (1976). Retrieval processes in recognition memory. *Psychological Review*, **86**, 190–214.

Raynard, R. H. (1977). Risky decisions which violate transitivity and double cancellation. *Acta Psychologica*, **41**, 449–459.

Reed, S. K. (1972). Pattern recognition and categorization. *Cognitive Psychology*, **3**, 382–407.

Regenwetter, M. (1996). Random utility representations of finite m-ary relations. *Journal of Mathematical Psychology*, **40**, 152–159.

Regenwetter, M., Falmagne, J.-C., & Grofman, B. (1995). *A stochastic model of preference change and its application to 1992 presidential election panel data.* Manuscript submitted for publication. Available as MBS 95–30 Technical Report at the IMBS, University of California, Irvine.

Regenwetter, M., & Marley, A. A. J. (1996). *Random relations, random utilities, and random functions.* Manuscript, Department of Psychology, McGill University.

Riskey, D. R., & Birnbaum, M. H. (1974). Compensatory effects in moral judgment: Two rights don't make up for a wrong. *Journal of Experimental Psychology*, **103**, 171–173.

Roberts, F. S. (1979). *Measurement Theory.* London: Addison-Wesley.

Roberts, F. S., & Sternberg, S. (1992). The meaning of additive reaction-time effects: Tests of three alternatives. In D. E. Meyer & S. Kornblum (Eds.), *Attention and performance XIV* (pp. 611–654). Cambridge, MA: MIT Press.

Robertson, T., Wright, F. T., & Dykstra, R. L. (1988). *Order Restricted Statistical Inference.* New York: Wiley.

Rockafellar, R. T. (1970). *Convex Analysis.* Princeton, NJ: Princeton University Press.

Rockwell, C., & Yellott, Jr., J. I. (1979). A note on equivalent Thurstone models. *Journal of Mathematical Psychology*, **19**, 61–64.

Ronen, J. (1971). Some effects of sequential aggregation in accounting on decision-making. *Journal of Accounting Research*, **9**, 307–332.

Ronen, J. (1973). Effects of some probability displays on choices. *Organizational Behavior and Human Performance*, **9**, 1–15.

Rosch, E. (1973a). Natural categories. *Cognitive Psychology*, **4**, 328–350.

Rosch, E. (1977). Human categorization. In N. Warren (Ed.), *Studies in Cross-Cultural Psychology* (pp. 1–49). Hillsdale, NJ: Erlbaum.

Rothschild, M., & Stiglitz, J. (1970). Increasing risk I: A definition. *Journal of Economic Theory*, **2**, 225–243.

Rounds, J. (1995). Vocational interests: evaluating structural hypotheses. In D. Lubinski & R. V. Davis (Eds.), *Assessing Individual Differences in Human Behavior: New Concepts, Methods, and Findings* (pp. 177–232). Palo Alto, CA: Consulting Psychologists Press.

Rounds, J., Tracey, T. J., & Hubert, L. (1992). Methods for evaluating vocational interest structural hypotheses. *Journal of Vocational Behavior*, **40**, 239–259.

Rumelhart, D. E., Hinton, G. E., & Williams, R. J. (1986). Learning internal representations by error propagation. In D. E. Rumelhart & J. L. McClelland (Eds.), *Parallel Distributed Processing. Explorations in the Microstructure of Cognition, Volume 1* (pp. 282–317). Cambridge, MA: MIT Press.

Samejima, F. (1984). *Plausibility functions of Iowa Vocabulary Test Items estimated by the simple sum procedure of the the conditional P.D.F. approach.* Available as Technical Report 84-1 at the University of Tennessee, Department of Psychology, Knoxville, TN.

Sarin, R. K. (1984). Some extensions of Luce's measures of risk. *Theory and Decision*, **22**, 25–141.

Sarin, R. K., & Weber, M. (1993). Risk-value models. *European Journal of Operations Research*, **70**, 135–149.

Savage, C. W., & Ehrlich, P. (1992). *Philosophical and Foundational Issues in Measurement Theory*. Hillsdale, NJ: Erlbaum.

Savage, L. J. (1954). *Foundations of Statistics*. New York: Wiley.

Schmeidler, D. (1989). Subjective probability and expected utility without additivity. *Econometrica*, **57**, 571–587.

Schneider, S. L., & Lopes, L. L. (1986). Reflection in preference under risk: Who and when may suggest why. *Journal of Experimental Psychology: Human Perception and Performance*, **12**, 535–548.

Schneider, W. (1988). Micro Experimental Laboratory: An integrated system for IBM PC compatibles. *Behavior Research Methods, Instruments, and Computers*, **20**, 206–217.

Schoemaker, P. J. H. (1982). The expected utility model: Its variants, purposes, evidence and limitations. *Journal of Economic Literature*, **20**, 529–563.

Schoemaker, P. J. H. (1990). Are risk-attitudes related across domain and response modes? *Management Science*, **36**, 1451–1463.

Schwarz, W. (1989). A new model to explain the redundant-signals effect. *Perception and Psychophysics*, **46**, 498–500.

Schwarz, W. (1994). Diffusion, superposition, and the redundant-targets effect. *Journal of Mathematical Psychology*, **38**, 504–520.

Schweizer, B., & Sklar, S. (1983). *Probabilistic Metric Spaces*. New York: North-Holland.

Scott, D. (1964). Measurement models and linear inequalities. *Journal of Mathematical Psychology*, **1**, 233–247.

Scott, D., & Suppes, P. (1958). Foundational aspects of theories of measurement. *Journal of Symbolic Logic*, **23**, 113–128.

Scurfield, B. K. (1996). Multiple-event forced-choice tasks in the theory of signal detectability. *Journal of Mathematical Psychology*, **40**, 253–269.

Senders, V. L., & Sowards, A. (1952). Analysis of response sequences in the setting of a psychophysical experiment. *American Journal of Psychology*, **65**, 358–374.

Sereno, M., Dale, A., Reppas, J., Kwang, K., Belliveau, J., Brady, T., Rosen, B., & Tootell, R. (1995). Borders of multiple visual areas in humans revealed by functional magnetic resonance imaging. *Science*, **268**, 889–893.

Shepard, R. N. (1957). Stimulus and response generalization: A stochastic model relating generalization to distance in psychological space. *Psychometrika*, **22**, 325–345.

Shepard, R. N. (1987). Toward a universal law of generalization for psychological science. *Science*, **237**, 1317–1323.

Shiffrin, R. M., & Nosofsky, R. M. (1994). Seven plus or minus two: A commentary on capacity limitations. *Psychological Review*, **101**, 357–361.

Shiffrin, R. M., & Thompson, M. (1988). Moments of transition-additive random variables defined on finite, regenerative random processes. *Journal of Mathematical Psychology*, **32**, 313–340.

Shin, H. J., & Nosofsky, R. M. (1992). Similarity-scaling studies of dot-pattern classification and recognition. *Journal of Experimental Psychology: General*, **121**, 278–304.

Shoenfield, J. R. (1967). *Mathematical Logic*. Reading, Mass: Addison-Wesley.

Shohat, J. A., & Tamarkin, J. D. (1943). *The Problem of Moments*. New York: Mathematical Surveys No. 1.

Skaperdas, S., & Grofman, B. (1995). Modelling negative campaigning. *American Political Science Review*, **89**, 49–61.

Slovic, P. (1964). Assessment of risk taking behavior. *Psychological Bulletin*, **61**, 330–333.

Slovic, P., Fischhoff, B., & Lichtenstein, S. (1986). The psychometric study of risk perception. In V. T. Covello, J. Menkes, & J. Mumpower (Eds.), *Risk Evaluation and Management* (pp. 131–156). New York: Plenum Press.

Slovic, P., & Lichtenstein, S. (1968). Importance of variance preferences in gambling decisions. *Journal of Experimental Psychology*, **78**, 646–654.

Slovic, P., & Lichtenstein, S. (1983). Preference reversals: A broader perspective. *American Economic Review*, **73**, 569–605.

Slovic, P., Lichtenstein, S., & Fischhoff, B. (1988). Decision making. In R. C. Atkinson, R. J. Herrnstein, G. Lindzey, & R. D. Luce (Eds.), *Stevens' Handbook of Experimental Psychology, Vol. 2* (pp. 673–738). New York: Wiley.

Smith, E. E., & Medin, D. L. (1981). *Categories and Concepts*. Cambridge, MA: Harvard University Press.

Smith, J. E. K. (1992). Alternative biased choice models. *Mathematical Social Sciences*, **23**, 199–219.

Smith, P. L. (1990). A note on the distribution of response times for a random walk with Gaussian increments. *Journal of Mathematical Psychology*, **34**, 445–459.

Sniderman, P. M., Glaser, J. H., & Griffin, R. (1990). Information and electoral choice. In J. Ferejohn & J. Kuklinski (Eds.), *Information and Democratic Processes* (pp. 117–135). Urbana-Champaign, Illinois: University of Illinois Press.

Sommer, R., & Suppes, P. (in press a). Dispensing with the continuum. *Journal of Mathematical Psychology*.

Sommer, R., & Suppes, P. (in press b). Finite models of elementary recursive nonstandard analysis. *Proceedings of the Chilean National Academy of Sciences*.

Stein, B. E., & Meredi'¹ M. A. (1993). *The Merging of the Senses*. Cambridge, MA: MIT Press.

Sternberg, S. (1969). Memory scanning: Mental processes revealed by reaction time experiments. *American Scientist*, **57**, 421–457.

Strauss, D. (1979). Some results on random utility models. *Journal of Mathematical Psychology*, **20**, 35–52.

Suck, R. (1992). Geometric and combinatorial properties of the polytope of binary choice probabilities. *Mathematical Social Sciences*, **23**, 81–102.

Suck, R. (1995a). *Random classification and clustering*. Manuscript, Fachbereich Psychologie, Universität Osnabrück.

Suck, R. (1995b). *Random utility representations based on semiorders, interval orders, and partial orders*. Manuscript, Fachbereich Psychologie, Universität Osnabrück.

Suppes, P. (1961). Behavioristic foundations of utility. *Econometrica*, **29**, 186–202.

Suppes, P., & Chuaqui, R. (1993). A finitarily consistent free-variable positive fragment of infinitesimal analysis. *Proceedings of the 9th Latin American Symposium on Mathematical Logic, Notas de Lógica Matemática,* **38**, 1–59.

Suppes, P., Krantz, D. H., Luce, R. D., & Tversky, A. (1989). *Foundations of Measurement, Volume II.* New York: Academic Press.

Suppes, P., & Zanotti, M. (1981). When are probabilistic explanations possible? *Synthese,* **48**, 191–199.

Swaney, K. B. (1995). *Technical Manual: Revised Unisex Edition of the ACT Interest Inventory (UNIACT).* Iowa City: American College Testing Program.

Tanner, Jr., W. P., & Swets, J. A. (1954). A decision-making theory of visual detection. *Psychological Review,* **61**, 401–409.

Taylor, M. A. (1973). Certain functional equations on groupoids weaker than quasi-groups. *Aequationes Mathematicae,* **9**, 23–29.

Taylor, M. A. (1978). On the generalised equations of associativity and bisymmetry. *Aequationes Mathematicae,* **17**, 154–163.

Teghtsoonian, R. (1971). On the exponents in Stevens' law and the constant in Ekman's law. *Psychological Review,* **86**, 3–27.

Thaler, R. H. (1985). Mental accounting and consumer choice. *Marketing Science,* **4**, 199–214.

Thaler, R. H., & Johnson, E. J. (1990). Gambling with house money and trying to break even: The effects of prior outcomes on risky choice. *Management Science,* **36**, 643–660.

Thissen, D. (1988). *MULTILOG User's Guide* (2nd. ed.). Mooresville, IN: Scientific Software, Inc.

Thomas, E. A., & Myers, J. L. (1972). Implications of latency data for threshold and nonthreshold models of signal detection. *Journal of Mathematical Psychology,* **9**, 253–285.

Thurstone, L. L. (1927). A law of comparative judgment. *Psychological Review,* **34**, 273–286.

Torgerson, W. S. (1961). Distances and ratios in psychological scaling. *Acta Psychologica,* **19**, 201–205.

Townsend, J. T. (1971a). Theoretical analysis of an alphabetic confusion matrix. *Perception and Psychophysics,* **9**, 40–50.

Townsend, J. T. (1971b). Alphabetic confusion: A test of models for individuals. *Perception and Psychophysics,* **9**, 449–454.

Townsend, J. T. (1974). Issues and models concerning the processing of a finite number of inputs. In B. H. Kantowitz (Ed.), *Human Information Processing: Tutorials in Performance and Cognition* (pp. 133–186). New York: Wiley.

Townsend, J. T. (1976). Serial and within-stage independent parallel model equivalence on the minimum completion time. *Journal of Mathematical Psychology,* **14**, 219–238.

Townsend, J. T. (1984). Uncovering mental processes with factorial experiments. *Journal of Mathematical Psychology,* **28**, 363–400.

Townsend, J. T. (1990). Serial vs parallel processing: Sometimes they look like tweedledum and tweedledee but they can (and should) be distinguished. *Psychological Science,* **1**, 46–54.

Townsend, J. T., & Ashby, F. G. (1982). Experimental test of contemporary mathematical models of visual letter recognition. *Journal of Experimental Psychology: Human Perception and Performance*, **8**, 834–864.

Townsend, J. T., & Ashby, F. G. (1983). *The Stochastic Modeling of Elementary Psychological Processes*. New York: Cambridge University Press.

Townsend, J. T., & Colonius, H. (in press). Parallel processing response times and experimental determination of the stopping rule. In C. Dowling, F. S. Roberts, & P. Theuns (Eds.), *Progress in Mathematical Psychology*. Mahwah, NJ: Erlbaum.

Townsend, J. T., & Fikes, T. (1995). *A beginning quantitative taxonomy of cognitive activation systems and application to continuous flow processes*. Indiana University Cognitive Science Program Research Report 131.

Townsend, J. T., & Landon, D. E. (1982). An experimental and theoretical investigation of the constant-ratio rule and other models of visual letter confusion. *Journal of Mathematical Psychology*, **25**, 119–162.

Townsend, J. T., & Nozawa, G. (1995). Spatio-temporal properties of elementary perception: An investigation of parallel, serial, and coactive theories. *Journal of Mathematical Psychology*, **39**, 321–359.

Townsend, J. T., & Schweickert, R. (1989). Toward the trichotomy method of reaction times: Laying the foundation of stochastic mental networks. *Journal of Mathematical Psychology*, **33**, 309–327.

Townsend, J. T., & Thomas, R. D. (1994). Stochastic dependencies in parallel and serial models: Effects on systems factorial interactions. *Journal of Mathematical Psychology*, **38**, 1–34.

Treisman, A. (1985). Preattentive processing in vision. *Computer Vision, Graphics, and Image Processing*, **31**, 156–177.

Tuckwell, H. C. (1989). *Stochastic Processes in the Neurosciences*. Cambridge, MA: Cambridge University Press.

Tversky, A. (1967). Additivity, utility, and subjective probability. *Journal of Mathematical Psychology*, **4**, 175–201.

Tversky, A. (1969). Intransitivity of preferences. *Psychological Review*, **76**, 31–48.

Tversky, A. (1972a). Elimination by aspects: A theory of choice. *Psychological Review*, **79**, 281–299.

Tversky, A. (1972b). Choice by elimination. *Journal of Mathematical Psychology*, **9**, 342–367.

Tversky, A., & Kahneman, D. (1971). Belief in the law of small numbers. *Psychological Bulletin*, **76**, 105–110.

Tversky, A., & Kahneman, D. (1974). Judgment under uncertainty: Heuristics and biases. *Science*, **185**, 1124–1131.

Tversky, A., & Kahneman, D. (1983). Extensional versus intuitive reasoning: The conjunction fallacy in probability judgment. *Psychological Review*, **90**, 293–315.

Tversky, A., & Kahneman, D. (1986). Rational choice and the framing of decisions. *Journal of Business*, **59**, S251–S278.

Tversky, A., & Kahneman, D. (1992). Advances in prospect theory: Cumulative representation of uncertainty. *Journal of Risk and Uncertainty*, **5**, 297–323.

Tversky, A., & Russo, J. E. (1969). Substitutability and similarity in binary choices. *Journal of Mathematical Psychology, 6*, 1–12.

Tversky, A., Sattath, S., & Slovic, P. (1988). Contingent weighting in judgment and choice. *Psychological Review, 95*, 371–384.

Tversky, A., Slovic, P., & Kahneman, D. (1990). The causes of preference reversal. *American Economic Review, 80*, 204–217.

Ulrich, R., & Giray, M. (1986). Separate-activation models with variable base times: Testability and checking of cross-channel dependency. *Perception and Psychophysics, 34*, 248–254.

van Daal, J., & Merkies, A. H. Q. M. (1987). The problem of aggregation of individual economic relations: Consistency and representativity in a historical perspective. In W. Eichhorn (Ed.), *Measurement in Economics* (pp. 607–637). Heidelberg: Physica.

van Santen, J. P. H., & Bamber, D. (1981). Finite and infinite state confusion models. *Journal of Mathematical Psychology, 24*, 101–111.

Varey, C. A., Mellers, B. A., & Birnbaum, M. H. (1990). Judgments of proportions. *Journal of Experimental Psychology: Human Perception and Performance, 16*, 613–625.

von Neumann, J., & Morgenstern, O. (1947). *Theory of Games and Economic Behavior*. Princeton, NJ: Princeton University Press.

von Stengel, B. (1991). *Eine Dekompositionstheorie für mehrstellige Funktionen*. Frankfurt/M.: Hain.

von Stengel, B. (1993). Closure properties of independence concepts for continuous utilities. *Mathematics of Operations Research, 18*, 346–389.

von Winterfeldt, D., Chung, N.-K., Luce, R. D., & Cho, Y. (1997). Tests of consequence monotonicity in decision making under uncertainty. *Journal of Experimental Psychology: Learning, Memory, and Cognition, 23*, 1–23.

von Winterfeldt, D., & Edwards, W. (1986). *Decision Analysis and Behavioral Research*. New York: Cambridge University Press.

Vorberg, D. (1990). *Within-stage independence, future-order independence, and realizability of parallel processing systems*. Manuscript, Institut für Psychologie, Technische Universität Braunschweig.

Wakker, P. P. (1989). *Additive Representations of Preferences: A New Foundation of Decision Analysis*. Dordrecht, The Netherlands: Kluwer.

Wakker, P. P. (1993). Additive representations on rank-ordered sets, II. The topological approach. *Journal of Mathematical Economics, 22*, 1–26.

Wakker, P. P., Erev, I., & Weber, E. U. (1994). Comonotonic independence: The critical test between classical and rank-dependent utility theories. *Journal of Risk and Uncertainty, 9*, 195–230.

Wakker, P. P., & Tversky, A. (1993). An axiomatization of cumulative prospect theory. *Journal of Risk and Uncertainty, 7*, 147–176.

Wallace, M. T., Meredith, M. A., & Stein, B. E. (1993). Converging influences from visual, auditory, and somatosensory cortices onto output neurons of the superior colliculus. *Journal of Neurophysiology, 69*, 1797–1809.

Wallsten, T. S. (1983). The theoretical status of judgmental heuristics. In

R. W. Scholz (Ed.), *Decision Making Under Uncertainty* (pp. 21–38). North-Holland: Elsevier Science Publishers.

Wanke, M., Schwartz, N., & Bless, H. (1995). The availability heuristic revisited: Experienced ease of retrieval in mundane frequency estimates. *Acta Psychologica*, **89**, 83–90.

Ward, L. M., & Lockhead, G. R. (1970). Sequential effects and memory in category judgment. *Journal of Experimental Psychology*, **84**, 27–34.

Weber, D. L., Green, D. M., & Luce, R. D. (1977). Effects of practice and distribution of auditory signals on absolute identification. *Perception and Psychophysics*, **22**, 223–231.

Weber, E. U. (1984). Combine and Conquer: A joint application of conjoint and functional approaches to the problem of risk measurement. *Journal of Experimental Psychology: Human Perception and Performance*, **10**, 179–194.

Weber, E. U. (1988). A descriptive measure of risk. *Acta Psychologica*, **69**, 185–203.

Weber, E. U. (1994). From subjective probabilities to decision weights: The effects of asymmetric loss functions on the evaluation of uncertain outcomes and events. *Psychological Bulletin*, **114**, 228–242.

Weber, E. U., Anderson, C. J., & Birnbaum, M. H. (1992). A theory of perceived risk and attractiveness. *Organizational Behavior and Human Decision Processes*, **52**, 492–523.

Weber, E. U., & Bottom, W. P. (1989). Axiomatic measures of perceived risk: Some tests and extensions. *Journal of Behavioral Decision Making*, **2**, 113–131.

Weber, E. U., & Bottom, W. P. (1990). An empirical evaluation of the transitivity, monotonicity, accounting, and conjoint axioms for perceived risk. *Organizational Behavior and Human Decision Processes*, **45**, 253–276.

Weber, E. U., & Hsee, C. K. (in press). Cross-cultural differences in risk perception but cross-cultural similarities in attitudes towards risk. *Management Science*.

Weber, E. U., & Kirsner, B. (1996). Reasons for rank-dependent utility evaluation. *Journal of Risk and Uncertainty*, **14**, 41–61.

Weber, E. U., & Milliman, R. (1997). Perceived risk attitudes: Relating risk perception to risky choice. *Management Science*, **43**, 122–143.

Weber, M. (1990). *Risikoentscheidungskalküle in der Finanzierungstheorie*. Stuttgart: Poeschel.

Westendorf, D., & Blake, R. (1988). Binocular reaction times to contrast increments. *Vision Research*, **28**, 355–359.

Wilcox, R. R. (1982). Some empirical and theoretical results on an answer-until-correct scoring procedure. *British Journal of Mathematical and Statistical Psychology*, **35**, 57–70.

Woldorff, M., Gallen, C., Hampson, S., Hillyard, S., Pantev, C., Sobel, D., & Bloom, F. (1993). Modulation of early sensory processing in human auditory cortex during auditory selective attention. *Proceedings of the National Academy of Sciences (USA)*, **90**, 8722–8726.

Wu, G. (1994). An empirical test of ordinal independence. *Journal of Risk and Uncertainty*, **9**, 39–60.

Wu, G., & Gonzalez, R. (1996). Curvature of the probability weighting function. *Management Science*, **42**, 1676–1690.

Yaari, M. E. (1987). The dual theory of choice under risk. *Econometrica*, **55**, 95–115.

Yates, J. F., & Stone, E. R. (1992a). The risk construct. In J. F. Yates (Ed.), *Risk-Taking Behavior* (pp. 1–25). New York: Wiley.

Yates, J. F., & Stone, E. R. (1992b). Risk appraisal. In J. F. Yates (Ed.), *Risk-Taking Behavior* (pp. 49–86). New York: Wiley.

Yellott, Jr., J. I. (1977). The relationship between Luce's Choice Axiom, Thurstone's Theory of Comparative Judgment, and the double exponential distribution. *Journal of Mathematical Psychology*, **15**, 109–144.

Yellott, Jr., J. I. (1980). Generalized Thurstone models for ranking: equivalence and reversibility. *Journal of Mathematical Psychology*, **22**, 48–69.

Yellott, Jr., J. I., & Iverson, G. J. (1992). Uniqueness properties of higher-order autocorrelation functions. *Journal of the Optical Society of America A*, **9**, 388–404.

Yermalov, S. M. (1971). *Method of Monte-Carlo and Related Issues*. Moscow: Nauka.

Zaller, J. (1992). *The Nature and Origins of Mass Opinions*. New York: Cambridge University Press.

Ziegler, G. M. (1994). *Lectures on Polytopes*. Berlin: Springer.

Choice, Decision, and Measurement
A. A. J. Marley (Ed.),
©Lawrence Erlbaum Associates, NJ, 1997.

AUTHOR INDEX

Choice, Decision, and Measurement
A. A. J. Marley (Ed.),
©Lawrence Erlbaum Associates, NJ, 1997.

SUBJECT INDEX